THE
SYNDICATE

THE STORY OF THE COMING
WORLD GOVERNMENT

Books published by Nicholas Hagger

The Fire and the Stones
Selected Poems
The Universe and the Light
A White Radiance
A Mystic Way
Awakening to the Light
A Spade Fresh with Mud
The Warlords
Overlord
A Smell of Leaves and Summer
The Tragedy of Prince Tudor
The One and the Many
Wheeling Bats and a Harvest Moon
The Warm Glow of the Monastery Courtyard

NICHOLAS HAGGER

THE SYNDICATE

THE STORY OF THE COMING
WORLD GOVERNMENT

BOOKS

Winchester, UK
Washington, USA

Copyright © 2004 O Books
O Books is an imprint of John Hunt Publishing Ltd., Deershot Lodge,
Park Lane, Ropley, Hants, SO24 0BE, UK
office@johnhunt-publishing.com
www.O-books.net

Distribution in:
UK
Orca Book Services
orders@orcabookservices.co.uk
Tel: 01202 665432 Fax: 01202 666219 Int. code (44)

USA and Canada
NBN
custserv@nbnbooks.com
Tel: 1 800 462 6420 Fax: 1 800 338 4550

Australia
Brumby Books
sales@brumbybooks.com
Tel: 61 3 9761 5535 Fax: 61 3 9761 7095

New Zealand
Peaceful Living
books@peaceful-living.co.nz
Tel: 64 7 57 18105 Fax: 64 7 57 18513

Singapore
STP
davidbuckland@tlp.com.sg
Tel: 65 6276 Fax: 65 6276 7119

South Africa
Alternative Books
altbook@global.co.za
Tel: 27 011 792 7730 Fax: 27 011 972 7787

Text: © 2004 Nicholas Hagger
Reprinted 2004

Design: Jim Weaver Design
Cover design: Krave Ltd., London

ISBN 1 903816 85 8

The rights of Nicholas Hagger as author has been asserted in
accordance with the Copyright, Designs and Patents Act 1988.

A CIP catalogue record for this book is available from the British Library.

Printed and bound by CPI Group (UK) Ltd, Croydon, CR0 4YY

NOTE TO THE READER

This book is an attempt to arrive at a view of twentieth-century history that explains the events. I have made available all my sources in the Notes. I am aware that the quality of the sources varies. Some are unimpeachable, others of more dubious reliability. The truth is that there is quite simply not always a good source for every judgment in this field. Government of any kind involves secrecy. I have put it all down, warts and all, and leave it to the reader's judgment as to whether it is all smoke and no fire.

My people perish for lack of knowledge.

Hosea 4:6

It will be enough for me ... if these words of mine are judged useful by those who want to understand clearly the events which happened in the past and which (human nature being what it is) will, at some time or other and in much the same ways, be repeated in the future. My work is not a piece of writing designed to meet the taste of an immediate public; but was done to last for ever.

Thucydides, History of The Peloponnesian War

ACKNOWLEDGMENTS

I am grateful to the authors of the books that appear in the Notes, many of whom had the courage to question the official line and describe current affairs as they saw them. I am grateful to many people who have shared my enthusiasm for finding out what is really happening in the world today, the story behind the news: the story the public is not told.

I acknowledge the memory of Charles Douglas-Home who, when Features Editor of the London *Times*, taught me to present statistics in the articles I wrote for his *Times'* center page, to let the facts speak for themselves and to leave it to the reader to draw conclusions. I am grateful to my learned friend Edward Garnier, QC, MP, a former Conservative Party Shadow Attorney General, for painstakingly reading through the text and offering valuable advice from his considerable knowledge of public life and world leaders. And also to John Hunt, who took on the responsibility of seeing this book into print and whose wise approach has been crucial to bringing it to birth in its present form.

CONTENTS

PROLOGUE

The Queen of England is alleged to have told her butler Paul Burrell a few months after Princess Diana's death in a car crash, "Be careful. There are powers at work in this country about which we have no knowledge." Misreporting? Or is she wrong? Or could it be true? The theme of this book is that it is.

The history and current affairs we are taught in schools, read in the newspapers, and read in books, tends to focus on public figures – kings, prime ministers, nations. It highlights the events that are most visible. But there are currents that determine these events, and figures hidden from the public eye that move them. It can be hard to discern these figures, and the sequence of events can be hard to unravel.

It's hard enough to unravel the events in front of our noses. Did Iraq for instance have weapons of mass destruction or not? You might think that with all the modern technology at the disposal of Western governments, down to satellites that can spot cigarette packets, there could be little room for doubt. If our governments can get it so wrong, what chance do we have? Who can we trust? What can we believe? It's easy to lose our bearings and believe any conspiracy theory. The opposite is equally true: it's easy to believe what the government says, that everything is open and above board. I believe the answer is to look at the broader picture, to look at patterns over decades rather than at single events.

Many of the conclusions here are tentative. They may sound impossible. But then many things do without the benefit of hindsight. Who would have guessed in 1930 that the following decade would see the attempt to create a New World Order involving the extermination of most of Europe's Jews and the overall deaths of 70 million? Who would have guessed in 2000 that the following year would see the politics of the West dominated by a war against terror, with troops now in Afghanistan and Iraq? Who is really behind this terror? How has it suddenly appeared, with such vigor and success, seemingly from nowhere?

There is a pattern behind recent events, which I attempt to uncover. The overall explanation is that these events are not random, not driven by individual acts of evil. They are the result of a gradual, inexorable drive on the behalf of certain parties to a world government. The dreams of past empires are not dead, but very much alive. The drive to world government is not a past fad, limited only by the lack of knowledge of how big the world is and the ability to get around it all, but present today. It is not the fantasy of alien cultures, of fundamentalists of different hues, but has been slipped into our own democracies by people and organizations we've never really understood were in our midst.

These dreams have driven the creation of the United States as well as the European Empires. They are behind the push to a united Europe, and many of the recent events in the Middle East. They will be realized, if we let it happen, in a United States of the World, a world government. With modern communications, in a small planet, this is inevitable. The question is whether this world government is going to work for the good of everyone, coming from a universalist, global democratic perspective, or whether it's going to be run in the interests of the few. This is the key question we face over the coming decades.

In covering so much ground in one book I realize it often makes assumptions and judgments that may seem questionable, particularly in the case of recent events. As in any court of law, some of the evidence for the Syndicate and its actions will be less than satisfactory – circumstantial, hearsay, and inadmissible. But a judgment has to be made. Otherwise the twenty-first century could prove even more violent than the twentieth. Wisdom with hindsight is easy, but too late for many. I leave it to you to decide.

1

THE QUESTION

There is no proletarian, not even a Communist movement that has not operated in the interests of money, in the direction indicated by money, and for the time being permitted by money – and that without the idealists among its leaders having the slightest suspicion of the fact.

Oswald Spengler, Decline of the West

In the West most people, even if they don't trust their politicians, see their system of government as essentially benign, working for the good of the nation, being firm and fair in its dealings with the world beyond its borders, offering peace and cooperation and only going to war if absolutely forced to. In the developing countries, particularly Moslem ones, that great spread from the Atlantic to the Pacific covering most of the ancient civilizations, people see the West differently. As devious and aggressive, if not outright evil.

I recognize their point of view. I think it has more accuracy than most Westerners realize. It may be because I find it easier to see the world through non-Western eyes than most academic historians. In 1966 I was among the first Westerners to witness the Chinese Cultural Revolution. In 1969 I was driving across Tripoli on the morning of the Libyan Revolution. I've lectured at the University of Baghdad and was Professor of English for four years at three universities in Tokyo, Japan.

So in these chapters I approach twentieth-century history in a manner that will be unfamiliar to most readers. They describe the dominant themes that determined the major events as money and oil rather than random assassination or government cock-up. Railroad and oil magnates are more significant than Lloyd George or the Kaiser.

1

The events of the last couple of years have brought increasing numbers around to this way of thinking. The pace of events is accelerating. The lies seem to get bigger, and the events seem more inexplicable. It's why we're increasingly suspicious of politicians. Why we suspect that they're not really working with our best interests at heart. Why we're more reluctant to go to war. They have to persuade us harder. They invent stories, or turn a deaf ear to the ones they don't want us to hear. Here's why.

I'll come straight to the point, offering four comments.

The first is that the world is running out of oil. Virtually all commentators agree there are 50 to 100 years of supplies left, overall, assuming current rates of production and consumption continue and newly industrializing and populous countries like China don't rapidly increase their demand (which seems inevitable).[1]

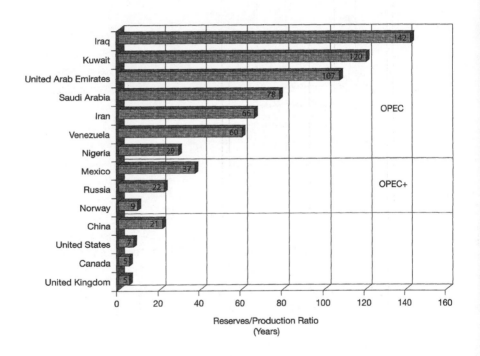

(Production for 1998. Reserves as at January 1, 1999)

The second is that the reserves are distributed as follows:[2]

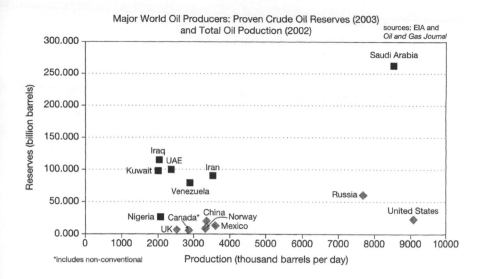

Major World Oil Producers: Proven Crude Oil Reserves (2003) and Total Oil Poduction (2002)

sources: EIA and *Oil and Gas Journal*

*includes non-conventional   Production (thousand barrels per day)

Both the USA and UK have around 5 years' oil supply left, or less. Their increasing reliance on imports is having a serious effect on the balance of payments. As a reflection of the UK's oil trade deficit, the UK's balance of payments is currently running at over £40b p.a. Harold Macmillan's Conservative government was thrown out of office in 1964 for having a balance of payments deficit of well under £1b. The US balance of payments in 2003 was running at a $542b deficit.[3]

The third is that oil and politics are increasingly intermingled. It's particularly apparent in the present US government. Vice-President Dick Cheney previously served as chairman and chief executive of Halliburton Co., the world's largest oilfield services company, which had operations in Azerbaijan. Cheney and Donald Evans, Commerce Secretary, both ran energy-related companies and earned millions of dollars from oil. Condoleezza Rice, national security advisor, was a director with Chevron from 1991 until January 2001 and had a company oil tanker named after her. Brent Scowcroft, advisor to Rice and national security advisor to Bush Sr., was a director of Pennzoil-Quaker State Co. and Enron Global Power & Pipelines, a unit of Enron Corp. Christine Todd Whitman, the administrator of the Environmental Protection Agency, owned interests in oil wells in Texas and Colorado. Donald Rumsfeld, Defense Secretary, had between $3.25m and $15.5m worth of investments in energy-related companies. James Baker, advisor to the Bush family and former Secretary of State, had a law firm which represented several oil companies with interests in Azerbaijan, including Exxon-Mobil Corp. Richard Armitage, Deputy Secretary of State, was a co-chairman of the US-Azerbaijan Chamber of Commerce.[4]

George W. Bush followed his father into the Texan oil business. He founded Bush Exploration in 1975. His Arbusto company did not always strike oil, and investors lost money when a dry hole was dug. By 1983 the oil industry was in decline and, with his father Vice-President of the USA, Bush sought financial help. Bill De Witt approached Bush and made him Chairman of his own successful firm, Spectrum 7 Energy Corporation and gave him a salary of $75,000 p.a. and more than a million shares. Eighteen months later the company began to founder and in 1986 it was taken over by Harken Energy. With his father campaigning for the Presidency, Bush was paid a salary of $120,000 as a consultant and given $600,000 worth of Harken Energy shares. In 1990 Harken Energy beat its rival Amoco to land an offshore drilling deal in Bahrain.

The fourth is that for the first time in our history we have gone to war on the basis of (apparently wrong) intelligence with a country, Iraq, who (it is now apparent) was no direct threat to the national security of either the US or the UK. No troops were massing on their borders prepared to attack the USA or cross the English Channel. No terrorists were being sent out from Baghdad to bomb New York or London. Of the 9/11 terrorists none were Iraqis. It was a poor country bled dry by sanctions, with part of its territory cordoned off by the Alliance, flown over regularly by US spy planes, and with UN inspectors crawling over the ground. But it does happen to have the world's longest-lasting oil reserves with 142 years' supply at the June 1998 production rate.[5]

Our oil is running out, Iraq has plenty. Our politicians are linked to oil. We've gone to war with Iraq. Maybe these facts are not directly connected. Maybe the USA and UK governments genuinely believed their citizens or soldiers were in imminent threat from Saddam's weapons of mass destruction. Or maybe they went to war in Iraq for humanitarian rather than geo-political reasons. Few would deny that the world is better off with Saddam Hussein behind bars. The difficulty with this argument, of course, is why we haven't gone to war with a dozen similar or worse despotic regimes in the last couple of decades; indeed, why do we more often seem to support them than attack them, as we supported Saddam himself through the 80s and early 90s.

The argument made here is that not only are these facts connected, but similar connections can be found through the history of the twentieth century and earlier.

Here, for instance, is a broader outline of recent history:

Date	Oilfields	US Conflict of Interests with	Event	Page reference
1905	Baku	Russia	Revolution	20
1910–34	Mexican	Diáz (Mexico)	Revolution	43
1916	Mosul	Britain	Alliance with Kaiser	16–19
1917	Baku	Russia	Revolution	20–1
1940	Saudi Arabian	Britain	World War Two	55–8
1942–5	Chinese	Japan	World War Two	304
1949–76	Chinese	Chiang Kai-Shek	Revolution	303–5
1952	Suez Canal, oil lifeline	King Farouk/ West	Nasser's revolution	71–2, 306–7
	S.E. Bolivian	Bolivian military	Revolution	81, 306,395
1955–75	Vietnamese	North Vietnam	Vietnam war	77–80, 306
		South Vietnam		
1958	Iraqi	King Feisal/West	Kassem's revolution	125, 307
			(Baathist *coups* in 1963,1968)	126
1959	Bolivian/other Latin American	Batista	Cuban Revolution to train Latin American revolutionaries	73–4, 306
1969	Libyan	King Idris/West	Gaddafi's revolution	82, 307–8
1975–9	Cambodian	Lon Nol	Khmer Rouge revolution	308
1979	Iranian	Shah/Regency's Bakhtiar	Iranian Revolution	123–4, 308–9
1980–88	Iran/Iraq	Iran	Iran-Iraq War	126–7
1982	Falkland Isles	Britain	Argentinian invasion of Falkland Isles	86
1984	North Sea	Britain	Scargill's revolutionary miners' strike	90, 398
1991	Rumaila	Kuwait	Saddam Hussein's failed invasion of Kuwait	125–130
1994–6, 2000	Chechnya/Baku	Chechnya	Russian siege of Grozny	111–114

Is it accident that war and revolution center around oilfields and pipelines? If it's no accident, how far are the instigators aware of their own motives? How far are they prepared to go to cover them up? How far are they responsible for the numbers of dead involved?

This is the first theme of the book: That we need to be more aware of the powers behind the powers. The pursuit of oil and money drives twentieth and twenty-first-century events as much as the protection of liberty and democracy. Of course there is nothing necessarily wrong in itself for a country to secure its supplies, any more than wanting to enlarge your business, to gain more control over your sources – every supermarket plays the same game. And it's natural that business at every level is one of shifting relationships and alliances. And at a basic economic level, much of the economy is now global. Citizens own stock in countries all round the world. Corporations are of necessity multinational.

You may be with me so far; opinion polls suggest that the majority in the West suspect we didn't go to war with Iraq for the right reasons, even if the majority applaud the (hoped for) outcome: a more democratic Iraq, freed from the specter of Saddam Hussein.[6] But I go further. The second theme of the book is that there is a deeper game being played. We're talking here of a level where countries and peoples are pawns in a game. The leaders we elect to serve us aren't necessarily working in our best interests. The logic of these global interests is to promote multinational, regional, even global government rather than national government. It could then eliminate differences in currencies, armies, import and export taxes. It could concentrate on increasing wealth without being subject to the vagaries of nation-states. After all, individual nation-states are erratic, unstable, and (generally) governed in the interests of the people in that country rather than multinational, global interests. Corporations with a global reach need global organizations to influence and operate through. These global interests, focused today around money and oil, act in concert. They form what we can call "The Syndicate."[7] It is bigger than any one individual, or any numbers of individuals. It is more powerful than individual "members" are aware. Its influence is so pervasive, its ideas so rational, that many – including presidents and prime ministers – act in its interest without considering the logical outcome.

I go still further. Whereas the intention of some in the Syndicate may be benign, the effect overall is malign. And some are driven by darker visions. They may sound incredible, but they form the backdrop to the history of the twentieth century. The events we read about tell us that the darkest visions do get put into practice. World domination is an ancient dream. The same ambition still drives individuals today. And in modern times they have the capacity to make these dreams come true. We can only fight them if we're aware of them. And usually, when we are, it's too late for millions. Come with me in the argument as far as you can.

2

THE GENESIS OF
THE SYNDICATE

The United States were sold to the Rothschilds in 1863.
Ezra Pound, America, Roosevelt and the Causes of the Present War

Most of us have a fairly naïve attitude to wealth. We think of its creation and maintenance as something separate from the corridors of power, from politics, particularly democratic politics. But the two are indivisible. It's money that rules. This chapter gives the background on who really rules the world today.

Our story starts with Mayer Amschel, a Frankfurt Jew,[1] someone you've probably never heard of. A clerk in a bank owned by the Oppenheimers, he worked his way up to junior partner and then left to take over the business his father started in 1750, buying and selling rare coins. In 1769 he became court agent for the Elector, William IX, Landgrave of Hesse-Kassel. William inherited the largest private fortune in Europe when his father died in 1785; the equivalent of $40 million, money paid by Great Britain for the use of 16,800 Hessian troops during the American Revolution. When Napoleon invaded Germany in 1806, William fled from Frankfurt leaving Amschel to guard the equivalent of $3 million,[2] which he buried in his garden. William gave a power of attorney to Budrus von Carlhausen, who made Amschel his banker with the responsibility of collecting interest on royal loans. That is how the Rothschild banking dynasty began. The name by which Mayer Amschel came to be known, "Rothschild," came from "rotschildt" or the "red shield" that hung over the door in the house in the ghetto where his ancestors once lived.[3]

When Mayer Amschel died in 1812 he was the richest man ever to have lived,[4] with a fortune of \$3.5m (£1,669m if related to GDP and not merely multiplied by 35.5 for inflation since 1836).[5] His will was never published, but he established the principle that his fortune would pass down through his male descendents through a dynastic line.[6]

Like the riches of monarchs, the Rothschilds' wealth was handed down untaxed. Their private banks were partnerships whose profits were distributed within the family, leaving little for the government. Indeed, they regarded themselves as monarchs in their own right, wealthier than all the crown heads of Europe put together. They had banks in London, Paris, Frankfurt, Vienna, and Naples, and from their huge profits had built no fewer than 42 great country houses throughout Europe.

Mayer had five sons,[7] and the lead in his banking empire was taken by the eldest, Nathan. He increased the fortune to \$7.5b by 1820 – he boasted he had multiplied his capital 2,500 times in five years, largely by speculating on the outcome of the Battle of Waterloo.[8] On June 20, 1815 his selling triggered a mass sale of stock and a price collapse, and his subsequent buying of the market and all government bonds left him owning the country's cash flow and the Bank of England.[9] Wellington won the battle of Waterloo, but the financial independence of the country was lost before most people heard the news. Nathan possibly had \$100b by 1840. It has been estimated that by 1940 the family fortune had reached \$500b (worth \$20 trillion at today's values), approximately half the wealth of America (including banks) at that time.[10]

It's hard to estimate the Rothschild wealth today. Frederic Morton, author of *The Rothschilds*, which was commissioned by the family, writes, "Today the family grooms the inaudibility and invisibility of its presence." It is concealed behind a network of merchant banks, gold dealings, investments in minerals, and land and property holdings. Under its 2003–formed Netherlands-based holding company Concordia BV, Rothschilds Continuation Holdings AG, a Swiss holding company for the worldwide Rothschild merchant banking business, was the parent of scores of industrial, commercial, mining, and tourist corporations, not one of which bears the family name.[11] Many were accumulated during the spread of the British Empire of which they were a driving-force.

Today the Rothschilds' merchant banks in London and Paris are probably the largest private institutions in the world. They helped fund and finance Royal Dutch Shell and De Beers. In the 1920s the banks were organized under the French house into a "noiseless international syndicate that reached from J. P. Morgan in New York to Baron Louis-controlled Creditanstalt in Vienna."[12] They bought a 50,000 square-mile tract of land in Canada, the biggest in the history of Canada, which included gold deposits. They influence the Bank of England, Bank of France, and the Reichsbank of Germany, all of which are known as government institutions-central banks regulating currency – but are in effect privately owned by the House of Rothschild as stockholder. They also influence the US Federal Reserve, the IMF, and Geneva finance: in short, the world's monetary policy.[13]

The primary business of the London-based N M Rothschild and Sons, the most influential of the Rothschilds' houses, has been to sell and buy treasuries and gold bullion. At 10.30am and 3pm each day they have helped fix the price of gold through the London Bullion Marketing Association. Five men have talked by phone for 10 minutes, then lowered tiny Union Jacks on their desks in a ceremony that has been performed daily since September 12, 1919. The Rothschilds have earned fees on every transaction involving treasuries and 42m ounces of gold a day – on transfers, calls, puts, trades, and leases.[14] Of the world's above-ground gold reserves (120,000 tons), one third (40,000 tons) is held in central banks and the remaining two-thirds are held privately. It is not known by whom.

It is difficult to quantify the world's wealth. This is the sum total of the wealth of all nations, and includes their GDP (gross domestic product), mineral and oil reserves, investments, and the gold bullion in the world's banks ($300b). According to a prestigious world wealth report[15] based on people with more than $1m, the combined GDP of the world in 2002 was $27.2 trillion. (Of this, North America accounted for $7.4 trillion and Europe for $8.8 trillion.) If we reckon that the world's wealth is ten times the world's GDP, then the world's wealth is $272 trillion.

An estimate of the Rothschilds' worth? The *Richest Men in the World* lists generally exclude dynastic families. If they had $6b in 1850 (a low estimate),[16] then, assuming no erosion of the wealth base, it could have been invested to bring in a conservative range of between 4% and 8% per annum, which gives figures ranging from $1.9 trillion to $491,409 trillion[17] (more than the world's wealth according to our estimate). Take a really conservative estimate of around $1 trillion.[18] In comparison, Bill Gates' worth was estimated in 2004 as $32 billion.[19] If you consider that a little over $300b would buy every ounce of gold in every bank in the world today,[20] and that the US national debt is currently (in 2004) $7.5 trillion (i.e. $7,500b),[21] the Rothschilds' position in the financial world can be grasped.

The Creation of the US Federal Reserve

I give a fuller account of the Rothschild story in the companion volume to this book, coming next year, *The Secret History of the West*.[22] The point of bringing it in here is that you don't get to be this enormously wealthy by making widgets, by buying and selling things. The Rothschilds got to be this wealthy through controlling the money supply of the nations of Europe. As President Garfield said in 1881: "Whoever controls a nation's money supply shapes its destiny."

But the Rothschilds were relatively weak in the New World. They tried to acquire an American central bank in the 1860s; Lincoln thwarted their efforts by opposing the National Bank Act of 1863, which gave federal banks the power to control the credit and finances of the US.[23] They made another attempt early on in the twentieth century. Central to their new attempt was another German Jew, Jacob Schiff, who had arrived in America in 1865. In 1873 they gave him financial backing that enabled him to buy into the German Jewish firm of Kuhn and Loeb.[24] Schiff married Solomon Loeb's eldest daughter Theresa and bought out Kuhn's interest. He was now effectively the sole owner of Kuhn, Loeb & Co. He became a millionaire by financing railroads, and (with "Rothschild" finance) helped Edward Henry Harriman, the American financier and railroad magnate, amass the greatest railroad fortune in the world. Schiff (again using "Rothschild" finance) also funded Carnegie's steel empire – and John D. Rockefeller's Standard Oil.[25]

Paul Warburg was also a key figure. He and his brother Felix, also German Jews, arrived from Frankfurt in 1902 and, financed by "Rothschilds," bought into Schiff's Kuhn, Loeb & Co. Paul married Solomon Loeb's younger daughter Nina – so he and Jacob Schiff were brothers-in-law – and Felix married Frida Schiff, Jacob's daughter, becoming his son-in-law. The Rothschilds sent Paul and Felix Warburg to New York to lobby for Congress to pass the central banking law, which would set up a central bank with the power to create money and regulate its value. Paul

Warburg was responsible for putting together the Federal Reserve Act, which was masterminded by Baron Alfred de Rothschild in London.[26] In 1903, instructed by "Rothschilds," Paul Warburg wrote a memorandum for Schiff on how the European Central Banking system applied to America's monetary system. Schiff passed it to the National City bank, where Rockefeller's agent Vanderlip contacted bankers, including J. P. Morgan, citing Paul Warburg's reputation as a world authority on central banking. In 1907 the *New York Times* ran an article by Paul Warburg on America's need for a central banking system. In 1908 Schiff contacted another "Rothschild" representative, Col. House, who was Schiff's chief representative and courier, and Bernard Baruch, a multi-millionaire from stock market speculation, whose advice was sought by the US President of the day.

In 1908 Senator Aldrich (another "Rothschildite") introduced a bill that proposed that banks would issue currency backed by Federal, state, and local government bonds (the first circulation of paper money by the federal government had taken place in 1861.) This was criticized, as it would not provide a monetary system that could respond to seasonal demand. Representative E. B. Vreeland then proposed basing currency on communal paper rather than bonds. This was passed, and the National Monetary Commission was established under Aldrich to approve all monetary legislation sent to Congress. In 1910 Paul Warburg made an influential speech calling for a United Reserve Bank with capital of $100m, and the power to circulate paper money.

A secret meeting was convened.[27] Those invited met on a railway platform in New Jersey and were taken by boat to a hunting lodge on Jekyll Island, off Brunswick, Georgia. The island had been bought in 1888 by J. P. Morgan, John D. Rockefeller's brother William, Vanderbilt and other bankers. Those present included Sen. Aldrich, Vanderlip, Paul Warburg, John D. Rockefeller, Bernard Baruch, Col. House, and Jacob Schiff. One way or another all were linked to the Rothschilds. Ten days later they had agreed upon the concept of what became the Federal Reserve System.

Theodore Roosevelt would make the ideal president for the Rothschilds, and the "Rothschild"-affiliated J. P. Morgan and Co. first financed his election bid in 1912.[28] At this early stage it may simply have been to pull votes away from President Taft, to help the election effort of Woodrow Wilson (much as Ralph Nader split the Democratic vote to allow Bush

Jr. to beat Gore, and is likely to do the same with Kerry).[29] Wilson won
the election, and the Democrats gained control of both houses. To avoid
mentioning a central bank, Wilson proposed that the new regional banks
should be called "Federal Reserve banks." The Federal Reserve Bill was
passed by the House of Representatives and Senate on December 23, 1913,
when many Congressmen and Senators were away for the beginning of
their Christmas break, and an hour after the Senate vote Wilson signed
the Federal Reserve Act into law. So in one day "Rothschilds" and their
supporters, notably J. P. Morgan's First National Bank and Kuhn, Loeb
& Co.'s National City Bank, had effectively taken control of the American
economy.

The Federal Reserve System was established in October 1914 and
began operating in 1915. It acted (and still acts) as a fiscal agent for the
US government; it guards the reserve accounts of commercial banks,
to which it makes loans, and controls the paper currency supply in the
USA. There was now a "Rothschild"-controlled central banking system
with inflatable currency, which meant that the money supply shrank with
each loan repayment and could only be kept going by ever-increasing
borrowing. Col. House began to lobby for a graduated income tax – two
recommendations in Marx's *Communist Manifesto*. The seven governors
of the Federal Reserve Board were picked by Col. House, the "Rothschild"
representative, and included the "Rothschildite" Paul Warburg.[30] The
American people began to discover that the Federal Reserve Banks
were privately-held corporations owned by stockholders, and agents of
("Rothschildite") foreign banks acting as part of a world system, and not
US government institutions.[31]

Whoever controlled the Federal Reserve Bank of New York controlled
the whole Federal Reserve system. Ninety of the 100 largest banks were
in New York, and of the New York banks' 200,000 shares, National City
Bank owned 30,000, Chase National 6,000, Morgan's First National Bank
15,000 and Morgan's National Bank of Commerce 21,000.

The Great Crash

"Rothschilds" manipulated the financial climate of the 1920s and early
1930s to their own advantage. The Federal Reserve Board held a secret
meeting on May 18, 1920.[32] Whatever the intention, the effect was to

take money from US farmers and make them more dependent on the government (which the bankers controlled). Small country banks in the Middle West and West, which had refused to be part of the Federal Reserve System, were broken. Large banks began calling in loans, and stocks dropped from 138.12 in 1919 to 66.24 in 1921. Government bonds plummeted, and banks called in more loans and, when customers could not pay, seized their assets.

After 1922 the Federal Reserve's profits rose and it was able to lend ten times more than its reserves. Credit was easily obtained, and between 1923 and 1929 the Federal Reserve expanded money supply by 62%. Following a bankers' meeting in 1926, the press reported that there were large profits to be made from the stock market. In July 1927 the New York Federal Reserve Board met the heads of European central banks at a secret luncheon.[33] The Federal Reserve Board introduced a cheap-money policy; it doubled its holdings of government securities, and as a result nearly $500 million worth of gold moved out of the US to Europe, notably France. This helped trigger the Depression. Details of the meeting were revealed in 1928 in the House hearings on the Stabilizing of the Purchasing Power of the Dollar. On February 6, 1929 Montagu Norman, Governor of the Bank of England and a close friend of Lord Rothschild who controlled the Bank of England, visited the US and met Andrew Mellon, the Secretary of Treasury.

The Federal Reserve Board then reversed its cheap money policy again and raised the discount rate. In March 1929 Paul Warburg tipped off the group of families around "Rothschilds." They took their money out of the stock market and put it into gold and silver.[34] Between 1929 and 1933 the Reserve reduced the money flow by a third. On October 24, 1929 the New York banking Establishment began calling in loans. Customers had to sell stock at low prices to pay off loans. Stock prices fell by 90%, US Securities lost $26b. Thousands of small banks and insurance companies went bankrupt; many millionaires found they were broke.

At home citizens now depended on the government. Unemployment was high, there were few job opportunities, and people looked to the government for handouts. The network of families finally brought Roosevelt to power in 1932, and people were dependent on Roosevelt's New Deal program. The Federal Reserve Board – "Rothschilds" – now ruled America.

The Rockefellers

There is another thread to be bought in here. Railroads dominated the nineteenth century. They opened up the vast interiors of North America and Asia. They enabled the migration of settlers and the mass-movement of goods, speeded up the process of Empire, were key to industrialization, and allowed large armies to be moved quickly. The twentieth century became a mechanized century. All these new machines needed power to drive them, and this was supplied by oil. Oil became the major source of money. It had been used as fuel for lamps in Berlin since 1853. In 1882 the British Captain Fisher (later Admiral) argued that the British fleet should be driven by smokeless oil fuel rather than coal, the burning of which made smoke that could be seen miles away. The best oil for this came from Russia.[35] By 1900 Russian oil – the oil of the Caucasus, i.e. Baku and, next in importance, Grozny – accounted for half all oil produced in the world. The French Rothschilds had been involved in the Russian petroleum industry since the 1860s and in partnership with a company known as Deutsch de la Meurthe had built a refinery at Fiume (then Hungary's only seaport).[36] The Rothschilds moved in on Baku, the largest Russian oilfield, and by 1890 "Rothschilds'" Baku-based operation controlled a third of Russian oil output. Of $214m invested in the Russian oil industry before the First World War, $130m came from foreign capital, 60% of which came from Great Britain.[37]

But the key figure in oil was the magnate John D. Rockefeller, and the rise of the Rockefellers to dominate the world's oil supplies had repercussions throughout the century. Rockefeller had German blood: he was descended on his paternal side from a Hessian mercenary (Roggenfelder, which means "rye field" in German),[38] who had Turkish ancestry and had come to America to fight for the British army during the Revolutionary war. He had deserted when offered a bribe of land in New Jersey. Roggenfelder changed his name to Rockefeller,[39] but it is important to remember the family's German origin. It explains its alliance with the German ruler of the day: the Kaiser, Hitler, most recently Kohl, and in particular with the Rothschilds.

John D Rockefeller had "Rothschilds'" financial help via Schiff.[40] In 1870 when Standard Oil of Ohio was incorporated, Rockefeller owned 21 out of 26 refineries in Cleveland. Next year Standard Oil (SO – our Esso) was the largest refining company in the world, and in 1879 Rockefeller controlled 90% of all the refined oil sold in the USA; he had 20,000 oil wells and 100,000 employees. By 1885 he controlled the oil industry in the US, and had branches in Western Europe and China.

By now Rockefeller was in partnership with "Rothschilds," and was granted a rebate on each barrel of oil he transported on the Kuhn, Loeb railroads of Pennsylvania, Baltimore, and Ohio.[41] In 1892 he moved to New Jersey because the oil trust he had formed was not acceptable to Ohio. He now began tax-avoidance schemes under the guise of philanthropy (such as the University of Chicago, Medical Research, General Education Co.).[42]

The German-American Rockefellers sought control of the world's oilfields. The main obstacle was the Royal Dutch Company, which was supported by the Dutch and British Empires. "Rockefellers" could not compete in the European markets with Royal Dutch (which was able to ship oil from its Baku and Ploesti fields at lower prices), so they began a propaganda war against their rival company. This led to a price war. The price war hurt the Royal Dutch Co., and Henri Deterding, its head, rescued it from bankruptcy by persuading "Rothschilds" to make a loan in return for a minority interest.[43] "Rothschilds" now had a stake in Royal Dutch.

John D. Rockefeller's wealth rose from $200m in 1899 to $1b by 1911 (equivalent to well over $13b in today's money).[44] He then benefited hugely through the break up of Standard Oil by the US Supreme Court in 1911, which gave Rockefeller 30 days to shed 37 subsidiaries. This led to the creation of 34 separate companies. Shares doubled, even trebled, and Rockefeller's wealth soared.[45]

By 1930 the profit of the Standard Oil Company was estimated at $900 million, a third of which went to Rockefeller personally.[46] It has been estimated that not long afterwards he had inestimable trillions, but that may be an exaggeration. What is clear is that by the time he died in 1937 "Rockefellers" owned a known fortune of at least $5b (worth about $200b now).[47] They were the richest family in America and some sources say had overtaken the Rothschilds as the richest family in the world. Rockefeller owned 20% of American industry and had given away $550m to "philanthropic" tax-saving projects,[48] leaving a tax bill of only $10 million. He had built the 14 buildings of Rockefeller Center in New York, had acquired his 4,180-acre family estate at Pocantico Hills north of

New York City, and was reconstructing Colonial Williamsburg.

The rapid rise of "Rockefellers" in the early 1900s was a wake-up call for the Rothschilds. The mouth they had fed was biting back. Rockefeller was now competing for their oil in Mexico, Russia, and the Middle East. In 1911 they exchanged their entire Russian operation for more shares in Royal Dutch Shell, and became the largest shareholder in the company.[49] The Rothschilds and Rockefellers were now in direct competition.

Like Mayer Amschel Rothschild's five sons, John D. Rockefeller's five sons (John III, Nelson, Laurance, Winthrop, and David) each went into a different sphere of "Rockefeller" enterprise: "philanthropy," government, business, oil, and banking. The five Rockefeller sons were a mirror image of the five Rothschild sons. They all worked within the commercial empire. Nelson Rockefeller became Governor of New York and Vice-President, while David Rockefeller became Chairman of Chase Manhattan Bank. The family now maintains 100 residences in all parts of the world.[50]

"Rockefellers" Fund the Kaiser

You don't make vast fortunes by tracking the Stock Market. You make them by outguessing it, manipulating it. Best of all, by writing the rules. The Rothschilds have made their fortunes on the backs of millions of people who have lost their savings. Similarly you come to dominate the world production of oil by controlling the ground the oil is lying in: by owning it or leasing it on good terms. This means dictating the politics of the region. This is why the Rockefellers are so important to the history of the twentieth century. It is their interests that determine the areas of conflict, their actions that drive events.

In 1900 the world's oil production was dominated by Britain – in Mexico, the Ottoman Near East, Saudi Arabia, and the Caspian region.[51] "Rockefellers" waged an economic war to wrest these territories from imperialistic Britain and the first half of the twentieth century was about their victorious campaign to replace Britain as the main oil empire in these regions. The story of how "Rothschilds" and "Rockefellers" funded different sides of the Russian revolution is told in *The Secret History of the West*. They were both also involved in the First World War.

When we think of the First World War it's of a long line of trenches through Belgium and France, from the North Sea right down to the Alps.

It's a bit of a mystery to us (and historians still debate the question) as to why it started. After all, there was no significant territorial dispute between France, Germany, and Britain to account for it, let alone one to draw in the USA and half the rest of the world. Dig underneath the surface politics, the individuals, and it's oil that led to the First World War, in particular Germany's attempt to seize British oil in the Near East. The German–American Rockefellers were closely involved in it. In 1904 the Germans had been given a concession by the Ottoman Turkish Sultan Abdul Hamid, with an option to drill the Baghdad-Mosul oilfields, which had previously been promised to Americans. Then in 1905 Britain, through the spy Sidney Reilly, acquired the right to drill for oil there, beating off competition from the French Rothschilds.[52] In 1912 the German government exchanged their concession for a quarter interest in Turkish Petroleum Co., which was 75% owned by the British government through Royal Dutch Shell and the Anglo-Persian Co. (thereby excluding "Rockefellers" from the Mosul field). "Rockefellers" fanned German resentment at being outmaneuvered.[53] The Kaiser then turned to "Rockefellers" and with their financial help built the Berlin-to-Baghdad railway so he could drill the oilfields under Ottoman control and wrest Near Eastern oil from his imperialistic competitor, the British.[54] The Kaiser was thus threatening to seize Egypt and eliminate British control of the Suez Canal and sever the British Empire's lifeline. This aim put Germany on a collision course with Great Britain.

The Rockefellers' distant Turkish ancestry also enabled them to approach the Ottomans. In 1914 Standard Oil loaned the Turkish government $35m, and in return were permitted to drill for oil in Ottoman territory. Through Chase National and Kuhn, Loeb, and in accordance with a deal they made with the Kaiser via Warburgs, "Rockefellers" gave the Kaiser $300m to finance the First World War through the Federal Reserve System, which stipulated that any bank losses would be financed by the US Treasury.[55] Their Standard Oil interests made a deal with the German government under which their holdings were taken over by the Reich with full compensation, and they supplied the Germans with the oil they required for the conduct of the war.[56] (A similar deal between "Rockefellers" and the Germans took place at the beginning of the Second World War and led to Senator Truman's charge of treason against Standard Oil.)

"Rockefellers" Wrest Oil in Near East

When a Serbian (who was also a Grand Orient Freemason) called Gabriel Princip assassinated the Austrian Archduke Franz Ferdinand events were running out of control in Europe, and the First World War began on June 28, 1914.

The Rothschilds, split between five countries, supported their own countries and found themselves on the sides of both Great Britain and Austro-Hungary. But Britain was going broke. In 1915 the New York banking-house J. P. Morgan and Co., the top American "Rothschild" representative, was named (with the approval of Woodrow Wilson) as the sole purchasing agent for all war supplies from the neutral US.[57] By 1917 Britain had ordered $20 billion worth of arms on Morgan's account (on which Morgans took 2%, making $400m). Britain had won the war and become the dominant world power on borrowed money. John Foster Dulles calculated that Britain, France, and the Allied Powers owed the US $12.5 billion at 5% interest, but were owed $33 billion by Germany in war reparations. By 1919 England owed the US $4.7b in war debts, and the British national debt had risen drastically from £650 million (1914) to the then huge amount of £7.4b.[58]

America loaned the allies $3b and another $6b for exports. Those who made the loans were J. P. Morgan, the top American "Rothschild" representative with new links to "Rockefellers," John D. Rockefeller, and Paul and Felix Warburg and Schiff.[59] Several "Rockefellerites" contributed funding, including a Federal Reserve Bank of New York director and "Rockefellerite" partners of J. P. Morgan, who gave $1m each.[60] All seven sought to protect their investments in Europe, making hundreds of million dollars out of the First World War, and it was their influence that finally took America into the war on the British side in 1917.[61]

After the bloodbath of Verdun in 1916 Winston Churchill realized that Britain could not win the war without more direct American help.[62] Supporting Britain was by no means certain, more Americans were of German ancestry than English. One factor that initially pushed the Americans to the British side was the sinking of the *Lusitania* by a German submarine in 1915. This was allegedly a British passenger liner carrying 1,201 people, including 128 Americans, who were all killed. But it seems more likely today that it was also carrying a large store of military weapons.

The ship's owners, Cunard Lines, had turned it over to the First Lord of the Admiralty, Winston Churchill. It was sent to New York to be loaded with 6 million rounds of ammunition owned by J. P. Morgan and Co. to be sold to England and France to aid the war against Germany. (On August 3, 1914 the French firm of Rothschild Frères cabled Morgan and Co. in New York suggesting a floating loan of $100m to pay for French purchases of American goods.)

In December 1914 England broke the German war code. When the *Lusitania* set sail for England Churchill knew where every U-boat was, including three in the *Lusitania*'s vicinity.[63] According to Commander Joseph Kenworth of British Naval Intelligence, "the *Lusitania* was deliberately sent at considerably reduced speed into an area where a U-boat was known to be waiting and her escort withdrawn."[64]

British Foreign Secretary Sir Edward Grey had asked Col. House, "What will America do if the Germans sink an ocean liner with American passengers on board?" House replied, "I believe that a flame of indignation would sweep the United States and that by itself would be sufficient to carry us into the war."[65]

The price for American involvement in the war was that British vassals in the Near East should grant concessions to "Rockefellers'" Standard Oil.[66] Jews had lobbied for such concessions. Some no doubt hoped that American involvement would advance Zionist aspirations of resettling in Palestine. In 1917 the British Foreign secretary, Lord Balfour, addressed a letter containing the Balfour Declaration, to Walter, Lord Rothschild, which promised a new Jewish homeland. The Rockefellers lobbied not because of any deep sympathy with Jews – as Roggenfelders they had been German Turks – but to advance their grip on world oil supplies.

The British agreed to let Standard Oil into the Near East.[67] Only when that had happened did America come into the war. The Near East gave "Rockefellers" a world platform. After the war, operating from the Near East, Standard Oil obtained access to Romania, Belgium, Ethiopia, Sumatra, Persia, Kamchatka, Turkey, Saudi Arabia, France, Czechoslovakia, and China.

By 1919, following the collapse of the Ottoman Empire, the Oil Empire was based on private corporations (Standard Oil, Shell, British Petroleum), rather than nations.

It was to seize Turkish oilfields that Britain had launched her disastrous campaign against Gallipoli.[68] After the war the victorious British took over the Baku oilfields from the defeated Turks and Germans. In exchange for French help in the Near East, Britain offered Syria a quarter interest in the Turkish Petroleum Co., and in 1920 Britain and France signed an agreement to this effect in San Remo. France however undid this agreement by signing a treaty with Turkey in 1921, whereupon Britain claimed Mosul for Iraq and made Emir Feisal King of Iraq.[69]

In 1920 "Rockefellers" moved to obtain British oilfields. Standard Oil bought half the Baku oil holding of Nobel Oil Co., having battled "Rothschilds"' Royal Dutch and Shell for Baku for eight years.[70] In December 1921 "Rockefellers"' Standard Oil made a deal with Britain for half the Mesopotamian and Palestinian oilfields and a quarter interest in the Turkish Petroleum Co. (formerly the French share) in exchange for half "Rockefellers"' North Persian oilfields.[71] Well satisfied, "Rockefellers" and the US State Department then withdrew their opposition to the League of Nations' willingness to grant mandates to Britain in Palestine and other regions.[72] "Rockefellers" were now well entrenched in the Near East. In 1927 engineers of the quarter-"Rockefellers"' Turkish Petroleum Company struck the first oil in Iraq, at Baba Gurgur, north of Kirkuk.[73]

Russia

The Rockefellers became involved with Russia as well as Germany. The Russian Revolution itself can be seen in part at least in terms of a battle between "Rothschilds"' Royal Dutch Co. and "Rockefellers"' Standard Oil for control of the Russian Baku oilfields. It was in fact a series of revolutions. (Full details of these revolutions can be found in *The Secret History of the West*.)

The first was in 1905, when "Rockefellers" funded Trotsky's abortive attempt via Kuhn Loeb.[74] "Rothschilds" then mobilized Lord Milner (a 33rd-degree Mason whose intransigence as High Commissioner in South Africa had precipitated the Boer War and who had become a minister in Lloyd George's First World War cabinet in 1916) and the British Embassy in Moscow to install Kerensky with a brief to depose the Tsar. Milner spent 21 million roubles financing (around $50 million in current values) to fund this second revolution by Kerensky and his Mensheviks.[75]

"Rockefellers," taken by surprise by Kerensky's revolution, struck back.

Following an emergency meeting at the Grand Orient Lodge in Hamburg, Jacob Schiff, the investment banker, ordered by cable: "Prepare Trotsky."[76] Trotsky (whose real name was Bronstein) was sent back to Russia from the "Rockefeller"/Standard Oil property he had been living on at Constable Hook, Bayonne, New Jersey with Grand Orient backing[77] to liaise with Lenin (real name Ulianov), and precipitate the third revolution which took place in October 1917. Jacob Schiff is alleged to have given $20m ($320m in today's values) to fund this third revolution.[78] It was set up (according to the consensus view) by Max Warburg and Co. of Hamburg, and the Rhineland Westphalia Syndicate, and the funds were placed in the Nya Banken at Stockholm, Sweden (a Warburg bank).[79] Max Warburg was Chief of the Secret Police in Germany,[80] brother to Paul Warburg who masterminded the Federal Reserve. There are also claims that $10 million went to Trotsky, and $15 million to Lenin, who took $5–6 million of that with him on a train on his famous return to Russia.[81]

A cartoon in the *St Louis Post-Dispatch* in 1911 sums it up. Karl Marx stands in Wall Street surrounded by an appreciative audience of financiers: John D Rockefeller, J. P. Morgan, John D. Ryan of National City Bank and Morgan partner George W. Perkins. It was well known that "Rockefellers"(having been thwarted by the Tsar over Baku) were "dee-lighted" (the caption on the cartoon) to be associated with revolutionary activity in Russia.[82]

In 1920 "Rockefellers"' Standard Oil bought half the Baku oil holding of Nobel Oil Co. from the Bolsheviks, as we have seen. When Lenin established his New Economic Policy in 1921, capitalists returned to Russia, whose economy was in chaos. The most notable of the capitalists were the Rockefellers. The Rockefellers' Chase National Bank (later Chase Manhattan) established an American–Russian Chamber of Commerce in 1922, through their representative Frank

Vanderlip and the Harrimans. In 1925 Chase National agreed to finance Soviet raw material imports to the US and export cotton and machinery to the Soviet Union.[83]

When Lenin died in 1924 there was effectively a fourth revolution in which Stalin seized the succession from his rivals, and in 1925 sold a half interest in Russian oil including Baku (which had been previously worked by "Rothschilds") to the Rockefellers in return for funding for his Five-Year Plans.[84] The first Plan was financed in 1926 through Schiff's Kuhn, Loeb & Co., who now acted for the Rockefellers and not for their original clients, the Rothschilds.[85] In March 1926 "Rockefellers'" Standard Oil of New York and its subsidiary Vacuum Oil Co. loaned $75m to the Bolsheviks, bought 800,000 tons of crude oil and 100,000 tons of kerosene from the Russian government and marketed Soviet oil throughout Europe.[86] In 1927 Standard Oil of New York built a refinery in Russia, which helped the Bolsheviks to restore the economy.[87] In 1928 Chase National sold Bolshevik bonds in the US to raise money for Stalin's regime.[88]

"Rockefellers" were now carrying out a twentieth-century policy of imperialism similar to but even more aggressive than the policy of the Rothschilds in the nineteenth century. Countries belonging to the League of Nations (see below) were seeking help from the US. However, as part of the Treaty of Versailles, John D. Rockefeller said that no country could receive a loan unless influential bankers controlled its central bank.[89] Countries without a central bank now set one up, and the east-coast network of banking families controlled all new central banks. The Bank for International Settlement was set up in 1930, and through it the network of families controlled the world's money.[90] In these early decades of the twentieth century we can see the pattern of money, oil, and intervention in the affairs of nations around the world which is still very much with us today.

3

THE NATURE OF
THE SYNDICATE

From the days of Spartacus Weishaupt to those of Karl Marx, to those of Trotsky, Bela-Kuhn, Rosa Luxembourg and Emma Goldman, this world wide conspiracy ... has been steadily growing.

Winston Churchill, Illustrated Sunday Herald, February 8, 1920

A number of individuals and families now controlled a significant proportion of the world's wealth, and were collaborating to promote their joint commercial interest – the Rothschilds, Rockefellers, Warburgs, Morgans, and Schiffs, the families of the influential men who devised the Federal Reserve System on Jekyll Island – and they can now be referred to collectively as "the Syndicate" (my word). The dictionary definition of a "syndicate" is "a combination of individuals or commercial firms to promote some common interest," and this combination of influential families had a common interest.

The Syndicate is dynastic. It has renewed itself from generation to generation, and as we shall see, it continues today. The Schiff, Warburg, Morgan, Harriman, and Milner families have given way to new names. A full list of the most influential corporate families would not be complete without the Astors, the Bundys, the Bushes, the Collinses, the du Ponts, the Eatons, the Freemans, the Kennedys, the Lis, the Onassises, the Reynoldses, the Russells, and the Van Duyns, as well as the Rockefellers, and the Rothschilds.[1]

It is now difficult to distinguish between the individuals and their commercial firms, conglomerates of companies or corporations which shared the common interest of the Syndicate. By placing inverted commas round family names ("Rothschilds," "Rockefellers") I seek to make clear that I am not referring to particular individuals but to a particular emphasis of a commercial pattern. When I have used, and from now on when I use, the terms "Rothschilds" or "Rothschildite," and "Rockefellers" or "Rockefellerite," I am defining an emphasis, a shade within the ethos and outlook on life of the Syndicate rather than the influence of a specific individual; in the case of the "Rothschilds," a commercial drive associated with their nineteenth-century financial dominance and imperialism, and in the case of the "Rockefellers," a commercial drive associated with their twentieth-century acquisition of oil and shaping of international events through revolutions. "Rothschildian" is a descriptive adjective meaning "belonging to" the commercial enterprise of "Rothschilds," as in "Rothschildian oil interests." "Rockefellerite" can similarly mean "belonging to" the commercial enterprise of "Rockefellers." A "Rockefellerite" means a follower of the "Rockefeller" faction within the Syndicate and its policies; a "Rothschildite" means a follower of the "Rothschild" faction within the Syndicate and its policies. "Rockefellerite" and "Rothschildite" mean "pertaining to the faction and policies" of "Rockefellers"/"Rothschilds." (Compare "Thatcherite," which can indicate a member of the Thatcher faction or a follower of a Thatcher policy; or even an economic or commercial direction.)

In the rest of this book I am not making any imputation against the specific behavior of any individual, family, company, or corporation among the Syndicate families and their institutionalized fortunes. Rather, I am presenting the achievements of the Syndicate families as part of a pattern.

I believe some of the corporate leaders and bankers among the élite families had a noble, altruistic vision of a unified world without war, disease, or famine: of a Utopia, a Paradise. Revolutions and ideas of new world orders frequently begin with a noble aim of banishing inequality, hunger, disease, and war. However, if this noble ideal was to be imposed by stealth without the consent of the people of the US, Europe, and other countries of the world, then it was fundamentally undemocratic and wrong in principle, no matter how well-intentioned.

Others had an ignoble, exploitative, self-interested, capitalist vision which was to maximize their billions and turn them into more billions.

To increase their profits, they desired sympathetic world leaders whose political policies would assist their commercial interests and who would be happy to install puppet presidents and prime ministers who would implement their commercial policies. They would use the political situation for their own commercial ends, and were not averse to assisting both sides in a conflict if it suited them

Each of the branches of the Syndicate has their own blend of idealism, practicality, and ambition. But the different branches of the Syndicate, particularly the two factions of the Rothschilds and Rockefellers, are not really in conflict. It's more like the number-one supplier of, say, washing powder, with competing brands of its own product on the shelf. We think we have a choice, but it's offered to us by the same company. We don't realize how powerful and how connected it is because it operates in secret. And your immediate response might be – then how do you know it's there? How does it work?

The first part of the answer is that it works through various inter-linked, often informal organizations, whose relative influence in the US and Europe varies over the years. The more secretive they are, the more significant they sometimes appear to be. When you look at their connections it's often surprising how close they are, despite the surface differences. At any one time in the twentieth century there have been no more than a few hundred individuals in the West who have shaped its history – financiers, politicians, diplomats, monarchs, revolutionaries, media barons, and they all tend to know each other through these groups.

The Round Table

The idea of a society throughout the world working for federal union fascinated Milner as it had fascinated Rhodes.
Carroll Quigley, Anglo-American Establishment

These secretive organizations mostly operate under "Chatham House Rules," an unwritten code (respected by journalists) referring to a forum in which individuals with "status position" can express their personal views confidentially, without future attribution or risk to their reputation, on certain occasions. One such formed in 1910 under the leadership of "Rothschilds" was the Round Table, which was named after a quarterly journal brought out that year. The idea was taken from the legend of King Arthur and his Knights. It originated in a secret group established in South Africa in 1891 by Cecil Rhodes.[2] An "Inner Circle of Initiates," "the Society of the Elect," included: Rhodes; Milner (who was appointed as the main trustee to carry out the terms of Rhodes' last will); Balfour; Nathan, Lord Rothschild; Arnold Toynbee; and Lord Grey. An Outer Circle, "the Association of Helpers," was established by Milner between 1909 and 1913 as the Round Table. This was divided into an Inner Circle that included Arnold Toynbee, and an Outer Circle.[3]

After 1902 it was funded out of the diamond fortune of "Rothschilds" protégé Cecil Rhodes, who expanded British rule in Southern and Central Africa.[4] In his first will, made in 1877 while he was an undergraduate, he left a fortune he had not yet made to the colonial secretary to found a secret society that would work for "the extension of British rule throughout the world ..., the foundation of so great a power as to hereafter render wars impossible and promote the interests of humanity." At Oxford University Rhodes had been taught by John Ruskin that Ruskin's élite students should eventually lead mankind, which would benefit from their rule. In his third will he left his wealth to Nathan Mayer, Lord Rothschild who, for strategic reasons was replaced by Lord Rosebery in the seventh will. Lord Rosebery (who was British Prime Minister in 1894–5) had married into the Rothschild family in 1878 (his wife Hannah was the daughter of Mayer Rothschild).[5] Rhodes's intention was that the £3m fund he left in 1902 should promote the concept of globalism and one-world government, and it set up the Rhodes Scholarships, whose beneficiaries have included Dean Rusk (US Secretary of State throughout the 1960s), Senator Fulbright, and President Bill Clinton.

The Round Table had come together at a time of rapid revolution in communications. The development of flight, which was demonstrated by the Wright brothers in 1903 and led less than a dozen years later to planes flying in the First World War, together with the development of wireless radio made the problem of great distances surmountable and a new round of pressure for world government seemed timely. The goal of the Round Table was "nothing less than to create a world system of financial control in private hands able to dominate the political system of each country and the economy of the world as a whole"[6] – in other words, a one-world government controlled by the international bankers. They saw England as an Atlantic power, not a European power and hoped for a federation of the English-speaking world.

Milner (who believed that "men should strive to build the Kingdom of Heaven here upon this earth, and that the leadership in that task must fall first and foremost upon the English-speaking peoples")[7] spread the Round Table groups to South Africa, Canada, Australia, New Zealand, India, and the US. They were all controlled from England, and their members included the most prominent politicians of the British government, all of whom were dedicated to a one-world government.[8] The Round Table is referred to,[9] by both participants and outsiders, as "the Milner Group," "the Committee of 300" (a separate organization), "the Illuminati" or "neo-Illuminati," and "the Olympians" (meaning, those equal to the gods of Olympus in Greek legend). (References to "the Order" with its "Skull and Bones" ritual indicate the American Templars.) The Illuminati refer to the private Order founded in Frankfurt by the first Rothschild in 1776, following his meetings with Adam Weishaupt. Following the oppression by the elector of Bavaria the Order was hidden in the "Grand Orient," a branch of Freemasonry. In due course the rich Syndicate families such as the Rockefellers and J. P. Morgans were among the Round Table's financiers. Through the Astor family the Round Table controlled the London *Times* newspaper. The parallel American Round-Table group, controlled by J. P. Morgan and Co., had an identical goal.[10] It included leaders of the Carnegie Endowment and other US-based foundations. According to the Carnegie Endowment's own documents, its leaders concluded in 1911 that the best way to alter a people's life is to involve it in war.

Fabian Society

Stealth, intrigue, subversion, and the deception of never calling socialism by its right name.

Shaw, on the Fabian Society

The Rothschilds have generally been identified after Waterloo with the imperial drives of Britain and other major European countries. The intellectual movement of internationalism reflected similar aims, though by different methods. The Rothschilds also had an interest in funding these movements. For instance they funded Karl Marx, author of the *Communist Manifesto*, to write *Das Kapital* in the 1860s.[11] The major expression of internationalism in the UK was the Fabian Society, a socialist society founded in London in 1883–4 by George Bernard Shaw, Sidney and Beatrice Webb, and others.[12] The Society believed in gradual revolution to bring about a socialist one-world government and was named after the Roman general Fabius Maximus, nicknamed "Cunctator" for his delaying tactics during the Second Punic War.[13] The Society's emblem was (and is) a wolf in sheep's clothing. Generally Fabian plans have not been presented under the names of individuals (George Bernard Shaw, Sidney and Beatrice Webb, Annie Besant, John Galsworthy, R. H. Tawney, H. G. Wells, and Harold Laski), but under the think-tanks and planning units they created as fronts: the LSE (London School of Economics, in 1895), PEP (Political and Economic Planning), and FU (Federal Union).[14] Among the LSE's major contributors were the Rockefeller Foundation and Mrs. Ernest Elmhirst, the widow of J. P. Morgan partner Willard Straight.[15] The Fabian Society's best-known publication is the *Economist*, but its tradition of *Fabian Essays in Socialism*, edited in 1899 by Shaw,[16] has been continued in the *New Fabian Essays*, edited in 1952 by R. H. S. Crossman, later a British Labour minister.

After the First World War Fabian influence spread to Europe, where Jean Monnet, a young French socialist sent to Canada in 1910 who had met the exclusive group of one-worlders round Woodrow Wilson's special advisor, Col. House, and had been made deputy secretary general of the League of Nations in 1919,[17] represented the message. Fabianism also spread to America, where the Supreme Court Justice and Communist sympathizer Felix Frankfurter[18] established an American version of PEP – the NPA (the National Planning Association) – which was followed by the BAC (the Business Advisory Council). These three organizations worked closely with the Council on Foreign Relations to promote a United States of Europe. Frankfurter's Fabian policy of amending the US Constitution has tilted it towards socialism. Frankfurter became a close friend of Harold Laski, a Marxist Professor at the LSE, and they frequently exchanged visits and ideas, and Laski became a friend of Roosevelt.

The League of Nations

Collective security.
President Woodrow Wilson to the Senate, 1917

The armistice that ended the First World War had been based on Woodrow Wilson's 14–point proposals for a post-war peace settlement, and this was included in the Treaty of Versailles. The clauses of the treaty were worked out at an international Grand Orient Masonic Congress held at their headquarters in Rue Cadet, Paris, in June 1917.[19] They had the idea for the League of Nations and worked out the clauses of the constitution. The minutes for a preliminary planning meeting in January 1917 speak of "elaborating the Constitution of the League of Nations." "Rothschilds'" representative Col. House (a 33rd-degree Grand-Lodge Mason) was in charge. President Wilson took the idea from Col. House,[20] and represented the US at the Peace Conference. Bernard Baruch, who had made $200m for himself while head of the War Industries Board,[21] was also in the American delegation to the Paris Peace Conference. The English delegation included Sir Philip Sassoon, a direct descendent of Mayer Amschel Rothschild; and the French delegation included Georges Mandel (who was also known as Jereboam Rothschild).[22]

The stated aim of the League was to solve international disputes and reduce arms. But the Grand Orient wanted the Treaty of Versailles between the Allies and Germany (1919) to transfer the wealth of the fallen monarchies to the Grand Orient nations in the form of war reparations.[23] War reparations would cripple Germany, and the Treaty of Versailles included a 20–year truce, which split up Europe. As Lloyd George pointed out: "We have written a document that guarantees war in 20 years .... When you place conditions on a people (Germany) that it cannot possibly keep, you force it to either breach the agreement or to war."[24] Lloyd George was prescient, almost to the year.

The US Senate, however, then rejected the League, and in 1921 made a separate peace treaty with Germany and Austria.[25] Maybe for oil and money interests peace was not such a good idea. Maybe a public organization like this, in the media spotlight, wasn't what they really wanted and needed.

The Royal Institute of International Affairs

The Royal Institute of International Affairs (RIIA) is nothing but the Milner Group "writ large."

Carroll Quigley, Anglo-American Establishment

When news of the rejection by the US of the League of Nations reached Col. House in Paris, where he was constructing the Versailles Treaty, pro-globalist Americans met their pro-globalist British counterparts and established in principle two organizations that would fulfill the plans of the Round Table.[26]

The first of these two organizations to be set up was the British one. In 1919 Lionel Curtis, secretary to Lord Milner, established a front system[27] for the Round Table known as the Royal Institute of International Affairs (RIIA), which was also known as the Chatham House Study Group as its headquarters (until 1961) were in Chatham House, Ormond Yard (which gave its name to the "Chatham House Rules"). Its first paid official was the world-government federalist historian Arnold Toynbee, who later became its Director. Its initial endowment was £2,000 from Thomas Lamont of J. P. Morgan,[28] and it has since received many millions of dollars from the Rockefeller Foundation and Carnegie Corporation.[29]

The American version was the Institute of International Affairs (IIA), formed in July 1919 by Col. House, following a year of meetings in New York.[30] House was an admirer of Karl Marx, and had written a novel (*Philip Dru: Administrator*) about establishing "socialism as dreamed of by Karl Marx" and about the creation of a one-world totalitarian government with a central bank and income tax. House implemented the philosophy of his book during his time as Wilson's advisor.[31]

In May 1919 Baron Edmond de Rothschild hosted a dinner in Paris for Colonel House's IIA (which was supported by a number of J. P. Morgan's associates) and the Round Table (Milner, Curtis, and others). It was decided that the two organizations should remain separate.[32]

In 1922 the RIIA apparently asked Major John Rawlings Reese to set up the largest brainwashing and psychological warfare facility in the world at the Tavistock Institute for Human Relations, part of Sussex University. Since then the US government has given contracts worth billions of dollars to Tavistock.[33]

The British RIIA's original aims were to extend the British Empire into a world government.[34] Its leaders in London were Lionel Curtis, secretary to Milner in South Africa and founder of the quarterly *Round Table* in 1910, and Lord Lothian (a relative of the current British Conservative Party Shadow Foreign Secretary, Michael Ancram, whose father inherited the title from a cousin), John Maynard Keynes, and Alfred Zimmern (an Oxford Professor and author of *The League of Nations and the Rule of Law*), who introduced his pupil Arnold Toynbee, the celebrated historian.[35] Meetings began in July 1920, and Toynbee wrote the first annual International Survey in 1924.[36] In a speech given in Copenhagen in 1931 Toynbee declared: "We are at present working with all our might to wrest this mysterious force called sovereignty out of the clutches of the local national states of our world. And all the time we are denying with our lips what we are doing with our hands."[37]

John D. Rockefeller made a contribution of £8,000 pa from 1932,[38] and was known to Toynbee. On the American CFR side, the leaders were Woodrow Wilson, Col. House, Christian Herter, Tasker Bliss (acting chief of staff to US troops during the First World War and US delegate to the Paris Peace Conference), and John Foster Dulles and his brother Allen Dulles. Walter Lippmann was influential, as were Robert Schuman and Paul Warburg.[39]

The link between Chatham House and the CFR (see below) was strong because of the friendship between John Foster Dulles, chairman of the Trustees of the Rockefeller Foundation, and Arnold Toynbee, who regularly exchanged visits. "Rockefellers" partly funded Toynbee through Dulles.[40]

When Toynbee went to the US, Dulles arranged speaking engagements for him through the CFR.[41] Both men believed that the nation-state should die, although they had differing political views: Dulles was a Republican who saw the end of Europe's nation-states as guaranteeing peace, while Toynbee was virtually a Marxist and was ideologically opposed to the nation-state.[42]

Toynbee was the central figure at Chatham House from 1925 until he retired in 1955; he was Director of Studies there (as well as being Professor at the London School of Economics, which had been founded by the Fabians in 1895) and he was central to the campaign for world federation.[43] His 12 volumes of *A Study of History* brought him international fame, and he exercised the influence this gave him by arguing that nation-states should be destroyed[44] and replaced by large blocs which would one day lead to a world government. He criticized Curtis's belief in Empire federation with sovereign states as "monomania," and ran a series of international study conferences that promoted internationalism. He argued that if Europe lost influence to China or South Africa, the new international society would be an outgrowth of Western civilization from European roots. The internationalist Clement Attlee, leader of the British Labour Party, told the Party's Conference in 1934 in words that echoed Toynbee's theme: "We are deliberately putting loyalty to a world order above loyalty to our own country."[45] Toynbee's friends were pioneers of the European Union, such as the Bolsheviks R. H. Tawney and William Temple (later Archbishop of Canterbury), who supported a federal and regional world structure and a united Europe that subsumed 25 sovereign states.[46] This view was supported by Visser t'Hooft, ecumenist and general secretary of the World Council of Churches, who in the spring of 1945 was given $1m by John D. Rockefeller Jr. to promote ecumenism.[47] Dulles sent American churchmen to visit Toynbee.[48] In due course the creation of Benelux, the union of Belgium, the Netherlands, and Luxembourg, took place as a result of planning by the Federal Union in London, Arnold Toynbee, and John Foster Dulles.[49]

Council on Foreign Relations

> The real rulers in Washington are invisible, and exercise power from behind the scenes.
>
> *Felix Frankfurter, justice of the US Supreme Court* [50]

A separate version of the RIIA in the USA was called the Council on Foreign Relations (CFR). This will crop up frequently during the book. It was a front[51] for the "Rothschild"-affiliated J. P. Morgan and Co., who controlled a small Round Table group, and it was incorporated on July 21, 1921 out of the IIA, which supported the League of Nations, and out of the Round Table, which wanted to weaken the League to strengthen Germany and isolate England from Europe so as to establish an Anglo-American Atlantic power of England, the British Dominions, and the United States.[52] The CFR also included participants of the Paris Peace talks. It was decided that now that America was growing in confidence and had intervened in Europe to win victory in the First World War, the American Round Table would in future be an American entity, based in the Institute of Advanced Study at Princeton University, and not connected with the British Round Table based at All Souls College, Oxford.[53] The ubiquitous Col. House wrote the CFR's Charter,[54] and it was financed by Paul Warburg, Jacob Schiff, Averill Harriman, Vanderlip, Baruch, Aldrich, J. P. Morgan, John D. Rockefeller, Kahn, Wiggin, and Lehman. Its 150 members had mostly worked on the Versailles Peace Treaty, and many were linked to J. P. Morgans.[55] The CFR's posture was to study international relations, but in fact its members were to infiltrate the American government and influence its agenda.[56] The CFR members, the financiers of the Syndicate, are known as "Insiders," "the Establishment," or "the invisible government."

In 1927 they were funded by the Rockefeller Foundation, fresh from its new involvement with Stalin – and Bolivia, where Standard Oil (New Jersey) had just located oilfields – and later by the Carnegie and Ford Foundations, and J. P. Morgans.[57] In 1929 the CFR's headquarters were moved to 58 East 68th Street in New York (where they still are).[58] This building was funded by "Rockefellers" and has been called "the Foreign Office of the Rockefeller Empire."[59] Beside it stand two other emblems of the "Rockefeller"–Soviet Axis: the building of the Soviet delegation to the UN and "Rockefellers" Institute of Public Administration, which controlled the city and State governments. By 1936 the CFR had 250 members. Almost every key position in every administration from Roosevelt to the present time has been held by a CFR member, and since 1945 practically every Presidential candidate has been a CFR member.[60] Today there are some 3,000 members.

Institute of Pacific Relations

The chief figure in the Institute of Pacific Relations of the U.S. was, for many years, Jerome D. Greene, Boston banker known to both Rockefeller and Morgan.

Carroll Quigley, Anglo-American Establishment

In 1925 Curtis established the Institute of Pacific Relations (IPR) in 12 countries.[61] By 1927, when the American Council of the IPR signed the group's Constitution, the IPR was dependent on "Rockefellers," which gave it grants totaling $2m over a period of 25 years.[62]

The IPR was organized at the same time as Standard Oil's deal to buy surplus Russian oil, the basis of the "Rockefeller"–Soviet Axis, which was underway in 1925–6.[63] Lenin had said, "Who controls Asia, controls the world."[64] Half the world's population is in Asia, which is rich in resources, and Hitler's expansionist-thinking Haushofer as well as Lenin sought conquest of the world through domination of the Eurasian land mass. The IPR's agenda was extending "Rockefellers'" influence in Asia, in particular taking control of South-East Asian oil from Royal Dutch Shell.[65] With this end in view it has been claimed that it controlled the moves that led to America's entry into the Second World War.[66] Information is now coming out that USS *Ward* provoked the attack on Pearl Harbor,[67] and that "Rockefellers'" Institute knew in advance when the attack would take place and that it would involve the US in war.[68]

The Japanese swept through Asia and seized all the oil holdings of Royal Dutch Shell in South-East Asia. With the defeat of Japan in 1945, most of Royal Dutch Shell's oilfields in South-East Asia came under the control of "Rockefellers'" Standard Oil.[69]

The Bilderberg Group

It is difficult to re-educate the people who have been brought up on nationalism to the idea of relinquishing part of their sovereignty to a supranational body.

Prince Bernhard

The degree to which some names crop up in many different organizations will have become apparent. Even ones seemingly on different sides of the political spectrum are linked, through contacts or financing. The one group that brings them together more than any other has been described as the Bilderberg Group.

It became known as this because they first met at the Hotel de Bilderberg in Oosterbeck, Holland, in May 1954. The participants called the group "the Alliance."[70] Journalists, unable to learn the group's name, dubbed them "Bilderbergers."

The host of the first Bilderberg meeting, Prince Bernhard of the

Netherlands (Queen Juliana's husband) had backed Hitler and become an SS officer during the Second World War.[71] At the end of the war he had returned to the Hague Grand Lodge, and was a major stockholder in Royal Dutch Shell, the "Rothschild"-dominated oil company.[72] A member of the House of Orange, Bernhard claimed descent from the Merovingian line which produced the Kings of Jerusalem.[73] In a sense, the Bilderberg Group was founded by a descendent of Godfroi de Bouillon, who became King of Jerusalem in 1099. As well as the German Prince Bernhard the "Bilderberger" group was organized by Dr. Joseph Retinger, a Polish Communist; Colin Gubbins, director of British Special Operations Executive; and Gen. Bedell Smith, former US Ambassador to Moscow and director of the CIA.[74] It is reputed to have been created by the Chairman of the RIIA, Alastair Buchan, son of author John Buchan (Lord Tweedsmuir), with input from Arnold Toynbee.[75] Its governing council included representatives of N. M. Rothschild, Schröder Bank, the *New York Times*, the RIIA, the CIA, and Henry Kissinger.[76] Its members, who were handpicked by Baron Edmond de Rothschild and Laurance Rockefeller, were 100 of the world's élite, many drawn from the CFR which now dovetailed with the Bilderberg Group, the English-Speaking Union, the Pilgrims Society, and the Round Table.[77] Every member of the Bilderberg Steering Committee was a member of the Council on Foreign Relations.[78] The Rothschilds were active through Edmond and Guy de Rothschild, both prominent Bilderbergers.[79]

"Rockefellers" and "Rothschilds" share power in the Group, which has met every year since 1954 – the Rothschilds hosting meetings held in Europe – and which has had a huge influence on world events. Out of their deliberations have come all the major developments of the last 50 years.[80]

Of course it might be that the Bilderberg Group is an academic body, a network that has met privately to discuss world issues. Of course it's natural for world players to have a private forum in which they can raise issues beyond those dictated for them by the public arena, where they aren't circumscribed by civil servants and local political agendas, where they can discuss longer term concerns and goals. If so, then why is the security so intense for their meetings, with helicopters, police cordons, and reporters being harshly treated? And why does it go to elaborate lengths to keep its name out of the press? Leading press barons either attend the meetings or send representatives; they have the knowledge to report meetings if so inclined. But they never do. On July 3, 2003 British radio (BBC4) aired a half hour program on the Bilderberg group. Reporter Simon Cox tried (unsuccessfully) to find out what was being discussed at the 2003 Bilderberg meeting, and concluded that the reluctance to speak about the Syndicate was akin to *omerta*, the Mafia code of silence.

At the 1993 Bilderberg meeting (attended among others by future English Prime Minister Blair – future Chancellor Gordon Brown having attended the June 1991 Bilderberg meeting),[81] David Rockefeller was reported as thanking newspaper editors who "have respected for nearly four decades their promises to remain discreet" for "it would have been impossible to develop *our project (or plan) for the world* if we had been subject to the full blaze of publicity during these years."[82] He is reported to have said, "The supranational sovereignty of an intellectual élite is surely preferable to the self-determination of nations practiced in past centuries. Hence we are obliged to keep the press abreast of our convictions pertaining to the historical future of the century."[83] If the Bilderberg Group makes policies rather than observations, this "project for the world" will require all who attend Bilderberg meetings to keep silent about plans to violate national sovereignty, which their allegiance to their sovereign monarch or president requires them to reveal. If they do not they are technically committing treason.

We need to bear these considerations in mind as the events unfold.

The Club of Rome

A new global community under a common leadership.

Club of Rome Report

The Club of Rome first met in April 1968 at Rockefeller's private estate in Bellagio, Italy.[84] It was officially founded in 1968 by Aurelio Peccei, Chief Executive Officer of Giovanni Agnelli's Fiat Motor Company and head of the Atlantic Institute's Economic council for three decades, though it's also claimed that the Grand Orient was the driving force. He told his close friend the former American Secretary of State Alexander Haig that he felt "like Adam Weishaupt reincarnated."[85]

The Club of Rome speaks on American affairs, Germany and Japan, and depopulation.[86] It is credited with having formulated NATO's post-1968 policies and as operating under cover of NATO.[87] It is composed of 100 prominent Anglo-American financiers and selected scientists, industrialists, and economists of the world.[88]

The Trilateral Commission

> The Trilateral Commission was David Rockefeller's idea originally.
>
> George Franklin, North American Secretary of the Trilateral Commission

Against the background of American retreat from Vietnam, a new Commission had been proposed[89] by David Rockefeller (Chairman of the CFR since 1970 and now a Director of the Federal Reserve Bank of New York) and Zbigniew Brzezinski, a "Rockefeller" advisor and specialist in international affairs, after they attended the Bilderberg conference of 1971 which led to President Nixon announcing great changes in international policy. The US was in economic difficulties, and pressured Japan and Western Europe into relaxing trade barriers. The new policy towards China was implemented, allowing the prospect of US trade with China, where "Rockefellers" owned oil.

In the early 1970s, during the creation of the Trilateral Commission, David Rockefeller spent much of his time flying round the globe in his private Grumman Gulfstream jet visiting world leaders to give advice. He kept a card index of 35,000 "personal friends" in high places round the world.[90] Rockefeller's power was now so great that it was said he was no longer subject to customs or passport controls (and according to a CFR journalist, "hardly pauses for traffic lights"). The result of his efforts was the creation of the Trilateral Commission.

This had been proposed at the Bilderberg meeting of 1972, when Brzezinski suggested[91] the creation of an International Commission of Peace and Prosperity, which later became the Trilateral Commission because it focused on North America, Western Europe, and Japan. David Rockefeller and the Kettering and Ford Foundations funded the new body.[92]

The Trilateral Commission was an offshoot of the Bilderberg Group, the CFR, RIIA, and IPR (Institute of Pacific Relations), which were in turn descended from the Round Table of the Syndicate and English Freemasonry. Its member nations are the G7 industrial powers: the US, Canada, Great Britain, France, Germany, Italy, and Japan. About 250 members attended the Trilateral Commission's first meeting in 1972.[93]

Is the idea that these groups are linked, that they act in cohort,[94] that they have aims that may run counter to the interests of the nation states of the different members, sheer fiction?

Dreams of world domination by secretive groups may seem like fiction to you. But it's not fiction to those involved. Read the novels of John Buchan, who became Governor-General of Canada, to get an idea of the way these people think. All I can do is point you to where the connections exist, and let you draw your own conclusions.

4

THE UNITED STATES OF ALL
THE AMERICAS – AND THE WORLD

The twenty-first century ... will be the era of World Controllers.
Aldous Huxley, Brave New World Revisited

The idea that there could be a small group of individuals working together to subvert nation-states, building regional blocs as a stepping-stone to world government, may seem bizarre to you. Even more so, that it may have a secret, even occultic side. But it's happening in front of our eyes. It finds its fullest expression in the US.

The Founding of the United States

I have dealt with the American Revolution fully in *The Secret History of the West*. In mid-1776 Congress adopted Richard Henry Lee's resolution "That these United Colonies are, and of right ought to be, free and independent States." Thomas Jefferson was asked to draft the Declaration of Independence, which was approved (with changes) in the State House (now Independence Hall), Philadelphia on July 4. Jefferson's words eloquently expressed the philosophy of the new federation.

On Lee's proposal, work began on the Articles of Confederation, the new country's first constitution. The Articles, passed in 1778, left Congress too weak to govern effectively. Once freedom had been won in 1783, and the Continental Army had been disbanded after Yorktown, an attempt was made to perfect the mechanism of the government. In May 1787 delegates in the Constitutional Convention met at Philadelphia's State House and wrote a new constitution.

With George Washington presiding and with help from the 81–year-old Benjamin Franklin, delegates scrapped the Articles of Confederation and created a charter for a "more perfect Union." They established three branches of government – executive, legislative, and judicial – and decided the issue of representation. Large states had fought for proportional representation, smaller states for an equal voice. The founding fathers of the constitution gave proportional representation to the House of Representatives and equal representation to the Senate. They were not specific enough on rights, and between September 1789 and December 1791 Congress passed 10 amendments guaranteeing personal freedoms, known as the Bill of Rights.[1]

The Great Seal

Most of the founding fathers were Freemasons: of 56 signatories to the Declaration of Independence, 53 were Master Masons.[2] Washington and Lee were Templar Masons, while Franklin was a Templar, a Rosicrucian, *and* a French Grand Orient Mason.[3] Benjamin Franklin was the Provincial Grand Master of the Rosicrucian Masons in Pennsylvania,[4] familiar with English Freemasonry's Great Plan to create a Baconian "philosophical Atlantis"[5] in America. Thomas Jefferson and John Adams were Rosicrucians and Freemasons.[6] The instigators of the Boston Tea Party, Joseph Warren, Paul Revere, and Samuel Adams, were all Templar Masons from St Andrew's Lodge.[7] George Washington was a Templar Grand Mason, and all his generals were Templars, as was Marquis de Lafayette.[8]

Even the constitution of the USA is parallel to the Masonic federal system of government.[9] Washington DC was laid out by the Masonic founding fathers to form Masonic symbols: a compass, square, rule, pentagram, pentagon, and octagon.[10] All the main federal buildings from the White House to the capitol have had a cornerstone and specific Masonic regalia laid in a Masonic ritual.[11]

The founding fathers had a Freemasonic-style Seal in mind. Late in the afternoon of July 4, 1776, after the Declaration of Independence had been signed, they passed a resolution: "Resolved, that Dr. Franklin, Mr. J. Adams, and Mr. Jefferson be a committee to prepare a device for a Seal of the United States of America."[12] The three men were Masons.

In September 1776 Congress agreed to send a commission to France to seek economic and military help. Franklin was one of three commissioners who arrived in Paris before Christmas. There he met a representative of the new Order of the Illuminati,[13] which had been created that year by Adam Weishaupt for Mayer Amschel Rothschild. The representative may have been Weishaupt himself; alternatively, the meeting could have resulted in another meeting with Weishaupt. Franklin was shown the Seal of the Illuminati, whose declared aim was a world federation. The Seal displayed an unfinished pyramid under a Masonic all-seeing Eye. The date 1776 in Latin was written on the lowest level of bricks in the pyramid, and the Latin tags "*Annuit Coeptis*" and "*Novus Ordo Seclorum*" appeared on the top and bottom of the round Seal.[14] Franklin incorporated the Seal of the Illuminati as the reverse of his two-sided design for the Great Seal of the United States, which was adopted in 1782. In other words, the founding fathers chose a Freemasonic Seal.[15]

The obverse side shows a tufted phoenix. It is a Freemasonic symbol. The reverse side of the Seal shows an unfinished building, the university in the old Atlantis: a pyramid of 13 layers of bricks symbolizing the 13 American Templar colonies that would become a New Atlantis under Sion's disembodied eye.[16] On the bottom layer of bricks is the year 1776, the year in which Weishaupt founded his organization, whose Seal represented the secret Doctrine of the Ages, the plan to build a New Atlantis in a New World.[17] Today the eagle-like nature of that phoenix[18] – it is a hybrid eagle-phoenix – suggests the virtue of the American people. It bears the escutcheon on its shoulders, calling on Americans to be self-reliant. It clutches arrows (war) and an olive branch (peace) and bears the

obverse   *reverse*

The Great Seal of the United States of America

inscription "*E Pluribus Unum*" in the lettering, suggesting "out of many, one," i.e. union, the unification of nations,[19] but also egalitarianism. The 13 stars in the glory cloud are gathered into a six-pointed star suggesting the Star of David, two overlaid equilateral triangles which Kabbalists used to ward off evil spirits, and which after the seventeenth century became the official seal of the Jewish communities.[20]

On the reverse side of the Seal over the spying eye of Sion[21] is "*Annuit Coeptis*," "Announcing the Birth," which signifies a divine blessing for America's new society. Underneath the land of Atlantis is the Latin phrase "*Novus Ordo Seclorum*" (which strictly means "new secular order" or "new order of the ages"). The whole means "announcing the birth of a new secular order" or of a new world order.[22]

The reverse of this Seal is now to be seen on the dollar bill. In 1933 or 1934 the "Rockefellerite" Templar[23] Mason Henry A. Wallace, Secretary of Agriculture (in charge of presenting the New Deal) and later US Vice-President, was impressed by the tag on the Seal, which he translated as "the New Deal of the Ages." He brought this to the attention of his fellow Templar Mason Roosevelt, who put them on the dollar bill, and after 153 years of obscurity the reverse of the Seal came fully into the public domain. The tag gave currency backing to his "New Deal" policy (adopted on advice from the young Nelson Rockefeller and first announced in July 1932).[24]

The Utopian pyramid on the reverse of the Seal has now come to be a symbol of the New World Order, the still uncompleted unity of a world government in which all nations are bricks. The meaning of the Seal is that it's America's spiritual destiny to complete its building, that the Templars have been given the task of building a world government under the watchful eye of Sion, that when the sun-rayed capstone – symbolizing the Merovingian successor to the ancient King of Jerusalem – is finally lowered onto the pyramid, the world government will be complete.[25]

This could all be coincidence. But if it looks like a duck, walks like a duck, and quacks like a duck, let's be open to the possibility at least that it is a duck. American republicanism was Templar. Its origins were secretive and occult as much as they were democratic and Christian. The USA, in part at least, and in intention, was a Templar-created Masonic state ruled by Templars.[26] Don't take my word for it, look at a dollar bill yourself, and see if you can come up with a better explanation for its strange images.

The Spread of the Federal Template

The founding fathers' work, spanning 15 years between 1776 and 1791, established a pattern or template for federalism – for turning individual colonies into a federated union with local autonomy and a degree of central control.

As America grew and more states were added between 1784 and 1854, the principle of regional government established by the Founding Fathers extended throughout the United States.

More recently the whole of North America has drawn together. Mexico had won its independence from Spain in 1821, and there was intense competition for its oil around 1910, when the British, who dominated Mexico's oilfields, were replaced by "Rockefellers"' Standard Oil. The United States has now drawn in Mexico and Canada, once a British dominion. All three are now members of the North American Free Trade Agreement (NAFTA).

The same process has been happening in Central America. The Central American Free Trade Agreement (CAFTA) covers US trade with five Central American nations: El Salvador, Guatemala, Nicaragua, Honduras and Costa Rica.

The Latin American Free Trade Association (LAFTA) was created in 1960 to establish a common market for its member nations, and it was replaced in 1980 by the Latin American Integration Association (LAIA), formed by Argentina, Bolivia, Brazil, Chile, Colombia, Ecuador, Mexico, Paraguay, Peru, Uruguay, and Venezuela to encourage free trade, with no deadline for the institution of a common market. Economic hardship in Argentina, Brazil, and other member nations has made LAIA's task difficult. This Latin American free trade area has been a stepping-stone to such a regional bloc (which will one day include the Falkland Islands).

There is a Caribbean Free Trade Association (CARIFTA). There are potential links between the Caribbean countries and Latin America: there is a 480–mile-long Occidental Petroleum pipeline from the second largest oilfield in Colombia (the seventh largest supplier of petroleum to the US) to the Caribbean coast.

Throughout South and Central America a network of oil and gas pipelines is being extended all the time, linking the states in Free Trade agreements through energy interconnections.

An effort is being made to unite the colonies of the Western hemisphere into a single free trade arrangement. This began at the Summit of the Americas held in December 1994 in Miami. The heads of state of the 34 democracies in the region agreed to construct a Free Trade Area of the Americas (FTAA) by 2005. The 34 states are: Antigua and Barbuda, Argentina, Bahamas, Barbados, Belize, Bolivia, Brazil, Canada, Chile, Colombia, Costa Rica, Dominica, Dominican Republic, Ecuador, El Salvador, Grenada, Guatemala, Guyana, Haiti, Honduras, Jamaica, Mexico, Nicaragua, Panama, Paraguay, Peru, St Vincent and the Grenadines, St Lucia, St Kitts and Nevis, Surinam, Trinidad and Tobago, Uruguay, the United States of America, and Venezuela.[27]

The FTAA is in partnership between the 34 governments and non-governmental organizations and multinational corporations in the private sector, such as: the Organization of American States (OAS), the World Bank, the Inter-American Development Bank, and the UN Economic Commission on Latin American and the Caribbean (ECLAC). A granite-and-marble building two blocks away from the White House, called the Organization of American States, is a "Congress" of all the 34 countries in the Western hemisphere. The US sends representatives to regional meetings there. Bush Jr. has continued Clinton's hemispheric policy: "My administration is committed to free trade – the first administration in a long time to achieve trade promotion authority from the Congress. And we're using that to promote free trade agreements on a bilateral basis, on a hemispheric basis" (joint press briefing with Blair, 2003).[28]

Regional thinking has already been implemented, and US business is being transferred to Central America. For example, the Maryland Crab Industry has been shut down allegedly because of conditions in the Chesapeake Bay and crabs are now brought into the area from Mexico or Chile. The dollar is to be integrated with the Chilean, Brazilian, and Mexican peso.

The political and economic integration of the Western hemisphere is already a *fait accompli*, and the US is no longer solely acting as the United States of America but as part of a greater unit, the Free Trade Area of the Americas – just as European states act as part of a greater unit, the European Union.

Ahead is the prospect of an American Union of all countries in North, Central, and South America.

The American Union is being strengthened by the Council of the Americas, a group of top bankers and businessmen founded by "Rockefellers" in 1965 to consolidate their financial operations throughout the Western hemisphere. Its most ambitious goal is the launch in 2005 of the Free Trade Area of the Americas (FTAA), the world's largest free-trade zone that will include every nation in North and South America except for Communist Cuba. "Rockefellerites" have been appointed to two key central banks in South America. The "Rockefellerite" Hernando Meirelles (former director of the Council of the Americas) has been appointed to front Brazil's central bank, and Alfonso Prat-Gay (former head of emerging market research for David Rockefeller's J. P. Morgan Chase) is President of the Argentine central bank.

The Council of the Americas' sister group, the Americas Society, which was also founded by David Rockefeller in 1965, has sought to strengthen the American Union's hold over South-American oil. On January 15, 2003 it convened a meeting of the leading members of the Venezuelan opposition in New York to topple President Hugo Chavez, the leader of Venezuela, which supplies 10 to 15% of the United States' oil needs, and bring about a "regime change." The meeting was hosted by Gustavo Cisneros, an advisor member of the CFR and the Americas Society with a $5.3b fortune and numerous links to "Rockefellers," who was suspected of bankrolling the failed April 2002 "Rockefellerite" *coup* against Chavez.[29]

The Syndicate's Federal Plan

Economically the whole of North, Central, and South America will be one market, and there is a plan for the federal form of government devised by the US's founding fathers to be extended to the entire American Continent, from north to south. It will be one massive regional bloc, the Western World, labeled on the map of the office of the US Trade Representative as the Western Hemisphere.

There is a plan[30] for the same principle of a "United States"-style constitution to be applied to other regional blocs – to Europe, Russia, the former Soviet Republics, the Middle East, and Africa. To advance towards this the plan is that there will be a regional United States of Europe (including Russia and the former Soviet Republics), a regional United States of the Middle East (or United Arab States), and a regional United

States of Africa. (In July 2000 an Organization of African Unity summit approved Gaddafi's idea that an African Union, a United States of Africa, should replace the OAU, and this was delivered in 2002.) Collectively it is planned that these will form the Central World. It is labeled on the US Trade Representative map as Europe and the Mediterranean, and Africa.

Similarly, the Eastern World – labeled by the US Trade Representative as Asia and the Pacific, and no doubt to be called in due course the Eastern Hemisphere – will comprise India, Pakistan, China, Japan, South and South-East Asia, Australia, and New Zealand. The South Asian Free Trade Area (SAFTA) was signed in January 2004 by 7 nations (India, Pakistan, Bangladesh, Bhutan, Nepal, Sri Lanka, and the Maldives).

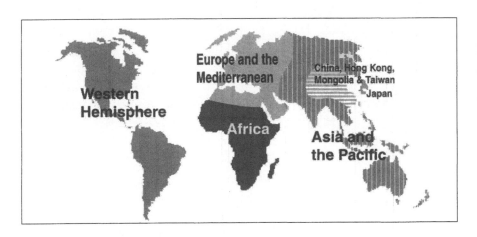

US Trade Representative's map of World Regions[31]

There are already signs that these three huge world blocs will be connected. India is encouraging the idea of an Asian Economic Community that would include ASEAN (10 countries in the Association of South-East Asian Nations which include Thailand, the Philippines, Malaysia, and Indonesia), China (which has undertaken to sign a Free Trade Agreement with ASEAN by 2010), Japan, and Korea. There is already a connection between Russia (Central World) and China and Japan (Eastern World).[32] Mutual self-interest had brought China and Russia together in the

'Shanghai Five' group of nations, along with Kazakhstan, Kyrgyzstan and Tajikistan. China plans to import Russian oil and gas. Despite being the world's fifth largest oil producer, China has become a net oil importing country due to its economic growth. China and Russia plan a web of pipelines crossing Central Asia and Russian Siberia to China's Pacific coast, so that by 2010 China could be a distribution hub for oil and gas exports to South Korea and Japan, two of the largest energy-importing states in the world. China is subduing separatists in the western province of Xinjiang, whence gas and oil pipelines are to run to the east-cost of Shanghai at a cost of $14.2b. Xinjiang will be the second-largest oil-producing region in China (after the north-east), with reserves of 20.9b tonnes. In October 2000 "Rockefellers'" US-based ExxonMobil purchased 19% of one of the Chinese oil companies, Sinopec; and two months earlier British-based BP Amoco purchased 2.2% of PetroChina. ExxonMobil is one of the largest foreign players developing Central Asian and Far Eastern oil and gas, with major oil interests in Azerbaijan and Kazakhstan and gas interests in Turkmenistan and on Russia's Sakhalin Island (north of Japan). It is preparing to pipe gas from east Turkmenistan to China. Both China and Japan are currently vying for pipelines to transport Russian oil from Angarsk in Siberia to Nakhodka (also in Siberia) for Japan, at a cost of £3.2b, and to Daquing in China, at a cost of £1.5b. Russia prefers the Nakhodka route as it would retain control over its pipeline and could export oil to China, South Korea, and the US from Nakhodka.[33]

That is the plan the Trilateral Commission are working towards: reducing 10 kingdoms drawn up by the Club of Rome in 1973 to three blocs.[34] Will the plan to extend the US founding fathers' concept to the entire world succeed? The plan assumes that the history of each world region can be interrupted and redefined in terms of its connection with the Western, Central, and Eastern Worlds, and eventually a unification of these three blocs.

In another work, *The Fire and the Stones*, I have considered the rise and fall of 25 dead and living civilizations, carrying forward the tradition and vision of Gibbon, Spengler, and Toynbee. I have concluded that all civilizations – for example, the Egyptian and Roman civilizations – have a lifecycle of 61 stages. It so happens that the North American civilization is currently in the same stage that the Roman civilization was in when it ruled the world.

I have considered whether the mold can be broken by a one-bloc world government and have concluded that the cycles of civilizations have to take their course to their end, and that any attempt to impose a "world government" pattern on all civilizations, some of which are thousands of years old (for example, the Indian civilization), is doomed to failure. For the internal organic life of each civilization will be too strong for the controlling authority. The UN (which takes its troops from the world's nation-states) is not strong enough to impose such a new pattern on all civilizations.

I have concluded that the only way such a one-world pattern can come into being is as an expression of one powerful civilization's globalist phase. If the North American civilization becomes openly imperialist and imposes an American-led confederate empire on the world, then such a pattern may last during the North American civilization's expansionist phase. It would be as when the Roman or British Empires subjugated other civilizations for a while, until they broke away and resumed their own life-cycle. Consequently, no civilization can abandon its rise-and-fall cycle to take part in such an external pattern unless it does so within a phase when it can be conquered by a foreign power. It would then revert to its previous cycle. Every town on earth belongs to a civilization, whose evolution through stages never ceases. See Appendix 1, 3, and 4 for a more detailed view.

Such a plan dominates the thinking of the Great Powers at the present time, and it appears to be having some success. We are therefore tracking the progress of a plan that is dictating regional developments, but whose end may never happen.

5

HITLER: A FAILED ONE-WORLD REVOLUTION?

We shall unleash the Nihilists and the atheists, and we shall provoke a formidable social cataclysm which in its horror will show clearly to the nations the effect of absolute atheism, origin of savagery, and of the most bloody turmoil. Then, everywhere, the citizens, obliged to defend themselves against the world minority of revolutionaries, will exterminate those destroyers of civilization, and the multitude, disillusioned with Christianity, whose deistic spirits will from that moment be without compass, anxious for an ideal, but without knowing where to render its adoration, will receive the pure light ..., brought finally into public view, through the universal manifestation which will result from the general reactionary movement which will follow the destruction of Christianity and atheism, both conquered and exterminated at the same time.

General Albert Pike, letter to Mazzini predicting three world wars, 1871[1]

It may be easy to overestimate the occult nature of the Syndicate today. I'm not suggesting that the Freemasons or the Illuminati have the same force in the same kind of way. Their nature has changed. In part it's simply that the few with money and power link together, like all groups with similar interests and backgrounds. It's a natural human instinct. They act to preserve and extend their influence. The organizations they form change over time. But you can trace their roots. And it may be equally easy to underestimate the occult nature, and the possibility that the original aims continue, in modified form.

These dark visions have driven the revolutions and wars of the twentieth century. The difference between the world stage and the lunatic asylum is only one of degree and success.

Maybe these dreams of world domination and government are just that, dreams. We may occasionally see traces of them cropping up in esoteric literature, in trappings and symbols, but assume they only have a marginal effect on real politics, real life.

Well, we don't need to look far back in our own time to see a vivid example of an attempt to realize the wildest, most evil of dreams. The middle years of the twentieth century were dominated by the Second World War. This is often seen as mostly the responsibility of one individual, Hitler, a mad genius who managed to turn the German people on their heads and single-handedly inspire them to visions of world domination and destruction. But it's not as simple as that. He didn't think his ideas alone, and he didn't do it alone. And all such visions need money.

"Rockefellers" Fund Hitler's Expansion/War Machine

From 1924 the Dawes Plan to reconstitute Germany, "largely a J. P. Morgan production,"[2] poured American capital into the country, loans totaling $800m[3] which enabled Germany to build a war machine.

It was natural for the German Roggenfelders/Rockefellers to ally with Germany again. The Syndicate financed Hitler through the Warburg-controlled Mendelsohn Bank of Amsterdam, and the J. Henry Schröder Bank (which was agent for the Nazi government and which also had branches in Frankfurt, London, and New York).[4] Schröder Bank's chief lawyer was John Foster Dulles of the CFR, a director of International Nickel Company. Dulles helped reach an agreement with I. G. Farben that enabled the Nazis to stockpile nickel (to be converted into armaments) for the coming war.[5] John F. Dulles's brother Allen was a director of the board. The Dulles brothers were cousins of the Rockefellers, who later acquired the controlling interest in I. G. Farben (a US company).[6] I. G. Farben was a key supplier of the German war machine, making high-grade fuel from coal. After the First World war it received a $30m loan from the Rockefellers.[7] Over the coming decades it became the largest corporation in Europe.

"Rockefellers" controlled I. G. Farbenindustrie's assets through a US holding company called American I. G. Farben. On the board were, among others, the Presidents of "Rockefellers'" Standard Oil, New Jersey, Walter Teagle, and of National City Bank in New York, Edsel Ford; and Paul Warburg, chairman of the Federal Reserve. In 1929 the Rockefeller-owned Standard Oil of New Jersey (now Exxon) made a cartel agreement with Rockefellers' I. G. Farbenindustrie, which had been created in 1926 out of the German chemical dye and drug companies previously controlled by the British (see p56), so that they would not be competing in each other's markets. Standard Oil supplied Hitler with petroleum, while I. G. Farben provided glycerin for munitions (from the fat of concentration camp victims). "Rockefellers'" Standard Oil regarded its agreements with 'Rockefellers'" I. G. Farbenindustrie as having priority over any questions of patriotism.[8] In 1933 Standard Oil Company of New York sent a loan to Germany of $2m, and after that earned $500,000 a year making *ersatz* gas "for war purposes"[9] but could not export its earnings. I. G. Farbenindustrie supplied 45% of the election funds used to bring the Nazis to power in 1933.[10] In 1933 the Syndicate financed Hitler through payments made by I. G. Farben (sourced by "Rockefellers") and General Electric.[11] In July 1934 "Rockefellers" assigned Ivy Lee, their top specialist in publicity, propaganda, and spin-doctoring (who had presented John D. Rockefeller as a philanthropist), to I. G. Farbenindustrie to advise Hitler on the rearmament of Germany[12] – in other words, to encourage German rearmament. (In the 1920s Lee had advised Stalin on Soviet publicity and propaganda.)[13] Plans to dismantle I. G. Farben at the end of the war were countermanded by General William Draper of Dillon Read, who had financed German rearmament in the 1920s (and was a member of the Council on Foreign Relations). [14]

On January 4, 1933 Hitler met the Dulles brothers in Cologne, at the home of Baron Kurt von Schröder (a partner of the Cologne bank J. H. Stein and Co. and Hitler's personal banker), to guarantee Hitler the funds that were needed to install him as Chancellor of Germany later that month.[15] The Dulles brothers were there as legal representatives of Kuhn, Loeb & Co., who had given short-term credits to Germany and needed a guarantee that they would be repaid.[16]

After being funded by Kuhn, Loeb via the Dulles brothers Hitler was invited to be Chancellor of Germany in January 1933. He needed a pretext to turn against the Communists and prepare for hostilities towards Russia. In February the Reichstag caught fire. A Communist was blamed, but there is a strong suspicion that Hitler ordered the blaze. It was the excuse for a decree overriding personal freedom and sanctioning mass arrests.[17]

In March 1933 Hitler was given full powers by the Reichstag and established an absolute dictatorship. In this same year the US, seemingly alarmed at the turn of events in Germany, recognized the Bolshevik regime in the Soviet Union. In June 1934 Hitler ordered the execution of his political opponents, including his old ally Röhm.

In August 1934 it was announced that Standard Oil, New Jersey had acquired 730,000 acres of oil land in Germany from the North European Oil Corporation. They built extensive refineries in Germany for the Nazis and supplied them with oil, payment (in June 1936) being millions of harmonicas (*sic*) and a number of ships.[18] It built a refinery in Hamburg that produced 15,000 tons of aviation gasoline each week and operated throughout the war.[19] Also before the war, Standard Oil's oil tankers manned with Nazi crews refueled German U-boats.[20] Standard Oil also sold the Nazis artificial rubber,[21] and ball-bearings for anti-aircraft guns.[22] The refineries were eventually handed over to Hitler.[23] From 1933 until 1944 Standard Oil of New Jersey ("Rockefellers") and Sosthenes Behn, a subsidiary of ITT, made payments to Himmler.[24]

Why were Standard Oil and other "Rockefeller" industries so keen to support Hitler? Maybe they saw him as a possible ruler of Europe and Asia, who would enable them to exploit 100% of the Baku oilfields rather than 50%. Ezra Pound, who was imprisoned in the USA after the war, believed that they lured Hitler into the war.[25] They suggested that England would not fight, and there would be no opposition in the Rhineland, Austria, Sudetenland, Czechoslovakia, and Poland, and he was indeed reportedly surprised by the lack of opposition.

The President of Standard Oil, New Jersey incidentally, who oversaw the payments to Himmler and the re-fueling of the U-boats, was William S. Farish I, grandfather of the US Ambassador to Britain during the second Iraq war. One of the richest men in Texas, he was a close friend of Bush Sr., and managed his personal wealth when he was elected Vice-President in 1980, cementing a link between the families that goes back to 1929. The Farishes were the only private family the Queen of England visited when she went to the US in 1984.[26]

Hitler became supreme when Hindenburg died in 1935. The army agreed to the merging of the presidency, the chancellorship, and the supreme command of the armed forces, and this was the basis of the oath of allegiance and personal loyalty to Hitler sworn by every German soldier from that time.

In 1936 "Rockefellers" entered into partnership with the key institution in the Fascist "economic miracle," the Schröder Bank of New York (and with their Schröder-employed cousins, the Dulles brothers).[27] In 1939 the "Rockefeller"-controlled Chase National Bank secured $25m for Nazi Germany and supplied Berlin with information on 10,000 Nazi sympathizers in the US.[28] Throughout the war (except for a break of a few months) the "Rockefeller"-owned Standard Oil of New Jersey shipped oil to the Nazis through Spain.[29] Hitler was also funded by Krupps and (indirectly) by "Rothschilds."[30] Dr. Hjalmar Schacht, the president of the Reichsbank, acted as go-between between Hitler and Wall Street.[31] Schacht's father worked in a Morgan-affiliated Trust Co. in Berlin.[32] There is thus evidence that both "Rockefellers" and "Rothschilds" indirectly financed Hitler through intermediaries,[33] and built up his army.

From 1935 to 1939 vast sums of money were poured into Nazi Germany by the Syndicate. US multinationals were profiting from Hitler's military construction program at least until 1942.[34] Germany's largest tank producers were Opel, a subsidiary of General Motors (controlled by J. P. Morgans and the DuPonts) and Ford AG, a subsidiary of the Ford Motor Company. ITT (International Telephone and Telegraph) had invested in Focke-Wolfe, producer of German fight aircraft. Hitler implemented his policy of expansion and conquest which led to the overrunning, one by one, of the Rhineland, Austria, the Sudetenland, Czechoslovakia, and Poland. He revealed his plan for expansion to his military leaders in 1937. While Hitler implemented his one-at-a-time occupations, he posed as the champion of Europe against Bolshevism, which was how "Rockefellers" saw him. While aggressing against his neighbors, Hitler claimed that his sole aim was to remove the inequalities of the Versailles Treaty, which had been pushed through by President Wilson, Col. House, Baruch, the Rothschild family, and other members of the Syndicate.

Hitler hoped that his successful invasion of Poland would lead to peace with Britain, which would allow him to turn his attention towards Bolshevik Russia – or what remained of it after Stalin's Great Purge. In England, the Syndicate shaped "the appeasement lobby" at country houses such as Cliveden, where Lord Milner's once young Round-Table advisors Lionel Curtis and Philip Kerr, the Marquess of Lothian, shaped the policies of Geoffrey Dawson, editor of *The Times*, and other influential opinion-makers at the seat of the Astors.[35]

"Rothschildite" Funds Churchill

The Syndicate is so all-pervasive it is rare to find it funding only one side in a conflict. After all, then it would risk losing. Across the Channel Winston Churchill had earlier received financial help from "Rothschilds".[36] In April 1897 when Turkey declared war on Greece, Churchill (then 22) had wanted to go to the front as a correspondent and had told his mother, "Lord Rothschild would be the person to arrange this for me as he knows everyone." He bought Chartwell at the end of 1921 for £5,000 on the strength of the £4,000 pa rent and revenues he would be receiving from the Garron Tower estate in County Antrim, which he had just inherited from a distant cousin, and from advances totaling £22,000 from publishers for volume one of his history of the First World War, *The World Crisis*. After bearing the massive refurbishing and maintenance costs throughout the 1920s and 1930s and after years of extravagant living, in February 1938 Churchill found himself £18,000 in debt with tax demands to meet. On the verge of bankruptcy, he turned to Brendan Bracken, who had first campaigned for him in 1923, for advice, and put Chartwell on the market.[37]

Bracken seems to have raised the alarm with "Rothschilds."[38] A close intimate of Lord Rothschild, Austrian-born Sir Henry Strakosch, a Moravian-Jewish financier of great wealth who had made his fortune in gold-mining in South Africa, appeared like a fairy godmother and agreed to take over Churchill's losses for three years, saving Churchill from bankruptcy. Strakosch had served as an advisor to the Bank of England throughout the 1920s and 1930s and was a close intimate of Governor Montagu Norman as well as of Lord Rothschild, the power behind the Bank of England. Churchill had worked closely with Montagu Norman when Chancellor of the Exchequer: in 1925 they had fixed sterling at an inflated rate and rejoined the link to gold.

Strakosch advanced Churchill a £150,000 interest-free, repayment-free "loan"[39] and became his "advisor," and Chartwell was taken off the market.

Churchill had privately written to Bernard Baruch of the Syndicate in early 1939: "War is coming very soon. You will be running the show over there."[40] Baruch, once a close advisor to President Woodrow Wilson, was by now a symbol of the power of wealth. In 1929 Churchill had traveled to the US and had visited Baruch before journeying in his railway carriage to the White House. Baruch was now the link between Roosevelt and the bankers.

Soon after his letter to Baruch, Churchill did a U-turn, probably on Baruch's "advice";[41] instead of opposing Zionism in the British Parliament (as on October 22, 1938) he spoke in favor of it, criticizing a White Paper he had issued as Colonial Secretary in the 1920s, which the Zionists loathed as "whittling down" the Balfour Declaration. This new outlook was warmly supported in the pro-Zionist US and, of course, by "Rothschilds." A few months after his self-criticism and change of heart, Churchill's "wilderness years" ended and he became Prime Minister. For his help, Churchill put Bracken in his war cabinet (where he was Minister of Information from 1941 and First Lord of the Admiralty in 1945). Strakosch, in his will (reported in the London *Times* on February 1, 1944) converted an interest-free loan to Churchill of £20,000 into a gift, and also a loan of £10,000 to Lord Simon, Lord Chancellor and Minister of War Transport in Churchill's war cabinet.[42]

Churchill signs Saudi-Arabian Oilfields to "Rockefellers"

Churchill became British Prime Minister following Germany's invasion of the Low Countries on May 10, 1940. He immediately delivered his famous "blood, toil, tears and sweat" speech, and after Dunkirk began trying to draw the Americans into the war. He implemented his new pro-Zionist outlook. On May 23 he gave orders that British troops should be withdrawn from Palestine and that the Jews should be "armed in their own defence and properly organized as rapidly as possible." He knew this would be sympathetically received in the US and be seen as a first step towards establishing the State of Israel of the Balfour Declaration. But he was reluctant to hand over British-guarded rights to oil under the ground in Saudi Arabia.

"Rockefellers" still saw their interests threatened. In 1933 a "Rockefeller" company, the Standard Oil Co. of California (Socal, later Chevron) obtained a 60–year lease for Saudi-Arabian oil (which would expire in 1993). In 1936 it sold a 50% interest to Texaco, another US company. Commercial production began in March 1938.[43] But the British controlled Saudi Arabia through the king, Ibn Saud, whose attempt to be leader they had backed in return for protection for the Suez Canal, the sea route to India. "Rockefellers" found that the British, including Royal Dutch and Shell, blocked their development. The British control of Arabia predates the First World War. Using Col. T. E. Lawrence of British Intelligence to befriend the Arabs and lead an independence movement against the Ottoman Empire, they encouraged Sharif Hussein, the ruler of Mecca, to attack the Turks. Ibn Saud granted the first Arabian oil concession in 1923 to a British investment group, the Eastern and General Syndicate. In 1913 the British armed the Abdul Aziz and Wahhabi families, and supported Ibn Saud Abdul Aziz. Ibn Saud captured Medina in 1925 and proclaimed himself King of Hijaz in 1926. When Arabia was renamed Saudi Arabia in 1932, the British were in full control of oil concessions in the country. This was a consequence of Lawrence of Arabia's work – and the British government's disregarding of promises Lawrence made to the Arabian leaders. [44]

The British government had controlled the Gulf's oil from before the First World War, and had a controlling interest in Anglo-Persian Oil Co. (a forerunner of BP)[45] and the London-based Iraq Petroleum Company. When the Ottoman Empire collapsed it was Britain (in the person of Sir Percy Cox, High Commissioner in Baghdad, acting for Winston Churchill, Colonial Secretary) who drew the boundary lines between Iraq, Kuwait, Jordan, and Saudi Arabia. The British had set up the Red Line Agreement of 1928, which restricted foreign oil companies. As the price for US intervention in the First World War, "Rockefellers" extracted a deal from the British whereby the British Saudi-Arabian oil concessions were made over to them. "Rockefellers" withdrew support from the Kaiser and through their puppet Woodrow Wilson engineered troop reinforcements funded by the Syndicate, at a cost of a quarter of a million US lives. "Rockefellers" then wrested control of the German chemical dye and drug companies from the British and merged them in 1926 into I. G. Farbenindustrie, A. G. Infuriated, Churchill blocked "Rockefellers" from developing Saudi-Arabian oil. Britain refused to grant visas to Standard Oil employees and to clear ships carrying much-needed supplies.[46] The British Empire still threatened the Turkish, Arabian, and Iranian oil reserves "Rockefellers" wanted to control. "Rockefellers" were apprehensive about Germany, which threatened to market a synthesizing oil, but they could contain this as they controlled the German Dye Trust, I. G. Farbenindustrie, which had developed the process.[47] "Rockefellers" wanted to reach an understanding that Britain would allow American oil companies to export Gulf oil without any hindrance from Britain or British companies. They wanted American entry on Britain's side to be conditional on her signing over (i.e. agreeing not to prevent the US development of) all the Saudi-Arabian oilfields and perhaps promising to de-colonize after the war.[48]

Hitler unleashed massive bombing raids on London in August and September 1940 to soften Britain up before a cross-Channel sea-borne invasion. To carry this invasion, Hitler massed sufficient barges to carry 50,000 troops and their equipment in ports from Ostend to Le Havre. [49]

Churchill, desperate for American help after the *débâcle* of Dunkirk, was now confronted with a stark choice between letting potential Saudi-Arabian oilfields go and promising de-colonization, or foregoing American help. It was a rerun of the choice he had encountered after the Battle of Verdun in 1916,[50] when he had signed the Baghdad-Mosul oilfields to "Rockefellers"' Standard Oil to introduce American help that would win the First World War. He realized that unless he now, once again, gave "Rockefellers" what they wanted, the British would lose the Second World War and the British Empire would be destroyed. He signed the Saudi-Arabian oilfields over to Standard Oil. He perhaps promised to de-colonize at the end of the war. Some time after Dunkirk, June 1940, Churchill asked Roosevelt, his cousin, to lend him the arms to defeat Hitler, payment to be deferred. Roosevelt agreed, stipulating three conditions: the surrender of all British assets in the US (see note 52); the surrender of British oilfields in Saudi Arabia; and (I believe) the surrender of British colonies in the future. In short, Churchill sold the British Empire to defeat Hitler. Most of this momentous decision is invisible. The tips of the iceberg appear here and there. One day it will be wholly revealed.[51] In return the Americans would supply convoy support and lend-lease, which was eventually authorized by Congress in March 1941. Roosevelt, having made a speech firmly keeping America out of the war, within a week, in a reversal of policy[52] committed America to helping Europe.

The US subsidized the Saudi government in the Second World War when production was affected. The two American companies working in Saudi Arabia, Socal and Texaco, founded a new company Aramco (Arabian American Oil Co.) in January 1944. "Rockefellers"' President Roosevelt, who had implemented the New Deal for them, secretly gave Aramco $165m out of a special fund allocated to him by Congress for the war effort.[53] "Rockefellers" did not have to account for this money, and they used it to buy concessions and construct a 1,000–mile-long pipeline from Saudi-Arabian oilfields to the Mediterranean, work done at the American taxpayers' expense.[54] The "Rockefeller"-influenced US Export-Import Bank paid $25m to King Ibn Saud to fund the building of a road from his main palace, and the US army built an airfield and military base at Dhahran near the Aramco oilfields; the base was turned over to Ibn Saud gratis.[55]

After the Yalta conference Roosevelt met King Saud on a US warship in the Suez Canal in February 1945 and promised the king US protection in return for privileged access to Saudi oil,[56] confirming Britain's "handing over" of Saudi Arabia to the US. In 1945 a State Department analyst described Saudi Arabia as "one of the greatest material prizes in world history."[57]

With the support of his financial backers via I. G. Farben, Hitler directed all his fire on Russia. The eastern front now had priority.[58] The Soviet Union had occupied eastern Poland and Bessarabia, and Hitler blocked further Soviet advances by confronting the Russians in Hungary and Romania, where there was oil. Urged on,[59] and financed, by the Syndicate, Hitler invaded the Soviet Union in June 1941. He was so confident of a quick victory that he had not provided his troops with winter clothing against the bitter Russian cold. The Germans failed to achieve a quick victory, and in December 1941 the Russians counter-attacked. Some 49 million Soviet people would die as a result of Operation Barbarossa.[60]

The Nazi Vision

So far the Second World War has similarities with the First. Oil was key to both, particularly the oilfields of the Middle East. Control of oil determines victory. Stakes in oil companies are the bargaining chips for the money that brings victory. But as we all know, there is a far darker side to the Second World War.

Did "Rockefellers" understand the full depravity of Hitler's vision? Maybe they were only interested in oil. But his motivations and ambitions were clear to those who knew him. It's well known that Hitler had an occult background. As a youth in 1909 he renewed acquaintance[61] with Jorg Lanz von Liebenfels, who two years earlier had founded the "Order of the New Templars," which used the swastika as its symbol. (It seems that Hitler first met him at school before 1900.)[62] Liebenfels wrote in a letter later in 1932 that Hitler would "develop a movement that would make the world tremble."[63] In 1919 Hitler is thought to have joined the Thule Society, which practiced black magic and worshipped Satan.[64] The Thule's leading figure was Dietrich Eckart, one of the seven founding members of the Nazi Party. This had begun as the German Workers' Party, founded in Munich in 1919 by Anton Drexler, another member of the Thule Society.[65]

The Thule Society sought the lost Nordic homeland of Thule (a northern Atlantis, as it were), and its members thought themselves political masters of the earth.[66] The Thule – and Hitler – worshipped *Rex Mundi*: Satan, who had equal status with God (Jehovah, the creator of the material world and therefore a demiurge).[67] From this Society Hitler learned to manipulate Vril, the hidden energy of the earth, in rituals.[68] Through the Ahnenerbe (the German Ancestral Heritage Organization) and Kurt Wiligut, the ex-Thule Nazis focused on the Externsteine, a group of awesomely high rocks with an eerie, primitive atmosphere, the highest part of which (Irminsul) held an ancient pillar of the Saxons.[69] At Schloss Wewelsburg, a school for SS leaders owned by Himmler, rituals were performed in a subterranean crypt with a stone stoup. This chamber was known as the Realm of the Dead, and it was intended that Hitler would be interred there.[70] In the Great Hall above the crypt, the 13 Knights of the Oak Leaf met at a round table.[71]

On his deathbed Eckart predicted that Hitler would make an impact on the world: "Follow Hitler. He will dance, but it is I who have called the tune! I have initiated him into the 'Secret Doctrine,' opened his centers in vision and given him the means to communicate with the Powers. Do not mourn for me: I shall have influenced history more than any other German."[72]

While in prison at Landsberg in the 1920s, Hitler had dictated the first volume of *Mein Kampf* to Hess. (It may actually have been largely written by Hess and Göring.)[73] The book held that the *Volk* (people) were the unit of mankind; the State merely served the people,[74] and the German people were greater than any other people. Hitler only served nine months of his sentence. Out of prison, Hitler lived in Eckart's house on the Obersalzberg, near Berchtesgaden.[75] As a result he came to love the area, and in due course built the Berghof nearby.

Nuremberg: Center of the World

Hitler had selected Nuremberg, the city of the Holy Roman Emperors, as his seat after the war. Conrad III, who was the first Hohenstaufen to be Holy Roman Emperor and German King, held court there before he left for the Second Crusade in 1147, and Otto IV convened the Imperial Diet there. To consolidate his rule, Hitler planned for the time when he would be crowned Emperor – Kaiser Adolf I – of Germany. And he would not just be Emperor of Germany. When he had accepted the surrender of the Soviet Union, the United States, the British Empire including India, and in due course his ally Japan, he would be Emperor of the whole world, whose representatives would have to be accommodated.

At Nuremberg Hitler began an impressive building program modeled on ancient Rome. He built the Coliseum, an open Congress Hall, to accommodate 50,000 representatives. This was never finished, but can be visited today. Near this neo-Roman Coliseum was the grandstand of the Zeppelinfeld, built between 1935 and 1937, where Hitler stood on a podium and addressed no fewer than 1.6 million people one day in 1938. Also nearby is a lake that was gouged out to be a stadium capable of accommodating a crowd of 350,000 to 450,000 people. A wide route, two kilometers long, was built to lead to the Castle. Hitler declared that Nuremberg would be the scene of party congresses "for all time." His election as Emperor, "Kaiser," would be completed by electors meeting in the Castle, as had happened throughout its long history. The Märzfeld ("march-field") at Dutzendteiches ("dozen ponds"), the Stadium and the New Congress Hall (or Coliseum) would make Nuremberg the center of the new pagan Holy Roman Empire. Hence the Roman symbolism: the Coliseum, the eagle (on the Nazi standard and in the name Eagle's Nest). Nuremberg would be the new pagan Holy City of the Thousand-Year Reich with a parade-ground covering 148 acres surrounded by 28 towers, each 40 meters high.[76]

This neo-Roman complex of buildings would be the ultimate political expression of Hitler's National Socialist revolution, which gave him absolute power. It would have been the center of the world had he won the Second World War and achieved world government. It is unlikely that Hitler would have felt beholden to the Syndicate if he had achieved his dream of world power; he had, after all, seized control of banks in Germany and canceled the national debt. The Syndicate no doubt reckoned that they could control him until they replaced him,[77] perhaps after assassinating him, and that through the partnership they would win control of all the world's oil.

The Final Solution

What distinguished Hitler was not his ambition, or its occult origin, but his commitment to carrying it through. He put the most horrific fantasies into action. He prepared for a new order in Europe that would follow his victory in the war. The concentration camps were expanded, and extermination camps were added to them, at Auschwitz and Mauthausen, for example. The "final solution" of the Jewish problem – first proposed in May 1941 at the time of the invasion of Russia and confirmed at the Wannsee Conference in Berlin on January 20, 1942 – was put into practice, and between July 1942 and January 1945 some 4.5 to 5.5 million Jews[78] (1.5 million on some counts) were gassed in 1,500 concentration camps across German-occupied Europe. The Zyklon B that gassed so many Jews in the holocaust was produced by a pest-control subsidiary of the German company I. G. Farben, Tesch/Stabanow and Degesch.[79]

Some 5 million Jews had been stripped of £2.7b during the Second World War (worth £102b in today's currency). The Nazis seized much of this money when they invaded France and the Low Countries – including much property of the French Rothschilds – and they removed it to Swiss bank accounts, where it has remained to this day. Much of this money was deposited in the Bank for International Settlements, which was dominated by Hitler.[80] The BIS board included Montagu Norman of the Bank of England, whose major stockholder was the House of Rothschild, but he was in a minority on the BIS board.[81] The Rothschilds are likely to have been unaware that they were benefiting from this money.

The Syndicate Now Back Stalin

In fact, Hitler was now losing the war. The Germans were running out of oil; they did not have enough to fly their planes. Hitler had planned to capture: the oilfields in Ploesti, Romania by 1939 so Germany would be self-sufficient in oil; the oilfields in Persia by 1941; and the oilfields in Russia by 1942. Instead, the Ploesti oilfields were insufficient; Rommel had seized the Suez Canal rather than British-Persian oilfields and the Japanese had attacked South East Asia rather than Russia.[82]

At the end of 1942 Hitler was defeated at el-Alamein and at Stalingrad, and his Empire began shrinking. He stayed in his headquarters in the east, the Wolf's Lair, fed optimistic news by Bormann, his secretary, his mood controlled by injections given by his physician, Dr. Morell. In July 1943 Mussolini was arrested and there was an armistice in Italy. The U-boat campaign was failing, and the Allies were bombing Germany to rubble.

In July von Stauffenberg nearly killed him when a bomb went off at his East Prussian headquarters, the Wolf's Lair. Stauffenberg had hoped to end the war and save 30m people from being killed in the final bloody stages of a German defeat.[83] He and 8,000 others were executed, and the army was placed under Nazi political control. The Allies made progress across France, and in December Hitler moved his headquarters to the Ardennes to launch a counter-offensive. This failed, and he withdrew to the Berlin Chancellery and its bunker – deep underground.

The Syndicate, seeing that Hitler was losing after 1942 and unlikely to seize any more British oilfields, switched their allegiance to Stalin,[84] who was winning and taking territories with new oilfields in them. They now intrigued the birth of a "United Nations," and backed Stalin to create an Eastern European Empire they could run following the destruction of the British and German empires. "Rockefellers," having backed Stalin in 1925 and having switched their support to Hitler in the 1930s, now abandoned him.

"Rockefellers" intrigued for Stalin to be the first to take Berlin. Under orders from Gen. Marshall and President Roosevelt, the "Rockefeller" puppet,[85] Eisenhower mystifyingly refused to send Allied troops to Berlin, despite Montgomery's urgings.[86] Through Roosevelt and Eisenhower, "Rockefellers" arranged for Stalin to arrive at Berlin before the British and Americans.

Underground living took its toll on Hitler. Exhausted and ill, senile beyond his years, he married his mistress Eva Braun and they both committed suicide in the bunker on April 30, 1945 as the Allies reached Berlin. Goebbels and his wife followed suit. At the war's end Eisenhower made his HQ in the old I. G. Farben head office in Frankfurt.[87]

*   *   *

Hitler's attempt to consolidate his Empire was a failure. He was assailed on three fronts (from Russia, Italy, and France), and although he tried to secure his revolution by executions and genocide, implementing his anti-Semitic program by killing over five-eighths (5 million out of some 8 million) of the Jewish race, and hoped to set the Americans against the Russians, he was defeated. He did not understand that his own Western backers, "Rockefellerites" and others in the Syndicate, had also backed Stalin.

There's little doubt about Hitler's connections with the occult, and the Syndicate's financing both of the German war-machine and Stalin. But was this simply a lone madness on the one hand, and a miscalculation on the other? Can that explain 70 million dead? Here's a possible scenario, which explains why the Second World War took the form it did.

Both Hitler and Stalin had ambitions to control the whole of the Eurasian land mass. Both believed their ideology would conquer the world. "Rockefellers" helped finance both because they saw them as potential world governors. "Rockefellers" controlled Stalin and had exclusive leasing rights over Soviet oil in return for financial help (their funding of Stalin's Five-Year Plans), and they now hoped that Hitler would confiscate the Baku oilfield on their behalf so that they could own Russian oil rather than lease it. They were commercially driven, and hoped Hitler would terrify Britain into surrendering the Saudi-Arabian oilfields, which he did. They had their eye on all the Near-Eastern territory between the Gulf of Aden and the Red Sea, the Black and Caspian Seas, the Mediterranean and the Persian Gulf, which was one vast oil basin. And they backed President Roosevelt, whom they controlled, to acquire it. In expectation of German "liberation" Persia had renamed itself "Aryan" ("Iran" in Farsi)[88] to align with Hitler. The Germans did not arrive, and at the end of the war, the Anglo-Persian Oil Company still controlled the vast oilfields in Iran.

The Second World War marks a shift in the balance of power between the Rothschilds and Rockefellers. Through the 1930s the Rothschilds had less influence on world finance, and the first head of the Bank of International Settlements, a joint creation of the world's banks in 1930, was a "Rockefellerite."[89] "Rockefellers" took the lead in financing both Hitler and Stalin, and profited accordingly.

6

THE TWO STATES;
THE COLD WAR

First we will take Eastern Europe, then masses of Asia. Then we
will encircle the United States, which will be the last bastion of
capitalism. We shall not have to attack. It will fall like a ripe
grapefruit into our hands.

Lenin

The Syndicate backed Hitler to an astonishing extent right through the war
years. Would they have been prepared to back a Hitler world government
based in Nuremberg? We don't know. They knew what was going on, they
were implicated, maybe they would have got cold feet. But it's rare for them
to put morality before money. They would probably have come to terms.

After the War, the most devastating ever, leaving over 70 million dead,
you would have thought the world would have settled down for a while. It
was time to forgive and forget, to rebuild, to turn swords into ploughshares.
There can have been few ordinary people in the late 1940s who didn't
want peace. Ordinary British and Americans had no desire to attack the
Russians, to get involved in Egypt, or later in Korea, Vietnam, or a dozen
other places. Nor had ordinary Russians, or Chinese.

But to others war means profit, and opportunity. We call the period from
1945 to around 1990 the "Cold War." It was "cold" because both sides had
such vast arsenals that to use them would have destroyed mankind. So it
was fought by proxy, in small, local wars. Churchill observed that a balance
of terror had replaced the traditional balance of power,[1] and it dawned on
smaller nations that if neither side was prepared to use nuclear weapons
there was a stalemate and local wars were possible.

In this chapter we look at some of the events in the Cold War and offer an interpretation.

The world of the 1930s was one of fading European Empires.[2] The Second World War destroyed them. Hitler had failed to establish a new European Empire. The Syndicate now took a new tack. They encouraged the division of the world into blocs, with individual national aspirations being suppressed.

The progress of the Cold War can be described in stages. From 1944 to around 1949, an Eastern European bloc was established under Stalin. Simultaneously a Western Empire bloc was created through Marshall Aid, and cemented with the EEC in the 50s. The European Empires in Africa and elsewhere were dismantled and leveled in the 50s to 70s by Cold War/local conflicts. Both Eastern and Western blocs attempted to use the newly created UN for their own ends. Their competition reached its height in the Kennedy/Krushchev era. The next twenty years saw a new phase of Soviet expansion. Around the world there's a series of messy conflicts, highlighted in Cuba, Vietnam, Congo, Iran, Afghanistan, and the former Yugoslavia. In 1989 the abolition of the Berlin Wall began to unify Eastern and Western European blocs into a United States of Europe. The rest of the world then began to develop into blocs. Oil interests remain key throughout.

The East European Empire

The key to controlling Eastern Europe after the war was whoever held Berlin. Montgomery had been ready to take it, but his commanding officer, Eisenhower, along with Roosevelt and General Marshall (who advised Roosevelt on army matters) wouldn't allow him.[3] As a result, the arrangements for these new blocs were confirmed at Tehran, Yalta, and Potsdam, where the world was split into three parts: a Russian zone (including Hungary), in which the Americans would not interfere; an American zone, in which the Russians would not interfere; and the Third World, for which Russia and America would be free to compete. The three leaders at Yalta were all Masons,[4] and had exclusively Masonic advisors.[5] They represented British, American, and Russian Freemasonry: Sionist Rosicrucianism; American Templarism; and the remnants of Grand Orient Bolshevism, much of which Stalin had eliminated for the Priory of

Sion in his great purge.[6] Freemasonry had established the basis for a new Cold War.

The CFR/Syndicate Create the UN

The foundation of the UN can be traced back to 1939, when the League of Nations ceased functioning and the American Council on Foreign Relations began planning its replacement. On its advice, the US State Department set up a "Special Research Division" in 1940, headed by the CFR's Leo Pasvolsky and totally staffed by the CFR.[7] The CFR's *Foreign Affairs* urged the creation of a "Commonwealth of Free Nations" a few months before Pearl Harbor in 1941.[8] The term "United Nations" was first used of the nations opposing the Axis powers (Germany, Italy, and Japan) on January 1, 1942, when 26 "united nations" made a declaration of war aims.[9]

The plan for a UN was conceived at the Moscow Conference in 1943 when Molotov, Litvinov, and Vyshinsky proposed it to Cordell Hull, US Secretary of State from 1933 to 1944 and a devotee of expanding world trade, and Averill Harriman as a means of bringing peace. Hull recommended approval, and the Senate approved the plan.[10] The idea of the UN was proposed at the 1944 Dumbarton Oaks Conference, where Molotov worked on the draft of the UN Charter with "Rockefellers" employee, and later Nelson Rockefeller's personal representative at the UN, Alger Hiss (a former State Department official who was convicted of perjury in 1950 and exposed as a Soviet spy, and who was therefore not acting on the Americans' side).[11] The Charter of the UN was written at Yalta in February 1945 by Molotov, who represented the Soviets, and Alger Hiss, who represented the "Rockefeller"-Soviet Axis and the CFR ("the Rockefeller Foreign Office").[12] Roosevelt, Churchill, and Stalin agreed at Yalta that the UN should be established.[13]

The CFR had taken over the State Department by 1939.[14] Funded by "Rockefellers" ($0.5m from both the Rockefeller Foundation and Carnegie Endowment after the war),[15] it has nominated most of the officials in every President's administration since the 1920s.[16]

The American delegation to the UN conference at San Francisco in 1945 contained at least 47 CFR members.[17] Under Alger Hiss, the founding conference's Secretary-General, the long-awaited organization was formally created and the US Senate approved the idea in days.[18] In

December 1946 the Rockefeller Foundation donated a check to buy 18 acres of land in Manhattan on which the UN building was built: John D. Rockefeller III contributed $8.5m, with the New York City contributing a further $4.25m.[19] (From 1970 to 1985 David Rockefeller was the chairman of the CFR.)[20] A year later two members of the CFR – one of them being James Warburg – established the United World Federalists, a merging of the Americans United for World Government, the World Federalists, the Massachusetts Committee for World Federation, the Student Federalists, the World Citizens of Georgia, and the World Republic.[21] All agreed to "strengthen the United Nations into a world government of limited powers, adequate to prevent a war and having direct jurisdiction over the individual."[22]

The UN, "open to all peace-loving nations and sovereign equals," claimed to maintain global peace and security,[23] though in effect it favored communism in the balance of power. (Right from the outset, the Soviet Union held three votes to America's one in the General Assembly.[24] At the Dumbarton Oaks Conference of August 1944 the Soviet delegation had shocked Roosevelt by presenting Stalin's demand for 16 votes, one for each republic. At the Yalta Conference in February 1945 this was reduced to three: the USSR, Ukraine, and White Russia.)[25] The UN's structure included a Security Council that then consisted of 11 members, which had responsibility for maintaining international peace and security. The permanent members, the five Great Powers, had a veto and seemed unable to cooperate or reach agreement, a weakness the USSR manipulated to fan the flames of de-colonizing wars. They pressed for incidents to be referred to the General Assembly, which required a two-thirds majority of all members, and were prepared to use the Soviet veto.[26]

Nelson Rockefeller agreed with Stalin that the UN would not interfere in Russian affairs.[27] In return Stalin would continue to supply Soviet oil to "Rockefeller" companies, and keep the Bolsheviks out of Saudi Arabia and Iran.[28]

The Western Empire

Soviet expansionism in Eastern Europe filled the West with foreboding. In 1945 Stalin had announced that the doctrine of world revolution still applied: "revolution in one country" meant building a base for world revolution. Flushed with victory and his earlier capture of Estonia, Latvia and Lithuania, and part of Finland, Stalin took part of East Prussia from Germany, sealed off Eastern Europe behind an "iron curtain"[29] and between 1945 and 1949 rapidly created Soviet satellites in Yugoslavia, Albania, Bulgaria, Rumania, Poland, Czechoslovakia, Hungary, and East Germany. A risky confrontation between the US and USSR came when the Russians blockaded Berlin, which had to be supplied from the West by air for over ten months.

In 1947 during a congressional debate Bernard Baruch, now a congressional advisor, was the first to describe the open but restricted rivalry between the US and USSR on political, economic, and propaganda grounds as "Cold War."[30] It was an appropriate term for Stalin's competition with the West. Taking advantage of the non-interference of the UN, Stalin had created a Russian empire of satellites.

Stalin also took advantage of UN non-interference to seek parity with the US following the Hiroshima and Nagasaki atomic bombs and turn the Soviet Union into a nuclear power. The Soviet Union rejected the Baruch Plan of 1946, which asserted that no nation could use its UN Security Council veto on atomic issues.[31] By 1949, largely through espionage, it had built its own atomic bomb. Alarmed by the growing Soviet might, the British became an atomic power in October 1952. To keep its lead (and with relatively few bombs) the US developed the hydrogen bomb, which was exploded in August 1953. An arms race began.

As a reaction to Stalin's moves in Eastern Europe, the US, Canada, and the UK and some of the free European and Scandinavian nations formed the North Atlantic Treaty Organization (NATO) in April 1949, funded for five years by the German Marshall Fund (i.e. "Rockefellers"). Under the Treaty an attack on one nation would be regarded as an attack on all. The US was the power behind NATO and supplied most of the aircraft.

The USSR retaliated by forming Comecon, an aid program for Eastern Europe, to promote trade between Iron Curtain countries. Western Europe countered by forging economic treaties. The economic union of Belgium, the Netherlands, and Luxembourg in 1949, and of France and Italy, led to the integration of Europe's coal and steel industries and a Western Europe economic treaty in 1951, which established the beginnings of a common market. The roots of this economic union, called the "Schuman Plan" but mainly the work of Jean Monnet, can be found in an essay written by Joseph Stalin in 1912, "Marxism and the National Question." Stalin called for "regional autonomy" to bring about the "eradication" of nationalism. In 1926 Stalin addressed the Politburo: "There should be a Federated State of Europe, to which the USSR would adhere and in which … Great Britain would be included. Once Great Britain had been absorbed the USSR would … become the dominant power."[32] Under the stress of Stalin's pressure, Europe had turned away from its old imperial system to a new political economy in the regional Stalin tradition which left the old European Empires vulnerable. During this weakening, the economic power of the US remained overwhelming.

As well as planning the establishment of the UN, the CFR reconstructed Europe. Through the CFR's Harry Hopkins, Jean Monnet became personal advisor on Europe to President Roosevelt.[33] The CFR and Monnet devised the Marshall Plan for European recovery after the Second World War.[34] From 1946 to 1947 David Rockefeller acted as secretary to a CFR study group on European reconstruction. The plan was largely funded by "Rockefellers," for whom Gen. Marshall acted as a proxy.[35] The Plan was conditional upon the re-establishment of capitalism, linked to the Truman Doctrine of blocking communism globally. It poured billions of American aid into Western Europe ($13b initially, $72.5b by 1959)[36] to combat Stalin's moves. CFR study groups planned the reconstruction of Germany and Japan, and the creation of the IMF and World Bank as well as aid to Europe.[37] Between 1943 and 1947, flushed with knowledge of America's nuclear supremacy, American leaders spoke confidently of US domination of the globe, which would extend the benefits of Western capitalism and representative government to all peoples – by establishing a New World Order.[38]

North Korea

By the 1950s, Western Europe is relatively secure. Russia looks to make progress elsewhere in the world, and switches its attention to the east rather than the West. As well as controlling half of Russian oil "Rockefellers" owned substantial reserves of Chinese oil. They encouraged rapprochement between the two countries, which led to a 30–year treaty with Mao in 1950. Emboldened by this, the North Koreans invaded South Korea. South Korea appealed to the Americans/UN for help. Around 50,000 American troops have been killed in South Korea, with 37,000 still tied down.[39] Ironically the North Koreans would not have been able to launch their war if they hadn't received their oil from "Rockefellers," supplied through the Caltex Co. at the American taxpayers' expense.[40] In 1953 Mao proposed to Stalin that every country in the world except the US should be Communist-controlled by 1973.[41]

Suez Canal

On the other side of the world an equally dramatic confrontation was shaping up, which clearly illustrates the changing balance of power and new roles of "Rothschilds" and "Rockefellers." In 1945 the Egyptian government demanded the withdrawal of British troops and the transfer to it of Sudan, which eventually (in 1953) voted for independence. Nationalists won the elections of 1950 and rescinded Egypt's treaty with Great Britain a year later. General Naguib overthrew King Farouk in 1952.

Colonel Nasser took over from General Naguib. He was of Jewish origin, his real name was Nasserbaum and his father is buried in the Orthodox Jewish cemetery in Cairo. He had good links with the Soviet Union, and was armed by them.[42] They in turn were funded, as we have seen, by "Rockefellers," who had financed Stalin's Five Year Plans since 1925.[43]

At the heart of the Suez crisis was the Aswan dam project. Bigger than the pyramids, the cost was over $1 billion. The World Bank was prepared to lend $200 million at one point if America and Britain lent $70 million. John Foster Dulles (a partner of "Rockefellers") issued a high-handed State Department statement saying that the American offer was withdrawn. Provoked, Nasser announced in July 1956 that he was nationalizing the Suez Canal (which had been bought by N. M. Rothschild and Sons for the Disraeli government from Egypt's debt-ridden Khedive for £3.68m in 1875), and that the revenues would pay for the building of the dam.

The three "Rothschildite" countries, Israel, France, and Great Britain, colluded to attack Egypt in October 1956.[44]

Eisenhower ("Rockefellers"' man) instructed John Foster Dulles to block the Israelites when they were about to seize the Suez Canal and save Nasser to fight another day.[45] Dulles went to the UN Security Council, and when that action failed, to the General Assembly. With a "heavy heart" he said: "The Israeli–French–British invasion is a grave error inconsistent with the principles and purposes of this charter."[46] He also exerted great pressure on the British and French, who withdrew their troops.[47] The Suez adventure, which was in the mold of nineteenth-century gunboat diplomacy, marked the end of British imperialism, which was so identified with the Rothschilds.

Hungary

At the same time as the Suez crisis Hungarians were rising against the Soviet Union, and appealed to the West for help. The Syndicate wanted the Eastern bloc to remain intact, and America was also bound not to interfere as it had agreed at Tehran and confirmed at Yalta the principle that Hungary was part of the Soviet sphere of influence. In contrast to their actions at Suez, when the Americans effectively forced the "Rothschild" countries to pull back, in Hungary they left it to the Soviets. The same happened in Czechoslavakia in 1968.

West European De-colonization

There were eight Western European Empires (the British, French, German, Dutch, Belgian, Italian, Spanish, and Portuguese Empires) all of which held territories tempting to the "Rockefellerite" Syndicate and opposed by the Soviet Union. The British Empire bore the brunt of insurgency at first.

1948 had seen anti-European insurgency in India, Burma, Malaya, Indonesia, and the Philippines. The first (anti-French) Indo-China war had already begun. Riots in West Africa led to a promise of independence for the Gold Coast, and in 1952 the Mau Mau terrorist organization began fighting in Kenya. There was three-way fighting in Cyprus. But the Cold War took on a new impetus after Suez. Britain no longer looked like providing the kind of World Government that Cecil Rhodes had envisaged. In 1957 the Earl of Gosford, Joint Parliamentary Under-Secretary of State for Foreign Affairs, presented Britain's retreat from empire in terms of being subsumed within a different kind of world government: "Her Majesty's Government are fully in agreement with world government. We agree that this must be the goal, and that every step that is humanly possible must be taken to reach that goal."[48]

Egypt hosted a Solidarity Conference of the people of Asia and Africa in 1957 with backing from the Soviet Union. A flood of independence movements followed. In Iraq Gen. Kassem overthrew King Faisal in 1958 and set up an anti-Western regime. There was a Communist revolution in Cuba in 1959.

After their Suez reverse "Rothschilds" went along with the plan[49] to offload the British Empire. Harold Macmillan, a member of RIIA in the 1930s, made his "winds of change" speech in February 1960. De-colonized governments would in future be responsible for their own financing – and the costs of keeping their starving populations fed and healthy. In Africa the "wind of change" turned many countries independent in the 1960s, and many had Marxist or semi-Marxist governments: Guinea, Mali, the Central African Republic, Algeria, the Republic of Congo, Ghana, Sudan, Tanzania, Uganda, Yemen (PDRY), and Somalia. Libya turned anti-Western with Gaddafi's revolution in 1969. Elsewhere in the Third World, Indonesia had already turned anti-Western, as had Peru. Chile turned Marxist in 1970. Soviet weapons entered the African countries from Algeria and Egypt in Soviet-built AM12 transporters.

There were Soviet-funded and supplied liberation movements in South Africa (ANC), Namibia (SWAPO), Rhodesia/Zimbabwe (ZAPU), Angola (MPLA), Mozambique (FRELIMO), Guinea-Bissau (PAIGC), and Eritrea (ELF). Money reached these organizations from the pro-"Soviet World Council of Churches" program to combat racism.

This post-Suez period reflects the diminishing influence of the "Rothschildite" countries, with their post-war exhaustion and depleted finances, and the increasing influence of "Rockefellers" as exercised through the US and Soviet governments, who now divided the world between them.

Cuba

President Batista was asked to abdicate by President Eisenhower, and did so in October 1958. Castro came to power in January 1959. He did not reveal that he had been a Communist since 1947. The US placed an embargo on Cuba, and at the end of January 1962 Cuba was expelled from the Organization of American States. Soviet arms poured into the island. The confrontation took place in October, by which time Cuba had 42 Soviet medium-range ballistic missiles (ultimately funded by the Syndicate) with sufficient range to reach New York, Chicago, Washington, and other major American cities. During the eyeball-to-eyeball confrontation between Kennedy and Krushchev a new world war seemed imminent. On October 28 Krushchev agreed to withdraw the missiles if the US promised not to invade Cuba at a later date.

The picture on Cuba is still confused, forty years later. Krushchev undeniably supported Cuba and intended to move missiles there. Did "Rockefellers" encourage him to threaten America because that would spur the US administration to spend more on arms, i.e. borrow from the Syndicate?[50] It was also a base for revolutionaries to seize oilfields throughout South America. Maybe "Rockefellers" wanted Cuba as a training-ground for subversion in Latin America and attempts on Latin American oil with Soviet support?

The "Rockefellerite" Kennedy was in office to do the arms spending/borrowing the Syndicate wished. But he lost the plot, and attacked Cuba, seeking to overthrow Castro. Then he lost his nerve, denying the Bay of Pigs operation air cover in April 1961 and refusing to follow it up. The Syndicate came to regard him as "a loose cannon," which is why Gov. Nelson Rockefeller thought it necessary to stand against him for the Presidency. He may have angered Rockefeller by contemplating withdrawing from involvement in Vietnam.[51]

The Height of Competition: Kennedy and Krushchev

Contemporary history writing tends to focus on the particular events, seemingly random. The prime example of this is the assassination of President Kennedy in 1963. The received opinion is that there was only one assassin involved in the Kennedy shooting, and he was assassinated himself. There was no deeper motive, no conspiracy.

I'd like to believe this, and of course it may be true. In a way it would make life simpler if random acts of evil were individual aberrations. Most Americans don't believe it, and President Johnson went to his grave convinced the Cubans were behind it, taking their revenge for the Bay of Pigs invasion. The trouble for me is that I've seen color footage of the murder in the possession of the late William Cooper, a former US Naval

Intelligence officer, taken from state archives.[52] The driver of Kennedy's car appears to turn and fire at Kennedy as he approaches the underpass – that is apparently why Jackie Kennedy scrambled over the back to the car to get away. It also seems that a shot came from a man in some bushes nearby.

Maybe this is just paranoia. But it troubles me that William Cooper was shot and killed by a sheriff's deputy while resisting arrest, allegedly for a traffic offence, on November 5, 2001, after he began showing this film.[53] It troubles me that Earl Warren, who headed the commission that looked into the evidence, was a 33rd-degree Freemason,[54] as was his deputy Allen Dulles, a CFR and CIA member.[55]

On the broader scale, J. F. Kennedy was making enemies. He himself had been educated at two "Rockefeller"-subsidized institutions, Harvard and the London School of Economics, where his teachers included the Fabians Harold Laski and John Maynard Keynes. As a senator he served "Rockefeller" interests.[56]

But maybe he fell out with the Rockefellers, which is why on November 9, 1963 Governor Nelson Rockefeller announced that he would be seeking the Republican nomination for President. After all, huge oilfields had been discovered off the coast of Vietnam in 1950, and "Rockefellerites" had fanned the fear that Vietnam might be lost to Communism. Kennedy wanted to end American involvement in Vietnam by 1965, and by 1963 he had withdrawn 1,000 troops. The day after the assassination President Johnson escalated the war in Vietnam.

Kennedy had also tried to strip the "Rothschildian" Federal Reserve Bank of its power to loan money to the government and receive interest. On June 4, 1963, Kennedy had signed executive Order no. 11110, which returned the power to issue currency against silver bullion in the US treasury's vault to the US government. He put $4.3b into circulation and was about to put the Federal Bank of New York out of business. This would have been a catastrophe for the Syndicate.[57]

Most of the current US national debt of more than $7.5 trillion has been created since 1963 and had Kennedy's attempt to eliminate the US debt – by eliminating the Federal Reserve's control over the creation of money – worked, the US national debt would now be on a far more manageable level. It could be repaid without paying interest on new money. In tackling the causes of US debt – war and the creation of money by a privately-owned bank – he had threatened to undermine the enormous fortunes of some very powerful people.

The assassination has been credited to the Cubans, the CIA, the Soviets, the Mafia, the Freemasons, and many others. Maybe some of these parties were linked. There's little doubt for instance that "Rockefellers" were heavily involved in Russia. A 1959 photograph shows a delighted Nelson Rockefeller pretending to box the widely beaming Nikita Krushchev. They were clearly on familiar terms. When David Rockefeller visited Moscow crowds lined the streets from the airport. The Politburo was run by the Central Committee of the CPSU and the Council of Elders. An extract from the Cominform weekly journal of February 11, 1955 quotes a speech by Krushchev: "Comrades deputies, on the instruction of the Central Committee of the CPSU and the Council of Elders, I wish ... "[58] This Council of Elders has never been explained. Are the elders the elders of Sion, or Zion? Is it a freemasonic Council? This might sound fanciful. But it's worth remembering that Lenin's Bolshevik administration had 447 Jews, most of whom were also Freemasons, out of a total membership of 545.[59]

The Ousting of Krushchev

Krushchev was ousted because of China rather than the Cuba crisis. Despite his blustering, larger-than-life dealings with America (which included removing a shoe and banging it on a table in the UN building), and although "Rockefellers" were funding an increase of missiles against Russia, "Rockefellers" expected Krushchev to advance their commercial interests in Asia.[60] Krushchev's prestige had suffered over Cuba, and his strong anti-Maoist policy had interfered with Soviet-Chinese trade, which was important to David Rockefeller, President of Chase Manhattan Bank,[61] who now had the rights to all oil exported from China.[62] "Rockefellers" had gone to great lengths to defend their Chinese oil interests against the Japanese, and in the past had made representations to President Truman and the US war cabinet (in which "Rockefellerites" were in the majority)[63] and influenced the decision to drop the first atomic bomb on Hiroshima to protect "Rockefellers"' oil interests in China from an invasion by Japan.[64]

In August 1964 trade between the USSR and China had broken down because of the feud between Krushchev and Mao, and to make matters worse on August 5, 1964 the US bombed several installations in North

Vietnam for the first time. David Rockefeller was holding a Bilderberg conference in Leningrad to urge Soviet trade with China – notably, the export of "Rockefeller" oil from the USSR to China.[65] (This could be handled by his new Hong Kong branch of Chase Manhattan Bank, which he had personally opened six months earlier.)[66] Krushchev phoned Rockefeller and implored him to go to Moscow immediately to discuss the matter in the Kremlin. It was a difficult meeting, the subject being Krushchev's failure to advance "Rockefellers"' oil interests. David Rockefeller's daughter Neva took notes.[67] In October Krushchev was ousted.

David Rockefeller seems to have been able to influence Soviet domestic politics, perhaps via the Council of the Elders,[68] in order to protect his oil interests in China. Despite the Cold War, it seems that Rockefeller's relationship with the post-Stalin leadership was such that he could go to Moscow, demand the replacement of the Russian leader and secure it two months later. The Soviet Union was now something of a "Rockefeller" satellite. Rockefeller was known as "the Czar of the New World Order."[69]

North Vietnam

Vast oilfields had been found off the coast of Vietnam in 1950. A month after Krushchev's departure, the political wing of the Viet Cong guerrillas in South Vietnam was invited to open an office in Moscow.

The North Vietnamese are thought to have been armed at the end of the Second World War by Laurance Rockefeller, Gen. MacArthur's assistant, who sold weapons and munitions from the US stockpile on Okinawa to Ho Chi Minh, leader of Vietnam.[70] Maybe Rockefeller hoped that Vietnam would drive out the French so that Standard Oil could develop the as yet undeveloped offshore oilfields. After the defeat of the French at Dien Bien Phu in 1954, Ho reneged on the deal to exploit the offshore oil for Vietnam.[71]

The whole of Indo-China stands on an oil basin. During the Indo-Chinese war of 1946–54, Standard Oil began – in 1950 – a search for oil off Vietnam. They conducted a seismic survey of the seabed that lasted 10 years.[72] By 1960 they had located vast oil reserves. They wanted to divide the seabed into oil lots and bid for the ones that had the most oil. There had to be a Vietnamese government they could deal with. Since the defeat of the French in 1954 Vietnam had been split into South and North Vietnam, divided by the 17th parallel, and South Vietnam was unstable.[73] The only way the oil could be removed was for there to be one stable government throughout the whole of Vietnam, with the prospect of long-term peace. In other words, for Vietnam to be unified.

To effect such unity, there had to be a war which would preferably lead to South Vietnamese victory; or failing that a North Vietnamese victory which would establish long-term stability. In early 1961 President Kennedy secretly sent 400 Special Operations Forces soldiers to teach the South Vietnamese how to fight counterinsurgency war against Communist guerrillas.[74] For the US to enter a new Vietnamese war, US public opinion would have to believe in resisting the Soviet Union in Asia. The threat of the USSR had to be built up.

Cuba was the Syndicate's way of influencing US public opinion. Sometimes in the Cold War the US and USSR got at each other in more than one region simultaneously. This was the case with Cuba and Vietnam. They are on opposite sides of the world, yet were linked in Cold War confrontation. Recently communized, Cuba was already an affront on the US's doorstep and the missile crisis magnified Soviet threat.

Now the American public had been alarmed by Soviet "expansionism" the way was clear for the Syndicate to intensify the war in Vietnam. Kennedy wanted to scale it down – in fact, pull out of Vietnam – for vote reasons. He was murdered. At the time of his death in 1963 there were 16,000 American advisors in Vietnam. Johnson, his successor, increased the US's military involvement. There were 3,500 US troops in Vietnam in March 1965, 75,000 by July 1965, and 510,000 by early 1968. They fought alongside 600,000 South Vietnamese. Collectively they were fighting 230,000 Viet Cong and 50,000 North Vietnamese army troops.[75]

The Soviet Union had decided to intervene in the Vietnam War following America's bombing of North Vietnam after a naval incident in the Gulf of Tonkin. On November 26, 1964 the Russians promised to help Vietnam. The war went badly for South Vietnam, and in February 1965 the US again bombed North Vietnam in the very week Kosygin, the Soviet premier, visited Hanoi. From now on there was regular bombing of North Vietnam.

The war was unpopular with the American public. But for the Syndicate the war was useful. It generated huge arms expenditure. This suited "Rockefellers"; they had gone into huge arms production before January

1967. Through the International Basic Economy Corporation, which was controlled by the Rockefeller brothers, they had joined with Tower International Inc.[76] This was headed by Cyrus Eaton, the US-Canadian founder of the Republic Steel Corporation and nuclear disarmer who was once John D. Rockefeller I's secretary.[77] His son Cyrus Eaton Jr. was a close acquaintance of Kosygin and Brezhnev.[78] "Rockefellers" and Eaton Jr. had joined forces to build arms production plants – in particular a \$50m aluminum plant in Russia – and to finance Soviet industry, commerce, and tourism.[79] The "Rockefeller"/Standard Oil-Stalin deal of 1925/6 was behind the new "Rockefeller"-Soviet Axis of the 1960s. Their arms production plant is believed to have kept the Viet Cong well supplied with arms.[80] "Rockefellers" owned a massive oil refinery in North Vietnam that was not bombed by US planes. Foreign banks controlled by "Rockefellers" funded the North Vietnemese war effort.[81]

In spring 1968 in the Tet offensive, the Viet Cong and North Vietnamese attacked more than 100 cities and military bases. Washington concluded that military victory was no longer possible and declined to send another 206,000 US troops.[82] On March 31, 1968 President Johnson announced that he would pursue a negotiated settlement with Hanoi and restrict the bombing of North Vietnam.

Kissinger's détente – a thawing of the Cold War – grew out of this new American realization in 1968–9. He began the strategic arms limitation talks (SALT) in 1969. President Nixon went to China in 1970 and negotiated an American withdrawal from Vietnam – which would be followed by a North Vietnamese invasion and victory.

The Syndicate, having wanted the unification of Vietnam from the South, now supported Vietnamese unification from the North. A ceasefire was signed in Paris in January 1973, and the US withdrew, abandoning military equipment worth \$5b[83] and leaving South Vietnam along with Laos and Cambodia undefended. Saigon eventually fell to the Communists in April 1975. Some 57,000 US troops and 500,000 Vietnamese had been killed fighting in Vietnam.[84]

The Standard Oil seismic survey had lasted 20 years in all, from 1950 to 1970. After 1964 jet planes that had taken off from aircraft carriers to bomb locations in North and South Vietnam, and had to dump unsafe or unused bombs in the ocean in accordance with normal military procedure before returning to their carriers, were guided to safe ordnance drop zones that would not interfere with the small explosions that took place daily in the waters of the South China Sea, and which seemed – even to close-up observers – to be part of the war. When the survey was completed, there was no need for the war to continue.[85]

As the Syndicate had wanted back in 1960, a strong and unified Vietnam divided the offshore coastal area into oil lots. BP, Royal Dutch Shell, Statoil of Norway, Russia, Germany, and Australia won bids, drilled but found nothing. The lots Standard Oil won, identified as a result of their 20–year survey, contained vast oil reserves.[86]

Between 1960 and 1963 did the Syndicate decide to escalate the conflict in Vietnam to gain it? And did "Rockefellers" back both sides for safety's sake – supporting Johnson's war effort between 1964 and 1967, and at the same time currying favor with the Soviet Union and North Vietnam by opening their arms factory in 1967 and refinery? (Compare how Standard Oil controlled the arms and oil supply to Hitler.) Did Standard Oil finally gain access to North Vietnamese oil in return for helping the Soviet Union win victory in North Vietnam?

Six-Day War

Col. Nasser had been armed by the Soviet Union with the backing of "Rockefellers."[87] But he had plotted to take over the Near Eastern Arab states including Saudi Arabia, seize their oil profits and turn on Israel.[88] The plan was that the states would break their oil contracts and demand increased shares in the profits. "Rockefellers"' Caltex and Aramco gave the ruler of Saudi Arabia 50%. Nasser pressed him and other Arab rulers to demand 75%.[89] So Nasser upset both sides of the Syndicate.

The Soviet Union escalated tension, accusing Israel of massing forces on the Syrian border. Moscow sent much of its Black Sea fleet into the Mediterranean, and supported Nasser when he blocked Israeli shipping in the Red Sea and demanded that the UN force in Sinai should be removed. Alarmed by the impending arrival of the Soviet fleet and Nasser's blockade, Israel launched a pre-emptive strike against its Arab neighbors on June 5.[90]

The third Arab-Israeli War of June 1967 (the previous two being in 1948 and 1956) began with Nasser closing the Gulf of Aqaba to Israeli shipping and ended with the chastening of Nasser and the expansion of

"Rothschilds"' Israel through the capture of the Syrian Golan Heights and Gaza.

Czechoslovakia

In 1968 Russian tanks rolled into Czechoslovakia to snuff out Dubcek's Prague Spring. It is likely that some of these tanks came from the "Rockefellers"-Eaton production line.

In April 1967 Ché Guevara, an Argentine-born Cuban citizen close to Castro, fighting in, or rather to acquire, oil-rich Bolivia, had called for new revolutionary fronts, "two, three ... many Vietnams."[91] There were now three revolutionary fronts in accordance with Ché Guevara's call – in North Vietnam, the Middle East, and Eastern Europe – and soon there would be numerous fronts throughout the world, notably in Africa, Asia, and Latin America.

Terrorism Increases

After the Six-Day War debacle terrorism began to spread, an Arab response to Israel's expansion. Palestinian terrorists trained in Soviet-backed training camps were responsible for 50,000 acts of terror between 1970 and 1985. In total there were 223 training camps, the biggest number being in the USSR. Fifty terrorist groups from the Soviet Union and its satellites were centrally coordinated by the Palestinians.

The Syndicate wanted to create a United States of the Middle East, which would give it access to oil. The process was furthered by the confrontation between Palestine and Israel, for it created two blocs within the Middle East, which could eventually become one regional bloc, with Israel and Palestine living harmoniously together, as conflict gave way to reconciliation.

Terrorism furthered this end and was an instrument of policy. For example, the terrorist Carlos "the Jackal," who lived in luxury in Libya in the early 1970s, kidnapped Sheikh Yamani in 1975, at the time Saudi Arabia's oil minister and the most powerful figure on OPEC, an act calculated to influence Saudi Arabia's and OPEC's oil policy. In 1973 the OPEC oil-producing countries of the Middle East had rebelled against the Western-owned oil companies, quadrupling the price of crude oil. [92]

Détente

When Richard Nixon, a member of the CFR since 1961, became President in 1969, Dr. Henry Kissinger left Nelson Rockefeller's employ as chief advisor on foreign affairs after working for him for 15 years. (He had graduated from Harvard in 1950 with the aid of a Rockefeller Foundation Fellowship for Political Theory.) Rockefeller gave him $50,000 in January 1969 before he joined the White House as national security advisor. (This gift was disclosed in 1970 during a tax investigation, and it is not known why it was made.)[93] In the course of Nixon's Presidency (from 1969 to 1974) 110 CFR members were given government appointments.[94]

Soon after he was appointed Secretary of State, Kissinger pursued a policy of détente. It was pursuing the same means under a different emphasis. The policy was welcomed by Brezhnev, who was trying to repair the damage caused to the USSR's image by the brutal repression of Dubcek's Prague Spring.

Following talks to limit nuclear missiles, Nixon for his part signaled that Asia must be defended by Asians, with Americans providing logistical and economic support. This led to Nixon's visit to China in 1972, which opened up trade, an aim of "Rockefellers," and made possible the settlement in Vietnam.

Soviet Satellites

In practice, détente didn't make much difference. No new Soviet satellites were created between the time of the Communization of China (1949) and the satellization of Cuba (1970), but following "Rockefellers" partnership with Soviet imperialism from 1967 and Kissinger's détente suddenly a string of Soviet satellites or pliant states emerged in parts of what used to be the European Empires: India and Bangladesh (1971); Egypt (which in 1969–70 had 17,000 Soviet advisors, who were expelled in 1972) and Iraq (1972); the Yemen, Somalia, and Afghanistan (1974); Guinea-Bissau, Mozambique, and Angola (by the USSR Friendship Treaty of 1976 following the Cuban-led conquest); and Libya (following a huge $12b Soviet arms deal in 1976 though it was already pro-"Rockefeller"/Soviet from the time of Gaddafi's 1969 revolution). It took a fundamental change in the USSR, which led to the tearing down of the Berlin Wall, to put an end to East–West confrontation and make possible a true coming-together (which had always been "Rockefellers"/Kissinger's ultimate aim) of Europe, the former USSR's East European satellites and Russia in a United States of Europe that might eventually include them all.

7

THE UNITED STATES OF EUROPE AND RUSSIA

Let us have the United States of Europe; let us have continental federation.
Victor Hugo, address to the Masonic Peace Conference, Paris in 1849[1]

The Cold War led to the development of regional blocs, which would have been inconceivable 50 years ago. The West European bloc has been gradually strengthened over the decades, slowly but inexorably turning into a formal federation, with individual nations releasing more and more sovereignty.

Lenin wanted Russia and Europe to be united in a "republican United States of Europe – if accompanied by the revolutionary overthrow of the three most reactionary monarchs in Europe, headed by the Russian."[2] As we have seen, Stalin echoed his call in 1926.[3] Churchill wrote an essay entitled "The United States of Europe," which was published in the February 15, 1930 issue of the American *Saturday Evening Post*. He wrote to his cabinet in October 1942, "Hard as it is to say now, I trust that the European family may act unitedly as one under a Council of Europe. I look forward to a United States of Europe." In 1946 in Zurich he said, "We must build a kind of United States of Europe."[4]

A United States of Europe (which included Russia) had been envisaged by Count Coudenhove-Kalergi in his *Pan Europa* in 1923 and three years later at his first Pan-European Congress. Coudenhove's ideas influenced Jean Monnet, deputy secretary general of the League of Nations from 1919. The idea of a United States of Europe was developed by Monnet in conjunction with the shadowy new American organization, the CFR. It's been on the agenda of the Round Table, the Bilderberg Group, and the Trilateral Commission for many years.[5]

A constitution for a "United States of Europe" was first proposed in a manifesto by a young Italian Communist Altieri Spinelli (after whom the main building in the EU Parliament in Brussels is now named) in 1944. Spinelli admitted that his United States of Europe could not come into existence democratically, but would have to be implemented gradually, without the peoples of Europe grasping what was happening until they were presented with a constitution. Jean Monnet carried the vision forward, becoming President of the European Coal and Steel Community in 1952. "This" he declared, "is the government of Europe." Monnet's proposal for a "United States of Europe" to Paul-Henri Spaak, the former Belgian Prime Minister, was returned to him with all references to a "United States of Europe" or "supra-national government" deleted.[6] The pretence was then adopted that it would be an economic community, and it was on that basis that the Treaty of Rome was signed in 1957, setting up the EEC.

The trend towards a united Europe seems unstoppable. The UK is a case in point. Having stayed out of the EEC in its early days the British Prime Minister Ted Heath won the election in 1970, and one of his first acts was to appoint Victor, Lord Rothschild as head of his think-tank, where he served from 1970 to 1974. As a result the UK was admitted into the EEC in 1972.[7] Even Margaret Thatcher signed up to the Europe that was later regulated by the Maastricht Treaty. But she also stood up for Britain's sovereignty and to retain the Falklands' oil. When the Bilderberg Group met at La Toja in Spain in May 1989 the "Rockefellerite" Henry Kissinger was reported as complaining that Thatcher was opposing the creation of a European Central Bank, which was crucial to the United States of Europe.[8] This Bank was a "Rockefellerite" concept and would counterbalance the Rothschilds' Bank of England, the American Federal Reserve System, and the City. The decision was taken to speed up a United States of Europe that would include the Eastern European nations just emerging from Soviet rule – another "Rockefellerite" concept, for "Rothschilds" did not want the republican Eastern European nations in its monarchist Europe. A whispering campaign was started against Margaret Thatcher, the British Prime Minister, because she opposed any further surrender of British sovereignty to the German-dominated European Union.

A call went out for Thatcher to be overthrown. The call was answered – perhaps by a coincidence of aim and timing rather than to do Bilderberg's bidding – by the "Rothschildites" Michael Heseltine and Sir Geoffrey Howe, whose crucial interventions and speeches created a loss of confidence in the Prime Minister and resulted in her failure to win the leadership contest, as a result of which she resigned. The "Rothschildite" Thatcher was overthrown and replaced not by the "Rothschildites'" first choice,[9] Michael Heseltine, but by the lesser-known, John Major. Though elected by the Conservative Parliamentary Party, many of whom had not heard of the Bilderberg Group and were certainly not operating under its control, he was expected by the Syndicate to do Bilderberg's business:[10] pass the Maastricht Treaty in the English Parliament and agree to a single European currency, a Central Bank, and a Court in Strasbourg that would order member nations to rewrite or cancel some of their laws.

Major disappointed his "Rothschildite" supporters as he had a tiny majority and was barely able to get the Maastricht Treaty bill through Parliament. He also prevaricated on the single currency, saying that the European countries could have one if they wanted but that the UK would wait and see.

British Devolution

In May 1997 John Major was replaced by another "Rothschildite,"[11] Tony Blair, who like a cuckoo in the nest took over Major's policies with the benefit of a large majority. His election was helped by the billionaire, Sir James Goldsmith, a relative of the Rothschilds, standing against Major.

Blair had attended the April 1993 Bilderberg meeting at Vouliagmeni in Greece – Gordon Brown, later to be his Chancellor, had attended the 1991 meeting – and he listed his visit two years later in the Commons Register of Members' interests (paras 1, 5, and 7 of the "Appendix to the Third Report of the Select Committee on Standards and Privileges," published in *Hansard*). In 1998 Blair denied that any member of his government had ever attended any Bilderberg meeting when challenged by Christopher Gill MP in a written Commons question (*Hansard*, March 30, 1998, cols. 375–376). Technically his answer was correct, as both Blair and Brown were not in the British government when in opposition.

Once elected, Blair made sweeping constitutional changes. In July 1996 Blair had visited Kissinger at his office in New York, shown on a TV clip at the time. Kissinger was reported later as saying, tongue in cheek, "The illegal we do immediately, the unconstitutional takes a little longer." Blair devolved Scotland, Wales, Northern Ireland (in which the victorious IRA share power with the Protestants), and London.[12]

One result of these changes was to loosen the ties between Scotland and England by giving Scotland its own Parliament, thus weakening the UK. If the Scottish National Party win a general election, then a sovereign independent Scotland will not join a United States of Europe. The ownership of dwindling supplies of North Sea oil will pass to Scotland in either case.

Blair is also prepared to split England into eight further regions with tax-raising powers.[13]

In July 2002 it was reported (in London's *Sunday Telegraph*, July 7, 2002) that according to Dr. Richard North, director for the Europe of Democracies and Diversities, Britain's local government system was to be replaced by a network of regional governments, which will control planning, education, and the police. The prototypes of these bodies were set up in the UK in 1994 to receive regional funds from Brussels, funds that would otherwise not have been paid.

The study by Dr. North revealed that John Prescott, Britain's Deputy Prime Minister, has masterminded the process of breaking Britain up into regions since 1970 when he was leader of the Labour group in the European Parliament and delegate to the Council of Europe. In 1996 Prescott outflanked New Labour's party policy by setting up his own "regional commission," chaired by former Brussels Commissioner for the Regions Bruce Millan. When Labour took power in 1997 this regional commission enabled Prescott to push through regional governments for Scotland, Wales, Northern Ireland, and London, but also "regional development agencies" for the eight remaining English regions, which became regional governments-in-waiting. According to Dr. North on the continent regional governments are able to bypass national governments by relating directly to Brussels, i.e. by receiving funds from Brussels and in return exercising powers granted by Brussels.[14] Europe is thus likely to become a political union that is a network of federal regional governments.

Currency

From January 2002 the euro circulated in 12 out of 15 EU countries, and by the end of February 2002 the euro replaced all 12 European currencies, except for Britain's, Sweden's, and Denmark's. The following currencies ceased to be legal tender: the French, Belgian, and Luxembourgian franc, the German mark, the Dutch guilder, the Italian lira, the Greek drachma, the Spanish peseta, the Portuguese escudo, the Austrian schilling, the Finnish markka, and the Irish punt. The British Prime Minister Blair, returned to power with a virtually unchanged majority in May 2001, declared (in the handed-out text of a speech to the Trades Union Congress in September 2001) that he would support a successful single currency and the campaign for the euro to replace the pound. Syndicate plans for Britain and an enlarged Europe to be fully "euro-ed" therefore look unstoppable. In his pre-budget address on November 27, 2001, the "Rothschildite" British Chancellor Brown[15] reported that Britain has paid off a substantial amount (£51b) of national debt (i.e. he has repaid money borrowed from "Rothschilds" and others, and old issues of stock), and has cut debt interest payments to their lowest level since 1918, to 31% of the government's total expenditure (against 40% in the US, Germany, and France and 95% in Italy). Seen from this perspective, Britain's economy falls within the Maastricht criteria, and although after a £6b surplus it faces four years of deficits (beginning with a predicted deficit of £12b), requiring more borrowing and a new issue of government stock and an increase in the national debt, it is stronger than the other economies of Europe. Alarm was expressed that this position might be weakening when in October 2002 Britain's foreign trade deficit was a record £3.56b, the largest monthly deficit since William of Orange ordered trade records to be kept in 1697.[16]

Industries

In 2003 Britain's fishing industry lost its self-sufficiency. In 1970 Britain, Norway, Ireland, and Denmark had fishing rights that extended 200 miles from their shores and owned 90% of Europe's fish. The day their applications to join the EEC arrived the Six (France, Germany, Italy, Belgium, the Netherlands, and Luxembourg) issued a law that all countries in the Common Market would have equal access to each other's fishing-waters. Heath sacrificed Britain's fishing-waters in return for entry into Europe, but concealed the truth from Parliament.[17] In 1982 a 20–year "transitional phase" of the Common Fisheries Policy came into force. Spain had only limited access to British waters, which were now designated "Community" waters, and was compensated by £4b of EU taxpayers' money (£500m from UK taxpayers) and invested this in modernizing its trawlers. On December 31, 2002 this 20–year phase ended, and thousands of British vessels had to be removed to make room for Spanish trawlers in 2003. Under the guise of "cod conservation" British ships were restricted to fishing nine days per month, forcing many fishermen into retirement, and some into bankruptcy.[18]

Britain's farming industry, which made the nation-state self-sufficient during the Second World War, is now facing the biggest crisis in its history as a result of the EU's Common Agricultural Policy (CAP). Subsidies have encouraged farmers to produce unwanted surpluses – eggs, poultry or sheep meat, beef, pigs, potatoes, wheat, barley, milk – that have to be destroyed. British farmers have had to compete with produce from Spain, which is cheap due to cheap labor and round-the-year sun. They have been paid in relation to their "hectarage" and compensated for "set-aside" (land left fallow). Prices have fallen, and some farmers' incomes have fallen to a quarter of what they were 10 years previously. Abattoirs are closing. CAP reforms in 1993 and 2000 imposed production controls and cut farm prices while compensating farmers through direct payments. However, reform has not put a stop to overproduction and collapsing livestock prices, and a drift away from farming can be expected. In comparison Britain will be even less self-sufficient.[19]

As a result of the British miners' strike of 1984, when Scargill opposed the closure of 20 pits, 170 pits were reduced to 12.[20]

Ten of the 22 nuclear power stations in the UK were designated for decommissioning. As a result Britain would cease to be self-sufficient in the production of electricity. In 2004 London was importing much of its electricity from France.[21]

As each industry (fishing, farming, coal, electricity) was eroded, national independence was diminished and European interdependence was advanced.

Policing

On May 22, 2002 the EC's President Romano Prodi, a Steering Committee member of the Bilderberg Group in the 1980s, called for "a giant step forward in European integration," an EU government with control over criminal justice, taxation, and foreign affairs – "a supranational democracy" in an enlarged union of 25 or 30 countries with common border controls, "an integrated European police force," and a public prosecutor to fight EU financial fraud. Under his proposal the bureaucracy in Brussels would implement tax and budgetary harmonization and would acquire a diplomatic and economic machinery that would enable the EU to compete with the US. All decisions would be made by majority voting, and no nation would retain the power of veto.

In early June 2002 it was revealed in London's *Observer* that the EU is drawing up a "common code" on data retention, and that Europol, the police and intelligence arm of the EU, compiled a document in The Hague in April 2002 that proposes that telephone and Internet firms should retain millions of pieces of data, including details of visits to Internet chat rooms and of calls made on mobile phones and text messages, for up to five years. All e-mails, other Internet information and telephone records should be made accessible to the European police and intelligence services. Britain has put pressure on other member states of the EU to put this legislation in place.

In Britain legislation was passed in 2000 permitting only the police, customs, intelligence agencies, and the Inland Revenue to obtain communications records. Under the Regulation of Investigatory Powers Act this power has been extended to two dozen ministries and quangos: seven more government departments including the Department of Health, every local authority, the Environment Agency, the Food Standards Agency, the Health and Safety Executive, and the Post Office. Ministerial assurances that the power was aimed at tackling crime and terrorism has been undermined by the extension of the power to the Food Standards Agency.

Army

In October 2003 it was revealed (in an 8–page dossier circulating in Germany's defense ministry) that the German military high command wanted to create a fully-fledged European army that would be financed by the EU Parliament and would report to the EU government. It would be a unified EU military army that would rival NATO. Under these plans German defense chiefs wanted the EU to seize control of Britain's nuclear weapons, which would be integrated within the EU defense system.[22] Britain would be forced to share its nuclear arsenal with Germany, which is banned from possessing its own nuclear weapons. MEPs would have the power to send UK troops into battle. France wanted the Euro-army to be based in Lille and to be flying 600 aerial sorties a day by 2006.[23] British troops would take orders from French generals. Blair has allowed the principle of a European army to be based on English soil.[24] In September 2003 he backed Franco-German plans to give the Euro-army the means to plan and carry out missions outside NATO's command.

Constitution

In October 2002, the European Commission gave the go-ahead for a "Big Bang" admission of 10 new states in early 2004. This would reunite Europe in a 25–state Union and add 73 million citizens from poor countries: Poland, the Czech Republic, Hungary, Slovakia, Slovenia, Lithuania, Latvia, Estonia, Malta, and Cyprus (but not Turkey) – with Romania and Bulgaria expected to follow by 2007. The admission would create a behemoth of 370m people stretching from Galway to Gdansk, the world's largest market. At the same time the constitutional convention based on the Philadelphian Convention of 1787 and chaired by former French President Valery Giscard d'Estaing proposed a "preliminary draft constitutional treaty." This was the "new Charter for the EU" that was urged by President Clinton when he visited the Bilderberg Group's meeting near Brussels in the summer of 2000 (see page 239) and that was adopted in Nice in December 2000. (Ireland ratified the Nice treaty at its second attempt.)

After months of discussion within the Convention on the Future of Europe, which was grappling with the task of charting the course of European enlargement, Giscard d'Estaing proposed: a set of rules for a united Europe that would give Europe a single constitutional structure with its own legal identity and bill of rights, and foreign and defense policy; moving power from the nation-states to Brussels; binding Britain and all Europe's states into a super-state: renaming the European Union "the United States of Europe" (an idea immediately opposed by the British, who wanted a Union of European nation-states and feared being dragged into a European super-state); giving all citizens "dual citizenship," i.e. both national and European citizenship – a proposal that in itself elevated the EU to statehood.[25]

The main consequence of these proposals was that all states including Britain would lose the right to veto plans for foreign and defense policy, and tax harmonization and the collection of taxes – measures needed to subsidize the economies of the 10 newly admitted poor countries. Brussels would decree the amounts that all nation-states, including Britain, should pay, and these amounts would be redistributed under international-socialist principles throughout the newly enlarged European Community. Really poor nation-states like Lithuania and Latvia would therefore be subsidized by the richer nation-states such as Britain.

In November 2002 Lord Tebbit, the British Minister injured in the IRA Brighton bomb in 1984, accused Blair of seeking "the destruction" of the UK and "its absorption within a foreign jurisdiction." In the Ian Gow Memorial Lecture he said: "The outrages in Yugoslavia and those of September 11 in New York have confirmed in the mind of Mr. Blair the need not merely to submerge the UK into a Euro-state but to create a wider world authority." He spoke of Blair's "attempted obliteration of the culture and history" of the UK – of social reforms that undermined the family, and criminal and civil law reforms that overturned a thousand years of English (i.e. post-Alfred) jurisprudence, and of "his resolution to cede our very currency to foreign interests." He said that initially he believed Blair's ambitions were confined to the creation of a European identity to replace an identity of Britishness, but that he now believed Blair sought the destruction of the UK and its surrender to European jurisdiction: "Never before have we had in office ... a Prime Minister who detests our history, our constitution, our institutions and indeed the very nation we are and whose intention is to subjugate us to foreign rule," i.e. Europe.

The draft text of the European constitution filled the British government with dismay in February 2003. Sweeping aside British objections, the document established the EU on a "federal basis" with "primacy over the law of its member states." Under its provisions all nation-states would lose control of their foreign policy and defense (a provision which would have made it impossible for Britain to fight a war in Iraq), and economic governance, and would be stripped of their sovereign power to legislate in almost all areas of national life. Instead there would be "shared competence." Britain's parliamentary democracy would be abolished, as everything would be within the competence of Brussels. No one state should be allowed to block the majority, the convention's president Giscard d'Estaing said. The British government accused an élite group of insiders on the convention's 13–member presidium of carrying out a "federalist" *coup*. The text of the constitution was drafted by a triumvirate of federalists: two commissioners, Michel Barnier of France and Antonio Vitorino of Portugal, and the former Italian prime minister Guiliano Amato.

Article 46 of the secret draft text of the new European constitution was leaked before it was presented to the 105–strong Convention on the Future of Europe by the presidium headed by Giscard d'Estaing. It contained a tough secession clause that would make it illegal for Britain to leave the European Union without permission. Secession would have to be approved by two-thirds of member states, and a minority bloc of states could impose conditions offering no guarantee that a departing country could keep its trading rights or reclaim currency reserves held by the European Central Bank. David Heathcoat-Amory, a British Conservative MP on the convention, called the text outrageous and said, "It's a prison clause, not a secession clause ... We're no longer talking about a voluntary union you can leave whenever you want. It is the final extinction of parliamentary sovereignty."

The significance of the new constitution now dawned on Britain. It threatened to usher in a new order that would overturn the governing basis of British parliamentary democracy for ever. The EU would become the fount of power with its own legal personality, and would delegate functions back to Britain. Article 9 in the draft stated, "The Constitution will have primacy over the law of member states." A European interior and justice ministry (Eurojust) would have power to launch raids across the EU, including Britain, and Westminster would be prohibited from legislating in public health, social policy, transport, justice, agriculture, energy, economic and social cohesion, the environment, internal and external trade, and consumer protection.

One worrying feature of the constitution was that the new state would have power over Europe's energy supply. If a majority of EU heads of state agreed, it would have the power to transfer the remnants of North Sea oil, gas, and coal to any EU state in a global energy crisis, to ensure the security of energy supplies in the EU. This would mean Britain surrendering control of multi-billion-pound oil stocks to Brussels. The new state would also be able to raid Britain's £600b pensions fund and distribute it to less provident European states.

At the Athens Summit on April 16, 2003, in the Stoa of Attalos, the 10 new members were welcomed to the EU.

Blair called for a President of the new enlarged Europe "who could speak regularly to President Bush," and it was felt that he may have been putting himself forward for the position in the future,[26] presumably as a reward for delivering Britain into the euro in the near future. It was confirmed that the convention would support Blair's idea that Europe should have a full-time (rather than a rotating) President and Foreign Secretary for the new super-state. Blair, fresh from cooperating with Bush in the Iraq War, apparently saw no contradiction between an Anglo-American alliance in war and a pacifist Europe in which Britain would be one of 25 states under a European President and Foreign Secretary who would dictate future relations with America. At Athens, however, European leaders failed to agree whether the EU should have a permanent chairman or president, and Blair went home early and was missing from the communal photograph.

Stirred by public opposition to the new constitution, Blair had to deny the United States of Europe in both name and deed. In the face of rising British resentment, he laid down a series of "red lines," which Britain would not cross. (If the new constitution was merely a "tidying-up exercise," why the need for "red lines"?) He said he would not allow British sovereignty to be put at risk. He said he would not allow a common foreign and security policy, with one European Foreign Minister deciding on all matters of British foreign policy, or tax and benefit harmonization.

In June EC President Romano Prodi demanded that national vetoes ("red lines") should be scrapped altogether. He also demanded an end to Britain's veto over key policies such as taxation. D'Estaing said that scrapping further national vetoes may be the only way of securing a deal on the new constitutional document, and that foreign policy issues and tax rates should be decided by majority voting. Britain would have more votes than minnows such as Luxembourg, but there was a real prospect that Britain could be outvoted on foreign affairs or tax matters.

In the final version, the preamble of the new constitution omitted the EU's former goal of "an ever-closer union" and the word "federal." It stated that "the people of Europe are determined to transcend their ancient divisions, and, united ever more closely, to forge a common destiny."

In horse-trading, Britain agreed to a new EU Presidency, elected by the Council of Ministers every two and half years from 2009, in return for having one commissioner rather than two with full voting rights for 10 years of every 15. The Commission would have an inner core of 15 with full voting rights. There would be 736 Euro-MPs. One Eurocrat, confirming that signing the constitution would mean renouncing vestigial sovereignty, said: "This is more important than Maastricht, Amsterdam, and Nice combined." As Beethoven's "Ode to Joy" celebrated final agreement on the draft proposals, Germany, Denmark, and Spain stated that the blueprint for an EU super-state was the most fundamental treaty since the Community was set up in 1957.

Britain's representative stormed out of a drafting meeting at a move by d'Estaing to allow future treaty changes without requiring ratification by national parliaments. An "escalator" clause slipped into Article 24 at the last moment allowed Brussels to insert future amendments without asking national parliaments for permission. This meant that Eurocrats could rewrite Europe's, and Britain's, constitution without Westminster being given a say.

At a summit in Thessalonika, Greece in June 2003 d'Estaing gave out leather-bound copies of the draft European constitution to EU leaders, which he called "a great leap forward." To Blair's mortification it was agreed that the German anti-Bush Foreign Minister Joschka Fischer, leader of Germany's Green Party, would be the first EU Foreign Minister and in charge of European policies towards weapons of mass destruction, terrorism, and rogue states. Blair caved in. Publicly, in the presence of the EU leaders, Blair welcomed the text, saying it struck the right balance; he made no mention of British red lines on defense, taxation, or foreign policy. In the British press he hailed the new draft constitution, which was on course to surrender as many as 26 British vetoes, "a victory for Britain" – and, blanked by the other European leaders and isolated, slipped away a day early without holding a press conference.

President Jacques Chirac of France and Chancellor Schröder of Germany stayed to the end of the meeting, and the irritated Prodi, in Blair's absence, warned the absent Blair that Britain would be forced to give up control over its tax, foreign, and defense policies and that his "red lines" policy was "doomed to fail." "It is up to the IGC [inter-governmental conference of October 2003] to do this," he said.

On June 27, 2003 d'Estaing said that Blair's promise to stop more powers being transferred from Westminster to Brussels was "doomed to fail." He boasted that Blair had left it too late to stop the EU seizing more powers. Asked if he thought the draft constitution would be adopted as it is, causing Britain to lose its "red line" vetoes, d'Estaing replied: "Almost as it is. At the start, the various groups had different approaches, but we ended with a common position. It is therefore very difficult to start all over again and encounter the same obstacles we have already overcome."

A Brussels summit had been arranged for December 12–13, 2003 so that the 25 countries could sign the new constitution. In the event it collapsed over voting rights. Poland (one of the new countries) and Spain, who had each been allocated 27 votes at the Nice summit in 2000, refused to accept less. Germany, with double Poland's population, only had 29 votes, and refused to accept Poland's 27. The Polish premier Leszek Miller had been badly injured in a helicopter crash 10 days previously.

Both engines of his government Soviet-era MI-8 helicopter stopped 12 miles from Warsaw on December 4. Witnesses said that the helicopter fell out of the sky, tilted sideways, and clipped trees before coming down in a field, and Miller broke two vertebrae in his back. The crash was blamed on frozen engines or contaminated fuel. The helicopter had been used by the Pope when he visited Poland and had recently passed a technical check-up and been declared airworthy. Miller attended the summit in a wheelchair, in pain from injuries to his spine, and refused to give way. All went home early on December 13. There was talk of a new attempt in May 2004 – or 2005, or even later according to some countries. Had "Eutopia" been postponed or abandoned?

The truth is, the courageous determination of the Polish government on one issue had saved the British people – albeit temporarily – from being betrayed by a deceitful British government into signing up to a constitution that would have destroyed British law, liberty, and democracy. I cannot help wondering how the Polish premier, who was already known to be opposed to compromising on voting rights at the conference, came to have a helicopter crash just 10 days before the conference. Was the crash a complete accident, or was the helicopter downed with assistance from the Syndicate?

After the collapse of talks on the constitution, the same heads of government, sitting as the European Council, in just two minutes agreed to the siting of 10 new agencies, each of which would be based in a different European country, take power from national governments, and have supranational control of: food (Italy); aviation safety (Germany); maritime safety (Portugal); railway safety (France); fisheries (Spain); Internet network security (Greece); chemicals (Finland); disease prevention (Sweden); racism and xenophobia (Austria); and the harmonization of criminal justice (Holland). (London was to be the site of a European Police College to promote the integration of European police forces, and the Public Prosecutor would be in Luxembourg.) An agency for border management was ahead.

The constitution was back on following an attack on Madrid by al-Qaeda in March 2004. Ten simultaneous bombs went off on Spanish trains killing 200 people. The explosions influenced the general election a few days later. Spanish voters returned the Socialist Party, who were committed to withdrawing Spanish troops from Iraq and immediately reversed Spain's alliances. The new Prime Minister elect, José Zapatero, spoke of renewing "a magnificent relationship" with France and Germany. Spain turned from supporting the Anglo-American alliance and war in Iraq to supporting the Franco-German alliance and opposing the war in Iraq, which it now regarded as illegal. Al-Qaeda had split the Western war alliance. The Polish Prime Minister, reacting to this new situation, said that it would be "very dangerous" for Poland to be isolated and that he would not continue to block the constitution. The German Chancellor went to Warsaw at the invitation of Leszek Miller, and the two men reached an understanding. Miller then announced his resignation.

The change of attitude in Spain and Poland's subsequent acceptance of the voting system meant that the constitution could be agreed sooner than expected. At a meeting in Brussels on March 25, 2004 Europe's leaders set a June deadline for an agreement to coincide with elections to the European Parliament. They were mindful that they had 450m people to protect from terrorism, and needed centralized uniformity to achieve this. A Franco-German-Spanish alliance could now force through the centralizing European constitution at an inter-governmental EU conference in Brussels in June 2004, and dominate Europe. Britain was isolated. Blair now removed one of his red lines (on criminal justice) and, hoping to ram it through, called for the EU to agree the constitution "as soon as possible." He then announced, in a U- (or EU-) turn, after a holiday in Bermuda and without consulting his cabinet, that there would be a referendum after the next General Election, i.e. perhaps in autumn 2005, and after parliament had completed its work on the new treaty. There were reports that the 10 new agencies would be running most of Britain by June 2004.

On June 18, 2004, no doubt to enormous "Rockefellerite"/"Roths-childite"/Bilderberg rejoicing, agreement was reached in Brussels on the EU constitution – but not on the identity of the President of the European Commission. According to Belgium's prime minister Guy Verhofstadt, the new constitution was the "capstone of a European federal state." The Belgian vice-chairman of the constitutional convention and author of the constitution, Jean-Luc Dehaene, confirmed that it was a blueprint for a European super-state and "marks the EU's passage from a socio-economic Europe to a more political Europe." It certainly came close to fulfilling Jean Monnet's Utopian vision. The EU was now a state in its own right with its own legal personality. As a constitution is by definition "the principles on which a state is governed" the EU state draws legitimacy from this. The new constitution was a legal framework for a new state, the book of rules for micro-management by the unelected Brussels bureaucracy, the Commission and Council.

It was now clear that the new constitution would be interpreted by the European Court of Justice, and its application would be decided by lawyers and judges. The new state would control all labour laws by a new charter of fundamental rights and would fulfil a new duty to "coordinate economic policy". According to senior lawyers EU law was now set to have precedence and primacy over parliamentary statutes/national laws and national constitutions, whether written or unwritten – and therefore over all British law and British representational democracy.

The myth-perpetuating Blair made much of Britain's retention of its red lines on tax, foreign policy, defense, and social security (all of which will be quietly discontinued a few years after the referendum, like his predecessor John Major's opt-out from the Social Chapter), and kept quiet about the 248 British amendments that were rejected – only 27 out of 275 British amendments were included in the final draft. A pattern had been perpetuated: the Maastricht Treaty had led to Britain's losing the right to govern itself in 30 areas; the Amsterdam Treaty to the surrender of another 20 areas;

and the Nice Treaty to the loss of more than 40 areas. The new constitution would lead to the British surrender of the right to veto in 43 new areas. Thirty-six other articles would result in Britain's ceding legislative powers to the European Parliament. If the constitution was ratified, Britain could be outvoted on asylum policy and its own legislation could be set aside by foreign judges. It seemed that Britain's seat on the UN Security Council would have to be surrendered to the new EU Foreign Minister when Brussels requested. Giscard d'Estaing, who led the constitutional convention, said that 90% of the original draft of the constitution had been left intact, with 13,500 out of the original 14,800 words unchanged.

It only later became clear that Britain had lost control of its economic policy, for in a last-minute sleight-of-hand amendment, the power to dictate economic policy was transferred from the European Council to the Council of Ministers, where decisions can be made by qualified majority voting. If the constitution was ratified, Britain could be forced to adopt economic policies that were against the British national interest and which were opposed by Britain.

Despite evidence of overwhelming opposition to Brussels in the European elections a few days previously, which saw the emergence of the UK Independence Party that seeks Britain's withdrawal from Europe, Blair, with no mandate from his people, had signed up to an extraordinary leap forward into a European federal super-state – while insisting that he had retained a Europe of nation-states. Britain had had experience of creating such a federal state, having created Canada, Australia, India, and the ill-fated Federation of Rhodesia and Nyasaland.

The super-state, a new entity, would finally arrive by stealth; the end of the process would be the covert rescinding of all red lines after full ratification. A 48-nation European Union/United States of Europe including all the ex-USSR territories was now a firm possibility. If any country voted against ratification (which had to be completed by the end of 2006), the constitution would fall. The way was clear for a European Constitution Bill to be brought before the British Parliament in the autumn of 2004 and for ratification to be the main issue in the impending British general election expected in 2005. This would be followed by a referendum, which had to be held by June 2006. The new constitution had to be ratified by 25 national parliaments and 6 referenda in all. Would it be greeted by a ferocious battle, or by an uncomprehending yawn?

Monarchy

In May 2003 it had been announced that Blair was to abolish the rights of the 92 remaining hereditary peers to sit and vote in the House of Lords. In a secret deal struck with Lord Cranborne (for which Cranborne was sacked by Hague), they had initially been allowed to stay until the second stage of reform was completed. Although this had not happened, Blair decided to press ahead with removing the last hereditary peers, and the new Lord Chancellor, Lord Falconer, announced the decision in September. Their removal would leave a Lords of "yes men" who could approve a new European constitution and entry into the euro. Blair's constitutional *coup*, whereby he removed the hereditary peers who could be expected to vote against the new European arrangements, was effected in two phases and spread over several years.

In June 2003 Blair announced in a reshuffle like a *coup d'état* that the 1,400–year-old office of Lord Chancellor (which can be traced back to 605), the "Keeper of the Queen's Conscience," the oldest secular office, would be abolished and replaced by a Ministry of Justice. Blair was supposed to consult the Queen, the judiciary, peers, and the Opposition, and was summoned to Parliament by the Speaker to explain his actions. The Queen was reported to be furious; the feeling was that the monarchy would be next. She sought independent legal advice on the threat to the role of her sovereignty under the new constitution.[27] In early 2004 it was announced in a parallel thrust that can be seen as mere smartening up of an image that the Crown Prosecution Service would be renamed the Public Prosecution Service.

It was claimed that the Queen broke her Coronation Oath to her people in 1972 when she allowed Parliament to pass[28] the European Communities Act and gave it the Royal Assent. According to District Judge Morgan in his judgment on the "metric martyrs" on April 9, 2001, the Act surrendered the sovereignty of the British people to the EU. Morgan was not subsequently rebuked or reprimanded, and so his interpretation stands. Therefore since 1972 Britain has ceased to be a sovereign nation, and the British have been without a Queen.[29]

For many centuries the Lord Chancellor has handed the Queen's speech to the Queen at the State Opening of Parliament. The abolition of the Lord Chancellor meant that this part of the State Opening ceremony could no longer happen, and it was now rumored that Blair planned to abolish the State Opening of Parliament. A rearguard action was fought by some peers who wanted the Lords Speaker to retain the title of Lord Chancellor and continue to perform ceremonial duties during the State Opening of Parliament.

Under the Laeken declaration of December 2001, it was proposed that the President of the EU should be elected – giving him/her an electorate of over 300m citizens and thus making him more powerful than any of the leaders of Europe's nation-states – and that a convention (based on the Philadelphian Convention of 1787) would consider a new constitution for an integrated United States of Europe with an elected President. In January 2003 Schröder and Chirac agreed that there would be two Presidents of the EU: one to chair the European Council of Ministers, elected by Euro-MPs (the French choice), and one to be President of the Commission, elected by the European Parliament (the German, more federal choice).

Rebellion

Now a group of members of the Convention on the Future of Europe, the body writing the new constitution, planned to publish a minority report opposing the main proposals. Some 12 politicians from eight countries (including Britain, France Sweden, Denmark, and Ireland) proposed to abolish the European Union and replace it with a "Europe of Democracies." European countries should not lose their veto on foreign policy, taxes should not be harmonized and the European Union should not be renamed "the United States of Europe."

There was now a campaign (launched by the Campaign for a Referendum on the European Constitution) to request the Queen to block the European constitution, which was modeled on the US constitution, to prevent the British way of life from being destroyed. A petition to the Queen urged her to withhold the Royal Assent from any Bill incorporating the constitution into British law. It was suggested that Britain should have associate membership of the new blocs so that it could be part of a single European market, but not a political union.

It emerged that the original version of the EU constitution had contained a section that said it should be approved by the people of Europe. Campaigners for a referendum could be expected to seize on this. It was reported that Sir John Kerr, a British official working with Giscard d'Estaing, supported its deletion from the first published version of the constitution.[30] A spokesman for d'Estaing's office did not deny the claim. The only British political figure with the resolve and determination to oppose the new European constitution in deed rather than in word was Iain Duncan Smith, who had been elected Conservative Leader by the rank and file membership of the party. A spate of negative stories in the press now suggested that the majority of Conservative MPs was calling for him to be replaced as Opposition Leader. A report alleging improper payments to his wife from public funds was submitted by an investigative journalist to the Parliamentary Commissioner for Standards, Sir Philip Mawer, who later cleared him. Ambitious women within the Conservative Party making the allegations perhaps hoped to gain by being rewarded by a replacement Leader, but the allegations were coincidentally to the advantage of those in the Bilderberg Group who championed the euro and the new European constitution. From their perspective, the allegations could only help secure a victory for their puppet Blair at the next General Election by splitting and weakening the Conservative Party, and if successful, might bring the additional benefit of replacing Duncan Smith with a pro-euro, pro-constitution Leader.

This is exactly what happened. After six weeks of turmoil and unsourced stories about plotting MPs in the press, on Thursday October 23 Duncan Smith launched a nationwide petition for a referendum on the new constitution (a policy vehemently opposed by Ken Clarke). Within days 25 (mostly unnamed) Conservative MPs forced a vote of no confidence in Duncan Smith under the new Hague rules. On October 29, 2003 Duncan Smith lost the vote 90 to 75 and was removed as Leader. He was replaced by Michael Howard (son of an European immigrant, a Romanian whose name when he came to Britain was Bernat Hecht) in a *putsch* by the Parliamentary Party. Duncan Smith had been elected by the 320,000 Conservative membership, and had defeated his rival Ken Clarke 61% to 39%. This electorate was not consulted. At his news conference (launched by "Rothschildite" Lord Lamont, a director of N. M. Rothschild & Sons who had attended the 1995 Bilderberg meeting as a British delegate along with Emma Rothschild, daughter of Victor, also a British delegate)[31] to declare his candidature for the Leadership, Howard said that the Conservative Party would be centrist and "internationalist" in outlook. Earlier in the day (at Denis Thatcher's memorial service) Lord Carrington, ex-Chairman of Bilderberg, was seen on television approaching him, beaming at him and patting him several times on the arm as if to say, "Well done," no doubt relieved that the Conservative Party now had a credible leader and delighted at the success of someone he knew.

The *coup* had been brilliantly organized as the participants were all thinking in the currency of effectiveness, leadership, and integrity, and the MPs and journalists involved – and probably even Howard himself – had little idea of the game plan behind the no-confidence vote.

It was later revealed that the part-time Shadow Cabinet Minister Oliver Letwin, son of a Ukrainian/American academic (who had worked at N. M. Rothschild & Sons since 1986 and been a director since 1991, and who at that time still worked there every morning) was instrumental in giving Howard a clear run.[32] He had visited David Davis immediately after Duncan Smith conceded – Letwin's office at the Commons was next door to Davis's – and had established that Davis would not be standing.[33] He took the message back to the Howard camp. Davis's decision not to stand colored the decisions of other rivals, who followed suit. It was reported that Ken Clarke decided not to stand following a meeting with Howard to establish his agenda, including his European policy. Having heard this, Clarke was happy to endorse Howard but elected to remain on the backbenches so he could criticize any deviation from a "Euro-centrist" position. From the Bilderberg/"Rothschildian" perspective, Letwin had delivered Howard's sole candidature, while Clarke had delivered the shaping of Howard's European policy (by threatening to stand if it was not acceptable to him).

Howard issued a credo of "I believes." It closely echoed John D. Rockefeller Jr.'s credo given in a 1941 radio broadcast and mounted on a plaque outside his complex in New York. A Conservative spokesman admitted that Howard's credo (written by a copywriter at M & C Saatchi) had been "partly influenced by the design of a commemorative plaque to John D. Rockefeller Jr." but Howard professed not to have known that Rockefeller had issued such a credo.

It seems that Howard had changed his outlook to an internationalist position. He could be expected to oppose but not block the new European constitution and the euro. It looked as if Bilderberg, using certain MPs and journalists, had had a *putsch* on the Conservative leadership and had replaced a nation-stater with an internationalist. All three parties in Britain now had internationalist leaders.

The Cost of British EU Membership

Britain's membership of the EU has been presented as winning increased prosperity, which has, together with the political considerations, compensated for any loss of British sovereignty. In fact, Britain's annual contribution to the EU budget was, at the beginning of 2003, £12b a year, and recent studies by the Institute of Directors and Institute of Economic Affairs have concluded that Britain would be better off by £10b a year if it ran its own farming policy and by a significant additional amount if it ran its own fisheries policy. British trade has been penalized by the Common External Tariff and over the last 30 years Britain has had a trade deficit with other member states in every year except 1980 and 1981.[34] Swiss, Icelandic, and Norwegian citizens outside the EU enjoy far higher standards of living than their EU counterparts. In Germany the euro is nicknamed the "teuro" (a play on the German word for "expensive," *teuer*). After a year of the euro, the EU suffered economic slowdown and strain as half its member states were destabilized by one-size-fits-all interest rates, which caused them to overheat or slump. Germany's Stability and Growth Pact, which was devised to stop debtors debauching the euro by reverting to inflationary deficits of more than 3% of GDP, was broken by Portugal. Germany (in slump and with 4.5 million unemployed) and France (pledged to tax cuts) were set to break the Pact.

For the three months to November 2003 the overall British trade deficit was a stunning £10.2b.[35] Exports to non-EU countries rose by 12.9% compared with a year before, whereas exports to the EU, which account for a far greater proportion of our trade, fell by almost the same amount. The widening balance of payments deficit was attributed to a fall in North Sea oil production.

According to the Treasury Pink Book (which gives detailed estimates of the UK's balance of payments) for 2000, Britain's payment to the EU budget was £8.433b and receipts were £4.241b, leaving a shortfall of £4.192b, and a total shortfall since 1973 of £27.323b. A less authoritative calculation has Britain's gross contribution as £10.719b and net contribution £3.854b.[36] It's likely to increase. In late 2003 French EU commissioner Pascal Lamy called for a Euro-tax, an EU tax or levy to fund the running of the EU. This would be on top of what businesses already pay to their government. He admitted that the tax will be raised only after the new EU constitution had been signed.

It had now become clear that under the new constitution Britain would be expected to surrender control of its North Sea oil reserves to the EU. Both BP and Shell wrote to Blair urging him to stand firm against the EU. The BP chief Lord Browne feared that the new constitution's Energy Chapter would give Brussels sweeping powers over Britain's $21b-a-year North Sea oil industry. The EU could control Britain's oil tax, licensing, security of supply, and regulation of pipelines as well as transfer British oil reserves to other EU states in an energy crisis.

An inexperienced Blair has delivered the UK to "Rockefellerites" by implementing "Rockefellerite-Rothschildite" devolution policies. Foreign rule will be imposed on a country that ruled a quarter of the world at the beginning of the twentieth century. A partition into 12 Euro-regions that have tax-raising powers, the abolition of England, and the annexation by "Rockefellerites" of all remaining oil and natural gas resources in the North Sea will set the seal on national extinction.

The consequence of all this for Britain was that the majority of Britons did not want to join the euro and, if faced with the choice of "full integration with euro" versus secession, tended to favor secession. They may be right. The internationalist "Rothschildite" Blair is doing a Gorbachev, breaking up the UK by devolution so that American oil companies will be able to export its assets of oil and gas.[37]

There are claims from groups that guard English sovereignty that an armed militia of 20,000 men is ready to fight Brussels on behalf of the English nation.[38] Maybe they're exaggerating. But given events in other parts of Europe over the last decade it might be a mistake to presume too much on an overall willingness to accept loss of sovereignty.

✩   ✩   ✩

Europe and Russia

Prior to 1917 there was not the kind of East/West split that we think natural today. Indeed if Kerensky's revolution, financed by "Rothschilds," had succeeded, West European nations and Russia may have been drawn closer together in the twentieth century rather than further apart. Having suppressed nation-states in the Western and Eastern blocs, the next logical step was to bring Europe and Russia together into one larger entity (see pages 117, 242–3). This has been the driving force behind many of the events of the last 20 years.

Gorbachev

In March 1985 on the death of Chernenko, a young and reform-minded Freemason[39] called Gorbachev became General-Secretary of the Communist Party. He started the process that will eventually see Russia and Europe together.

In 1984, around the time he became a Grand Orient Freemason, Gorbachev had met Otto von Habsburg, Pretender to the thrones of Austria, Hungary, and the Holy Roman Empire and an MEP fluent in some 40 European languages. Habsburg was supremely well qualified to speak for Europe. It is said[40] that the two made an agreement that if Gorbachev came to power he would release four East European nations to the West (East Germany, Poland, Hungary, and Czechoslovakia), and in return Habsburg would uncouple Europe from the US by promoting an integrated European Union. Europe's uncoupling from the US was plain for all to see during the second Iraq War of 2003.

One of his first acts[41] after assuming the leadership of the USSR was to permit Zionist Jews to leave Russia for Palestine, a "Rothschildian" policy, and to permit the return of Grand Orient Freemasonry (and therefore of revolution) to Russia – where it is still a force. His talk of economic restructuring (*perestroika*) and openness (*glasnost*) in due course came to be seen as adopting decentralized capitalism and democracy. In 1986 he met Reagan at the Reykjavik Summit and proposed dramatic cuts in long-range missiles; more followed in 1988.

Following the Syndicate ambition to combine Eastern and Western Europe into one United States of Europe, which had been worked out by Bilderberg and the Trilateral Commission, Gorbachev began to dismantle the Soviet Empire from within. He withdrew Soviet troops from Afghanistan and cut off aid to the warring Afghans. In 1989 he voiced his support for reformist Communists in Eastern Europe, and when the Communist regimes collapsed in East Germany, Poland, Hungary, and Czechoslovakia, Gorbachev agreed to phased troop withdrawals. It may seem bizarre, but the one condition was that Grand Orient Masonic lodges should be opened in each country (including Budapest), and he asked French Masonic leaders to facilitate this.[42] In late 1989 the Berlin Wall came down and by 1990 Gorbachev agreed to the reunification of East and West Germany and allowed it to join NATO.

There was civil unrest in the USSR and Gorbachev used military force to suppress ethnic strife in the Central Asian republics and forced Lithuania back into the Soviet fold. In 1990 he was elected President of the USSR and he abolished the Communist Party's monopoly of political power, opening the way for the legalization of political parties. At the end of 1991 he stepped down from power, toppling Communism with the Masonic words, "I hereby discontinue my activities at the post of President of the Union of Soviet Socialist Republics. We're now living in a New World!"[43]

Mikhail Gorbachev, during a visit to London, on March 23, 2000 described the European Union as being "the new European Soviet" (reported in the London *Daily Telegraph*'s Peterborough column, March 24, 2000). It has been a long-term covert Soviet aim to establish "Europe from the Atlantic to Vladivostok." This partially coincides with the current pan-German hegemony from the Atlantic to the Urals. Meanwhile the European Union collective now coordinates two strategies within it: the ongoing covert Soviet strategy of pursuing a "Europe from the Atlantic to Vladivostok" (i.e. Soviet hegemony from the Atlantic to the Pacific); and the parallel pan-German strategy, which has not changed since the days of Hitler and is still continuing, of pursuing a "Europe from the Atlantic to the Urals." The combination of these two strategies in "the new European Soviet" isolates and corrals the former Moslem Soviet republics into an "arc of Islamic extremism."[44]

Gorbachev's talk of "openness" (*glasnost*) and "restructuring" (*perestroika*) had now turned into the collapse of the Soviet Empire in Eastern Europe and of Communism itself and the introduction of democracy. There would soon be little to choose between the right-wing policies of the Eastern European nations, who now embraced the free market and private ownership, and the left-wing policies of the Western European nations.

After Gorbachev was ousted following the attempted *coup* by his apparently anti-*perestroika* Vice-President Gennadi Yanaev, which placed him under house arrest in the Crimea and which brought Boris Yeltsin to power, a Foundation was set up in America, the funding of which reveals

Gorbachev's alignment. The Gorbachev Foundation, USA, was capitalized with $3m from the Carnegie Endowment for International Peace, the Ford Foundation, the Rockefeller Brothers Fund, and the Pew and Mellon Funds.[45] As this suggests, Gorbachev was backed by "Rockefellers" to loosen the union of the USSR and make possible a regional world government, in which Europe would be uncoupled from the US. Gorbachev was linked to "Rockefellers," the Syndicate, and the Bilderberg Group all along, and to French Grand Orient Freemasonry. His allegiance and outlook put him in the tradition of the French and Russian revolutionaries and their Utopian dreams. He was a Templar Mason like the Americans, and an internationalist who dismembered the Soviet Empire and part of the USSR and handed them over to the Syndicate for further loosening.

Yeltsin

In 1995 at the Gorbachev State of the World Forum held in San Francisco, Brzezinski, the co-founder (with David Rockefeller) of the Trilateral Commission, said: "We cannot leap into world government in one quick step ... The precondition for eventual globalization is progressive regionalization."[46]

Gorbachev had half-done what the Syndicate wanted. He had dismantled the totalitarian structure of the Soviet State (a practical meaning of *perestroika*) and he had brought in representational democracy (a practical meaning of *glasnost*). But he was being slow in freeing the Soviet economy from the grip of centralized State direction and in handing it over to private entrepreneurs and a free market of the Western European kind. He had kept the Soviet Union together as a single state.

The Syndicate, the CFR, and the Bilderberg Group envisaged Western Europe and the USSR merging into one vast free market. There were obvious benefits in replacing Gorbachev with a man who would carry the revolution forward – and allow "Rockefellers" to buy up huge chunks of the USSR. This meant splitting the USSR into regional blocs.

To the Syndicate, Boris Yeltsin must have seemed just their man. A Communist, he had been made Mayor of Moscow in 1985; Gorbachev had known him for some years. He had become a member of the Politburo in 1986, and was strongly critical of Gorbachev, speaking out in favor of more reforms and complaining that Gorbachev had not gone far enough.

As a result he was forced to resign from the Moscow party leadership in 1987 and from the Politburo in 1988. He was elected President of the Russian Republic in 1990, and supported the right of all republics to greater autonomy within the Soviet Union, which meant control over their own resources and a multi-party, market-oriented economy. He favored replacing the USSR with a confederation, i.e. he favored breaking up the Communist union in favor of a commonwealth of regions. Yeltsin left the Communist Party in 1991.

Gorbachev lingered on for four months, trying to preserve the USSR as a single state without using force. Only seven of the 12 republics appeared at the twice-postponed opening of the USSR parliament, and Belorussia and Ukraine declared the USSR dead. Russia (through Yeltsin) announced the takeover of the union parliament and then of the Kremlin, and Gorbachev resigned.

"Rockefellers" Buy Russia's Natural Resources

The CIS (Commonwealth of Independent States) was denationalized by having its assets stripped and sold to "Rockefellers." It was reported in *Spotlight* on April 22, 1996 that Yeltsin's Prime Minister Viktor Chernomyrdin was in partnership with David Rockefeller and his Chase Manhattan Bank, and agreed to sell Russia's natural resources to "Rockefellers" via Moscow banks that acted as fronts for "Rockefellers" at give-away prices (based on currency exchange rates that suited "international investors").[47] One economist described the transaction as "the most profitable piece of plunder since World War 2."[48] To privatize Russia's State-owned economy, Yeltsin sold some of the world's largest oil and gas deposits and gold and diamond mines. Gazprom, worth $3.4b according to a 1993 World Bank study,[49] was sold in Moscow for $228m, a tenth of its market value. Lukoil, Russia's largest petroleum conglomerate, worth at least $3.4b, was sold for $294m. United Energy Systems, the Soviet bloc's main power and utility generator, said to be worth more than $3b was sold for $467m. Under a deal between Chase Manhattan and Yeltsin's government in 1991, 85% of the world's diamond output, including Russia's diamond exports, was to be exclusively handled by de Beers, which had originally been funded by "Rothschilds," long a secret ally of Chase Manhattan.[50] "Rockefellers" had an interest in all these transactions. And a great prize of the break-up was the Caspian oil of the Baku oilfields

Oil: Baku/Chechnya/Ceyhan

Besides owning much of the former USSR's oil, gas, and electricity, "Rockefellers" had their eye on the westward flow of oil from Baku through pipelines near the oilfields in Chechnya, the backbone of whose economy is petroleum. Drilling is in the oilfields in the Sunzha Valley and Sunzha and Terek mountain ranges, especially around Malgobek, while refining is at Grozny, where there is a network of refineries. Pipelines run to the Caspian and Black Seas. (Natural gas is also found in the area.)

According to geologists 200b barrels of oil lie under the Caspian, from whose Baku oilfields two pipelines serve the West. Both pump oil to the Black Sea under the control of the British-led consortium, the Azerbaijan International Oil Co. (AIOC), which is headed by the BP Group (a new name for Standard Oil's takeover of BP as BP Amoco, which during the 1990s invested £300m in Azerbaijan, whose capital is Baku). An American pipeline, which was opened in April 1999, passes from Baku through Georgia to Supsa on the Black Sea (see map 2), and a Russian pipeline that is important to BP runs from Baku through Chechnya to Novorossiysk on the Black Sea (see maps 1 and 2). Chechnya declared independence in 1991. Russia denied it not because of its oil refineries but because of the traversing pipelines from Baku.

After Yeltsin's abrupt return to Moscow from the OSCE summit in Istanbul, the AIOC consortium have proposed an alternative new $2.4b pipeline branching off from Georgia to the Turkish Mediterranean port of Ceyhan, which would remove Moscow's political control over the flow of oil to the West and prevent Moscow from earning millions of pounds in tariffs. A treaty has been signed by Turkey, Georgia, Azerbaijan, and the US. Turkey's proposed admission to the EC has gone forward, and with Turkey pro-Western the flow of oil from Baku to the West will doubtless be guaranteed.

In the summer of 1999 the Russian Baku-Chechnya-Novorossiysk pipeline was closed by Chechen nationalists, and Russia proposed an alternative new pipeline well north of Chechnya, which would branch off

1. *Pipeline from Chechnya to Novorossiysk.*
See http://www.hermes-press.com/impintrol.htm

the pipeline from Tengiz (see map 2).[51] In November 1999 the "Rockefellerite" Yeltsin ordered Russian forces to attack Grozny in an all-out war to
retake the oilfields and oil refineries and to control the Baku pipeline. In
early 2000, victory in Chechnya restored Russian (and therefore "Rockefellerite") control over the northern pipeline from Baku to Novorossiysk
and allowed the Russians to disrupt the Georgian pipeline, thus giving
Moscow (and therefore "Rockefellers") complete control over all oil flowing to the West.

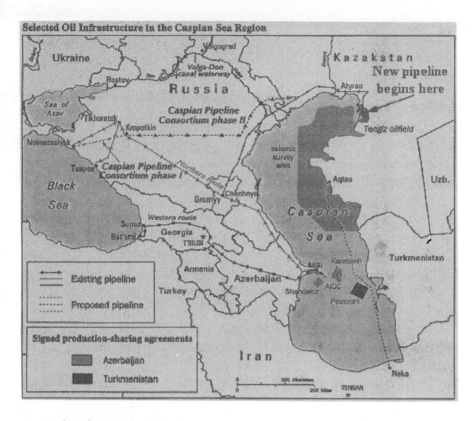

2. *Pipeline from Baku to Supsa.*
See http://www.hermes-press.com/impintrol.htm

In January 2004 it was announced (*American Free Press*, January 26, 2004) that the US had defeated competition from Russia, China, and Iran and would implement the pipeline from Baku and Tbilisi (the Georgian capital) to Ceyhan (see map 3). The pipeline would run through Azerbaijan (where power passed in December 2003 from Aleyda Aliyev, who died in an American hospital, to his son, the first dynastic successor in an former Soviet Republic) and Georgia (where the pro-Russian leader Eduard Shevardnadze was replaced in December 2003 by the young pro-American Mikhail Saakashvili). Rumsfeld visited Azerbaijan in December 2003, and proposed that NATO troops should guard the pipeline. BP owns 35% of the pipeline and will be its operator, the Azeri Oil Co. Socar owns 25%, and Unocal owns 9%.

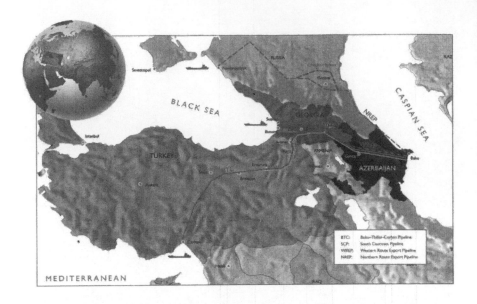

3. Pipeline from Baku and Tbilisi to Ceyhan.
See http://www.peaceplangroup.assets.org.uk/app4.htm

BP leads the consortium that will build the pipeline. The consortium will pay 30% of the estimated \$3.3b cost; the remaining 70% is to come from banks, including the World Bank, which is in turn funded by the taxpayers of contributing countries. The British taxpayer is to contribute.

"Rockefellers"' power in the USSR had increased with each decade. From an oil-for-cash arrangement with Stalin in the 1920s, they had progressed through diverting Japan from attacking the USSR in 1941 to intriguing Stalin's Eastern European Empire and to Nelson Rockefeller's more formal arrangement with Stalin (UN non-interference in Russia in return for Soviet non-interference in Saudi Arabia and Iran, and exclusive rights to Soviet oil). "Rockefellers" now own a huge part of Russia's natural resources.

Serbia/Kosovo/Croatia/Bosnia

The New World Order Revolution has also been behind the conflict in former Yugoslavia. A pipeline easement was to carry oil from the Caspian

Sea through Kosovo to the Adriatic, whence it could be shipped to Western European markets. Yugoslavia refused to cooperate with the IMF.[52]

After Tito's death in 1980 and the collapse of European Communism, the pulling down of the Berlin Wall, and German reunification, nationalism resurfaced in Yugoslavia. Slobodan Milosevic called for a Greater Serbia (an echo of Yeltsin's Greater Russia) that would return the Balkans to their pre-1915 borders and include Croatia, which has rich oilfields. The Serb aim was to seize as much territory as possible, driving out Croatians and Moslems – this was the origin of ethnic cleansing – so that eventually the UN could be called in to "adjudicate" and award all land held by Serb nationals to Serbia.

Civil war broke out, and Yugoslavia was broken up into statelets that would be more cooperative. The aim was to effect the US occupation of Kosovo to guarantee the flow of Caspian oil.

With a third of ethnic Serbs living outside the Serbian republic, Serbia resisted the break-up of the Federation, removed the autonomy of the Kosovo province, and opposed independence in Slovenia and Croatia. In June 1991, the Yugoslav federal army moved into Slovenia and in July fighting spread across Croatia. The US and EC were focusing on the Gulf War, and could not give the problem their undivided attention. After lengthy diplomatic efforts fighting stopped in Slovenia in September.

In 2001 work began on a $1.2b, 920k-long trans-Balkan pipeline due to be operative in 2005. Oil piped from the Baku region of the Caspian to Ceyhan on the Black Sea is to be conveyed by tanker across the sea and then piped from Burgas in Bulgaria across the Balkans and Macedonia to the Adriatic port of Vlore in Albania.[53] See map 4 for three corridors connected with this pipeline. The pipeline is being built by the US-owned Albanian-Macedonian-Bulgarian Company (AMBO). The pipeline will be guarded by KFOR according to its commander Gen. Michael Jackson. It will transport 750,000 barrels of oil per day.[54]

Oil giants working under AMBO include Texaco, Chevron, Exxon, Mobil, BP, Amoco, Agip, and Total Fina Elf. Camp Bondsteel, the largest US military base since Vietnam, was built by Halliburton (the company linked with Cheney), who are servicing the troops in the Balkans. The feasibility study for the AMBO pipeline was conducted by Brown and Root Ltd. of London, Halliburton's British subsidiary.[55]

4. *Trans-Balkan Pipeline.*
See www.scarabee.com/EDITO2/070699.html

Along the pipeline corridor are to be a number of protectorates. The US has promised a "Greater Albania," which reaches into Greece.[56] The AMBO line branches into Greece. There are ethnic Albanian populations in Kosovo and Macedonia, and non-Albanians are attacked by ethnic Albanian KLA and NLA terrorists seeking to spread "Greater Albania." Each pipeline corridor is to have a highway, railway, electricity, and telecommunications. Macedonia, Bulgaria, and Albania are to be integrated into the EU. The US wants to distance the three countries from Germany-EU by cocooning them in US protectorates.[57]

It can now be seen that the break-up of the USSR has released Caspian oil to the West. It is reasonable to conclude that the USSR was broken up so that this oil could be piped. And that Yugoslavia was broken up so that the pipeline could be well protected.

Expansion

At NATO's Prague Summit in November 2002 seven former Communist Eastern Empire countries were invited to join NATO: Bulgaria, Romania, Slovenia, Slovakia, Estonia, Latvia, and Lithuania. Full membership was scheduled for 2004. The Czech Republic, Hungary, and Poland had entered NATO at the outbreak of the war in Kosovo. The enlargement extended NATO's territory to Russia's borders in the Baltic and Black Sea, and formally marked the end of the Soviet Empire.

There were plans to expand the EU to include all Russia and the former Soviet republics. As a stepping-stone to this, Putin went to Yalta, and at a meeting with the Ukraine President called for a common market that linked the EU with Russia, Ukraine, Kazakhstan, and Belarus. This raised the prospect that the European constitution would dominate a bloc even larger than the Soviet Union, in which former Soviet territories would play the largest part. Effectively the whole land mass of Europe and Euro-Asia would be sovietized under the European constitution.

Hitler's Europe was envisaged in the form of a German Reich stretching from the Atlantic to the Urals with a single currency. It included a European Economic Community ("Europaische Wirtschaft-gemeinschaft"), collective access to basic commodities, a European industrial economy, a European Regional Principle, a common Labour Policy, economic and trading agreements, a European currency system, and a Eurobank in Berlin. Our Europe has a European Economic Community, common energy and agricultural policies, a Common Industrial Policy, a Committee of the Regions, a Social Chapter, a Single Market, a European Exchange Rate Mechanism, and a European Central Bank in Frankfurt that controls the single European currency (which is effectively a German currency). Almost word for word, the collectivist, statist, trade-protectionist, and corporatist ideas of Germany in the 30s have re-emerged in our European Union.[58]

8

THE UNITED STATES
OF THE MIDDLE EAST

I do not need to justify my subject: "America and the World
Revolution." There can be few contemporary questions that
are of such outstanding importance and interest as this one is.
Arnold Toynbee[1]

The last years of the twentieth century were ones of optimism. The Soviet Empire had crumbled with surprising speed at the end. Literally, walls were being pulled down. Nuclear arms were being reduced. The West looked forward to years of stability and trade. Hopes were expressed of spreading democracy and prosperity around the world. A few years later and it all seems to have changed. As if from nowhere, a new enemy has appeared, "terrorism." And it largely originates from problems in the Middle East – Israel's occupation of Arab land and the insecurity of supplies of Middle Eastern oil.

Middle Eastern oil is crucial to the West's survival. Western multinationals discovered the oil in the first half of the twentieth century and kept it flowing when Arab colonies became independent. But at the very time when the US and Britain were running out of their own oil, many of their main oil suppliers – countries like Saudi Arabia and Iraq – had become politically unreliable, and could no longer be taken for granted. Israel, a Western enclave and the West's principal ally in the Middle East, helped maintain the balance of power in the troubled region, but was also the main source of Arab discontent. The West had now reached a point where a reinstatement of the Ottoman Empire would be attractive: a United States of the Middle East including North Africa that would toe the Western line and guarantee Western access to oil for decades to come. And now that the Great Power rivalry of the Cold War had ended, the post-Cold-War New World Order run by the US was in a position to impose it by Syndicate interventions.

The New World Order

The term "New World Order" was first used in the modern media by New York Governor Nelson Rockefeller, who was quoted in *AP* (July 26, 1968) as saying "he would work toward international creation of 'a new world order.'" In the AP report Nelson Rockefeller pledged that "As President, he would work toward international creation of a new world order." In fact he had called for world federalism in his *The Future of Federalism*, 1962, claiming that current events compellingly demanded a "new world order" as the old order was crumbling. "There will evolve the bases for a federal structure of the free world." In 1967 Richard Nixon echoed this call for a New World Order. In the October 1967 issue of *Foreign Affairs*, the CFR journal, Nixon wrote of nations' dispositions to evolve regional approaches to development needs and to the evolution of a "new world order."[2]

The roots of the New World Order can be found in the French Revolution, the storming of the Bastille in 1789 that was organized by the Illuminati within the Grand Orient under the Duke of Orléans as I have shown in *The Secret History of the West*, and culminated in the beheading of Louis XVI. The 200th anniversary of this revolutionary act was celebrated on March 30, 1989,[3] when President Mitterand (then the most powerful 33rd-degree Grand Orient Freemason in Europe)[4] unveiled a glass pyramid designed by the American architect I. M. Pei outside the Louvre.[5] The pyramid is an Illuminati symbol found on the American Great Seal and dollar bill above the tag *"Novus Ordo Seculorum,"* "Secular New Order," as we have seen. It was clear to all who took part in the ceremony that the purpose of the New World Order was to finish the business begun by the Illuminatist French Revolution: to bring about a universal republic that would rule the world. This relaunching in Paris of the New World Order called for by Nelson Rockefeller in 1968 was swiftly followed by Gorbachev's pulling down of the Berlin Wall on November 9, 1989 – and the tearing down of the Iron Curtain.

On September 11, 1990, after Bush Sr. had said that "a New World Order can emerge"[6] that could "shape the future for generations to come," Secretary of State James Baker said that "it would set an extremely unfortunate precedent for the New World Order" if aggression were rewarded and that "if we really believe that there's an opportunity here for a New World Order, and many of us do believe that, we can't start out by appeasing aggression."[7] Bush supported the "Rockefellcrite" UN Secretary-General Boutros-Ghali's call for a permanent UN Army and pledged America's economic and military support for this "revolutionary" attempt to create a New World Order.

President Bush made a number of references to the New World Order in January 1991. In an interview in *US News & World Report* (January 7) he said: "I think that what's at stake here is the New World Order. What's at stake here is whether we can have disputes peacefully resolved in the future by a reinvigorated United Nations." In a press conference (January 9) he said: "[The Gulf crisis] has to do with a New World Order. And that New World Order is only going to be enhanced if this newly activated peace-keeping function of the United Nations proves to be effective." In a televised address (January 16) he said: "When we are successful, and we will be, we have a real chance at this New World Order, an Order in which a credible United Nations can use its peace-keeping role to fulfill the promise and vision of the UN's founders." In the *National Security Strategy of the United States* (August 1991) issued by the White House and signed by Bush, he said: "In the Gulf, we saw the United Nations playing the role dreamed of by its founders .... I hope history will record that the Gulf crisis was the crucible of the New World Order."[8]

On February 6, 1991, President Bush spoke at the Economic Club of New York City in the presence of the ex-Chairman of the CFR, David Rockefeller. He was asked a question by a reporter: "You have talked several times about basing the future on a New World Order. Can you give us a definition of a New World Order, and if it depends on the collaboration between the Soviet Union and the United States, how do events in the Soviet Union affect this concept?" Bush replied: "Well, it doesn't depend entirely on it, but it would be greatly enhanced by a Soviet Union that goes down the line with its commitment to market reform, to private ownership of land, to a free economic system, to a system that resists, and does not use force to assure order amongst the republics, that goes farther down the road with elections, and all the openness that I give President Gorbachev credit for .... Now, my vision of a New World Order foresees a United Nations with a revitalized peace-keeping function."[9] It is clear from this exchange that Bush envisaged the New World Order as a world democracy that would include the former Soviet Union.

Maybe "New World Order" is a vague description of a new arrangement of the balance of power. Or maybe Bush, a Skull and Bones Templar Freemason[10] (Skull and Bones is a Yale Order which has getting on for 600 living initiates among its graduates), was aware he was drawing on a Freemasonic tradition of an Order originally linked with the New World, America, by the Elizabethan Francis Bacon (see *The Secret History of the West* for more on this).

In either case, disputes over oil have driven events in the twentieth century. The Syndicate has intervened continuously in the affairs of nation-states to move the world to global government, leveling the European Empires and crushing the independence of smaller nations. Acting in conjunction with US diplomacy, they have managed Eastern and Western Europe in such a way that they have both been leveled sufficiently to meet within a broadly socialist Europe. At the same time, on the fringes of Europe and further afield, the UN and NATO have been used successively as a world army to carry out leveling procedures against dictators in the Middle East, Africa, and the Balkans. The two parallel policies of the Syndicate have prepared nation-states for world government. The first Iraqi War demonstrates an increasing momentum on both counts. The reason is – the world is running out of oil. The Arabs tried to exploit this shortage.

OPEC

In 1953 an internal US document[11] declared, "United States policy is to keep the sources of oil in the Middle East in American hands." However, by the 1960s most Middle-Eastern countries had gained a measure of independence, and OPEC (the Organization of Petroleum Exporting Countries) was founded by Venezuela, Iran, Saudi Arabia, Kuwait, and Iraq. Since then the United Arab Emirates, Qatar, Nigeria, Libya, Algeria, and Indonesia have joined. During the 1950s production exceeded demand and oil prices sank.

In the 1970s the main oil-producing countries of the Middle East resented being controlled by the large Western-owned oil companies, and decided to take control of their own oil and use it as a political weapon.

OPEC aimed to push up oil prices by cutting production and weaken the oil companies. OPEC raised the price of crude oil 70% and quadrupled it; and Arab states placed an embargo on supplies to countries that supported Israel's expansionism. In the fourth quarter of 1973 the Western companies had enormously increased their profits: Exxon by 59%, Texaco by 70.1%, Standard of California by 94.2%, Mobil by 68.2%, Standard of Indiana by 52.8%, and Gulf by 153%. The oil companies overcharged some $2b during 1973–4.[12]

OPEC profits were invested in special high interest 20– and 30–year certificates of deposit in American banks. Huge amounts of OPEC money, multiplied by the methods of fractional reserve banking (in which a one billion-dollar reserve expands into more than $30b in loans) were then loaned by the American banks to developing countries so that they could afford oil at the new price. This was known as petro-dollar recycling. For example, Standard Oil bought $1b worth of crude oil for its refineries from Saudi Arabia, who then placed that money in Chase Manhattan Bank, which was partly owned by "Rockefellers" who also owned Standard Oil. Chase Manhattan then loaned the money to developing countries, and received many multiples of $1b (the original cost of the crude oil).[13]

The large oil companies are now making huge profits. BP's profit in the second quarter of 2000 was $3.6b (164% up from the previous year, making its half-year profit up 197%). Exxon Mobil's profit rose 123%, and Royal Dutch Shell's 95%.[14]

Iran

Most of the world's oil reserves are in the Middle East, and its recent history reflects the desire of the West to get their hands on it. In the first half of the twentieth century Iran was controlled by the British. In 1952 the Iranian premier Dr. Mosaddeq nationalized the Iranian oil industry and the Shah's royal estates, and the Shah fled the country. The next year a CIA-backed *coup* against him restored the Shah, who expelled the British. "Rockefellers" Standard Oil now controlled the British-Persian oilfield.[15] Occidental Petroleum (founded by Armand Hammer, who had close ties with Russia) and Russia built two large pipelines from the Russian oilfields along both sides of the Caspian to reach the oilfields in Iran, and Standard Oil received the oil and sold it on the world market as Iranian oil for nearly 50 years.[16]

From 1954 onwards Chase Manhattan had received all money due from the sale of Iranian oil in the West (approximately $30b a year), and had acted as banker for the Pahlavi Foundation.[17] In 1978 there was a revolution in Iran, and the Standard Oil-backed Shah fled in January 1979. Through the influence of David Rockefeller and Kissinger he was allowed to go to Mexico.[18] Immediately both Iranian and Saudi Arabian oil exports were cut, and oil prices soared. The resulting energy crisis in the US contributed to the fall of President Carter.

Ayatollah Khomeini, a Moslem Islamic Shi'ite cleric who had opposed the Shah's reduction of religious land, flew back from exile in Paris to rule Iran. The flow of Russian oil through Iran stopped. Other pipelines were constructed through Iraq and Turkey to convey Russian oil to the West. Russian oil was called OPEC Arabian-Middle Eastern oil.[19]

The "Rockefeller"-influenced US government threatened to seize $7.9b of Iranian assets in the US. To increase his leverage on the West, Khomeini encouraged "students" to seize the US Embassy in Tehran in November 1979 and held 52 hostages for nearly 15 months against the return of the dying Shah.[20]

In April 1979, meeting in Austria, the Bilderberg Group endorsed a theocratic state under Khomeini.[21] Did this endorsement become Western policy? In 1981 the $7.9b was transferred electronically to Iran.[22]

Afghanistan

In December 1979 the Soviet Union invaded Afghanistan, another of "Rockefellers"' new fronts, as Standard Oil/Russia tried to secure a short and safe oil pipeline route through the country.[23] Besides implementing the pipeline the invasion offered an opportunity to export oil by a pipeline to Pakistan, and the prospect of eventual access to a port on the Indian Ocean whence the oil of the Persian Gulf, and of Iran, could be exported.[24]

This invasion put an end to further arms reduction (SALT II) and signaled that *détente* was now dead. Carter (a protégé of David Rockefeller's who had more than 70 members of the CFR – 291 members of the Trilateral Commission and CFR combined – in his administration)[25] pledged in January 1980 (in his State of the Union address) that any attack on the Persian Gulf – or anywhere in Brzezinski's "arc of crisis"[26] – would be regarded as an attack on the US and would be met by a Rapid Deployment Force.

Soviet troops failed to conquer Afghanistan and the pipeline project was abandoned.[27]

Iraq

Iraq was on the receiving end of the biggest Syndicate intervention following years of intrigue concerning Kuwait.

Kuwait had been founded in the eighteenth century. In 1880 the British Government made Emir Abdullah al Salem al Sabah its representative outside the southern border of Iraq, near where the Rumaila oilfields had been discovered inside Iraq. In 1899 al Sabah ceded to England and British Petroleum land inside Iraq, including part of the Rumaila oilfields, which he had no right to do.[28] In 1915 – after the building of the Berlin–Baghdad railway – the British invaded Iraq and set up a mandate in North Iraq and a puppet regime under King Faisal of Syria in Basra and South Iraq.[29]

In 1923 Britain had to agree to grant Iraq independence when Iraq joined the League of Nations, to the anger of the oil companies. Iraq became independent in 1932. In the same year the Mosul oilfields were discovered, and in 1935 British Petroleum built a pipeline from there to Haifa (in modern Israel).[30] In 1961 Abdul Karim Kassem claimed that Kuwait was Iraqi, as the Ottoman Empire itself had recognized for 400 years. In 1965 Britain granted Kuwait independence, which meant that Kuwait could not be given back to Iraq and that Iraq's claims could be ignored. The British ruled Kuwait through the al Sabah family for another 30 years.[31]

Saddam was trying to recover part of the Rumaila oilfields – the north Rumaila field produces 750,000 barrels per day, the south Rumaila field 500,000 bpd – and to seize the al-Burqan oilfields in Kuwait itself, the second largest in the world.[32]

Saddam Hussein was a criminal before he entered politics and had been on the run after attempting to assassinate the dictator Abdul Karim Kassem. According to Richard Sale, intelligence correspondent for UPI, Saddam was recruited by the CIA in 1959 to do this, following Iraq's withdrawal from the anti-Soviet Baghdad Pact in 1959.[33] This withdrawal prompted Allen Dulles, CIA Director, to say that Iraq was "the most dangerous spot in the world." Sale wrote that Saddam lost his nerve and began firing too soon, killing Kassem's driver but only wounding Kassem in his shoulder and arm.

US Arms Saddam against Iran

Saddam rose with the Baath Party's *coup* of 1968, and he took supreme power in 1979.

He now milked Iraq for his family and ran a brutal regime based on torture and execution: on one estimate three million Iraqis were executed after 1968, and Saddam may have been responsible for two million of these.[34] Saddam modeled himself on Stalin and admired Stalin's treatment of his Russian people. He used chemical weapons on the Iraqi Kurds to avenge their collaboration with Iran.

Saddam had nevertheless been a good friend of America. His relationship with the CIA intensified after the start of the Iran–Iraq war in September 1980. The US were alarmed at the extremism in Iran, and courted him as an ally.

During the 1980s the "Rockefellerite" Syndicate through US diplomats had encouraged[35] Saddam to abrogate the 1975 agreement with Iran and send his armored units into south-west Iran, thus precipitating the Iran–Iraq war, which was to weaken both sides and set back their respective drives for nuclear weapons so that they would not be a threat to British and American oil interests or to Israel. It was also to keep the British and American oilfields out of Iraq's and Iran's grasp. Henry Kissinger said at the time, "The ultimate American interest in the war is that both should lose," and throughout the war Israel supplied Iran with at least $500m worth of arms a year.[36] In July 1985 Reagan authorized Israel to sell TOW anti-tank missiles to Iran, and in January 1986 approved direct US arms sales to the Khomeini government in Iran.[37] During the eight years of the Iran–Iraq war, each side lost a million men.[38]

Did "Rockefellerites" who organized the overthrow of the Shah in the hope of securing Iranian oil also arm Saddam Hussein in the hope of securing Iraqi oil? In 1983 the US Agriculture Department loaned Iraq $365m officially to buy agricultural products, although the money was in fact spent on arms.[39] The Banco Nazionale de Lavoro, whose Brescia branch had given credit in 1981 so that Iraq could buy mines from an Italian company, made a $2.1b commercial loan through its Atlanta branch. In all the Bush administration provided Saddam with loans totaling $5.5b.[40]

Prelude to War

In 1989, when global demand for Gulf oil had increased, the US Department of Energy reported, to considerable consternation, that Iraq had begun to build an atomic bomb, using US technology.[41] Had the program been unknowingly funded by the US? Be that as it may, the US government made it clear that this was not acceptable.

In November 1989, allegedly in response to this nuclear test, the CIA Director met the head of Kuwaiti State Security and promised US cooperation if Kuwait pressed Iraq on the border dispute, thus taking advantage of Iraq's deteriorating economic position.[42] A memo of this meeting was later seized by the Iraqis when they invaded Kuwait, and was angrily shown to the Kuwaiti Foreign Minister at an Arab Summit meeting in mid-August 1990.[43] Both US Secretary of Defense Dick Cheney and Undersecretary of Defense for Policy Paul Wolfowitz stated that the US was committed to defending Kuwait. (Both later served in the administration of George W. Bush.) Even so, joint US-Iraq military maneuvers were planned for late 1991.

Saddam was broke following the Iran–Iraq war. He had borrowed extensively from Kuwait. He felt he had defended other Arab states including Kuwait from the Iranian threat, and he asked Kuwait to pay its share – by canceling the $17b debt Iraq owed from the time of the Iran–Iraq war. Kuwait refused. Saddam was outraged. Moreover, Iraq had long accused Kuwait of stealing oil worth $10–14b by slant-drilling in the 1980s.[44]

In February 1990 Saddam condemned the US military presence in the Persian Gulf and warned that growing US power in the region might lead to the US's dictating the price, production, and distribution of the region's oil. In April he called for a pan-Arab troop build-up; if the Arab states remained weak, he claimed, they would never expel Israel from the occupied territories and establish a Palestinian state.

The response from the USA was confused. In April 1990 the US White House hosted a meeting of advisors at which it was proposed that there should be a change in US attitude to Iraq.[45] The Interagency Deputies

Committee of the National Security Council was headed by Robert Gates, a "Rockefellerite" and descendent of John D. Rockefeller's right-hand man Robert Gates I. He was instrumental in carrying through the change in the US's attitude.[46] In May the National Security Agency blocked a loan of $500m due to be made to Iraq by the Department of Agriculture.[47]

On the other hand, on July 25, 1990 on Bush's instructions, April Glaspie, the US ambassador to Iraq, met Saddam Hussein and assured him that America had no quarrel with him and would not intervene in any inter-Arab border disputes.[48] She said that the US had no opinion about inter-Arab conflicts. Saddam took this as a green light to invade Kuwait and reclaim the Rumaila oilfields. 90% of the Rumaila oilfields were owned by Iraq; 10% by Kuwait. It was the 10% Saddam was after. [49] Four days after the meeting Saddam began moving troops. Shortly afterwards Glaspie denied her assurance – perhaps President Bush had changed his view following the invasion – and then "resigned" from the State Department and headed for obscurity, out of the public eye.[50] On August 2 Saddam's troops invaded Kuwait and annexed it as the nineteenth province of Iraq in "a comprehensive and eternal merger."[51]

On August 2 the UN Security Council demanded that Iraq should withdraw from Kuwait.[52] Four days later sanctions were imposed, including an embargo on Iraqi and Kuwaiti oil. The "Rockefellerite" Secretaries James Baker and Dick Cheney flew to Saudi Arabia, convinced King Fahd that Saddam was about to invade Saudi Arabia and threaten his oil, and persuaded him to agree to have American troops in his kingdom, although the CIA reported to Bush that Iraq had no plans to invade Saudi Arabia.[53]

Saudi Arabia and Kuwait would pay most of the costs of a war with Iraq, with Germany and Japan (Trilateral partners) contributing. (In fact, Saudi Arabia paid $16.8b, Kuwait $16b, Germany $6.6b, and Japan $13b.) The war wouldn't cost the US a dollar.

This was the basis for Operation Desert Shield. In fact, the war cost around $61b, and the US contributed some $7b on top of the contributions from its four partners.[54] An alliance was put together of America, Saudi Arabia, and other Arab countries to control Saddam. The American troops were sent on August 7 and were joined by troops from Egypt, Morocco, and Syria. When Saddam turned US and Western European hostages into a human shield against American attack, Edward Heath, a "Rothschildite" pro-European British ex-Prime Minister, went to speak to him.

Between August 10 and 19 Iraq made three proposals for resolving the Gulf crisis: Iraqi withdrawal from Kuwait in exchange for Israel's evacuation of the West Bank and Gaza and Syria's evacuation of the Lebanon; replacement of US by UN troops; and Iraqi control of the Rumaila oilfields.[55] The US ignored these proposals and continued building up troops in Saudi Arabia.

From the outset Bush signaled that only unconditional surrender would enable Saddam to survive. The US secured UN authorization for a war against Iraq on November 29 by offering other Security Council member states economic assistance packages. The Soviet Union received a pledge of $6b. Colombia, Ethiopia, and Zaire received new aid and access to World Bank and IMF loans. China's post-Tienanmen Square isolation was ended when the Chinese ambassador was called to a meeting at the White House and told that withheld World Bank credits would now be released. Yemen, which voted against the resolution, found that $70m in US aid was cancelled.[56]

The UN set a deadline for Iraq to withdraw from Kuwait and accept UN demands, or be attacked under a resolution that permitted "all appropriate measures." In Congress Senators supported this by 52 votes to 47. The Desert Shield force was more than doubled to 550,000 men as Desert Storm was unleashed under Gen. Schwarzkopf.

Desert Storm

Desert Storm began on January 17, 1991. Fighter bombers using "smart" bombs attacked the presidential palace, the airport, oil refineries, nuclear reactors, and electrical plants in Baghdad. B-52s bombed the Republican Guard, who were positioned in trenches all along the Kuwait–Saudi border. Over 100 Tomahawk Cruise missiles were launched from the sea. Saddam retaliated with Scud missiles against Israel (which infuriated "Rothschilds") and one Scud (which was destroyed in the air) against the US base in Dhahran, Saudi Arabia. For six weeks a coalition air force destroyed the Iraqi air force and had the freedom of the skies. The US and allied forces reduced Saddam's power by bombing his infrastructure and culling his army.

Saddam retaliated by spilling oil from five tankers in the Persian Gulf and creating the largest oil slick in history (35 miles long by 10 miles wide).

But on the same day, 80 Iraqi pilots flew their planes to Iran and gave themselves up. The army was battered and without air cover.

Saddam's position was desperate and he sent Tariq Aziz, his Foreign Minister, to speak to Gorbachev. Gorbachev's peace plan was never implemented. Bush warned Saddam to leave Kuwait by February 23. Saddam did not comply.

The ground attack was launched on February 24. On the 25th Saddam gave the order for withdrawal from Kuwait. The next day the retreating Iraqis set fire to 100 Kuwaiti oil wells in the Rumaila oilfields, all the property of British Petroleum, one of Standard Oil's main British competitors

On February 27 Bush declared, "Iraq's army is defeated and Kuwait is liberated." The coalition immediately ceased hostilities, pleading that the UN mandate to expel Saddam from Kuwait had been fulfilled.

In fact, some of the Iraqi-owned Rumaila oilfields would now be unofficially within Kuwaiti territory; Iraq had in effect lost some of its territory to Kuwait. By the end of the Iran–Iraq war, Kuwait had accumulated 900 square miles of Iraqi territory by advancing its border with Iraq northward. This was presented to Iraq as a *fait accompli* and it gave Kuwait (and the Syndicate) access to the Rumaila oilfield. The Kuwaiti Sheikh had bought the Santa Fe Drilling Corporation of Alhambra, California for $2.3b, and used its slant-drilling equipment to gain access to the Iraqi Rumaila oilfield. The first Iraq war was fought to control the Rumaila oilfields. Saddam tried to take back the 10% Kuwaiti oilfields and effectively lost full control of the Iraqi-owned oilfields. Kuwait had been accused of slant-drilling in the 1980s and would now have greater access to Iraqi oil – and so, presumably, would the Syndicate. It looks as if Saddam was lured into seizing Kuwaiti Rumaila oil: the US, through April Glaspie, professed to have no opinion on inter-Arab conflict.[57]

The decision came as a great shock. The road to Baghdad was open, and Saddam could have been taken prisoner. A friendly successor regime could have been installed. It was rumored that Saddam had agreed to make a payment to have the war stopped.[58] A figure of $2b was mentioned. To whom was payment supposed to have been made? For some reason Bush had decided that he was not going to risk his troops on the ground, or fracture the international alliance by installing a regime that would have no domestic support among the Sunnis of Central Iraq. He was counting on the Iraqis to overthrow Saddam.

Saddam Still in Charge

Whatever the reason, the Americans stopped short of deposing Saddam, and following an agreement between Boutros-Ghali, Secretary-General of the UN, and Saddam they left him in place. Saddam continued to function with Russian support, and found ways of avoiding implementing the next 12 UN resolutions, which demanded reparations and imposed UN inspection teams on Iraq so that weapons of mass destruction could be destroyed. Most of Saddam's weapons of mass destruction were probably destroyed – no one knows for sure – but Saddam seems to have encouraged the belief that he still retained some, fearing an attack from Israel which he had Scud-attacked during the war. Saddam's defiance meant that the Iraq War of 2003, if not inevitable, was always a probability.

A year after the Gulf War Saddam was more firmly in power than ever before. But the West had obtained access to a significant part of the Rumaila oilfields by unofficially expanding the boundaries of Kuwait after the war.[59] As a result Kuwait, which has heavy American and British oil-company investments, was able to double its pre-war oil output. America had won a victory that had laid to rest the Vietnam defeat, and there was a feeling of pride and unity throughout the US that had not been felt since 1945. But the decisive action was not repeated when Iraq attacked the Kurds and Shi'a, or when Serbia attacked Croatia and Bosnia – which were not oil-rich states.

UN sanctions imposed on Iraq in August 1990 remained in force until 2003. They were tied to Iraqi compliance with Security Council Resolution 687, which requires the demolition of Iraq's weapons of mass destruction and compliance inspections at 60-day intervals. The sanctions could not be lifted until there was unanimity among the Security Council's permanent members. The US and Britain have remained firmly opposed to lifting them. Iraq's sufferings were slightly alleviated by UN humanitarian aid and, since 1996, the Oil for Food Program, which permitted Iraq to resume oil exports. Sanctions have caused massive migrations from the south of Iraq to Baghdad, inflation, unemployment, and a huge rise in child mortality. The first Iraq War was another invasion that would place a nation-state's sovereignty under the authority of the UN. It again demonstrated that the foreign policy of the US was controlled by commercial and security considerations.

Later Developments

The 70s and 80s had seen the Rockefellers and Rothschilds coming closer together. Their rapprochement must be understood in terms of oil. During the First and Second World Wars, "Rockefellers" were in competition with "Rothschilds" and secured the British "Rothschildian" oilfields in Iraq and Saudi Arabia. A stalemate developed in which "Rockefellers" could not take any more of "Rothschilds'" oil – though there was still oil to take in the Caspian region and the Middle and Far East.

At the same time "Rockefellers," who were behind both Stalin and his successor Krushchev, continued to dominate the Soviet Union. Following the creation of the Alliance, as a counter to NATO, the Warsaw Pact strengthened the Soviet Union's position in Eastern Europe by providing a unified military command for 6 million troops under Soviet control.

When we speak of "Rockefellerites" organizing revolutions to further an American empire based on oil, of course what is meant is that the US President, diplomats, and armed forces have conducted official international relations with the country involved, but that "Rockefellers'" enormous commercial interests at the level of banking and oil production, and through the CFR (which they set up) have influenced the American and local incumbents behind the scenes. The same considerations apply as applied with the Bilderberg Group.

The Cold War was a means to split the disparate, warring nation states into two blocs, to sell arms to each bloc for huge business profits, and then unify them all into one world.

On January 30, 1976 a new "Rockefellerite" document called *The Declaration of Interdependence* (varying the "Declaration of Independence" of the US constitution) was signed by 32 Senators and 92 Representatives in Washington DC. It stated: "Two centuries ago our forefathers brought forth a new nation; now we must join with others to bring forth a New World Order ... To establish a New World Order of compassion, peace, justice, and security, it is essential that mankind free itself from the limitations of national prejudice, and acknowledge that the forces that unite it are incomparably deeper than those that divide it – that all people are part of one global community."[60]

Both the Rockefeller and Rothschild families were involved in instigating the chain of revolutions which have brought into being the New World

Order. It is meaningful now to identify a New World Order Revolution, the sum total of a number of revolutions in different countries in different parts of the globe; for such a Revolution has been the *means* to bring about the New World Order.

Within this revolution, the conflicts and Syndicate interventions involving Iran and Iraq were supposed to level the two states into a regional bloc within the intended global community. However, the development of a United States of the Middle East received a setback when an Islamic fight-back took the American government by surprise.

9

THE MIDDLE EAST
REBELLION

Let him who desires peace, prepare for war.

Vegetius[1]

The election in 2000 of a new Republican President, George W. Bush, raised the question as to what influence his father would have over American policy. We have seen that Bush Sr. had spoken of the New World Order a lot shortly before the Gulf War. Bush Jr. did not mention it. Did the son have the same globalist mindset as his father? Would Saddam Hussein be paid back for surviving the Gulf War? Bush Jr. indirectly answered these questions by appointing to key positions many of those who had served his father, notably Dick Cheney as Vice-President, Donald Rumsfeld, and Colin Powell.

September 11: Facts

Comfortable liberal progress was soon shattered by the spectacular and dreadful events of September 11, 2001. Two hijacked planes flew into the Twin Towers of the World Trade Center, causing both (and other buildings) to collapse. A third hijacked plane on course for the White House, which was obscured by trees, changed course and crashed into the Pentagon, which *was* visible, hitting its least important side but still causing severe damage; and a fourth crash-landed, perhaps on its way to the Capitol's Rotunda. In all, just over 3,000 people lost their lives. The targets were symbols of Anglo-American industrial, commercial, military, and political power.

135

Bin Laden: The Background

Many of the reported hijackers were soon linked with the 44–year-old Osama bin Laden. Osama's Yemeni father had emigrated from South Yemen to what would become Saudi Arabia around 1930 and had some 54 children by 30 wives. He made a fortune in construction, renovating the royal palaces, improving the mosques of Mecca and Medina – and rebuilding al-Aqsa mosque in Jerusalem. Osama bin Laden's mother was Syrian and he was born a Saudi-Arabian, his father's seventeenth son. According to one view (despite having some 53 brothers or sisters with a claim on his father's wealth) he inherited $300m when his father was killed in an air crash in 1967.

The family company was then run by Osama's eldest brother Salem (who was 10 years older than Osama). Salem turned the core construction business into an international conglomerate that embraced industrial and power projects, oil exploration, mining, and telecommunications. Salem was killed in 1988 when an ultra-light plane he was piloting inexplicably turned right instead of left during take-off and crashed into power lines in San Antonio, Texas.

The family company is now run by another of Osama's brothers, Bakr, who is Chairman of the Saudi Binladen Group (SBG) which by the mid-1990s was worth $5b and employed 37,000 people. SBG projects include renovating and reconstructing airports (in Cairo and Aden), constructing suburbs (in Cairo), hotels (in Amman), and a seaside resort (in Latakia, Syria). The family has also built a mosque (in Kuala Lumpur), a thirty-story office building (in Riyadh), and a $150m base for 4,000 US soldiers in Saudi Arabia (built after Osama organized the bombing of US troops in Riyadh and Dhahran). There are also businesses that manufacture spare car parts and manage resorts in Saudi Arabia, own property in Dubai, distribute drinks and cars in the Middle East, produce books in Arabic based on Disney feature films, distribute hamburgers, and that have been involved in a mobile phone venture. The family continues to maintain and renovate the mosques at Mecca and Medina, having expanded them so that they can hold up to a million worshippers each.[2]

The financial assets of SBG are managed by the Carlyle Group, which was created in 1987 and now oversees a portfolio worth $12b. It holds a majority of shares in Seven Up (bottlers for Cadbury Schweppes),

Federal Data Corporation (who equipped Federal Aviation Authority with its surveillance system for civilian air traffic), and United Defense Industries Inc. (major suppliers of the American, Turkish, and Saudi Arabian armies). It is the 11th largest American armaments company, and is presided over by Frank C. Carlucci (ex-deputy-director of the CIA and Secretary of Defense). James Baker (Secretary of State under George Bush Sr.) is an advisor, and the Carlyle Group is represented abroad by George Bush Sr. and John Major, former British Prime Minister.[3]

According to a report in the *Wall Street Journal* and other reputable sources, in the 1970s Salem was a business partner of George W. Bush before Bush Jr. became President, and co-founder with him of the Arbusto Energy oil company ("arbusto" means "bush" in Spanish) in Bush Jr.'s home state of Texas.[4] The position is unclear. The two are reported to have been connected through Bush Jr.'s friend from the Texas Air National Guard and neighbor, airplane broker James R. Bath of Houston, who represented at least four wealthy Saudis as business agent. The story is that Bath put up $50,000, channeling the money (via the Bank of Credit and Commerce International) of two Saudi sheikhs, Khalid bin Mahfouz and Salem bin Laden, and receiving a 5% interest in Arbusto '79 and Arbusto '80, limited partnerships controlled by George W. Bush.[5] (When on the point of going bankrupt, Arbusto was bought by Spectrum 7, which in 1986 was in turn bought by Harken Energy Corporation; which kept Bush Jr. on the board for his contacts, mainly his father, and put James R. Bath on its board apparently as a representative of Salem.)[6] Was Bath's investment on behalf of Salem bin Laden or others, or was it a personal holding? The White House has made an unsourced denial.

So bin Laden is an international pariah accused of masterminding the September 11 attacks, yet one of his brothers was a business partner of Bush Jr. in the 1970s and his family's assets are still represented abroad by Bush Sr. – a combination of circumstances that bemuses.

Bin Laden: Recent History

Between 1979 and 1989 Osama helped drive the Russians from Afghanistan, making grenades from landmines and shells from rusty tin cans. In the late spring of 1986, using the name "Tim Osman," he traveled to the US to see if Reagan's administration would help Afghan rebels combat Soviet aircraft, according to the *American Free Press* of January 7, 14, 2002. He attended a meeting at the Hilton Hotel in Sherman Oaks, California. The *American Free Press* claims that the CIA brought him to the US. He was accompanied by an American businessman identified as Ralph Olberg, who was procuring American weapons and technology for the Afghan rebels. The two men met a retired FBI top executive (Senior Special Agent), Ted Gunderson, who has revealed the meeting, and a CIA explosives, armaments, and computer electronics expert named as Michael Riconosciuto. "Osman" (bin Laden) sat in silence throughout the 90–minute meeting.

In 1989 bin Laden founded al-Qaeda, which would eventually merge with Ayman al-Zawahiri's Jihad group (which planned the assassination of President Anwar Sadat of Egypt in 1981).[7] Mohammed Atta, the alleged ringleader of the hijackers, was a pupil of Zawahiri's at university. Al-Qaeda was run like a multinational holding company that can operate without its Chief Executive, and had an independently organized shadow structure in Europe that made individual terrorists very hard to trace.

When the Russians withdrew from Afghanistan Osama returned to Saudi Arabia but fell out with the royal family over Saddam Hussein's invasion of Kuwait. Known to want to rid Mecca, Medina, and Jerusalem of non-Moslems, Osama wanted Saudi Arabia to expel Americans and side with Saddam. He was utterly disenchanted when Saudi Arabia invited the Americans in and opposed Saddam in the Gulf War. In 1991 Osama fled to Sudan, vowing to overthrow corrupt Arab governments like the House of Saud and establish a new, pure theocracy in the Arabian peninsula.[8]

In Sudan Osama created a business empire by investing in banks and agricultural projects, and by building a major road. At the same time he organized training camps to train al-Qaeda followers in paramilitary tactics. His companies were the Wadi al-Aqiq trading company; Ladin International Company; Al-Hijra Construction, which built roads and bridges in conjunction with the Sudanese government; Al-Themar agricultural company, which had 4,000 employees working on a million-acre farm; Taba Investment Ltd., which exported gum, corn, sunflower, and sesame; The Blessed Fruits company, which grew fruit and vegetables; Al-Ikhlas, which produced sweets and honey; Al-Qudurat trucking company; Khartoum Tannery, a leather company; a bakery; a furniture makers; and Al-Shamal Islamic bank in Khartoum, into which he put

$50m of his own money.[9] It has been alleged that a business associate of bin Laden's, presumably during these Sudanese enterprises, was Sharon Percy Rockefeller, the wife of John D. ("Jay") Rockefeller IV.[10]

From Sudan Osama waged war against America with attacks on US troops in Saudi Arabia, US warships off the Yemen, and the US Embassies in Kenya and Tanzania, causing hundreds of deaths. He was expelled from Sudan in 1996 and returned to Afghanistan following a car bomb in Riyadh that was blamed on him.[11]

At this stage, Osama's financial dealings had become something of a mystery. Osama's share of his father's estate was $300m according to some sources, $35m to others. In 1994, according to a former al-Qaeda member, he was saying he had lost all his money; there was some sort of a financial crisis. When Sudan expelled him in 1996 he may have lost as much as $150m in assets he was unable to take with him. Nevertheless, when he arrived in Afghanistan in 1996 at the invitation of Younus Khalis, he gave the Taliban millions of dollars for construction projects round Kandahar: for a large mosque, a dam, and agricultural projects.[12]

In Afghanistan he was supported by Younus Khalis, who later became a major figure in the Taliban in Jalalabad, and whose military commander (Awal Gul) held the road that led to the al-Qaeda base in the White Mountains, Tora Bora (a network of caves and tunnels accessible only on foot). The fanatical Moslem Taliban regime swept to power in late 1996. Mullah Omar was bankrolled by Osama (to the extent of £68m according to an American intelligence estimate),[13] sheltered him in gratitude for his financial support and for his achievement in helping to expel the Russians and gave him control of large areas of Nangarhar province as a gift. This eastern province between Kabul and Pakistan's North-West Frontier province has many poppy fields. Afghanistan produces three-quarters of the world's supply of opium, the basic ingredient of heroin, and Osama now had all the drug revenues from the poppy-rich province.[14]

Osama established training camps there for 2,000 terrorists, at which Clinton ordered cruise missiles to be fired in 1998. It was at one of these camps in Afghanistan that he met Mohammed Atta personally in December 1999.[15] He had 11,000 trained fighters in 50 countries round the world, and between early 2000 and July 2001 spent $800,000 a month on buying small arms and ammunition from stockpiles within the former Soviet Union. He is reputed to have received $1b from Afghan-related heroin deals.[16] According to another view, such money, if it exists, has come from another (unknown) source, and Osama bin Laden had merely a few million dollars to his own name.

According to papers filed in a $1 trillion lawsuit in America in 2002, senior members of the Saudi royal family, deeply worried by Islamic fundamentalist attacks on a US army training facility in Riyadh in November 1995 and on the Khobar Towers barracks in June 1996 (in which 19 US airmen died), paid at least $200m to Osama's terror group and the Taliban in return for an agreement that his organization would not attack Saudi Arabia. This "protection money" was arranged following meetings in Paris in 1996 and in Kandahar, Afghanistan, in July 1998, both of which Osama attended. This protection money covered some of his expenditure after 1998.[17]

Al-Qaeda, initially a guest, became a cuckoo and took over the Afghan nest, successfully demanding that Mullah Omar should rename the country "The Islamic Emirate of Afghanistan." In February 2001 bin Laden is alleged to have planned to kill all 625 Euro-MPs and hundreds of officials by releasing sarin gas (nerve gas) into the European Parliament building in Strasbourg, using Algerian proxies funded by his source fund. The plot was foiled by German police, who made a number of raids.[18]

Bin Laden's Responsibility

The *Washington Post* of December 23, 2001 reported that the CIA paid a team of Afghans to track bin Laden for four years. The article says that the CIA had their eyes on bin Laden most of that time, but that just before September 11 they lost track of him.

Bin Laden conveniently appeared on a video broadcast by al-Jazeera, the Arabic satellite station in Qatar, to insist that "the war against Afghanistan and Osama bin Laden is a war on Islam," suggesting that *he* was the leader of all Arabs, not the "corrupt regimes" he has often criticized, such as Saudi Arabia. He praised the attacks on New York and Washington and said that their perpetrators were martyrs who have gone to Paradise. His support fell short of admitting responsibility for the attacks. He said the attacks took place because of American support for Israel, and that there would be no peace until Palestine is free. He complained that a million of Iraq's children had been killed. The Arabs must throw the Americans out of Arab territory – which meant expelling Jews from Israel and all Americans from the Middle East, the "Arab nation."

In his video, speaking confidently and clearly expecting to win, bin Laden made three historical allusions. He called for "a new battle, a great battle, similar to the great battles of Islam, like the conqueror of Jerusalem." He was referring to Salah-ad-Din Yusuf ibn-Ayyub, or Saladin, the Kurdish-born Moslem leader who liberated Jerusalem from the Crusaders in 1187. Bin Laden was speaking as if he were a new Saladin who was trying to widen the war to cover all Islam: "I envision Saladin coming out of the clouds carrying his sword, with the blood of unbelievers dripping from it." He also said: "What America is facing today is a little of what we have tasted for decades. Our nation, for nearly 80 years, had tasted this humiliation." He was referring to the break-up of the Ottoman Empire during the First World War, which ended Moslem rule over Jerusalem in 1917 and the loss of Palestine in 1922. He also referred to Moslem Spain: "Let the whole world know that we shall never accept that the tragedy of Andalusia would be repeated in Palestine." From the eleventh century the Moslems were gradually driven out of Spain, and Moslem cultural superiority was eroded by the conquest of Ferdinand and Isabella in 1492.

Calling for *jihad* (holy war), bin Laden invoked the Crusades: "The crusader forces became the main cause of our disastrous condition." Pope Urban II urged in 1095: "Enter upon the road to the Holy Sepulcher, wrest that land from the wicked race .... God wills it." Bin Laden was echoing such religious fanaticism a millennium later.

With Mullah Omar, the Taliban leader, reinforcing his call for a holy war, Arabs and Pakistanis flocked to Afghanistan and were sent to the front line whence Afghans, who might defect to the Northern Alliance, were withdrawn. The prospect loomed of a war between the Arabs and Israel, and perhaps even between Pakistan and India (both nuclear powers). In December 2001 an attack on the Indian parliament by Kashmiri militants linked to al-Qaeda left 14 people dead. The prospect of nuclear war seemed close. It was said that 12 million might be killed and 7 million critically injured.[19]

On November 3, 2001 bin Laden, perhaps sensing that the Americans were closing in on him, appeared on another video smuggled out to Qatar and denied that there was any evidence linking Afghanistan (or himself) to the attack on America of September 11. He accused the UN (which had supported the American bombing) of being a "tool of crime against Moslems," and said that Arab leaders who seek UN help (such as the Pakistani leadership) are infidels. With Pakistan's religious leaders urging Pakistanis to volunteer for *jihad* (holy war) against the wish of Pakistan's military dictatorship, he was clearly trying to split the Global Coalition in the hope that Pakistan (and possibly Saudi Arabia) would insist that the American bombing should be stopped.

Bin Laden's denial was compromised by a training video for al-Qaeda followers. In it bin Laden said that the Twin Towers were "legitimate targets, they were supporting US economic power." The people known to have died in them were "not civilians" but were working for the American system: "supporters of the economic power of the US who are abusing the world." The Twin Towers were thus icons of American power. This video was taken as an admission of responsibility for the attack on September 11.

The War[20]

The American response was as the perpetrators could have predicted. President Bush Jr. proclaimed the attack the first act of war in the twenty-first century, and there was talk of an incident worse than the Japanese attack on Pearl Harbor.

The Americans declared war on world terrorism (a globalist agenda) and Bush refused to make public the evidence he had against bin Laden. Following a round of frantic diplomatic activity during which British Prime Minister Blair visited Pakistan and India, on October 7 American and British forces retaliated by striking al-Qaeda training-camps and Taliban military installations in Afghanistan. There were air attacks on Kabul, Jalalabad, and Kandahar. It was announced that 15 bombers and 25 strike aircraft were used, and that 50 Tomahawk cruise missiles were fired from submarines.

President George W. Bush implied that this was the first stage of a long "self-defense" war that would include more countries – perhaps Iraq, Syria, Somalia, Yemen, Libya, and Iran.

US planes bombed the Red Cross warehouse that stockpiled food for refugees twice, in the Kabul region. Not long afterwards a UN warehouse in Kandahar stockpiling food was bombed. These strikes could only worsen the chances of the Afghan refugees, estimated to be approaching 7.5 million.

The Northern Alliance swept the country. Mazar-i-Sharif fell. Kabul was vacated, its defenders having been routed by American carpet-bombing. It fell to Tajik *mujahideen*, and there were uprisings by tribesmen in Kandahar and Jalalabad, which fell, leaving pockets of Taliban to be mopped up, most notably at Kunduz, where 10,000 Taliban were surrounded along with 600 fanatical al-Qaeda ideologues: Chechnyans, Arabs, Pakistanis, even Chinese Moslems, all of whom had fled from Mazar-i-Sharif. Al-Qaeda fanatics executed 470 Taliban for planning to defect so as to escape the siege.

Bin Laden's military chief, Mohammed Atef, who was thought to have planned the September 11 attack and the attacks on the US embassies in Kenya and Tanzania, was killed in a bombing raid on Kabul. An abandoned al-Qaeda safe house in Kabul allegedly revealed plans to manufacture the biological poison ricin together with printed matter about the building of an atomic bomb.

Kunduz fell after a siege of two weeks. The captors discovered that, though surrounded, of the 600 al-Qaeda hardliners some had been airlifted out with their weapons by Russian Antinov planes at 2 am, on three successive nights, between bombing raids and under the noses of the Northern Alliance and under the scrutiny of American Awacs planes. Probably to Pakistan. In early December 2001 Kandahar fell, after some 10,000 troops and civilians had been killed by relentless bombing. All weapons were handed in, but Mullah Omar had fled to mountains near Baghran with a fighting force of around 2,000 Taliban and al-Qaeda troops. When this force was surrounded he escaped by motorbike. On the run, he telephoned the BBC world service and chillingly warned that America faced "extinction."

For some while the press had carried reports that bin Laden was hiding in the al-Qaeda headquarters, alleged to comprise a vast multi-storey complex inside the White Mountains at Tora Bora, 13,000 feet up and sheltering in the virtually impregnable network of tunnels built with American money to resist Russian onslaughts. It was said that the passages slope upwards from the entrance as a precaution against air strikes, that it sleeps over

2,000, and has its own electricity supply from a generator worked by a mountain stream.

The battle for Tora Bora lasted nearly a fortnight. The Americans bombed the mountainside with daisy-cutters that wipe out everything within 600 yards. B-52s pounded the mountain ridges and slopes, killing many al-Qaeda. Some were captured, the rest were dispersed. Bin Laden's deputy, al-Zawahiri, who merged his Jihad group with al-Qaeda, was wounded. It was believed that bin Laden himself had fled across the border into Pakistan. Other sources say the Himalayan Mountains, sheltered by the Harkat-ul-Mujahideen Islamic guerilla group, funded by the CIA in the 1980s to fight the Russians. Others say back in the Arabian peninsula, in his ancestral Yemeni region of Hadhra Maug. Others say he was in Kashmir, China, Cairo ....

The campaign continued against small pockets of resistance. The US military rounded up captured al-Qaeda fighters and flew them for (possibly illegal) detention at Guantanamo Bay, Cuba. They were interrogated, and the press reported that an execution chamber was being built in readiness for military tribunals.

In September 2002 two al-Qaeda men claimed to have masterminded the September 11 attacks: Khalid Sheikh Mohammed, the uncle of Ramzi Yousef who is now serving a life sentence for attacking the World Trade Center in 1993, and Ramzi bin al-Shibh, a Yemeni citizen from Hadramawt, the hometown of bin Laden, Khalid's aide and a former flat-mate of Mohammed Atta. The two gave an interview to Yosri Fouda of al-Jazeera television (reported in London's *Sunday Times* of September 8, 2002) in Karachi. They said they organized and executed the death flights with the approval of bin Laden, who was "alive and well." They revealed that the fourth plane *was* targeting Capitol Hill and not the White House; and that the initial plan was to crash the hijacked jets into nuclear power plants. The decision to launch a massive suicide attack on the US was taken in early 1999. Bin al-Shibh wanted to be the twentieth hijacker, but was refused entry into the US.

Within days of the release of this interview bin al-Shibh was captured alive after a long and bloody gun and grenade battle lasting three to four hours targeting a fifth-floor apartment in a well-to-do suburb of Karachi. Two suspected al-Qaeda men were killed, five surrendered. In all 10 were arrested: one Egyptian, one Saudi, and eight Yemenis following a joint raid by Pakistani forces and US special force commandos. It seems that bin al-Shibh was trapped when he used a satellite phone that was picked up by a US satellite programmed to recognize his voice after his al-Jazeera appearance, although it is possible that Pakistani and US agents tailed Fouda as he traveled to meet bin al-Shibh for the interview. Apparently Pakistani and US surveillance teams waited until two men left the apartment and police arrested them in the street. One of them shouted a warning, and the others opened fire from the top floor. The two men were killed in the flat after their colleagues had climbed on to the roof. When the police eventually stormed the flat they found "There is no God but Allah" written in Arabic in blood on the kitchen wall (possibly by bin al-Shibh). It transpired that bin al-Shibh had masterminded the September 11 attacks by sending coded instructions on the Internet to the hijackers via Atta, posing as Atta's German girlfriend. They referred to the targets as university departments. The World Trade Center was the "faculty of town planning" (Atta's academic specialty).

It later emerged that bin al-Shibh was to have piloted a fifth plane on September 11. He applied to take flying lessons within the US but was unable to obtain a visa. After four unsuccessful visa applications he settled for an organizational role.

In February 2003, the Kuwaiti-born Khalid Sheikh Mohammed, al-Qaeda's no. 3 who was suspected of masterminding the September 11 attacks as bin Laden's military advisor, was arrested with Mustafa Ahmed Hawsawi, the alleged financier of the attacks, in Rawalpindi, Pakistan. They had apparently been betrayed by the son (Mohammed Abdul-Rahman) of the Egyptian convicted of planning the first bombing of the World Trade Center in 1993, Sheikh Omar Abdul-Rahman, the "blind cleric." Khalid had a bounty of $25m on his head. According to an interview he had given to al-Jazeera, it was he who dreamed up the idea of flying planes into the WTC towers. Khalid is alleged to have told his interrogators that bin Laden was responsible for recruiting the hijackers.

The case seems clear cut. Bin Laden and his lieutenants were responsible for September 11. Bin Laden wanted a holy war that could drive America from the Middle East. The significance of the symbolism behind the September 11 date has been overlooked. Extremists often select an anniversary for their deed. Thus Gavrilo Princip chose the date of Serbia's fourteenth-century defeat in Kosovo (June 28, 1914) to assassinate the Austrian archduke, the act which triggered the First World War, while Timothy McVeigh chose the anniversary of the bloodbath at the Branch Davidian compound at Waco, Texas, to carry out the bombing of the government office in Oklahoma that he held responsible. September 11 was the anniversary of September 11, 1683, when the conquering armies of Islam were thrown back from the gates of Vienna, a humiliating defeat from which the Ottoman Empire never recovered and which allowed the Western Christian powers to dominate the Moslem world.[21] Bin Laden (if he was involved) and the hijackers who planned to die were presumably seeking to reverse a period of Islamic history that began with this date and were signaling that Arab Islam would again move against the West.

Intelligence sources also believe that some of the terrorists – many of the 19 hijackers who were to overpower passengers and crew – passed through bin Laden's camps in Afghanistan. Evidence for bin Laden's personal involvement in the September 11 attacks is strengthened by reports of a personal meeting Mohammed Atta (the alleged ringleader of the hijackers) had with him in Afghanistan in December 1999. Film has surfaced showing four of the hijackers planning the attacks, studying a map of the Pentagon, and reading their wills. It is thought that bin Laden's voice can be heard in the background, off camera.

On March 11, 2002 President Bush Jr., in a speech marking the six months since the September 11 attack, made it clear that he was trying to reassemble the international coalition for the next stage of the war against terrorism. On the same day Vice-President Dick Cheney and British Prime Minister Blair raised fears that weapons of mass destruction – nuclear and biochemical weapons – might fall into the hands of terrorist groups such as al-Qaeda. In signaling forthcoming action against Iraq they suggested that Saddam might supply al-Qaeda with nuclear or biochemical weapons with which they could attack America. The position of international ogre and main global threat had passed from bin Laden to Saddam Hussein.

Iraqi Oil[22]

While there was a certain amount of score-settling in George W. Bush's decision to attack Iraq, there was also calculation, for Saddam had been sold weapons and weapon parts – by the Americans themselves and the French – that could be converted into weapons of mass destruction and endanger the Middle East, particularly Israel. At a time when al-Qaeda was a ubiquitous danger and oil-rich Saudi Arabia's support for the West was deemed unreliable, Iraq's huge oil reserves were tempting. The 2002 Bilderberg Group's meeting in Virginia had recognized that a UN tax on all world citizens would be resisted, and had considered a world tax on oil at the wellhead instead. Military action against Iraq was a way of achieving this.

Western oil companies have long had their eyes on Iraq, which has 11% of the world's known oil reserves. Huge new reserves have been discovered in the south (which is dominated by Shia Moslems linked to Iran). US Vice-President Dick Cheney, who like President George W. Bush had his own commercial interests in the Middle East before holding office, said at the beginning of August 2002 of Saddam: "He sits on top of 10% of the world's oil reserves. He has enormous wealth being generated by that. And left to his own devices, it's the judgment of many of us that in the not too distant future he will acquire nuclear weapons." If Saddam were toppled, the Western oil companies, led by Exxon, would have access to Iraq's oil reserves and become less dependent on Saudi oilfields and the future stability of the Saudi royal family.

To put it more starkly, the American way of life is dependent on 20 million barrels of oil per day (19.7 million to be exact, a quarter of the world's consumption of oil), and half has to be imported (some, despite UN controls, from Iraq, resold as low-sulfur Syrian oil). Until recently the two main suppliers (recently overtaken by Canada) were Saudi Arabia, now considered unreliable, and Venezuela, unstable as a result of permanent demonstrations to oust President Chavez. Since September 11 the US had made approaches for oil to Russia and African nations, but the cheapest alternative was Iraqi oil as it sits just below the desert sands. Facing its most chronic shortage in oil stocks for 27 years as a result of the loss of 1.5 million barrels per day of Venezuelan production and with net liabilities to the rest of the world of more than $2.3 trillion, America desperately needed reserves of oil at minimal cost. In early 2003 America doubled its import of oil from Iraq. Russia (in five oilfields) and France (in two) made oil deals with Iraq, and both countries consequently initially opposed a Western attack on Iraq.

In early September 2002 Cheney said, "The risk of inaction [is] far greater than the risk of action." The Bush administration seemed to have taken a decision to effect a change of regime in Baghdad at a cost estimated at $80b (to be recouped from reduced future expenditure on oil). The leader of Britain's internationalist government, Blair, supported this Bilderberg line, citing the threat of Saddam's weapons of mass destruction, which had been developed in breach of nine UN resolutions: Iraq had not fulfilled 23 out of 27 demands. He promised that a dossier of evidence on Iraq would be published within a few weeks. He said that Iraq was just as much an issue for Britain as for America, and urged the US to seek a Security Council resolution to justify military action. America had seemed ready to "go it alone" and attack Iraq without UN approval, risking being accused of what many felt would be an illegal act. (Any leader who declares that another nation is terrorist and then attacks it risks being accused of a criminal violation of international law.)

At a summit at Camp David, Bush and Blair agreed to topple Saddam by military means even if the UN did not pass a resolution authorizing the use of force. Saddam was reported to be buying North Korean ballistic missile technology to carry weapons of mass destruction to their targets. It was claimed that he had enough chemical and biological weapons to wipe out everyone on earth, and that he was on the verge of having nuclear weapons. He could assemble an atomic bomb "within months" and was close to a nuclear capability. He was reputed to have a $3b-a-year fund to finance al-Qaeda terrorists. What was the balance of concern here between Saddam as a threat and Iraqi oil as an opportunity to be grasped? You'll have to decide.

UN

On September 12, 2002 President Bush went to the UN General Assembly and called Saddam "a grave and gathering danger." There was unease that if Saddam was attacked, he would fire nuclear weapons at Israel, and that if Israel attacked back, the Middle East could become an inferno. If he fired ICBMs at the US, there could be a global inferno. Saudi Arabia decided to allow British and US planes to launch air strikes from its soil if they received UN authority. On September 16 Iraq sent a letter to the UN agreeing to readmit the UN weapons inspectors, who had been expelled four years previously, "without conditions," but making no mention of disarming or destroying weapons stocks. Iraq now technically complied with all UN resolutions, and this appeared to satisfy Russia. The US and Britain, however, felt that Saddam was playing for time.

UN Secretary-General Kofi Annan had married into the Bilderberg Wallenberg[23] family, which dominates Sweden's industry and economy. His wife, the Swedish Nane Lagergren, was a niece of the diplomat who went missing at the end of the Second World War, Raoul Wallenberg. Annan relied on an élite of "neutral" Swedish diplomats to oversee the globalist agenda in places such as the Balkans and Iraq. In January 2000 a Swedish diplomat, Hans Blix, was appointed the new chief weapons inspector and head of UNMOVIC, the new inspections regime for Iraq, and John Stern Wolf, was appointed as a special advisor to the President and secretary of state for Caspian Basin Energy Diplomacy, to serve on a College of Commissioners for UNMOVIC.

On September 20, 2002 Bush's administration announced a new post-September 11 foreign policy doctrine that emphasized pre-emptive action against "hostile states" and terrorist groups alleged to be developing weapons of mass destruction, to defend American interests rather than the old priorities of deterrence and containment. The US, the doctrine insisted, would never allow its military supremacy to be challenged as it was during the Cold War. This ambition seemed to be in conflict with the internationalism of the UN, and indeed seemed to assert that the UN would no longer have a role if it did not pass a tough resolution on Iraq.

On November 8 the UN Security Council unanimously (by 15 votes to nil) approved a resolution "bringing the civilized world together to disarm Saddam Hussein." It authorized the use of force without the need for another resolution, and gave Iraq until November 18 to comply and December 11 to provide a complete declaration of all its weapons of mass destruction. The inspectors were to start work in Iraq by December 26 and report to the Security Council by February 24, 2003. The unanimity of the decision confirmed the US's status as a "hyperpower" (Russia's word) with an unprecedented mastery of sea, land, and air and a global reach. Iraq responded by presenting a declaration in Arabic exceeding 11,000 pages. It denied possessing any weapons of mass destruction, and the declaration amounted to a nil return.

The Iraqi declaration left open what happened to 8,500 liters of anthrax (allegedly destroyed without record in 1991), 50 warheads (allegedly destroyed), 550 mustard-gas-filled artillery shells (declared lost), and 400 biological weapon-capable aerial bombs. Apparently 6,000 fewer chemical gas bombs were used in the Iran–Iraq war than Baghdad claimed, and these were not declared. The UN Special Commission concluded that 26,000 liters of anthrax might be unaccounted for, together with 1,200 liters of botulinum toxin and 5,500 liters of *Clostridium perfringens*. Iraq had disclosed manufacturing new fuels suited to a class of missile it does not admit to possessing, and had not disclosed why it sought to procure uranium from Niger. Nearly 30,000 empty munitions that could be filled with chemical agents were unaccounted for, and there was no mention of the unmanned Mig-21 remote-piloted vehicles that can carry a biological weapon spray system, which Iraq admitted possessing in 1995. Iraq had not accounted for quantities of VX nerve gas and many parts used in the manufacture of nuclear bombs.

Part of the West's concern was that they thought they knew Saddam had these weapons because they had been involved in financing and supplying them. It was revealed by the *Washington Post* that the US's arch-hawk in advocating going to war with Saddam, Donald Rumsfeld, as an envoy of Reagan had secret meetings with Saddam in 1983 to arrange for the Iraqis to receive billions of pounds in loans to buy weapons for his war with Iran. On November 1, 1983, a month before Rumsfeld's visit, the CIA officially informed Secretary of State George Shultz that Iraqis were resorting to "almost daily use of chemical weapons" against Iran. The assistance is alleged to have been given a year after the UN had passed a resolution calling on countries not to supply arms to either side in the Iran–Iraq war.

According to the *Washington Post* in the mid-1980s, following the Rumsfeld visit dozens of biological agents including anthrax were shipped to Iraq under license from the US Commerce Department. It has been alleged on television that Saddam's 11,000–page declaration included a laconic section listing all the American companies that supplied these biological agents during the 1980s – and that these pages were omitted from the 5,000–page edited version supplied by the US (which had charged itself with both the copying and distribution of Iraq's declaration) to such countries as Syria. US intelligence experts hit back at these allegations by claiming that Saddam was hiding two nuclear and chemical experts in his presidential palaces, and that all his weapons of mass destruction had been moved to a secret underground bunker in the desert north of Baghdad.

The UN Fails to Act

In his New Year message for 2003 Blair said that Iraq posed a threat that demanded the ultimate sanction of "defensive aggression." In other words, the West must attack him first to defend itself. Many Western citizens were now perturbed to discover that, having spent much of their lives on the "good" side, having regarded the Anglo-American alliance as a defensive force for good against Hitler and then, with NATO, against Soviet aggression in Budapest and Prague, they were now on the side of the aggressors, "the baddies." Although Orwellian Newspeak presents aggression as defense, many Western intellectuals felt that their regime's policies were now morally ambivalent at best, and morally compromising at worst.

On January 16, 2003, following information supplied by American and British intelligence, the UN weapons inspectors searched a large group of bunkers in a relatively new ammunition storage area and found 12 empty 122mm chemical warheads (warheads designed to carry chemical warfare agents) that were "in excellent condition." They had not been included in Iraq's 11,000–page declaration and their discovery suggested that Saddam had not been sincere in what he had declared. They represented a "false statement or omissions ... and failure by Iraq to comply" that constituted a "material breach" of UN resolution 1441. An Iraqi spokesman claimed that the warheads were not linked to any banned arms program, and had expired and been forgotten about.

At the January 2003 meeting in Davos, Switzerland, of the World Economic Forum (WEF), a private meeting of the global élite of business leaders, the post-war distribution of Iraqi oil was discussed behind closed doors: "carving up the Iraqi black gold cake" according to one of the participants, Tony Juniper of Friends of the Earth (press conference, January 26). The head of nearly every major oil company was present, including Peter Sutherland, chief executive of BP and a leader in the Bilderberg Group and Trilateral Commission, and Philip Watts, chairman of Royal Dutch Shell. There were discussions on the BP-operated oil pipeline from

Baku on the Caspian to Ceyhan, Turkey. Bill Clinton attended and Gen. Wes Clark explained how a US-led assault on Iraq might develop.

Hans Blix, the UN's chief weapons inspector, reported to the Security Council on February 28. He said that Saddam had not accounted for 6,500 chemical bombs and "several thousand" chemical rocket warheads, 550 shells filled with mustard gas, chemicals used to make VX nerve gas, and 8,500 liters of anthrax virus, all of which were known to exist in 1998. In addition 380 rocket engines illegally smuggled into Iraq were missing, along with manufacturing equipment that could be used in making a nuclear bomb. Blix was told that he must report back to the Security Council by February 14. Seizing on Blix's report in his State of the Union (actually State of the World) address, President Bush declared that thousands of Iraqis were moving the missing missiles, chemical weapons, and mobile germ warfare units ahead of the UN inspectors' visits. He said that Saddam was not disarming but deceiving, and that only war would disarm him. He announced that Secretary of State Colin Powell would be laying evidence linking Iraq to al-Qaeda before the UN. A day after Nelson Mandela made a scathing attack on Bush, claiming that all America wanted was Iraqi oil, Bush received Blair at the White House and agreed that if Saddam did not disarm war would follow in weeks. A second UN resolution (sought by Blair) would be desirable but was not necessary.

On February 5, 2003 Colin Powell (drawing on a new and since discredited British dossier) made a dramatic 75–minute presentation to the UN of declassified satellite pictures of chemical weapons and facilities being sanitized, and of communications intercepts of Iraqi officers ordering the concealment of weapons programs. In one of these an Iraqi officer gave instructions for all references to "nerve agents" to be deleted. Powell claimed that Iraqi scientists were threatened with death if they cooperated with the UN, and the officer responsible for liaising with the UN was the architect of Iraq's concealment effort. Terrorists affiliated to al-Qaeda were operating freely from Baghdad, and a senior al-Qaeda leader in Iraq, Abu Musab al-Zarqawi, a Palestinian born in Jordan, was masterminding the European terror network, including the gang that had attempted to manufacture ricin in Britain. Were the US and UK deliberately spinning "the facts" to justify the coming war on Iraq? Iraqis had visited al-Qaeda training camps in Afghanistan. Eighteen biological weapons laboratories were hidden in lorries or train carriages, and up to 500 tons of chemical weapons agents were unaccounted for. Iraq was continuing to attempt to obtain nuclear weapons components, including special magnets needed for a centrifuge system, and was developing missiles with a range of 1,200 kilometers and planes with a range of 500 kilometers to deliver chemicals or germs. Prisoners were used as guinea pigs for chemical and biological agents. Powell's powerful presentation failed to persuade key members of the UN Security Council to back military action to disarm Iraq, but it had an impact on world public opinion, much of which tentatively swung behind a US attack on Iraq.

In February 2003 the UN weapons inspectors found a banned al-Samoud 2 missile system, which, independent experts ruled, could fly beyond the permitted 150k range and threaten Israel. Iraq was given until the end of the month to destroy the 100 to 120 missiles, which, with their diameter of 760mm instead of the original design's 750mm and the 600mm permitted by a UN letter of 1994, could be adapted to contain two Volga engines instead of one. The two engines could carry a larger payload (1,000kg, sufficient to transport a nuclear device) or convey it a longer range and certainly put Israel (300k away) well within reach. The Iraqis destroyed more than thirty of these missiles in the course of March. The UN weapons inspectors also found an R400 bomb that had been banned and may have contained biological weapons.

Blix reported again to the Security Council on March 7 in balanced, neutral terms, praising Saddam for cooperating and glossing over his failure to account for chemical and biological stocks he was known to possess in 1998. Kofi Annan, the UN's Secretary-General, then warned that military action in Iraq without international backing from the UN would be illegal. This was a judgment on his part. Frustrated at the prospects of further delay, and aware of Blair's difficulties with his party, the "Rockefellerite" Rumsfeld declared that the US was ready to launch a war without Britain. To him, the US's superpowerdom was the main reality in world power, and the UN had marginalized itself and been revealed as a diplomatic *souk* in which competing big powers offered bribes to tin-pot dictators of small countries (like Guinea) with appalling human rights records, to secure their votes. Like the League of Nations, the UN was designed to preserve peace. It had been exposed as a forum in which tyrannies had equal status with democracies, and in which democracies were powerless to enforce the will of the free democratic world against anti-American despots such as Saddam Hussein and Kim Jong-Il who were bent on developing their own weapons of mass destruction. To him, the UN had been shown to have lost its credibility.

The truth of the situation was that in consequence of the "Rockefellerite" Blix–Annan–Chirac line, the US and "Rothschildite" Britain had difficulty in carrying the second resolution, which was abandoned. They embarked on military action on the strength of resolution 1441, which many interpreted as being without UN approval.

According to Peter Foster, a convicted conman and former boyfriend of Blair's lifestyle advisor Carole Caplin, in April 2002 Bush Jr. told Blair at his Texas ranch that he had decided to go to war in Iraq – a year before it happened. If this is true, Blair's case for war had been a justification for a decision made by Bush Jr. a year before the second Iraq war.

In view of the diplomatic difficulties, a plan for which Bilderberg would have preferred to have multilateral endorsement became unilateral. The "Rockefellerite"-"Rothschildite" Bilderberg design on Iraq was implemented and forced through and sugarcoated with talk of democratic self-government for Iraq after the fall of Saddam. "The New World" Blair explained in an interview, "faces a new threat of chaos. If the threats all come together all nations are targets." The main threats to the New World Order, which after the fall of the Berlin Wall had given hope of universal peace and security (under American hegemony), were terrorism and rogue dictators' weapons of mass destruction.

Anglo-American Victory in Iraq

At 2.30 a.m. on March 20 the US carried out an opportunistic attack that was designed "to decapitate" the regime before the beginning of the war. Saddam appeared to survive: a figure purporting to be Saddam appeared on television, wearing battledress, a beret, and horn-rimmed spectacles and looking disheveled, to denounce the "criminal" raid.

On March 21 American and British forces spread up to Umm Qasr, Basra, and Nasiriyah in the south, and Operation Shock and Awe was unleashed on Baghdad by B52s, striking Saddam's palace complex and intelligence headquarters in an attack of unprecedented ferocity involving 1,000 missiles, creating fireballs, mushroom clouds, and a firestorm that left parts of central Baghdad in flames. At the same time Mosul and Kirkuk were bombed by B52s.

Shock and Awe was designed to leave the world in awe of American superpower. The codename was taken from the title of a study of Gulf War strategy by Harlan Ullman, which was published by Washington's National Defense University in 1996. It recommended intimidating an adversary into losing the will to fight. Shock and Awe was originally programmed to last eight days. In fact, intensive bombing would last for no more than a few hours. Even so, the attacks on Baghdad would require a multi-billion dollar (at least $100b, probably $330b and perhaps as much as $500b) reconstruction program with contracts to make a start being awarded to Syndicate companies with links to the Republican Party (including a contract to blow out wellhead oil fires worth about $50m to Kellogg Brown & Root, a subsidiary of Halliburton, the oil company that used to employ Dick Cheney). There would also be opportunities for the Syndicate to loan money on favorable terms, as in the case of the Balkan wars of the 1990s.

The Americans captured two bridges intact at Nasiriyah and crossed the Euphrates. One tank force made its way to Kut, another remained on the west bank of the Euphrates and reached Kerbala. The tanks prepared a hundred-mile-long line between those two towns to attack Baghdad.

Perhaps sensing that complete victory would be less quick than he had first thought, President Bush asked for $74.7b (around three and a half years of revenue from Iraqi oil) to replace high-tech munitions, a sum that would cover a month's fighting, and Congress voted to give nearly $79b to the war, foreign aid, and domestic security, of which $63b was to pay for the war. There were suggestions that with post-war reconstruction Iraq could cost the Americans over several years as much as $550b. (The costs of the occupation alone would be $17b a year, with several billions more to be spent on humanitarian assistance.) It was likely that such amounts, if allocated, would be raised by borrowing, which would further increase the national debt. It was difficult to see how such amounts could be spent without some compensation from Iraq's oil (which has an annual revenue of $20b) for incurring the costs of the war. A flow of cheap Iraqi oil to the US would pay for the war over a period of time.[24]

The Coalition's operation brought world-wide condemnation – from Arab countries, of course, and from France, Germany, and Russia, where the "Rockefellerite" Gorbachev branded Britain a "satellite" of the US and said, "If you sow the wind, you reap the whirlwind." Commentators observed that the Axis of Evil policy had wrecked the US economy, doubled oil prices, undermined the dollar, decimated the value of American assets, diverted energy from the War against Terror, intensified global hatred of Israel, and fueled anti-US feeling in a way that must have delighted bin Laden. War against Iraq had split the UN, the European Union, NATO, and Blair's New Labour Party (over 120 MPs of which had opposed the war in the Commons). Although her trade deficit for 2002, £34.3b,[25] was the worst figure since William III ordered records to be kept in 1697, Britain had allocated £1.75b for the war on Iraq (later raised to £3b). War also seemed to have split Bilderberg into hawks and doves – doves who wanted the New World Order to be peaceful and secure while they traded with Saddam.

It had been announced that the reconstruction of Iraq would not be run by Gen. Franks but by Jay Garner, a retired US General and supporter of Israel, who would head the Office for Reconstruction of Humanitarian Assistance, the Pentagon agency preparing to govern Iraq's 24 million people after the war. He would act as President, King, Viceroy, Governor, Vizier, and Sheriff in one. Britain urged that the transitional governing of Iraq by the US-led Coalition should be backed by a UN resolution and that Coalition rule should be as short as possible so that a government of Iraqis could be installed. On April 6 Paul Wolfowitz announced that the interim period before Iraqi self-government would be at least six months and probably longer, plenty of time in which to allocate business and oil contracts to US companies. This forecast was later extended to a year.

Chaos, and No Saddam

From April 5 to 8 US tanks pushed into first western, then eastern Baghdad and toppled the 20–foot-high statue of Saddam on a plinth in Firdos Square. The Iraqi people discovered that they were free, and immediately celebrated in an orgy of looting from government buildings. There was then a rumor, which Russia would neither confirm nor deny, that Russians were helping Saddam flee Baghdad. This raised the prospect that Saddam was holed up in the Russian embassy in Baghdad, or in Russia itself (having traveled by convoy, which was unsuccessfully bombed by the US, with the Russian Ambassador).

This rumor raised the prospect that "Rockefellerite" Russia was looking after its own agent. During his dictatorship Saddam had looted Iraq's oil revenues and spent them on palaces, weapons of mass destruction, his family, and a $40b hoard for himself. Saddam used more than 50 bank accounts and 300 offshore companies to channel a fortune overseas. (One of his accounts, no. 70513, at the Banco del Gottardo in Nassau, the Bahamas, was in the name of "Satan.") He had built more than 50 palaces with expensive, albeit tasteless, fittings. It was later revealed that he had authorized his son Qusay to rob the Central Bank of $1b, which was driven away in three trucks hours before the bombing began, at 4 a.m. on March 8. Since 1981 he had paid France some £13b for arms used in the Gulf War and the Iraq War. At the time of his fall Saddam had incurred Iraqi debts to foreign lenders of around $65b.

How far had Russia helped Saddam? Two retired Russian Generals, Vladislav Achalov, a specialist in urban warfare, and Igor Maltsey, an expert in air defense, had visited Iraq on twenty occasions, the last time when they were awarded medals by Saddam six days before fighting began. Former Russian Premier, Yevgeny Primakov, visited Baghdad on February 23, 2003 on Putin's orders and met Saddam in one of his palaces to arrange the transfer of Iraq's secret service files to Moscow in the event of Saddam's defeat, and to discuss an exit strategy for Saddam and his sons. (He had made a similar visit to Saddam shortly before the first Iraq War.)

In a startling move, the US Total Information Awareness office (TIA), which spies on US citizens to fight terrorism, employed two former KGB heads, Gen. Aleksandr V. Karpof and this same Gen. Yevgeny Primakov, who had previously worked with the Center for Strategic and International Studies, a private company that is consulted by the US government on issues of terrorism and domestic security. Primakov's appointment was covered in the *American Free Press* on April 21/May 12, 2002 ("Get Ready for the Sovietization of America"). It seems that Primakov (who was born Finkelstein) was in the employ of the US government at the time of his visit to Baghdad to meet Saddam.

Documents in Arabic obtained from the bombed Iraqi Intelligence Service headquarters in Baghdad on April 12, 2003, and made available to London's *Sunday Telegraph*, show that Russia provided Saddam with assistance in the months leading up to the Iraq War, including intelligence on private conversations between Blair and Western leaders, lists of assassins available for hits in the West, and details of arms deals to countries adjoining Iraq. The two nations, Russia and Iraq, signed agreements to share intelligence, help each other to obtain visas for agents to go to other countries, and to exchange information on the activities of bin Laden – suggesting that Russia expected Saddam to know about bin Laden's activities. Iraq owed Russia $8b for arms shipments and Russian (i.e. "Rockefellerite") oil companies had been trying to develop Iraq's oil resources.

The US now targeted Tikrit, Saddam's hometown, and threatened to drop the massive 21,000–lb bomb known as MOAB (nicknamed "The Mother of All Bombs" but actually standing for "Massive Ordnance Air Blast"), which wipes out everything within a mile radius. On April 13 US tanks were reported in Tikrit, and on April 14 US troops entered the main palace there without much resistance and were in control of Tikrit. There was no sign of Saddam Hussein.

10

DOUBTS ON SEPTEMBER 11:
KNOWLEDGE IN ADVANCE?

A monster, which the Blatant beast men call,
A dreadful fiend of gods and men ydrad.

Edmund Spenser[1]

It is now clear that there are difficulties with the official version of the attack on the Twin Towers.

The Event[2]

The Bush administration accused Bin Laden within hours of the September 11 outrage. War in Afghanistan began just over three weeks later. The speed with which the US invasion was mounted was impressive. It was also surprising as it left little or no time to assess the responsibility for the collapse of the Twin Towers and the other attacks. For a war in as remote a country as Afghanistan to have been begun so swiftly, mobilization must have begun with the announcement after just a few hours that bin Laden was responsible. The speed with which the American retaliation happened must be considered alongside a plan to attack Afghanistan that Condoleezza Rice had before her on September 10.[3] (The plan may have been a response to a Presidential Daily Briefing memo dated August 6 2001, titled "Bin Laden Determined to Attack Inside the United States" and claiming that bin Laden's "followers would follow the example of World Trade Center bomber Ramzi Yousef and 'bring the fighting to America,'" and that they were "casing" buildings in New York. Condoleezza Rice, denying a complaint by Richard Clarke, Bush Jr.'s counter-terrorism advisor, that both Bush Jr. and she had ignored warnings regarding al-Qaeda in the weeks before September 11, told a congressional hearing that the memo was not specific as to time or place – hence, perhaps, a plan made in August to attack Afghanistan.) Quite simply, the Bush administration jumped to conclusions and *assumed* that bin Laden was responsible without sifting evidence.

According to CNN, both President Bush and Vice-President Dick Cheney have personally intervened and asked Senate Majority Leader Tom Daschle to "limit the congressional investigation into the events of September 11." Cheney made his appeal to Daschle on January 25, 2002. Bush made his request at a private meeting with congressional leaders on January 29, 2002. Bush asked that the focus should be on "the potential breakdowns among federal agencies that could have allowed the terrorist attacks to occur" rather than on a comprehensive inquiry.

According to the *American Free Press* of July 21, 2003 Larry Silverstein sold 99–year leases on the Twin Towers shortly before September 11 and insured the two properties and their future income against terrorism. He was seeking $7.2b. Silverstein had built WTC-7, the 47–story building that mysteriously collapsed on September 11. This had been mortgaged in October 2000 to the Blackstone Group of Peter G Preston, Chairman of the CFR and Federal Reserve Bank of New York. Silverstein had insured the building and received $441m in insurance payments, although the cause of the collapse was still unexplained.

The Hijackers

There are also doubts as to who the hijackers were. According to a BBC report on September 21, there is a discrepancy between the seat numbers of the four hijackers reported in the final desperate words of a flight attendant, Madeline Amy Sweeney, to air-traffic control, and the seats of the five Arab hijackers the FBI say were involved, including Mohammed Atta, who is believed to have been the ringleader. Atta's father is adamant that his son was not an Islamic fundamentalist, and claims that he was kidnapped and is still alive, having had his identity stolen. Atta had reported his passport as having been stolen long before September 11, and it reappeared unburned on top of a pile of rubble near the World Trade Center, according to Attorney General John Ashcroft, although the crash and explosion destroyed the fire-proof cockpit recorders. The FBI later retreated from Ashcroft's announcement, claiming that the report of the discovery of Atta's passport was only "a rumor." Was some evidence planted to suggest that Atta was to blame?

If Atta was the ringleader, why did he take a connecting flight from Portland to Boston on the morning of September 11 that was scheduled to arrive only minutes before it was time to board the plane that was hijacked? If the plane from Portland had been delayed by a few minutes, he would not have caught the doomed flight. Why did he cut the timing so fine?

The FBI have incriminating evidence on Atta, as we shall see, but at least six, possibly seven, of the purported terrorists are still alive and had nothing to do with the attacks, apparently having had their identities wrongly used. Investigations have shown that most of the Arab terrorists involved, including Atta, drank hard and went after girls in a way that contradicted Islamic fundamentalism. Did the suicide-terrorists have anti-Islamic lifestyles? Was evidence planted to implicate certain sections of the Arab world as opposed to other nationalities?[4]

It has not been widely reported that at 1 p.m. on September 11 the Japanese Red Army, which has hijacked several planes, called al-Jazeera Television and claimed responsibility for the attacks, which, they said, were in retaliation for the atomic attacks on Nagasaki and Hiroshima. The only identification of the September 11 hijackers by passengers using cell-phones was that they wore red headbands; no mention was made of the language, nationality, or appearance of the terrorists. The Japanese Red Army wear red headbands. Perhaps this claim was false; perhaps the Japanese Red Army were opportunistically claiming credit for a feat they had nothing to do with, for propaganda purposes.

In June 2002, following comments that the discoveries of letters and documents in their belongings "proved" they were "on a mission for Allah," FBI Director Robert Mueller said that the 19 Moslem hijackers had left no paper trail: "In our investigation, we have not uncovered a single piece of paper – either here in the United States or in the treasure trove of information that has turned up in Afghanistan and elsewhere – that mentioned any aspect of the September 11 plot." Suicide notes aside – six left notes, 13 left no notes – no evidence has been found of actual plotting by the 19 or indeed their involvement in the September 11 plot. It left open the possibility that others carried out the September 11 attacks, using the identities of the 19 Moslem men who have apparently disappeared.

It has been claimed (in London's *Daily Mail* of December 21, 2001) that there was a plan for two planes to crash into London's Houses of Parliament and Tower Bridge, but that the eight hijackers heard about the scale of the disaster in the US while waiting to board the London–Manchester planes, panicked, and fled. One of them, Mohammed Afroze, was held in Bombay after claiming that al-Qaeda paid for him to train at a flying school in England. According to another source, the Golden Gate Bridge, San Francisco, was also supposed to have been a target on September 11.

It had been reported (in *Le Figaro* and on radio France International, reports covered in London's *Times* of November 1, 2001) that bin Laden was treated secretly for kidney disease: that he flew from Quetta in Pakistan to Dubai on July 4, 2001, and checked into the American hospital there with his personal physician and al-Qaeda's second-in-command Dr. Ayman Zawahiri. He stayed in hospital for 10 days according to *Le Figaro* and was visited by a CIA agent "who was recognized taking the main lift in the hospital to go to Osama bin Laden's room."

The hospital denied that he was a patient there. However, intelligence sources reported that he was using a dialysis machine that was shipped to Kandahar earlier in the year. He could not walk without a stick because of an old back injury, and was reported to be dying of a kidney disease (caused by an attempt to poison him) that had infected his liver.

It now seems that the anthrax scare, which was linked to the hijackings and contributed to the hysteria before the invasion of Afghanistan and war on Iraq, had a domestic origin. Genetic testing of samples has since revealed that the source of the spores was probably the US army's Medical Research Institute in Utah, the only known center to have processed the poison into a fine powder and where the CIA has carried out bio-weapons research. Were the anthrax letters the work of a lone extremist involved in the program, for an unknown motive, and was he perhaps himself killed by the anthrax, hence the cessation of incidents? Or was it CIA/Syndicate related?

In March 2002 a biochemical arms expert, Barbara Hatch Rosenberg, a microbiologist at State University of New York who heads the biological arms-control panel of the Federation of American Scientists, said that the FBI had a "prime suspect," "a particular person ... a member of the biochemical community ... a middle-aged American who works for a CIA contractor in the Washington DC area" and had an up-to-date vaccination against anthrax, but was reluctant to arrest this person for fear of exposing secret US government biochemical projects and operations.

The anthrax incidents stopped after Professor Don Wiley, a microbiologist of global renown, inexplicably plunged to his death into the Mississippi from Hernando de Soto Bridge, which links Tennessee to Arkansas, on November 16, 2001. It seems that he had unaccountably taken a series of wrong turnings, and that he may have been unconscious when he fell over the side of the bridge as he bounced off the structure. It probably wasn't a suicide, as all those have avoided the angled structure and have jumped directly into the water.

Who was Responsible?

Who had been responsible for striking at the heart of American military, financial, and political power? The perpetrators of the attack genuinely wanted to damage America. Maybe, in addition, they wanted to lure America into a retaliation against Arabs/Moslems to cause uproar in the Arab world and another war or *jihad* (holy war) between the West and Islam.

Who was capable of organizing such an attack that triggered such swift Anglo-American retaliation? Who, bearing in mind all the circumstantial evidence we have gleaned so far, were the immediate suspects?

Bin Laden?

No elaborate, multi-cave complex was ever found. Eleven days after the Americans began bombing the Tora Bora Mountains they released another video, apparently found in a house in Kandahar. It showed bin Laden meeting a sheikh, since identified as Sheikh al-Ghamdi, a militant Saudi cleric paralyzed from the waist down, apparently on November 9, 2001, laughing as he said that the attack on the World Trade Center had been more successful than he had expected. He had calculated that a few floors would collapse, not the entire buildings. He said that he had had knowledge of the attack since the Thursday before it happened, and had tuned in to listen to it on the radio. "They were overjoyed when the first plane hit the building, so I said to them: 'Be patient.'" He said that Atta was the leader of the hijackers, and that the 19 hijackers were not aware of the precise nature of their mission until shortly before they boarded the planes. So did six have time to write suicide notes? And why didn't the other 13 write notes?

The tape appeared to be genuine. The video had poor sound quality and looked as if the camera were eavesdropping. There was no obvious propagandizing about Israel, and the dialogue did not appear to have been tampered with. Bin Laden looked healthy. Did he know he was being filmed? Was one of his sons the amateurish cameraman? Was he putting his thoughts on the record as he was a Moslem icon?

If so, why did he confess to responsibility for the attack? Elsewhere he said there was only circumstantial evidence to connect him with the attack. Why had he broken his tight security to talk? Why was there no mention of the war and of the US bombing, which had started a month before November 9?

The Pentagon's translation of the Arabic used in the tape has been found to have been manipulated and is judged to be inaccurate by Arabic language experts interviewed on the German state television show *Monitor* on December 20, 2001. According to one of the experts, Dr. Abdel El Husseini, "At the most important places which have been presented as proof of bin Laden's guilt, the Pentagon translation does not agree with the Arabic heard on the video." Bin Laden says in the English version "We calculated in advance the number of casualties from the enemy" but the words "in advance" are not said in Arabic. In the Arabic version bin Laden says not "We had notification since the previous Thursday that the event would take place that day" but "We had notification since Thursday." Notification of what?

According to the *American Free Press* of December 31, 2001 a specialist in Islamic affairs, Hani al-Sibaei, said that the tape showed bin Laden being congratulated on the pre-arranged marriage of his child to the child of Ayman al-Zawahiri in 1997 rather than discussing the attack. Did clever sound editing string together past words and impose them on a conversation to do with marriage? If so, there are only 20 people in the US who are good enough to fool everybody, according to Sean Broughton, the director of London-based production company, Smoke and Mirrors. Did one of these work for Mossad or the CIA? Bin Laden looked a lot fitter than in his previous videos, when he had to support himself on a cane. Does he seem relaxed and fatter in the face than in the other videos of autumn 2001 because this video was shot in 1997?

Al-Qaeda/Iraq's Joint Involvement?

The link between al-Qaeda and Iraq was tenuous. In an interview with Tony Benn, the left-wing British MP, Saddam said, "We have no relationship with al-Qaeda." But documents found in the destroyed Iraqi Intelligence HQ after the fall of Baghdad and publicized in the British *Sunday Telegraph* (April 27, 2003) show that Saddam's intelligence chiefs were seeking to establish links with al-Qaeda in March 1998. An unnamed al-Qaeda envoy traveled clandestinely from Khartoum – bin Laden was based in Sudan until 1996 – to Baghdad, and the documents show that the visit went so well that it was extended by a week. The relationship was so covert that bin Laden's name was taken out of the documents with white correcting fluid, though it was still readable underneath.

It has been confirmed by the Czech Interior Minister Stanislav Gross, according to the London *Times* of October 27, 2001, that a meeting in Prague took place on April 22, 2001 between Atta and the Iraqi consul in Prague, Mohammed Khalil Ibrahim al-Ani, a very senior Iraqi agent. It was alleged that Atta in all made four visits to Prague to see al-Ani, who was deported from Prague to Iraq in April 2001 for "activities incompatible with his status as a diplomat" (in fact, taking a close interest in the Prague headquarters of Radio Free Europe, a possible bomb target). It was alleged that Atta was given a vacuum flask of anthrax spores at his last meeting with al-Ani in Prague (April 22). There have been persistent denials that Atta ever met al-Ani. The existence of their April 22 meeting has subsequently been denied by Czech President Vaclav Havel, who contradicted his own Interior Minister.

In July 2001, one of Saddam's intelligence agents, Habib Faris Abdullah al-Mamouri, who had been sent to Rome as headmaster of a school for Iraqi diplomats in Italy, took a holiday with Atta. They were seen together in Hamburg (where his flat-mate was Ziad Samir Jarrah, the pilot of the plane that crashed in Pennsylvania, who had links with a Palestinian terror group run by Abu Nidal and sponsored by Iraq) and Prague. Atta was also spotted in Spain with an Iraqi envoy known to be one of Saddam's agents. Perhaps Atta was unaware of his associates' intelligence links? The attack on September 11 could in theory have been a shared operation.[5] Intelligence sources believe that half the $500,000 the hijackers used came from al-Qaeda sources. While Mounir al-Motassadeq has been accused in Hamburg of running the bank accounts of Atta and other pilots and sending them money for flying lessons (for which he was sentenced to 15 years' imprisonment), all of this $500,000 has been traced back to the United Arab Emirates, and Atta received $100,000 from money-changers in Sharjah, one of the emirates. The pilot of the second plane to hit the World Trade Center also received money from Sharjah. There was clearly UAE involvement in financing the pilots, and Sharjah clearly acted as a conduit that conveyed funds to the West from a source elsewhere that has yet to be identified. The UAE had diplomatic links with the Taliban, and established a free trade area with Iraq in June 2001. But it seems unlikely that Iraq had a direct connection with it.

Israel?

It is a strange coincidence that the Twin Towers of the World Trade Center were originally built by the Port Authority of New York and New Jersey with "Rockefeller" assistance. David and Nelson Rockefeller were respectively prominent international banker and Governor of New York. David took up a 1946 idea to regenerate Manhattan; he proposed the formation of the Downtown-Lower Manhattan Association, which by January 1960 proposed a Trade Center, and Nelson helped the idea through. The Twin Towers opened in 1970 after an eight-year construction program. They were then 100 feet taller than the Empire State Building, and were the highest Towers in the world until they were surpassed by Chicago's Sears Towers and the Petrona Towers in Kuala Lumpur. The North Tower had a 347–foot-high radio tower, which allowed the World Trade Center to retain its claim to being the world's tallest building despite the completion of the later taller towers. The two Towers in New York were originally jokingly nicknamed after David and Nelson Rockefeller, one after each brother. The names may have been "affectionate names" (nicknames).[6] These Towers were leased by the Port Authority of New York and New Jersey to Silverstein Properties, the company of a new owner, Larry Silverstein, a prominent Jewish businessman born in Manhattan, two months before they collapsed (on July 24), for $3.2b. They were thus not connected with the Rockefellers at the time of the attack, although at the level of image they were still historically associated with them.

It was revealed by the *American Free Press* of December 10, 2001 that an Israeli company, Zim American Israeli Shipping Co., Inc., whose parent company Zim Israel Navigation Co. is nearly half-owned by the State of Israel, broke its lease of rented offices on the sixteenth and seventeenth floors of the World Trade Center's north tower at the beginning of September, as a result of which it lost $50,000. Was it tipped-off? This action contributed to rumors that Israel was behind the attack, and that the pilots who carried out the attack were Israelis (Jewish terrorists) who had assumed Arab identities.

The *American Free Press* (December 24, 2001) quotes Horst Ehmke, who coordinated the German secret services under Brandt in the 1970s, as saying, "Terrorists could not have carried out an operation with four planes without the support of a secret service." Also Andreas von Bülow, who served on the parliamentary commission that oversees the three branches of the German secret service, is quoted as believing that Mossad was behind the September 11 attacks. Its motive? To turn public opinion against the Arabs and boost military and security spending.

It must be observed that on December 3, 2001, citing the parallels between the most recent suicide-bombings in Jerusalem and the September 11 attack, with Anglo-American support Israel launched a small war on Palestine, striking at buildings and helicopters personally used by President Arafat in Gaza City and in towns on the West Bank. In March and April 2002, exasperated that the Palestinian killers of an Israeli government minister had sought refuge in Arafat's headquarters in Ramallah, they besieged the building. (The six men were taken under Anglo-American guard to a prison in Jericho.) By insisting that Israel was in the same predicament as the US, Sharon seemed to be opportunistically cashing in on America's outrage against terrorists.

Reports of Israeli involvement may be strengthened by reports (e.g. in the *American Free Press*, February 10, 2003) that bin Laden had access to the Inslaw computer company's PROMIS surveillance software after it was stolen from the US and made available on the Russian black market. Through this software bin Laden would have been able to monitor the US efforts to track him down and to have access to the computer data bases of other nations' intelligence services. It has been alleged that bin Laden used this software to carry out the September 11 attacks. Anyone using the software would have his own activities monitored by those from whom the software was received, and it is suggested that Mossad was behind the supply of PROMIS from Russia to bin Laden. If this is correct, Mossad knew from their monitoring of the PROMIS software what bin Laden was planning. Could Israel have "overheard" bin Laden's planning of the September 11 attacks and helped them into action?

On December 12, 2001 Fox News with Brit Hume carried a report by Carl Cameron, who said (according to the *American Free Press* of December 24, 2001): "There is no indication that Israelis were involved in the September 11 attacks, but investigators suspect that they may have gathered intelligence about the attacks in advance and not shared it." Cameron was asked, "What about this question of advance knowledge of what was going to happen on 9/11? How clear are investigators that some Israeli agents may have known something?" Cameron replied: "It's very explosive information, obviously, and there's a great deal of evidence that they say they have collected. None of it necessarily conclusive. It's more when they put it all together. A bigger question, they say, is 'How could they not have known?' [That is] almost a direct quote [from the investigators]." On October 1, 2001 the *American Free Press* carried a story that the FBI had arrested three groups of Israeli Jews suspected of working for Mossad who were seen "acting suspiciously" and videotaping the WTC disaster from varying angles. In all, 60 Israeli Jews were taken into custody following the terrorist attacks and were held because the FBI suspected that they had material knowledge about the attacks. On another view they faced immigration charges unconnected with terrorism. There are allegations that an Israeli spying ring operated in the USA without the knowledge of the US authorities and gathered information on the impending September 11 attacks, which the ring did not share with the US authorities.

Israel is said to be America's best Middle-East source on bin Laden and al-Qaeda and regularly supplies intelligence to the CIA (*American Free Press*, November 12, 2001). Israeli intelligence is said to finance Islamic fundamentalists and Arab terrorist groups to advance Israel's strategic aims (*American Free Press*, October 29, 2001).

Did Israel hand the US the video found in a house in Kandahar that shows bin Laden admitting to prior knowledge of the attack at least 11 days before the US began the bombing of Tora Bora? According to one view, Sheikh al-Ghamdi, the Saudi cleric, knew the tape was being made, and the operation may have been a CIA-controlled sting, using a secondary intelligence service: Saudi, Pakistani, or Egyptian. It is possible that Mossad, and not the CIA, instigated the taping or at any rate the "voices over." Was that why bin Laden barely refers to Israel in the tape?

It may be that the Israelis came by the tape. If so, was it filmed by an Israeli agent, or did they acquire it? Had Mossad been watching and filming bin Laden? The surfacing of the tape coincided with Sharon's visit to the US on December 2, 2001. The relationship between Bush and Sharon was not good, and Bush was still smarting at being accused by Sharon of appeasing the Palestinians just as Chamberlain appeased the Nazis. Was the tape passed to the White House by Mossad/Sharon? The White House have confirmed having received the tape on November 29, and Bush saw it on November 30. The tape could therefore have been discussed at the Bush–Sharon summit on December 2. If so, was it partly to reciprocate this favor that Bush permitted Israel to target Arafat during their attacks on Palestine that followed Sharon's visit, on December 3–4, 2001?

CIA? How Much did the CIA Know in Advance?

According to Sherman Skolnick[7] the American CIA knew of the attack on America a week in advance, having been told by Mossad and the French CIA who had both penetrated the plot. Did the American authorities know the attack was coming and do nothing? Was that how the planes came to be filmed from all angles as they flew into the Twin Towers?

On May 17, 2002 it was reported that Bush was facing the prospect of a congressional investigation after admitting that he had received warnings of possible al-Qaeda plans to hijack a US aircraft shortly before September 11. The information was contained in a CIA intelligence report of August 6, prior to which there was a CIA warning of al-Qaeda attacks on June 28 based on material gathered since May, and a warning by Richard Clarke, of the US government's counter-terrorism office, on July 5 that "something really spectacular is going to happen ... soon." During the congressional hearing in March 2004 Clarke was critical of the administration's failure to prevent the attacks.

The FBI had been told on August 6, 1998 that a group of unidentified Arabs planned to fly an airplane loaded with explosives into the World Trade Center from a foreign country. In July 2001, the CIA warned senior intelligence officials that "based on a review of all-source reporting over the last five months, we believe that UBL (bin Laden) will launch a significant terrorist attack against US and/or Israeli interests in the coming weeks. The attack will be spectacular and designed to inflict mass casualties against US facilities or interests. Attack preparations have been made. Attack will occur with little or no warning." The August-6 information, which had been passed by MI6 to liaison staff at the American Embassy in London's Grosvenor Square, was handed to Bush at a meeting at his ranch in Crawford, Texas. The memo left little doubt that hijacked aircraft would be used as missiles against targets within the US, and, according to White House spokesman Ari Fleischer, was headlined "Bin Laden Determined to Strike the United States." An FBI report said that bin Laden might be sending Middle-Eastern terrorists for pilot training at US flight schools, and that Zacarias Moussaoui, the suspected 20th hijacker, "might be planning to fly a plane into the World Trade Center." Dick Cheney, the Vice-President, and Condoleezza Rice, the National Security Advisor, were also party to the information, which was said by a White-House source (Condoleezza Rice) to be of a general, not a specific nature and did not warrant shutting down the American civil aviation system. The report said that al-Qaeda might hijack an aircraft to demand the release of prisoners such as Omar Abdel Rahman, who tried to blow up the World Trade Center in 1993.

Could the August 6 information have prevented the September 11 attack? And why did Bush not disclose this for nine months? As a result of calls for a congressional investigation, Bush faced the biggest scandal to blight the presidency since Watergate thirty years previously.

It was also revealed that a US plan to topple bin Laden had been approved by Bush the day before the September 11 attacks. The plan to remove bin Laden was dated September 10 and placed on Condoleezza Rice's desk for Bush to review. It recommended thwarting bin Laden "through work within the Northern Alliance to dismantle al-Qaeda and the Taliban." The September 10 memo outlined a £140m CIA program to arm the Northern Alliance and anti-Taliban forces. According to a preliminary report by a joint congressional intelligence committee, the US government had so much information about a forthcoming attack that the CIA director had "declared war" on Osama bin Laden.

At the congressional hearing in June 2002 Bush blamed lack of communication between the FBI and CIA and maintained, "I have seen no evidence to date that said this country could have prevented the attack." However, a consensus has emerged on Capitol Hill that the US intelligence community did have enough information to be able to prevent the September 11 attacks. Senator Richard Shelby, senior Republican on the Senate intelligence committee said: "If they had acted on the information they had and followed through, maybe things would be different. There were massive intelligence failures."

It has since come to light, according to *The American Free Press* (August 12, 2002), that Lt. Gen. Mahmoud Ahmad, head of Pakistan's Inter-Services Security Agency (ISI), which had been linked to the CIA for more than a generation, was dismissed on the insistence of US authorities for being involved in wiring £100,000 from banks in Pakistan to the hijacker Mohammed Atta's accounts in two banks in Florida through one Ahmad Sheikh. According to the *Times* of India this was exposed by Indian sources. The sending of the money had been reported by ABC's Brian Ross on September 30, 2001. It also came to light that, according to the *New York Times*, on the morning of September 11, 2001 the co-chairmen of the Joint-Intelligence Committee, Bob Graham and Porter Goss, met Lt. Gen. Mahmoud Ahmad for breakfast in Washington while the attacks were in progress. Three days after the attacks, according to the *New York Times*, Secretary of State Colin Powell, Deputy Secretary of State Richard Armitage, Under Secretary of State Marc Grossman, Chairman of the Senate Foreign Relations Committee Senator Joseph Biden, and CIA Director George Tenet, and other members of the Senate and House Intelligence committees, met Lt. Gen. Mahmoud Ahmad. On May 16, 2002 Dr. Condoleezza Rice denied having seen the report that Lt. Gen. Mahmoud Ahmad was in Washington on September 11 and that £100,000 was wired from Pakistan to the hijackers on September 10. Is there any truth in these allegations in such reputable papers? Did these officials meet the Pakistani General in the hope of learning about al-Qaeda? It is surely unlikely that they were aware at that time of financial links between Pakistani banks and the hijackers?

In a speculative work, *The CIA and September 11*, Andreas von Bülow, a former research minister in the German government, wrote that the September 11 attacks could only have happened with the support of the CIA, and that they were staged to justify the subsequent wars in Afghanistan and Iraq.

Fourteen months after the event it was reported in the *American Free Press* (November 11, 2002) that a US intelligence agency, the National Reconnaissance Office in Chantilly, Virginia (about four miles from the runways of Dulles airport), which operates US reconnaissance satellites, had planned a simulated security exercise on September 11 in which a plane would crash into one of the four towers of the agency's headquarters. The Pentagon and CIA were aware of the planned "contingency response" exercise – which may be why three of the planes were unchallenged by fighters. However, the location of the agency was too far from the Twin Towers for the exercise to explain why the planes were filmed from all angles on September 11. The US government said it was a "bizarre coincidence" that this security exercise was planned for September 11, but the truth may be that the "game" was hijacked by agents who overlaid it with a lethal scenario. (In the same way, during a security exercise in Israel Yitzhak Rabin was assassinated.)

Was Saddam linked with al-Qaeda or not? The lack of any weapons of mass destruction in Iraq do not by themselves suggest that he was not. There is, however, evidence that he hated al-Qaeda and could, like Gaddafi, have been an "ally" in the war against al-Qaeda (as he was against Iran). Bush Jr. and Condoleezza Rice were criticized in a book by his former counter-terrorism organizer Richard Clarke, *Against all Enemies,* for not taking the threat of al-Qaeda seriously enough before September 11 and for being obsessed with targeting Saddam, who had affronted the Bush family by surviving the first Iraq War waged by Bush Sr., and for not preventing the attacks. This was the thrust of the congressional hearing before which Rice testified. Clarke's view was that Saddam was not linked with al-Qaeda. This view was borne out up to a point by the finding of the US commission investigating September 11: "We have no credible evidence that Iraq and al-Qaeda cooperated on attacks upon the United States" – although the commission found that al-Qaeda *had* approached Iraq as when bin Laden apparently met an Iraqi intelligence official in the Sudan in 1994 and requested space to establish training camps in Iraq. This led to Iraq's explosives expert Brigadier Salim al-Ahmed meeting bin Laden on his Khartoum farm in September and October 1995 and in July 1996 to discuss technical assistance in making bombs, according to Stephen Hayes' *The Connection*. It can probably safely be said that al-Qaeda made overtures to Saddam, who mostly ignored them and did not collaborate with them in any terrorist outrage.

We can now reconstruct a theoretical scenario for what could have happened before, during, and after September 11. Israeli intelligence, Mossad, had been watching bin Laden and filming his conversations, having infiltrated the group around him. They had advance information of the September 11 attack possibly before June 28 and July 5, probably before August 6, and definitely by the Thursday before (when bin Laden knew, if the Ghamdi video *was* shot in 2001 and not 1997). Either they kept the information to themselves, or they told the US CIA in confidence, perhaps in general rather than specific terms, but not the political leadership (Bush). If the latter, the US CIA, privy to this information and wanting a pretext to attack Afghanistan and bin Laden, did nothing, but made sure that on September 10 there was a plan to topple bin Laden. Mossad, and perhaps the CIA, arranged for the attack to be filmed (just as 60 years earlier someone with prior knowledge had arranged for the bombing of Pearl Harbor, which killed 2,300 American servicemen, to be caught on film to fuel outrage across the US).

There was a preconceived plan to invade Afghanistan, before the attack on the Twin Towers. The Syndicate, some of them, knew an attack was likely, and that if it happened it would suit their purposes. Osama bin Laden is a pawn in the game rather than some master-evil genius. Could a man living in an Afghan mountain cave without a mobile phone – he was reported as not allowing any electronic or electrical equipment near him for fear of giving away his whereabouts, though videos and a satellite phone later feature – really achieve so much devastation in New York and Washington? It's not so much him that is the threat, as the war-like situation Syndicate policies have produced.

11

DOUBTS ON IRAQ:
A MILITARY STRATEGY?

Rule the peoples of the world with empire, Roman: these are
your arts, your mission, which you should take to heart; make
peace and secure it with law; spare the vanquished and use
war to unseat the proud.

Anchises' version of PNAC in Virgil's Aeneid

A first dossier on Iraq released by the British government on September 24, 2002, written by the Joint Intelligence Committee, stated that Saddam had created a massive network to procure banned technologies that would rebuild his nuclear and ballistic missile programs. He had missiles that could threaten a radius of 650k, and had secretly begun to develop ballistic missiles with a range of more than 1,000k. He was trying to acquire the material to make a nuclear device, including attempts to buy uranium from Africa. Iraq was one to two years away from producing a nuclear device if it succeeded in obtaining material from abroad. The dossier did not mention al-Qaeda.

In February the British government brought out a second dossier. It was later found to have been cobbled together from various sources, including a student's PhD thesis written some years before and plagiarized from the Internet, as a briefing note for six Sunday newspaper journalists, and although Blair had told MPs it was "an intelligence report" it came to be known as "the dodgy dossier."

Lt. Gen. Amer Hammoudi al-Saadi, the top Iraqi weapons specialist, surrendered to the coalition in front of a German television crew, denying Iraq held any chemical or biological weapons. More than anyone al-Saadi would have known where the weapons of mass destruction (if any) were. No such weapons were found by the US.

In September 2003 a CIA report on Iraqi weapons of mass destruction claimed that Saddam had placed his missile and nuclear development programs "in hibernation" to prevent UN inspectors from identifying them. Allegedly Gen. Primakov had loaded them onto two former Soviet warships at Umm Qasr and had buried them deep in the Indian Ocean. Maybe they were hibernating in the Indian Ocean. In early October David Kay, the civilian head of the 1,200-strong Iraq Survey Group charged with making an interim report to Congress, found that while the search had been hindered by an elaborate concealment operation, Iraq had probably had no large-scale chemical weapons program since 1991. He reaffirmed this position in January 2004 in the course of resigning "because there are no more weapons to find in Iraq." He claimed that some components were moved to Syria before the war.

Rolf Ekeus, a Swedish diplomat who directed the UN weapons inspections commission (UNSCOM) in Iraq from 1991 to 1997, confirmed Iraq's claims that the US had staffed UNSCOM with spies and manipulated the inspections to provoke Baghdad. He doubted that the US had any hard evidence that Iraq possessed weapons of mass destruction as "practically everything was found and destroyed."

It is possible that Saddam was bluffing all along – that there were weapons of mass destruction programs without weapons of mass destruction, to deter the US from invading Iraq. It is equally possible that weapons of mass destruction programs were a bluff by Saddam's minions, who were too terrified to tell Saddam that in fact they didn't have any weapons.

Or, perhaps, whatever weapons of mass destruction Iraq had had indeed been destroyed, as they claimed. After all, it's hard to prove a negative, that you haven't any weapons when you haven't any.

PNAC

There seemed to be other motives for attacking Iraq. And they were soon made clear. In December 2002 it emerged in the *American Free Press* that the huge increase in US defense spending that occurred after September 11 ($40b to fund the war on terrorism) and an attack on Iraq were both planned *before* George W. Bush was elected in January 2001 – by the men who have promoted the war on terrorism and the invasion and occupation of Iraq. The Washington-based "neo-conservative" PNAC (Project for the New American Century) was founded in spring 1997 by "Rockefellerites" Robert Kagan (a US State Department advisor from 1984 to 1998 and author of *Paradise and Power: America and Europe in the New World Order*, which argues that the US provided "free security" which enabled the EU experiment to proceed), William Kristol (an influential US editor), and Richard Perle (a senior US Pentagon advisor).

PNAC was an independent, i.e. non-government, organization, and was funded by three foundations closely linked to Persian Gulf oil and weapons and defense industries. It drafted a war plan for US global domination through military power, and called for a huge increase in defense spending as the first step in the PNAC's long-term plan to transform the US military into a global army that would enforce a *Pax Americana* round the world. PNAC believe that peace can be imposed by war, and that freedom, democracy, the tenets of the American Revolution, and American values can be spread through liberation.

On June 3, 1997 PNAC's Statement of Principles was signed by Dick Cheney, Donald Rumsfeld, Jeb Bush (George W. Bush's brother), and Paul Wolfowitz, and by many of the other members of Bush's "war cabinet." Rumsfeld, Wolfowitz (US Deputy Defense Secretary and Bush's top advisor, a pupil of Leo Strauss), and Perle had close ties to Israel and viewed Iraq as a threat to Israel.

Nine members of this semi-secret body which urged the war on Iraq were linked to companies which won defense contracts worth more than $50b in 2000/1. Richard Perle, co-founder of PNAC and critic of the UN, Saudi Arabia, and France, resigned as chairman of the Defense Policy Board, a Pentagon advisory panel, to avoid embroiling defense chiefs in a "distracting" controversy over his business interests.

The purpose of the planned increase in defense spending was "to carry out our global responsibilities today and modernize our armed forces for the future"; "to challenge regimes hostile to our interests and values"; and "to accept responsibility for America's unique role in preserving and extending an international order friendly to our security, our prosperity, and our principles." A subsequent PNAC document, dated September 2000 and entitled *Rebuilding America's Defenses: Strategies, Forces, and Resources for a New Century*, shows that before the presidential election of January

2001 members of Bush's cabinet planned to take military control of the Gulf region whether Saddam was in power or not: "The United States has for decades sought to play a more permanent role in Gulf regional security. While the unresolved conflict with Iraq provides the immediate justification, the need for a substantial American force presence in the Gulf transcends the issue of the regime of Saddam Hussein. Even should Saddam pass from the scene," the plan says, US military bases in Saudi Arabia and Kuwait should remain as Iran "may well prove as large a threat to US interests as Iraq."

The PNAC document says that a "core mission" for the transformed US military is "to fight and decisively win multiple, simultaneous major theatre wars." Defense spending should be increased "to a minimum level of 3.5 to 3.8% of gross domestic product, adding $15b to $20b to total defense spending annually." The PNAC plan says, "The process of transformation is likely to be a long one, absent some catastrophic and catalyzing event – like a new Pearl Harbor."

Christopher Maletz, assistant director of the PNAC, clarified this: "They needed more money to up the defense budget for raises, new arms, and future capabilities." He added that "without some disaster or catastrophic event" neither the politicians nor the military would have approved.

Of the $40b allocated after September 11, $17.5b went to defense.[1] The 2002 defense budget was $345.7b, including a $14.5b supplement. This was 12% above the 2001 defense budget. The 2003 defense budget was set to be $364.6b, and the 2004 defense budget request was for $379.9b (excluding the costs of the Iraq war). The Pentagon projects that the defense budget for the financial year of 2009 will be $483.6b. All these figures are in line with the PNAC plan.[2]

Richard Perle, one of PNAC's founding members, said in an interview with John Pilger: "No stages. This is total war. We are fighting a variety of enemies. There are lots of them out there. All this talk about first we are going to do Afghanistan, then we will do Iraq …. This is entirely the wrong way to go about it. If we just let our vision of the world go forth, and we embrace it entirely and we don't try to piece together clever diplomacy, but just wage a total war … our children will sing great songs about us years from now."

In response British MP Tam Dalyell said, "This is a blueprint for US world domination – a new world order of their making." On television

Dalyell described the US leadership around Dick Cheney as "a small group of people who've taken over the government of a great country." In an interview with *Vanity Fair*, he controversially said that Bush's policies on the Middle East had been influenced by Jewish people in his administration, including Richard Perle, a Pentagon advisor; Paul Wolfowitz, the Deputy Defense Secretary; and Ari Fleischer, the President's press secretary. He said that Blair's policies on the Middle East had been indirectly influenced by these same men, and more directly by Lord Levy (Blair's personal envoy to the Middle East), Peter Mandelson, and Jack Straw, all of whom had Jewish ancestry.

Is the Jewishness of these influential men coincidental? What is more important is their membership of, or links with, the Syndicate. The PNAC is an independent, non-governmental organization with strong Syndicate links. PNAC is an example of how the Syndicate is using the governments of nation-states to fund its operations in bringing about a world government, which entails the abolition of these same nation-states. Individually and collectively, in the name of "freedom" all American taxpayers are unwittingly digging the grave in which their freedom will be buried.

The Iraq War and Oil: Haifa Pipeline

Lukoil was sold, as we've seen, by Yeltsin's Prime Minister Chernomyrdin, who was in partnership with David Rockefeller, to "Rockefellers" for $294 (although valued at $3.4b in 1993). In 1997 they signed a 23–year, $3.7b contract to refurbish the huge West Qurna oilfield in Iraq in 1997.

In February 2003 Saddam cancelled the deal. The Lukoil vice-president maintained the deal still stood, and threatened to sue for $20b anyone who tried to take over the oilfield, and threatened to arrest tankers which conveyed crude oil in Iraqi waters. (Under the contract Lukoil would get half, Iraq a quarter, and the Russian government agencies a quarter of the field's 667m tons of crude, a $20b deal – and Iraq still owed Russia $8b for arms.)[3]

Putin's budget for 2003 had assumed oil would not fall below $19 a barrel; during the Iraq War oil dropped from $34 to $24 a barrel, and was set to plunge further. If Iraq withdrew from OPEC it could undercut the price-fixing of the OPEC cartel. In the short term, America and Britain wanted the pumping of Iraqi oil to be resumed as soon as possible. A new Iraqi government could then privatize Iraqi oil by selling concessions to the highest bidders, and Russian and French companies like Lukoil who had made deals with Saddam – $40b had been allocated in contracts – would have to reapply and compete for concessions anew.

When the US announced the end of fighting on April 30 it also announced its intention to withdraw its military bases from Saudi Arabia, as bin Laden had demanded. This would cut out a plank in al-Qaeda's platform. The truth was, Saudi Arabia had become too dangerous for US troops because of the intensification of Wahhabism. The September 11 hijackers, the Taliban, and al-Qaeda had all emerged from a single Islamic fundamentalist movement, Wahhabism, which had originated in Saudi Arabia. Wahhabism, a puritanical Moslem sect, spread in 1744 when Mohammed Ibn Saud, the emir of the region round modern Riyadh, married the daughter of Mohammed ibn Abdul Wahhab, founder of the Wahhabi movement. From that time the Saudi royal family promoted ibn Abdul Wahhab's fanatical ideas, and recently Saudi clerics have preached terrorism and financial *jihad*.

Russia responded by wooing Saudi Arabia, holder of the world's largest oil reserves. In September 2003, in a little publicized visit, Saudi Arabia's *de facto* ruler Crown Prince Abdullah visited Moscow for talks with President Putin. The oil ministers of the world's two biggest oil exporters were also present. A Russian–Saudi agreement was reached to provide Russian gas pipeline building to develop Saudi gas fields. Russia now had access to Saudi oil.[4] Saudi Arabia had pulled billions of dollars out of the US and was set to re-invest them in Russia. Russia may have severed Saudi backing for the Chechen Moslem Separatist rebels. Russia, having lost some of its access to Iraqi oil, had recouped its position by switching to Saudi oil. "Rockefellerite" Russia/Saudi Arabia looked set to be on a different course from "Rothschildite"-PNAC US/UK/Iraq. But the prosperity of both sides was grounded in oil.

In June 2004, however, the Saudis were keen to be seen to be pro-American. Alarmed that the beheading of an American hostage in Riyadh might panic Western oil workers into leaving Saudi Arabia *en masse*, a Saudi spokesman held a press conference in the US to announce the shooting of four top al-Qaeda men who had been responsible for the killing, and to emphasize Saudi determination to work with the US to defeat al-Qaeda.

Russia had not given up over Iraq. In December 2003 President Putin agreed to write off more than half of Iraq's debt to Russia (which would be cut from $8b – part of Iraq's overall debt of $120b – to $3.5b) in return for favorable treatment of Russian companies. Lukoil would now be allowed to implement the $3.7b West Qurna deal. Contracts allowing several Russian companies to drill wells in Iraq would be honored.

It now became clear that the Iraq War *was* about oil. As US marines left Baghdad, a plan to build a pipeline to bring oil from Iraq to Israel (see map 5), and thence to the US, was being discussed between Washington and Tel Aviv, according to the London *Observer* (April 20, 2003). The plan involved reconstructing the old pipeline that, as we have seen, was built by British Petroleum from the Mosul oilfields to Haifa in 1935. This pipeline had been inactive since the end of the British mandate in Palestine in 1948, when the flow from Iraq's northern oilfields to Palestine was redirected to Syria. Now Syria would be cut out, and this would solve Israel's energy

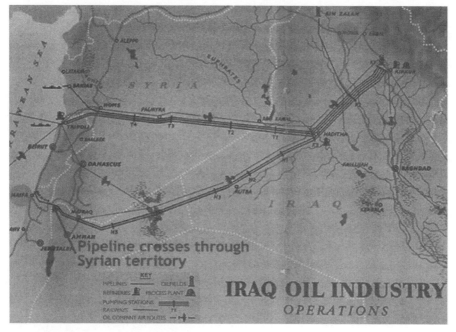

5. Kirkuk (near Mosul)-Haifa Pipeline
http://www.cooperativeresearch.org/wot/iraq/mosulhaifapipeline.html

crisis at a stroke (cutting Israel's energy bill by 25%) and, as the flow of Iraqi oil would once again end at the Israeli port of Haifa, create an endless source of cheap Iraqi oil for the US which would be guarded by its reliable ally Israel. The project would require Iraq to recognize Israel, an idea to which Ahmad Chalabi, the Pentagon's early choice of ruler of the new Iraq, was committed.[5]

The plan was first proposed by Henry Kissinger in 1975, when he signed a Memorandum of Understanding whereby the US would guarantee Israel's oil reserves and energy supply in times of crisis. It was proposed again more recently by Defense Secretary Donald Rumsfeld. Over the years the cost to the US of supporting Israel has been colossal. Research by Thomas R. Stauffer, published in the June 2003 issue of *The Washington Report on Middle East Affairs*, shows that since its inauguration Israel has cost the US taxpayer $3 trillion, the largest costs being caused by a series of oil-supply crises that accompanied the Israeli–Arab wars, particularly after 1973, and the construction of a Strategic Petroleum Reserve. The $3b reserve for Israel's energy supply in the 2002 US budget would be slashed by the plan. The pipeline would be rebuilt by the Bechtel Company, to which the Bush administration awarded a $680m contract for the reconstruction of Iraq in mid-April.

James Akins, a former US ambassador to Saudi Arabia, said, "There would be a fee for transit rights through Jordan, just as there would be fees for Israel from those using what would be the Haifa terminal. After all, this is a New World Order now. This is what things look like particularly if we wipe out Syria. It just goes to show that it is all about oil, for the United States and its ally."

It was also revealed that the Bush administration planned to keep and maintain at least four permanent bases in Iraq: at the International Airport outside Baghdad; at Tallil, near Nasiriyah; at H1, an airstrip in the western desert near Jordan; and at the Bashur airfield in the Kurdish-held north. These bases and the US troops' facilities in Afghanistan would virtually surround Iran.

In the early 1990s Zbigniew Brzezinski, President Carter's former National Security advisor, a "Rockefeller" advisor and co-founder with David Rockefeller of the Trilateral Commission, wrote that the US had to gain control of key areas of energy production and supply in order to survive. Since then the US has concentrated its military strength on parts of the world where oil and gas are produced or regions through which they are piped.

Was this pipeline the motive for the attack on Iraq from the outset, and were fears of weapons of mass destruction part of an elaborate deception on the part of both Washington and London? Was the true aim of the Iraq War to establish US military and economic influence in the Middle East?

The US occupation of Iraq meant that the US had, in effect, become a member of OPEC (the Organization of the Petroleum Exporting Countries). US control of pipelines across the Balkan peninsula, the Caspian region of Central Asia, and the Middle and Near East would enable America to compete with its biggest, newly industrialized rival, China. None of this was any consolation for Iraq.

Occupation/Restructuring

Iraq was broke. Besides owing $65b, perhaps as much as $100b, to foreign lenders, it owed $200b in reparations claims following the 1991 invasion of Kuwait. The cost of the initial reconstruction of Iraq was estimated at $20b a year for several years by the Council on Foreign Relations. In the event, Washington limited its initial funding to $2.4b in the first phase. Iraq had $383b of international debt (unpaid loans, legal claims, and outstanding contracts), more than any other country, and France and Russia (both owed about $8b), and Germany, refused US requests that they should write off debts owed to them. (We have seen that Russia more-than-halved its debt in return for oil agreements.) Iraq's oil infrastructure needed heavy investment of between $10b and $30b to bring production back to the level of 3.5 million barrels a day in 1989. If Iraq's oil production could rise to 3 million barrels a day, there would be an income of $27b a year, but $5b would have to be invested in modernizing Iraq's dilapidated oil extraction and refinery infrastructure. In the short term Iraq's oil dues would be absorbed by this cost. However, the Center for Global Energy Studies has predicted that with new finds (such as the West Qurna field and the untapped Western Desert) oil production could rise to 8 million barrels a day by 2011 and certainly by 2020.

In May 2003 the US and Britain asked the UN Security Council to give them the authority – a sweeping mandate – to rule Iraq as "occupying powers" for at least a year. They proposed that 12 years of sanctions should be lifted and that oil revenues should be used to fund reconstruction. Oil-for-food should be phased out over four months. The UN's role would be purely advisory. The Security Council voted 14–0 in favor of the resolution.

At the same time, plans by America and Britain to rebuild Iraq – promises that had been announced – were scrapped after the Spanish government revealed that there was a gaping hole in funding reconstruction. It had been hoped before the war that the sale of Iraqi oil would largely pay for reconstruction. Figures produced by Spain's Ministry of Economic Affairs and sent to the World Bank showed that oil revenues would fall short of the reconstruction figure the West originally envisaged, $41b. This was likely to be over $80b over 10 years, and international aid agencies believed that $250b would be more realistic. In 2002 Iraq pumped $13b worth of oil, but since then wells had been fired by Saddam's troops and the cost of renovating and modernizing Iraq's oil industry was, according to Spain's figures, $3.5b. The $2.4b Congress approved for Iraq was thus only a tiny fraction of the amount needed to remedy the chaos caused by the war. The rebuilding of Iraq was under-resourced and lacking in strategic direction. Defense sources said that British troops could be in Iraq for four years due to hit-and-run attacks by pro-Saddam militias.

Around the same time, the finance ministers for the Group of Seven countries met in Deauville to pave the way for a restructuring of Iraq's $60b-$100b foreign debts. The G7 countries agreed not to press for repayment of Iraqi debts for at least a year. Much of the debt was owed to Germany and France, who resisted the write-off policy urged by the US.

In August 2003 it emerged that America planned to mortgage Iraq's future oil supplies to pay for expensive post-war reconstruction work. Under proposals promoted by the US Export Import Bank and a lobbying group including the American contractors Bechtel and Halliburton, loans of $30b over 10 years would be made on the security of Iraq's oil reserves, the second largest in the world. Anne Pettifor, head of the Jubilee Plus debt relief campaign, said: "It is outrageous that the poor people of Iraq will be lumbered with billions of dollars of debt that will be used to boost the share prices of Wall Street financiers and US construction giants." She warned against the coalition "using the instrument of debt to control Iraq," pointing out that such a motive would repeat the mistakes made with Germany after the First World War.

It was revealed that Blair had at least three private meetings with Clinton during the Iraq War. Clinton acted as his advisor – presumably on behalf of the Bilderberg Group. It seems that Bilderberg's wishes were communicated to Blair via Clinton during these meetings.

There were now voices suggesting that Britain's future lay with America rather than with Europe. September 11, followed by Afghanistan and Iraq, had changed the post-Cold-War thinking, which, under Clinton, held that economic and trade issues should be ahead of military and diplomatic concerns, and that Britain had to find a way of relating its economy to a world of four blocs – America, the EC, Japan, and China – through economic links with the EC. Now the War against Terror made military and diplomatic concerns more important than economic and trade issues, and Britain's political links were with America, not France and Germany. Voices were raised suggesting that Britain should retain economic links with Europe, but not proceed to political union. Instead, there should be a more formal political link between Britain and the US.

The Recriminations

The world had split into two camps: "Rothschildite" England and a "Rothschildite" pro-Israel faction in America (PNAC) on the one hand; and the UN, Russia, France, Germany, and China, the traditional "Rockefellerite" empire, on the other hand. This view is borne out by the attitude of Senator Jay Rockefeller, the Senate Intelligence Committee's senior Democrat and would-be presidential candidate who appeared on television to call for televised hearings into the "accuracy" of intelligence used by Bush to justify the war: "We have found nothing of significance. We went into the war based on the fact that Saddam's ties to al-Qaeda and weapons of mass destruction were posing an imminent threat to our country. We need to know if this was accurate." Suggesting that Cheney's many visits to the CIA during the previous year were to put pressure on CIA officials to make their assessments fit the administration's policy aims, Senator Rockefeller asked, "What was he doing there?" In July 2004, Rockefeller, introducing the Senate's report into the "flawed" intelligence of the CIA, said that Congress would not have voted to go to war had it known of the intelligence shortcomings.

Many Europeans and Westerners asked, "Why Iraq, when North Korea is worse? Why now, when containment has been working? And where next, after Iraq is liberated?" To the last question American hawks would reply: Pakistan, North Korea, Syria, Iran.

Anglo-American forces had won the war, but they were losing the peace. The Iraqi Shi'ite leader, Ayatollah Mohammed Baqer al-Hakim, returned to be greeted by breast-beating crowds of more than a million Shi'ites in the holy city of Najaf. His call for foreign forces to leave and for a Shi'ite Islamic Iran-style state alarmed the US. He was killed in August 2003 by two massive 1,500lb bombs outside the Holy Imam Ali shrine in Najaf. Both Jay Garner and Barbara Bodine were recalled to Washington as being ineffectual. Garner was replaced by L. Paul Bremer III, a Yale graduate and former diplomat and counter-terrorism expert, who became the new US civilian administrator of Iraq. Until recently he had served as managing director of Kissinger Associates (Henry Kissinger's consultancy business).

Bremer swiftly postponed the creation of a 300–member national congress to select an interim government that would take over the day-to-day running of Iraq because a body could not be assembled that represented Iraqi society. He then abandoned the idea. Instead the US would appoint a council of 25 to 30 senior figures across the religious and ethnic spectrum who would shadow the existing US administration. This group would begin drafting an Iraqi constitution. Unsurprisingly John Sawers, Blair's special envoy charged with bringing democracy to Iraq, also concluded that Iraq's political culture was too weak, and radicals too powerful, to proceed with elections for an interim government. Iraq was simply not ready for democracy.

Donald Rumsfeld said that it was possible that Saddam had destroyed the weapons of mass destruction before the war began. This was barely credible and, if true, meant that Saddam had complied with the UN resolution. Paul Wolfowitz, the US Deputy Defense Secretary who had signed PNAC's Statement of Principles in 1997, revealed that the coalition exaggerated the threat from weapons of mass destruction for "bureaucratic reasons" before going to war: "The truth is that for reasons that have a lot to do with the US government bureaucracy we settled on the one issue that everyone could agree on, which was weapons of mass destruction as the core reason." It was revealed that in September 2002 the Pentagon's Defense Intelligence Agency (DIA) had said that there was "no reliable information" that Iraq had chemical weapons or even the ability to make them.

The idea was now openly expressed on television (for example, by British MP Tony Benn) that Bush had wanted Iraqi oil, that he and Blair had thought up a pretext – weapons of mass destruction – and that they had deceived the world's public; and that nothing Blair said from now on (for example, on the European constitution) could be believed or trusted. Clare Short, the British minister who resigned after the Iraq War, accused Blair of duping the British public by doctoring intelligence reports – to exaggerate the imminent danger from Iraq. Charitable interpretations in the press spoke of Blair's having seized too uncritically on pieces of intelligence that supported conclusions he had jumped to, and that he had misled the public.

According to the *American Free Press* of July 28, 2003 the US Vice-President Dick Cheney was behind one of the deceptions that pushed the US into the Iraq War. In January 2003 he had ordered CIA director George Tenet to insert into a speech by Bush Jr. that there was "credible" British intelligence that in 2001 Saddam tried to buy uranium ore (yellow cake) from Niger, the poor West African nation. Tenet had told Bush the previous October that he could not support this claim, but, the *American Free Press* asserts, Cheney overruled him. The British Foreign Secretary Jack Straw later told the US that the British government had independent intelligence corroboration of the Niger story. This confirmation later appeared to have come from a French source – Niger was formerly a French colony – and to have been subsequently discredited.

The Kelly Inquiry

The pressure on Blair increased dramatically after Andrew Gilligan, the BBC's defense correspondent, reported on the BBC's *Today* program on May 29 that the September dossier had been "sexed up" against the wishes of the intelligence service by material inserted by the government, notably that Saddam could "deploy" weapons of mass destruction within 45 minutes. On June 1 Gilligan asserted in an article that Blair's director of communications and strategy, Alastair Campbell, was responsible for this. The inference was that Blair had exaggerated the case for war and had taken Britain into the Iraq War on false pretences.

The British Parliament's "High Court," the Foreign Affairs Select Committee, then summoned Gilligan (on June 19) and Campbell (on June 25). Campbell denied the allegations and demanded a BBC apology, saying forcefully that the BBC had "not a shred of evidence for their lie." The Committee cleared Campbell.

The British government's attack on the BBC was a smokescreen, a deliberate "distraction" from the issue of why Blair led Britain to war against Iraq. Nevertheless, the following day, on July 8, Dr. David Kelly, the British UN weapons inspector and British government's biological warfare expert and advisor, a scientist and Ministry-of-Defence civil servant, volunteered to his MoD line manager that he may have been *a* source for Gilligan's report and article

On July 17 Gilligan was recalled to the Foreign Affairs Select Committee. Perhaps sensing that Gilligan would contradict his own evidence, Kelly left his home to go for a walk. He did not return.

That evening Blair addressed a combined Congress and House of Representatives and received 17 standing ovations for his support for the Iraq War.

The next day Kelly was found dead on Harrowdown Hill, Oxfordshire, not far from his home. A packet of co-proxamol painkilling tablets and a knife were found near him. His left wrist had been slit and the *post-mortem* established that he had bled to death. Kelly's Baha'i faith, which he had adopted in 1999, forbids suicide.

It was very convenient for the British government that Kelly had died as it silenced an authoritative voice that had questioned the need for the Iraq War and had inferred that Blair had taken Britain into war on false pretences. Kelly's death had also eliminated a top UN weapons inspector who had made 37 visits to Iraq up to 1998 (when he was excluded by Saddam) and had knowledge of where weapons of mass destruction might be hidden. His ambition was to return to Iraq as soon as possible and spend the last year of his working life finding these hidden weapons.

One of Kelly's last e-mails named "many dark actors playing games with my life." He may have thought that these "dark actors" were national figures. Could the "dark actors" have been internationalist figures?

Blair swiftly ordered a Judicial Inquiry under Lord Hutton to establish the facts regarding Dr. Kelly's death. This absolved him of the need to answer questions as the matter was now *sub judice*. The reason for the Iraq

War was supposed to be outside Hutton's remit. In a sense, the Inquiry was a continuation of the "deliberate distraction" from the main issue of why Blair led Britain to war. The suggestion was that Kelly's expertise was in the past, but in fact he was intimately involved in compiling the war dossier with the most up-to-date intelligence. He was a biological weapons guru: he had been nominated for a Nobel Peace Prize, and had accompanied British Foreign Secretary Jack Straw at an appearance before the Foreign Affairs Select Committee. He was advisor to the top-level task force in the MoD, which processed intelligence on all aspects of Saddam's weapons, and as Britain's leading expert in biological weapons he was crucial to the group's work.

It was revealed in the *American Free Press* (August 4, 2003) that although Kelly was not employed by MI5 or MI6 or any other intelligence service he was consulted by the intelligence agencies of Britain, France, Germany, the US, Japan, and Australia. He knew about the types and strains of microorganisms, and the numbers of shells and aerial bombs filled with botulinum toxin. Kelly was also in charge of the program to dismantle Russia's biological warfare weapons program under the trilateral agreement between Russia, the US, and Britain

In Moscow he met Russia's top microbiologist, Pasechnik, who was then director of the Ultrapture Biopreparations Institute in St. Petersburg. Pasechnik told Kelly that he was part of the Biopreparat, a large secret program which is developing biological weapons like plague and smallpox. Plague (which is propelled by coughing) had brought on the Black Death that wiped out a third of the population of Europe in 1348. Kelly reported what Pasechnik was doing to MI6, and weeks later Pasechnick defected to Britain while at a Paris science conference. Kelly supervised his interrogation. Pasechnik was later employed in the Centre for Applied Microbiology and Research, run by the Department of Health, and he founded a company (Regman Biotechnologies). Kelly often visited him and often took him to Porton Down, entrance to which is restricted to those who have signed the Official Secrets Act. He was found dead at his home near Salisbury, England on November 2, 2001 – officially of a stroke. Kelly did not attend the funeral.

It was then claimed, in the *American Free Press* of August 18, 2003, that Dr. Kelly had worked with two other microbiologists who suffered unexplained deaths and who were, like Pasechnik (and Dr. Kelly himself), experts in DNA-sequencing (a vital element in developing biological weapons). In November 2001 Benito Que left his laboratory after receiving a phone call and was found in a coma in the parking lot of the Miami Medical School; he was found by the inquest to have died of natural causes. A few days later Don Wiley left a banquet for fellow researchers in Memphis and, after abandoning his car with his ignition key left in it and the lights left on, plunged off a bridge over the Mississippi River. There was no autopsy, and a local medical examination found he had suffered a dizzy spell, which caused him to fall off the bridge. Pasechnick was found dead in bed 10 days after he had met Wiley in Boston to discuss the latest developments in DNA-sequencing.

The *American Free Press* of August 18 suggested that the deaths of Pasechnik, Que, Wiley, and Dr. Kelly were linked to the deaths of five unnamed Russian – or perhaps Israeli – microbiologists whose commercial Siberian Airlines plane was shot down by a Ukrainian surface-to-air missile while flying from Israel to Novosibirsk in Siberia shortly before October 2001. It revealed that from October 2001 Dr. Kelly was involved in ultra-secret work at Israel's Institute for Biological Research, and that he had met Institute scientists several times in London during the next two years. Israel has not signed the Biological Weapons and Toxins Convention, an international treaty that forbids the possession and use of offensive biological weapons and which has been ratified by over 140 countries. The *American Free Press* of August 18 suggested that the Institute had been engaged in DNA-sequencing research. A member of the Knesset, Dedi Zucker, had caused a furor in the Israeli Parliament when he claimed that the Institute was "trying to create an ethnic specific weapon." Such an Israeli weapon could target Arabs. If dropped in Palestine it would attack the genetic structures of Arabs but would not touch Jews.

In all, 25 scientists (including Kelly) had died mysteriously between 2001 and 2003 – 10 in plane crashes, five after being mugged at home, three after being shot, two as a result of suicide, one after being stabbed, one after being gassed, one after being run over while jogging, and one after falling off a bridge. Had all these microbiologists been killed covertly because they knew too much about this "ethnic specific weapon," and in Dr. Kelly's case was it feared that he might be "a source" on *that* weapon of mass destruction?

On the last day but one of the Hutton Inquiry's public hearings, when confronted with a memo e-mailed from Jonathan Powell, the Prime Minister's chief of staff, to Alastair Campbell and John Scarlett of MI6, John Scarlett admitted omitting from the dossier the idea that Saddam would only use chemical weapons if he was attacked first. The government had in effect ordered this idea to be deleted, and Scarlett, who had had commanding control of the dossier, transformed the dossier by omission at the non-presentational insistence of the government. This admission was extremely damaging to the government. Scarlett was later appointed by Blair to head MI6.

Hutton's Report did not change the public's perception that Blair had been "led up the garden path" by Bush, and had led his own party and the Conservative Opposition up the garden path, and had found out from intelligence briefings too late that this was the case. Former British Foreign Secretary Robin Cook claimed in his published diaries that Blair had privately confided to him on March 5, 2003 that he knew Saddam had no weapons of mass destruction that would be ready for use in 45 minutes. If Cook was reporting his conversation with Blair accurately and was not distorting it to exact revenge for the events that led him to resign on March 17, the implication was that Kelly was right: Iraq was not "a real and present danger" for Britain, and Britain had gone to war on exaggerated evidence, a circumstance the Establishment – some of those interviewed by Hutton – had sought to cover up.

A secret file was deposited with the Hutton Inquiry marked "Not for Release. Police Information Only." It was about a tactical support operation by Thames Valley Police, strangely called Operation Mason, which began an hour *before* Kelly left his house for his last walk. Detectives searched Kelly's house, where the tablets and knife originated, before his body was found. The contents of the Operation Mason file were read by Hutton but have not been disclosed.

More Terrorism

By going to war with Saddam, besides being responsible for killing or maiming thousands of civilians and soldiers, Bush and Blair provoked a new al-Qaeda campaign of bombings in Saudi Arabia, Chechnya, and Morocco. Multiple explosions devastated areas of Riyadh and Casablanca. A call (in an audiotape aired by al-Jazeera) by bin Laden's no. 2, Ayman al-Zawahiri, to attack the missions (embassies) of the US, UK, Australia, and Norway made such terrorist attacks more likely and therefore made it harder for the US to fight the war against terrorism. The Saudis then foiled an attempt by three Moroccans to fly a plane into a Saudi skyscraper in a re-run of September 11. It was estimated that there were some 17,000 al-Qaeda operatives still free and ready to act against the West, although Rohan Gunaratna, author of *Inside al-Qaeda: Global Network of Terror*, claimed that following the Afghanistan and Iraq wars the hardcore members who act directly in the name of al-Qaeda had been reduced to about a thousand men. Looser groupings of organizations may make up the difference.

It seemed that like bin Laden, Saddam was constantly one step ahead of those trying to capture or kill him. On the eve of the Iraq War, documents originally in the possession of Saddam's half-brother, Barzan al-Tikriti, which had been copied by the French intelligence service, the DGSE, reached Washington. They suggested that Saddam was benefiting from state-of-the-art US computer software, a tracking program that the CIA and FBI depended on, which had enabled him to avoid capture. The software was capable of pinpointing Saddam's and bin Laden's every move, and so they could see themselves as the Americans saw them.

According to the *American Free Press* of July 21, 2003 President Bush Jr. brought Paul Redmond, America's top spy-catcher, out of his 1998 retirement to investigate how bin Laden and Saddam Hussein obtained PROMIS. He was told to investigate how Robert Hanssen, the FBI computer specialist and long-term Soviet mole, handed a copy of the PROMIS software to his KGB controllers for $2m. According to MI6 and Germany's BND PROMIS, which had been developed by a small company called Inslaw, was installed by the FBI in its headquarters to track terrorists. Hanssen had stolen a copy of the software and handed it to the KGB. The USSR then used it for computer-based espionage against the US, with great success. After the collapse of the USSR PROMIS found its way on to the Moscow black market, and in a Moscow hotel room a redundant KGB officer approached one of bin Laden's representatives, who paid $4m for the PROMIS software shortly before the attacks on the Twin Towers and the Pentagon. Hanssen is now serving a life sentence for his treachery. According to MI6 and Germany's BND there is credible evidence that bin Laden then sold PROMIS to Saddam and to Kim Jong-Il of North Korea, and used the money he received to finance his alleged terrorist attacks on Bali and Kenya in 2002.

In mid-July Redmond suddenly resigned due to "ill health" – although his health was reported to be fine. According to the *American Free Press*, Redmond's findings shocked Bush Jr. for they probed business links involving "the mobilization of trillions of dollars" in 1989–91 by Bush Sr. and his brother, Neal. The *American Free Press* reports that documents in Redmond's possession and seen by Christopher Story of the *International Currency Review*, a London-based newsletter, show that the PROMIS software was provided to Saddam on the authority of Bush Sr. – at a time when relations between Baghdad and the US were close, during Iraq's war with Iran. Confronted with evidence that his father supplied PROMIS to Saddam, Bush Jr. sacked Redmond. Hours after Redmond cleared his desk, Bush Jr. placed a $25m bounty on the head of Saddam, and $15m on each of the heads of his two sons, in an attempt to put an end to the hit-and-run attacks – and to terminate their use of PROMIS. Bush wanted both Saddam and bin Laden "dead or alive."

On balance, the West appeared to be winning its war against terrorism. Following Bush's doctrine of pre-emption, the US had targeted terrorist groups that possessed a "global reach" and any country that gave a safe haven to terrorists. In January 2002 the policy was extended to "terrorists and regimes who seek chemical, biological or nuclear weapons." The US had overthrown the Taliban regime in Afghanistan, uprooted bin Laden's operational infrastructure, killed or captured many terrorists, and discovered details about al-Qaeda's methods, as a result of which more terrorist attacks had been foiled. Israel had begun to build a 370–mile-long, 25–foot-high steel security fence to keep out Palestinian suicide-bombers.

Despite numerous threats there had been no major terrorist attacks on the West in the two years following September 11. In Afghanistan and Iraq, which had become an al-Qaeda base and battleground, thousands of terrorists had been killed and terrorist activities had been disrupted. Bin Laden and Saddam had been forced into hiding and their ability to operate had been severely reduced. Saudi Arabia had become the epicenter of terrorist financing, with some of the 5,000 members of the Royal Family bankrolling terrorists. But now the West had found an alternative supply of oil in Iraq. Iraq was to be declared "independent" on June 30, 2004 – in the event, the "hand-over" was brought forward to June 28 because of the bad security situation, and Bremer's furtive departure recalled the scuttle from Vietnam and brought press accusations of cutting and running and of military defeat – but the number of Western troops involved has increased and the West would control the oil of its client-state. Under the terms of a UN resolution of June 1, 2004, US and British forces were to remain in Iraq until January 2006. The withdrawal of US forces would not affect the continuation of the four bases the US would retain in Iraq.

Oil

The West's policy towards the Middle East meant that America and Britain were more in control of the world's oil supplies than before, despite the frequent attacks on Iraq's oil pipelines.

However, from the perspective of the American economy, issues of security, containment, and ideology were almost irrelevant. The September-11 attacks made a move on Iraqi oil nearly inevitable. The American economy had suffered as a result of September 11. A $127b budget surplus was transformed into a $165b deficit in less than twelve months between 2001 and 2002. By July 2003 the budget deficit had risen to $455b (against $304b forecast in February). Bush's 10–year $1.3 trillion tax cut and the war in Afghanistan (which cost $900m-$950m a month, over $10b a year) both contributed to this result. Peacekeeping was costing a further $3.9b a month, of which around $1b a month could be attributed to Iraq. During this time the US boosted its oil reserves, making large payments while increasing the world demand for oil in 2002. US leaders must have found the attraction of seizing Iraqi oil to alleviate this expenditure very tempting. President Bush's economic advisor Larry Lindsey said in an interview with the *Wall Street Journal* that the removal of Saddam would be a great boost for the world (and therefore the US) economy, even though a war in Iraq might cost America up to £140b, as increased oil production in a free Iraq would bring down oil prices.

The British economy had also been damaged by the war as the initial budget of £1.75b had risen to £3b and was now approaching £4b, which could have been spent on schools and hospitals.

In September 2003 Iraq's interim finance minister Kamel al-Keylani announced at the annual meeting of the International Monetary Fund and World Bank in Dubai that foreign investors could buy complete control of all Iraqi enterprises except the oil industry. To raise $90b of investment for reconstruction, everything from power stations to banks would be up for sale. We have seen that "Rockefellers" bought the former USSR's industries at knock-down prices. Would they now move in on Iraq in a big way? Was this sale the final proof that the war was to secure oil and other natural resources and assets?

Capture of Saddam

At 8.30 p.m. on 13 December 2003 Saddam Hussein was captured alive in a targeted operation involving 600 troops following information from either a detainee or from a bodyguard (who may have drugged him). He was found, with a pistol he did not use, down a 6–8 foot deep hole covered by a slab, bricks, and dirt in Al-Dawr, 10 miles from his native Tikrit by the River Tigris. (One of Saddam's personal bodyguards, Ma'ad al-Nasuri, later revealed that Saddam had left Baghdad on April 10 in a white Oldsmobile and reached the environs of Tikrit.) The hole was next to a mud-hut farmhouse, and was clearly a hiding place he went into when Coalition troops were in the area. He had $750,000 in a suitcase but no cell-phones or communications equipment. His two bodyguards had run away.

He had been betrayed by a tip-off at 10.50 that morning. Would the resistance now crumble and give up? He was shown video footage of his crimes. Mass graves had been found. He was set to face trial in Iraq for crimes against humanity and war crimes. (He is estimated to have been responsible for killing somewhere between 1 and 4.5 million Iraqis). There were calls for him to face hanging. There were reports that he was defiant towards his captors but had admitted creaming off £25b from the profits of illicit oil sales and sending it through bogus companies to Switzerland, Germany, and Japan. He still denied having weapons of mass destruction.

So the US forces finally "got him" (Bremer's words). The sight of the pathetic captured Saddam, a broken man with his matted hair, unkempt beard, and furrowed (frightened?) brow, looking like a tramp, who put up no resistance, and the pictures of his primitive hole demystified his image as a fearless strong man who ruled Iraq by terror. They made it more difficult to believe that he controlled weapons of mass destruction and was a danger to the West. Arabs were openly calling him a coward and a fraud; the story that he had been drugged may have been spread by Saddamites. Be that as it may, Saddam's disheveled appearance and solitary hole confirmed the impression that the US had been after his oil.

The US still had to contend with daily terrorist incidents. In early January 2004 a bin Laden emissary, Hassam Ghul, was captured in the Kurdish border area bearing a letter from Abu Musab al-Zarqawi (a notorious Jordanian-born terrorist with links to al-Quaeda) outlining his terrorist operations in Iraq. The Americans put a price of $10m on al-Zarqawi's head as the ringleader of the terrorism in Iraq. In early March 2004, after fraught negotiations between Sunnis, Kurds, and Shias, the Iraqi Governing Council signed a draft constitution. A fragile Iraqi government now confronted terrorism with US backing. In April American troops were fighting on two fronts as simultaneous uprisings of Sunnis and Shi'ites evoked memories of the Tet offensive in Vietnam.

Terrorist incidents (including beheadings of US hostages) increased following the revelation that US guards had mistreated and sexually abused Arab prisoners at Baghdad's Abu Ghraib prison. Following the announcement of a 33-member Iraqi government to run Iraq from June 30, 2004 under a Sunni president, Sheikh Ghazi al-Yawer – the US had dumped Chalabi for duping the American administration into believing that Saddam had weapons of mass destruction – there were daily car-bombs that killed scores of Iraqis. Sabotage attacks on Iraq's two main pipelines feeding crude oil from storage tanks to offshore terminals at Basra and Khor al-Amaya halted Iraq's oil exports (normally 1.7m barrels a day) in mid-June 2004.

Bin Laden offered to treat with European countries who detached their troops from the US forces in Iraq. The Western forces hoped that al-Qaeda felt near to defeat and were looking for a truce in which they could regroup. More likely, there was an attempt to split the Western forces and press home the advantage their offensive had brought them.

Syria

America was now a new imperial power in all but name, and Baathist Syria, deemed to have given support to Saddam, now seemed at risk.

Wolfowitz said, "There will have to be a change in Syria." The Palestinian Hamas and Shi'ite Hizbollah militias based in the Lebanon were protected by Syria. The US was under pressure from PNAC to move against Syria and cut off aid to Hizbollah. An American *imperium* in the Middle East was in the sights of PNAC.

The US put pressure on Syria. Rumsfeld said that Syria had conducted a chemical weapons test within the last 12 to 15 months. In fact, Syria, Iran's closest ally for the last 15 years, was regarded by the Pentagon as the sole Moslem state possessing "a chemical systems capability in all critical elements" for chemical weapons. Press reports now appeared asserting that Syria had refused to sign the chemical weapons convention and had spent $1b-$2b annually on ballistic, chemical, and biological weapons. They claimed Syria could fire any of its 1,000 Scud-C missiles with chemical warheads at Israel, and that at any time Syria could make a first strike against Israel's nuclear reactor in Dimona. There were claims that the Scud-3 and Scud-4 missiles (range 300 miles and 450 miles respectively) were housed in at least 15 tunnels built with North Korean and Chinese assistance; and that Syria had manufactured aerial bombs with sarin and had thousands of other chemical aerial bombs carried by Su-22, Su-24, and MiG-23 planes. Press reports attacked Syria's Scientific Studies and Research Center (SSRC), which was in control of its chemical weapons program. How many of these claims were in the nature of propaganda to justify an attack on Syria? In early May 2003 it was reported by United Press International that Pentagon plans to expand the Iraqi ground war to Syria in the form of cross-border raids had been blocked by the White House national security advisor, Condoleezza Rice.

Iran

In fact, Iran, which is between Afghanistan and Iraq and whose hostility prevents a pipeline connecting the two, was now in the US sights. This switch of focus was linked to the PNAC plan of September 2000, which states that US military bases in Saudi Arabia and Kuwait should remain as Iran "may well prove as large a threat to US interests as Iraq."

In May 2003 it was revealed that at a three-day session of the American Israel Public Affairs Committee which ended on April 1, attended by 5,000 supporters of Israel-first policies (including half the Senate), John Bolton,

US Undersecretary of State for Arms Control and International Security, said that the US would place "an extremely high priority" on halting Iran's secret nuclear weapons program. The feeling at the conference was that Iran would be next.

Israeli sources stated that Iran's nuclear program would be "irreversible" unless it was stopped by the end of 2004.

Iranian oil now tempted the Syndicate. In mid-June 2003 there were demonstrations against the government in Iran. Were these engineered by the US/Syndicate as a deliberate "softening-up" process in a coordinated attempt to oust the Islamic fundamentalist government? Also in mid-June (according to the *American Free Press* of July 7, 2003) an aide to Donald Rumsfeld, Secretary of Defense, rang a Prince of the Kuwaiti Royal Family and asked if the Royal complex where secret meetings were held during the Iraq War was available. The next day a Hercules transport landed at Kuwait's international airport and a group got out, carrying laptops and bulky briefcases. These were the forward-planners for the coming war against Iran. Within an hour of arriving at the complex, which was guarded by US forces, they had unpacked their maps of Iran, downloaded their computer maps of its terrain and were planning "Target Iran," an operation expected to start in 2004 despite misgivings in the State Department.

The plan was to use Iraq's and Afghanistan's military airfields as bases for a pincer air attack that would be supported by US carriers and missile-launching battleships in the Gulf. Turkey was to be pressured into allowing its air space to be used by US planes. The aim was to ensure that Iran could no longer pose a threat to Israel.

John Bolton, US Undersecretary of State for Arms Control and International Security, speaking at the American Israel Public Affairs committee in Washington, had issued a new warning to Iran: "In the aftermath of Saddam, dealing with the Iranian nuclear weapons program will be of equal importance to dealing with the threat that North Korea continues to pose." In other words: after Iraq – Iran. Bolton was speaking for Cheney, Wolfowitz, and others, and had received a standing ovation. At the end of June British Foreign Secretary Jack Straw visited Tehran and urged the Iranians to sign up to a new protocol agreeing to enhanced IAEA (International Atomic Energy Authority) inspections by September. The Iranian Foreign Minister Kamal Kharazi bluntly told Straw that Iran would not permit the IAEA to conduct surprise visits to facilities unless it received concessions from the international community.

In a highly critical report delivered to the IAEA in Vienna in September 2003, UN weapons inspectors made clear that they had uncovered inconsistencies in Iran's nuclear program. They had found particles of weapons-grade enriched uranium at Natanz, which has an underground complex capable of holding 1,000 personnel, and also at the Kalaye electric plant on the southern outskirts of Tehran, which the Iranians admitted using as a testing center between 1997 and 2002. Many weapons inspectors concluded that Iran was working hard to develop an atomic bomb and would have a nuclear arsenal by 2005. Scientists questioned in Pakistan (including Dr. Khan, father of the Islamic bomb) admitted giving Iran crucial technical information on building an atomic bomb, probably in return for large payments. At a meeting of the board of 35 governors of the IAEA, the US argued that Iran should be found in breach of the nuclear Non-proliferation Treaty (NPT). The IAEA gave Iran an ultimatum to come clean on its nuclear weapons program: Iran had 45 days to comply. The implication was that there would be UN Security Council action if Iran refused to comply. The Iranian delegates angrily stormed out of the Vienna meeting. The US and Israel were reported to be considering a pre-emptive strike against the plants at Natanz and Arak (a heavy-water plant).

Following meetings with the foreign ministers of Britain, France, and Germany, Iran agreed to accept IAEA inspections of its entire nuclear program and to give assurances that it had no plans to develop nuclear weapons under the cover of a project for civil nuclear power. Iran promised to suspend all uranium enrichment and processing. Could Iran be believed? John Bolton said that Iran's offer to cooperate with the international community did not mean that Tehran had abandoned ambitions to build an atomic bomb. Each of Israel's fleet of three Dolphin-class submarines was now aiming 24 US-supplied Harpoon missiles armed with nuclear warheads at Iran's nuclear sites. These missiles had been sent by the US to Diego Garcia in the Indian Ocean for loading onto the three submarines.

It transpired that Pakistan had provided Iran (and Libya and North Korea) with the expertise and materials to construct a nuclear device. The head of the IAEA, El Baradei, said that Iran had undertaken nuclear experiments it had failed to declare and there were fears that Iran was still trying to build an atom bomb. In June 2004 the IAEA's board of governors drawn from 35 countries met in Vienna and delivered a sharp rebuke to

Iran for threatening to restart the most controversial part of its nuclear program, but stopped short of referring Iran to the Security Council. Such a referral would result in sanctions or military strikes.

Fourth World War

Foreign wars require a dramatic event to outrage public opinion, which will then approve of troops being committed abroad. The Americans were led into joining the First World War in Europe after the sinking of the *Lusitania*; into the Second World War in Europe and the Pacific by the bombing of Pearl Harbor; into the Cold War by the blockade of Berlin and subsequent airlift; into the Vietnam War by the Cuban crisis, for which the Soviet Union (perceived aggressor in Vietnam) was blamed; into the first Iraq War by Saddam's invasion of Kuwait; into the "War against Terror" by the September 11 attacks; and into the second Iraq War by the perception that Saddam had weapons of mass destruction. Close scrutiny and careful analysis can demonstrate that all these outrages were choreographed from within the US by the dynastic Syndicate, whose representatives followed a luring-and-then-bombing script.

There were now press reports that a new World War had already begun. About the same time CIA Director James Woolsey, in a speech in Los Angeles to college students, described the Cold War as the Third World War and spoke of a new Fourth World War: "This fourth world war, I think, will last considerably longer than either World Wars One or Two did for us. Hopefully not the full four-plus decades of the Cold War." He said that the new war is actually against three enemies: the religious rulers of Iran, the "fascists" of Iraq and Syria, and Islamic extremists like al-Qaeda. In fact, the planners of "Target Iran" had with them a list of targets across the world, including Pakistan, Libya, Saudi Arabia, Burma, Cuba, North Korea, and eventually (despite the huge Western investment in new projects there during the 1990s) China. In a briefing paper on global strategy for Bush Jr. they had with them, CIA Director George Tenet had written: "By 2015 China will have deployed many missiles with nuclear warheads targeted against the United States, mostly more-survivable land and sea mobile missiles."

There was considerable shock round the world when the classified US Nuclear Policy Review (NPR) of January 2002 was leaked. The Review recommended that the Pentagon should be prepared to use nuclear weapons during an Iraqi attack on Israel or its neighbors, a North Korean attack on South Korea, or a military confrontation between China and Taiwan. Written a year before the invasion of Iraq, the document states that an invasion of Iraq would be for oil reasons and to protect Israel and its occupation of Arab lands. Countries such as Iran, Syria, and Libya could be involved in immediate, potential, or unexpected contingencies that might require "nuclear strike capabilities." The NPR recommended that the US should develop a new generation of nuclear devices that could be integrated within the US war-fighting strategy.

In October 2003 John Bolton, US Undersecretary of State, announced that Syria, Libya, and Cuba were new members of America's "axis of evil," which had expanded. All three countries were intent on developing weapons of mass destruction and were a threat to the US and her allies. "We're now turning our attention to Iran, Syria, Libya, and Cuba," he said. Bolton accused Libya of making increased efforts to buy components for biological and chemical weapons after UN trade sanctions were lifted in September. The US already had sanctions in place against Iran, Libya, and Cuba, and were now bringing in punitive measures against Syria, who it accused of building weapons of mass destruction and occupying the Lebanon.

In the light of the apparent absence of weapons of mass destruction in Iraq, it looked as if the US was similarly exaggerating the threat of weapons of mass destruction in North Korea, Iran, and the "axis of evil" states. It looked as if the US was being pushed by the Syndicate into a series of conflicts across the globe to strengthen the US economy by seizing oil and to enable the Syndicate to fund a lot of missiles and a global defense shield.

12

THE PAY-OFFS

A certain class of dishonesty, dishonesty magnificent in its proportions and climbing into high places, has become at the same time so rampant and so splendid ... that it will cease to be abominable.

Anthony Trollope, The Way We Live Now

Cicero, when arriving at the innocence or guilt of an accused, asked the question, "*Cui bono?*" "To whose advantage was it?" Or, "Who benefited?" There are three pay-offs as a result of the September 11 attacks.

Pay-Off Number 1: Oil

The non-OPEC oil companies have long formed a cartel that controls the oil (and gas) that flows to the US and the world. Known as the "Seven Sisters," the cartel originally comprised: Exxon ("Rockefeller"-controlled, previously known as Standard Oil of New Jersey, or Esso); Mobil (Standard Oil of New York, which merged with Vacuum Oil); Chevron (Standard Oil of California or Socal); the Mellon's Gulf Oil; Shell; Texaco; and British Petroleum (Anglo-Iranian). These seven companies controlled 90% of crude oil exports to world markets and every important pipeline in the world – the TransArabian pipeline from Qaisuma in Saudi Arabia to the Mediterranean Sea, the inter-provincial pipeline in Canada, the main pipeline in Venezuela, and the Alaskan pipeline – and could limit oil supplies to refineries and restrict the flow of oil throughout the world. Oil companies' names are always changing, but the dominance of these seven companies has been maintained.[1]

Afghanistan is rich in mineral resources.[2] But more importantly the invasion of Afghanistan brought a potential oil benefit. This is of a transit, pipeline nature; it is not "in the ground." To grasp it, we need to look at the broad picture. See map 1 on p 112 as we consider this.

The US and UK were beginning to run out of secure hydrocarbon energy supplies, and were mindful of the fact that the Moslem world would control 60% of the world's oil production by 2010 and 95% of remaining global oil export capacity. They were looking for oil-providers who could replace the "unreliable" flow of Saudi oil. Gorbachev's withdrawal of Soviet troops from Afghanistan and his break-up of the USSR meant that they could focus on the newly independent republics round the Caspian, including Baku. The Commission on America's National Interests reported in July 2000 that the Caspian region held the most promising new source of world oil, and it was proposed that to diversify supply routes, a pipeline should run eastwards through Afghanistan and Pakistan to near the Indian border where Enron had invested $3b in a power plant at Dabhol. This needed cheap gas to survive.

It was reported (in the London *Times* of February 26, 2002) that President Bush had used the attacks of September 11 to further the cause of opening Alaska's Arctic National Wildlife Refuge (Anwar). He argued that the US should not rely on the Middle East or its volatile states to provide America's energy requirements: "This dependence on foreign oil is a matter of national security ... Sometimes we rely upon energy sources from countries that don't particularly like us." The US at present imports nearly 55% of its total oil consumption, some 10 million barrels a day. "This is dependence on foreign oil."

For decades a 762–mile gas pipeline has been planned to run from the Turkmen Dauletabad fields through Afghanistan to Multan in Pakistan, at a cost of $1.9b. To take it to India would cost another $600m. The Soviet invasion of Afghanistan in 1979 would have resulted in the opening of the oil pipeline if the USSR had succeeded in subduing the country.

Before the Soviet invasion, Afghanistan supplied 70–90% of its natural gas to the Soviet Union's natural gas grid via Uzbekistan. Plans to build an oil refinery in Afghanistan were terminated by the Soviets, who abolished the Afghan National Oil Company.

There have long been rumors that the Taliban were created in 1994 by the CIA and Pakistan. If this is so, it can now be seen that the US and Pakistan created the Taliban as a strong force that would guard the oil and gas pipelines they envisaged building between the former Soviet republics and Pakistan – hence the Taliban's visit to Unocal (see below). The US and British governments plan to control the Caspian's oil and gas. To the west a pipeline has to cross Chechnya. To the south, as Iran is hostile, it has to cross Afghanistan, which is therefore critical to the Anglo-American plan.

It was reported in the *American Free Press* of January 21, 2002 that the US have established military tent bases in 13 locations in nine countries encircling Afghanistan and the Caspian, including Bulgaria, Uzbekistan, Turkey, and Kuwait. The Arab media have seen the development of these bases as an American plan for hegemony and control of the region.

Unocal
International oil interests were – and are – in fierce competition to build pipelines through Afghanistan to transport the Caspian Sea's $5 trillion oil and gas reserves. The *American Free Press* (October 8, 2001) has revealed that Enron (a Texas-based gas and energy company), Amoco, British Petroleum, Chevron, Exxon, Mobil, and Unocal are all engaged in a multi-billion-dollar round of negotiations to extract the resources of Azerbaijan, Kazakhstan, and Turkmenistan, the three newly independent Soviet republics that adjoin the Caspian. The oil companies have sent members of George Bush Sr.'s administration to negotiate with these former republics: James Baker, Brent Scowcroft, John Sununu, and Dick Cheney (George W. Bush's Vice-President). In 1998 Cheney, then Chief Executive Officer of Halliburton, the world's biggest oil drilling equipment manufacturer, told oil industry executives: "I cannot think of a time when we have had a region emerge as suddenly, to become as strategically significant, as the Caspian." In 2001 Halliburton signed a major contract with the State Oil Company of Azerbaijan to develop a 6,000–square-meter marine base to support offshore oil construction in the Caspian.

A supply of oil has already been planned (by the "Rockefellerite" Syndicate) to reach the West from the former USSR: there is already a new 990–mile-long pipeline from the Tengiz field in Kazakhstan to Novorossiysk on the Black Sea (see map 1 on p 112), and another pipeline is planned to run from the Baku oilfield in Azerbaijan to Ceyhan on the Mediterranean coast of Turkey (see map 3 on p 114). Both these pipelines run from east to west, and oil can thus be brought from the former USSR to the West without dependence on Saudi Arabia.

There has already been a major attempt by an American company to build the 762-mile pipeline across Afghanistan to Central and South Asia. When the Taliban (which was created from Pakistani refugee camps and strict conservative religious schools in 1994) took Kabul in 1996, Unocal were quick to make an approach. The State Department's attitude to the new Afghanistan was summed up by a spokesman (Glyn Davies), who said that the US found "nothing objectionable" in the steps being taken by the Taliban to impose Islamic law. In February 1997 a delegation of Taliban leaders flew to Unocal headquarters at Sugarland, Texas for corporate hospitality. Unocal opened an office in Kandahar.

In May 1997 Unocal, the spearhead for Standard Oil interests, secured a $2.5b pipeline deal with the Taliban, Turkmenistan, and Pakistan. The Taliban made two conditions: that Unocal should reconstruct the country's infrastructure and that the pipeline should be open for local consumption at some point. From 1997 Unocal was a member (with Birdas) of a multinational consortium, Central Asia Gas (CentGas), which envisaged a pipeline from Turkmenistan's Chardzhou oilfield through Afghanistan to Pakistan and eventually India. There were reports that Unocal offered to pay the Taliban $100m a year as rent for oil and gas pipelines.

Unocal suspended its participation in August 1998 following the attacks against the US Embassies in Kenya and Tanzania, and withdrew from the consortium in December 1998 following the US cruise missile attack against Afghanistan. The pipeline was never constructed, and Birdas filed a $15b suit against Unocal, which was not successful. The size of the claim indicates the scale of the project. On September 14, 2001 Unocal denied "supporting the Taliban in Afghanistan" or having any project or involvement in Afghanistan. Was there a burning American desire to "get bin Laden dead or alive" as a result of the consortium's pipeline fiasco? Pakistan tried to keep the project alive by looking for a new sponsor, but no one was interested in investing in Afghanistan now.

The French authors Jean-Charles Brisard and Guillaume Dasquie say in *Bin Laden, la Verité Interdite* ("Bin Laden, the Forbidden Truth") that the US government saw the Taliban "as a source of stability in Central Asia that would enable the construction of an oil pipeline across Central Asia" from the rich oilfields in Turkmenistan, Uzbekistan, and Kazakhstan through Afghanistan and Pakistan to the Indian Ocean. They say that

Russia had controlled the oil and gas reserves in Central Asia until the advent of Bush's administration; and that Bush, wanting to seize them for the US, began to negotiate with the Taliban in February 2001. The US met the Taliban in Berlin in July 2001 and pressed them to form a government of national unity in return for aid. Niaz Naik, a former Pakistani Foreign Minister, who attended the meeting, said on French television that Tom Simons, the US representative at these meetings, put the situation clearly to the Taliban and Pakistan: "Either the Taliban behave as they ought to, or Pakistan convinces them to do so, or we will use another option, a military operation." Brisard said in an interview in Paris that the US representatives told the Taliban, "Either you accept our offer of a carpet of gold, or we bury you under a carpet of bombs."

Was a Taliban-ruled Afghanistan perceived as a threat to this flow of alternative oil to the West? Could it be that the Taliban were perceived as an obstacle, and that there should therefore be an incident that would give a pretext to replace the Taliban with a government sympathetic to the five partners involved: Russia (representing the suppliers); Pakistan and India (representing the consumers); and America and Britain (representing the providers and commercial beneficiaries)? If this was the case, the incident chosen created a Pearl-Harbor enthusiasm for bringing about change in Afghanistan. It swept America following the attack on the Twin Towers, and the war in Afghanistan was essentially about oil.

Significantly, at the end of November 2001 bin Laden was reported to have ordered al-Qaeda to attack "US oil and gas pipelines" if he or Mullah Omar were captured or killed. As a result, air patrols increased over thousands of miles of gas and petrol pipelines, and locations were removed from websites. Bin Laden's order suggests that he knows that the war in Afghanistan was really about oil and gas pipelines. The one reconstruction project underway in Afghanistan in 2003 was the construction of a gigantic gas pipeline from Turkmenistan to the Indian Ocean.

According to the *American Free Press* (October 8, 2001) Unocal plan to build a 1,030–mile Central Asian Oil Pipeline from Chardzhou in Turkmenistan, via Russia's Siberian oilfield pipelines, to Pakistan's Arabian coast. This would run parallel to the gas pipeline through Afghanistan and branch off in Pakistan to the Indian Ocean terminal in Ras Malan, and would transport one million barrels of oil a day from other areas of the former Soviet Union.

Unocal's top advisor during the negotiations with the Taliban to construct the CentGas (Central Asia Gas) pipeline from Turkmenistan through western Afghanistan to Pakistan was none other than Hamid Karzai, installed by the Bush Jr. administration as the new ruler of Afghanistan.[3] He had links with the CIA and Bush Sr. while fighting the Soviet Union in the 1980s. The north–south pipeline is guarded by US soldiers while UN forces police Afghanistan. The Afghani-American CentGas member Zalmay Khalizal, who liaised between Unocal and the Taliban, was made Bush Jr.'s Special National Security Assistant and Special Envoy for Afghanistan.[4] He has worked on risk analyses in connection with the pipeline for Condoleezza Rice, US National Security Advisor. The US now has a permanent military base in Afghanistan as well as Uzbekistan.

Bush Jr.

Meanwhile, in 1989 when his father was on the brink of winning the Presidency and while still working in the oil business, George W. Bush was approached by Bill De Witt, the owner of Spectrum 7, who suggested they should put together a consortium to bid for the Texas Rangers, a baseball team. De Witt and Bush found 70 investors, two of whom put in $7m. Bush put in $606,000, some of the proceeds from the sale of his Harken Energy shares,[5] and was selected to be the public face of the team on a salary of $200,000 p.a. The prominence the position gave him throughout Texas prepared the way for him to become State Governor. After threatening to move the team to a new home Bush and his fellow investors were controversially given a $135m subsidy by local taxpayers to build a new stadium.[6] In 1998 the consortium sold up and Bush received $14.9m. Bush therefore had a lump sum with which to fund his candidature for the Presidency in 2000.[7]

By now Bush Jr. was a born-again Christian. Before announcing his candidacy for the presidency, he told a Texan evangelist James Robinson: "I feel like God wants me to run for President. I can't explain it, but I sense my country is going to need me. Something is going to happen .... I know it won't be easy on me or my family, but God wants me to do it." He appointed a number of apparently evangelical Christians to his administration on becoming President, including Gen. William Boykin who headed the hunt for bin Laden and once said that the war on terror was a fight against Satan.

Although the Bush–Cheney administration was fronted by former oil employees – George W. Bush (on the board of Harken Energy, successor to the prospecting company Arbusto); Dick Cheney, Halliburton (the world's largest oilfield services company); Condoleezza Rice (on the board of Chevron); Donald Rumsfeld, Occidental; and George W. Bush Sr., the Carlyle Group, which has ownership in 164 companies worldwide – there did not appear to be any direct connection between Harken Energy, the successor to George W. Bush's Arbusto oil company, and Unocal or the other companies involved in the Caspian region. Personnel in both companies were undoubtedly business associates, however.

In December 2001 the Houston-based Enron, which had been valued at $77b earlier in the year, went bankrupt with debts of $40b in the biggest financial collapse in modern US history. Once the seventh largest US corporation, Enron had made political donations totaling $5.8m, of which nearly $2m went to Bush's campaigns. Kenneth Lay, Enron's chief, had close ties with Bush, and Enron had had an influence on Bush's energy strategy, successfully pressing for greater deregulation. Bush came to power promising to deregulate the oil and energy industries.

In April 2002 Representative Cynthia McKinney called on Congress to initiate an investigation of September 11 to find out if some of the government had foreknowledge of the terrorist attacks or profited from America's growing war on terrorism. She alleged (*American Free Press*, April 29, 2002): "It is known that President Bush's father, through the Carlyle Group had – at the time of the attacks – joint business interests with Bin Laden Construction Company and many defense industry holdings, the stocks of which have soared since September 11."

Blair/BP/Russia

It is interesting that, with all this pipeline activity going on, Blair's New Labour government had close links with British Petroleum, Britain's biggest oil company. BP has a "Rockefellerite" influence: in January 1987 Standard Oil bought out, and merged with, British Petroleum. The new company was called BP-America. In 1998 BP-America and Amoco merged and the new company was briefly known as BP Amoco. In 1999 it changed its name to BP. London's *Sunday Times* investigated the British government's links with BP in an article on December 9, 2001 ("Labour faces questions on links to BP"). In November 2001 Anji Hunter, a senior advisor to Blair, was appointed BP's director of communications. Lord Browne, the chief executive of BP (formerly executive vice-president and chief financial officer of Standard Oil in Ohio and chief executive officer of Standard Oil Production Co.), has had breakfasts and made opera visits with Blair; Lord Simon, ex-BP Chairman, is a Blair advisor; and Baroness Smith, widow of former Labour leader John Smith, is a member of BP's Scottish board and is BP advisor for Scotland. Five more links were revealed in the *Sunday Times* article. Could it be that commercial considerations are driving the British government's policy in Afghanistan? It is interesting that during a visit to London by the Russian leader Putin, Blair made a statement supporting Putin's war against the Chechens, arguing that the unsolved explosion in Moscow (blamed by some on the KGB) which killed 73 people in 1999 was similar to the September 11 outrage. The Blair–Putin alliance seems to be largely based on oil.

In June 2003 Blair (on behalf of "Rothschilds") and Putin brokered a £4.3b joint venture between BP and the Russian oil firm TNK, which was facing allegations of extortion in the US courts: it was alleged that a business rival was forced to abandon a Siberian oil plant when the Russian firm sent in guards armed with machine-guns. Lord Browne worked on the BP end of the deal, and there was concern in the British press over the role of Anji Hunter, Blair's advisor who was a BP employee on the communications side (as opposed to the commercial side which did the deal). Also on the BP payroll were former Blair advisors Nick Butler (BP's policy chief) and Philip Gould, formerly Blair's pollster. The BP–TNK deal was completed at a ceremony at Lancaster House, London that coincided with a State visit by President Putin, who became the first Russian President to be received by the reigning monarch for more than a hundred years.

Israel

Azerbaijan and Turkmenistan have close links with Israeli commercial interests and military intelligence. Yosef Maiman, President of the Merhav Group of Israel, was made a citizen of Turkmenistan and has been the official negotiator for the development of Turkmenistan's energy resources. He dominates all foreign business there. Turkmenistan and Russia are competing in a price war to supply gas to Turkey, and one of Maiman's proposed pipelines would bring Turkmenistan's gas and oil to Turkey via Azerbaijan and Georgia.

There are a number of projects that have been thrown up by this ferment. The Merhav Group has a $100m project that would divert water from the Tigris and Euphrates rivers in South East Turkey and reduce the flow of water to Iraq. An Israeli company, Magal, has an excellent relationship with Azerbaijan and has a contract to improve security at Baku airport. (The Baku oilfields featured greatly in the competition between "Rockefellers" and "Rothschilds" in the early twentieth century.) Enron conducted the feasibility study for a trans-Caspian gas pipeline, which is to be built under an agreement signed in February 1999 between Turkmenistan and two American companies, Bechtel and General Electric Capital Services.

The New World Order did not want the Taliban "fundamentalizing" Uzbekistan, Tajikistan, Kazakhstan, and Turmenistan and threatening their supply of oil, gas, and other resources which are to be transported throughout Asia. Just as in the nineteenth century European imperialism grew commercially through the spread of railways, so in the twenty-first century American imperialism is growing commercially through the spread of oil and gas pipelines and the mining of mineral resources. The war on terror is designed to control Middle Eastern, Caspian, and South Asian oil.

Pay-Off Number 2: A Global Defense System

The invasion of Afghanistan brought another potential benefit: an $80b global defense system[8] to counter the nuclear-bomb threat posed by rogue states and the "dirty-bomb" threat imposed by terrorists.

The September 11 attack emphasized American vulnerability and brought home to the American people the strategic, long-term need for a missile defense shield. Although such a shield, previously announced by Bush Jr., could not have stopped the attack by planes, the demolition of the World Trade Center had made Americans feel insecure and had made the adoption of the shield more likely.

A shield requires an enemy against whom the public must be shielded. One of the consequences of the attack was a flurry of articles in the press urging the shield, some by Dr. Kissinger, others saying Dr. Kissinger was right all along to say that American defense needed to be improved.

The shield is already being constructed. In December 2001 Bush announced America's unilateral withdrawal from the 30–year-old Anti-

Ballistic Missile Treaty, and by June 2002 five missile silos were being dug by hundreds of silo construction workers at Fort Greely, a few miles outside Delta Junction, Alaska to implement the missile defense shield program. A command and control center was scheduled to follow, with the work to be finished by autumn 2004.

If any time after 2005 a rogue Middle-Eastern state were to fire a long-range missile at the US traveling at 15,000 mph through space, within seconds the US radar base at Fylingdales, Yorkshire would pick this up and warn US commanders in Colorado who would fire interceptors. These would rise above the sub-Arctic forests of Fort Greely and the snow-capped Granite Mountains and, traveling at 5,000 mph, 10 minutes after firing would smash into the missile above the Arctic Ocean. On June 13, 2002 Bush said: "As the events of September 11 made clear, we no longer live in the Cold-War world for which the ABM Treaty was designed. We now face new threats from terrorists who seek to destroy our civilization by any means available to rogue states armed with weapons of mass destruction and long-range missiles." He called on Congress to fund his missile defense budget in full.

Congress's funding of much of the global defense system in 2003 must be seen against an $80b federal deficit for 2003 projected by the White House Office of Management and Budget. (The projected deficit for 2002 was $106b.) Partly as a result of the defense system the national debt was projected to rise.[9] The Syndicate are involved in the funding of the national debt through the Federal Reserve System, and therefore in the funding of its increase of $80b in 2003, exactly the cost of the defense system. It can therefore be said that, indirectly, the Syndicate provided the global defense system.

But who is this shield really meant to protect us from? We can detail in turn the threat from each group or nation/rogue state that has the capacity to impact on the West.

Al-Qaeda

It was known before September 11, but not publicized until disclosed in reports from "intelligence sources" on October 25 (to coincide with news of the committal of ground troops to Afghanistan), that Osama bin Laden and his al-Qaeda network had acquired nuclear materials for possible terrorist use in their war with the West. We have seen that Saddam may have successfully tested an atomic bomb in 1989, and since then he is reputed to have amassed a menacing nuclear, chemical, and biological arsenal. Before the second Iraq War Saddam seemed a likely source for bin Laden's nuclear materials.

In fact, however, the materials seem to have been obtained from Pakistan where the father of Pakistan's nuclear bomb, Dr. Abdul Qadeer Khan, was found to have sold nuclear expertise to Libya, Iran, and North Korea. Earlier in 2001 10 canisters of radioactive material were seized on the border between Uzbekistan and Kazakhstan. They were bound for Quetta in Pakistan, allegedly for bin Laden's organization. A dirty bomb created from nuclear waste material and conventional explosives, detonated in Manhattan at noon, could kill 2,000 people and leave many thousands more with radiation poisoning. Although a US Defense Spokesman (General Tommy Franks) confirmed on November 27, 2001 that no evidence had been found that al-Qaeda had produced any nuclear, chemical, or biological weapons, he reported that Americans had identified 40 laboratories where they may have conducted tests to develop such weapons, and that each site was being checked as it fell into the hands of the Northern Alliance.

On December 24, 2001 it was reported that uranium had been found in a vast underground workshop outside Kandahar. It was in an area known as Turnak Farms that abutted Kandahar airport. Here was al-Qaeda's principal military camp and training ground in southern Afghanistan, and it held 1,800 people. Several hundred Arabs lost their lives fighting to the death when tribal forces attacked the base. Low-grade uranium 238, which could be used to make a "dirty bomb" was found stored in underground concrete tunnels along with cyanide in hundreds of different containers: small and large jars sealed with metal lids and containing white and yellowish powders and liquids. These were labeled in Chinese, Russian, Arabic, and English. There were large drums and metal boxes with sides eight inches thick. American officials said that Russia, the states of the former Soviet Union, China, and Pakistan were all possible sources of the uranium. Two Pakistani scientists admitted to having had long discussions about nuclear, chemical, and biological weapons, with bin Laden in Kabul in August 2001.

Documents discovered by the London *Times* in abandoned houses in Kabul and printed on December 29, 2001 show that al-Qaeda cells were examining how to make a low-grade "dirty" nuclear device and that their bomb-related electronic circuitry exceeded that of the Provisional IRA's experts; that they had tested chemical weapons, including cyanide gas, on rabbits; and that they were training terrorist units to assassinate Middle-Eastern leaders sympathetic towards the West.

But al-Qaeda by itself does not warrant a missile defense shield. There are many cheaper and easier ways of delivering a dirty bomb into the US than firing it into space.

China

It was reported in the *American Free Press* of December 31, 2001 that Bush Jr. and the Russian leader Putin reached agreement for a missile defense system to be sited in the Afghan mountains. This would be directed against China, and would protect the US, Britain, and Russia against a Chinese ballistic missile attack. This system would protect the flow of oil and gas across Afghanistan.

It was reported in the London *Times* (January 10, 2002) that China has increased its nuclear missiles aimed at the US, according to a CIA analysis, *Foreign Missile Developments and the Ballistic Missile Threat Through 2015*. In 2015 China will have 100 long-range missiles pointing at the United States. An accelerated Chinese nuclear build-up is the likely result of Bush's determination to push through a missile defense shield for the US. This shield system could bring down 20 missiles from China if they were launched simultaneously. But 100 Chinese missiles launched at the same time would overwhelm the shield system. The Chinese military is developing three new missile systems, two truck-launched and one submarine-launched, which would be active by 2010. At the same time it was revealed that most of the 4,000 American nuclear warheads Bush told Putin he wanted to destroy would be kept in storage.

It was also reported in the *American Free Press* of September 16, 2002 that a former American chairman of the Joint Chiefs of Staff, Admiral Thomas Moorer, has warned that China is preparing for a major war with the US by 2005. China plans to take Taiwan. In July 2004 China staged a rehearsal for a D-Day-type invasion of Taiwan when 18,000 men, supported by Russian-built fighter jets and submarines, landed on the beaches of Dongshan island 150 miles west of Taiwan. China is prepared to use nuclear weapons in a war that such a seizure would trigger. Red Chinese secured American nuclear and missile technology in an espionage *coup* from the Clinton administration. Taiwan-born scientist Wen Ho Lee was jailed for passing US nuclear weapons secrets from the US nuclear laboratories at Los Alamos to Red China, although it has been alleged that China's secret service, the CSIS, had independently penetrated Los Alamos, some say – for example Gordon Thomas in *Seeds of Fire* – in conjunction with Israel's Mossad.

According to Thomas's book, on September 11, 2001, the very day of the attacks, a Chinese People's Liberation Army transport aircraft from Beijing landed at Kabul bearing a Chinese delegation that had come to sign the contract that would provide the Taliban with missile-tracking and advanced communications equipment and air-defense systems requested by bin Laden, in return for the Taliban's promise to end attacks by Moslem extremists in China's north-western regions. Hours later, George Tenet, CIA director, received a message from Mossad that China was prepared to use bin Laden as a surrogate to attack the US. China was certainly using the aftermath of the crisis to launch itself as a new superpower and act as the US's major enemy. Bin Laden had clearly requested the equipment before September 11; is it conceivable that China encouraged the September-11 attacks, or even promised the equipment if the attacks took place – hence the timing of the delegation's visit? Or is Chinese involvement in the attacks, which on the face of it seems very far-fetched, a fabrication, part of a Syndicate campaign to justify regarding China as an enemy in order to influence the decision to buy the missile defense shield?

China is apparently at enmity with the US. It was reported in the *American Free Press* of January 20, 2003 that China has promised North Korea its continued support and has increased aid in the hope that the US will be stretched on two fronts at the same time (North Korea and Iraq) and that China will be able to reunite Taiwan with the mainland while the US is preoccupied. China has purchased modern Sovremmeny-class destroyers from Russia, which, if armed with Russian-made Sunburn missiles, could attack US warships opposing Taiwan. The Chinese purchase includes the *Varyag*, a Soviet super-carrier capable of launching 60 jet fighters and 15 anti-submarine helicopters. This super-carrier will give China a deep-water global naval presence.

China has built bases[10] at *both* ends of the Panama Canal and in the Bahamas, and has leased the decommissioned Longbeach Naval Station (a naval base) on US soil in California; it can use these bases to strike every

US city with atomic weapons that can be delivered by short- and medium-range missiles. China has already ringed America to the east, south, and west with bases that could each be new Cubas.

But in reality, as anyone who has visited Shanghai in 2002 will have immediately grasped, China is undergoing a peaceful economic boom. Under a treaty of 1990 following Deng Hsiao-ping's opening of China in 1978 and his harsh suppression of the Tiananmen students' democracy movement in 1989 (when the central committee signaled that it dictated strategy without being directed by students), the World Bank and foreign investors have made a huge investment in Shanghai, which now resembles a mini-Manhattan. Its high-rise banks, hotels, and Oriental Pearl building dwarf London's Canary Wharf. The Chinese pay interest on these huge foreign loans. (Foreign investment in China reached $52.7b in 2002, an increase of 12.5%.)

This building began in 1990, seemingly as a Western response to Tiananmen, as an attempt to encourage China to take the democratic path. It was implemented in 1993 and has accelerated since 1996 when Dr. Kissinger met the Mayor of Shanghai at the Peace Hotel in Shanghai's Bund on September 12, 1996. The US pressured Britain into giving up Hong Kong in 1997, and the 2008 Olympics have been awarded to China; athletic events will take place in Shanghai. In return China has on occasion taken the US side against North Korea and Saddam.

It seems that there was a deal in 1996. China would allow Hong Kong to function as before so that the West would notice no change of ownership; in return China would be helped with World Bank investment in developing Shanghai and, to a lesser extent, Beijing. There would also be help with the $110b required to develop the Yangtze River: $70b for the Three Gorges dam projects and another $40b for the diversion of the Yangtze to the north.

The sequence of events behind this contradiction of investment and enmity is as follows:

- America agreed to help China's projects (Yangtze and Shanghai) via intermediaries in return for normality in Hong Kong after 1997;
- America was shocked to learn that China had acquired US nuclear technology through espionage;
- America decided to have a missile defense shield against China to

be on the safe side, and conveniently the attacks on September 11 took place to convince the American public that the US needed such a shield;

- China has demanded the return of Taiwan by the end of 2004, and America may be in no mood to grant it following the theft of nuclear information.

It can thus be seen that an attempt to democratize Red China has been overtaken by confrontation, following the nuclear theft. Some advisors to Bush Jr. were reputed to favor regime change in China, a policy linked to their promotion of a global defense shield. It was a measure of China's stunning progress since the early 1990s that in October 2003 it became the third country (after the US and the USSR) to launch a man into space. The event may also have been a measure of how much rocket technology China had stolen from the US.

It was reported on February 7, 2002 that US military might had secured a stronghold in Kyrgyzstan, north of China. Three thousand foreign troops were expected to occupy the Manas air base by the spring. A Kyrgyz military expert, Alexander Kim, was quoted as saying: "There is one great power in this region which can oppose the US. I don't think that this base is connected to strategic plains to the south as much as to China."

Did the Americans see a war in Afghanistan as a preparation for a missile defense system against China, a system the Syndicate would help finance? Will such a system defend the US from states that resist the Syndicate's drives for new oil?

North Korea

In October 2002 North Korea admitted that it had a secret nuclear weapons program that violated an agreement it signed with ex-President Bill Clinton in 1994 to freeze its nuclear program. In a stormy meeting US Assistant Secretary of State James Kelly, visiting a month after Bush Jr. announced his policy of pre-emptive strikes, confronted North Koreans with evidence of their nuclear activities during a visit to Pyongyang, and the North Koreans acknowledged that their program involved enriched uranium, which could be used in nuclear weapons. It is believed that Pakistan supplied Pyongyang with both uranium and technology during the 1990s, and that North Korea may now have as many as three to five nuclear weapons. (Some have said the tally can only be, at the most, one or two.) If fitted to one of North Korea's 30 Nodong-1 medium-range missiles tested in 1993, which have a range of 650 miles, these would be able to reach the 37,000 US troops in South Korea and US bases in Japan. The Americans do not know where these weapons are; they are likely to be in one of the 11,000 caves excavated below Pyongyang since the outbreak of the Korean War in 1950. (There are 15,000 underground military-industrial sites in all.) North Korea also has 500 Scud missiles and stocks of anthrax, cholera, and plague, and eight chemical production plants for mustard gas and nerve agents. There was concern as the new dictator of North Korea, Kim Jong-Il, had the reputation for being unstable and "dangerous" (Chinese leader Jiang Zemin's word).

There was enormous US concern when in December 2002 the UN seals and surveillance cameras at North Korea's Yongbyon five-megawatt nuclear reactor 56 miles north of Pyongyang were removed, the reactor having been shut down in a deal (the Agreed Framework) with the US in 1994. The reopening of the reactor was allegedly to generate electricity, but it was capable of producing weapons-grade plutonium for nuclear bombs. The International Atomic Energy Agency reported that fresh fuel (1,000 uranium fuel rods) had been added to the reactor but that no work was being done at the reprocessing plant, which produces plutonium. As North Korea has fissile material the reactor could make four or five additional nuclear weapons within months. North Korea is developing an inter-continental missile system, which would put Europe and North America within range. The US missile defense shield had partly been conceived as a defense against North Korea's missile program, although until now the program did not warrant a system of the magnitude of the missile defense shield. In a chilling briefing at the Pentagon, US Defense Secretary Donald Rumsfeld warned the North Korean regime that the US military was prepared to take them on at the same time as Iraq. He said that the US was able to wage two regional conflicts at the same time: "We are capable of winning decisively in one and swiftly defeating in the case of the other." As much of North Korea's military complex is underground, Rumsfeld has revised the war plan for Korea ("Operations Plan 5030") and has planned a pre-emptive strike on Yongbyon followed by nuclear strikes against multiple targets. In February 2003 North Korea threatened a pre-emptive nuclear strike against the US. North Korea withdrew from the Nuclear Non-Proliferation Treaty, and the IAEA reported North Korea to the UN Security Council as being in breach of UN resolutions, raising the prospect of further action.

In January 2004 it was revealed that North Korea has offshore oil. Oil reserves of 8–10b tons (73 billion barrels if 10b tons) were claimed in three documents published by North Korea in 1997.[11] North Korea also has gas reserves. Halliburton (the company linked with Cheney) are involved and say that Korea has significant but quite unmeasured reserves of offshore oil.

It seems that since the arrival of Bush Jr. as President, the US has exaggerated the threat of North Korea, which had previously been contained for nearly 50 years, to help justify the US missile defense shield – and control North Korean oil.

The "Axis of Evil"

On January 29, 2002 President Bush, in his State-of-the-Union address, spoke of the US as being at war with an "Axis of Evil," a collection of terrorist states, the foremost of which he named as Iran, Iraq, and North Korea. The inclusion of Iran in the firing line followed the seizure by Israel of a boat full of Iran-sponsored weapons on its way to Palestine. By using the word "Axis" Bush was echoing the globalist Axis of Evil during the Second World War – Germany, Italy, and Japan – and signaling a return to the globalist outlook of the Allies during the Second World War. The language used by Bush Jr. subliminally suggested that a new world war (the Fourth World War if the Cold War was the Third) had already broken out. His administration let it be known that the war against world terrorism may last for years. Condoleezza Rice told the congressional hearing into "9/11" that America was now "at war." Action against North Korea may precipitate conflict with China, and provides scope for presenting China as a hostile state that justifies expenditure on a missile defense system. If such action is planned, then the next World War may already have begun, its theatres being the Moslem territories of the Middle East which threaten Israel and Saudi-Arabian oil; North Korea; and perhaps China, where there are huge "Rockefellerite" oil interests.

It was reported on March 10, 2002 that a Pentagon report had been leaked revealing that Washington has contingency plans to use nuclear weapons against seven countries: China, Russia, Iran, Iraq, North Korea,

Libya (since welcomed as an ally), and Syria. It should be noted that all seven countries are producers of oil or strategically important as pipeline terminals. (The Mosul–Haifa pipeline was redirected to Syria.) The report, signed off by Donald Rumsfeld and sent to Congress on January 8, 2002, stated that nuclear weapons might be used: against targets able to withstand conventional attack; in retaliation for the use of nuclear or biochemical weapons; or "in the event of surprising military developments" (presumably more incidents like those of September 11). The report envisages nuclear weapons being used in a Chinese confrontation over Taiwan; a North Korean attack on South Korea; an attack by Iraq on Israel or another neighbor; or in an Arab-Israeli conflict. This nuclear strategy and the missile defense system are two sides of the same coin: aggressive and reactive self-defense.

Pay-Off Number 3: A World Government

The invasion of Afghanistan brought a further potential benefit, of world peace. For as a result of the attack on America, a Global Coalition was assembled to conduct a global war for freedom against world terrorism: a war for civilization against barbarism in which Moslems would fight with Christians against mass destruction. The aim of the Global Coalition was to line up on America's side as many countries as possible – as many as 60 were mentioned – in a "New World Order" to which pan-Arabism is a great threat. Maybe the ulterior aim of the September 11 attack was to create a global issue, to find a universal cause that would align on the same side and unite the great majority of humankind, to evince a global response. Perhaps globalists used the attack to increase global awareness, promote global thinking among all nations, and secure the victory of the globalists over the nationalists.

Crucial to the globalist agenda was the election of Bush Jr. to implement the Syndicate's expansive oil program. His controversial election had hinged on 170,000 Florida votes rejected as unreadable. On September 11, 2001 an investigation was in process. A study, commissioned by a consortium including the *Wall Street Journal*, the *Washington Post* and the *New York Times* and costing more than £700,000, had reached its final phase: the counting of the votes. The effect of the September-11 attacks was that this final phase was postponed indefinitely, now that a strong

President had led America into war. Possible evidence of a Gore victory was suspended in the interests of "patriotism." Bush was closer to the Syndicate and its oil agenda than Gore. (Gore is, however, related to the family of Jacob Schiff by the marriage of his daughter to Drew Schiff.)

The Syndicate has always used Middle-Eastern potentates and guerilla leaders as pawns in their grand design. We have seen that although "Rockefellers" and "Rothschilds" have different emphases in the Middle East – "Rockefellers" being more pro-Palestine, "Rothschilds" more pro-Israel, for example – they both share the same umbrella, just as the British politicians Blair and Brown (one pro-euro, the other pro-pound) make common cause although they differ in emphasis.

Maybe the Syndicate is not involved at all. Each individual member probably abhors such attacks. But their maneuvering for oil has created the situation where terrorism takes root and flourishes. The effect of terrorism is to provide them with an excuse to increase their grip rather than loosen it. But would we really face terrorism on the scale we do today if there were no commercial Western interests across the Middle East? If we left those nations to follow their own destinies? The way it's turned out, isn't the "war against terrorism that will last for years" a convenient way of imposing the will of the world government and of securing the victory of the globalists over the nationalists?

In December 2002 it was announced that Dr. Kissinger, "Rockefellers" and Bilderberg's globalist general factotum, would chair an inquiry into the September 11 attacks (spy agency failures, and aviation and immigration issues). Kissinger was scheduled to announce his findings within 18 months, at the peak of Bush's campaign for re-election in November 2004. At this stage it could confidently be expected that the Syndicate would not feature in the 79–year-old Kissinger's report, and that there would be a denial of Bush's alleged complicity in the September 11 attacks, and a vindication of America's war against terror. Two weeks after his appointment, however, Kissinger resigned as chairman of the inquiry to shield his private consultancy company from controversy. Reports stated that he faced intense pressure from Democrats in Congress to divulge his client list, which is believed to include some of the world's largest multinational firms and a number of governments.

The guardians are in a strong position because we *want* to be protected from terrorists' misuse of nuclear, biological, and chemical warfare. The great majority of world citizens would assert that any country capable of delivering nuclear, biological, or chemical weapons against the Western public should have its capability closed down, regardless of whether it is small like Afghanistan or vast like Communist China. We will gladly give up freedoms in return for being safe. If a world government can make us safe, we will welcome it. If it can shield three-quarters of the world against the truculent quarter and over a period of time root out its terrorism and make the whole world safe, we will go along with it.

Welcoming the announcement of a new interim government for Afghanistan that would replace the Taliban, the British Foreign Secretary said, "This really is One World." Few viewers would have grasped the real meaning of these words, that the New World Order had removed a government that was unsympathetic towards globalism, and replaced it with a government that would be internationalist in outlook.

The attacks on New York and Washington had the effect of advancing the Syndicate's cause of creating a world government that will replace nation-states – an eventuality the North American civilization must resist if it is to survive. It should remain in control of its global stage as did Rome during the period of its world *imperium*, and not be dismantled to be ruled by globalists. North American civilization has two enemies. One is Arab extremism and Islamic fanaticism. The other is an enemy within, Syndicate extremism and Masonic fanaticism. Both enemies would merge the North American civilization into a global one for their own purposes.

Conclusion

In September 2003 former British minister Michael Meacher, citing the PNAC blueprint, wrote a controversial article claiming that the US deliberately let the September-11 attacks happen to launch Bush's master plan for world domination. He claimed that the American plan included regime change in China. There was an outcry from the US embassy in London and the British press. He was right. The attack was caught on camera because it was expected. Bin Laden and Saddam were put up to it by Westerners, they were proxies. It was planned to trigger an attack in return on Afghanistan.

In February 2004 Blair said in a speech that the war against terror was "approaching the end of the first phase" (i.e. "the end of the beginning" as

Churchill said of a phase in the Second World War). It was thought that he was referring to a planned spring offensive against al-Quaeda within Pakistan, to squeeze bin Laden between Pakistan and Afghanistan. This was trumped by a spring offensive against American troops in Iraq.

War does not eradicate terrorism. If the criterion for success is eradication, the war against terrorism has failed. Many feel that the Islamic militancy has gained in strength, judging by the bombings of relatively soft targets in Morocco, Kenya, Saudi Arabia, India, and Indonesia, and of course Iraq. Bush Jr. probably shared this view in private. In an abrupt reversal of policy in September 2003 he turned to the spurned and derided UN, seeking to extricate the US from its costly post-war plight. While the US was asking the UN to share the financial and human burden of reconstructing Iraq, Britain agreed to send 1,400 more troops. Britain agreed to send 3,000 more to support the new Iraqi government after June 30, 2004.

Robin Cook, former British Foreign Secretary and later leader of the House until he resigned because he disagreed with the Iraq War, had concluded at the Foreign Office that containment of Saddam was working. Was he right? Al-Qaeda had come through Afghanistan and its aftermath and had survived. But it was committed to reversing history, to destroying westernization, and restoring a seventh-century Islamic caliphate, the central idea of the Arab civilization. For al-Qaeda, the source of human perfection is strict adherence to Sharia law and religious war (*jihad*) against the West. Its Utopian perfectibility is a myth, but once the September-11 attacks had shattered the myth of Western invincibility and pre-eminence, perhaps the West was powerless to contain the traditional beliefs at the core of Arab civilization.

It looks as if the US is being pushed by the Syndicate into a series of conflicts across the globe to strengthen the US economy by seizing oil and to enable the Syndicate to fund a lot of missiles and a global defense shield. The world is turning into a network of oil pipelines, and Western policy is driven by a deceitful imperialism, snaffling oil under the guise of seeking terrorists and pre-emptive strikes.

Through Bush Jr. the US has played on "pan-Arabism" to create an atmosphere of fear, which it has then exploited by presenting the world with a choice between (a) a reign of global terror whose goal is the creation of a series of anti-Western fundamentalist Islamic nation-states; or (b) a war against terrorism followed by a reign of global peace.

The real pay-off is that the threats need to be perpetuated so that the world can be "protected" into world government. (In Orwell's *1984*, the Party's enemy Emmanuel Goldstein is displayed on public screens each day and all citizens have to express two minutes' hate, so that his threat can be perpetuated and the Party's "protection" reaffirmed. Bin Laden's role is not unlike Goldstein's.) The reign of global peace will be under a pro-Western New World Order – controlled by the Syndicate – that reaches into every continent, including darkest Africa.

13

THE UNITED STATES
OF AFRICA

There is always something new from Africa.

Pliny[1]

In early July 2003 it was announced that Bush Jr. had ordered the military to plan for a massive expansion of its presence in Africa to reinforce America's commercial interest in the continent's oil. The Pentagon wanted to set up bases in Algeria and Mali, strengthen ties with Morocco and Tunisia, and secure refueling agreements with Uganda and Senegal. There was already a US presence in Djibouti for counter-terrorist activities in the Horn of Africa. Such plans indicate the nature of the global agenda ahead.

In 2002, an African Union came into being after some 30 African heads of state had voted for it two years earlier. The inspirer of the African Union was Libya's Gaddafi,[2] who as Africa's longest surviving statesman – he had been in power since 1969 – seemed to have inherited Nelson Mandela's mantle as leader of Africa. Subsequent events in Libya must be seen against the background of an emerging United States of Africa.

Libya

The US policy in Africa received a boost when the oil-rich Libya (which has the seventh-largest oil reserves in the world), one of the new members of the "Axis of Evil," announced on December 19, 2003 that it would give up its nuclear and chemical weapons of mass destruction and permit UN weapons inspections. The first approach had been made in March at the time of the build-up to Anglo-American action in Iraq. Wanting to be accepted back in the international fold, Libya had admitted being responsible for the Lockerbie bombing and agreed to pay nearly £2b in compensation. Kusa Musa, head of Libya's External Security Organization, contacted the British Embassy in Tripoli to invite a team from the British SIS (MI6) to visit and see stocks of weapons of mass destruction and help dispose of them. In June Gaddafi made Dr. Shukri Ghanem, a pro-West ex-deputy secretary general of OPEC, his Prime Minister.

A team of CIA and MI6 inspectors went in October and again in December, and discovered that Libya was far more advanced in creating a nuclear program than had been realized, perhaps as a result of links with Iran and North Korea. At 10 sites with dual-purpose laboratories they found chemical weapons and bombs filled with chemicals, some 100 tonnes of mustard gas and nerve agents including sarin allegedly sold by North Korea, and attempts to create biological weapons with deadly toxins and viruses. Libya had been working with North Korea to develop Scud missiles.

Under the deal announced in December, Libya's missiles would be limited to 300k (186 miles) and would therefore not reach Israel. Libya would also supply intelligence on hundreds of al-Qaeda and other Islamic extremists. Libya would sign the non-proliferation treaty. Shukri Ganem said, "We are turning our swords into ploughshares, and this step should be appreciated and followed by all other countries." He no doubt meant "including Israel" which has 100–200 nuclear warheads.

This was a stunning decision on Libya's part. At first sight it seemed to be a result of Shock and Awe, and a vindication of the US's line on Iraq. It was said that Col. Gaddafi had watched what happened to Saddam and had realized he could be deposed just as easily. The decision raised the question, "If diplomacy could work on Libya, why had it not been made to work on Iraq?"

However, Gaddafi did not voluntarily opt to renounce his weapons, although that was the implication of the wording of his announcements in Libya, Britain, and the US. His hand had allegedly been forced by the interception of transport carrying banned weapons. The operation was carried out by the US-led Proliferation Security Initiative (PSI), which aimed to halt the spread of weapons of mass destruction by seizing them in transit. PSI, which had been proposed in May 2003 by Bush Jr. and launched in September, had "netted several seizures" of Libyan weapons of mass destruction by December, according to the US State Department. John Bolton US Undersecretary of State, said that since the lifting of UN sanctions in September, "Libya has been able to be more aggressive in pursuing weapons of mass destruction." Gaddafi's son revealed that Libya had bought plans to make a nuclear bomb from Pakistani scientists – notably the father of "the Islamic bomb," Dr. Khan – for $40m and other material from Malaysia and various Asian countries. Libya was closer to building a bomb than the UN believed but still had a long way to go.

In fact, Gaddafi had not given up what was being claimed. Mohammed El Baradei, head of the International Atomic Energy Agency (IAEA) visited Tripoli and said that Libya had a small uranium enrichment facility, which had already been abandoned, and was not close to building a nuclear weapon. Gadaffi had renounced something he was not close to having. The threat from Libya had been exaggerated by the US and the Syndicate to manipulate Western public opinion so that Gaddafi's renunciation of the threat would turn him from a "baddy" into a "goody."

Gaddafi had in fact sought his rapprochement for the lifting of UN and US sanctions before the war in Iraq. It had been revealed in August 2002, for example, that the UN had chosen Libya to chair the UN Commission on Human Rights, the body that condemned the US prison system for permitting capital punishment. (Poacher turned gamekeeper, indeed.) He was trying to buy his way out of international pariahdom and into the prospect of economic growth after 17 years of crippling sanctions. He would then be able to use his oil riches to advance the wealth of his backward people, and this would increase his chances of survival. In return the US would have access to his Middle-Eastern and African intelligence and the Syndicate would have renewed access to Libyan oil by peaceful means, and would be able to pursue Africa's oil without impediment from Libya. The US and Syndicate would be able to open up Africa. Gaddafi had been the main provider of oil to Zimbabwe, for instance, and a pro-Western oil-denying Gaddafi could force Mugabe to fall.

As a reward for siding with the Anglo-American West against al-Qaeda, the British Prime Minister Blair flew to Tripoli and shook Gaddafi's hand to welcome him back into the international fold.[3] Shell, which had been reported as going through a difficult time, stood to gain oil concessions, and agreed an initial $200m (potential $550m) gas exploration deal. France and Italy had already sunk $6b into a Western Desert gas export pipeline that would link Libya and Italy, and Libya's foreign minister claimed to have 180 more oil and gas contracts worth $30b to hand out. Gaddafi would now supply oil via Shell to keep the British and American economies running – in Britain's case, replacing North Sea oil. The consequence of the West's *rapprochement* with Libya was a gain in the West's oil and gas.

It was later revealed that in June and August 2003, Gaddafi had personally met an American Moslem activist, Abdurahman al-Amoudi, to discuss the killing of the *de facto* ruler of Saudi Arabia, Crown Prince Abdullah. Al-Amoudi had been discovered boarding a flight from London to Syria with $340,000 in a briefcase. He told British police the cash came from a Libyan charity. Held in remand in Virginia since September, al-Amoudi was trying to negotiate a lighter sentence. Was he telling the truth? And given Gaddafi's new importance, would it make any difference if he was?

Defenders of the second Iraq War now argued that it ended Libya's nuclear, biological, and chemical weapons program; brought Iran back under the control of the inspectors of the International Atomic Energy Agency; resulted in North Korea's talking to the US (for a while) about its weapons of mass destruction; ended the nuclear trade of Dr. Khan; and ensured that there was no repetition of the September-11 attacks on the West's cities. The reality was that the rehabilitation of Gaddafi made possible the Syndicate's dream of a United States of Africa. The task was to integrate within one African regional bloc all those countries whose oil had caused civil wars and UN interventions, and which were now emerging as major oil producers.

Congo/Burundi/Rwanda

The former Belgian Congo is immensely wealthy in mineral resources: coal, cobalt, copper, diamonds, germanium, gold, manganese, zinc, and uranium. (The mining town of Shinkolowe, which is now teeming with North Korean uranium miners, provided uranium for the Hiroshima bomb.) By 1960 these assets had attracted "Rockefellers'" attention. In June the Congo became independent under President Kasavubu and pro-Communist Prime Minister Lumumba, and was split into Congo (Kinshasa) and Congo (Brazzaville). In July Tshombe, pro-American

President of the Province of mineral-rich Katanga which possessed 50% of Congo's wealth, seceded from the Communist central government with support from Belgian mining interests rather than accept Wall Street control of Katanga. Belgian troops took Leopoldville airport. Kasavubu and Lumumba appealed for help.

The UN supported Kasavubu, the Soviet Union Lumumba. UN Secretary-General Dag Hammarskjöld sent troops and opposed Tshombe. Kasavubu staged an army *coup*, dismissed Lumumba, and later handed him over to Katangans, who murdered him in February 1961. A UN investigating commission found he had been killed by a Belgian mercenary in Tshombe's presence. US and Belgian involvement has been alleged.[4] The Soviet Union was outraged and demanded Kasavubu's resignation. In September 1961 Hammarskjöld was killed in a plane crash on his way to meet Tshombe and there was suspicion that the Russians had had him murdered in revenge for Lumumba's death.

The conflict between the UN and USSR had made the Congo even more volatile. "Rockefellers" and the Syndicate were on the side of the UN and Kasavubu and against Lumumba and were maneuvering to seize Katanga from Tshombe, but had links with the USSR which supported Lumumba and Tshombe. As in the case of Vietnam, the Syndicate backed one side but maintained a link with the other side to ensure it would achieve its aims no matter who won.

David Rockefeller moved in. At a series of Bilderberg meetings – for example the Bilderberg reunion in Burgenstock, Switzerland – Kissinger and David Rockefeller spoke of the need to dislodge Tshombe. Pressed by American officials, UN forces stationed in the Congo attacked Tshombe in January 1963 and drove him into exile. Shortly afterwards Chase Manhattan and Standard Oil of Indiana won a joint concession to take over the huge copper-mining complex at Tenke-Fungurume.

The Democratic Republic of the Congo (formerly Belgian Congo and then Zaire) is across the border from Rwanda and Burundi. It has produced oil since 1976. From 1890 to 1962 Rwanda and Burundi were one nation, Rwanda-Urundi, under the control of first Germany and then Belgium. Independence did nothing to reduce tension between the Tutsis and Hutus.

In 1990 fighting broke out in Uganda between the Tutsi-dominated Rwandan Patriotic Front (RPF), which was based in Uganda and supported by the US and Britain, and Hutu Rwandese, the Rwandan government supported by France. The UN were involved as observers. The Tutsis felt the UN was encouraging them to impose order in mineral-rich Burundi. A military *coup* there in October 1993, when Tutsi soldiers (led by the head of the army, who was later acquitted) overthrew and killed the Hutu President, led to rival massacres between Tutsis and Hutus and caused 800,000 refugees to flee to neighboring countries. The UN condemned the *coup* but remained detached, and mounted an emergency operation to save the refugees. In January 1994 Maj. Gen. Romeo Dallaire, the French-Canadian commander of a UN peacekeeping force in Rwanda, sent an urgent telegram to Kofi Annan, then head of peacekeeping in New York. The telegram was ignored.[5]

In April 1994 an aircraft carrying the Hutu President of Rwanda and the new Burundian President was shot down by a missile as it came in to land at Kigali, the Rwandan capital. According to a UN report commissioned by UN Secretary-General Boutros Boutros-Ghali in April 1994, three members of an "elite covert strike team" confirmed that the attack had been sanctioned by the leader of the Tutsi RPF to seize power and cancel power-sharing arrangements between Tutsis and Hutus. Three years later the UN report was suppressed. Rwandans maintained that the plane had been shot down by Hutu hardliners opposed to the government's attempts to settle with the RPF.

The deaths of the two Presidents triggered a bloodbath in which the Tutsi Prime Minister was killed by the Presidential Guard along with 10 Belgian UN soldiers. The Tutsi RPF forces marched on the capital and fought Hutu government troops, and the UN withdrew. In the ensuing war officially 800,000 were killed. There is a problem with the official figures in Rwanda[6] and the death toll for 1994 has also been put at a million.

A UN embargo on arms sales to Rwanda was imposed on May 17, 1994, five weeks after the genocide began, when soldiers of the Rwandan army and Hutu militia slaughtered Tutsis and moderate Hutus. In September 1994 the head of a UN team of four investigating the genocide, Karen Kenny, resigned, apparently because she felt she was not receiving support from the UN in Geneva, New York, and Rwanda itself.

A huge oilfield was discovered off the shores of the Democratic Republic of the Congo in 1998. The consortium operating offshore concessions includes Congo Gulf Oil (Chevron), 50%; and Union Oil of California

(Unocal), 18%.[7] The target for 2002 was 21,000 barrels per day.

1998 Congolese rebel forces led by ethnic Tutsi in east Congo who were backed with arms by Rwanda and Uganda attacked the forces of President Laurent Kabila, who had ousted Mobutu. The rebels gained most of the country but were driven back by Angolan, Namibian, and Zimbabwean troops called in by Kabila. In 1999 the Lusaka Accord was signed. In January 2001 Kabila was assassinated, allegedly by a bodyguard. He was succeeded by his son Joseph, who agreed to share power with Ugandan-backed rebels. In July the presidents of the Congo and Rwanda signed an accord, followed (in September) by Uganda. The civil war involving seven foreign armies and numerous rebel groups was over. In the Democratic Republic of the Congo's four-year civil war from 1998 to 2002 at least 2 million, possibly as many as 2.5 million were killed.[8] In 1997 the UN's refugee agency was ordered to leave, and the Congo military forced Rwandan refugees (Hutus) back across the border, killing many. In 2001 a further 80,000 died. In April 2003 there were more massacres and several hundred, perhaps a thousand died according to UN staff.

In 2004 Rwanda's President Kagame told a rally marking the tenth anniversary of the genocide that France had trained and armed the Hutu perpetrators, in the full knowledge that they were intent on committing genocide. The French Junior Foreign Minister Renard Muselier, who attended the rally, cut short his visit and flew home in protest at the allegation, which Paris strongly denied, claiming that the French military had prevented a total genocide.

In all 3 million are thought to have died in the Congo's Great Lakes region (on Rwanda's and Burundi's western borders) since the 1994 conflict. The problem in quantifying the numbers killed in massacres is obvious: no one can have precise knowledge. On another view, the total number thought to have died is 4 million. This is not far short of the 5 million Jews thought to have been killed under Hitler.

It is hard to disentangle what happened in a region where life is notoriously cheap but at the root of the massacres a pattern can be found: arms sales, a green light, failure by the UN, a cull of the population, and US control of the Congo's oil. From being Conrad's "heart of darkness" the Congo has progressed to being an oil-rich state (the fourth largest producer of oil in sub-Saharan Africa) in the growing United States of Africa.

Somalia /Liberia/Sierra Leone

Other potentially oil-rich states have been pacified into the new regional bloc. As usual, oil was at the bottom of their civil wars and Western interventions. According to documents obtained by *The Times*, nearly two-thirds of Somalia was allocated to the American oil giants, Conoco, Amoco, Chevron, and Phillips[9] before civil war broke out in 1988 and the Marxist President Mohammed Siad Barre was overthrown in a popular revolt in January 1991 (*Los Angeles Times*, January 18, 1993). Their interest went back to the mid-1980s when geologists found that Yemeni oil reserves arced into and across northern Somalia. In April 1986 Bush Sr. officially dedicated a new $18m refinery near the Yemeni town of Marib.[10]

After the overthrow of the president, the country was plunged into turmoil and to "safeguard humanitarian shipments of aid" 20,000 US troops went in during late 1992 and protected the substantially "Rockefellerite" oil companies' investments there. In the civil war between 1991 and 1993 400,000 died.

Oil exploration has since resumed, the companies involved being the US Chevron, French TotalFinaElf, and UK Seminole Copenhagen Group.[11] There will be an announcement in due course that the region has been pacified and the US corporations' position will be strengthened following the intervention of US government troops.

As much as 15% of America's imported oil now comes from West Africa, about the same amount as is imported from Saudi Arabia. The key area there is the Gulf of Guinea, where vast oil reserves have been discovered which could result in a 25% increase in US oil imports from Africa. Nigeria, home to a quarter of all people living in sub-Saharan Africa, has one of the world's largest oil reserves.[12] It has had a long civil war and Chevron-Texaco and Shell are now installed in the pacified country and exporting oil. So is Ivory Coast, which is in the middle of a civil war. Nearby Liberia and Sierra Leone are good jumping-off places for the US Syndicate operation to control this region, and the US can benefit from a presence in both countries. Both have been plunged into civil war.

Liberia's civil war began when President Samuel Doe was ousted in 1989 and assassinated in 1990. The US-educated Charles Taylor, leader of the rebellion against him, was entrammeled in an inconclusive civil war until 1995, and though he was eventually elected president in 1997 he faced armed opposition from 1999 and was forced into exile in 2003. According to the Liberian Embassy 150,000 were killed, although other estimates suggest 100,000.

Sierra Leone's own oil has been shrouded in mystery. Tennessee (Sierra Leone) Inc. arrived to start a marine seismic survey for oil in 1962, according to the chief inspector of mines' report of May 25, 1963. The Sierra Leone oil refinery was opened in 1970 as a joint venture between the government and BP, Mobil, Texaco, Shell, and Agip.[13] In 1980 it was rumored that Prime Minister (later President) Siaka Stevens invited BP to investigate the possibility of new oil deposits. In 1982 he gave the go-ahead for more prospecting. The oil operation in Sierra Leone has been very secret. Civil war broke out in 1991, since when at least 50,000 have been killed. Some estimates reckon 100,000. In May 2000 1,000 British troops intervened to help the evacuation of foreign nationals but stayed on to assist the UN operation and train government forces.[14] They captured the rebel leader Foday Sankoh and forced his Revolutionary United Front (RUF) to retreat. American troops moved in via Nigeria in August 2000.

Somalia, Sierra Leone, and Liberia do not feature in the Table of World Production of Crude Oil (see page 334), but Nigeria is the seventh largest world oil net exporter and the civil wars in all three countries can be seen as part of a pacification program to secure the oil reserves in the Gulf of Aden and in Nigeria and the Gulf of Guinea.[15]

If you reflect that I have examined just a few of the oil states that will form the coming United States of Africa – we have not touched on the potentially oil-rich Angola and Namibia – then it is obvious why the US government, led by the Syndicate, is moving in on Africa – and why they both need Gaddafi, "inspirer" (with Syndicate encouragement?) of the African Union, to coordinate the political structure of an oil-rich United States of Africa, which is a vital region in their wished-for world government.

14

THE SYNDICATE TODAY

*The simple step of a courageous individual is not to take part
in the lie. One word of truth outweighs the world.*
Alexander Solzhenitsyn's Nobel Prize Speech

The Balance of Power within the Syndicate

How close are we to world government? The answer to this question may
lie in the nature of the balance of power between the Rothschilds and
Rockefellers.

Historical Tussle

While they steered the world toward world government, "Rothschilds"
encouraged "Rockefellers" to act as an agent of change, a catalyst.

It may be that "Rothschilds," who created the Syndicate to take America
over,[1] set up the Federal Reserve to return America to the British Empire
so that it could more easily be controlled. If so, then "Rockefellers" did a
reverse take-over and tried to run Britain through Germany (their native
country): first by manipulating the Kaiser during the First World War until
they put their energies into carrying out the Soviet revolution through
Lenin; then by manipulating Hitler during the Second World War; then
by manipulating Stalin and his successors into reunifying Germany; and
finally by intriguing a German-centered United States of Europe under
which Britain is about to be subsumed.

"Rockefellers" wanted a German-centered Europe. The Rothschilds, on
the other hand, were German Jews from Frankfurt who were mistreated

235

by Hitler along with all other Jews during the Second World War. The Rothschilds were anti-Hitler and pro-Jew, whereas "Rockefellers," though far from being anti-Jew, were pro-German: they wanted to restore the Thousand-Year Reich in Germany. Hence the reunification of Germany and their insistence that the central bank of Europe should be at Frankfurt. Their ambition to rule the world from Germany brought them into conflict with the anti-German Rothschilds and into a battle for the world's oilfields.

Readers who have the conventional account of recent history firmly in mind – that the nation-state of Germany has sought to dominate and rule Europe (or even the rest of the world) and has attempted to do this through the Franco-Prussian War, two World Wars, and Germany's dominant position in the EU – will naturally see "an ambition to rule the world from Germany" as another example of "*Deutschland über Alles,*" for which they will blame "the Germans," and not those exploiting them and their nation-state to achieve their own ends. Similar blame may be laid at the door of "the Americans" and "the British" following their foreign adventures in Afghanistan and Iraq. It may be that the creation of "enemies" and "hate figures" is a deliberate ploy exploited by the Syndicate to divert people's attention away from their own behind-the-scenes activities. The recent conflict between Britain and France may be seen in this light. Grasping this involves realizing that the apparently democratically elected governments of nation-states are little more than fronts/puppets whose strings are pulled by the Syndicate, while their citizens are possibly regarded as little more than "factory-workers" in an industry whose output is geared towards the establishment of a world government.

In 1945 "Rothschilds" wanted a United States of Europe and a United States of the World, and used their influence as the world's bankers on Churchill and (through "Rockefellers") Roosevelt and Stalin to set the post-war world on a globalist course at Yalta and Potsdam. So Churchill, a "Rothschild" nominee (through Baruch)[2] and recipient of "Rothschild" money in 1938, spoke out at Zurich in favor of a United States of Europe in 1946. As a follower of Coudenhove-Kalergi's *Pan Europa,* he had written an essay entitled "The United States of Europe" in 1930, but in this instance he was speaking for "Rothschilds," not the British Conservative Party which has sought to play down this speech ever since.

"Rothschilds" (in conjunction with the early "Rockefeller"-funded CFR and Monnet) took steps to create a common market in Europe as a half-way house to a United States of Europe. They had seen before the end of the Second World War that the European Empires had become a drain on the European powers, which could no longer sustain them. The Suez *débâcle*, the watershed of the British and French Empires, was a signal to the colonies that Britain could not defend them and that they could have their independence without a fight.

"Rockefellers" pressed on towards a communized European Union with Frankfurt replacing London as the world's financial center. Through their links (originally via Schiff and Col. House) with the Grand Orient they had links with Gorbachev in Russia and Mitterand in France (both of whom belonged to the Grand Orient).

Meanwhile the City – London, the center of "Rothschilds"' activities – prospered. Whoever was British Prime Minister had to be at least partly a "Rothschildite." Edward Heath understood this when he put Victor, Lord Rothschild in charge of his think-tank. Some Prime Ministers were pro-Europe (like Heath), while some were pro-Britain (like Margaret Thatcher), and different emphases suited the Syndicate at different times. It seems that "Rothschilds," the bank manager of governments, to whom the American and most European governments are in debt, ordered the British government to advance "Rockefellers"' United States of Europe, in the principle of which (currency details aside) they believed. The British government duly ratified the Maastricht Treaty.

Blair

But then something went wrong around the time of Blair's arrival in 1997. There were clearly misgivings about the sale of Bank of England gold, which was transferred to Frankfurt. "Rothschilds" pulled away from Europe and resolved to keep London out of it and out of the single currency, in order to preserve the status quo on eurobonds. The pro-English "Rothschildite" British Chancellor Gordon Brown, who had handed control of interest rates to the "Rothschild"-controlled Bank of England on his arrival in office in May 1997, announced in *The Times* on October 18, 1997 that Britain would not enter the single currency during the lifetime of that parliament. It has since been revealed that Prime Minister Blair was not aware that this policy announcement would be made, even though it bound him.

The London Stock Exchange, a limited company within "Rothschilds" sphere of influence, later told the Frankfurt stock exchange Deutsche Börse that it was not interested in an amalgamation, which would have seen "Rockefellers" wrest control of the financial center of Europe from "Rothschilds." It may be that "Rothschilds" detected that "Rockefellers" were making an onslaught on North Sea oil by breaking up the UK, and they may have gone slow on Europeanization to retain North Sea oil, which has been vital to their Shell interests. The Europhile Tony Blair has had to live with the contradiction of their blowing hot and cold on Europe.

Bilderberg Meetings

1999[3]

The Bilderberg meeting of June 1999 was held at Caesar Park Hotel, Penha Longa, Portugal and attended by David Rockefeller and Henry Kissinger. Its minutes were leaked in the British sub-culture magazine *The Big Issue* (though hardly an authoritative source) of November 15–21, 1999. They purport to reveal that the Bilderberg Group was advised after Kosovo that NATO has given Russia *carte blanche* to bomb Chechnya. They reveal that NATO is now operating in an environment in which international law has become obsolete, and is in danger of mimicking a colonial power such as the Ottoman and Habsburg Empires in creating a permanent protectorate, Kissinger is reported to have said. He pessimistically described Kosovo as "this generation's Vietnam" as troops could be there for 25 years. Britain's Peter Mandelson is reported to have said that NATO can be either an enforcer in an ethnocentric Europe, or the agent for the world's cooperating Great Powers.

Dollarization (with the US controlling the world's monetary policy) was raised as the next step after the single European currency; in other words, the world is to move towards a world currency of a world dollar. According to the report, the Bilderberg minutes also revealed that in Britain it would be easier for welfare cuts to be made by socialists rather than by Conservatives. Britain's Prime Minister Tony Blair attended the Bilderberg meeting near Athens in 1993, and the report suggested that it would be easier for (nominally) socialist New Labour, who are "consolidating the victories of the Right," to implement the cuts as "it might be easier for somebody who claimed to be a socialist to impose change." If the Bilderberg meetings are the backdrop against which policy is made worldwide, and if secret policy groups work on what has been discussed in the more open, talk-based Bilderberg meetings and arrange for them to be implemented as government policy within each nation-state, then from these leaks – if they are accurate – we can gauge the Syndicate's thinking about world population at this present time.

2000

The 2000 Bilderberg meeting for a reduced number of delegates (the so-called "steering committee") was held near Brussels at the Château du Lac. Having attacked the illegal NATO bombing of Serbia in the House of Lords when Kissinger supported it, Lord Carrington had either retired or been retired as Chairman of the Bilderberg Group. Martin Taylor (advisor to Goldman Sachs, the largest investment bank in the world, along with Romano Prodi, President of the EU Commission) acted as Honorary Secretary-General.

According to reports in that part of the press that feels able to discuss such matters, during their meeting Bilderberg communicated with President Clinton, who was 50 miles away in Aachen receiving the Charlemagne Prize for his contribution to creating the United States of Europe. In his speech he urged the EU to write a new Charter or constitution (see page 92). At the same time, "the Convention" (62 men) were preparing a new Charter for the EU (which was adopted in Nice in December 2000) that turns the EU into a single super-state with an American-style President and Cabinet as well as a European Parliament and Court. It is alleged that Clinton dropped in on Bilderberg in "private time." This Bilderberg–Clinton initiative was intended to consolidate a key region within the coming United States of the World.

From the press reports it seems that oil had again become a Bilderberg weapon to squeeze the West into deflation and reduce Western aid to the Third World. OPEC was again delivering "Rockefellerite" policy. Between 1999 and 2000 the price of oil trebled from $10 per barrel to more than $35. This price rise had been effected by the Venezuelan President Hugo Chavez, who has influenced OPEC. He has argued that the West should pay more to the developing nations for its oil, and toured Iraq and Libya to lobby for support for reducing oil production so as to increase prices. Chavez's oil minister, Ali Rodriguez, was then President of OPEC. In

2001, however, the price of oil fell in spite of the US military action in Afghanistan and OPEC's attempts to raise it. At the end of 2001 OPEC cut the worldwide production of oil by 1.5 million barrels a day and pump prices began to rise. As in the 1970s will the rising price of oil plunge the West into recession while further enriching "Rockefellers" and "Rothschilds," and demonstrate that talk of a computer-led (i.e. Bill-Gates-led) new era in the world economy is over-optimistic? World deflation as a result of rising oil prices can only assist depopulation in the Third World.

2001

The 2001 Bilderberg meeting was held in Stenungsund in Sweden in May. The American newspaper *The Spotlight,* reported that the Bilderberg Group was determined that the Western hemisphere (see pages 43–6) should become a single economic and political entity like the EU, whose member states have already surrendered most of their own sovereignty. In the 10.30 a.m. slot on May 26 Richard Perle spoke on "European Security, Defense Identity, and Transatlantic Security," while in the 4.15 slot Kissinger spoke on "the Rise of China, its Impact on Asia and the World."

2002

The 2002 Bilderberg meeting held at the Westfields luxury hotel in Chantilly, Virginia on May 30–June 2 pressed for a "UN Financial Action Task Force" to promote a global levy, a world tax by stealth. It is perceived that a UN tax on all people on earth would be met by outrage, and so the Bilderberg Group is considering a 10%-per-barrel tax on oil at the wellhead, a surcharge on international travel by air and sea, and a charge for cross-border financial transactions. It also wants tax harmonization between Europe, America, and elsewhere so that high-tax countries can compete with low-tax nations for foreign investment. The tax rate in the US and other low-tax countries would rise to Sweden's high-tax 42% level. At the same time – and there is linkage – it is calling for the "transparency" of all bank accounts and credit cards to a UN agency – which means that a Bilderberg-controlled UN agency would be able to access all bank accounts and credit card transactions, thus eliminating financial privacy for all people on earth.

It now seems that the 2002 Bilderberg meeting was perhaps the most divisive ever. The American and European delegates did retain their common goal of creating a world government in which the international élite will dominate, but European Union delegates were angry that Bush has protected the US steel industry from overseas dumping and that agricultural subsidies have increased. They were angry that the US has rejected the International Criminal Court and the Kyoto Treaty on global climate control, and that American foreign policy is so pro-Israel. America's long-planned attack on Iraq was delayed until 2003 in the face of opposition from European leaders.

It was reported in *Portman Papers* (July 2001) that some Bilderbergers (a minority faction) are more interested in corporate governance than in world governance. To this faction, financial and business interests are paramount and if the financial costs of the EU prove too high and the loss of nations' sovereignty too great, then Britain should leave the EU and join the North American Free Trade Agreement (NAFTA).

2003

The 2003 Bilderberg meeting was held from May 15 to 18 in the Trianon Palace Hotel in Versailles (the French Rothschilds' home territory). The hotel was sealed off with armed guards and all employees were told to see and hear nothing under penalty of being fired and blacklisted. As part of the security, bewildered residents' cars were towed away without warning. The hotel, where the Treaty of Versailles was handed to the defeated Germans, is adjacent to the park or grounds attached to the château or palace of Versailles, to which there is normally free access. The entry to the hotel is near the Grille de la Reine, a gate to this palace park. The entrance to this park at the Grille de la Reine, through which the people of Versailles are normally allowed to pass, was closed without explanation.

Those attending of course included David Rockefeller (listed as representing J. P. Morgan International Council), but there was no member of the Rothschild family present. Giscard d'Estaing was present, along with Paul Wolfowitz, Richard Perle, and John Bolton (US Under-Secretary of State for Arms Control and International Security) from the US. The UK attendees included Peter Sutherland (Chairman and Managing Director of Goldman Sachs International and Chairman of BP), Martin Taylor (Hon. Secretary-General and International Advisor, Goldman Sachs International), Ed Balls (Chief Economic Advisor to the Treasury), Mervyn King (Governor of the Bank of England, who would be affected by the adoption of the euro), Philip Gould (Public Relations Advisor to Blair), and Kenneth Clarke (the former Chancellor). Royals included Queen Beatrix of the Netherlands, the Queen of Spain, and Prince Philippe (Crown Prince of Belgium).

Jacques Chirac, the French President, delivered a welcoming speech designed to calm tensions. He pointed out that Americans and West Europeans are traditional allies. At the 2002 Bilderberg meeting Europeans extracted a promise from Rumsfeld not to invade Iraq in 2002. Now some Europeans asked tauntingly, "Where are all these weapons of mass destruction?" And of US plans to control Iraq's oil for the "benefit" of the Iraqi people, "Who are the 'other' beneficiaries?" On the agenda was the plight of Bilderberg-connected companies based in France and Germany that had lucrative contracts supplying arms to Saddam's Iraq, contracts that had now lost most of their value.

Emotions ran even higher on the Middle East peace plan. Sharon had just dismissed dismantling Israeli settlements in Palestine as "not on the horizon," and in the *Jerusalem Post* ridiculed any idea that in consequence US aid might be reduced. (US aid to Israel is normally $10b a year. In 2003 Israel demanded $12b because there was less tourism and the economy was depressed.) One European told a grim-faced American, "You are too stupid to know when you've been insulted by a moral midget." The will of Bilderberg prevailed and within three weeks Sharon was publicly promising at Aqaba to dismantle the settlements – after being threatened with monetary punishments and with having to give up land Israel acquired in the 1967 war. It is unprecedented for a US president to come under such hostile Bilderberg fire.

An independent UN army was also discussed. Some wanted it controlled by NATO, others (excluding the Secretary-General of NATO, George Robertson) wanted a separate EU force in addition. Europeans urged Britain to embrace the euro on June 9, but it was accepted that the British people were opposed and that it would be politically dangerous for Blair to do this without a referendum.

Also on the agenda was the expansion of the EU to include Russia and all the former Soviet republics (see pages 106–7, 117) – a prelude to the EU–Russian summit on May 31 in St Petersburg, where the city's 300th anniversary celebrations were attended by Bush. At a meeting in Yalta with the Ukrainian President, Putin called for a common market linking the

EU with Russia, Ukraine, Kazakhstan, and Belarus by September 2003. The prospect therefore was that over half the enlarged EU would comprise former Soviet territories – all under the new European constitution and funded by taxation across this Greater Europe. Europe would also control oil in the former Soviet territories.

The Council on Foreign Relations acts as the propaganda ministry of the shadow world government, and within months produces scholarly papers on the causes discussed at the annual May/June Bilderberg meetings. It is a measure of the extent to which Bilderberg meetings determine shadow world government policy that Sharon could be prevailed upon to announce a reversal of Israeli policy towards the settlements. The 2003 Bilderberg meeting effected a U-turn in Israel's policy. It can therefore confidently be expected that all the Bilderberg recommendations will be implemented.

The Bilderbergers did, however, receive a setback when Donald Rumsfeld later announced that the US would not be paying an expected 22% of the $342.4m cost of a new "futuristic" NATO headquarters building in Brussels so long as Belgium claimed worldwide jurisdiction to try anyone for "war crimes" committed anywhere. (Lawsuits under Belgian law have been brought against Gen. Tommy Franks, President Bush Sr., Colin Powell, and Gen. Norman Schwarzkopf for their activities in the first Iraq War. All could be arrested if they set foot in Belgium.) At the same time the UN was forced to extend immunity from the International Criminal Court (ICC) at The Hague to US troops serving on UN-sponsored overseas "peace missions." Meanwhile, British Prime Minister Blair, who had endorsed the ICC at The Hague, found himself facing "war crimes" charges brought by the Greek Bar Association for his support of the US-led invasion of Iraq. It was widely felt that if Blair were convicted President Bush Jr. may be next. If Blair were to ignore this criminal prosecution, he would have difficulty in traveling to countries that might hand him over to the court – including Belgium, the seat of the new European Union of which he onced hoped to be President. It looked as if Blair's European ambitions would be dogged by Iraq.

2004

The 2004, 50th-anniversary Bilderberg meeting was held at the Grand Hotel des Iles Borromees on the lakefront of Stresa, Italy on 3-6 June, and focused on European-American relations. Britain was harshly criticized for supporting the invasion of Iraq and for failing to embrace the euro, despite Blair's promise to do so at the 1998 Bilderberg meeting at Turnberry, Scotland. There was annoyance at the British clamour to leave the EU. The US was criticized because its foreign aid was a smaller percentage of GDP than that of other nations. Europeans tried to dissuade the US from reducing American troops in Germany. For the third Bilderberg meeting running, congeniality gave way to recriminations, accusations and divisions. However, all agreed that the UN role in regulating global relations should be strengthened.

It was decided that British élites should be urged to press on with full membership of the European Union, despite growing opposition. It was decided that the Free Trade Area of the Americas should be enacted and include the entire Western hemisphere except for Cuba, which would join on Castro's departure. It should evolve into "the American Union," a replica of the European Union. It was decided that an "Asian-Pacific Union" should emerge as the third super-state. The world would be split into three super-states – the American, European and Asian-Pacific Unions – for the convenience of banking and corporate élites, and the US should facilitate these global trade pacts. It was decided that there would be three global currencies: the dollar for the American Union, the euro for the European Union, and another for the Asian-Pacific Union. All these would of course eventually merge into a world-dollar, and the three Unions would eventually merge into one United States of the World that would mirror the United States of America. It was decided that as a means of imposing a UN tax on all the world's citizens there should be a tax on oil at the wellhead (ie on cars, buses and planes), and a tax on international financial transactions – which would suit both "Rockefellers" and "Rothschilds." As regards Iraq, the Europeans were indignant that Iraq had been invaded without the UN's blessing, and Rumsfeld sent a message promising that US troops would behave more defensively and less provocatively now. Rumsfeld was represented by Douglas Feith (his undersecretary for policy) and William Luti (deputy undersecretary for Near Eastern and South Asian affairs). Richard Perle, one of the advocates of war in Iraq, and Robert Kagan, both of PNAC, were present. Henry Kissinger was present along with David Rockefeller (listed as Member, J P Morgan International Council, and Chairman of the Council of Americas). Martin Taylor was once again Honorary Secretary-General. The Honorary Chairman was Etienne Davignon (Vice-Chairman,

Suez-Tractebel). It was suggested that President Bush, who was in Rome
on June 4, would drop in on June 5. The conference ended with a ferry ride
to a luxury island on Lake Maggiore.

The Succession

In September 2002 Sir Evelyn de Rothschild, head of the British arm of the
Rothschild banking dynasty who then chaired N. M. Rothschild & Sons, its
merchant bank, was revealed in the British press as donating £250,000 to
Policy Network Foundation, a charity set up by a group of young Blairites
in 2000, a "super think-tank" that has some of 10 Downing Street's
senior policy advisors (Andrew Adonis, Roger Liddle, Lord Levy, and Adair
Turner) on its board and is chaired by Peter Mandelson. Mandelson was
a guest at de Rothschild's remarriage and was flown to Albania, where de
Rothschild and Lord Sainsbury were taking steps to preserve the city of
Butrint, a world heritage site. In June 2002 de Rothschild attended Policy
Network's "progressive" leaders' conference at Brocket Hall, Hertfordshire
along with Clinton and Blair, and in the evening the gathering moved to
de Rothschild's Ascott House, Buckinghamshire for a seated banquet for
100. It is clear that "Rothschilds" are in a good position to influence the
British government behind the scenes.

Blair has furthered the "Rothschildite"-Bilderberg vision of the world
by working for world unity through appeasement. Blair's role as an
appeaser has required him to surrender Northern Ireland to the IRA; the
Straits of Gibraltar to Spain; an independent British foreign policy (over
Afghanistan and Iraq) to America; and Britain to Europe. He has obscured
his appeaser's role by wrapping himself in the Union Jack, by assuming
an image of toughness towards Kosovo, Afghanistan, and Iraq. Blair has
been a good "Rothschilds' man." It looks as if "Rockefellerites" have a plan
to unite the whole Western hemisphere, and as if "Rothschilds" are going
along with it while seeking to protect their British financial and business
interests. However we regard the Rothschilds in the past, it is clear that
their empire is now crumbling. Gone are the days when Baron Edmond
Rothschild of the Paris Rothschilds, who died in 1997, shared power
behind the Bilderberg Group with David Rockefeller.

There have been problems with the "Rothschildian" succession.
Amschel Rothschild, son of Victor, Lord Rothschild (and Evelyn's heir to

the British "Rothschild" fortune after David, first in the line of succession) was found strangled. He was kneeling under a flimsy towel-rail with a dressing-gown girdle round his neck in his Paris hotel suite in July 1996 after a meeting to discuss merging "Rothschilds"' international asset management operations. After initial reports that he had committed suicide there was soon speculation that he had in fact been murdered. He was reported to have been laundering the £500b illegally sent to Europe each year by Russia's central bank since 1991, and he had taken over from Robert Maxwell the task of bribing Soviet officials to send Soviet archives on Zionist agents to Israel. (Maxwell was a prominent "Rothschildite" who acted as go-between for Israel, who honored him by burying him in Jerusalem's most prestigious cemetery after his mysterious drowning.) The supply of discounted money from the Bank of England to the British banks has always been the Rothschilds' preserve. Now, at the beginning of the twenty-first century, the right to issue discounted money has been awarded outside the Rothschild family to a new name. This is a measure of the difficulties caused by the problem of the "Rothschildian" succession.

In February 2003 it was announced that Sir Evelyn de Rothschild would be replaced as head of N. M. Rothschild by his distant French cousin, Baron David de Rothschild, in a deal thought to bring Sir Evelyn (who would continue as non-executive chairman) some £300m. A consequence of the death of Amschel has thus been that the London-based Rothschild bank has passed to the French branch of the Rothschild family. In July it was announced that David, then 60, would take control of the whole family-held business. A new company, Concordia BV, domiciled in the Netherlands, would hold the controlling interest in Rothschild Continuation Holdings, the Swiss company thought to be worth around £560m and which is the parent of most companies bearing the Rothschild name (including N. M. Rothschild). It was announced that David de Rothschild would run the business from Paris but spend more time in London; his appointment would bind the English and French families more closely. Has David replaced Sir Evelyn as the current Rothschild "King"?[4]

The Rulers Today

Today "Rothschilds" remain the capstone of the Masonic pyramid.[5] But the position appears confused because "Rothschilds" are behind both sides of another division in English politics: the pro-Europeans like Ted Heath (who put Victor, Lord Rothschild in charge of his think-tank) and John Major (deliverer of the Maastricht Treaty); and the anti-Europeans like John Redwood and Norman Lamont, who both worked for "Rothschilds." Both sides have their uses at different times.

"Rockefellers" would like to be supreme in their partnership with "Rothschilds" in the Syndicate, in Bilderberg, and in the proposed world government,[6] but they have had no political empire and so have had to create revolutions to secure a world oil empire, using proxies. "Rothschilds" do not want to alienate "Rockefellers" as they need the American economy to work well in view of their investment in both the American and English central banks.

To quantify the respective wealth of "Rockefellers" and "Rothschilds" today is probably impossible. There are networks of tangled front companies worth trillions. It may be fair to say that "Rothschilds" (inheritors of the largest estate the world has ever known, which may still require 300 top people to manage it in the political arena)[7] have more money, "Rockefellers" more power and influence. The two share power in the Bilderberg Group and other such bodies, as we have seen, and despite their rivalry and different emphases are still a formidable combination.

But if the nineteenth century belonged to "Rothschilds," the twentieth century has belonged to "Rockefellers." Ian Fleming, who was no. 2 in British Intelligence, portrayed the main Rockefeller of his time as "Goldfinger." Goldfinger was opposed by a "Rothschildite" spy – "Rothschilds" are reputed to control MI6 – codenamed "007." (Fleming derived his character's codename from the two eyes and ear – 007 – in a pattern on a dress worn by Elizabeth I in a portrait in Hatfield House, which symbolized the intelligence service of Lord Burleigh, Walsingham and Heneage.)[8] The Rothschilds of the European civilization are still present as a huge force and control the British and (to some extent) American central banks, and the Federal Reserve System (once their exclusive domain), to which the American government is in debt to the staggering figure (in 2004) of $7.5 trillion.[9] But the Rockefellers, operating within the American civilization are the thrusting organizers of revolutions. They have the energy, and their wealth is more concrete, consisting of natural resources rather than paper or figures on computer screens. It may even be that they are now the major power in the Federal Reserve System, as according to Standard and

Poor (leading market analysts) 53% of the shares in the Federal Reserve System (and 22% of the shares in the influential Federal Reserve Bank of New York) are owned by the "Rockefeller" banking group.[10] But as ownership of the Federal Reserve central banks is secret there are many different views.[11] It is likely that Rockefellers now dominate the Federal Reserve System and that it is Rockefellers, not Rothschilds on whom they used to be financially dependent, who in theory have the power to force cutbacks and loan repayments, bankrupt the United States and compel the US President to pull out US troops from all round the world.

"Rothschilds," historically the richer of the two, went along with "Rockefellers"' drive for world government and backed the status quo. "Rockefellers," on the other hand, knew the new order would be a universal republic and that they would have more control over shaping governments and world events. "Rockefellers" have a higher profile in the media, and there are tensions as they emphasize their own agenda in their own sphere of influence. Both need each other to bring in the world government that has driven their actions for the last 130 years. Both "Rothschilds" and "Rockefellers" have to stay together to survive.

The balance of power between "Rothschilds" and "Rockefellers" is such that one faction is always pulling against the other in a never-ending tug-of-war in which we, the citizens of the world, are the rope on which they are pulling.

The vastness of US indebtedness to the Central Bank is mind-boggling. The figures need to be taken in. In 1918 this debt was $1 billion; in 1974 it was $1 trillion; and by 1984 it was over $4 trillion. The amount owed by the US government to the Federal Reserve System/the Syndicate is now correspondingly larger. The so-called "debt-ceiling" (the limit to the amount of debt the Treasury can carry under federal law) of $6.43 trillion was reached, and in June 2003 Congress raised it by a further $984b to $7.414 trillion. There is a view that the true figure was $14 trillion. This is now $15 trillion. If the lower figure is taken as true, America is broke, with a debt of around $7,500b.[12]

Net liabilities to the rest of the world are more than $2.3 trillion,[13] nearly 30% of GDP. Capital flooded into America in the 1990s when it had the reputation for being the world's richest country, while financial crises rocked Russia, Asia, and Latin America. This left Americans living off the rest of the world's savings – and being the world's largest debtor. At the end of 2001 foreign investors owned $9.2 trillion of US assets while US investors owned $6.9 trillion worth of the equivalent foreign assets, leaving a net debt to the rest of the world of $2.3 trillion.

America imports more than it exports, and the gap between foreign earnings and foreign spending is 5% of GDP, a trend that has lasted for 25 years. And this is at a time when the US federal government budget has never been higher: President Bush's budget proposal for the fiscal year 2003 was a staggering $2.128 trillion, over a third of the huge national debt. (In 2003 New York was facing a deficit of $6.4b, and California $21b.)

At the same time, President Bush has authorized a huge increase in the Pentagon's budget which would see US defense spending increase from $382.2b (2003) to $399b (2004) and more than $500b by 2010.[14] According to Stephen Kosiak, US director of budget studies at the Center for Strategic and Budgetary Assessment, "We've come to the point where we're spending more money than we spent during the Cold War. Whether this is sustainable over the next six years is questionable."

We saw in the opening pages of this book that whoever controls the Federal Reserve Bank of New York controls the whole Federal Reserve System, which makes loans to commercial banks, controls their reserve accounts, and controls the supply of paper currency in the USA. A large part of America's $7,500b indebtedness is to "Rockefellers," who have nearly a quarter of the Federal Reserve Bank of New York stock and more than half of all Federal Reserve stock. "Rockefellers" (and to a lesser extent "Rothschilds") can bankrupt the US at any time if it suits the Syndicate to turn the USA into regions of the United States of the World.

The Syndicate has clearly used (and continues to use) its powerful position as the US's chief creditor (and its subsequent ability to bankrupt the US at any time) to serve its own ends by forcing the US to follow Syndicate policies. The inference of this is that the Syndicate is using the US, its allies, and other nation-states, as tools to arrive at a US which is a world government in all but name. If it then makes the US bankrupt, the world economy will collapse and the Syndicate could emerge from the shadows to establish its own world government.

However, in the world of the Syndicate where the chess master plays for both sides, appearances can be deceptive. It is now clear that the Rothschilds have cemented their alliance with the Clintons and seem more influential than ever. In July 2003, Lynn Forester de Rothschild (the new wife of Sir Evelyn, who was present) threw a party at the Orangery, Kensington Palace for Hillary and Bill Clinton, to promote Hillary's book *Living History*. Peter Mandelson was of course present, along with Labour Minister and ex-Communist John Reid, Tory MP Nicholas Soames (Churchill's grandson), spin-doctor Alastair Campbell, and Sir Ronald Dearlove, the retiring Director of MI6. Mrs. Clinton (who in her speech referred to "President Blair") is generally acknowledged to be the "Rothschilds"' candidate for President in 2008. Meanwhile, there was press speculation that Condoleezza Rice, Bush Jr.'s national security advisor, would like to run for the White House in 2012. If she were to win, she could perhaps replace Hillary Clinton and be the incumbent in 2016, the date set for the USA to be subsumed under a world government.[15]

In late July 2003 it was revealed that Lynn Forester, now Lady de Rothschild, the wife of Sir Evelyn, had volunteered to be fundraiser for the British Labour Party's General Election campaign, which was expected to be in 2005. She had been one of the US Democrats' most successful fundraisers and had paid for, and organized, all President Clinton's Third Way conferences. (She had made over $100m by selling two communications companies she had started.) She and Sir Evelyn spent their wedding night in Clinton's White House in 2000. It was also revealed that Blair would fight the next election committed to serve as Prime Minister for a full third term, according to his friend, the new Lord Chancellor, Lord Falconer. It was not clear where this intention left the plan for Blair to become President of Europe; perhaps that had now been abandoned. It was also revealed that "Rothschildite" Peter Mandelson, Alastair Campbell, and Philip Gould would form a new "kitchen cabinet" to advise Blair on his General Election strategy. In September 2003 it was announced that Mandelson was already drafting the manifesto for the General Election with help from ex-ministers Stephen Byers and Alan Milburn. We have seen that New Labour's opponents would be a new, centrist, "internationalist" Conservative Party, following a change of leadership that would effectively guarantee "Rothschildite" policies.

Besides seeking to control the American and British leaderships, it became apparent that "Rothschilds" were heavily involved in attempting to control the Russian Presidency. "Rothschilds"' attempt to replace President Vladimir Putin with their own man came to light when at the end of October 2003 Putin ordered the arrest of Russia's then richest man, Mikhail Khodorkovsky, chairman of the Russian giant oil company Yukos. (In 1995 he had bought the state oil company for $300m. It is now thought to be worth more than $30b, and his fortune has been put at £4.72b.) Khodorkovsky was seized at a Siberian airport and was sent to prison by Russian prosecutors on charges of obtaining $1b by fraud and tax evasion. Prosecutors tried to freeze a 44% $15b stake in Yukos to protect Khodorkovsky from selling the shares on. Khodorkovsky was said to be the beneficial owner of 59.5% of the shares of Yukos (although some reports put the figure at a third, attributing some of the shares to his business partner Platon Lebedev). They found that as Khodorkovsky was unable to "act as a beneficiary of the shares," voting rights had been transferred to an unnamed foreigner who turned out to be Lord Jacob Rothschild. The son of Victor, Lord Rothschild, he had left N. M. Rothschilds in 1981 when control of the bank passed to his cousin Sir Evelyn Rothschild, causing a family rift, and was thought to be worth £400m. Rothschild was one of a number of people who had been asked to take on the voting rights.

Khodorkovsky and Rothschild had put a trustee agreement in place when Khodorkovsky realized he was facing arrest and a possible 10 years in jail. The shares were held in the Menatep Group, based in Gibraltar. It seems that Khodorkovsky had political ambitions, which were backed by Rothschild, to succeed the "Rockefellerite" Putin as Russian president. Through Khodorkovsky's patronage of Opposition politicians he had come to control 200 MPs. It seems that the arrest was to put an end to these political ambitions – and to "Rothschilds"' controlling a country whose utilities had been bought by "Rockefellers." It seems that Putin had struck to prevent a situation described in a *Sunday Times* headline: "Rothschild, New Power in Russia."

It was reported that Putin had turned against capitalism generally, and that the prosecutors would turn their fire on Yukos's rival (with which it was merging), Sibneft, and its major shareholder Roman Abramovich, who had bought Chelsea Football Club in London. (In 1995 Abramovich had paid $100.3m for the state oil company that is now worth $12b, and he was now thought to be worth around £7.2b, having overtaken Khodorkovsky.) Abramovich was linked with Lord Rothschild through the Yukos-funded Open Russia Foundation, founded in 2001, of which both Lord Rothschild and Khodorkovsky were trustees. But the central issue was a "Rothschild"-

backed plan to wrest the presidency from Putin.

In the same week that news broke of his involvement in Russia, Lord Jacob Rothschild learned that he would be sued for £1.5b in damages by a former business partner, David Elias, whose fuel card empire collapsed after a joint venture with RIT Capital Partners, Rothschild's fund management group whose headquarters were at Princess Diana's former family home, Spencer House, in London. An RIT employee was also being sued. Lord Rothschild was also appointed non-executive deputy chairman of BSkyB. Rupert Murdoch was Chairman and his son chief executive.[16]

It seemed, then, that with "Rothschild" money behind him for a third term, Blair was set to be returned, albeit with a substantially reduced majority. The prospect was that "Rothschilds" might control Hillary Clinton in the White House from 2008 and Blair in Downing Street from 2005 and be influential in news management. There was a chance that "Rothschilds" might also control Khodorkovsky in the Kremlin after the next presidential elections.

Meanwhile "Rockefellers" were regrouping and putting the Syndicate into a strong position. Chase Manhattan, their retail group bank which operated in 52 countries, had merged with the originally "Rothschild"-affiliated investment bank J. P. Morgan in 2001 to create J. P. Morgan Chase. Now, on January 15, 2004 it was announced that J. P. Morgan Chase was to buy Bank One in a $60b deal to create the world's second largest bank after Citigroup, the financial services chain. J. P. Morgan Chase would manage assets of $759b, Bank One assets of $277b. The new bank would therefore control assets of more than $1 trillion. The "Rockefellerite" Syndicate were now well positioned to fund global projects.

The second Iraq War split Europe. A Franco-German-Russian alliance at the UN denied the US and Britain a second resolution, and Jacques Chirac, the President of France, and Putin, the President of Russia, were very vocal in opposing the war as the Saddam regime had granted French and Russian companies oil contracts in Iraq, which were to have taken effect as soon as sanctions were lifted. Chirac and Putin were presumably mouthpieces for the French/Russian "Rockefellerite" financial and business interests. The US-led attack on Iraq was fundamentally a "Rockefellerite" US/Syndicate operation to secure Iraqi oil. A PNAC faction wanted to bring some respite to Israel at the same time. "Rothschildite" Britain made common cause with the US to secure a new supply of oil that would replace the North Sea and to improve Israel's position. A consequence of the Anglo-American action was the cancellation, with the fall of Saddam, of some contracts with French and Russian oil companies and their replacement by Iraqi contracts with US companies. A year after the war a Sunni-Shia uprising caused general chaos and anarchy across the country, but the withdrawal of US and British forces (the Vietnam scenario) before January 2006 was not an option.

The West has nearly run out of oil. The Syndicate are scooping up alternative supplies in the Middle East (Iraq) and North Africa (Libya). The Western peoples have to make up their minds: do they want the oil that will keep their lifestyle going or not? If they do, then Western peoples must put up with self-interested foreign policy and condone the Syndicate's smash-and-grab imperialistic raids on the oil of others, under the guise of spreading liberty and democracy.

The second Iraq War presumably carried forward the Bilderberg agenda of eventually achieving a tax on oil at the wellhead and reducing aid to the Third World. One thing we can be sure of: that the Syndicate made progress towards its goal of an extended United States of the World.

15

THE UNITED STATES
OF THE WORLD

A United States of the World (not of Europe alone) is the
state form of the unification and freedom of nations which we
associate with socialism – until the time when the complete
victory of communism brings about the total disappearance of
the state, including the democratic.

Lenin, Collected Works, vol 21, pp. 339–43; 1915

"Rockefellers" and the "Rockefellerite" faction in the Syndicate tried, and
failed, to unite Europe and the world through Hitler's empire. Its second
attempt to unite Europe and part of the USSR by diplomacy and Cold War
and integrate them with North America and Japan looks like succeeding
– even if "Rothschilds" joins forces with the English monarchy to fight for
the continuation of the nation-state.

The "Rockefellerite" Syndicate have abandoned the Cold War, which
has served its purpose. In May 2002 Bush agreed with Putin that the US
and Russia would slash nuclear weapons by up to two thirds to rule a
line under the Cold War. The Americans and Russia will cut their nuclear
arsenals from levels of between 7,000 and 6,000 nuclear weapons each
side to between 1,700 and 2,200 by 2012.[1]

It may have become apparent that there are, in effect, two New World
Orders: the essentially benign New World Order of popular imagination,
a "new Utopian" idea reborn at the end of the twentieth century; and
the malign New World Order of the Syndicate, a world government that
has been "in waiting" for several generations and that is motivated by
commercial considerations and the profit motive. The first seeks to improve

255

things for the many, the second for a few. The first seeks to abolish war, disease, famine, and unrest and turn the earth into a paradise; the second rewards those who serve it with multi-billion contracts and positions of great power. The New World Order mentioned by Nelson Rockefeller (in 1968) and Bush Sr. is the second one masquerading as the first.

This New World Order, which is perceived to have been born in 1989 with the collapse of the Berlin Wall but which in fact was on the tongues of Cecil Rhodes and Adolf Hitler, kept a world-wide peace of sorts until September 2001. The first Iraq War and the Balkan wars came and went and were localized. Indeed, these wars were the means by which world peace was maintained, for they sent out signals to all tyrants that aggressive behavior would not be tolerated. Despite occasional terrorist incidents that strained relations in Northern Ireland and in Jerusalem, peace was – just – maintained in the most troubled spots and there were attempts to bring lasting peace to Ireland and Palestine.

Since September 2001, peace has looked fragile in Israel and Palestine and non-existent in Afghanistan and Iraq, where the US is still "at war." The War on Terror has put the New World Order on a war footing. (On the eve of the second Iraq War Peter Ustinov said, "War is the terrorism of the rich; terrorism is the war of the poor.")

We have a choice. Either we can continue to be manipulated and exploited by those who are currently running the world and steering it towards a world government under which our freedom will be curtailed; or we can – both collectively and as individuals – take our power back from them and with freedom regained take responsibility for the unfolding destiny of the human race and create a world free from war, famine, suffering, disease, unrest, and civil strife.

The UN reflects the ideology of the old Round Table. In January 2000, UN Secretary-General Kofi Annan said, "State sovereignty, in its most basic sense, is being redefined by the forces of globalization and international cooperation." Such globalism is the ideology of the new Round Table/ Committee of 300. These "Olympians" have set up the naked figure of Zeus, the Greek father of the gods, in the main lobby of the UN building, and have shaped the meditation room in the UN like a pyramid laid on its side – a Weishauptian, Illuminati symbol.[2] The UN is the headquarters of the new Olympian Illuminati, who embrace "Rothschilds'" Sionist organization and the Templars with their "Skull and Bones" offshoot at Yale.

Structure of a United States of the World

The first map of a world government was adopted in London in 1952 by the World Association of Parliamentarians for World Government. It showed eight zones and 51 regions; there would be a World Director, and no zone directors or region directors would serve in their own country. Aliens would therefore command troops and police in each region to prevent regions from "sheltering behind national allegiance."

Ten Zones

A revised plan for a world government was outlined in 1973 by the "Rockefellerite" Club of Rome, which split the world into 10 political/economic regions or zones that would unite the entire world under one government (see map 6). These were originally called "Kingdoms" to reflect the 10 kingdoms within Atlantis in Plato's account in *Critias* that is honored by Freemasons. The word "Kingdoms" was omitted when the plan was published in a book, *Mankind at the Turning Point*, which argued that the world's problems could only be solved "in a global context."[3] These zones are:

1. North America
2. Western Europe
3. Japan

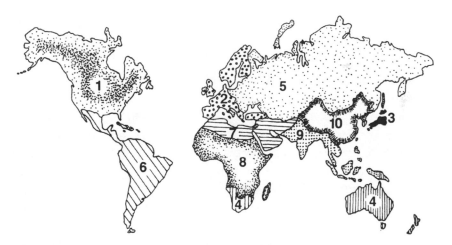

6. *Ten Kingdoms from The Club of Rome*

4. The rest of the developed market economies (Israel, Australia, Tasmania, New Zealand, Oceania, South Africa)
5. Eastern Europe including the free Soviet Union
6. Latin America
7. North Africa and the Middle East
8. Main Africa
9. South and South Eastern Asia including India
10. "Centrally-planned Asia," meaning Communist Asia (Mongolia, N. Korea, N. Vietnam, and China).

This is part of a pattern. It's reported that Bilderberg policy is to establish regions around the world, and islands, like Hong Kong, Gibraltar and the Falklands, are to be reunited politically with the mainland.

A few moments' thought will remind us of how the 10 zones are progressing:

1. *N. America.* The North American Free Trade Agreement (NAFTA) which embraces the US, Canada, and oil-rich Mexico,[4] has gone ahead and is fast creating a regional bloc. There is now a Free Trade Area of the Americas and a Western hemisphere (see pages 43–6).

2. *W. Europe.* Following the Maastricht, Amsterdam and Nice Treaties and the agreement of the new European constitution, a United States of Europe is progressing. The Eastern European states and Turkey are now associated, and some have already joined the European Union. By 2010 there may be a 48–nation Europe stretching from the Atlantic to the Urals, comprising 700 million inhabitants: a nine-region England, Wales, Scotland, Ireland, Denmark, the Netherlands, Belgium, Luxembourg, Germany, France, Liechtenstein, Monaco, San Marino, Portugal, Spain, Italy, and Greece; Norway, Sweden, Finland, Switzerland and Austria; Iceland, Malta, Cyprus, Poland, Czechoslovakia, and Hungary; Estonia, Latvia, Lithuania, Romania, Bulgaria, Slovenia, Croatia, Bosnia, Serbia, Montenegro, Macedonia, Albania, and Turkey; and Belarus, Ukraine, Moldova, Georgia, Armenia, Azerbaijan, and Russia. There may eventually be 111 regions and 666 sub-regional districts. The wars in former Yugoslavia have to be seen within this context; they were to break up a union into new states.

3. *Japan.* Linked to North America and Western Europe by the Trilateral Commission, Japan is advancing toward an Asian-Pacific Community

and Union – currently called an Asian Economic Community (see page 46).

4. *The rest of the developed market economies.* Israel is now more integrated with its Middle Eastern neighbors following agreements with Egypt, Palestine, and the US.

Australia and Tasmania have narrowly missed becoming a republic, and can be expected to become republican soon. Australia, New Zealand, and Oceania are advancing towards a federation of Oceanian states within Asia and the Pacific (see page 46).

South Africa has ended apartheid and is multi-racial and democratic. South Africa is advancing into a pan-African Federation of African states, a United States of Africa. The Syndicate has been looting South Africa, which has gone democratic under Nelson Mandela, whose power base was strengthened by the Bilderberg Group as a result of a visit to South Africa by Kissinger and Lord Carrington in April 1994.

5. *Eastern Europe.* The Eastern European states have already joined the European Union.

The Soviet Union is now known as the Russian Federation having moved from Union to a looser federation, a commonwealth of independent states.

6. *Latin America.* South America has been in America's sphere of influence since Yalta, and is advancing into a pan-Latin American Federation of South American states. Another attempt will be made to return the Falkland Islands to Argentina, as all offshore islands have to be returned to their mainland (as Hong Kong was returned to China). There is a Latin American Free Trade Association (LAFTA, see page 43).

7. *North Africa and the Middle East.* In 1969 Col. Gaddafi of Libya tried to create an organization of Arab states. The Arab states are advancing into a pan-Arab federation of Arab states; a United States of the Middle East. There is more unity in the Arab world than ever before.

8. *Main Africa.* Wars, starvation, and disease have depopulated main Africa, but the liberation and independence movements have now virtually accomplished their goals and Africa is ready to dissolve into a pan-African Federation of African states; a United States of Africa. The African Union, unveiled at an inaugural summit in Durban on July 8, 2002, replaces the moribund, bankrupt, and discredited

Organization of African Unity, which was owed money by 45 of its 53 members and failed to stand up to the continent's dictators or stop the Rwandan genocide.

9. *South and South-East Asia including India.* The de-colonizing Indo-Chinese wars are finished and the states are dissolving into a new regional bloc, a pan-South East Asian federation of South East Asian states; Asia and the Pacific.

10. *Centrally-planned (i.e. Communist) Asia.* China has now received Hong Kong and is in touch with the US. It has influence on Mongolia, and is advancing into a regional bloc that includes North Korea and perhaps Vietnam.

Eventually each of the 10 regions will have a President, and all 10 Presidents will communicate through live link-ups in a regional United States of the World (USW). At least, that is the plan. The Internet is therefore a network to facilitate communication between the governments and citizens of a USW. The successful testing in March 2004 of a US plane that can fly at seven times the speed of sound (nearly 5,000 mph) promised to revolutionize air travel, for the opposite ends of the earth could be reached in the time it takes to check in. Technology has kept pace with globalization, overcoming distance and cutting communication times. In the meantime, each region is making progress in relation to its goal. Western Europe for example is trying to make its single currency, the euro, work in each state, with all member-states taking part, and there is much presenting to do as nation-states are abolished into regions and agree to be ruled from Brussels. Each region will eventually be traversed by a network of oil and gas pipelines. An image for the coming world government is: a network of pipelines seen criss-crossing the earth from outer space.

Three Regions

The world has undergone enormous developments in the 30 years since the 10 zones were identified in 1973, the year of the Trilateral Commission's inception. The speed with which we are being frog-marched into world government is staggering. Where will we be in 30 years' time? The broad plan now is to turn the United Nations into a world government by splitting the world into three great regions for the administrative convenience of a world government, with the dollar as a common currency. These regions reflect the 1973 Trilateral Commission's original focus on North America, Western Europe, and Japan. They will be:

1. An American Union of all countries in North, Central, and South America.[5] President Bush is fast-tracking the expansion of NAFTA (the North American Free Trade Agreement) throughout the Western hemisphere. In 2003 there were talks to speed up CAFTA (the Central American Free Trade Agreement, which will cover US trade with five Central American nations: El Salvador, Guatemala, Nicaragua, Honduras, and Costa Rica); and LAFTA (the Latin American Free Trade Association), see page 43. This region will cover zones 1 and 6.

2. An expanded European Union, which will eventually include Russia, the former Soviet republics, the Middle East, and Africa[6] (all the former European colonies, most of which retain links with Europe through the Commonwealth or trade). See page 45. The African Union was inaugurated in July 2002 and a Middle East Free Trade Area was mentioned in a speech by Bush in early May 2003.) This region will cover zones 2, 4 (Israel), 5, 7, and 8.

3. An Asian-Pacific Union,[7] which will eventually include Japan, Australia, South and South-East Asia, and China. This region is already bound together as APEC (the Asia-Pacific Economic Co-operation forum) and there are meetings of Asian-Pacific defense ministers. Seven nations including India and Pakistan are bound together as SAFTA (the South Asian Free Trade Area). It is moving towards an Asian Economic Community. See pages 46–7.This region will cover zones 3, 4 (Australia, etc), 9, and 10.

Any war in the Middle East (for example, Iraq) or involving the "Axis of Terror" of 60 countries will advance this process. The American, European, and Asian-Pacific Unions thus defined will collectively form one World Union: a United States of the World. The three regions coincide broadly with the three blocs Orwell foresaw in *1984*. (He called the Asian-Pacific Union Oceania.) These regions are the Trilateral Commission's tripartite girdle round the world that has found embodiment in the G7 (Group of Seven) meetings, the seven – the most powerful industrial nations in the world – being: the US, Canada (1); Great Britain, France, Germany, Italy (2); and Japan (3). The G7 have become the G8 with the addition of Russia.

It must be pointed out that the capital of the European Union, Brussels – indeed, all Belgium – has had a strong link with the Rothschilds ever since the Belgian branch of the family under Baron Leon Lambert financed Leopold I's Belgian Empire from the Banque Lambert de Bruxelles.[8] (The Congo Empire was created in 1885 after Leopold – and therefore the Belgian Rothschilds – financed Stanley's explorations.) The siting of the United States of Europe in Brussels, Strasbourg, and Frankfurt is in cities that have long had strong links with "Rothschilds" and the Syndicate.

The European dream is of a united Europe that is designed to prevent war, in which nationalism will be tamed and with an economy as large as America's. It is a political vision with an economic angle that masks the dream. The three central pillars of political European integration are the single market, the single currency, and regional governments being able to bypass national governments. (Regional governments are federated to the European Union inasmuch as they receive regional funds from Brussels and exercise the powers granted by Brussels.) The great paradox of Europe – one that the Syndicate is well placed to exploit – is that unelected EU officials in the European Central Bank give instructions on how to bring down budget deficits to politicians of former nation-states' regions who have been elected. The future direction of Europe depends on whether the EU bureaucracy, notably the European Central Bank's, will be made more democratically accountable. Will Europe become a true democracy or remain a collective?

The European single currency will have truly arrived when all the states of an expanded European Union have the euro as their currency. The new European constitution was duly agreed by mid-2004, the fiftieth anniversary of the inauguration of the Bilderberg Group in 1954. The agreement of the constitution by this date was seen as a fitting fiftieth-birthday present to Bilderberg.

The plan now is for all the Eastern European and ex-Soviet states to embrace the free market and privatization as they prepare to join the EU, and for all the Western European states to be permanently socialist. The Conservative parties in Western Europe and the Communist parties in Eastern Europe and Russia have to be kept divided to maintain a uniform socialist European System. As the plan to create a three-Union United States of the World is implemented, America and Japan will also have to be kept socialist; Israel too. And the liberalization of China will have to continue so that China has a place in the coming United States of the World.

World Institutions[9]

The Syndicate have already taken steps to create a world army. The European Army is to contribute to this world army; European troops will be based in every European state including the regions of England. The UN has already begun to set up a world police force, which will have the power to move into any country, including the United States, at short notice.

In 1998 the "Rothschildian" world government arranged for the setting-up of the International Criminal Court (ICC), which was endorsed by 120 nations in Rome, but not the US. The ICC was officially set up by the UN, but is outside the control of the "Rockefellerite" UN Security Council. If the Security Council were to control which cases come before the court, Washington could use its UN veto to block the prosecution of Americans. The "Rockefellerites" are alarmed that the court could bring politically inspired prosecutions, for example against Henry Kissinger on charges arising from his role in the Vietnam War and against Donald Rumsfeld on charges connected to the War on Terror. Both men could be arrested while traveling abroad like the former Chilean dictator Augusto Pinochet. Alternatively, there could be attempted legal action like that in Belgium against Israeli Prime Minister Ariel Sharon.

Some American conservatives have seen the creation of the ICC as "another step towards world government" that threatens US sovereignty. If it were true that President Bush Jr. had sided with the defenders of US sovereignty against the world government, this would be dramatic and encouraging news. In fact, as we have seen, Bush Jr. and Kissinger are deeply idcntified with the "Rockefellerite" world government, and they are using the language of US sovereignty to extricate themselves from a European-"Rothschildite" initiative which could lay some past activities open to prosecution and act as a brake on future global operations. Congress has passed legislation authorizing military action to free any ("Rockefellerite") American taken into custody to be brought before the ICC.

A United States of the World will have a single world currency, which will be an "earth-dollar." The euro has already converged with the dollar, and should strictly be called a "euro-dollar." The single European currency is a stepping-stone to a single world currency, which the Bilderberg Group anticipate will be implemented around 2015. 2010 is regarded as being too early.[10] It is intended that the world currency will be in place by what the Syndicate hope will be the last US Presidential elections of 2016, by which time the United States is to be dissolved either by treaty or executive order, with July 4, 2016 being the last Independence Day.[11]

An Illuminized Grand-Orient United-States-of-Europe Republic

But above all the Syndicate has secretly poured money into creating a United States of Europe. The head of Grand Orient Freemasonry at the time of the inauguration of the United States of Europe at Maastricht on December 31, 1992 was France's President Francois Mitterand, who was the most powerful 33rd-degree Freemason in Europe.[12] He helped inaugurate Freemasonry's long awaited United States of Europe. In 1983 he had hired the Japanese architect I. M. Pei to create a glass pyramid with 673 windows (presumably representing, besides world government, the intended 666 districts of the completed United States of Europe, plus 7 Masonic/Syndicate leaders) in the courtyard of the Louvre (the old royal castle),[13] a triangular Illuminati monument whose design is linked with that of the meditation room in the UN.

It was Mitterand of the Grand Orient who, according to media reports (angrily denied by Kohl), channeled £10m to Chancellor Kohl's 1994 re-election campaign, via Elf-Aquitaine, the State-owned French oil company which (thanks to Kohl's acting as facilitator) bought the East German oil refinery of Leuna and obtained the right to buy petrol stations in Eastern Germany. The supplier of the £10m used a multinational oil company to promote France's interests in East Germany, and Mitterand and Kohl were his proxies. A Corsican businessman has alleged that, with the knowledge of Mitterand and Kohl, he allowed the former head of Elf to use his letterbox for companies in Liechtenstein to channel DM85m (£27m) to German political parties including Kohl's when Elf bought the Leuna oil refinery.

Chancellor Kohl, the architect of the German–American Axis that led to the founding of the United States of Europe and the re-unifier of Germany, was accused in late 1999 of accepting DM1m from an unnamed oil refinery and "international backers" while in power. The money was received in August 1991, six months after he bent Germany's arms export rules and sent 36 armored vehicles to Saudi Arabia during the Gulf War, an action that would have pleased "Rockefellers" whose CFR (the "Rockefeller Foreign Office") was responsible for the German–American Axis and for implementing it through a Franco-German alliance and special relationship. The Syndicate secures its aims in the United States of Europe created in December 1992 by a clientilist system of patronage. The Grand Orient were behind the French and Russian Revolutions, and now they are behind the New World Order Revolution in Europe; a process that has happened before is happening all over again.

But it has not happened yet. It is an idea whose time is coming. Lenin spoke of a United States of the World, and, if public opinion can be manipulated into agreeing, it may happen in our lifetimes.

How a United States of the World May Be Consolidated

If the New World Order were being conducted by saints as a Utopian replica of Heaven on earth, then it would lead to the abolition of war, disease, famine, and unrest, the Four Horsemen of the Apocalypse, and would be wholly good. It would be an outcome the whole of mankind would long for, and it would be consolidated by the enthusiastic assent of all who place the interests of mankind above those of the nation-state.

But what would a Syndicate New World Order be like? The danger is it would be a socialist state in which there would be a redistribution of wealth and a reduced standard of living for all Westerners. (There would be howls of rage as their hard-earned pensions and savings are shared with the poorest among mankind who have paid no contributions.) There would be regimentation and restriction on movement, with no freedom of worship, no freedom to buy or own private property, no free speech, and no freedom to publish. From a personal point of view, most Westerners would not want to give up such freedoms, and make such sacrifices. From the point of view of the whole, however, they might well come to regard a system that brings equality to all the world's citizens as worthy of such sacrifices. (One of the objects of the Fabian Society has been to make equality and justice synonymous, whereas equality and justice are not identical.) Such trust would be misplaced.

Mind Control

Could it involve mind control? Such an idea may seem preposterous. Some of Aldous Huxley's ideas in *Brave New World* (1932), such as "test-tube babies," seemed preposterous at the time and have since become a reality. Modern advertising techniques and political spin are two examples of the way our minds are controlled today and mind-control techniques such as NLP (Neurolinguistic Programming) and Silver Mind Control are widely promoted in the New Age and business fields. The consolidation of the United States of the World could be achieved through mind control in the coming decades. When bombarded with microwaves of 425 megacycles, people lose the power to resist and become zombies. It could be possible to turn the world's population into a slave race, a new technologically created underclass, by beaming microwaves at them from cell-phone masts and other sources of microwaves. A central world computer will know everything about us and will monitor our movements on digital cameras as we drive around the country, passing beneath gantries that can take 60,000 pictures an hour. (This has already begun to happen in a few parts of Britain.) The ring roads round cities could be turned into "moats" that keep the urban population in and the rural population out, with the help of tanks sitting on roads like the M25 and of centrally controlled cameras. The *Grand Boulevards* in Paris were laid out by Haussmann in the nineteenth century to allow rapid access across the city so that the forces of law and order could quickly quell riots. The concept of ring roads as moats is therefore not really far-fetched.

There is already much in place that with a little tweaking could bring in George Orwell's "thought police." Amateur computer hackers are already able to access the computers of the unwary – what could professional hackers do? There is a legal move afoot to compel ISPs (Internet Server Providers) and mobile phone companies to retain all e-mails and mobile phone conversations for five years. This is being promoted as part of a campaign against criminal activity. There were howls of outrage when it was discovered that Microsoft had inserted a hidden module into their Windows operating system, which would have enabled them to monitor the use of their software. The module was "locked" and could only be accessed by Microsoft. Those who apply for credit are already aware of the amount of information stored about them in their "credit rating" –

how much more information could be collated on a centralized computer from other computerized records? According to the *American Free Press* of May 6, 2002, a Bilderberg-controlled UN agency is to have the power to have access to all bank accounts and credit card transactions. With all this already in place, the infrastructure of a world government is already present in embryonic form.

Depopulation

The vision of the inspirers of world government surfaced on July 24, 1980, when the results of a two-volume study begun by the CFR, the Trilateral Commission, and the IMF when Jimmy Carter took office, and involving hundreds of consultants, were unveiled at a press conference by Secretary of State Edmund Muskie: *The Global 2000 Report to the President*.[14] This projected the global economic trends of the next 20 years, from 1980 to 2000. Hundreds of outside consultants contributed, as did scores of task-force personnel from the State Department and White House Council on Environmental Quality. The study predicted a world endangered by overpopulation, food shortages, and environmental hazards, and by implication forecast 170 million deaths through disease and famine in the developing countries by 2000.

The Report built on "Rockefellerite" policies. Population control was given prominence by John D. Rockefeller III's establishment of a Population Council in 1952 to issue manifestos in favor of "zero population growth"; by the Club of Rome's 1971 report (published in 1972), *Limits to Growth*; and by Laurance Rockefeller's 1972 report on population growth.

The Report predicted (on pp. 1 and 3) that the world population would rise from 4.1 billion in 1975 to 6.35 billion in 2000, 10 billion by 2030 and 30 billion by the end of the twenty-first century (by 2091, p. 428 of the Report). After 2000, "100m people (will be) added each year compared with 75m in 1975" (p. 1). The Report lowered the figure of 6.35 billion to 6.18 billion (p. 12) as 170 million were expected to die: "In the years ahead, lack of food for the urban poor, lack of jobs and increasing illness and misery may slow the growth of LDC (less developed countries) cities and alter the trend. Difficult as urban conditions are, conditions in rural areas of many LDCs are generally worse. Food, water, health and income problems are often most severe in outlying agricultural and grazing areas

.... An updated medium-series population projection would show little change from the *Global 2000 Study* projections. World population in 2000 would be estimated at about 6.18 (as opposed to 6.35) b."

The scaled-down figure of 6.18 billion was too pessimistic. In fact, the world's population reached 6 billion on August 5, 1999, just a few months before 2000, which suggests that the true number of deaths due to disease and famine may have been 350 million, not 170 million. (There was no fall in the world's birth rate: by 2003 the world's population had crept up to 6.3 billion.)

The Report raised the question of how great a population the earth can "carry" (p. 41): The *Global 2000* Study does not estimate the earth's carrying capacity, but it does provide a basis for evaluating an earlier estimate published in the US National Academy of Sciences' report, *Resources and Man*. In this 1969 report the Academy concluded that a world population of 10b "is close to (if not above) the maximum that an *intensively managed* world might hope to support with some degree of comfort and individual choice ...." Nothing in the *Global 2000* Study counters the Academy's conclusions. If anything, data gathered over the past decade suggest the Academy may have underestimated the extent of some problems, especially deforestation and the loss and deterioration of soils.

The Report wound up (pp. 41–2): "At present and projected growth rates, the world's population would rapidly approach the Academy's figures. If the fertility and mortality rates projected for 2000 were to continue unchanged into the twenty-first century, the world's population would reach 10b by 2030 ... This same rate of growth would produce a population of nearly 30b before the end of the end of the twenty-first century ... As the world's populations exceed and reduce the land's carrying capacity in widening areas, the trends of the last century or two toward improved health and longer life may come to a halt. Hunger and disease may claim more lives – especially lives of babies and young children. More of those surviving infancy may be mentally and physically handicapped by childhood malnutrition."

Six months later, in January 1981, the Council on Environmental Quality published policy recommendations on this document: *Global Future: A Time to Act*. It was subtitled *Report to the President on Global Resources, Environment, and Population*.[15] Its Preface, co-signed by Secretary of State Edmund Muskie, stated that the *Global 2000 Report* "was the US government's analysis of probable changes in world population, resources and environment through the end of the century. The Report indicated the potential for progressive impoverishment of world resources and degradation of the global environment – if present trends and policies continue. Unless nations of the world take prompt decisive action to alter the trends, the Report concluded, the next 20 years may see a decline in the earth's capacity to support life, while rapid population growth continues." It says: "The *Global 2000 Report* to the President identified the problems; it did not attempt to find solutions."

Global Future published policy recommendations on the problems defined by the *Global 2000 Report*. Its cornerstone was "population control" through an aggressive program of family planning, sterilization, contraception, and abortion, which might reduce the world population by 4.2 billion (more exactly, 4.16 billion) (p. 50): "This effort could also mean that global population would eventually stabilize at 8b, versus the 12.2b that would result if higher fertility rates continued over a longer period of time. The difference of 4.2b is almost equal to the *total* current world population." ("Current" meant "in 1981.") If such a program was not implemented, millions of people would die by famine and violence. If rising standards of living and health care, high economic growth rates, developing nuclear energy resources, advanced infrastructure, and other industry in developing countries were to allow the 170 million victims of famine and war to survive, then mankind would exceed the "carrying capacity" of the globe. The globe could not "carry" mankind, according to the Reports. "The key concept is *sustainable* development" (p. 12).

The *Global Future* report sets no targets, contains no tables. It speaks in very general terms. Is it to be taken at face value? Or is it between-the-lines stuff? "Unless population growth can be brought under control" (p. 19), wretched consequences will follow for mankind.

"The opportunity to stabilize the world's population below 10 billion, for example, is slipping away." We have just seen that a declared aim of the Report was "that global population would eventually stabilize at 8b" (p. 50). There is a half-declared ambiguity regarding 2 billion people (i.e. 6.18 billion minus 4.16 billion) – a third of mankind on its present total of just over 6 billion.

Did this scaled-down figure represent a prediction, an informed guess? Or did it represent an objective, a target to be achieved as an effect of policy?

The *Executive Intelligence Review*'s critique of the Report (August 1982) is in no doubt as can be judged from its title: *Global 2000, Blueprint for Genocide*.[16] The *Executive Intelligence Review*'s critique states: "Committees have been formed to promote the reports' recommendations, including the Committee for the Year 2000 chaired by the former Secretary of State Cyrus Vance.[17] And now the British publishing firm Penguin has published the *Global 2000 Report* in paperback, to afford it even wider circulation. Just what is going on here? The *Global 2000 Report to the President* and *Global Future: A Time to Act* are correctly understood as political statements of intent – the intent on the part of such policy-centers as the Council on Foreign Relations, the Trilateral Commission, and the International Monetary Fund, to pursue policies that will result not only in the death of the 170m cited in the Reports but in the death of upwards of 2b people by the year 2000."[18] (Penguin of course acted as any responsible and reputable publisher would in publishing an important forecast about the next 20 years, and would in no way have regarded the *Global 2000 Report* as a "political statement of intent.")

The language of the Reports appears positive and harmless, but the Reports do not advocate technological progress in developing countries to counter the effects of the projected increase in population. On the contrary, scientific development is to be restricted, as is food production. Nuclear energy development is to be prevented. After 1980 the loans to developing countries made by the IMF, World Bank, and Bank for International Settlements in Basel became conditional on those countries reducing their imports of food and fuel, cutting investments in industry, and decreasing food subsidies while increasing their crop exports.

The *Global Future* Report focuses on family planning rather than on wars, famine, and disease to reduce population. The reality is that wars destroy crops and promote famine and diseases, and encourage refugees whose resistance is weakened and who can succumb to their wretched circumstances. The *Global Future* Report makes it clear that "controlling population growth" should be central to the US government's response to the *Global 2000 Report*. "The experience of these (developing) nations illustrates the possibilities of slowing or halting population growth" (p. 50).

Both Reports purport to have mankind's best interests at heart. At the same time we have seen a host of crises in developing countries have led to wars, famine, and disease. These crises have combined and have had the effect of "slowing or halting" the population growth. Were they encouraged? The two Reports call for population control. The history of the twentieth century, much of which has been aimed at building a world government, has produced two world wars and many other local wars that have caused many tens of millions of deaths.

Both Reports were accepted by President Carter. Hundreds of conferences and discussions took place about these two Reports, and Cyrus Vance of the Trilateral Commission chairing the Committee of the Year 2000, announced his vision of "a new world order based on environmentalism." The main thrust of the Committee's outlook was that if the world population carried on growing at its then rate of growth, the world's resources would not be able to sustain it.

All the West's leaders claim to know the best way forward and believe they are improving the world. Are these people individually or collectively showing the world that there is a problem of sustainability through these Reports? Do the Reports contain observations on what might happen, state a likelihood? Or can it be that these people individually or collectively are setting out policies that have the effect of reducing the world population? Are they setting out policies that advocate an intention to kill billions of human beings? Are the policies they are pursuing going to have the effect of more Cambodias, Rwandas, and Vietnams – of more droughts, famines, and diseases? And if this is the case, do the world leaders know this? Are the world leaders being carried along like flotsam on a river, or are they in control of the channel, are they digging the path of the river?

The effect of the policies focused on in the two Reports would be an increase in the likelihood of the 170 million deaths forecast in the Reports (which have happened, the true figure perhaps being 350 million as we have seen) and of the deaths of more than 2 billion people by 2030. The policies of the reports would reduce the world population from 10 billion, forecast for 2030, to 8 billion by 2030. In 2003 the UN Population Division expected the world's population in 2050 to be 8.9 billion instead of 9.3 billion (2000 figure) and 9.9 billion (a decade earlier).

The *Global 2000 Report* and *Global Future* have guided the economic and foreign policies of the US since 1980 and have been accepted by every President since then. If these Reports are policy rather than statements of likelihood, it follows that to achieve the targets of the *Global 2000 Report* and *Global Future* the world population has to be reduced by 2 billion. This figure is not an abstraction, like a telephone number. It refers to human beings – each one an individual, like you and me.

There's surely something strange going on. In Europe we throw fish back into the sea, farmers are paid to "set aside" cropless fields and plough crops back into the ground without harvesting them – we implement fishing and farming quotas. At the same time one fifth of the world's population is on the starvation line, or under it.

Forced depopulation has undoubtedly happened. One third of the Cambodian population was killed by the Khmers Rouges between 1975 and 1978: officially 1.7 to 2.2 million people although other informed estimates suggest 3 to 4 million people. As many as 4 million may have been killed in the Congo's Great Lakes region. Contrived wars, famines, and diseases can control the growth of populations, as is happening most clearly in Africa. More than 25 million have died from Aids in Africa alone. In all, 38 million have died from Aids throughout the world. By 2050 it is expected that 278 million will have died from Aids throughout the world, and 178 million fewer babies will have been born because of the impact of the epidemic on women of childbearing age.

Poor living standards also depopulate. In Africa droughts followed by the after-effects of disease and economic dislocation have threatened to kill 250 million out of 450 million Africans from the west in Senegal, through south Tunisia and Algeria to the Sudan, Kenya, Tanzania, Uganda, Mozambique, and South Africa. In Sudan in 1980 more than 100% of the national income went on oil payments and debt-servicing; in Uganda tens of thousands starved to death in drought; in Zaire the population was slowly starving on an average of 800 calories a day. In 1981 Tanzania was about to run out of food after the failure of the *ujamaa* system. There has been a famine in Ethiopia that threatened 8 million. In 1982 a Fusion Energy Foundation study[19] found that 115 million people died prematurely over 15 years due to the denial of nuclear energy (which Britain is now phasing out).

In 2002 the US was blocking an international plan to halve, by 2015, the 2.4 billion people around the world who lack even a bucket for their wastes – one of the main causes of world disease. The US gave no clear reason for their objection to the sanitation plan at a meeting at Bali, which was to prepare for an environmental Earth Summit in Johannesburg in

September 2002. More than 2.2 million, mainly children, die in the Third World each year from diseases caused by lack of sanitation and by dirty drinking water. The US Bush Jr. administration had already agreed to halve the number of people without clean drinking water by 2015.

Depopulation can also be achieved by less drastic means. Deng Hsiao-ping envisaged reducing the Chinese population from over 1 billion to 600 to 700 million by restricting couples to one child, through programs of sterilization, contraception, and abortion, and though they're not there – the population of China today is double the target, 1.26 billion against 1.2 billion in 1995 – a substantial increase has been prevented – for the time being. The UN Population Projection shows that China's population more than doubled from 556.7 million in 1950 to 1.2267 billion in 1995,[20] with 1.3805 billion forecast in 2010 and 1.4881 billion in 2025.[21]

The presence of fluoride in Western water supplies has already helped to reduce male sperm count, and therefore to control fertility. There is suspicion that genetically modified foods, ostensibly being produced in the West to make "good food" available throughout the world at the cheapest possible price, are in fact another manifestation of a depopulation program. If the World Bank restricts aid to Third World countries and controls their government's policies, malnutrition sets in and there are many deaths from natural causes resulting from the effects of poverty on the human body. Debilitated in such ways, human bodies are frail and susceptible to germs released among them. The heating-up of the earth's atmosphere through Western carbon dioxide emissions has caused some 100,000 deaths through droughts, torrential rain, and hurricanes in poor countries during the three years before 2000.[22]

If the world-government-in-waiting is operating a system of quotas and culls, and if these cannot be achieved by such traditional "gradualist" methods and it is a question of wiping out 2 billion (of today's population) and as many as 4 billion (of a stabilized population of 8 billion) "useless eaters"[23] to make policy work – if that is the case, then we can expect depopulation targets to be achieved by nuclear war. Both India and Pakistan now have nuclear weapons and dispute Kashmir. A nuclear war between these two countries might deposit radiation on parts of China and South East Asia and, if properly (or rather, improperly) managed, could reduce the population of mankind to target levels.

Can the Syndicate, with its pursuit of Freemasonry, manage the world population problem sensitively, without harming human beings? Or is the chilling reality that the consolidation of their world government cannot take place without harming a third, perhaps two thirds, of mankind? If the Syndicate's wish is to implement the Four Horsemen of the Apocalypse as policy, then its ideas could be described as neo-Hitlerian. If they seek a Malthusian replica of Hell on earth, with 2 billion dead, and if the world population rises from 6 billion (now) to 10 billion by 2030 as forecast, and the aim is to keep the world's population at its 2000 level, then another 4 billion must die within three decades. This conclusion must fill all with deep unease, if not dread.

Deaths on such a scale cannot be allowed to happen. Courageous people everywhere must mobilize, build "flood defenses," and influence public policies to make sure they are not allowed to happen. It would be better to be assassinated or liquidated than to tolerate – consent to – a world in which 2 billion, let alone an additional 4 billion in the future, are systematically slaughtered as a result of revolutionary thinking. Right-thinking and morally sound people everywhere must oppose such a preposterous scenario, no matter what the cost to their job prospects or their lives.

Is there a covert drive towards a world government? In order to help us make our choice we need to review the evidence.

The Case for the Prosecution

The Syndicate worked for world revolution before, during, and after the First World War, and during the Second World War. Their descendants were very active during the Cold War and during the reunification of Europe in our own time, and have used the UN and NATO as a world army. Are they pursuing the same traditions and aspirations that drove their forebears during the first half of the twentieth century? There must be a strong presumption that they are. Do these considerations include controlling the world population? Are the *Global 2000* reports policy rather than forecasts? They were accepted as policy by President Carter, and their recommendations have the effect of reducing the world's population. They were policy, members of the jury.

The drive towards world government (the Global Plantation) has been achieved at the cost of numerous local wars, the collapse of the European Empires, and the dismantling of many nation-states to pave the way for a United States of Europe. There have been millions of deaths in wars of de-colonization and independence as liberation movements have conducted guerilla warfare to bring in what they thought would be a new nation but which is turning out to be the creation of a new regional bloc in the world government.

Are not Western leaders opposed to Europe's nation-states? Are they not bringing in a new European constitution while concealing their real intentions? Are they not creating a world government for a few, the Syndicate, to prosper commercially while the many are disenfranchised? Are not the poor of the world to be made victims of war merely so that the oligarchic Syndicate can flourish?

George Orwell saw the greatest threat to our well-being as totalitarianism. The greatest threat is not totalitarianism but covert oligarchy masquerading as democracy and manipulating it and hiding behind it in a totalitarian way.

Has a secretive shadow world government enmeshed world leaders in their schemes, and are the Western publics and voters being deceived, even on what has happened in Afghanistan and Iraq? Members of the jury, Western military action in pursuit of a hidden commercial agenda connected with oil was disguised as action against terrorists. And this pattern is ongoing and is openly being called by key Western leaders "The Fourth World War." (Their assumption is that the 40–year-long Cold War was the Third World War.) Are some Western leaders knowingly deceptive? Are they building a political United States of the World which is to have a one-world currency and a world government? Is the European Union a dummy run for a world union? That is for the jury to decide. If what they are doing is open and above-board, why the secrecy and over-the-top security?

Now the defense make their closing statement.

The Case for the Defense

Under British law a defendant is innocent until proved guilty 'beyond reasonable doubt'. There are many doubts. The world leaders who worked for a better world during the First and Second World Wars were driven by philanthropic, humanitarian (*and* commercial) considerations. Their Foundations are evidence of that. Their descendants who set up the United Nations have worked to break down the divisions of the Cold War, to bring East and West Europe together in the interests of peace, and have only had mankind's good at heart. A united world is far better than the war-torn world of two world wars. Any projections made about future population growth are sensible planning, good management of the world, being ahead of trends. World leaders should be ahead of things and should not suddenly discover that the world's food cannot sustain a rapidly growing population that cannot be stabilized. Any formal world union ahead is difficult to organize – look how hard it has been to sustain the Global Coalition over Afghanistan, a single-issue problem – and so has to be done behind closed doors. The discussions of the various bodies have the status of conferences that share ideas, no more. The security has to be tight because those who attend have a high profile. No small cohort of mega-billionaires has seized the reins of the world in secret. The conferences throw up ideas that prominent entrepreneurs and academics can discuss, and understanding is promoted between countries as relationships are formed.

A European Union is good for European security and will make for a better standard of living for the peoples of Europe. Good leadership requires that the peoples of Europe should be led to union in their own better interests. A world union will be good for all the peoples of the world, and there can be redistribution of wealth from the richer to the poorer countries. The commercial activities of the Syndicate are creating jobs and prosperity all round the world.

The Verdict

So now it is decision time. Have the Syndicate dynastically planned a long-term world revolution, and have all subordinate local revolutions painstakingly made changes to their regions to prepare for the long-term plan of global union? Or are the twentieth-century revolutions – such as the Russian Revolution and the rise of Stalin, and the rise of Nazi Germany – local revolutions that have nothing to do with the Syndicate? Have the Syndicate been writing "forecast papers" to brief themselves, or have they been making policy?

Have the Syndicate held meetings to understand the world and comment on likelihoods, or have they shaped events? Have world leaders been carried along by the current, or have they dug the channel?

Much of the evidence we have been considering is circumstantial. In a matter like this, there is not going to be an answerable "smoking gun" that clinches proof. But there have been enough glimpses of the Syndicate at work during the twentieth century for us to find that there is a case to answer, and to have laid it before the jury.

What is the verdict? Has the prosecution established its case? Or is there still reasonable doubt? It must be emphasized that if the verdict is "Not proved beyond all reasonable doubt," there is enough circumstantial evidence to present an extremely worrying picture.

How do you find? There are two standards of proof, which must not be confused. Either you, the members of the jury, are sure and have been satisfied by the evidence I have deployed beyond doubt; or you are merely persuaded on the balance of probabilities that the case has been made. It is the difference between the criminal and the civil standard of proof. I submit that at the very least, on the balance of probabilities the pattern speaks for itself: the case has been made.

EPILOGUE: WORLD GOVERNMENT VERSUS GLOBAL DEMOCRACY

We are not with you but with him (i.e. the Devil): that is our secret! ... We took from him what you rejected with scorn, the last gift he offered you, after having shown you all the kingdoms of the earth: we took from him Rome and the sword of Caesar and proclaimed ourselves the rulers of the earth, the sole rulers ... Why did you reject that last gift? By accepting that third counsel of the mighty spirit, you would have accomplished all that man seeks on earth, that is to say, whom to worship, to whom to entrust his conscience and how at last to unite all in a common, harmonious, and incontestable ant-hill, for the need of universal unity is the third and last torment of men. Mankind as a whole has always striven to organize itself into a world state ... By accepting the world and Caesar's purple, you would have founded the world state and given universal peace.

Dostoevsky, The Brothers Karamazov,
the Grand Inquisitor addressing Christ

If the case *has* been made, the US, with the UN behind it, has been inching the long New World Order Revolution towards world government, and the UN has been acting as an instrument of the Syndicate, sanctioning its use of "world army" alliances (as in the first Iraq War) and NATO (as in the case of Serbia), and has shown masterly inactivity when inactivity suits the Syndicate's purpose (as before September 11, in the case of Afghanistan). The UN can contribute UN armies, but its authority was ignored and diminished over Iraq, and realistically only the US hyper-power can sort out future defiance like the Taliban's or Saddam's.

Following the "Rockefellerite" Syndicate's creation of a world empire based on oil, natural resources, and military might, the US now has the means to deliver a world government. The Bush/PNAC leadership and Syndicate have tipped the balance of the world government's leadership from the UN to the US. The world government is now a possible consequence of American hegemony, and can make use of UN-related initiatives encouraged during the Clinton years.

In a sense the world government has already begun to function behind the scenes as many of the institutions have been quietly put in place. Global policies have been discussed and decided behind the closed doors of exclusive groups such as the G8, the OECD, the Bank of International Settlements, the World Bank, the International Monetary Fund, and the World Trade Organization. Networks of their officials have already created the institutions of world government, which in turn are readily influenced by transnational corporations – such as the oil companies – that pursue their own world strategies.

The UN Millennium Assembly and Summit of world leaders, meeting in September 2000 to discuss the future of the world and world government, put global democracy firmly on the international agenda. The Assembly, opened by former Soviet dictator (now turned environmentalist) Mikhail Gorbachev before 149 participating heads of government and officials from 31 other nations, with only 14 world leaders missing, ushered in the age of global governance and adopted a revised version of the UN Charter, known as the Charter for Global Democracy,[1] which had already been signed by the leaders of 56 nations.

The new Charter calls for a massive restructuring and strengthening of UN authority throughout the world. There is to be a standing UN army (called for by the Bilderberg-linked "Rothschildite" Blair and Schröder) to enforce international law, violators of which will be prosecuted in the UN International Criminal Court. There is to be a global constabulary and intelligence service licensed to kill, and a global tax on e-mail communications, international money transfers, and energy products. The UN is scheduled to unveil plans to expedite the implementation of world government. The Charter for Global Democracy vows to make the existing processes of world administration operated by these groups and agencies accountable to the peoples of the world. Many of these changes have been called for by the World Federalist Association, whose stated aim is to abolish war.[2]

It's not going to work. It won't affect the reality that the resulting worldwide authority will be manipulated just as before by those who seek to dominate world government.

Universalism

Global democracy is rooted in political Universalism. Universalist thinking sees all mankind, in all cultures and civilizations and at all periods of recorded history, in terms of the spiritual and metaphysical One, which pervades all religions and unifies the universe. It differs from globalism, which is merely spatial/geographical, not spiritual. Just as religious Universalism holds that God and the universe are One and that the souls of all Mankind, not just Christians, can be saved, so political Universalism holds that all mankind is One and promotes the rule of all mankind with the participation of all mankind, as all human beings have souls.

Moves towards political Universalism have taken place during the 1990s. The Commission on Global Governance[3] has sought a framework for global politics and decision-making. The Earth Summit in Rio, Agenda 21, The Earth Charter, the Real World Coalition, Earth Action's Call for a Safer World, the One Planet Initiative, and the Citizens' Public Trust Treaty have all made global declarations on development. The Hague Agenda for Peace has sought to eliminate war: the campaign against landmines has changed international law, and international conferences at New York, Vienna, Cairo, Copenhagen, Beijing, and Istanbul have focused on gender equality, family, employment, and social rights. The Inter-Parliamentary Union, which includes over 130 national parliaments,[4] adopted the Universal Declaration of Democracy, which has been endorsed by most parliaments in the world, while Jubilee 2000 has campaigned for the cancellation of unpayable debts owed by the world's poorest countries. The International Chamber of Commerce, the World Business Council for Sustainable Development, and other agencies have promoted high standards in international business. The Human Development Report has focused on global governance. A United Religious Initiative has accompanied progress towards a one-world government, and in June 2000 the constitution for a one-world religion was signed at the Carnegie Hall, New York. Much has been written on how a new way of governing the world (which world government supporters call "governance") can democratize international affairs.

A new Utopian hope has grown out of the New World Order Revolution –
the hope that global democracy can bring every agency of world government
to account, including the Bilderberg Group, the Trilateral Commission,
international economic alliances (OECD), international military alliances
(NATO), the central banking systems (the Federal Reserve System and
"Rothschilds"' Central Banks), and all the agencies for environmental,
financial, social, and sporting activities. The UN has been sidelined in the
quest for global democracy, but it too could be made more accountable.
In particular the UN's mandate "to save succeeding generations from the
scourge of war" could be applied equally to all peoples in the world.

Since the UN Charter was signed, over 30 million people have been
killed in war, millions more have died in genocide and ethnic conflict,
and over 100 million have fled their homes, of whom 20 million remain
refugees today. The UN has proved inadequate but is better than nothing,
and is the only arena in which all countries sit together.

For global governance to be accountable, the decision-takers of each
country must be answerable to the public of each country (i.e. each state
within the United States of the World). All decisions should be compatible
with public criteria of environmental suitability, the principles of equality
and human rights, and social and economic justice. Problems that can
be tackled at a global level include the environment, biodiversity, food
security and climate change, international security and disarmament,
international trade, finance and labor rights, epidemics, communications,
and international crime. The view is growing that global problems can
only get worse if international decision-making is left in the hands of
undemocratic, exclusive institutions such as the Bilderberg Group and the
Trilateral Commission.

Such Universalist thinking will be an increasing feature of the twenty-
first century as a move towards world government accelerates. The
gropings towards Universalist democracy show that the New World Order
Revolution does not have to end in dictatorship; nor does it have to pursue
a policy of depopulation.

Opponents of the Charter for Global Democracy will say that it is a charter
for the abolition of individual freedom; that it gives the UN the power to
tax aircraft and shipping fuels, and the use of outer space, the atmosphere,
and the high seas. It effectively eliminates the power to exercise national
vetoes in the Security Council and sanctions a standing UN army. It orders

the reduction of all national armies and the registration of all arms (which could be used to secede from the world government). Opponents argue that the Charter for Global Democracy is financed by none other than David Rockefeller, and is intended as a veneer to be superimposed on the Syndicate's hegemonistic New World Order, to make it acceptable.

A Choice of New World Orders?

This view may be too pessimistic. The New World Order Revolution can in fact proceed in one of two directions.

Ahead of us is a stark choice between two New World Orders. There are two New World Orders – one in the revolutionary image of Lucifer and one in the spiritual image of Christ.[5] Which will triumph? The answer to that question will determine the health of the North American and European civilizations during the next millennium.

Just as there are two New World Orders, so there are two Universalisms: the good kind I have developed in my philosophy, which thinks globally about the whole of mankind and sees globally in terms of the souls of human beings, each of which has equally emerged from the One (the metaphysical Fire or Light); and the bad kind which owes much to Freemasonry and is dominated by the occult, particularly Luciferianism. For some, the revolutionary Lucifer is the god of worldly wealth and the flesh, and is a secular metaphor for "bad and malevolent."

The tension between these two Universalisms is shaping the growing heresy of our time, which can be contacted through the New Age movement and proliferating Eastern sects. The good Universalism enshrines the vision of the mystics of all cultures and civilizations in global purity. The bad Universalism purveys the cynical and corrupt Luciferian vision of the Illuminati, which has been adopted by the Syndicate.

Christ's New World Order – and I use Christ as a secular metaphor to mean "good and benevolent," not in any sense of evangelical fundamentalism exported round the world – will embrace and enfold an Islam purged of terrorism within its globalism. It holds out the prospect of a Utopia to end all Utopias: all humankind living at peace, free from war, famine, and disease through globally planned resources, each world citizen in touch with his or her inner nature and metaphysical reality. Will the New World Order leaders recreate Christ's Heaven on earth? That is the question that will dominate the twenty-first century.

The New World Order Revolution can open up and become accountable. Wars, famines, and diseases can be eliminated by global planning, by a truly Universalist (i.e. spiritual pan-human but non-Masonic) outlook that sees all mankind as the constituency of the world's leaders. This is (to use a contrasting personifying symbol and free it from its Christian-fundamentalist associations) Christ's New World Order, a compassionate order, which liberates the poor and feeds and frees all mankind.

One day such global planning may mean that every citizen of the world is governed by the principles outlined by St Paul in *The Acts of the Apostles* (2:44–5): "Now the company of those who believed were of one heart and soul, and no one said that any of the things which he possessed was his own, but they had everything in common .... There was not a needy person among them, for as many as were possessors of lands or houses sold them, and brought the proceeds of what was sold and laid it at the apostles' feet; and distribution was made to each as any had need." Such a physical consolidation of the spiritual vision of the oneness and harmony of humankind would spread contentment throughout the earth and turn Universalism into a positive creed of human love.

The spiritual vision which sees "all is One, all mankind is my brother" (as can be known in the poetic vision) also grasps that when "the Kingdom of God" is literalized it degenerates or steps down and becomes physical in globalization. Nevertheless, as above, so below, and a world government that mirrors the spiritual idea will be more perfect than its more corrupt, occult copy of a group of marauders running the world self-interestedly, to suit themselves, and seeking world domination while claiming to be acting for the good of mankind. A world government run by saints will be better than one run by self-interested bandits.

It is not easy to establish a world government of saints. Cromwell found it impossible to create a national Parliament of saints, let alone a world Parliament of enlightened men. In the course of my research I have established that all revolutions have begun as occult visions and have degenerated into less-than-ideal political and physical regimes as the original occult vision steps down to political government.

The revolutionary dynamic of the ideas (and methods of government) behind the pure Universalist New World Order Revolution can be stated as follows:

Spiritual inspiration	Intellectual expression	Political expression	Physical consolidation
Universal Christ	Universalism reflecting God as divine Light/World religion[6]	Consenting world government	World Paradise: abolition of war, famine and disease
Christ's method of government: representation	Universalist democratic movement	Council of world leaders	Free liberal democracy, liberty under the law

The Corruption of a Spiritual Vision

Will the New World Order Revolution for a world government corrupt and enslave people? Will the New World Order leaders take the view of Dostoevsky's Grand Inquisitor in the story told by Ivan Karamazov, that people are happiest when they give up their freedom and responsibility to an authoritarian dictator who turns stones into bread to feed them, enslaves them with miracles, and rules all the kingdoms of the earth – the three temptations Satan offered Christ, which the Grand Inquisitor insists Christ should have accepted? Will the New World Order leaders apply the thinking of Satan as interpreted by the Grand Inquisitor, or will they jettison Lucifer's New Age with its emblem of the All-Seeing Eye over an unfinished pyramid (the occult hieroglyph of the New World Order Revolution so far)?

On the one hand, the New World Order can remain enclosed and secretive, avoiding publicity and (if the recommendations of their meetings have the force of policy) in effect governed by the Bilderberg Group and the Trilateral Commission, a hidden hand behind world leaders. If such a model is being proposed, it is a dictatorial, Freemasonic model.

This possible direction for the New World Order is accompanied by a disquieting belief system. We can now state the revolutionary dynamic of the ideas (and methods of government) behind the Luciferian New World Order Revolution as follows:

Occult inspiration	Intellectual expression	Political expression	Physical consolidation
Luciferianism	Freemasonry reflecting Lucifer as Great Architect/Deism/atheism	Tyrannical government	World Hell: world depopulation by 2 billion by genocide?
Satan/Lucifer's method of government: boundless power	Secretive intellectual élite/oil imperialism	False messiah as world dictator, council of elders	World police state

The "stepping down" process from the original vision, through its intellectual and political expression to its physical consolidation, can be found in the revolutionary dynamic of both New World Orders. It seems that in the case of the Luciferian model each stage of the "stepping down" process also involves progressively bringing out what is most base in human nature. There is therefore another sense in which the vision "steps down" into the physical world. On the other hand with the dynamic of the Universalist New World Order, it seems that each stage of the "stepping down" process also progressively involves bringing out what is the highest in human nature. In effect, it is a "stepping up" process for humankind.

The revelation that the New World Order's progress towards a political one-world government is an occult corruption of a Universalist spiritual vision should not come as a great surprise. However, although there have been many clues the reader may not be prepared for the revelation (an alarming "twist in the tale") that the God the Freemasons serve is none other than Lucifer.[7] The composite god of the Masonic quasi-religion, known as Je-Ho-Vah Jah-Bul-On, is believed by Christians to refer to an incarnation of Satan. The syllables combine four names of God: the Hebrew Jehovah, the Chaldean Jah, the Syriac-Canaanite Baal, and the Egyptian On or Osiris-Re, a reference to the Temple of Re at Heliopolis. The four names mean that Jehovah, God, is Chaldean-Canaanite-Egyptian, i.e. horned like Baal, i.e. Lucifer.[8] This is only revealed to 30th, 31st, 32nd, and 33rd-degree Freemasons and may come as a shock to many lower-ranking Freemasons who joined to do good works and support charitable causes.[9]

In fact, a number of US presidents have been 33rd-degree Freemasons, including such organizers of the contemporary New World Order as George W. Bush (who though a born-again Christian asked to be sworn in as president on the same Masonic Bible his father had used), his father Bush Sr., Bill Clinton, and Gerald Ford. Other influential New World Order Freemasonic organizers are reputed to include John D. Rockefeller IV, David Rockefeller, Bob Dole, Newt Gingrinch, Al Gore, Jesse Jackson, and Ross Perot.[10]

The reader may be equally surprised at the revelation (and again there have been many clues) that if the New World Order is controlled by influential Freemasons, then consequently its outlook is actively Luciferian, indeed Satanist. Besides being taught that Lucifer is the true God, 32nd- and 33rd-degree Masons have their own Luciferian calendar, based on *Anno Lucis* (or the Year of Light/Lucifer).[11] It will now be fully understood why the Freemasonic tradition of several revolutions is referred to as "occult" for the knowledge it has hidden and kept secret is that it follows Lucifer.

Lucifer/Semiramis

According to legend, Lucifer, the Angel Satanail or Satanael, was the elder son of God (Christ being God's second son).[12] Although he had great power, he sought to be greater than God, his Father, and attempted to overthrow him and become ruler of Heaven and Earth. The archangel Michael flung him into the abyss, and as he fell an emerald became detached from his diadem and landed in the Hindu Kush Mountains (near bin Laden's mountain hideout). Those who follow Lucifer hold a dualistic rather than a unitary vision of the universe as they champion Satanail against his brother Christ and work for a "one-world government" in which Lucifer is in control of the world at God's expense. They have divided the unity of creation.[13]

At a practical, physical level members of the Syndicate admire the Luciferian tradition. Worshipping money and world revolution, seeking an alternative to the Christian nation-states of medieval Europe, the main members of the Syndicate have turned to Freemasonry and have followed the example of Weishaupt and Pike in placing themselves beneath the figure of Satan/Lucifer.

The implications of this belief system for the Syndicate's New World Order are profound. The Syndicate regards the coming United States of Europe as the seat of the Antichrist. It is rumored that it will eventually have III regions, each with 6 zones, totaling 666 districts or counties – the number of the mark of the Beast.[14] In preparation for this finished creation, the central (NATO) computer in Brussels, on which every European citizen's records are placed, is called "The 666" or "The Beast." (It is three storeys high and has the capacity to house numbers – all prefixed "666" – for all persons in the world.)[15] Such Satanic imagery is not accidental.

Similarly, the 12 golden stars on the blue flag of Europe and the New World Order are Satanic.[16] The flag was unveiled in Paris on July 14, 1989, the 200th anniversary of the French Revolution which was orchestrated by Freemasonic secret societies. The flag appeared to be patterned after the Miraculous Medal of the Virgin Mary made in 1832, a billion of which had been sold by 1876, and to represent the crown of Mary, Queen of Heaven. The symbol is drawn from the Woman (see below) clothed with the sun, standing on the moon with a crown of 12 stars on her head (Revelation 12:1),[17] whom Catholics teach is Mary. The message appears to be that the Queen of Heaven is a symbol around which predominantly Catholic Europe can unify. The poster of the uncompleted Tower of Babel under 12 stars (see below) was released at the same time as the flag. The poster announces that the Tower of Babel will now be completed despite the confusion of tongues visited on its inhabitants by God. The completion of the Tower is thus an act of rebellion against God, i.e. Luciferian.[18] The stars appear upside down. In astrology the upside-down star represents the Goat of Mendes, who is Satan.[19]

The official poster of the Council of Europe

The Queen of Heaven is thus *not* the Virgin Mary but Queen Semiramis, Nimrod's licentious wife who introduced sacred prostitution and became known as the Whore of Babylon.[20] Semiramis was the prototype of the Woman with "Mystery" on her forehead (Revelation 17), for she founded the mystery religion in Babylon. Later she was worshipped as Vesta and

Venus.[21] The mysterious Queen of Heaven is thus a harlot pretending to be a virgin.[22] The 12 stars have nothing to do with the number of countries in the EU, but represent the crown of this Semiramis associated with impurity: Satan's bride and Queen.[23] This Semiramis is shown on old coins with spoked rays on her head[24] and appears as the Statue of Liberty, a gift from Freemasons in Paris to Freemasons in New York.[25] She holds the torch of liberty representing the knowledge of the illuminated – the Illuminati – but also stands as the bride of Lucifer.[26] The statue copies a Masonic statue on an island in the Seine.[27] This is Satan's, or Lucifer's, New World Order. If the *Global 2000* reports are policy, its Malthusian goals include extermination for a third of mankind by planned wars, famines, and diseases.

For Freemasons Babylon has a special significance[28] because under the rule of Nimrod mankind was united, a unity symbolized in the Tower of Babel. It had been known for some time that occultists behind the New World Order have sought to control the Babylonian ruins that gave rise to the Whore of Babylon and the Tower of Babel,[29] and the Sumerian ruins of the ziggurat of Ur, the birthplace of Abraham, which was built by 4000 BC and restored by Nebuchadnezzar II in the sixth century BC.

Babylonian religion developed round traditions concerning the "ungodly" rule of Nimrod, which was in Babel, Erech, Akkad, and Calneh (Genesis 10:10), and his wife Semiramis and her child Tammuz. Semiramis was also known as Semele, who was identified with the moon (and so, later, Diana); after his death, Nimrod's body was cut into pieces and burnt, and his ashes were sent to different parts of his kingdom and he became known as the sun-god.[30] Around 2400 BC northern Akkad dominated Sumer, and the rites of Tammuz held on the top of ziggurats such as Ur invoked the moon-goddess, who had a shrine on the ziggurat's top, but also invoked the sun-god. The rites focused on the death of Tammuz, the vegetation god; his imprisoning in the Underworld; and his rising in the spring after the Queen of Heaven descended to reclaim him. There was then a Royal Sacred Marriage between the risen Tammuz and the Queen of Heaven (who was later known as Inanna).[31]

Oil aside, were members of the Syndicate (Freemasonic Illuminati) partly drawn to Iraq, using American and British troops, because of the occultist significance of Babylon and Ur? The Garden of Eden is traditionally located at al-Qurna in the lush vegetation where the Tigris and Euphrates meet. Babylon, with its Hanging Gardens and Tower of Babel, saw Hammurabi's legal code. The city of Ur knew Abraham; the city of Uruk was where the epic of *Gilgamesh* was situated. Nineveh was the Assyrian capital and Baghdad was where caliph al-Mansour built his circular City of Peace in 762.

Will world leaders put aside their national interests and place themselves beneath a world government? Or will a *Pax Americana* backed by strength enforce a New World Order by subduing any leader that seeks to threaten it by acquiring weapons of mass destruction?

The earth can be a paradise for enlightened people; it does not have to be a Hell, a Luciferian Auschwitz, a Freemasonic death factory.

Regardless of whether it lives in a universal republic or a universal monarchy,[32] can humankind rise above the killing and exploitation of his or her neighbor's oil to the noble vision of the best world government that controls international relations, food supply, medicine, and outlaws war, starvation, and disease? A new century and a new millennium bring hope.

Our study has shown that for more than a hundred years Western statesmen have pursued the elusive dream of world peace – through wars and violent revolutions. The dream is revolutionary and Utopian.

In the twentieth century, because they were inspired by the Syndicate, all revolutions can be seen to belong to a single world revolutionary movement committed to the creation of one-world government. Particularly in the twentieth century revolutions have been manipulated by the Syndicate for its own purposes. We have seen that the New World Order seeks to free humankind from established religion and (on the wishes of one faction) replace it with a Freemasonic religion of Lucifer. Nevertheless, it is still possible that Christ's New World Order of global democracy will emerge like a butterfly from its present chrysalis.

Will this noblest of hopes for a better world be fulfilled? If so, the nation-state is doomed, but humankind will enter a new Golden Age, free from repression, torture, despotism, and genocide; free from the Four Horsemen of the Apocalypse: unrest, famine, war, and disease. If so, would the 100 million victims of revolutions be found not to have died in vain? Will harmony finally prevail where there was once discord and contradiction? And an Age of Peace where there was once conflict and revolution?

Benevolence

It may appear that I am more in favor of nation-states than of the regional blocs created by the Syndicate or of the breaking-up of nations (such as the USSR and Yugoslavia) into smaller regions; and that I am unduly sympathetic towards the British Empire.

In fact, I see civilizations as progressing through phases, during some of which (in expansionist phases) they create regional blocs. The North American civilization is passing through an expansionist phase and is "conquering" the world and imposing on it the philosophy of its own founding fathers: democracy, freedom, federalism, and capitalism. The Byzantine-Russian civilization, by contrast, is older and more advanced and has entered a phase in which a union (the Communist USSR) has broken up into smaller components that are linked federally.

It is not that I prefer nation-states and empires to regional blocs and fragments, but that I see nation-states, empires, blocs, and fragments as consequences or symptoms of specific phases in the rise and fall of specific civilizations. A civilization's globalist phase/new world order that is good for mankind – like the best traditions of the British Empire, with its educative mission – and abolishes war, famine, and disease is preferable to one that promotes war, famine, disease, depopulation, and its own brand of terrorism to widen its power.

The management of civilizations in relation to each other depends on the degree of benevolence of the dominant civilization and the degree of benevolence of civilizations that oppose it. States have to organize themselves through global institutions. The global institutions are only as good as the dominant civilization – at present the North American civilization. The UN, like the League of Nations, has its faults: it can be manipulated by the dominant civilization and more powerful nations. Despite the Syndicate's plan for it, the UN will never impose a world rule on nations as it is not strong enough – for it is merely a reflection of the forces of its member states. The only way states can cooperate is through global institutions, short of world government.

Given the support of a benevolent dominant civilization, the UN could represent Christ's New World Order and intervene more aggressively and prevent massacres, in which case it will need an active world army. It can remain a talking-shop and not have an active world army. The kind of

UN that is most desirable requires the dominant civilization, the globalist North American civilization, to impose a benevolent New World Order. If America is benevolent, then the UN's world army would be a force for good. If America is malevolent, the UN should remain a talking-shop and not conquer other nations. As regimes go, the US administration appears from the outside to be reasonably decent. From what we have seen in this book, the Syndicate is a pressure on the US administration within the North American civilization that is not a benevolent force for universal good.

The Syndicate wants world dominance and has reacted against the Arab civilization, which has challenged it. This challenge has clothed itself in terrorist methods. How the UN responds to terrorism depends on the nature of the challenge. Bin Laden wants the Arab civilization to become strong and pay the West back for past humiliations: pay Spain back for ending the Moorish Andalus; Britain and America for allowing Israel to be planted in its midst; and Europe for sending crusaders to the Middle East and driving the Arabs back from the gates of Vienna. He has awakened the spirit of Saladin during the Crusades. Hence he refers to Western armies as "the Crusaders." The truth is, there is a bitter struggle between Wahhabist extremists within the Arab civilization against the North American civilization – the Middle-Eastern rebellion in which death is glorious and suicide-bombers are martyrs.

The Syndicate's plan is to defeat and conquer the Arab civilization and take its oil. It involves a clash between the North American and Arab civilizations as I predicted in *The Fire and the Stones*: a war between civilizations. The Syndicate wants to blur this by speaking of an alliance against terrorism. It will be said that there is an Anglo-American-Libyan alliance against al-Qaeda (like a Roman alliance with an African client-state against Jugurtha). This is false. Libya is not committed to exterminating al-Qaeda but to getting on the right side of the US and Britain so that the Libyan economy can be re-floated, which will help Gaddafi to survive. It is an alliance of convenience.

We are living through a clash between two civilizations, a war picked by the US to further its expansionist phase and world dominance and called a war against terrorism. The regional blocs and break-ups that have already happened or are coming into being have to be seen within this aggressive intention. They are not being created with altruistic benevolent intentions but out of self-interest. Because the US is in a powerful, expansionist phase if its development, the globalist groupings promote US self-interest, though they are hailed by Americans as being for the good of mankind. Today, the language of national self-interest is couched in altruism.

An expanding civilization is, by its very nature, governed by self-interest rather than benevolent altruism. (The same was true of the British Empire, which nevertheless managed to include an astonishing degree of altruism.) Therefore each time such a civilization intervenes aggressively, it is something of a disaster for the rest of mankind – although there can be universal benefits when tyrants are brought low. What should be happening is the spreading of a benevolent New World Order that combines freedom and justice for all mankind with freedom from famine, disease, and war. This is the (probably unattainable) goal and ideal, and it is worth giving up nation-states for such a utopian paradise. When a malevolent New World Order, motivated by acquisitiveness and greed, threatens to sweep aside our traditional freedoms, national groupings, and culture for reasons of self-interest, the nation-state is preferable to the regional bloc.

It is not globalism itself that is wrong but unbenevolent globalism dedicated to the self-interested widening of power and influence and acquisition of natural resources and oil. And yet, we cannot really say that such self-interested globalism is "wrong" for it is a product of the rise and fall of civilizations, a manifestation of a phase. It happens, and is arguably no more "wrong" than the swoop of a large bird of prey. Nevertheless, enlightened globalism is preferable. A democratic globalism within a benevolent civilization in an expansionist phase would be a boon for mankind, as was (for some of the time and in parts, but not in places such as Amritsar, the scene of a dreadful massacre in India) life under the generally remarkably enlightened British Empire.

Some individuals among the Syndicate's leaders may have such enlightened good intentions and aspire to an idealistic and benevolent view of mankind, and hope to benefit mankind through the UN. We have seen enough in this book to conclude that the majority of the Syndicate pursue an agenda of accumulating oil reserves and natural resources, fomenting civil wars, and manipulating the UN into rooking mankind. They either do not aspire to good intentions or disguise their real self-interested motives with altruistic-sounding lies.

Taming the Phoenix

My study of revolutions has established that they are not merely destructive mechanisms. Revolutions are within civilizations and act as corrective adjustments. They help them to change; they are a means of bringing speedy transformations which are urgently needed and which have to take place abruptly. They yank their civilization forward and are a vital part of the pattern of growth and decay. They destroy the old so that new growth can come through, just as a storm removes dead leaves and prepares for new buds. It must be said, however, that they contribute greatly to the "stepping down" of a civilization from its original spiritual vision to its eventual disintegration.

I am aware that this is something of a pioneering work. When the history of the growth of the world government comes to be written in the twenty-first century, reference will have to be made to the growth of the "Rockefeller Empire" in the twentieth century and its use of revolutions, which in turn requires the study of previous revolutions. The foregoing pages, and those in their companion volume *The Secret History of the West*, are fundamental to an understanding of the expanding world government in our time, which, even though it is ignored by the news media, is the biggest story of our lifetimes. Its growth is inextricably linked with the continuing ascendancy of the North American civilization.

The world's revolutionary spirit is like the mythical phoenix. There is only one of it, and it is reborn every 500 years. Nesting in Arabia (not far from "Rockefellers,"' and bin Laden's, Saudi Arabia) it emerged from its anti-Catholic predecessor's body and was nurtured on Rosicrucianism and first flew in 1776. Its birth sent shock waves round the world, causing seismic activity that has disturbed the oceans. The earthquakes have continued during its growth to maturity.

Now the gigantic phoenix, beautiful though it is, has become a menace. Each time it has stirred it has made waves.

Since 1450 each of the world's revolutions has been accompanied by small waves. By the end of the twentieth century the small waves have multiplied in each regional bloc (Europe, Latin America, Africa, the Middle East, and South East Asia), and the sea level has risen. Each small wave has been gathering into one universal, ocean-wide tidal wave (the accumulation of 550 years of revolutions), which is curling to crash onto our shores and destroy our heritage.

Fundamental changes to our nation-state are taking place in our time. A seismic shift is happening before our eyes: the national characteristics which Churchill and Montgomery fought so hard to defend are being submerged in a tide of multiculturalism, Europe-driven changes that have affected our currency, and globalist thinking which has created a Global Coalition.

The nation-state leader feels powerless to confront the approaching tidal wave. Frustrated by the expectations of his court, King Canute sat on the shore to demonstrate to his courtiers his powerlessness to control the sea (or the weather, or harvests). He was a wise man and was graphically demonstrating to his courtiers the limitations of his sovereign power in relation to the universal tidal force of the sea by getting his feet wet and having to move his throne further up the beach.

Confronting the tidal wave on the beaches (to use Churchill's phrase) will mean suffering Canute's fate. The only wise course is to shackle its cause – the monstrous phoenix. A Beowulf is needed to seek out Grendel and tame the monster. "*Wyrd oft nereth unfaegne eorl thonne his ellen deah*": "fate often preserves the undoomed warrior when his courage is strong." Or so the *Beowulf* poet, writing in England in the early Anglo-Saxon period, informs us.

History never ends. Each of the world's civilizations continues to unfold new stages, and no New World Order can arrest the never-ending, rise-and-fall pattern of individual civilizations with a world government. It is a global phase or stage within a civilization. It can now be seen that one of my aims, if not my principal aim, has been to place recent events within the context of a larger, unfolding picture – the end is not nigh, and the Syndicate need not rule the world. An alternative solution lies within us all – in that part of us which is "the best (or highest)" we can aspire to.

The pressing task is to produce a world philosophy – Universalism – that accords all world citizens dignity and genuinely democratic rights, but has no truck with the secret agendas of Freemasonry or Luciferianism. Such a philosophy must be based on the good, mystic way of Light that seeks to do its best for all humankind rather than the evil, occult way of darkness that seeks to destroy a third of humankind.

This phoenix's allotted time is nearly up. We have to believe that its destructive antics can be tamed, that its successor can be reared in harmless captivity without causing world-wide havoc, and that the world can become a Utopian paradise without the hideous massacres that have defiled revolutions.

It is patriotic for Americans to love the US and for Britons to love Britain. Something wrong is happening. The US is being stolen by the Syndicate via the abolition of US elections after 2016. Britain is also being stolen by the Syndicate via the new European constitution. Patriots regard the prospect of constitutional theft with dismay. What should they do?

Patriots should press Western (ie North American and European) leaders and the leaders of the world's living civilizations and their nation-states to inform themselves of the Syndicate's plan for "world union." This book has briefed them. Once they are alert to the Syndicate's real aims and policies they can be urged to stop serving global interests at the expense of their own national governments, and resist the Syndicate's darker visions and its unelected, self-interested drive to create a particular, wrong kind of United States of the World that will enable it to dominate and subjugate our pure earth and all who dwell on it. Many in the current US, British and European administrations will applaud if the serpent-like Syndicate is bound in a great chain, that it "should deceive the nations no more."

APPENDICES

Appendix 1: The 4–part revolutionary dynamic of the Syndicate's New World Order Revolution

Stepping-Down

In my study of all the revolutions between 1453 and the Russian Revolution, *The Secret History of the West*, I offer a new and original theory as to why revolutions happen: a 4–part revolutionary dynamic. In all the revolutions before the twentieth century, an idealist has an occultist vision, which others state in intellectual terms. This becomes corrupted by a political regime, and results in physical suppression (such as Stalin's purge). There is a "stepping down" process from the original vision, through its intellectual and political expression to its physical consolidation. All revolutions have promised greater freedom for their peoples and have ended up enslaving them. The New World Order Revolution, though unfinished, is no exception and conforms to the pattern.

Early Dynamic of the Syndicate's New World Order Revolution

The first two phases of that dynamic can be stated more fully in terms of a sequence of five sub-phases:

1. The occultist vision is heretical, in the sense that it is outside the orthodoxy of the Christian religion. In the New World Order's case it is Freemasonic.
2. This vision is then interpreted to others so that it reaches an audience. In the New World Order's case the "interpreting" was performed by the Round Table.
3. A revolutionary originator then takes the interpretation and by his energy, teaching, and/or funding spreads it and turns it into a

revolutionary program of concealed action. In the New World Order's case this role has been performed by the Council on Foreign Relations (CFR).

4. The heretical vision that has been interpreted and covertly turned into action is then interpreted by a thoughtful intellectual. He expresses it within a group or groups and promotes the revolutionary idea in a new way. In the New World Order's case this role is performed within the Bilderberg Group and Trilateral Commission.

5. This intellectual expression of the revolutionary idea is then taken up by a new thinker, who puts it into practice outside the political system. In the New World Order Revolution this semi-political action is the tearing down of the Berlin Wall.

The formula of the full early revolutionary dynamic will enable us to review the evidence we have assembled in greater detail:

1. The heretical occultist vision of the New World Order Revolution is found in the Sionist Rosicrucian – and also Grand Orient Templar – Adam Weishaupt, who was funded by Mayer Amschel Rothschild.

2. The occultist interpreter was Cecil Rhodes'/Lord Milner's Round Table, which was backed by the Weishauptian "Rothschilds" and the Syndicate of Western capitalists; the main interpreter was eventually the historian Arnold Toynbee, who dominated Chatham House for 30 years and produced *A Study of History*, which interpreted Weishaupt's vision.

3. The occult revolutionary originator was John D. Rockefeller I, the richest man in the world. He supported the CFR and created a worldwide oil empire through revolutions and interpreted Weishaupt's and Toynbee's vision in terms of his hidden Freemasonic tradition which kept the knowledge secret. His son, John D. Rockefeller II, continued his policy and donated a sum to pay for the land for the UN building. By influencing the selection of UN and government personnel through the CFR he controlled the UN and many governments.

4. The thoughtful intellectual interpreter who gave the vision a new slant was his grandson, David Rockefeller of the Bilderberg Group and Trilateral Commission, considered the most powerful man in the

world. Did he control the USSR? He has arguably been the Weishaupt of our time.

5. The semi-political intellectual interpreter who later became political was Gorbachev, who became a Grand Orient Mason in 1984 and then brought down the Berlin Wall and ended the Cold War, paving the way for the successors to the British, German, and Russian Empires to join the US in a post-nation-state world government.

The early revolutionary dynamic of the Syndicate's New World Order Revolution can be stated (or summarized) as follows:

Heretical occultist vision	Occultist interpreter	Occult revolutionary originator	Thoughtful intellectual interpreter	Semi- political intellectual interpreter
Weishaupt/Mayer Amschel Rothschild	Cecil Rhodes'/ Milner's Round Table/Arnold Toynbee ("Rothschilds")	John D. Rockefeller I/II	David Rockefeller	Gorbachev

Dynamic of Nazi Revolution

We need to relate this pattern to the Syndicate's failed attempts to achieve world government in the twentieth century. The evidence laid out suggests that representatives of the Syndicate made two attempts: first by financing Hitler, and then by sustaining and ending the Cold War.

The five sub-phases of the first two stages of the dynamic of the Nazi Revolution were as follows:

1. The heretical occultist vision of the Nazi Revolution can be found in Weishaupt and his Bavarian Illuminati.
2. The occultist interpreter was the anti-Semitic von Liebenfels, whose New Templars revived the Templar republican side of Weishaupt's vision under the emblem of the swastika.
3. The occult revolutionary originator was Dietrich Eckart, leading figure of the Thule Society and a Manichean.
4. The thoughtful intellectual interpreter who gave the occult vision a new slant was Anton Drexler, founder of the German Workers' Party, which Hitler renamed the Nazi Party.
5. The semi-political intellectual who later became political was Adolf Hitler, whose *Mein Kampf* stated Nazism as a political program.

The early revolutionary dynamic of the Nazi Revolution can be summarized as follows:

Heretical occultist vision	Occultist interpreter	Occult revolutionary originator	Thoughtful intellectual interpreter	Semi- political intellectual interpreter
Weishaupt	von Liebenfels	Eckart	Drexler	Hitler

The intellectual expression of the Nazi Revolution was through Goebbels' propaganda ministry and Himmler's SS, who were trained at Schloss Wewelsburg. Rosenberg, a Manichean, and Wiligut, Himmler's guru, were important at a theoretical level.

The political expression of the Nazi Revolution can be found in Hitler's Third Reich, 1933–45. The physical consolidation of the Revolution was through world war (the Second World War) and genocide in concentration camps.

The full revolutionary dynamic of the Nazi Revolution and its ideas can be stated as follows:

Occult inspiration	Intellectual expression	Political expression	Physical consolidation
Weishaupt/von Liebenfels Eckart	Goebbels, Himmler and the SS, Rosenberg Wiligut	Hitler's Third Reich	Hitler's attempt at world government through world war and genocide

Full Dynamic of the Syndicate's New World Order Revolution

The full dynamic of the Syndicate's, New World Order Revolution incorporates the failed Nazi and Soviet attempts to establish a world government.

The intellectual expression of the Syndicate's New World Order Revolution can be found in those who have propagandized attempts to achieve a world government in the twentieth century: Goebbels, propagandizer of Hitler's Nazism; Monnet, who propagandized the European Union; and Yeltsin, who propagandized a de-Communized Russia.

The political expression of the world government has not happened yet, but Round Table followers have made failed or half-completed attempts. The first failed attempt was Hitler's anti-Bolshevik Empire in Europe, and its attempted consolidation in the Second World War. The second failed attempt was the expansionism of Stalin and his successors during the

Cold War. The half-completed attempt has been the coming European federal super-state or United States of Europe, which is a stepping-stone to this political expression.

Its consolidation involves "controlling" and thus reducing the world's population. If the *Global 2000 Report* is policy rather than a forecast of a likelihood, then the reduction, so far 170–350 million, will be 2 billion. The aim of the revolutionary Utopia is clear; the extent of depopulation required is not.

The full revolutionary dynamic of the New World Order Revolution so far, and of its failed and half-completed attempts to achieve world rule, can be stated as follows (failed attempt above half-completed attempt):

Occult inspiration	Intellectual expression	Political expression	Physical consolidation
Weishaupt/Round Table ("Rothschilds"– "Rockefellers") Syndicate	Hitler's Nazi anti-Bolshevism (Goebbels)	Third Reich's rule of Europe	Attempted Nazi world rule/Second World War
Same as above	Globalization (UN, Rockefeller): unification of Europe (USE, Monnet) and "de-Communized" Russia (Gorbachev/ Yeltsin); via Fabian Society, RIIA, CFR, Bilderberg, Trilaterals	(European super-state; world government, United States of World)	(Malthusian depopulation by 2 billion?)

Dynamic of Two British Empires

Something happened to the drive for world government in the course of the twentieth century. At the beginning of the century, Milner, Curtis, and others tried to turn the British Empire, on which the sun would never set, into a world government that would be an extension of the British Empire. By the 1950s, this approach had faded into the outlook of Toynbee and Dulles: all nation-states should end so that regional blocs could come into being and eventually be transformed into a world government. Towards the end of the century, the "Rockefellerite," CFR view had taken over: there was to be an American-led world government. In short, the "Rockefeller" Empire had replaced the British Empire. All the main events since 1989 – the collapse of a unified Soviet Union for a federation in which newly autonomous countries like Turkmenistan can reach deals with Western oil companies, the demolition of the Berlin Wall, the reunification of Europe, and the wars waged against Arab/Islamic countries – have advanced an expanding American commercial oil empire: in large measure, the "Rockefeller" Empire.

The dream of the New World Order is based on the victory of socialism masquerading as capitalism, the UN and triumphant US forces. "Rothschilds" have always been supreme. Their efforts – their funding of railways and search for diamonds – helped to create the Second British Empire, which was in effect a world empire. There is a view that they rode on the back of what was essentially a spiritual movement to Christianize and civilize the world, and transformed a benevolent Commonwealth into a commercial, exploitative empire. This view regards the Rothschilds as corrupters of the occultist vision that created the Second British Empire, just as the Cecils and Walsingham were corrupters of the occultist vision of Pierre D'Ailly and Columbus that created the First British Empire.

We can express the revolutionary dynamic of the two British Empires as follows:

First British Empire (built on the rejection of Catholicism)			
Occult inspiration	Intellectual expression	Political expression	Physical consolidation
D'Ailly/Columbus	John Dee/Raleigh/ Bartholomew Gosnold/ Bacon	Elizabeth I, Cecils/ Walsingham	Seventeenth-eighteenth century colonies of the New World
Second British Empire (built on the rejection of Republicanism)			
Occult inspiration	Intellectual expression	Political expression	Physical consolidation
Weishaupt	"Rothschilds"/ Palmerston/Ruskin/ Syndicate	Disraeli/Cecil Rhodes/ Syndicate intelligence services	Colonial exploitation in nineteenth century colonies

(*Burke and Ruskin expressed the occultist vision in intellectual terms. "Rothschilds" corrupted the occultist vision.)

Appendix 2: An analysis of some twentieth-century Cold War revolutions: the dynamic within the events and the Syndicate

A sample of the revolutions conducted during the Cold War shows that in each case their revolutionary dynamic accords with the pattern of events and of "Rockefellerite" activity we have found.

The revolutionary dynamic of the Cold War revolutions is as follows:

Revolution	Occult inspiration	Intellectual expression	Physical expression	Physical consolidation
Chinese	Marx	Sun Yat-sen/ Chou En-lai	Mao Tse-tung	Deng Hsiao-ping
Vietnamese	Marx	Viet Minh	Ho Chi Minh	Ho Chi Minh
Cuban	Marx	Ché Guevara	Castro	Castro
Egyptian	Marx	Free Officers	Naguib	Nasser
Iraqi	Marx/Nasser	Free Officers/Arif	Kassem	Saddam Hussein
Libyan	Marx/Nasser	Free Officers/ Jaloud	Gaddafi	Gaddafi
Cambodian	Marx	Chinese	Pol Pot	Pol Pot
Iranian	Marx	Rafsanjani	Khomeini	Khamenei

Behind Marx was his paymaster, the Rothschilds, who carried on the Weishauptian vision in the 1860s and paid him to write *Das Kapital* and thereby perfect socialism.

It is instructive to consider the extent to which the "Rockefellerite" Syndicate may have been behind the dynamic and events of these revolutions.

Chinese Revolution

The Chinese Revolution began after the overthrow of the Manchu dynasty in 1911. "Rockefellers" competed with "Rothschildite" Britain for China. In February 1914 Standard Oil loaned China $15m in return for a 75-year oil concession in Shensi and Chi Li, in partnership with the Chinese government. There was bitter opposition in China, Japan, and England, and "Rockefellers" conducted a propaganda campaign.

In 1918 the Russian Communists announced that they were marching to free the people of China and in 1921 Mao declared he was a Marxist after reading Marx's *Communist Manifesto*. A Russian agent was sent that year to Peking and then Shanghai to plan the First Congress of the Chinese Communist Party. Russians infiltrated the government in 1922, and by 1924 reorganized the Chinese armed forces along Soviet army lines. Chiang Kai-Shek (1887–1975) was the Commandant and Chou En-Lai was in charge of political affairs. Chou gave intellectual expression to the revolution. Chiang attacked Shanghai with Soviet troops and robbed the "Rothschild"-affiliated Soong bank. He then did a deal with Soong, changed sides, and married Soong's sister in 1927. He ejected the Russians and Mao fled and began training rebels. Chiang obstructed the revolution as President from 1927 to 1949.

By the 1920s, the Socony-Vacuum (now Mobil Oil) and Standard Oil subsidiaries had a monopoly of the sale of kerosene for the lamps they had "philanthropically" given the Chinese peasants, and "Rockefellers" sold small amounts of kerosene at more than a dollar a gallon compared with the US domestic price of five to ten cents. It was vital to "Rockefellers" that no oil should be produced in China, which could bring the price down and threaten their high-price monopoly. The Soongs and Chiang's National government saw to that. But the warlord of Shansi province granted a concession to the Japanese, who drilled and found oil, threatening Standard Oil's monopoly. In 1927 Chiang's Nationalist government cancelled the concession and ousted the Japanese.

In 1931 the Japanese took their revenge, seizing part of China and destroying "Rockefeller"/Standard Oil property. (In 1905 the Japanese received Kuhn, Loeb funding for the Russo-Japanese War.) In 1937 the Japanese shelled the *Panay*, a US gunboat that was escorting two Standard Oil tankers.

"Rockefellers" countered by making the Mitsuis, who with the Zaibatsu controlled Emperor Hirohito and Japan's policies, their agents in China. They then asked the US to rescue "Rockefeller" property in China, which would mean declaring war on Japan. This in turn would mean luring Japan into an attack on US property. The Roosevelt government was subservient to the Rockefellers – as "principal advisor" to President Roosevelt, Nelson Rockefeller had put forward the idea of the "New" Deal and had urged Roosevelt to take part in the Second World War – and J. P. Morgan's nephew Joseph Grew was appointed US Ambassador to Japan. The Japanese were persuaded to attack the US fleet in Pearl Harbor, and the Americans were then able to invade China and conquer Japan.

In 1949 "Rockefellers" delivered China to the Communists through their agent Gen. Marshall. After the Second World War, Gen. Marshall sent a special envoy to urge Chiang to include Communists in his government. Chiang refused, so Marshall stopped American aid, which meant Chiang had no fuel for his tanks and planes. The Russians then gave Mao military supplies they had captured from Japan and diverted American Lend-Lease material to him. America withheld funding until Chiang was defeated and had fled to Taiwan.

Mao gave political expression to the revolution. In 1950 he signed a 30–year friendship treaty with Russia. In 1953 he proposed to the Soviet Union a plan for world conquest, called "Memorandum on a New Programme for World Revolution," in which every country save the US would be Communist by 1973. Chou En-Lai took this plan to Moscow. The first phase was to be completed by 1960; Korea and Indo-China were to be under Chinese control. During the revolution's brutal physical phase, Mao is estimated to have killed 25 million Chinese.

In February 1966, afraid that the Chinese Revolution was being derailed by the bourgeoisie, Mao mobilized the young Red Guards and activists to purge all "bourgeois reactionaries" who favored traditional culture or the past. The ensuing violent "Cultural Revolution" against what was foreign and traditional was more a purge than a revolution, like Stalin's Great Purge, with young fanatics deciding who should be on the purge list. All institutions suffered violent clashes – schools, factories, and communes – and those affected by "corrupt" foreign or traditional attitudes either made public self-criticisms or were executed. The extreme iconoclasm amounted to a form of collective brainwashing.

In 1971 Mao called on the world to "unite and defeat the US aggressors and all their running dogs," but later in 1971 US–Chinese relations dramatically improved with Nixon's "Rockefeller"-inspired visit. Did Mao have "Rockefellers" in mind as the US "running dogs," and was the subtext of the Cultural Revolution his attempt to reclaim possession of Chinese oil? China's oilfields are in the northeast and in Sinkiang, Kansu, Tsinghai, Czechwan, Shantung, and Honan provinces. The most important oil-producing area, the Ta-ching field in Heilungkiang, was discovered in the late 1950s and soon produced a third of China's oil output. China had engaged Western oil companies to develop oil deposits in the China Sea, the Yellow Sea, the Gulf of Tonkin, and the Po Hai. The principal Western oil company involved belonged to "Rockefellers." As a result of this new policy, China exported some crude oil while keeping most of it for herself.

Deng Hsiao-ping further consolidated the Chinese Revolution, and as during the Thermidorean Reaction in the French Revolution, he led China away from world revolution to co-existence with the West and in the direction of the free market and privatization.

Vietnamese Revolution

The Vietnamese Revolution is different from the other revolutions in this group as it was against French colonization in Indo-China, which collapsed in 1954. "Rockefellers" were after Vietnamese oil from 1950. To what extent did they contribute to this collapse? Like the American Revolution it has no obvious brutal physical phase; other than repressive, tyrannical rule in the 1950s, 1960s, and 1970s. Ho Chi Minh was inspired by Marx. He gave it political expression during its conflict with America, and was in power long enough for him to be in charge of both a political and a physical phase.

Cuban Revolution

The 1958 Cuban Revolution against Batista began in 1947 when Castro became a Communist. The occult vision was Marx's. Castro attempted a revolt with guerillas in 1953, but was captured and paroled. Guevara rebuilt the guerilla forces and gave intellectual expression to the revolution. Castro received financial backing from Russia and bribed many military leaders. After denials that he was a Communist, he won ("Rockefellerite") American support. As a result of US pressure Batista left Cuba and Castro took control in 1959, giving political expression to the revolution. He was then able to train revolutionaries under Ché Guevara and Regis Debray, using Cuba as a training camp, and send them to oil-rich Latin American states to foment revolution with a view to seizing oilfields on behalf of "Rockefellerites" (most memorably, Bolivia, where Standard Oil of New Jersey located oilfields in 1927; Nicaragua, El Salvador, Guatemala, and the Honduras). Guevara fought in Bolivia in 1966 and was executed there in 1967.

In the 1960s and 1970s Castro sent troops to Ghana, Algeria, Morocco, and the Congo, and he sent 20,000 troops to Angola in 1975 and 16,000 troops to Ethiopia a year later. By 1980 he had more than a thousand troops in a dozen countries and had become a major destabilizing force. Did he have Syndicate masters? Castro's long tenure of power has meant that he has presided over both political and physical/consolidation phases – the first extreme, the second more moderate.

Egyptian Revolution

To turn briefly to the four Arab revolutions on our list, the Egyptian

Revolution was inspired by the occult vision of Marx. After Colonel Nasser's overthrow of King Farouk, his puppet Gen. Naguib gave the revolution political expression with his pro-Russian Arab Socialism.

In 1954 Nasser emerged from the shadows to assume full political power, which he consolidated all through the Soviet-backed extremism of the Suez crisis and the wars with Israel. To what extent did he have "Rockefellerite" assistance?

After Nasser Egypt passed to Sadat, one of the 12 Free Officers who helped carry out the 1952 *coup*, until he was assassinated for agreeing to peace with Israel. Egypt has now settled back into a comfortable relationship with the West and has declared war on the Islamic Brotherhood.

Iraqi Revolution

The Iraqi Revolution took its inspiration from Marx and Colonel Nasser. After the overthrow and murder of King Faisal, the military dictator General Kassem, who had been trained in Russia, gave the revolution political expression. He moved troops to Iraq's border with Kuwait and had designs on Kuwaiti oil. His revolution torpedoed the Baghdad Pact. To what extent did he have "Rockefellerite" assistance? The brutal, physical phase has been under Saddam Hussein. He was supported by the "Rockefellerite" Syndicate – armed by Donald Rumsfeld – at the beginning of the Iran–Iraq war.

Libyan Revolution

The Libyan Revolution also took inspiration from Marx and Colonel Nasser. As in the case of Egypt, there were 12 Free Officers. Gaddafi and the other 11 members of the original Revolutionary Command Council discussed the idea of the revolution in 1956 at the time of Suez when they were on a school picnic. They all agreed to go into the army and work for revolution. Later they regarded themselves as pan-Arab Nasserites, and the intellectual expression of the revolutionary idea took place between 1956 and 1969. Rich oil deposits had been discovered in Libya. As in the case of North Vietnam, where there is new oil there is "Rockefellerite" interest.

Col. Gaddafi led a military *coup* against King Idris, who had earlier told his Ministers that he would abdicate, thus creating a power vacuum. Being against the American and English bases, Western exploitation of

Libyan oil, and even against Western lettering, the Libyan revolutionaries looked to the Soviet Union for protection. Col. Gaddafi gave the revolution political expression. The first revolutionary slogan was "Freedom, Unity, Socialism," i.e. freedom from the Western bases, unity with other Arab states, and radical (Marxist) socialism. After Nasser's death in 1970, Gaddafi assumed the mantle of the radical Arab cause. He gave the terrorist Carlos a base in Libya; in 1975 Carlos took Sheikh Yamani, the Saudi-Arabian oil minister, hostage in Vienna, having been assisted in his preparations by members of Libyan intelligence. Did "Rockefellers" control Gaddafi (and keep him in power) via the Soviet Union? Did the pro-Soviet Gaddafi back "Rockefellerite" interests in Libya? He sided with Russia against the West and armed the IRA. There have been executions but the brutal phase has not really happened in the same way that it happened in Iraq or in China. Nevertheless, like Ho Chi Minh and Castro, Gaddafi has presided over both political and physical phases, and as a result of his arms policy Libya was expected to be a nuclear power by 2005. Following his dramatic renunciation of weapons of mass destruction, Gaddafi has been rehabilitated to oversee the growing African Union/United States of Africa.

Cambodian Revolution

The origins of the Cambodian or Kampuchean revolution can be found in 1970, near the end of the Vietnam War, when the pro-US Lon Nol deposed Prince Sihanouk, the ruler since 1941. Did both men have "Rockefellerite" assistance? In 1975 his government was overthrown by the Chinese-backed Khmers Rouges under Pol Pot, who exterminated between 1.7 and 2.2 million people – or 3 to 4 million according to some – by driving them out of cities into the countryside.

Iranian Revolution

The 1978 Iranian Revolution, which deposed the "Rockefellerite" Shah, was overtly an Islamic one. Was the driving force behind it in fact a Syndicate one: "Rockefellers" Chase Manhattan bank and BP, which wanted to seize the Iranian oilfields, perhaps by intriguing an Iran–Iraq war and supporting Saddam Hussein? Disciples of Khomeini, such as Ali Akbar Hashemi Rafsanjani, gave it intellectual expression. When Khomeini was exiled from Iran in 1962, Rafsanjani became his chief fund-raiser, and he was imprisoned from 1975 to 1978.

On Khomeini's return to Iran Rafsanjani helped found the Islamic Republican Party, served on the Revolutionary Council, and was Interior Minister during the early years of the Revolution. Khomeini gave it political expression. After he died Rafsanjani became President. He and other Ayatollahs consolidated the revolution, notably Ayatollah Ali Khamenei, later Iran's supreme leader.

Iran is now emerging into its post-revolutionary, Thermidorean phase, with free elections for seats in Parliament. In September 2001 President Khatami considered siding with the US and joining the Global Coalition against terrorism, and the British Foreign Secretary visited Iran.

Foreign Hidden Hand

All these twentieth-century revolutions have been intrigued from abroad with the involvement of a hidden hand, as can be seen from the following table which lists the political "outside generator" and the brotherhood who effect the revolution:

Political Revolution	Country of Outside Generator	Outside Agency/Brotherhood
Chinese	US ("Rockefellerite"); Russia	CFR
Vietnamese	US ("Rockefellerite"); Russia/China	CFR?
Cuban	US ("Rockefellerite")	CFR?
Egyptian	US ("Rockefellerite"); Russia	KGB?
Iraqi	US ("Rockefellerite"); Russia	KGB?
Libyan	US ("Rockefellerite"); Russia/Egypt	KGB?
Cambodian	US ("Rockefellerite"); China	CFR?
Iranian	US ("Rockefellerite")	CFR?

If you care to apply the 4–part revolutionary dynamic outlined in Appendix 1 to revolutions other than those covered above, you will find that they too contain the 4–part structure of the revolutionary dynamic.

Appendix 3: Islam, the Syndicate's globalism and the North American and European civilizations

A Clash of Civilizations

In my comparative study of the history of 25 civilizations, *The Fire and the Stones* (1991),[1] I demonstrated how all 25 civilizations progress through nearly identical stages. Of the 61 stages I defined, the North American civilization is currently passing through stage 15 – i.e. a quarter of the way through its evolution as a civilization.

After the shock of a military blow, which arrests growth (stage 14) there is a counterthrust and expansion into global empire (stage 15). In my view, the shock that befell Rome was the Celts' capture of Rome in 390 BC; the shock that befell America was the invasion of the secessionist Confederacy in 1861–2, which led to the American Civil War. In my view the North American civilization, recently shocked by defeat in Vietnam and more recently by the September 11 attacks, is in the same stage the Roman civilization was in after the shock of Hannibal's military blow at Lake Trasimene in 217 BC before it had an empire. Rome then had many imperial centuries ahead of her. In my view, so has America. In short, America has just begun a globalist phase, the equivalent of Rome's expansion into empire.

I demonstrated that the European civilization was passing from a period of de-colonization to stage 43, which involves loss of national sovereignty to a secularizing conglomerate that is a union (i.e. the coming United States of Europe). The Arab civilization, on the other hand, is further on, in stage 46, having emerged from a period in which all its nation-states lost their sovereignty to the European colonial empires to re-assert its sovereignty through an attempt at counterthrust.

In my study, which appeared two years before Samuel Huntington's *The Clash of Civilizations*, I predicted a clash between the North American and European civilizations on the one hand and militant Islam within the Arab civilization on the other.

In *The Fire and the Stones* I predicted that there would be conflict between the West and the Arab civilization: "Viewed from 1991 AD, the chief threat to the European and North American civilizations, then, is Islam, both from the ex-Khanate Soviet Islam which can be expected to secede from the Soviet Union and join the coming Federation of Islamic States, and from a revivified, fanatical, nuclear-armed Arab civilization which is determined to eliminate Israel." This was written two years before Samuel Huntington's *The Clash of Civilizations and the Remaking of World Order* appeared.

The war in Afghanistan was provoked by an Islamic section of the Arab civilization and was directed against Islamic militant extremists. The September 11 attack was different only in degree from previous attacks by Islamic sections of the Arab civilization against the West. In 1947

Arnold Toynbee warned that Islam was a "sleeping giant," and in 1952 the Egyptian Revolution brought Nasser to power. During the last 50 years, the Arab civilization has asserted itself against the West. Arab nationalism was responsible for seizing the Suez Canal in 1956, for using the oil weapon against the West in 1973, and arousing worldwide anti-Western Islamic fervor through the Iranian Revolution in 1979.

Such political, economic, and religious manifestations of Islamic anti-Westernism suggest that though he did not rule a country, bin Laden was in the tradition of Nasser, Ayatollah Khomeini, and Saddam Hussein. During the last 50 years Islam has seethed with internal and external conflicts: the eight-year-long Iran–Iraq war; Syria's occupation of Lebanon; Iraq's attack on Kuwait; murders of Christians in Sudan, Egypt, Nigeria, and Pakistan; conflicts between Moslems and Moslems in Egypt and Algeria; and Moslem attacks on the Chinese, Indians, and Russians.

The attack on America must be seen within this context. The aim of the Syndicate's New World Order and PNAC is to bring pressure to bear on the North American civilization to suppress expressions of Islamic anti-Western resurgence within the Arab civilization. Islamic insurgency could be expected to continue after the deaths of bin Laden and Saddam Hussein and even if Israel were handed over to the Arabs. Such insurgency is the continuation of "anti-Zionism," "anti-Westernism," and "anti-Americanism," which have been rife since the First World War, when the sleeping giant stirred over the creation of Israel. The West is in denial if it disregards this historical perspective.

Objectively, the 2001 conflict between the US and the Taliban cannot be anything other than a conflict between the leaders of the North American civilization and a section of the Arab civilization embodied by the Taliban and their Arab and Pakistani followers and al-Qaeda allies. A massacre in a Catholic church in Bahawalpur that left 18 dead sought to polarize the conflict into "Moslems versus Christians," groupings the Crusaders would have understood. In fact, in early November 2001 bin Laden issued a letter urging his followers in Pakistan to confront "the Christian Crusade against Islam," contrasting infidels "under the banner of the Cross" and true believers "under the banner of Islam."

Conversely, the spokesmen for the Syndicate's New World Order, which seeks to dismantle all civilizations, frame the conflict in terms of the hunting-down of an outlaw rather than in terms of a conflict between two civilizations. On the evidence of what has been said publicly by US government officials, influential figures in the CFR do not think in terms of separate civilizations which can clash – even though bin Laden spoke for a vast number of Arabs by calling for global Islamic law, which must bring about a clash with the Christian West – but (as we have seen) in terms of a "Global Coalition," with many nation-states joining a global alliance.

Despite these two attempts to interpret or "spin" the conflict to the advantage of either side, the conflict is essentially an encounter between two civilizations. A clash need not be a head-on-collision; it can be a side-on glancing blow, as when two cars bump into each other when converging side by side. The head-on collision scenario is one in which anti-Islamic factions within the North American civilization (or New World Order) clash with the anti-Western (or anti-Christian) factions within the Arab civilization. The side-on glancing blow scenario may be a truer representation of the encounter. The conflict, officially over weapons of mass destruction but really about oil, has provoked the involvement of the rank-and-file of the two civilizations, not just the anti-Islamic and anti-Western factions.

From my comparative study I stated a law, that in any clash between civilizations, the younger always triumphs. The Arab civilization is three-quarters through (in stage 46 of the 61 stages), and is slightly older than the European civilization (currently entering stage 43, a union). The quarter-through North American civilization, formally founded with the founding of the Jamestown Settlement in 1607, can therefore be expected to triumph in clashes with the Arab civilization.

It follows that the imminent collapse of the North American civilization, predicted in Paul Kennedy's *The Rise and Fall of the Great Powers*, could not be anticipated as a result of the torching of the Twin Towers of the World Trade Center. Nor could it be expected that young North America would lose a war against older Islam in Afghanistan. In fact the episode rallied America's spirit of defiance and strengthened her resolve and resilience.

Globalism and the New World Order Revolution

But if there was an obvious threat from an external Islamic enemy without, the main threat to the continuing ascendancy of the North American civilization comes from within, from globalist factions within the Council on Foreign Relations and the Bilderberg Group. The main threat is a reported agenda for the last American election to be in 2016,[2] after which, the intention is, there will be a world government and all nation-states will have ceased to exist.

This book has argued that if there is a globalist threat to end the American nation-state it can be seen off. The "Rockefellerite" revolutions throughout most of the twentieth century were instrumental in taking America to its present position of supremacy and superpowerdom, but the American people will not allow the American state to be shut down once they are in possession of the facts. Knowledge of the situation will give the American people strength, and be their salvation.

Is Europe also threatened from within? In my comparative study I predicted the end of Soviet Communism in 1991 and the beginning of a United States of Europe in 1997. Through "Rothschilds'" influence, full European integration is part-and-parcel of the Bilderberg agenda. Both "Rockefellerite" and "Rothschildite" factions within the Syndicate have made common cause to remove Europe's independence and place Europe under a coming world government. The internal threat to North America is also an internal threat to Europe.

The New World Order is inevitable. In good hands, as a democracy serving and therefore *beneath* the North American and European civilizations, a *Pax Americana* that extends round Europe's borders and across the world, it is welcome. It can do immense good in preserving the peace and improving humankind's lot. In the wrong hands – if it were a dictatorship *above* the North American and European civilizations that demanded population reduction – it would be a nightmare.

From my research into the subject it has become clear that true revolutions take place *within* civilizations; they are not imposed from without. Moreover, they act as corrective adjustments to civilizations; they do not shut them down or seek to control them. In the same way the New World Order arose as a stage *within* the North American civilization. So long as it remains a supportive dynamo of the North American civilization's continuing growth and spreading of democracy by peaceful, lawful means, it is a good thing, depending on the degree of benevolence it exercises towards other nation-states. If it were to take over the American nation-state, subordinate it to a world government comprising all civilizations, use it as a base from which to acquire the world's oil and natural resources, terrorize mankind, and develop an extremist and dictatorial agenda for population control, then it would be, and is, a bad thing.

If the North American civilization and its president can retain national independence despite the pressures from global internationalism, the North American civilization can prosper and go from strength to strength. If as a result of a military blow as shocking as Hannibal's first victory was to Rome, the North American civilization caves in to the globalist CFR within it and allows itself to lose its national independence, then the North American civilization will have broken down.

In my comparative study, I locate the breakdown of a civilization at the end of its growth. The North American civilization is not at the end of its growth. Breakdown takes place when there is a transfer of power from the people who have hitherto ruled a civilization to a "new people" who follow a heresy. The turning point is a military blow, which destroys the confidence of the old people and secularizes their religion, which ritualizes their experience of the Fire or Light.

In Rome's case, the breakdown did not occur with Hannibal, who was eventually defeated, but with the Roman defeat by the external Germanic tribes, the Cimbri and Teutones who defeated a Roman army in 113 BC. This blow helped to encourage the new heresy of the deified leader, which was transmitted to the Caesarian principate, the new people. The old Roman religion of Jupiter and Apollo gave way to this new heresy and to the new eastern cults of Cybele, Dionysus, and Mithras.

In North America's case, the breakdown will not occur as a result of the Islamic attack on New York and Washington, which may have a strong internal motivation, but as a result of a future defeat at the hands of external barbarian invaders and occupiers.

The Universalist "Heresy"

A "heresy" is a non-orthodox sect that has the potential to develop into a religion. Just as Christianity was once a heresy within Judaism, so the "heresy" of Universalism (an internationalist spiritual vision that is acceptable to all mankind, not just Christians or Moslems) may one day replace Christianity.

We are moving towards a time when the free, independent, and nationalist "old people" of the North American civilization may be replaced by a globalist "new people" who bring in a heresy that replaces the orthodoxy (orthodox Christianity). This "new people" will either work within the North American civilization to revivify it, as the Caesars revivified Rome through the Roman Empire where Christianity was itself a "heresy" emerging from within Judaism, or the "new people," Americans who think globally, can seek to take the North American civilization into a world empire so that it flows underground until it eventually surfaces again as itself, the North American civilization.

My comparative study shows that the first of these two possibilities is what has happened in all previous civilizations, and that the second would break the mold, and is without precedent. For this reason it is unlikely to succeed. In short, the ascendancy of the North American civilization will depend on its retaining control over its supporters and creative dynamo, and not surrendering to them.

I cannot emphasize this point enough, and I close with a warning. The North American civilization has a choice. It can either continue to be part of the pattern of civilizations I have unfolded in *The Fire and the Stones*, to which revolutions contribute. Or it can subordinate itself to a world government that is not a part of any civilization, and which is therefore a completely untried international experiment that is unlikely to succeed for long.

Europe and the North American Civilization
The European civilization, too, has a choice. It is entering a union with a single currency. My comparative study shows that the stage of union (stage 43) is always accompanied by Universalism and a yearning for the lost past of the civilization – in the case of Britain, for the Tudor-Renaissance time – and for a revival of cultural purity. The European soul is at present divided between the old traditional, national culture and the new union it has just joined. This division reveals itself as a fissure in the soul, and as self-division, to which it is important to bring unity.

If the North American civilization remains independent, the United States of Europe will still cease to be a Europe of nation-states in each of which there is a union stage, and will become a fully integrated union as has happened to all the other civilizations that have reached stage 43. If the North American civilization is subordinated to a world government, then so will an integrated Europe be, and there will be little national survival and rootedness; only regional variations within a new culture of a globalized Europe.

We are in a critical time on both sides of the Atlantic. Will there be a good New World Order or a bad one? Will there be a good United States of Europe or a bad one? Will we retain our separate cultures or be in the melting-pot?

I have seen the continuing ascendancy of the North American civilization and, for a shorter span, of the European Union, and I answer both questions optimistically. I therefore see all the revolutions we have been studying not as flowing into one-world government, as the Syndicate have seen them, an end they appear to have sought to intrigue, but as means of bringing speedy transformations to their civilizations which are needed urgently and which have to take place abruptly.

The visions of those who began the revolutions transformed their civilizations; the massacres perpetrated by those who corrupted the revolutions scarred their civilizations while the corrective adjustments were being made. Revolutions are within civilizations and help them to change constructively. They are not destructive mechanisms that allow Lucifer to be held up as ruler of the world.

Appendix 4: The Syndicate's New World Order as a global phase in the evolution of the North American civilization

In the West we have come to accept a view of modern global history in which the USA plays an increasingly dominant role. According to this view, the US liberated itself with the aid of the French in the eighteenth century (just as the British had liberated themselves with the aid of the Dutch in 1688). Since then the US has driven global liberation to democracy for more than a hundred years. The US brought freedom to Cuba in 1898 when the US battleship *Maine* exploded in Havana Harbor, and freedom to France and Germany from Prussian militarism in 1917, Nazi occupation in 1944, and Soviet occupation from the mid-1940s to the late 1980s. As a result of US activity, democracy has spread to most of the former Soviet countries and all the Warsaw Pact nations, which are now democracies, and democracy is spreading in Africa: in 2003, 17 of 54 African nations were democracies. US support for foreign revolutions has been a vital part of the long-term plan to bring liberty and democracy to the entire world.

In fact, the secret history of the West in the twentieth century was the hidden progress to a one-world government, the New World Order, through revolutions that have dismantled the old Europe, Middle and Far East. The Spanish Civil War, for instance, was an attempted Communist revolution. There have been revolutions in China, Vietnam, Cuba, Egypt, Iraq, Libya, and Iran. The revolutions have suddenly happened; their causes remain something of a mystery, their consequences enormous.

It has dawned on many that the startling changes in Europe following 1989, which saw the structures of Communism dismantled and Western Europe turn Socialist, were in fact no accident but had been planned. The Cold War did not end abruptly because the Russians collapsed. Rather, it gave way to a new scenario that was orchestrated.

All the main revolutions (the English, French, American, and Russian Revolutions) have happened within a civilization – the European, North American, and Byzantine-Russian civilizations – and the New World Order Revolution is no exception.

All civilizations have had a global phase – as did the Roman civilization whose territorial expansion gave Rome hegemony over the western Mediterranean (c341–218 BC) and later over much of the known world (c30 BC-AD 270). There are therefore strong reasons for regarding the New World Order Revolution as being created by a world government phase within the North American civilization. The rationale for this view – that the emerging world-wide phase of civilization is a consequence of a development or phase within the North American civilization – is that there has never been a world government before and that if it does happen it will be a result of pressure from the only surviving superpower, the US, and its supporting agencies, the UN, the CFR, and the Trilateral Commission.

To some extent this movement towards a world culture is a natural and inevitable consequence of an organic process within a civilization. Just as the Roman civilization achieved a world phase under Augustus, which ruled the known world including past empires (the Egyptian, Carthaginian, Greek, *et al.*), so the North American civilization will achieve a world phase that will create an American-led world government. This will be a result of an American initiative and will include the past empires of the European nations, including Great Britain and the USSR.

On this view, just as the Roman Empire absorbed the old Greek Empire, so the American-led world government will absorb the former European Empires including the British Empire (and the former colonies in their post-liberation-movement states) within a federal world structure, a United States of the World. De-colonization has fostered multiculturalism throughout the world – especially in India and Africa where different races and religions co-exist – and a new universalist world government will be multicultural while focusing on the indigenous cultures of local regions.

Prominent Europeans who have contributed to the world government, such as the Rothschilds, will therefore be seen as contributors to the creation of a global phase in the North American civilization, as did refugee scientists like Einstein and von Braun who gave their expertise, honed under the Nazis, to the US. In the same way, the British Rothschilds, German Jewish economic migrants from Frankfurt, helped create the British Empire after Waterloo.

We should therefore reject the view that "Rothschilds" are creating the world government for the European civilization, that the CFR is under the RIIA and beholden to the English Queen, who is therefore the originating force of a world government. Clearly the British Commonwealth would be subsumed in a world government and the Queen is therefore a force to be reckoned with, but we cannot regard a world government as originating in Europe or Great Britain, with America subservient to London. It may have been like that in 1900, it is not like that now. Such a view would be a misreading of twentieth-century history.

The only other alternative to the US-led view is to see all civilizations as coming to an end in world government, which will therefore not be a phase (lasting perhaps 100 years on past precedent) but a permanent creation. This view entails maintaining that all revolutions have advanced the Freemasonic Luciferian one-world global dictatorship – or "Christ's" free global democracy – and that the new stage will be a permanent entity, unlike the Roman Empire and all the other universalist empires that have ever been.

The End of History?

A form of such a view has recently been advanced by Francis Fukuyama, a New World Order apologist and policy-planner with the US State Department in Bush's administration. When he read in a speech by Gorbachev in 1988 that socialism equals competition, he rang a friend and said of the global triumph of capitalism, "If this is true we've reached the end of history" – in the sense that history, understood as a single evolutionary process that includes all peoples, has reached an end in liberal democracy (competitive socialism) and can go no further, having freed itself from the Hegelian dialectic and contradiction (i.e. competition versus the workers leading to a synthesis, socialism). Hegel had claimed that history ended in 1806 when revolutionary France under Napoleon beat the Prussians at Jena and ensured that the rights of man would triumph. Fukuyama wrote an essay *The National Interest* in 1989 and then a book, *The End of History and the Last Man* in 1992.[3]

Liberal democracy and market-oriented economic order are the only possibilities for modern societies and lead to the non-ideological outlook of Clinton and Blair; liberal democracies do not fight each other. Or so the theory goes. Therefore history as a process from lower to higher forms of human social organization has ended. Take Fukuyama's ideas further, and he is saying that the New World Order is a permanent world liberal democracy into which all civilizations have poured their identity, emptying themselves of all residual nationalism: the world government as a global democracy not attached to, and indeed, independent of, all particular nation-states.

This view has been adopted by the British historian Andrew Roberts in an article in the *Daily Telegraph* of October 9, 2000, which argues that the fall of Milosovic in Serbia proves that capitalist liberal democracy has finally swept the globe and is the "final form of human government," "the end of history." Arguing that since 1989 capitalist liberal democracy has replaced authoritarianism in Nicaragua, Chile, Ecuador, Guatemala, South Africa, Sierra Leone, Taiwan, Fiji, Mongolia, the Baltic states, Bangladesh, Poland, Croatia, Slovenia, Kenya, Armenia, Albania, Honduras, and Algeria – even "Rockefellers" Saudi-Arabia has had to give its subjects new constitutional rights since the Gulf War – Roberts claims that the only countries that deny the victory of global liberal capitalist democracy, "the former American president Woodrow Wilson's dream of 1918," are personal fiefdoms of anti-Americanism: Castro's Cuba, Gaddafi's Libya, Kim's North Korea, Saddam's Iraq, and of course China. The headline of the article screamed "Fukuyama was right about the rise and rise of capitalism." The article, staggeringly, claims that the end-state of history has been reached: global democracy, which will be world-wide and for all time.

This view was blown to pieces by the planes that caused the World Trade Center Twin Towers to collapse on September 11, 2001 and heralded in a clash between the Islamic and North American civilizations. The view was anyway naive inasmuch as it does not relate "Woodrow Wilson's dream of 1918" to the operation of the Syndicate and "Rockefellerite" oil imperialism, and it does not see the hand of "Rockefellerites" in the creation of dictators in Cuba, Libya, North Korea, Iraq, and China who can stampede many of the smaller states into change. The real story is not how democracies replace authoritarian regimes and live for ever, but, as we have seen, how a world government is being created by "Rockefellerites" through the use of proxies, a technique perfected by "Rockefellers" in their dealings with and for the Soviet Union and now applied throughout the world.

In short, capitalism is triumphing globally because of the world government lobby, the "Rockefellerite"-Bilderberg Syndicate. In fact, global capitalism is a smokescreen for the Syndicate's piecemeal achievement of a world government by stealth. Global liberal capitalist democracy is not a permanent end-state but a stage in the history of the North American civilization, a counterpart to the Roman civilization's global stage when Rome ruled the world.

Global liberal capitalist democracy will no more be "for all time" than was the Roman Empire. All empires are prone to the illusion that they will last a thousand years – including the German Third Reich and the British Empire on which the sun would never set – and the coming world empire is no exception in being immune from this illusion, or, rather, delusion. Heady statements that history has ended should be treated with great suspicion. History never ends; the pattern of civilizations continues to unfold as the stages of living civilizations echo the similar stages of civilizations that have died.

Careful thought reveals further difficulties with Fukuyama's view. It is like Marx's view of history: too materialistic. It does not take account of Hegel's life of the spirit. Can we really rule out the possibility that nationalism will re-emerge somewhere for all time? Can we rule out the consequences of mass migration? Do we really believe that there will be optimism forever, and no more nasty events like the two world wars that blew a hole in the Utopian optimism of 1910 and 1919?

Weishaupt's destructive agenda still has followers – notably, the Syndicate. America owes more than $7.5 trillion to the Syndicate-controlled Federal Reserve System, much of it to "Rockefellers," and if any of this were called in America would have to withdraw her forces worldwide.

Nuclear proliferation has been contained only so far – the first Iraq War set back Saddam's attempts to become a nuclear power – and the anticipated population explosion to 10 billion by 2030 may create destabilization, poverty, and militarization. The south may threaten the north with long-range nuclear weapons.

May there not be a New World Disorder rather than a New World Order? Such a view has been expressed by the Frenchman Pierre Lellouche, foreign policy advisor to Jacques Chirac in *The New World, From The Order of Yalta to the Disorder of Nations*.[4]

A for-all-time world government can be ruled out; there will be no permanent breaking of the mold. But a world government can be achieved for a while, as a phase. I have argued elsewhere[5] that this is to be expected in the next phase of the North American civilization. America's central bank (the Syndicate-dominated Federal Reserve System) wants it, and is therefore unlikely to have plans to call in America's overdraft of more than $7.5 trillion.

Another former senior advisor to the White House has produced a new apology for the New World Order. Philip Bobbitt in *The Shield of Achilles* maintains that the nation-state, successor to the nineteenth-century imperial state, is ending and being replaced by the market state, a new order that will embrace human rights, limit weapons of mass destruction, adjust to global and transitional threats (damage to the environment, migration, population expansion, disease and famine), and accommodate a world economic regime and communications network. The consequences of the market state – that governments are more driven by markets than morality – have been taken up by Britain's new Archbishop of Canterbury.

Immanuel Wallerstein[6] sees the US as having begun to suffer in 1967 from the same imperial overstretch that caused decline in Venice around 1500, in Holland around 1660, and in Britain around 1873. Paul Kennedy saw America as a victim of military top-heavy imperial overstretch in *The Rise and Fall of the Great Powers*[7] and likely to suffer the same problem as Philip II's Spain, Nicholas II's Russia, and Hitler's Germany, but he did not appreciate that the decline in America's share of the world's GNP is not continuous, as has been shown by Charles Wolf of the Rand Corporation,[8] who demonstrates that it has remained constant in the region of 22–24%.

The US's World Dominance

Meanwhile the co-founder of PNAC, Robert Kagan, argues in a short book, *Paradise and Power*, that the US and Europe are diverging. Recoiling from the bloodshed of two world wars, Europe is bent on creating a post-modern peaceful paradise and sees the US as high-handed, unilateralist, and recklessly belligerent. The US, a *hyperpuissance* (a term coined by Hubert Védrine, French foreign minister during the Clinton years), sees Europe as spent, unserious, and weak. There is a power gap, and the US affords Europe military protection while Europe conducts its peaceful experiment in European union. During the Cold War the term "the West" represented a unified alternative to Communism. Now, the US is achieving a hegemony to defend and advance international freedom and order.

As Bush Jr. put it in a speech on April 23, 2003, "We believe in peace, we understand we have an obligation to keep our nation secure ... We have applied our might in the name of peace and of freedom." The US sees itself as defending the democratic universal values enshrined in the UN's Universal Declaration of Rights, to which the whole world has signed up. This means opposing tyrannical regimes everywhere.

A world dominated by the US may appear to be unipolar. In fact it has moved from being bipolar (with the US and USSR at opposite poles) towards being more multipolar with Russia, China, nuclear India, and Europe all becoming economic, political, and military powers in their own right – in which three regional blocs stand out: Europe (including Russia), the American hemisphere, and East Asia. A world government would ostensibly diffuse power and create a polyarchy, in which there are many spheres of influence without alignment to any central agency. This multipolar, polyarchist tendency would be present under a world government, and the US would still be powerful – a superpower – in relation to other states.[9] Multipolarity is within the context of unipolarity.

What would be the relationship between the US, which now has a tendency to world hegemony, and the New World Order formed round the UN? During the last years of Clinton's presidency, the concept was clear. Overtly the US would place itself under the New World Order, the controller of all oil-and-money power, as would all nation-states. The sovereignty of all nation-states would be ended in every part of the world, and all human beings would be first and foremost citizens of the world ("cosmopolitans" with roots in their local hometown). US troops would join the world army along with other nations' troops. The UN would use American soil for its maneuvers – along with other soils.

But the funding of the world government would come principally from the surviving superpower, the US, through its controlling agency the CFR, and it would be clear who was in charge. Bush Jr. asked Congress for over $74b to fund the war against Iraq, and it was clear who was in charge of the world government's drive against Saddam Hussein. It would be as if Augustus's Rome had hosted a UN-like organization for representatives of all the known world, who had contributed to Roman legions composed of various nationalities; had sent them out, funded the lion's share, and, as its most influential member, manipulated peace-keeping to achieve Roman ends.

Nationalists, Globalists, and Universalists

The main tension of our time is between the globalists and the nationalists. In 1991 President Bush Sr. was opposed for the Republican nomination by Pat Buchanan, a typical nation-stater, who said of the President in his New Hampshire speech announcing his candidacy (December 10): "He is a globalist and we are nationalists. He believes in some *Pax Universalis*; we believe in the Old Republic. He would put America's wealth and power at the service of some vague New World Order; we will put America first."

The globalists, on the other hand, see the nation-staters as living in the world of the past, the world of the old order. As Hitler put it: "The present world is near its end. Our only task is to sack it." The twenty-first-century globalists no longer seek to sack the old world, but to dismantle it area by area, gradually, until a world government is in place. But whereas the nation-staters are open and forthright in their aims and philosophy, the globalists have preferred stealth, secrecy, and deception.

A globalist world empire is universalist (with a small "u," in the sense that it geographically covers the whole globe but is not spiritual). Western globalists see liberal democracy as becoming a universalist empire (with a small "u"). (To Moslems such a "universalism" would be a new imperialism, which is why bin Laden called for a Moslem "universalist" world empire.) Absolute Universalism (with a capital "U," the geographical spread with a spiritual vision acceptable to all humankind, not just to Moslems) involves a world government and world leaders totally removed from all civilizations. That is a Utopian ideal that will not happen. Limited universalism involves a world government set up by the CFR, ostensibly placing the US under the UN while policy is largely determined by the CFR and therefore the US. The CFR may become to some degree accountable to the world public.

It is this limited universalism that will form the world government. The more such a world government is linked dynastically to the Syndicate, the more Luciferian it will be and the more malevolent will be its New World Order. The more it frees itself from the Syndicate and becomes publicly accountable, the more Christ-like it will be and the more benign its New World Order.

Philosophical (true) Universalism sees each human being from all perspectives – including the spiritual and religious as well as the political. Philosophical Universalism therefore sees humankind in relation to the metaphysical Light from which (according to the tradition of many religions) the created universe came. Philosophical (true) Universalism holds that all human beings are equal in relation to the Light that can fill their souls like one sun that shines on all the phenomena of Nature. Secular political universalism is only a pale shadow of metaphysical Universalism, the philosophy of the twenty-first century and of the start of the new millennium.

NOTE TO THE READER ON THE QUALITY OF THE SOURCES

I have approached my sources with certain requirements. I have required that they should show evidence of years, if not decades, of deep thinking in this area, impressive research, and a measure of balance and, where possible, impartiality. I have borne in mind that what has driven people to spend decades researching has often been growing indignation and outrage, and that sometimes these feelings have colored the impartiality of their work.

A word about the sources that crop up most often. I could find alternative sources for all their points, but have narrowed the field to assist the reader. All these have to be seen in the round.

Sutton is very sound and scrupulous, and gives all his sources. His range is limited: he focuses on Wall Street's funding of the Bolshevik Revolution and Hitler.

Rivera and Daniel are both extremely well informed, but although they try to disguise it both write from a Christian position. Rivera ends before Gorbachev and (though he manages to mention him) so does Daniel.

On his own admission Rivera presents "a series of files" "crammed with facts" that have taken hundreds of hours of research to assemble, but does not annotate and therefore does not give us his source for each point. He draws extensively on Quigley's *Anglo-American Establishment*. Daniel sees contemporary history as a series of wars between Freemasonic sects, and while he adds a valuable additional perspective he risks being thought to say that the Second World War (for instance) was exclusively Masonic in its origin and development.

Coleman, an ex-MI6 officer, writes with inside knowledge; his main book is a gigantic leak, the only one by an ex-MI6 officer of its kind. Or is it a misreading? I have relegated his main perception (that there is a Committee of 300) to these Notes, as it is not corroborated by other authoritative sources. As with all such predominantly single-source books, caution should be exercised along with open-mindedness at the revelations. Coleman stops around the Gulf War.

Mullins wrote his main work in 1984. He was originally funded by the poet Ezra Pound to look into the actions of the Syndicate (not his word) that resulted in Pound's incarceration. His research made some valuable inroads. Josephson was very well informed but had a tendentious (anti-Rockefeller) bent and stops in the 1950s.

Armstrong is extremely authoritative on the Rothschild finances of the nineteenth century, but also had a tendentious bent: he stops in 1940, and overestimates the Jewish involvement in the Second World War. Were he writing today he would have a different view of his time.

All are very knowledgeable but their books reveal structural weaknesses. Events pop up in unexpected places, and they do not always make it easy for the reader. All except for the last two owe a debt to Quigley, who in *Tragedy and Hope* surveyed the twentieth century in 1350 pages, and stops in 1964. His approach is very academic, and places this field within mainstream contemporary history. By connecting to the broad sweep he sacrifices detail, and many of the events in this book are missing in Quigley's. However, his account of the Round Table is excellent, although the focus is narrow in relation to the sweep of this work.

The Internet is a valuable source, especially for very recent events, but is of varying quality. I have steered clear of the cranky sites. I have only recommended websites after satisfying myself that the writer is writing with authority, expertise, and knowledge, whether financial, historical, or political. The sites I have drawn on impressed with their thoughtfulness, balance, and determination to arrive at the truth.

I have carried the story forward to 2004. The last 20 years have seen some dramatic progress toward world government. I have gone to some pains to ground the thesis and argument of the book in fact. Hence the many notes. However, a work of this scope is necessarily also interpretative. I have tried to achieve a balance between fact and interpretation, and have consciously avoided speculation, leaving it to the reader to draw conclusions.

I have subscribed to the American weekly, *Spotlight*, for more than 10 years, and to its replacement, *American Free Press* – the only two weeklies that have followed the day-to-day activities of the hidden groups this book deals with. Many of the following notes are supported by articles in these papers, which are too numerous to list. They may be hard for a reader to obtain and I have only referred to them when they are a fundamental source.

It is a pity that Rivera, Daniel, Coleman, Mullins, and Josephson could not have adopted Quigley's meticulous approach and balanced thinking. If they had, we would not have the thousand or more events and perceptions that they have conveyed in their structurally flawed but probing works. They, more than Quigley, have made it possible for this book to arrive at the truth.

All websites were active when these notes were compiled.

NOTES / SOURCES

1. The Question

1. Reserve to Production Ratios for Top Ten Oil Producing Nations. See Office of Transportation Technologies website – www.ott.doe.gov/facts/archives/fotw125.shtml. Calculations by J. Mapla, Transcom Inc., using data from US Department of Energy, Energy Inspectorate Administration, International Energy Records 1998, Production for 1999: Table 8.1, original source *Oil and Gas*.

The 2002 statistics are revealing. The world's largest producers of oil were the US (9.08m barrels per day) and Saudi Arabia (8.54m b/d). Russia was third (7.65m b/d), Iran fifth (3.54m b/d) and the UK tenth (2.55m b/d). Iraq was thirteenth (2.04m b/d). See Table 1 below, graph on p. 3, Table 5 below.

Table 1. Top World Oil Producers, 2002* (OPEC members in italics)
See EIA (Energy Information Administration).
http://www.eia.doe.gov/emeu/cabs/topworldtables1_2.html

	Country	Total Oil Production** (million barrels per day)
1)	United States	9.08
2)	*Saudi Arabia*	8.54
3)	Russia	7.65
4)	Mexico	3.61
5)	*Iran*	3.54
6)	China	3.37
7)	Norway	3.33
8)	Canada	2.94
9)	*Venezuela*	2.91
10)	United Kingdom	2.55
11)	*United Arab Emirates*	2.38
12)	*Nigeria*	2.12
13)	*Iraq*	2.04
14)	*Kuwait*	2.02

*Table includes all countries total oil production exceeding 2 million barrels per day in 2002.
**Total Oil Production includes crude oil, natural gas liquids, condensate, refinery gain, and other liquids.

The world's two largest net exporters of oil were Saudi Arabia (7m b/d) and Russia (5.03m b/d). The third largest was Norway (3.14m b/d). Iran was the fifth largest (2.26m b/d) and Iraq the tenth largest (1.58m b/d). See Table 2 (below).

329

Table 2. Top World Oil Net Exporters, 2002 (OPEC members in italics)
See EIA (Energy Information Administration),
http://www.eia.doe.gov/emeu/cabs/topworldtables1_2.html

Country	Net Oil Exports (million barrels per day)
1) *Saudi Arabia*	7.00
2) Russia	5.03
3) Norway	3.14
4) *Venezuela*	2.46
5) *Iran*	2.26
6) *United Arab Emirates*	2.07
7) *Nigeria*	1.85
8) *Kuwait*	1.73
9) Mexico	1.68
10) *Iraq*	1.58
11) *Algeria*	1.34
12) *Libya*	1.17

*Table includes all countries with net exports exceeding 1 million barrels per day in 2002.

The world's largest consumer of oil was easily the US (894.3m tonnes), with a 25.39% share, followed by China (245.7m tonnes), with a 6.98% share. The UK was thirteenth (77.2m tonnes), with a 2.19% share. See Table 3 (below).

Table 3. Energy: Oil Consumption (in million tones)
See http://www.geohive.com/charts/linc.php?xml=3n-oilcons&xsl=en-res

Rank	Country	1992	2001	2002	Share
1.	USA	782.2	896.1	894.3	25.39%
2.	China	129.0	232.2	245.7	6.98%
3.	Japan	257.5	247.5	242.6	6.89%
4.	Germany	134.3	131.6	127.2	3.61%
5.	Russian Federation	224.4	122.3	122.9	3.49%
6.	South Korea	72.3	103.1	105.0	2.98%
7.	India	62.1	96.7	97.7	2.77%
8.	Italy	94.5	92.8	92.9	2.64%
9.	France	94.4	95.5	92.8	2.63%
10.	Canada	76.8	88.7	89.7	2.55%
11.	Brazil	62.1	87.5	85.4	2.42%
12.	Mexico	71.2	83.4	80.9	2.30%
13.	United Kingdom	83.6	77.3	77.2	2.19%
14.	Spain	52.8	72.7	73.5	2.09%
15.	Saudi Arabia	51.4	62.7	63.4	1.80%
16.	Iran	50.0	54.0	53.2	1.51%
17.	Indonesia	35.1	52.1	51.2	1.45%
18.	Netherlands	36.5	43.9	43.8	1.24%
19.	Taiwan	28.4	39.2	38.8	1.10%
20.	Australia	30.9	38.1	38.0	1.08%
21.	Singapore	24.7	36.4	35.5	1.01%
22.	Thailand	23.6	33.1	35.3	1.00%
23.	Belgium & Luxembourg	27.1	32.2	32.9	0.93%
24.	Turkey	23.5	30.5	29.9	0.85%
25.	Egypt	22.7	26.1	26.1	0.74%
26.	South Africa	17.3	23.0	23.6	0.67%
27.	Venezuela	19.7	22.2	22.9	0.65%

Rank	Country	1992	2001	2002	Share
28.	Malaysia	14.0	20.6	22.5	0.64%
29.	Greece	16.1	21.7	21.8	0.62%
30.	Poland	13.6	19.2	19.7	0.56%
31.	Pakistan	12.4	18.4	17.9	0.51%
32.	Argentina	19.6	19.0	16.8	0.48%
33.	Philippines	13.7	16.5	15.6	0.44%
34.	Sweden	16.4	15.2	15.0	0.43%
35.	Portugal	12.8	14.6	14.9	0.42%
36.	China - Hong Kong SAR	8.1	11.7	13.1	0.37%
37.	Austria	11.3	12.8	13.0	0.37%
38.	Ukraine	42.6	12.7	12.9	0.37%
39.	Switzerland	13.1	13.1	12.4	0.35%
40.	United Arab Emirates	16.9	12.3	12.4	0.35%
41.	Finland	10.3	10.5	10.9	0.31%
42.	Romania	12.7	10.6	10.9	0.31%
43.	Chile	7.4	10.6	10.8	0.31%
44.	Kuwait	5.6	10.5	10.7	0.30%
45.	Colombia	10.6	11.1	10.0	0.28%
46.	Algeria	9.1	9.1	9.9	0.28%
47.	Denmark	9.0	9.8	9.8	0.28%
48.	Norway	9.0	9.7	9.4	0.27%
49.	Republic of Ireland	5.1	9.0	8.7	0.25%
50.	Czech Republic	6.8	8.3	8.2	0.23%
51.	Peru	5.6	7.0	7.0	0.20%
52.	New Zealand	5.2	6.4	6.8	0.19%
53.	Uzbekistan	9.1	6.5	6.6	0.19%
54.	Kazakhstan	20.3	6.8	6.5	0.18%
55.	Hungary	8.1	6.7	6.4	0.18%
56.	Ecuador	4.6	5.9	5.9	0.17%
57.	Belarus	21.2	5.9	5.8	0.16%
	World	3,170.4	3,517.1	3,522.5	

Saudi Arabia had the world's largest oil reserves (261.8b barrels), a 24.99% share. Iraq had the second largest oil reserves in the world (112.5b barrels), a 10.74% share. Iran was fifth (89.7b barrels), an 8.56% share. Russia was seventh (60b barrels), a 5.73% share. The US was eighth (30.4b barrels), a 2.90% share. China was eleventh (18.3b barrels), a 1.75% share. The UK was twenty-fourth (4.7b barrels), a 0.45% share. See Table 4 (below) and graph on p. 3.

Table 4. Energy: proved oil reserves (in 1000 million barrels)
See http://www.geohive.com/charts/linc.php?xml=3n-oilcons&xsl=en-res

Rank	country	end 1992	end 2001	end 2002	share
1.	Saudi Arabia	260.3	261.8	261.8	24.99%
2.	Iraq	100.0	112.5	112.5	10.74%
3.	United Arab Emirates	98.1	97.8	97.8	9.33%
4.	Kuwait	96.5	96.5	96.5	9.21%
5.	Iran	92.9	89.7	89.7	8.56%
6.	Venezuela	62.7	77.7	77.8	7.43%
7.	Russian Federation	48.5	48.6	60.0	5.73%
8.	USA	32.1	30.0	30.4	2.90%
9.	Libya	22.8	29.5	29.5	2.82%
10.	Nigeria	17.9	24.0	24.0	2.29%

Rank	country	end 1992	end 2001	end 2002	share
11.	China	24.0	24.0	18.3	1.75%
12.	Qatar	3.7	15.2	15.2	1.45%
13.	Mexico	51.3	26.9	12.6	1.20%
14.	Norway	8.8	9.4	10.3	0.98%
15.	Algeria	9.2	9.2	9.2	0.88%
16.	Kazakhstan	5.2	8.0	9.0	0.86%
17.	Brazil	3.0	8.5	8.3	0.79%
18.	Azerbaijan	1.3	7.0	7.0	0.67%
19.	Canada	7.5	6.5	6.9	0.66%
20.	Oman	4.5	5.5	5.5	0.52%
21.	Angola	1.5	5.4	5.4	0.52%
22.	India	6.0	4.8	5.4	0.52%
23.	Indonesia	5.8	5.0	5.0	0.48%
24.	United Kingdom	4.1	4.9	4.7	0.45%
25.	Ecuador	1.6	2.1	4.6	0.44%
26.	Yemen	4.0	4.0	4.0	0.38%
27.	Egypt	6.2	3.7	3.7	0.35%
28.	Australia	1.8	3.5	3.5	0.33%
29.	Malaysia	3.7	3.0	3.0	0.29%
30.	Argentina	1.6	3.0	2.9	0.28%
31.	Syria	1.7	2.5	2.5	0.24%
32.	Gabon	0.7	2.5	2.5	0.24%
33.	Colombia	1.9	1.8	1.8	0.17%
34.	Rep. of Congo (Brazzaville)	0.8	1.5	1.5	0.14%
35.	Brunei	1.4	1.4	1.4	0.13%
36.	Denmark	0.7	1.1	1.3	0.12%
37.	Romania	1.6	1.0	1.0	0.10%
38.	Trinidad & Tobago	0.6	0.7	0.7	0.07%
39.	Italy	0.7	0.6	0.6	0.06%
40.	Uzbekistan	na	0.6	0.6	0.06%
41.	Sudan	0.3	0.6	0.6	0.06%
42.	Thailand	0.2	0.5	0.6	0.06%
43.	Vietnam	0.5	0.6	0.6	0.06%
44.	Turkmenistan	na	0.5	0.5	0.05%
45.	Cameroon	0.4	0.4	0.4	0.04%
46.	Peru	0.4	0.3	0.3	0.03%
47.	Tunisia	1.7	0.3	0.3	0.03%
48.	Papua New Guinea	0.3	0.2	0.2	0.02%
	World	1,006.7	1,050.3	1,047.7	

source: 'Statistical Review of World Energy June 2003', BP.
note: a barrel is equal to 159 litres (42 gallons).

Iraq's oil reserves have risen from 29.7b barrels in 1981 to 112.5b barrels in 2002. Iraq has been sitting on proven oil reserves worth US $3 trillion. The French, Russians and Chinese positioned themselves to exploit this and regarded Exxon, Chevron, Texaco and other US giants as competitors. See website http://www.crikey.com.au/business/2003/01/31–oilandiraq.print.html

The Middle East produced 28% of total world oil production; North America 20%; East Europe and the former Soviet Union 13%; the Far East and Oceania 11%; Africa 11%; and West Europe 9%.

Table 5. World Production of Crude Oil, NGPL, and Other Liquids, 1992–2001 *(Thousand Barrels per Day)*
See http://www.eia.doe.gov/emeu/iea/tables.html

Region/Country	1992	1993	1994	1995	1996	1997	1998	1999	2000	2001
North America										
Canada	2,065	2,186	2,275	2,386	2,432	2,558	2,632	2,560	2,676	2,738
Mexico	3,123	3,132	3,146	3,064	3,278	3,411	3,495	3,345	3,450	3,590
United States	8,996	8,836	8,645	8,626	8,607	8,611	8,392	8,107	8,110	8,054
Total	14,185	14,154	14,066	14,076	14,318	14,580	14,519	14,012	14,236	14,382
Central & South America										
Argentina	583	629	694	757	800	882	897	850	809	829
Barbados	1	1	1	1	1	1	2	2	2	1
Bolivia	28	29	30	34	37	37	43	43	40	44
Brazil	793	806	858	890	1,001	1,068	1,229	1,391	1,530	1,561
Chile	26	26	24	23	21	14	15	15	14	14
Colombia	439	461	455	593	631	661	743	828	703	614
Cuba	18	22	26	28	32	33	34	40	42	50
Ecuador	324	353	374	401	405	393	379	377	398	421
Guatemala	5	7	8	10	13	16	24	23	21	21
Peru	117	127	129	131	121	119	117	107	101	95
Suriname	5	5	6	7	7	5	7	10	10	10
Trinidad and Tobago	142	141	138	139	138	132	130	135	133	125
Venezuela	2,484	2,593	2,734	2,899	3,088	3,423	3,312	2,996	3,330	3,080
Total	4,967	5,200	5,479	5,913	6,295	6,785	6,931	6,816	7,132	6,866
Western Europe										
Austria	24	22	22	24	22	20	21	19	20	21
Denmark	163	174	185	186	208	230	238	300	363	346
France	70	68	69	62	55	46	40	37	36	35
Germany	85	81	79	78	78	75	77	76	88	86
Greece	14	12	11	10	9	10	7	1	6	6
Italy	86	86	89	97	105	114	110	86	94	79
Netherlands	67	67	103	87	81	77	79	59	55	46
Norway	2,324	2,450	2,624	2,905	3,242	3,282	3,149	3,139	3,317	3,408
Spain	31	24	21	17	11	8	11	6	5	7
Sweden	0	0	0	0	0	0	0	0	0	0
Turkey	84	76	72	67	67	68	65	59	53	48
United Kingdom	1,986	2,084	2,593	2,756	2,827	2,751	2,856	2,922	2,508	2,541
Croatia	42	43	46	40	36	37	38	32	30	29
Yugoslavia	23	23	24	22	22	20	18	18	16	15
Total	4,999	5,210	5,938	6,350	6,764	6,736	6,710	6,754	6,588	6,667
Eastern Europe & Former U.S.S.R.										
Albania	11	11	12	10	10	9	6	6	6	6
Bulgaria	1	1	1	1	1	1	1	1	1	1
Former Czechoslovakia	2	0	0	0	0	0	0	0	0	0
Czech Republic	0	2	3	3	4	3	4	4	6	7
Slovakia	0	1	1	1	2	2	1	1	1	1
Hungary	46	45	50	46	42	50	43	40	42	41
Poland	3	5	5	5	5	6	7	9	13	17
Romania	143	137	142	141	142	141	138	132	128	127

Region/Country	1992	1993	1994	1995	1996	1997	1998	1999	2000	2001
Azerbaijan	222	208	192	182	182	180	237	283	286	307
Belarus	40	40	40	38	36	36	36	37	37	37
Estonia	0	0	0	0	0	7	4	3	5	5
Georgia	3	2	2	1	1	3	2	2	2	2
Kazakhstan	530	490	415	414	457	521	526	604	718	798
Kyrgyzstan	2	2	2	2	2	2	2	2	2	2
Lithuania	0	2	3	3	3	4	5	5	6	5
Russia	7,862	6,950	6,335	6,175	6,035	6,115	6,074	6,310	6,711	7,286
Tajikistan	1	1	1	1	1	1	1	0	0	0
Turkmenistan	110	90	85	81	88	106	127	155	157	162
Ukraine	95	87	85	85	81	85	82	98	88	86
Uzbekistan	66	85	115	160	165	157	161	147	151	143
Total	9,137	8,159	7,487	7,349	7,256	7,428	7,458	7,837	8,361	9,035
Middle East										
Bahrain	44	53	54	51	45	52	48	48	48	43
Iran	3,479	3,595	3,673	3,703	3,746	3,734	3,709	3,632	3,771	3,804
Iraq	425	527	573	585	599	1,175	2,165	2,523	2,586	2,452
Israel	0	0	0	0	0	0	0	0	0	0
Jordan	0	0	0	0	0	0	0	0	0	0
Kuwait	1,092	1,905	2,110	2,152	2,147	2,116	2,200	2,013	2,194	2,117
Oman	746	781	816	861	893	910	906	916	974	964
Qatar	478	468	465	497	560	620	781	776	870	864
Saudi Arabia	9,045	8,902	8,818	8,933	8,915	9,074	9,144	8,499	9,109	8,711
Syria	483	562	568	584	590	571	561	546	528	523
United Arab Emirates	2,410	2,305	2,343	2,393	2,438	2,476	2,515	2,329	2,568	2,566
Yemen	182	220	335	345	340	362	388	409	440	438
Total	18,384	19,318	19,754	20,104	20,273	21,091	22,417	21,691	23,088	22,483
Africa										
Algeria	1,354	1,307	1,320	1,347	1,392	1,437	1,401	1,392	1,484	1,520
Angola	526	509	536	646	709	714	735	745	746	742
Benin	6	6	6	3	2	1	1	1	1	1
Cameroon	140	127	108	111	108	124	121	100	85	77
Congo (Brazzaville)	174	181	180	188	201	253	265	270	280	275
Congo (Kinshasa)	26	25	26	30	30	28	26	22	26	24
Cote d'Ivoire (Ivory Coast)	2	1	7	8	16	19	20	15	11	11
Egypt	926	945	954	980	987	927	909	927	850	817
Equatorial Guinea	2	5	5	5	17	52	83	102	168	181
Gabon	298	313	329	365	368	370	352	331	315	301
Ghana	1	2	1	- 4	6	5	5	6	7	7
Libya	1,473	1,402	1,419⁻	1,430	1,450	1,506	1,450	1,379	1,470	1,429
Morocco	0	0	0	0	0	0	0	0	0	0
Nigeria	1,943	1,960	1,931	1,993	2,001	2,132	2,153	2,130	2,165	2,256
South Africa	129	183	183	192	195	196	199	182	189	196
Sudan	0	0	0	0	2	5	10	69	186	209
Tunisia	114	102	96	90	88	85	81	84	82	73
Total	7,113	7,067	7,100	7,392	7,572	7,856	7,812	7,755	8,065	8,119
Asia & Oceania										
Australia	591	558	592	614	632	659	614	611	792	731

Region/Country	1992	1993	1994	1995	1996	1997	1998	1999	2000	2001
Bangladesh	1	1	2	1	2	2	2	2	3	4
Brunei	177	178	180	176	166	175	179	204	215	217
Burma	15	14	14	10	8	9	11	10	12	14
China	2,845	2,890	2,939	2,990	3,131	3,200	3,198	3,195	3,249	3,300
India	589	564	635	750	731	760	751	743	736	732
Indonesia	1,579	1,589	1,590	1,579	1,627	1,605	1,605	1,559	1,513	1,451
Japan	20	19	18	18	18	17	17	16	18	17
Malaysia	666	657	662	702	715	750	810	778	755	729
New Zealand	55	58	55	45	45	66	55	50	45	42
Pakistan	64	63	58	62	58	60	58	57	58	63
Papua New Guinea	53	126	110	100	103	80	79	97	70	68
Philippines	8	9	6	3	2	1	1	1	1	8
Taiwan	3	2	2	2	2	2	1	1	1	1
Thailand	65	67	78	89	96	122	135	145	170	174
Vietnam	106	120	141	173	175	191	246	290	316	357
Total	6,838	6,916	7,081	7,315	7,513	7,699	7,763	7,757	7,954	7,908
World Total	65,625	66,024	66,905	68,499	69,991	72,176	73,610	72,623	75,424	75,461

Eleven members of the Organization of Petroleum Exporting Countries (OPEC) collectively supplied about 40% of the world's oil and had 77.8% (811,526m barrels) of the world total of oil reserves (1,042,536m barrels). The 11 OPEC members are: Algeria, Indonesia, Iran, Iraq, Kuwait, Libya, Nigeria, Qatar, Saudi Arabia, United Arab Emirates and Venezuela. The OPEC countries made ten announcements of cuts in production and/or exports between 1999 and 2002, to keep the price of oil high and conserve reserves. Russia, which has attended many of OPEC's meetings since 1997, has made three commitments to cut production and/or exports, but there is ambiguity in Russia's statements. In 2002 production in Russia and the states bordering the Caspian Sea, and in China, was expected to rise during the next two years, and it seemed that Russia may become the world's leading oil producer.

See http://www.crikey.com.au/business/2003/01/31–oilandiraq.print.html, also EIA http://www.eia.doe.gov/emeu /cabs/topworldtables1_2.html

2. Major World Oil Producers: Proven Crude Oil Reserves (2003) and Total Oil Production (2002). Sources: EIA and Oil and Gas Journal.

3. Bureau of Economics, Analysis, www.bea.doc.gov/bea/di1.htm
   The US was the world's largest oil producer in 2002 because of a refinery gain of 750,000 b/d. 24% of the country's oil was produced in Alaska. The US was easily the world's largest consumer of oil, with 25.39% of the world's consumption, four times more than the second largest, China, which has four times the US's population. The US consumes its own oil, which accounts for more than 45% of its total consumption; and imports nearly 55% of its total consumption. Much of this was supplied by four or five countries: 15% from Canada, 14% from Saudi Arabia and Venezuela, 12% from Mexico, 5–6% from Iraq. More precise figures suggest that the US is a net oil importer of 52% of its requirements. See Table 1.

See EIA (Energy Information Administration). http://www.eia.doe.gov/emeu/cabs/topworldtables1_2.html

The US's proven oil reserves have fallen from 36.5b barrels in 1981 to 30.4b barrels in 2002. NAFTA's reserves fell from 102b barrels to 64.8b barrels due to excessive US consumption. If the US were to rely solely on NAFTA North America would be dry in less than ten years from the end of 2002.

The table on p. 2 shows that the US had only seven years of oil left from the supply known to exist in 1999, not taking account of new finds. On the basis of the 1999 prediction, the US was set to run out of oil in 2006 if there were no new finds. For NAFTA see website http://www.crikey.com.au/business/2003/01/31–oilandiraq.print. html.

For the table on p. 2 see Office of Transportation Technologies' see http://www.ott. doe.gov/facts/archives/fotw125.shtml

The US monthly trade deficit climbed to $41.77b for October 2003, from a deficit of $41.34b in September 2003. For the 2003 year the US trade deficit in goods and services was running at an annual rate of $490.8b, far more than 2002's record $418.04b. The October 2003 trade report showed that while US exports to China increased ($2.87b), imports from China were $16.43b – a trade deficit for the month of $13.57b.

See http://www.usatoday.com/money/economy/trade/2003–12–12–october-trade_x.htm

As regards the UK, in 2002 the UK was the tenth largest world oil producer, with 2.55m barrels per day. The UK was the twelfth largest world oil net exporter, with 0.83m b/d. Oil exports brought in some £400m p.a. The United Kingdom exports most of its high-quality crude oil and imports cheaper, lower-quality crude oils for refining (mainly from the Middle East). The UK is the thirteenth largest consumer of oil in the world, and has the twenty-fourth largest oil reserves (4.7b barrels).

But all is not as well as it seems. The North Sea (which the UK shares with Norway) is a 'mature' oil and natural gas area. Few large discoveries are likely to be made. As in the case of Norway, stocks of oil and natural gas are running out. The UK's production declined from a high of 2.95m b/d in 1999 to 2.55m b/d (or 2.53m b/d) in 2002. Production was expected to decline further in 2003. The domestic UK oil and gas industries are expected to decline and UK reserves to be depleted in the coming decade.

See http://www.eia.doe.gov/emeu/cabs/uk.html

The UK faced industrial problems. Following the replacing of Britain's coal industry by imports from abroad, nuclear reactors were set to be decommissioned and nuclear electricity generation was to be replaced by wind-turbines, with the possibility of nuclear-generated electricity being imported from France. In East Anglia, Sizewell and Dungeness were set to be decommissioned in 2006; Bradwell was closed in 2002. With no clear indications as to their replacement, black-outs or rationed electricity could not be ruled out.

The prospect was that much of the UK's oil and gas would come from Russia and be at risk from terrorist targeting or political interference. Wind, wave and solar power, and hot-rock heating, were being explored as alternatives. Have we all moved from a fossil to a solar century? See article in the *Western Morning News*, 'Solar Century a 'Great Chance for Business', January 14, 2004.

See http://www.westernmorningnews.co.uk/displayNode.jsp?nodeId=103354&comm and=displayContent&sourceNode=10331&contentPK=8488558 for this and the previous paragraph.

The table on p. 2 shows that the UK had five years' oil left in 1999 if there were no new finds, i.e. that the UK's oil was due to run out in 2004 if there were no new finds.

In September 2003 the UK suffered its first monthly oil trade deficit since 1991. This was later amended to a small surplus. Usually the UK's monthly oil surplus has been around £400m. By 2030 the swing from net oil exports to net oil imports would burden the balance of trade by £20–25b p.a., or possibly as much as £25–30b p.a., and add 65–85% to the UK's trade deficit. See Reuters article 'Analysis – UK Faces Future Without North Sea Oil', see website:

http://www.forbes.com/markets/newswire/2004/01/14/rtr1210361.html for this and previous paragraph. The £20–£25b and 65–85% figures came from Peter Odell, Professor Emeritus at Rotterdam's Erasmus University.

North Sea oil has contributed hundreds of billions of pounds to the UK economy since 1980. When the UK's oilwells run dry there will be an impact on tax revenues, which have received over £200b from oil since the late 1960s; on the service industry and employment; and trade figures. Oil has helped balance the UK's trade and has supported hundreds of thousands of jobs. The UK will soon join the US, Germany and Japan as net energy importers.

As a partial reflection of the UK's oil trade deficit, the UK's balance of payments showed a deficit of £10.2b for the three-months to November 2003, and was running at over £40b p.a. Harold Macmillan's Conservative government was thrown out of office in 1964 for having a balance of payments deficit of well under £1b, yet a deficit of £40b scarcely attracts any comment forty years later. The UK's oil has already begun to run out. As if blind to all this, Brown, the Labour Chancellor had thrown huge amounts of cash at the public services, and ministers were quoted in the press as privately admitting that £70b had been wasted, money swallowed up by the hospitals/schools black hole with no visible improvement to show for it.

What all this means is that both the US and the UK were desperate for oil in 2001. If the US was to continue to lead Western civilization for the Syndicate, it required additional long-term cheap sources of oil. If the UK was to continue to provide a supporting role, so did the UK. The Syndicate had access to many other countries' oil but needed the US and the UK to maintain their oil supplies so that they could play their part in implementing a world government.

In 2001 the US was the second largest oil producer (7.717m b/d) to Saudi Arabia (8.768m b/d). According to the US Department of Energy own projections, the US and its major trading partners (Canada, Venezuela and Mexico) would have to become more dependent on Gulf oil over the next two decades.

Bush Jr.'s administration has strong links with the oil industry. Many of the large energy-oil companies donated money to the Republican Party. Given the statistics we have been looking at and the background of Bush Jr.'s administration, it could be expected that oil would be the hallmark of a Bush Jr. administration.

With its own oil running out and Saudi Arabia, holder of the world's largest oil reserves, looking increasingly unstable, economic self-interest demanded that the US should control a significant source of Middle Eastern/Caspian oil. It was in the UK's economic self-interest to provide support.

The war with Iraq and the rehabilitation of Gaddafi's Libya – which until 1969 had supplied a quarter of Europe's crude oil – should be seen in this light.

Graph: U.S. Oil Consumption See www.ott.doe.gov/facts/archives/fotw191.shtml

The United States consumed 19.7 million barrels of oil per day in 2000, more than half of which (10.4 million barrels per day net) came from imports. Imports from the

Persian Gulf in 2000 were 2.5 million barrels per day, which amounts to 12.6% of U.S. consumption.

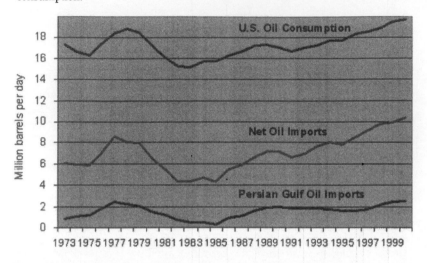

4. See http://www.crikey.com.au/business/2003/01/31–oilandiraq.print.html

5. See 1 above.

6. See BBC News, 11 Feb 2003, http://news.bbc.co.uk/1/hi/world/europe/2747175.stm

7. See p. 23 (i.e. ch 3, para 1) for a definition and full description of the Syndicate.

2. The Genesis of The Syndicate

1. Derek Wilson, *Rothschild, a Story of Wealth and Power*, pp. 9–33. Frederick Morton, *The Rothschilds*, pp. 17–36. Also Count Egon Caesar Corti, *The Rise of the House of Rothschild*, pp. 1–26; and George Armstrong, *The Rothschild Money Trust*, pp. 21–2. Also Niall Ferguson, *The World's Banker, The History of the House of Rothschild*.

2. Armstrong, *op. cit.*, p. 21; Wilson, *op. cit.*, p. 32.

3. Corti, *op. cit.*, p. 402; Morton, *op. cit*, p. 17: "Mayer's ancestors had once lived in a house with a red shield (Rothschild) at the more prosperous end of Jew Street."

4. Armstrong, *op. cit.*, p. 24.

5. Ferguson, *op. cit.*, pp. 1034–5.

6. Ferguson, *op. cit.*, pp. 78–9. The principle was established in September 1810 in a partnership agreement and Mayer Amschel confirmed it on his deathbed, hastily revising his will to reinforce the 1810 agreement.

7. Rothschild had five sons, all of whom participated in the new banking empire. Nathan Mayer Rothschild dealt in bullion and moved to Great Britain. He headed the new Rothschild bank in London, England, which was known as N. M. Rothschild and Sons. James Mayer Rothschild was in charge of the Rothschild bank in France, known as Messieurs de Rothschild Frères. The Rothschild bank in Germany was known as M. A. Rothschild and Söhne after Mayer Amschel Rothschild. The Rothschild bank in Austria was known as S. M. von Rothschild after Solomon Mayer Rothschild. The Rothschild bank in Naples (the last of the five to be set up, in 1821) was known as C. M. von Rothschild after Carl Mayer Rothschild. By the Congress of Vienna (1814–15) the House of Rothschild were hugely powerful international bankers, and most of the European nations were in debt to them.

8. Armstrong, *op. cit.*, p. 35. Also John Reeves, *The Rothschilds, Financial Rulers of Nations* (1887), p. 167, quoted in Armstrong, *op. cit.*, p. 27. Armstrong describes Reeves as a 'Rothschild partisan', and Reeves clearly wrote with inside knowledge of the family.

9. See www.wealthstudy.com/studentsonly/Strategic_Wealth/secII/sec2mod8.htm.

10. Armstrong, *op. cit.*, p. 36.

11. Morton, *The Rothschilds*, p. 11. Before the 2003 arrangement for Concordia BV, domiciled in the Netherlands, to hold the controlling interest in Rothschild Continuation Holdings (see p. 8 of text), "Rothschilds" structure was as follows: at the top of the pyramid was Rothschilds Continuation Holdings AG, a Zurich-based holding company whose main investments are 19 firms, here grouped geographically (see Ferguson, *The World's Banker, op. cit.*, p. 1029).
    - N. M. Rothschild & Sons Ltd, Rothschilds Continuation Ltd, N. M. Rothschild Corporate Finance Ltd and Rothschild Asset Management Ltd (UK)
    - N. M. Rothschild & Sons (CI) Ltd and Rothschild Asset Management (CI) Ltd (Channel Islands)
    - Rothschild & Cie Banque and Rothschild & Cie (France)
    - Rothschild Bank AG (Switzerland)

- Rothschild Europe BV and Rothschild Asset Management International Holdings BV (Netherlands)
- Rothschild North America Inc. and Rothschild Asset management Inc. (US)
- N. M. Rothschild & Sons (Australia) Ltd, N. M. Rothschild Australia Holdings pty Ltd and Rothschild Australia Asset Management Ltd
- N. M. Rothschild & Sons (Hong Kong) Ltd and Rothschild Asset Management (Hong Kong) Ltd
- N. M. Rothschild & Sons (Singapore) Ltd.

The N. M. Rothschild group was also controlled by the family through another Swiss company – Rothschild Concordia AG – which has a majority (52.4%) stake in Rothschilds Continuation Holdings AG. The Paris – Orleans (accent) holding company controlled 37% of Rothschild Canada and 40% of Rothschild Europe. The financial involvement of the Compagnie Financière was smaller.

In June 2003 the British and French counterparts of Rothschilds banks established a new equally owned holding company, Concordia BV.

12. Morton, *op. cit*, p. 251.

13. Markus Angelicus, *Gold Digest*: www.gwb.com.au/gwb/news/banking/rothschild.html

14. Morton, *op. cit.*, p. 297–8. See also note 13. In mid-April 2004 it was announced that N. M. Rothschild would withdraw from all its commodity trading activities, which accounted for 2.2% of "Rothschilds" operating income, including the gold market and its chairing of the London meetings that have set the world gold price since 1919 and including an oil trading business set up very recently. The change was due to restructuring by Baron David de Rothschild, who had taken control of the bank from his cousin, Sir Evelyn de Rothschild. See report in *Daily Telegraph*, Business section, April 15, 2004. In June 2003 N. M. Rothschild had set up a new oil business with a new range of derivative products to attract customers from the oil and power generation industries. One of Baron David's first acts was to commission finance director Andrew Didham to conduct a strategic review of the business. He implemented Didham's findings that the commodities business did not fit in with the bank's private and investment banking business. Two-thirds of the world's gold is privately owned. It is not known how much of this is owned by "Rothschilds." See *Daily Telegraph*, Business section, April 17, 2004.

15. Merrill Lynch/Cap Gemini, Ernst & Young, *World Wealth Report* www.cgey.com/finance/pubs/WWR2003.pdf .

16. Morton, *op. cit.*, p57, quoted by Markus Angelicus in *Gold Digest* see: www.gwb.com.au/gwb/news/banking/rothschild.html. I have checked the dollar-pound exchange rate from 1800 to 1900 from a table provided by Miami University: http.//eh.net/hmit/exchangerates/exchange.answer.php . It is around $5 to the £1 (£0.20/21/22 for most of the 19th century, with £0.10–0.18 from 1862 to 1876). Morton's low $6b is, he says, equivalent to "400 million pounds." On the above exchange rate $6b was equivalent to £1.2b. If the figure were £400m, each of the figures in the 4%-8% range should be cut by two-thirds. However, £1.2b is a more realistic base for the Rothschilds' wealth after Waterloo, and is much lower than other estimates. Morton's book was commissioned by the Rothschild family, who are known to play down their wealth and to hide behind their legend. (Morton writes, p. 11: "Today the family grooms the inaudibility and invisibility of its presence. As a result, some believe that little is left apart from a great legend. And

the Rothschilds are quite content to let the legend be their public relations.") So when Morton tells us that the Rothschilds' wealth was $6b for much of the nineteenth century, i.e. after Waterloo/ c.1820, we may feel that the family is his source and we should be aware that there may be understatement.

See also "The History of Money": http://www.xat.org/xat/history2.html, "The 19th century became known as the age of the Rothschilds when it was estimated they controlled half of the world's wealth ... They only apply the Rothschild name to a small fraction of the companies they actually control. Some authors claim that the Rothschilds had not only taken over the Bank of England but they had also in 1816 backed a new privately owned Central Bank in America called The Second Bank of the United States." Around 1900 the Rothschilds' wealth was held to be greater than that of all the crown heads of Europe put together. Griffin, *Descent into Slavery?*, p. 52.

17. Markus Angelicus in *Gold Digest*, www.gwb.com.au/gwb/news/banking/rothchild.html.

18. It has been asserted that the Rothschild family today is worth in excess of $100 trillion. CIO Newsletter: http://comment.cio.com/comments/13854.html

19. In 2004 Microsoft's stock was worth $32.28b. See Bill Gates' Net Worth Page: http://www.quuxuum.org/~evan/bgnw.html .

20. John Kutyn, *Gold Digest*, www.gold-eagle.com/gold_digest/kutyn111597.html .

21. The US federal national debt was $7.112 trillion on April 19, 2004 ($7,112,312,957,447). In June 2003 Congress raised the "debt-ceiling" to $7.414 trillion. See text for ch 14, note 12. At its present rate of increase it was expected to reach $7.5 trillion by the end of 2004. The interest payments on the US federal national debt were estimated at over $409b during the federal fiscal year from October 2003 to September 2004. As the Syndicate is responsible for the Federal Reserve System, in one form or another Syndicate banks receive this interest. It can be said that the Syndicate now receives some $400b a year from the Federal Reserve System. See next section. See: http://www.uwsa.com/uwsa-usdebt.html

22. *The Secret History of the West* shows that all the revolutions from 1453 to the Russian revolution lead to the New World Order. The Rothschild story is traced in relation to Mayer's collaboration with Adam Weishaupt, the Rothschilds' contribution to the development of the British Empire and their role in the first Russian revolution. I detail their control over the central banks of England, France, Austria, Naples and the US.

23. The National Bank Act is widely called the National Banking Act. Rivera, *Final Warning, A History of the New World Order*, p. 41. The National Bank Act prohibited states' creation of money. Federal banks were now in control. The post-1863 system was a forerunner of the Federal Reserve System. Lincoln may have been murdered because he tried to issue interest-free money in opposition to the new federal system.

24. Rivera, *op. cit.*, p. 44.

25. Rivera, *op. cit.*, p. 44.

26. Col. Ely Garrison, *Roosevelt, Wilson and the Federal Reserve Act*.

27. See G. Edward Griffin, *The Creature from Jekyll Island*, Appleton W. I.: American Opinion Publishing Inc, 1994. And book review by Jane Ingraham in *The New American*: http://

www.homevideo.net/dna/review.htm: "We are taken to the super-secret meeting of Insider financiers and Rothschild agent Paul Warburg on Jekyll Island in 1910 where the basic plan for what became the Federal Reserve Act was formulated." Also, Josephson, *The "Federal" Reserve Conspiracy and Rockefeller*, pp. 41–3.

28. Rivera, *op. cit.*, p50.

29. The same tactic was used in America in 1992 when Ross Perot pulled votes away from the Bush Sr. to let in the "Rothschildite" Clinton, and in Britain in 1997 when Sir James Goldsmith pulled votes away from Prime Minister Major to make sure Blair would be let in. As we shall see "Rothschilds" were also behind these tactics.

30. The first Federal Reserve Board is shown below. See Federal Reserve Bank of Minneapolis: http://minneapolisfed.org/pubs/region/99–12/when.cfm

The Federal Reserve Board originally included the Secretary of the Treasury and the Comptroller of the Currency. This 1914 photo of the first Board includes (clockwise from left) H. Parker Willis, Secretary to the Board; W. P. G. Harding; Paul M. Warburg; W. G. McAdoo, Secretary of the Treasury and Chairman; Charles S. Hamlin, Governor; John Skelton Williams, Comptroller of the Currency; Adolph C. Miller; and Frederic A. Delano, Vice Governor.

31. Rivera, *op. cit.*, pp52–54. The agents of "Rothschildite" foreign banks included Schiff, the Warburgs and J. P. Morgan. For the next paragraph, see Rivera, *op. cit.*, p55.

32. *America, The Agricultural Depression*: http://www.weekendonline.net/317/articles/agdepression.html

33. The central banks included the Bank of England and German Reichsbank. Details of the 1927 meeting were revealed in 1928 in the House hearings on the Stabilizing of the Purchasing Power of the Dollar. Rivera, *op. cit*, pp. 55, 80. Also Eustace Mullins, *The Secrets of the Federal Reserve*, ch 6, "The Great Depression": http://www.cephas-library.com/nwo/federal_reserve_chapter_12.html , pp. 55, 80. Also Josephson, *The "Federal" Reserve Conspiracy and Rockefeller*, *op. cit.*, p. 41.

34. Rivera, *op. cit.*, p80.

35. Josephson, *Rockefeller "Internationalist"*, p187; F. William Engdahl, *A Century of War, Anglo-American Oil Politics and the New World Order*, p. 29.

36. Ferguson, *op. cit.*, p. 880.

The background to Rothschilds' early domination of oil can be expressed in a timeline:

• "Rothschilds" Russian kerosene sold in Europe through their Industrial and Commercial Caspian and Black Sea Kerosene Company. (Société Industrielle et Commerciale de Naphte Caspienne et de la Mer Noir)

• "Rothschilds" in partnership with Russian shipping firm Pollack & Co and the International Bank of St Petersburg to form Mazout, in competion with nobels Standard Oil, Asian market

• 1891 origin of Shell Transport & Trading Company (formed 1897) when Marcus and Samuel Samuel acquired the right to market BNITO's kerosene east of Suez, in competition with Royal Dutch Company

• 1902 "Rothschilds" took a third share of the Asiatic Petroleum Co

• 1911 "Rothschilds" exchanged their entire Russian operation for shares in Royal Dutch and Shell (which had amalgamated in 1907). (Rothschilds' shares in BNITO and Mazout then valued at £2.9m.)

The following oil companies were related to "Rothschilds" at some point in their timelines: (see Petroleum Archives Project, Arabian Peninsula and Gulf Studies Program, University of Virginia, www.virginia.edu/igpr/apagoilhistory.html):

1. **Shell**

1833: Marcus Samuel starts import export business in London

1890: Royal Dutch Company launched

1892: Marcus commissions the first special oil tanker and delivers 4,000 tons of Russian kerosene to Singapore and Bangkok

1897: Samuel's company begins to operate under the name Shell Transport and Trading Company, Limited

1903: Shell and Dutch company N.V. Koninklijke Nederlandsche Maatschappij tot Explotatie van Petroleum-bronnen in Nederlandsch-Indië form the Asiatic Petroleum Company

1903: Royal Dutch and Shell group begins joint marketing campaign under name 'British Dutch'

1906–1914: British Dutch Group acquires producing interests in: Romania (1906), Russia (1910), Egypt (1911), Venezuela (1913) and Trinidad (1914)

1907: Royal Dutch/Shell partnership is extended worldwide, with the creation of the Royal Dutch / Shell Group of Companies

1912: Trading in the US starts after the acquisition of the American Gasoline Company, an American marketing company

1912: Turkish Petroleum Company founded with 50% ownership by Turkish National Bank, 25% Deutsche Bank, 25% Royal Dutch/Shell

1915: Formation of the Shell Company in California

1918: Royal Dutch/Shell buys Mexican Eagle

1922: Shell Union Oil Corporation [later Shell Oil Company] formed to consolidate Shell interests in the US with those of the Union Oil Company of Delaware

1937: Shell, Total, and Partex form the consortium Petroleum Development (Oman and Dhofar) later, Petroleum Development Oman

1945–55: Exploratory drilling in Tunisia, Algeria, Nigeria, Trinidad and offshore in British Borneo; Production from the Iraq Petroleum Company increases dramatically

1949: In 1949 Royal Dutch shortens its corporate title the name "Shell." "Rothschilds" agents began to sell their holdings in Royal Dutch Shell shortly before the death of Edouard de Rothschild in 1949 to drive down the value of his estate for taxation purposes, and bought them back at depressed prices after his death.

1954: Consortium of oil companies, including British Petroleum, Exxon, Socony, Texas Oil, Socal, Gulf, Royal Dutch/Shell Group, and CFP form the Iranian Oil Participants Ltd. (IOP) and negotiate agreement with Iranian government and for oil production in Iran

1956: Shell discovers oil in the Sahara

1959: Joint Shell/Esso exploration company called N.V. Nederlandse Aardolie Maatschappij (NAM) discovers gas fields in Groningen in the Netherlands

1974: Omani government claims 25% interest Petroleum Development Oman

1975: Omani government raises its interest in Petroleum Development Oman to 60%

1979: Shell acquires Belridge Oil

1984: Shell buys minority interest (30%) in Shell Oil US

Mid-1980s: Royal Dutch/Shell buys remaining 31% of Shell Oil USA (the remainder that it did not yet own)

1998: Shell Oil Co., Texaco Inc. and Saudi Aramco initiate joint venture combining their eastern U.S. refining and marketing assets under the name Motiva Enterprises LLC, paralleling a joint venture launched by Shell and Texaco under the name Equilon Enterprises LLC for their Midwest, Southwest and West Coast downstream assets; Shell to own 35% of Houston-based Motiva, while Texaco and Aramco will each own 32.5%

1998: Occidental and Royal Dutch/Shell, Anglo-Dutch oil group complete a $1bn global asset swap

2. **Union Oil/Unocal**

1890: Union Oil formed in California by merger of Hardison & Stewart Oil Company, the Sespe Oil Company, and the Torrey Canyon Oil Company

1917: Union purchases Pinal-Dome Oil Company

1922: Shell buys 25% of Union Oil of California

1922: Shell Union Oil Corporation formed to consolidate Shell interests in the US with those of the Union Oil Company of Delaware

1965: Union acquires Pure Oil

1983: Union Oil changes name to Unocal

1992: Ashland Chemical acquires most of Unocal's chemical distribution business, establishing the IC&S Division

3. **Gulf Oil (to 1984)**

1901: Guffey Oil founded

1901: Gulf Refining Company founded

1907: William Mellon reorganizes Guffey Oil and Gulf Refining under name of Gulf Oil Corporation

1922: Gulf Oil Corporation forms Eastern Gulf Oil Company

1928: Gulf joins Turkish Petroleum Company

1929: Gulf buys Paragon Refining Company

1934: Gulf sells its share of Iraq Petroleum Company to Socal

1934: Anglo-Iranian and Gulf Oil Corporation establish Kuwait Oil Company as a 50–50 joint venture to compete for Kuwait concession (which they obtain); Subsequent agreement establishes British control of KOC

1954: Consortium of oil companies, including British Petroleum, Exxon, Socony, Texas Oil, Socal, Gulf, Royal Dutch/Shell Group, and CFP form the Iranian Oil Participants Ltd. (IOP) and negotiate agreement with Iranian government and for oil production in Iran

1955: Acquires Warren Petroleum

1971: Gulf purchases 10% in Syncrude Canada Limited

1984: Chevron buys Gulf

4. **Iraq Petroleum Company**

1912: Turkish Petroleum Company founded with 50% ownership by Turkish National Bank, 25% Deutsche Bank, 25% Royal Dutch/Shell

1914: Turkish Petroleum Company reorganized, with Anglo-Persian holding 50%, Deutsche Bank and Shell each holding 25%

1914: Ottoman Grand Vizier promises Mesopotamian concession to Turkish Petroleum Company, but final concession agreement is not signed

1922: CFP joins Turkish Petroleum Company

1925: Turkish Petroleum Company gains oil concession in Iraq

1928: Gulf joins Turkish Petroleum Company

1928: Royal Dutch/Shell, Anglo-Persian, CFP, Exxon, Mobil, Atlantic Richfield, Gulf Oil Corporation, Standard Oil of Indiana [Amoco], and Participations and Explorations Corp., establish a joint venture called the Near East Development Company; The Near East Development Company signs "Red Lines Agreement" binding participating companies to cooperate with Turkish Petroleum Company in any ventures in Turkey, the Levant, Iraq and Arabian Peninsula (Atlantic, Gulf, and Standard eventually sell their shares to other participants)

1929: Turkish Petroleum changes name to Iraq Petroleum Company

1932: Mosul Petroleum Company formed to hold northern portion of IPC's Iraq concession

1938: Basrah Petroleum Company formed to hold southern portion of IPC's Iraq concession

1939: IPC establishes Abu Dhabi Petroleum Company Ltd. (ADPC) to hold Abu Dhabi concession

1939: British government seizes IPC shares held by CFP

1966: Iraq revokes portions of IPC concession and nationalizes these concessions

1972: Iraq nationalizes remaining IPC concessions

1973: Iraq nationalizes assets of foreign assets in Basrah Petroleum Company

5. **Occidental Petroleum**

1910: Cities Service Company formed

1920: Occidental Petroleum founded

1953: Cities Service Company obtains Dhofar province concession in Oman

1956: Armand Hammer buys Occidental Petroleum

1965: Cities Service Company begins marketing products under the brand name

'CITGO'

1965: Occidental wins oil concession in Libya

1983: Occidental acquires Cities Service Company

1983: Occidental reorganized Cities' assets and sells newly formed "CITGO Petroleum Corporation" to Southland Corporation

1980s: Libya nationalizes 51% of Occidental's operation in Libya

1986: Occidental acquired the Midcon Corporation,

1994: Occidental Petroleum Corp. completes acquisition of Placid Oil Co., which was founded in 1936 by H.L. Hunt

1995: Occidental purchases 19% stake in Clark USA

1998: Occidental and Royal Dutch/Shell, Anglo-Dutch oil group complete a $1bn global asset swap

1998: Occidental sells Occidental Netherlands Inc. unit to TransCanada Pipelines Ltd.

6. **Kuwait National Petroleum Company (until 1974)**

1934: Anglo-Iranian and Gulf Oil Corporation establish Kuwait Oil Company as a 50–50 joint venture to compete for Kuwait concession (which they obtain); Subsequent agreement establishes British control of KOC

1934: Sheikh Ahmed grants 75-year concession to KOC

1951: KOC oil concession extended for additional 17 years

1960: Kuwait National Petroleum Company established as a shareholder company owned by the government and the private sector

1968: KNPC commissions Shuaiba Refinery, the world's first all hydrogen refinery

1974: Kuwaiti government acquires 60% ownership of KOC

1975: KNPC becomes a fully state-owned company

1980: Kuwait Petroleum Corporation created, KNPC becomes fully owned by KPC; KNPC takes charge of the three oil refineries; Mina Al-Ahmadi, Mina Abdulla and Shuaiba, in addition to the LPG plant in Mina Al-Ahmadi

1981: Kuwait Oil Company purchases the Santa Fe International Corp., of California.

The following oil companies have less clear affiliations:

1. **Ashland Oil**

1924: Ashland Refining Company of Ashland, Ky., founded as a refining arm of Swiss Oil Company of Lexington

1930: Ashland Purchases Tri-State Refining

1931: Acquires Cumberland Pipeline Company's eastern Kentucky pipeline network

1936: Ashland Refining merges with Swiss Oil to form Ashland Oil & Refining Company

1946: Ashland Oil & Refining Company products first sold under the brand name "Ashland"

1948: Ashland and Allied Oil merge

1949: Ashland and Aetna Oil merge, Ashland acquires Kentucky retail marketing operation Freedom-Valvoline, including Valvoline Motor Oil brand and also acquires Southern Pipe Line Company

1950: Frontier Oil Refining of Buffalo, N.Y., and National Refining of Cleveland, Ohio, join Ashland

1956: Acquisition of R. J. Brown Company of St. Louis.

1963: Ashland acquires United Oil

1966: Ashland acquires Warren Brothers construction company

1967: Ashland purchases ADM Chemical Group and forms Ashland

1969: Ashland forms Ashland Petroleum operating division and Arch Mineral

1970: Ashland changes name to Ashland Oil, Inc.

1970: Ashland acquires Northwestern Refining of St. Paul, Minn. and the SuperAmerica retail marketing chain

1971: Exploration and production activities are consolidated into Ashland Exploration

1975: Construction division is formed, and Ashland Coal is created

1991: Ashland acquires The Permian Corporation and merges with Scurlock Oil Company

1992: Ashland Chemical acquires most of Unocal's chemical distribution business, establishing the IC&S Division

1994: Ashland's Valvoline acquires Zerex

1995: Ashland changes company's name to Ashland Inc.

1997: Ashland signs agreements with Marathon to combine the refining, marketing and transportation assets of the companies. Ashland acquires 38% of Marathon Ashland Petroleum LLC

2. Phillips Petroleum Company

1905: Phillips brothers begin oil exploration

1917: Phillips Petroleum Company founded by Frank Phillips

1922: Phillips forms the predecessor to what today is GPM Gas Corp

1925: Research and Development Group formed

1969: Phillips' Kenai LNG Plant begins operation

1985: Phillips successfully fends off hostile take-over attempts

1992: GPM Gas Corporation formed

3. Mesa Petroleum

1956: After resigning as a geologist with Phillips Petroleum Co., T. Boone Pickens forms development and production company called Petroleum Exploration

1959: Altair Oil and Gas is established to conduct oil and gas exploration in Canada

1964: Petroleum Exploration, Inc., and Altair merge to form Mesa Petroleum Co.

1967: Mesa Petroleum Co. shares began trading on the American Stock Exchange

1969: In hostile takeover, Pickens merges larger Hugoton into Mesa

1979: Mesa sells holdings in Canada and the North Sea to reduce debt and buy additional Hugoton reserves; Mesa also creates the Mesa Royalty Trust

1983: Mesa forms Gulf Investors Group (GIG)

1984: Mesa repurchases nearly 90% of the GIG units in a $500 million public tender offer

1985: The Mesa Petroleum Company changes its name to the Mesa Limited Partnership

1986: Mesa purchases Pioneer Corporation

1988: MESA partnership acquires gas reserves from Tenneco Inc.

1991: Mesa Limited Partnership changes name to MESA Inc.

4. Sun Company Inc.

1886: Robert Pew founds Sun Oil Company

1901: New Jersey Oil and Gas incorporated

1968: Sun buys Sunray (DX)

1971: Sun Oil Company reorganized and renamed Sun Company Incorporated

5. Elf Aquitaine

1941: Societe Nationale des Petroles d'Aquitaine (SNPA) incorporated at the initiative of the French government

1966: French government merges gas and oil interests into Enterprise de Recherches et d'Activities Petrolieres (ERAP), giving ERAP majority ownership of SNPA

1974: ERAP begins onshore and offshore exploration in Iran

1976: ERAP is reorganized and increases share of SNPA ownership to 70%

1976: ERAP changes name to Societe Nationale Elf Aquitaine, known as Elf Aquitaine Group

6. Ente Nazionale Idrocarburi (ENI)

1953: Enrico Mattei founds Ente Nazionale Idrocarburi [ENI] as a conglomeration of 36 subsidiaries including AGIP, with government sanction

1956: Signs 50–50 oil cooperation deal with National Iranian Oil Company

1970–75: Founds Agip (Qatar) Ltd,

1980s: Libya gains control of 50% of ENI Libya

1981: Enoxy, a joint ENI Occidental petrochemical and mining venture founded

1985: ENI wins contract to construct pipeline in Iraq

1986: ENI wins portion of a pipeline contact for Yemen

1992: ENI transformed into joint stock company traded on Italian and NYSE

7. Total Oil (CFP)

1924: Foundation of the French Compagnie Francaise Des Petroles (CFP), which assumes French shares of Turkish Petroleum Company

1927: Discovery of the first oil field near Kirkuk in Iraq

1954/5: Creation and registration of the trademark TOTAL, and foundation of the first companies marketing TOTAL products

1954: Consortium of oil companies, including British Petroleum, Exxon, Socony, Texas Oil, Socal, Gulf, Royal Dutch/Shell Group, and CFP form the Iranian Oil Participants Ltd. (IOP) and negotiate agreement with Iranian government and for oil production in Iran

1956: Discovery of the Hassi-Messaoud oil field and Hassi R'Mel gas field, in the Algerian Sahara

1960: CFP absorbs the OFP (Omnium Francais Des Petroles) group

1970: French Petroleum Company of Canada founded. The company is renamed Total Petroleum (North America) later that year

1973: First listing of CFP shares on the London Stock Exchange

1978: CFP signs an agreement with Abu Dhabi covering development of the Upper Zakum field and production of butane and propane as well as the condensates associated with the oil produced by ADPC (GASCO)

1980: TOTAL acquires Vickers Petroleum Corp., expanding TOTAL's presence in the United States

1985: CFP changes company name from CFP to TOTAL CFP

1985: TOTAL CFP acquires all United States hydrocarbon assets of Lear Petroleum Partners

1987: TOTAL CFP acquires hydrocarbon assets held by TIPCO in the United States as well as those of Francarep Italia, and divests of all refining assets and most of the Group's marketing interests in Italy

1988: TOTAL CFP acquires CSX OIL & GAS in the United States

1991: TOTAL CFP changes company name to TOTAL

1991: Reduction of the French government's direct share holding in TOTAL from 31.7% to 5.4%

1995: TOTAL signs agreements for establishing the Yemen gas liquefaction project and a development contract for the Iranian offshore fields Sirri A and E

1996: Divestment by the French State of a further 4% of TOTAL's capital, reducing the government's stake to 0.97%; TOTAL signs a production-sharing agreement for development of Algeria's Tin Fouyé Tabankort field

1998: TOTAL announces details of its development plans for Iran's giant South Pars gas field in coordination with the National Iranian Oil Co.

8. American Independent Oil Company (AMINOIL)

1947: Consortium of Phillips, Ashland, Signal Oil and Gas, J.S. Abercrombie, Sunray Mid-Continent Oil Co., Globe Oil and Refining Co., and Pauley Petroleum Inc formed to bid on Neutral Zone concession; Consortium is named American Independent Oil Company [Aminoil]

1948: Aminoil wins Neutral Zone concession from Kuwait

1970: Aminoil acquired by R. J. Reynolds Industries, Inc.

9. Eastern and General Syndicate

1919: Major Frank Holmes establishes Eastern and General Syndicate

1925: Eastern and General Syndicate wins al-Hasa Concession

1925: Eastern and General Syndicate awarded oil concession in Bahrain.

37. Robert E. Ebel, "The History and Politics of Chechen Oil", *Caspian Crossroads Magazine*: http://ourworld.compuserve.com/homepages/usazerb/3.htm.

38. Josephson, *The "Federal" Reserve Conspiracy and Rockefeller, op. cit.*, p. 75.

39. Josephson, *The Truth about Rockefeller, Public Enemy no. 1, op. cit.*, pp. 2, 54.

40. Rivera, *op. cit.*, p. 44. Morgan was the top American Rothschild representative. Schiff, a partner of Kuhn & Loeb in 1873 with financial backing from the Rothschilds, rivaled him by financing Harriman's railroad empire, Carnegie's steel empire and Rockefeller's oil empire: Standard Oil. Also William Still, *New World Order: The Ancient Plan of Secret Societies*, p. 136: "Working through the Wall Street firms Kuhn, Loeb & Co. and J. P. Morgan Co., the Rothschilds financed John D. Rockefeller so that he could create the Standard Oil empire."

41. Rivera, *op. cit.*, p. 64. Rockefeller's goal was for Standard Oil to be the world's only refinery.

42. Rockefeller gave the Rockefeller Foundation over $182m; the Laura Spelman and Rockefeller Memorial Fund over $74m; the Rockefeller Institute for Medical Research over $60m; and the General Education Co. over $129m. On his death his taxable estate was assessed as $26,410,837.10, and it paid just over $10m in inheritance tax. See Myer Kutz, *Rockefeller Power*, pp. 42–7; Josephson, *The "Federal" Reserve Conspiracy and Rockefeller, op. cit.*, pp. 82, 92; Rivera, *op. cit.*, p. 66.

43. Josephson, *Rockefeller "Internationalist", op. cit.*, p. 188.

44. Rivera, *op. cit.*, p. 65.

45. Ron Chernow, *Titan, The Life of John D. Rockefeller Sr*, p. 557. Rockefellers made $200m
    out of the First World War; see Curtis Dall, *My Exploited Father-in-Law*, p71, quoted in
    Perloff, James Perloff, *The Shadows of Power, The Council on Foreign Relations and the
    American Decline*, p. 29.
    Also http://www.threeworldwars.com/world-war-1/ww1.htm.
    The background to the break-up of Standard Oil can be summarized in a timeline (see
    http://www.US-highways.com/sohist1911.htm):
    1870: John D. Rockefeller and Henry Flagler found Standard Oil
    1882: Rockefeller organizes his various oil holdings into the Standard Oil Trust, with
    headquarters in New York
    1886: Standard Oil founds Natural Gas Trust
    1901: Standard establishes regional affiliate, Republic Oil
    1907: Standard establishes Standard Oil of California
    1911: Standard dissolved under court order, creating Standard Oil of New Jersey (Exxon),
    Standard Oil of New York (Mobil), Standard Oil [California] (Chevron), Standard Oil of
    Ohio (Sohio, arm of BP), Standard Oil of Indiana (Amoco), Continental Oil (Conoco),
    Atlantic (ARCO)
       Before the 1911 break-up of the Standard Oil Trust led by John D. Rockefeller I, there
    were 37 Standard Oil subsidiaries:
    - 1868: **Standard Oil Company (Pittsburg, Pennsylvania)** is organized. This was the first
      Standard Oil.
    - 1870: **The Standard Oil Company** is incorporated in Ohio. This would later become
      Sohio, and was the leading organization in the Trust for many years.
    - 1877: **The Standard Oil Company of California (Ventura)** formed by local businessmen
      in Ventura County, California, hoping for a future connection to the eastern company;
      Baltimore United Oil Company formed of parts of many smaller firms, including
      Camden Consolidated.
    - 1879: **The Standard Oil Company (Ohio)**'s marketing area included Ohio, Indiana,
      Illinois, Wisconsin, Michigan, the Rocky Mountain States, and California. **Vacuum
      Oil Company** (est. 1866) added to the Trust. **Pacific Coast Oil Company** acquired The
      Standard Oil Company of California (Ventura).
    - 1882: **Standard Oil Company of New Jersey ("Standard")** was formed to take advantage
      of New Jersey laws that allowed corporations to own stock in other corporations. It
      provided administrative coordination to the Trust. **Standard Oil Company of New York**
      also formed this year, and administered most of the foreign territories. **The West India
      Oil Company** formed to handle refining in Cuba & the Caribbean.
    - 1885: **Standard Oil Company of Iowa** was formed to handle marketing along the
      Pacific coast. **Solar Refining Company** formed. **Buckeye Pipe Line** formed.
    - 1886: **Standard Oil Company of Kentucky** was formed to absorb the assets of **Chess,
      Carley, & Company**. Also, **Standard Oil Company of Minnesota** was formed to absorb
      Bartles & Richardson in Wisconsin, Minnesota, North Dakota and South Dakota.
      Remaining assets of **The Standard Oil Company of California** (Ventura) liquidated.
    - 1889: **Standard Oil Company of Indiana** was formed, centered around the Whiting,
      Indiana refinery, and was only in the production end of the oil business. The Ohio
      Oil Company purchased by the Standard Trust, its only customer. **South Penn Oil
      Company** was formed to explore and produce oil in Pennsylvania and West Virginia.
    - 1890: The Trust purchased the remaining shares of P.C. Hanford and transferred its

assets to the newly formed **Standard Oil Company of Illinois**
- 1896: Indiana Standard purchased the marketing rights to Iowa, Nebraska, Kansas and Missouri from Kentucky Standard. **(The) Standard Oil Company of Kansas** and **Standard Oil Company of Missouri** organized due to anti-Standard sentiment in those states. SO (Kan.) was only a refining concern.
- 1906: **Standard Oil Company of California** was formed to take over the Pacific coast marketing area of Pacific Coast Oil and Iowa Standard. Iowa Standard was liquidated prior to the Trust breakup, despite being mentioned in court papers. Also that year, **Standard Oil Company of Nebraska** was formed from Indiana Standard assets in response to an anti-monopoly campaign in that state. Republic Oil was dissolved and its assets sold to Indiana Standard, Ohio Standard, and Waters-Pierce.
- 1909: **Standard Oil Company of Louisiana** organized by Jersey Standard. **Navarro (Corsicana) Refining Company** & **Security Oil Company** severed from Standard in a Texas court decision. Manhattan Oil Company absorbed by Anglo-American Oil Company
- 1910: **Standard Oil Company of Brazil** organized, absorbs Empreza Industria de Petroleo.

After 1911, Standard Oil was declared a monopoly and **broken up**. Among the company assets that were divided up was the right to use the well-known "Standard" brand name. Most of these "Baby Standards" kept using the popular "Red Crown" and "White Crown" gasoline brands, as well as "Polarine" Motor Oil. When the *"Ethyl"* additive became popular, most Standards adopted it. "Mobiloil" was commonly used by many Standards. The former Standards banded together in 1930 to form the Atlas Corporation, maker of tires, batteries, and other automotive accessories that were provided to Standard Stations of all stripes from the Atlantic to the Pacific.

Standard Oil Company of New York (a.k.a. **Socony**) was awarded Maine, New Hampshire, Vermont, Massachusetts, Rhode Island, Connecticut, and New York. The company was very expansion-minded and in 1918, Socony purchased a minority interest in Corsicana, Texas based Magnolia Petroleum in and completed the purchase in 1925. In 1926, California's General Petroleum was purchased. Socony purchased White Eagle of Minnesota in 1930.

Atlantic Refining (Atlantic) was awarded Pennsylvania and Delaware

Standard Oil of New Jersey (Jersey Standard a.k.a. 'Standard') was awarded New Jersey, Maryland, D.C., Virginia, West. Virginia, North Carolina, and South Carolina, and retained Stanocola, Carter Oil, Imperial Oil, many overseas properties, and Gilbert & Barker Manufacturing. Jersey purchased a controlling interest in Houston, Texas's Humble Oil & Refining in 1919.

Standard Oil of Ohio (The Standard Oil Company a.k.a. Sohio) was awarded Ohio. They expanded to neighboring states under the Fleet-Wing name.

Standard Oil of Kentucky (Kyso) was awarded Kentucky, Georgia, Florida, Alabama, and Mississippi. It was supplied by Jersey Standard.

Standard Oil of Indiana (Stanolind) was awarded Indiana, Michigan, Illinois, Wisconsin, Minnesota, North Dakota, South Dakota, Iowa, Kansas, and northern Missouri. To provide the company with a source of crude oil, it purchased Louisiana's Dixie Oil Company in 1919 and interest in Wyoming's Midwest Oil Company i 1920. In 1925, Indiana Standard purchased a large interest in the large, new Pan-Am with its crude reserves and transport network. Pan-Am itself had recently purchased an interest in a small Baltimore refiner and marketer, American Oil (and its signature product, high-quality Amoco Gas). Mexican Petroleum's northeastern and international operations were now open to Indiana Standard as well as Pan-Am's southeastern marketing operation. With the completion of the Midwest Oil purchase in 1928, Utah Oil Refining's Vico-Pep 88 stations in Utah and Idaho came under the Indiana Standard umbrella.

Standard Oil Company of Louisiana (Stanocola) was awarded eastern Louisiana (New Orleans and vicinity) and Tennessee - This company was completely under the control of Jersey Standard before the 1911 breakup. The Stanocola name fell into disuse in 1924 except for a hospital in Louisiana.

Waters-Pierce was awarded southern Missouri, western Louisiana, Arkansas, Oklahoma, and Texas, and used the name Pierce Petroleum before being purchased by Sinclair in 1930.

Standard Oil of Nebraska was awarded Nebraska.

Continental Oil Company (Conoco) was awarded Idaho, Montana, Wyoming, Utah, Colorado, and New Mexico. Marland Oil purchased Conoco in 1929, keeping its own triangle logo and Conoco's name and its rights to market Standard products.

Standard Oil of California (Socal) was awarded Washington, Oregon, Arizona, California and the territories of Alaska and Hawaii. It used Calol (California Oil) as an early appendage to the Standard products line. Socal expanded slower than other Standards, entering New Mexico and Texas under the Pasotex name in 1926.

The Other 24 Companies that were broken off from the Standard Oil Trust:

Anglo-American Oil Company (purchased in 1930 by Jersey Standard – now ESSO UK), Buckeye Pipe Line Company (transport), Borne-Scrymser Company (later Borne Chemical Company), Cheseborough Manufacturing Company (later Cheseborough-Ponds), Colonial Oil Company (merged with *Beacon Oil* in 1928 to form Colonial Beacon Oil Company), Crescent Pipe Line Company (Liquidated 1925), Cumberland Pipe Line Company (transport), Eureka Pipe Line Company (transport), Galena-Signal Oil Company, Indiana Pipe Line Company (transport), National Transit Company (transport), New York Transit Company (transport), Northern Pipe Line Company (transport), Ohio Oil Company (a.k.a. "The Ohio") (purchased *Mid-Kansas Oil & Gas* in the 1920s) (purchased *Lincoln Oil "Linco"* in 1924) (purchased *Red Fox Oil Co.* in 1928) (purchased *Transcontinental Oil "Marathon"* in 1930), Prairie Oil & Gas Company (production), Solar Refining Company, Southern Pipe Line Company (transport), South Penn Oil Company (purchased a controlling interest in the recently formed *Pennzoil Company* in 1925, acquiring a gasoline marketing operation in the process), Southwest Pennsylvania Pipe Lines Company (transport), Standard Oil of Kansas (refining), Swan & Finch Company, Union Tank Lines (transport), Vacuum Oil Company (introduced Gargoyle Mobiloil in 1904) (marketed Mobilgas in the 1920s) (purchased *Lubrite Refining Company* in 1929) (purchased *Wadhams Oil Company* and *White Star Refining Company* in 1930) and Washington Oil Company (production)

There were later Standard Oils:

Standard Oil of Colorado was chartered in Denver in 1922, the unused charter was rescinded in 1926. In 1927, it was re-incorporated as Standard Oil Company of Colorado and sold stock by 1930 to small investors trying to get a piece of the fractured Trust as the demand for gasoline increased. The company had no oil wells, no refineries, and no gasoline stations. In 1930, Indiana Standard was extending its 'Standard' marketing area into Conoco territory – Colorado and other Rocky Mountain states. After much confusion, in 1931 Indiana Standard sued Colorado Standard over the use of the Standard Oil name and won. In 1934, the suit was upheld and Colorado Standard was relegated to the footnotes of history.

Standard Oil of Connecticut was chartered as Standard Coal and Charcoal Company in Stratford, CT in 1915. The company's local focus and lack of an oil connection at the time left it beneath the radar of Socony. The company survived the Great Depression and became Standard Fuel after WW II. After the great re-branding of Esso as Exxon in the US, the local copyright to Standard Oil became available. Standard Fuel took the opportunity and became Standard Oil.

Standard Oil Company of Galicia, Ltd. briefly existed in France, probably in the 1890s, with no connection to the Trust except wishful thinking.

46. Ida Tarbell, *The History of the Standard Oil Company*, 1904; updated and reissued in two volumes 1931, ch 18. See: http://www.bilderberg.org/whatafel.htm#Ida.

"Rockefellers" oil supremacy was stunning. The following well-known oil companies with names other than Standard Oil were related to 'Rockefellers' at some point in their timelines:

1. **Amoco**

    1889: Standard Oil (Indiana) founded as subsidiary of Standard Oil Trust

    1911: Standard Oil of Indiana founded with dissolution of Standard Oil

    1910s: Standard Oil of Indiana purchases Pan American Petroleum

    1914: Standard Oil of Indiana licenses 'thermal cracking' process for producing gasoline to competing oil companies

    1925: Standard Oil of Indiana acquires controlling interest in Pan American Petroleum and Transport Company

    1932: Standard Oil of Indiana sells Venezuela operation to Jersey

    1954: Pan American and Standard of Indiana merge, new company is called American Oil Company [Amoco]

    1957: Begins joint venture with Iran independent of Iranian Oil Consortium

    1958: Amoco signs agreement with Shah of Iran

    1960s: Amoco Egypt Oil Company, Cairo, founded

    1980s: Amoco Sharjah Oil Company, Sharjah, U.A.E., in partnership with UEA, produces natural gas and natural gas liquids in Sharjah

    1990s: Amoco Oman Oil Company begins oil and gas exploration program

    1998 Amoco merges with BP to form BP-Amoco plc

2. **Chevron**

    1879: Pacific Coast Oil Company established

    1900: Pacific Coast Oil purchased by Standard Oil, but remains separate operation

    1906: Pacific Coast Oil consolidated with other Western US operations of Standard Oil into Standard Oil Company (California)

    1911: Dissolution of Standard Oil Trust makes Standard Oil of California (Socal) independent

    1926: Socal merges with Pacific Oil Company

    1929: Socal establishes Bahrain Petroleum Company to hold Bahrain concession

    1932: Bahrain Petroleum strikes oil in Bahrain

    1933: Socal wins Saudi Arabia concession; Socal establishes California-Arabia Standard

Oil Company, Casoc, to hold concession for Saudi Arabia

1933: Socal discoveries oil in Saudi Arabia

1936: Texaco joins with Standard Oil of California (later Chevron), to found the Arab-American Oil Company [Aramco]

1936: Texaco purchases half interest in Bahrain Petroleum and California-Arabian Standard Oil Company (Calarabian) from Socal

1936: California-Texas company, Caltex, founded as a joint venture between Socal and Texaco as outlet for future oil production in Bahrain and Saudi Arabia

1954: Consortium of oil companies, including British Petroleum, Exxon, Socony, Texas Oil, Socal, Gulf, Royal Dutch/Shell Group, and CFP form the Iranian Oil Participants Ltd. (IOP) and negotiate agreement with Iranian government and for oil production in Iran

1961: Socal buys Standard of Kentucky

1974: Bahraini government acquires 60% interest in BAPCO

1980: Bahraini government acquires remaining interest in BAPCO

1984: Socal buys Gulf Corporation and after restructuring changes name to Chevron Corporation

1993: Chevron undertakes a joint venture with the government of the Republic of Kazakhstan forming a new company named Tengizchevroil

1993: Pennzoil Company assimilates Chevron

3. **Exxon**

1882: Standard Oil of New Jersey formed by Standard Oil Trust

1888: Standard Oil of New Jersey establishes Anglo-American Oil Co. (predecessor of Esso Petroleum Co.) to market oil in the British Isles

1899: Standard Oil of New Jersey becomes a holding company for Standard Oil Interests, a subsidiary of Standard Oil

1898: Standard Oil of New Jersey gains control of Imperial Oil Limited of Canada

1928: Standard Oil of New Jersey acquires interest in Turkish (now Iraq) Petroleum Co.

1911: Standard Oil of New Jersey [Jersey] becomes independent with dissolution of Standard Oil Trust

1911: Humble Oil Company formed

1919: Jersey acquires majority ownership of Humble Oil

1930: Anglo-American acquired by Jersey

1933: Socony-Vacuum and Standard of New Jersey merge their Far East facilities and interests into a 50–50 venture called Standard-Vacuum Oil Co., or Stanvac

1947: Jersey affiliate, Imperial, strikes oil in Canada

1947: Anglo-Iranian, Jersey and Socony sign 20–year contract with Iran

1948: Jersey (30%) and Socony-Vacuum (10%) join Socal (30%) and Texaco (30%) in Aramco venture

1954: Consortium of oil companies, including British Petroleum, Exxon, Socony, Texas Oil, Socal, Gulf, Royal Dutch/Shell Group, and CFP form the Iranian Oil Participants Ltd. (IOP) and negotiate agreement with Iranian government and for oil production in Iran

1959: Jersey buys remainder of Humble Oil

1959: Jersey strikes oil in Libya

1960: Jersey begins to market gasoline under the brand name Esso

1960: Jersey purchases Monterey Oil

1961: Jersey buys Honolulu Oil

1962: Assets of Stanvac split between Jersey and Socony Mobil

1972: Jersey changes name to Exxon

1972: Iraq nationalizes Iraq Petroleum Company, of which Exxon is 12% owner

1972: Saudi Arabia, Abu Dhabi, Kuwait and Qatar acquire 25% interest in Exxon's production operations (in country), with right to increase stake to 51% by 1982

1980: Exxon buys Colony Oil Shale Project

1981: Exxon sells Esso Standard Libya to Libyan government

1982: Exxon ends Colony Oil Shale Project

1985: Exxon acquires 48% of Hunt Oil Company's production sharing agreement in North Yemen

1998: Exxon and Mobil announce plans for merger

4. Gulf Oil

1984: Chevron buys Gulf (see "Rothschild"-related list in ch 2 note 36 for earlier)

5. Mobil

1866: The Vacuum Oil Co. incorporated

1879: Standard Oil Co., headed by John D. Rockefeller, purchases a three-quarter interest in Vacuum

1870: Rockefeller and four partners organize Standard Oil Company in Ohio

1882: Rockefeller organizes his various oil holdings into the Standard Oil Trust, with headquarters in New York

1882: Standard Oil of New York formed

1911: Standard Oil Company of New York (Socony) founded with dissolution of Standard Oil

1918: Socony purchases a 45% interest in Magnolia Petroleum Co.

1926: Socony purchases the properties of General Petroleum Corp. of California

1929: Vacuum acquires the Lubrite Refining Co., a refining and marketing company based in St. Louis

1930: Socony acquires White Eagle Oil & Refining Co.

1930: Vacuum acquires Wadhams Oil Corp., and the White Star Refining Co.

1931: Socony acquires all the assets of Vacuum Oil Co. and changes its name to Socony-Vacuum Corp.

1933: Socony-Vacuum and Standard of New Jersey merge their Far East facilities and interests into a 50–50 venture called Standard-Vacuum Oil Co., or Stanvac

1934: Socony-Vacuum Corp. changes its name to Socony-Vacuum Oil Co., Inc.

1947: Anglo-Iranian, Jersey and Socony sign 20–year contract with Iran

1948: Jersey (30%) and Socony-Vacuum (10%) join Socal (30%) and Texaco (30%) in Aramco venture

1954: Consortium of oil companies, including British Petroleum, Exxon, Socony, Texaco and Socal, Gulf, Royal Dutch/Shell Group, and CFP form the Iranian Oil Participants Ltd. (IOP) and negotiate agreement with Iranian government and for oil production in Iran

1955: Socony-Vacuum changes name to Socony Mobil Oil Company

1959: Magnolia Petroleum and General Petroleum merged with other domestic subsidiaries into Socony Mobil Oil Company; Two major operating divisions created within the company: Mobil Oil Co. for the U.S. and Canada, and Mobil International

Oil Co. for the rest of the world (except the areas in which Stanvac had interests)
1960: Mobil Chemical Co. formed
1960: Mobil Petroleum Co. Inc. formed to oversee Socony Mobil's 50% interest in
Stanvac
1962: Assets of Stanvac split between Jersey and Socony Mobil
1966: Socony Mobil Oil Co. changes name to Mobil Oil Corporation. Mobil Oil Co.
becomes the North American Division; Mobil International becomes the International
Division, with coordinating responsibility for Mobil Petroleum Co. Inc.
1971: Mobil enters joint venture with Iranian Oil Company
1972: Mobil's 11.875% stake in Iraq Petroleum Company is nationalized
1975: Mobil increases its share of Aramco from 10% to 15%
1976: Mobil completes acquisition of Marcor, the holding company for Montgomery
Ward Department Stores
1976: Mobil Corporation formed as holding company
1979: Mobil sells 51% of its Turkish refinery to Turkish Petroleum
1984: Mobil acquires 100% of Superior Oil
1985: Yanbu Petrochemical Company (YANPET), a joint venture petrochemicals
complex at Yanbu, Saudi Arabia plant begins operation; Mobil and Saudi Basic
Industries Corporation (SABIC) are 50–50 partners in YANPET
1996: The Qatargas project, in which Mobil has a 10% interest, comes on line
producing first LNG from Qatar
1996: Mobil commissions two new plants in Yemen and Syria
1997: Second Qatargas liquefaction train completed
1998: Exxon and Mobil announce plans for merger
1972: Mobil's 11.875% stake in Iraq Petroleum Company is nationalized
1975: Mobil increases its share of Aramco from 10% to 15%
1976: Mobil completes acquisition of Marcor, the holding company for Montgomery
Ward Department Stores
1976: Mobil Corporation formed as holding company
1979: Mobil sells 51% of its Turkish refinery to Turkish Petroleum
1984: Mobil acquires 100% of Superior Oil
1985: Yanbu Petrochemical Company (YANPET), a joint venture petrochemicals
complex at Yanbu, Saudi Arabia plant begins operation; Mobil and Saudi Basic
Industries Corporation (SABIC) are 50–50 partners in YANPET
1996: The Qatargas project, in which Mobil has a 10% interest, comes on line
producing first LNG from Qatar
1996: Mobil commissions two new plants in Yemen and Syria
1997: Second Qatargas liquefaction train completed
1998: Exxon and Mobil announce plans for merger
1972: Mobil's 11.875% stake in Iraq Petroleum Company is nationalized
1975: Mobil increases its share of Aramco from 10% to 15%
1976: Mobil completes acquisition of Marcor, the holding company for Montgomery
Ward Department Stores
1976: Mobil Corporation formed as holding company
1979: Mobil sells 51% of its Turkish refinery to Turkish Petroleum
1984: Mobil acquires 100% of Superior Oil
1985: Yanbu Petrochemical Company (YANPET), a joint venture petrochemicals

complex at Yanbu, Saudi Arabia plant begins operation; Mobil and Saudi Basic Industries Corporation (SABIC) are 50–50 partners in YANPET

1996: The Qatargas project, in which Mobil has a 10% interest, comes on line producing first LNG from Qatar

1996: Mobil commissions two new plants in Yemen and Syria

1997: Second Qatargas liquefaction train completed

1998: Exxon and Mobil announce plans for merger

6. Texaco

1897: Joe Cullinan founds Texas Fuel Company

1903: Joe Cullinan and Arnold Schlaet found The Texas Oil Company in Beaumont, Texas

1906: Texas Oil Company registers the trademark name, 'Texaco'

1930s: Texas Oil Company joins with Standard Oil of California (later Chevron), to found the Arab-American Oil Company [Aramco]

1936: Texas Oil Company purchases half interest in Bahrain Petroleum and California-Arabian Standard Oil Company (Calarabian) from Socal

1936: Texas Oil Company joins with Standard Oil of California (later Chevron), to found the Arab-American Oil Company [Aramco]

1936: California-Texas company, Caltex, founded as a joint venture between Socal and Texas Oil Company as outlet for future oil production in Bahrain and Saudi Arabia

1954: Consortium of oil companies, including British Petroleum, Exxon, Socony, Texas Oil, Socal, Gulf, Royal Dutch/Shell Group, and CFP form the Iranian Oil Participants Ltd. (IOP) and negotiate agreement with Iranian government and for oil production in Iran

1956: Texas Oil Company acquires Regent Oil, a British company

1959: Texas Oil Company purchases the Paragon group of companies

1959: Texas Oil Company adopts the name Texaco for all of its businesses

1962: Texaco acquires White Fuel Corporation

1964: Purchases Superior Oil Company Venezuela

1984: Texaco acquires Getty Oil Company

1988: Texaco Forms Star Enterprise, a 50/50 joint venture with Saudi Refining Inc., to refine, distribute and market Texaco-branded products in the Eastern U.S.

1995: Texaco and Norsk Hydro formed a joint venture, Hydro Texaco, to market petroleum products throughout Scandinavia

1998: Texaco acquires Monterey Resources, a California based independent oil and gas producer

1998: Texaco and Shell Oil form downstream alliance in the Western U.S.

1998: Shell Oil Co., Texaco Inc. and Saudi Aramco initiate joint venture combining their eastern U.S. refining and marketing assets under the name Motiva Enterprises LLC, paralleling a joint venture launched by Shell and Texaco under the name Equilon Enterprises LLC for their Midwest, Southwest and West Coast downstream assets; Shell to own 35% of Houston-based Motiva, while Texaco and Aramco will each own 32.5%

7. British Petroleum (formerly Anglo-Persian Oil) – until 1998, when it merged with Amoco to form BP

1886: Burmah Oil founded in Scotland

1901: Shah of Iran signs concession agreement with William D'arcy

1904: Burmah Oil signs agreement to supply oil to British Admiralty

1905: Burmah Oil and D'arcy oil merged into Concession Syndicate

1908: Oil struck in commercial quantities in Iran

1909: Anglo- Persian Oil formed and Burmah Oil buys majority (97%) of shares in initial public offering

1914: British government becomes majority stockholder in Anglo- Persian Oil

1918: Anglo- Persian Oil purchases British Petroleum from British Government, which in turn had seized the company form Deutsche Bank during First World War

1932: Shah cancels Anglo-Persian concession

1933: Anglo-Persian wins back Iran concession

1934: Anglo-Iranian and Gulf Oil Corporation establish Kuwait Oil Company as a 50–50 joint venture to compete for Kuwait concession (which they obtain); Subsequent agreement establishes British control of KOC

1935: Anglo-Persian renamed Anglo-Iranian Oil Company Ltd.

1947: Anglo-Iranian, Jersey and Socony sign 20–year contract with Iran

1951: Mossadeq nationalizes Anglo-Iranian assets in Iran and founds National Iranian Oil Company (NIOC, see 8 below) to administer nationalized assets

1954: Anglo-Iranian re-named British Petroleum, previously the name of one of its subsidiaries

1954: Consortium of oil companies, including British Petroleum, Exxon, Socony, Texas Oil, Socal, Gulf, Royal Dutch/Shell Group, and CFP form the Iranian Oil Participants Ltd. (IOP) and negotiate agreement with Iranian government and for oil production in Iran

1962: British Petroleum begins commercial development in Abu Dhabi

1966: British Petroleum begins commercial development in Libya

1969: British Petroleum signs agreement with the Standard Oil Company of Ohio, which became effective in January 1970; According to the agreement Standard takes over BP's leases in Alaska; In return, BP acquires 25% of Standard's equity, a stake that would rise to a majority holding in 1978

1970: BP sells 33% of El Bunduq oilfield to a Japanese consortium in exchange for access to Japanese markets

1972: BP sells 33% of Abu Dhabi Main Areas Ltd. to Japanese oil company

Mid-1980s: BP buys 53% of Sohio, Sohio becomes BP's American arm, eventually buying all of the outstanding stock

1987: British government sells off its stock in BP

1987: British Petroleum acquires remaining stock of Sohio as well as British company Britoil

1987: Sohio merged with other BP interests to form BP America

1988: Kuwait Investment Office holding of BP stock reaches 21.6%

1989: British government forces reduction in KIO holding to 9.9% of BP stock

1998: BP announces merger with Amoco, new company will operate under the name BP Amoco p.l.c. BP is reported to have bought Amoco for $54b. The company is British-owned.

8. National Iranian Oil Company

1951: Iran nationalizes National Iranian Oil Company

1954: Consortium of oil companies, including British Petroleum, Jersey, Socony, Texaco and Socal, Gulf, Royal Dutch/Shell Group, Iricon Agency Ltd., Richfield Oil

Corp., Signal Oil and Gas, Aminoil, Sohio, Getty, Atlantic Oil, Tidewater Oil, San Jacinto Petroleum Corp., and CFP form the Iranian Oil Participants Ltd. (IOP). IOP then negotiates agreement with Iranian government and for oil production in Iran
1973: Oil Services Company of Iran (Osco) formed by NIOC to take over operations of IOP
1957: National Iranian Oil Company signs deal with ENI for oil production
1971: Mobil enters joint venture with National Iranian Oil Company
1990: National Iranian Oil Company signs agreement to import about 200,000 barrels a day of gas oil and kerosene from Bahrain, Qatar and Abu Dhabi refineries ending embargoes established during the Iran–Iraq war

9. Saudi Aramco
1933: King Abdul Aziz Bin Abdul Rahman Al-Saud signs agreement authorizing Standard Oil of California (Socal) to explore for oil in what is now the Eastern Province of the Kingdom
1933: Saudi government signed a concession agreement with the Standard Oil Company of California, predecessor of today's Chevron
1938: Commercial oil production begins in Saudi Arabia
1944: Calarabian a joint venture of Socal and Texaco changes name to Arabian – American Oil Company [Aramco]
1948: Jersey and Socony-Vacuum join Socal and Texaco in Aramco venture
1949: Saudi Arabia builds Tapline through northern Saudi Arabia, Syria, Jordan and Lebanon to the Mediterranean
1973: Saudi Arabian Government begins purchasing Aramco's assets from its shareholders, Socal (later Chevron), Texaco, Exxon and Socony-Vacuum (Mobil)
1975: Aramco initiates work to design, build and operate twin industrial cities at Jubail on the Gulf and Yanbu on the Red Sea
1980: Saudi Government acquires 100% of Aramco's shares, although Aramco partners continue to operate and manage Saudi Arabia's oil fields
1985: Yanbu Petrochemical Company (YANPET), a joint venture petrochemicals complex at Yanbu, Saudi Arabia plant begins operation; Mobil and Saudi Basic Industries Corporation (SABIC) are 50–50 partners in YANPET
1988: Royal decree establishes the Saudi Arabian Oil Company [Saudi Aramco] to take over the management and operations of Saudi Arabia's oil and gas fields from Aramco
1988: Saudi Aramco forms a joint venture with Texaco called Star Enterprise; Under the agreement, a Saudi Aramco subsidiary acquires a 50% share in Star's three refineries in the United States
1991: Saudi Aramco acquires a 35% interest in SangYong Oil Refining Company, South Korea's third-largest refiner and leading lubricant manufacturer,
1993: Royal decree merges all of the Kingdom's state-owned refining, product-distribution and marketing operations, as well as the Government's half-interest in three joint-venture refineries into Saudi Aramco
1994: Saudi Aramco enters joint venture with the Philippine National Oil Company (PNOC) purchasing a 40% stake in Petron Corp
1996: Saudi Aramco acquires a 50% interest in Motor Oil Hellas and Avin Oil, the refining and distribution affiliates of Greece's Vardinoyannis Group
1998: Shell Oil Co., Texaco Inc. and Saudi Aramco initiate joint venture combining

their eastern U.S. refining and marketing assets under the name Motiva Enterprises LLC, paralleling a joint venture launched by Shell and Texaco under the name Equilon Enterprises LLC for their Midwest, Southwest and West Coast downstream assets; Shell to own 35% of Houston-based Motiva, while Texaco and Aramco will each own 32.5%.

These well-known companies were also related to "Rockefellers" at some point in their timelines:

1. **Arco**
1866: Atlantic Petroleum Storage Company founded
1870: Atlantic Petroleum Storage Company establishes Atlantic Refining Company (Atlantic)
1874: Atlantic sold to John D. Rockefeller's Standard Oil Trust
1905: Richfield Oil Corporation founded
1911: Standard Oil Trust dissolved under Sherman Antitrust Act, and Atlantic is spun off as independent company
1916: Sinclair Oil Corporation, founded by Harry F. Sinclair
1931: Richfield goes into receivership and Sinclair merges with Rio Grande Oil and Prairie Pipeline and Prairie Oil and Gas Companies
1936: Richfield Oil Corporation emerges from receivership
1952: Atlantic begins offshore Gulf Coast production
1963: Atlantic purchased the Hondo Oil & Gas Company
1966: Richfield Oil Corporation merges with Atlantic Refining Company, creating Atlantic Richfield Company [ARCO]
1968: ARCO partners with Exxon for Alaskan North Slope production
1969: ARCO acquires Sinclair Oil Corporation
1972: ARCO headquarters moves from New York City to Los Angeles
1977: ARCO acquires the Anaconda Company
1985: ARCO divests East Coast marketing and refining operations
1988: Tricentrol acquired by ARCO
1988: ARCO completes merger with Houston based Union Texas Petroleum Holding Inc
1989: ARCO forms anew publicly held company, Lyondell Petrochemical
1993: ARCO's U.S. oil and gas business restructured and divided into four business units – ARCO Permian, ARCO Western Energy, ARCO Long Beach, Inc., and Vastar Resources, Inc.
1994: Vastar Resources Inc. initiates a public offering of 17 million shares of its common stock
1996: ARCO signs Production Sharing Contract with Sonatrach, the Algerian state oil company, to undertake major Enhanced Oil Recovery project in Algeria's second largest oil field, Rhourde El Baguel
1997: ARCO and Russia's largest oil company, LUKOIL, sign joint venture agreement to invest in oil and gas projects in Russia and other countries
1998: ARCO subsidiary (Western Midway Co.) and a unit of Mobil Corporation reaches agreement to exchange oil and gas properties in California's San Joaquin Valley and the Gulf of Mexico; The California properties owned by Western Midway go to Mobil, while Mobil oil and gas properties in the Gulf go to Western Midway. Upon completion of the exchange, Western Midway will be sold to Vastar Resources

Inc. (82.2% owned by ARCO)

1998: ARCO sells majority interest in ARCO Chemical Company and divests its coal assets in the U.S.

2. Conoco

1875: Continental Oil and Transportation Company founded

1885: Continental Oil and Transportation Company reincorporated as Continental within the Standard Oil trust

1913: Continental Oil reincorporated after breakup of Standard Oil Trust

1917: Marland Oil Company founded

1929: Continental Oil company merged with portions of Rocky Mountain (a former component of Standard oil) and Marland

Mid-1950s: Continental joins partnership with Marathon and Amerada, called Oasis Group

1981: Conoco becomes a wholly owned subsidiary of by E.I. Du Pont de Nemours & Company

1981: Conoco reorganized as Continental Group

3. Getty

1928: Pacific Western Oil Corporation incorporated as a holding company for Edward L. Doherty and family which subsequently came under the control of J. Paul Getty

1930s: Rocky Mountain division of Pacific Western, a Getty subsidiary, begins oil exploration in Saudi Arabia

1933: Pacific Western wins Saudi Arabia concession

1949: Getty's Western Pacific Oil Corporation signs concession for Saudi half of the Neutral Zone with Saudi government

1956: All of J. Paul Getty's oil holdings organized under Getty Oil

1953: Getty acquires Tidewater Oil

1984: Texaco acquires Getty

4. Marathon

1887: Ohio Oil Company founded

1889: Ohio Oil Company purchased by J.D. Rockefeller subsequently consolidated into the Standard Oil Trust

1905: Marathon headquarters moved to Findlay, Ohio

1911: Standard Oil Company of Ohio [Sohio] separated from Rockefeller's "Standard Trust"

Mid-1950s: Sohio joins partnership with Continental and Amerada, called Oasis Group

1962: Ohio Oil Company renamed the Marathon Oil Company

1962: Marathon buys Plymouth Oil

1982: Marathon becomes a wholly owned subsidiary of United States Steel Corporation, which has since become USX Corporation

1991: USX issues separate shares of common stock to reflect the performance of its two major businesses (steel and oil) and reinstates Marathon's symbol (MRO) on major stock exchanges

1990: Marathon Oil Company headquarters moved to Houston

1997: Ashland signs agreements with Marathon to combine the refining, marketing and transportation assets of the companies; Marathon Ashland Petroleum LLC formed Ashland acquires 38% of Marathon Ashland Petroleum LLC

5. Pennzoil

1889: South Penn Oil Company organized as a unit of Standard Oil Company

1916: Name 'Pennzoil' trademarked by Pennsylvania Refining Company, a predecessor to Pennzoil

1954: Bill Liedtke, John Overby, and George Bush Sr. form Zapata Offshore Oil Company

1963: Pennzoil Company is formed through consolidation of South Penn Oil Company, STETCO Petroleum Corporation and Zapata Offshore Oil Company

1965: Pennzoil Company acquires United Gas Corporation

1993: Pennzoil Company assimilates Chevron

1994: Pennzoil Company signs oil development deal with Qatar

1995: Pennzoil Company agrees to concession agreement with Egypt for Gulf of Suez

1998: Pennzoil-Quaker State Company was formed with merger of Pennzoil and Quaker State

1998: Simultaneous with the Pennzoil-Quaker State merger, the Pennzoil Company's marketing, manufacturing and fast oil change businesses (Pennzoil Products Group) is spun off and renamed the PennzEnergy Company.

In 1935 the stock Rockefeller held in Standard Oil of New Jersey, Standard Oil of California and Socony Vacuum Co. was reckoned to be $245m, according to the *New York Times* of January 10, 1935. Quoted in Sutton, *Wall Street and the Rise of Hitler, op. cit.*, p. 198.

47. Josephson, *Rockefeller "Internationalist", op. cit.*, p. 24. See also Kutz, *op. cit.*, p. 87 note.

48. Rivera, *op. cit.*, p. 66. See also Kutz, *op. cit.*, p. 86.

49. Ferguson, *op. cit.*, p881.

50. John D. Rockefeller Sr. had transferred $1b in oil holdings to his son John D. Rockefeller Jr. in 1920. See Josephson, *Rockefeller "Internationalist", op. cit.*, p. 24.

51. Josephson, *Rockefeller "Internationalist", op. cit.*, pp. 183–190. In 1910 huge petroleum reserves were discovered on the Gulf of Mexico. The Mexican regime was in league with British interests. Rockefellers' Standard Oil ran guns and money to Carranza, opponent of the regime, in conjunction with troops sent by President Wilson, and wrested Mexican oil from the British. They engineered the Mexican revolutions and Mexican War to oust Royal Dutch and other rivals from Mexico. See Josephson, *Rockefeller "Internationalist", op. cit.*, p. 204.

52. Engdahl, *op. cit.*, pp. 31–2. Also Josephson, *The "Federal" Reserve Conspiracy and Rockefeller, op. cit.*, p. 74.

53. Josephson, *Rockefeller "Internationalist", op. cit.*, p. 191.

54. Josephson, *Rockefeller "Internationalist", op. cit.*, p. 191; Engdahl, *op. cit.*, pp. 34–5.

55. Brewing & Licker Interests & German Bolshevik Propaganda vol. II, 1913. Senate documents 62.65 Congress, 2nd Session. Government Printing Office, Washington, 1919. And Cordell Hull, *Memoirs of Cordell Hull*. Both quoted in Josephson, *The "Federal" Reserve Conspiracy and Rockefeller, op. cit.*, pp. 74–5.

56. Josephson, *Rockefeller "Internationalist"*, *op. cit.*, p. 191.

57. Engdahl, *op. cit.*, p. 61.

58. Engdahl, *op. cit.*, p. 60. Also James Grant, *Wall Street Week with Fortune*: http://www.pbs. org/wsw/opinion/jimgranto718.html.

59. Rivera, *op. cit.*, p. 78.

60. Sutton, *Wall Street and the Bolshevik Revolution*, pp. 18, 97–8. The director of the Federal Reserve Bank of New York was William Boyce Thompson and the partner of J. P. Morgan was Thomas W. Lamont. In fact, Thompson had persuaded Lamont to support Kerensky in Russia for commercial reasons, to continue the war against Germany and keep Germany out of Russia. His goal was to capture the post-war Russian market. The two men visited British Prime Minister Lloyd George in London in late 1917. Thompson cabled requesting $1m from Morgan in New York on December 2, 1917, and he invested $1m of his own money to convince Russian peasants to support Kerensky. The Thompson-Lamont $2m was thus earmarked for preserving commercial markets in Russia. See also Rivera, *op. cit.*, p. 127.

61. Morgans made $400m out of the First World War; John D. Rockefeller Sr and Bernard Baruch each made $200m. The Warburgs and Schiff also made huge amounts.

62. Josephson, *The "Federal" Reserve Conspiracy and Rockefeller*, *op. cit.*, p. 75.

63. Rivera, *op. cit.*, p. 78. Daniel, *op. cit.*, pp. 461–2. See also Three World Wars: http://www. threeworldwars.com/world-war-1/ww1.htm.

64. Clive Simpson, *The Lusitania*, p157; quoted in Perloff, *op. cit.*, p. 31.

65. See: http://www.threeworldwars.com/world-war-1/ww1.htm. Also for *Lusitania*.

66. Josephson, *The "Federal" Reserve Conspiracy and Rockefeller*, *op. cit.*, p. 75.

67. Josephson, *The Strange Death of Franklin D. Roosevelt*, p. 71. Also Engdahl, *op. cit.*, ch 4, "Oil Becomes the Weapon, the Near East the Battleground."

68. Engdahl, *op. cit.*, p. 48.

69. Josephson, *Rockefeller "Internationalist"*, *op. cit.*, p. 376; and Engdahl, *op. cit.*, pp. 69–70.

70. Josephson, *The "Federal" Reserve Conspiracy and Rockefeller*, *op. cit.*, pp74–5; Josephson, *The Strange Death of Franklin D. Roosevelt*, *op. cit.*, pp70–1; Josephson, *Rockefeller "Internationalist"*, *op. cit.*, p. 205.

71. Josephson, *Rockefeller "Internationalist"*, *op. cit.*, p. 376.

72. Josephson, *Rockefeller "Internationalist"*, *op. cit.*, pp. 376–7.

73. Niall Ferguson, article in *New York Times*, April 27, 2003, 'The Empire Slinks Back': http://www.agitprop.org.au/nowar/20030427_ferguson_empire_slinks_back.htm

74. Josephson, *The Truth About Rockefeller, Public Enemy No. 1*, p. 19; Josephson, *Rockefeller Internationalist*, *op. cit.*, p. 204.

75. Josephson, *The Truth About Rockefeller, Public Enemy No. 1*, *op. cit.*, p. 44. For the inflation calculator see also *The Inflation Calculator*: http://www.westegg.com/inflation. Milner

spent $3m. Documents show that J. P. Morgan organization gave at least $1m, according to a report issued by the Committee of Public Information, Washington DC, quoted in Daniel, *op. cit.*, pp. 498–9; see Rivera, *op. cit.*, p. 127.

76. Daniel, John, *Scarlet and the Beast, A History of the War between English and French Freemasonry*, p. 498.

77. See: http://jerusalem.indymedia.org/news/2004/02/130046.php. Trotsky was living in Standard Oil property. John D. Rockefeller I obtained a special passport for him from Woodrow Wilson and sent Lincoln Steffens with him to ensure his safe return from Russia. Rockefeller put a purse containing $10,000 in Trotsky's pocket for travelling expenses. Daniel, *op. cit.*, pp488–9. I have a section on the Duke d'Orléans, founder of the Grand Orient, in *The Secret History of the West*. Trotsky was sent back to Russia with 275 Communist revolutionaries on the *SS Kristianiafjord*.

78. Rivera, *op. cit.*, p. 127. Also, "Today it is estimated by Jacob's grandson John Schiff, that the old man sank about 20,000,000 dollars for the final triumph of Bolshevism in Russia," *New York Journal-American*, February 3 1949; quoted in Réne Wormser, *Foundations, Their Power and Influence*. Also, "The important part played by the wealthy American banker Jacob Schiff in the events in Russia, though as yet only partially revealed, is no longer a secret," Arsene de Goulevitch, *Czarism and the Revolution*, p. 78. See *Newswatch Magazine*, March 2001 issue, http://www.newswatchmagazine.org/mar01/mar01.htm. See also *The Inflation Calculator*, note 75 above.

In 1904–5 Schiff's Kuhn, Loeb & Co. loaned the Japanese government $30m and made possible the Japanese victory over Russia. This anti-Tsar move was linked to Trotsky's abortive revolution in 1905. Schiff's/Rockefeller's attempt to overthrow the Tsar predated Kerensky's attempt by 12 years.

79. Daniel, *op. cit.*, p. 499.

80. Daniel, *op. cit.*, p. 498.

81. *Bankers and the Russian Revolution*: http://wsi.matriots.com/Bankers/RussRev.html.

82. Cartoon by Robert Minor.

83. Rivera, *op. cit.*, p. 130.

84. Josephson, *Rockefeller "Internationalist"*, *op. cit.*, pp. 204–31, particularly p. 212; Josephson, *The Truth About Rockefeller, Public Enemy No.*, pp. 44,133.

85. Rivera, *op. cit.*, p. 130.

86. Josephson, *Rockefeller "Internationalist"*, *op. cit.*, p212.

87. Mullins, *The World Order, Our Secret Rulers*, p77. Standard Oil of New York agreed to build the refinery after being promised 50% of all oil production in the Caucasus region (which is between the Black and Caspian Seas).

88. Gary Allen, *The Rockefeller File*:
http://www.mega.nu:8080/ainpp/garry_allen_rocker/ch9–11.html . See also Rivera, *op. cit.*, p. 130.

89. Rivera, *op. cit.*, p. 80.

90. Rivera, *op. cit.*, p. 80. The Bank for International Settlements was a private institution owned by the seven chief central banks and operated by their heads – see Carroll Quigley, *Tragedy and Hope*, pp. 309, 324. It was set up as an agency of the League of Nations. It came out of the Young Plan, which was named after a lawyer, Owen D. Young, who was a J. P. Morgan agent. It was therefore the brainchild of J. P. Morgan, and its first President, Thomas McKittrich, was an associate of Morgans. See Charles Higham, *Trading with the Enemy*, p. 29; quoted in Daniel, *op. cit.*, pp. 583–4. The network of families controlled the world's money by controlling all the central banks which applied to the BIS for US (i.e. Federal Reserve) loans, a condition of which was that (as in the case of the later IMF) the BIS would control their finances and economies.

3. The Nature of the Syndicate

1. Most of these names are included in Fritz Springmeier's *The Top 13 Illuminati Bloodlines*.

2. Rivera, *op. cit.*, p. 89; Quigley, *Anglo-American Establishment*, pp. 117ff.

3. See Quigley, *Anglo-American Establishment*, pp. 311–15 for lists of the Society of the Elect and the Association of Helpers. Arnold Toynbee, listed as a Helper (Inner Circle), may have been one of the Elect. See also Rivera, *op. cit.*, pp. 89–91 for a fuller account. Walter, Lord Rothschild was the Rothschild to whom Balfour wrote promising a Jewish homeland in Palestine. The system of inner and outer circles was used by the Anarchist movement in G. K. Chesterton's 1908 novel, *The Man Who Was Thursday*.

4. Daniel, *op. cit.*, p. 533. The Round Table was initially funded by the English Rothschild family. The House of Rothschild financed Rhodes' purchase of de Beers diamond mining company and Consolidated Gold Fields in South Africa.

5. For Rhodes' wills, see Rivera, *op. cit.*, p. 90; and Daniel, *op. cit.*, pp. 532–7.

6. Quigley, *Tragedy and Hope*, p. 324. The full quotation is: "The powers of financial capitalism had another far-reaching aim, nothing less than to create a world system of financial control in private hands able to dominate the political system of each country and the economy of the world as a whole. This system was to be controlled in a feudalist fashion by the central banks of the world acting in concert, by secret agreements arrived at in frequent private meetings and conferences." Quigley (p. 950) also writes: "This network, which we may identify as the Round Table Groups, has no aversion to co-operating with the Communists, or any other groups, and frequently does so." Quigley is very sympathetic towards the Round Table, and writes as its commissioned historian, emphasizing the gentlemanly qualities of the participants.

7. Quoted in Rivera, *op. cit.*, p. 91.

8. Rivera, *op. cit.*, p. 90.

9. Rivera, *op. cit.*, p. 90.

10. Rivera, *op. cit.*, p. 90.

11. Rivera, *op. cit.*, Internet version: http://user.pa.net/~drivera/fw7.htm. Nathan Rothschild gave Marx two checks for several thousand pounds while he was writing *Das Kapital* in the British Museum, to finance the cause of Socialism. The checks were put on display in the British Museum after a trustee, had willed his museum and library to the British Museum. In a letter to his uncle in June 1864 Marx announced that he had made £400 on the Stock Exchange. It was presumably Rothschild's money he had invested.

12. Rivera, *op. cit.*, p. 84.

13. Rivera, *op. cit.*, p. 87.

14. Rivera, *op. cit.*, p. 84.

15. Rivera, *op. cit.*, p. 84. See also: http://www.spartacus.schoolnet.co.uk/Pfabian.htm, which states that by 1886 the Fabians had 67 members and an income of £35.19s. See

also The Fabian Society, http://www.adsamai.org/files/fabian.html, for the Rockefeller Foundation and Mrs Elmhurst.

16. Shaw's mistress Florence Farr was a "witch" in the Order of the Golden Dawn, which was founded by "Rothschilds" in the 1880s. See Rivera, *op. cit.*, p. 87.

17. http://lboro.ac.uk/research/eurocentre/BIO.11TM.

18. Felix Frankfurter was an advisor to Roosevelt who was heavily involved with Rexford Tugwell and Bernard Baruch in renewing national planning institutions for the New Deal. See http://www.asu.edu/caed/proceedings01/HEMMENS/hemmens.htm. In 1943 an eyewitness described Auschwitz to him, but although Jewish, he refused to believe the report. See http://www.spiritone.com/~gdy52150/betray1p9.htm.

19. De Pincins, *Freemasonry and the Vatican*, pp. 51–2, quoted in Daniel, pp. 541–2. See also *Mackey's Encyclopedia of Freemasonry*, 'League of Nations and Masonry', quoted in Daniel, *op. cit.*, p. 541: "It [French Masonry's Grand Orient] held conferences for discussing a League of Nations." These references also cover the minutes of January 1917.

20. Daniel, *op. cit.*, p. 541; Perloff, *The Shadows of Power*, p. 31.

21. Rivera, *op. cit.*, p. 79.

22. Rivera, *op. cit.*, p 79.

23. Daniel, *op. cit.*, p. 547.

24. Quoted in Griffin, *Descent into Slavery?*, *op. cit.*, pp. 119–120.

25. Rivera, *op. cit.*, p. 79.

26. Perloff, *op. cit.*, pp. 36–7.

27. Rivera, *op. cit.*, p. 91.

28. Engdahl, *op. cit.*, p. 66 for both Toynbee and Lamont.

29. Mullins, *The World Order*, *op. cit.*, p. 52.

30. Rivera, *op. cit.*, p. 91.

31. Rivera, *op. cit.*, p. 91.

32. Rivera, *op. cit.*, p. 91.

33. Coleman, *Conspirators' Hierarchy*, p. 48.

34. The Round Table always wanted to turn the British Empire into a federal system that would eventually include the United Kingdom and the United States, perhaps with Washington as the capital of the whole organization. Such thoughts were in the minds of the Round Table group from 1884 to about 1915. See Quigley, *Tragedy and Hope*, *op. cit.*, p. 133. The Round Table had many discussions on developing the British Empire into an imperial, Anglo-American or world federation. These discussions eventually led to the Commonwealth of Nations, but world government was the eventual aim. See Quigley, *The Anglo-American Establishment*, *op. cit.*, p. 150. The RIIA reflected these Round-Table policies, and sought to establish a one-world government. See Rivera, *op. cit.*, p. 90.

35. Lindsay Jenkins, *Britain Held Hostage*, p. 46.

36. Jenkins, *op. cit.*, p. 47.

37. Jenkins, *op. cit.*, p. 51.

38. Jenkins, *op. cit.*, p. 47; and Adrian Krieg, *July 4th, 2016, The Last Independence Day*, p. 26.

39. Jenkins, *op. cit.*, pp. 46–7.

40. Jenkins, *op.cit.*, pp. 47, 100. For 40 years Toynbee was deeply involved in the RIIA's moves towards world Government. In his writings Toynbee sought to demonstrate that nation-states were in decline and that a "Rockefeller"-backed world government would replace them. Fascinating though Toynbee's total vision is, it is therefore sadly unreliable. Spengler's equally tendentious study, *Decline of the West*, is equally unreliable. It was a knee-jerk reaction to the devastation of the European nation-states during the First World War, and did not appreciate how Europe would recover with a new sense of *élan*.

41. Jenkins, *op. cit.*, p. 100.

42. Jenkins, *op. cit.*, pp. 47–8.

43. *Arabian Gulf Oil Concessions, 1911–1953*: http://www.archiveeditions.co.uk/Leafcopy/210–5.htm; Jenkins, *op. cit.*, pp. 49–50.

44. Jenkins, *op. cit.*, p. 50.

45. For Attlee's 1934 speech see www.nsec-88.org/knihy/protocols.doc.

46. Jenkins, *op. cit.*, pp. 52–5.

47. Jenkins, *op. cit.*, p. 102.

48. Jenkins, *op. cit.*, p. 98. It has been suggested that Churchill promised to de-colonize after the war in return for US entry on Britain's side. Until the Churchill-Roosevelt correspondence and papers are made public, there can be no proof of this.

49. Jenkins, *op. cit.*, pp. 102–3.

50. Quoted in Curtis B. Dall, *FDR: My Exploited Father-In-Law*, p67.

51. Quigley, *Tragedy and Hope, op. cit.*, p. 952; quoted in Perloff, *op. cit.*, p38. The US entry into the war spurred Hess into flying to Scotland (possibly with the connivance of the Duke of Windsor, who knew the Duke of Hamilton), allegedly to make peace with Britain. German generals had offered to eliminate Hitler so that Britain and Germany could join forces to attack Communist Russia; Britain was to give Germany a free hand in Europe and in return Hitler would guarantee the British Empire once Churchill had left office (King, *Satan and Swastika*, p. 229) and set up a joint Anglo-German attack on Russia. See Griffin, *Fourth Reich of the Rich*, pp. 97–8. Had Churchill agreed to this proposed deal, he might have saved the British oil assets in Saudi Arabia and prevented Stalin's East European Empire – but risked the enmity of the US and the taint of allying with Hitler.

52. Rivera, *op. cit.*, p. 92.

53. For Aramco, see Caltex: http://www.ianbyrne.free-online.co.uk/caltex.htm; and all refer: http://reference.allrefer.com/country-guide-study/saudi-arabia/saudi-arabia57.html. For $165m, see Rivera, *op. cit.*, p. 92. See also: http://www.mises.org/econsense/ch93. asp.

54. Rivera, *op. cit.*, p. 92.

55. Rivera, *op. cit.*, p. 92. See: http://www.mises.org/econsense/ch93.asp.

56. Allen and Abraham, *None Dare Call It Conspiracy*, pp. 82–3; Rivera, *op. cit.*, p. 93.

57. Rivera, *op. cit.*, p. 92.

58. Rivera, *op. cit.*, p. 92.

59. Josephson, *Rockefeller "Internationalist"*, *op. cit.*, p. 4; Allen and Abraham, *None Dare Call It Conspiracy*, *op. cit.*, p. 83.

60. Rivera, *op. cit.*, p. 92.

61. Rivera, *op. cit.*, p. 94.

62. Josephson, *Rockefeller "Internationalist"*, *op. cit.*, pp. 290–291, where the exact grants are listed. They total $2,167,433.83. The American Branch of IPR received funding from Standard Oil, Vacuum Oil, Shell Oil, Chase National Bank and J. P. Morgan among others. The Round Table IPR was funded by the Rockefeller, Carnegie, and Ford Foundations.

63. See ch 2, note 84.

64. Josephson, *Rockefeller "Internationalist"*, *op. cit.*, p274.

65. Josephson, *Rockefeller "Internationalist"*, *op. cit.*, p274.

66. Josephson, *The Strange Death of Franklin D. Roosevelt*, p. 196; also Josephson, *Rockefeller "Internationalist"*, *op. cit.*, p. 384. Crucial to this entry was a spy ring operating in Tokyo and monitoring the Japanese intention to attack Pearl Harbor. The ring's purpose was to encourage the Japanese to attack the US instead of "Rockefellers'" Soviet partners. After Roosevelt's embargo on all shipping to Japan – in retaliation for Japan's invasion of the French Indo-China – cut off Japan's oil supply and shut down its economy, the Japanese were told in effect, "Destroy the US Fleet at Pearl Harbor, and you have won the war from the start."

67. Oliver Lyttelton, Minister of Production in Churchill's war cabinet, told Parliament on July 20, 1944: "Japan was provoked into attacking America at Pearl Harbor. It is a travesty on history to say that America was *forced* into the war." Henry Stimson, Roosevelt's Secretary of War, later said that "the question was how we should maneuver them (the Japanese) into the position of firing the first shot without allowing too much danger to ourselves."

    At 6.45 a.m., 62 minutes before the Japanese attack on December 7, 1941, the American destroyer *USS Ward* fired at, and sank (with depth charges), a Japanese midget submarine whose periscope had earlier been observed above the water (by the minesweeper *Condor*) at 3.42 a.m. According to *Attack at Pearl Harbour 1941: The Japanese View Eyewitness* (www.eyewitnesstohistory.com), at 6.10 a.m. a first wave of 183 planes took off from Japanese aircraft carriers 230 miles north of Pearl Harbor. Did these planes leave then? Or were they called into action by the attack on the submarine? As was reported in the British press, the wreck of this submarine has been found 61 years later, in 2002, with a bullet hole clearly visible in its tower. Will Lehner, a sailor on the USS *Ward*, later reported, "We, in reality, had fired the first shot of World War Two by sinking an unidentified submarine in restricted waters." If the *Ward*'s attack on the submarine happened an hour earlier than officially reported, and if the submarine radioed to the Japanese aircraft carriers, then this was the shot that *started* the Pacific War. It was fired by America to provoke the Japanese, and as a result the Japanese sank the US battleship *West Virginia* in the Pearl Harbor attack, with the loss of 2,341 US soldiers' lives.

68. Josephson, *Rockefeller "Internationalist"*, op. cit., pp384–6: "The (Japanese) proceeded to seize China ... They could not forget the role played by the 'Rockefeller'-Standard Oil crowd in the cancellation of the concessions. They avenged themselves ... by destroying 'Rockefeller'-Standard Oil property first ... To accomplish the destruction of Japan, it was necessary to bring the American Army to the rescue of their property in China. But it would have been futile for the 'Rockefeller'-Standard Oil interests to ask Congress to declare war on Japan because it was destroying their property in China ... If, however, Japan could be induced to attack US – that would be a different story ... The appointment of Joseph Grew, nephew of John Pierpont Morgan, as Ambassador to Japan was dictated. The plan was to induce the Japs to attack the United States ... The conspirators were impatiently waiting and working to bring about an attack on the United States that would force Congress to declare officially the war that Roosevelt already was waging unofficially ... Rockefeller's Institute of Pacific Relations agents working under Sorge precipitated the Japanese attack on Pearl Harbor that the conspirators sought in order to bring the US into the war....As early as October 1941 the conspirators knew that the Japanese definitely planned an attack on Pearl Harbor." Richard Sorge, a German press correspondent, ran a Soviet spy ring in Tokyo during the Second World War. He was executed for informing the Russians of Japan's impending entry into the war. A letter from E. C. Carter, secretary general of the IPR, to William Lockwood, editor of *Amerasia* makes it clear that Rockefellers' IPR controlled Sorge's spy ring that instigated the attack on Pearl Harbor.

69. Norman Livergood, *The New US-British Oil Imperialism*: http://www.hermes-press.com/impintro1.htm, p. 3.

70. Rivera, *op. cit.*, p. 177.

71. Daniel, *op. cit.*, p. 581.

72. Daniel, *op. cit.*, p. 581.

73. For Bernhard as a member of the House of Orange, see Epperson, *The Unseen Hand*, p206. As a 5% stockholder in Royal Dutch Shell, his wife ex-Queen Juliana was worth around $2b in 1978. See Epperson, *op. cit.*, p. 206. For Bernhard's descent from the House of David through the Merovingian dynasty and the House of Orange, see Fritz Springmeier, *Merovingian Bloodline and the Black Nobility*: http://home.tiscali.de/alex.sk/A_Springmeier.html. Bernhard was also related to the Khazars, and was therefore a Gentile (same website). For a full explanation on how the Merovingian line produced the

Kings of Jerusalem, see Baigent, Leigh and Lincoln, *The Holy Blood and the Holy Grail*, *passim*.

74. Rivera, *op. cit.*, p. 177.

75. Rivera, *op. cit.*, p177. Toynbee's input was not surprising as he had been such an influential figure in the RIIA for so many years, and would have been regarded as a sort of 'Professor Emeritus' by the then Chairman of the RIIA, Alastair Buchan.

76. Rivera, *op. cit.*, p. 177.

77. Rivera, *op. cit.*, p. 177.

78. Rivera, *op. cit.*, p. 179.

79. Rivera, *op. cit.*, p. 177.

80. One of the main goals of the Bilderberg Group immediately after its official formation in May 1954 was to install a European super-state with a central bank and currency. See: http://iaehv.nl/users/lightnet/world/awaken/spider.html, which states: "The European Union we see today has been designed from the very beginning by those who control the Bilderberg Group – the House of Rothschild, the Rockefellers and the 'blue blood' families (tribes) of Europe." The European common market was discussed at Messina, Sicily in 1955 and implemented through the Treaty of Rome of 1957. This brought into being the European Economic Community (EEC) of 1958 and inspired another grouping of nations outside the EEC, the European Free Trade Association, which came into operation in 1960. The EEC was thus a combined "Rockefeller"-"Rothschild" enterprise. See *Spotlight*, numerous issues.

81. Blair's attendance was reported in *Spotlight* of May 24, 1993. Brown's attendance was reported in *Portman Papers*, July 2000.

82. Harvey O'Connor, *The Empire of Oil*, p. 38.

83. See 82.

84. Rivera, *op. cit.*, p. 186.

85. For the Grand Orient, see Daniel, *op. cit.*, p. 287: "Grand Orient Freemasons founded the Club of Rome to expressly study the future over population of the earth." For Peccei's comment, see Coleman, *op. cit.*, p. 15.

86. See Club of Rome's: http://www.clubofrome.org/about/index.php.

87. Coleman, *op. cit.*, p. 13.

88. Rivera, *op. cit.*, p. 186. The Club of Rome's website – see 86 – claims to have a 100 members.

89. David Rockefeller spoke at Chase Manhattan International Financial Forums in London, Brussels, Montreal and Paris in early 1972 and proposed the creation of an International Commission of Peace and Prosperity (which later became the Trilateral Commission). He wanted to "bring the best brains in the world to bear on problems of the future". See Rivera, *op. cit.*, p. 190.

90. Robert Eringer, *The Global Manipulators*, p. 73.

91. Brzezinski spoke after Rockefeller's addresses. He took up the idea of a Commission in mid-1972, after Rockefeller. He had proposed a tripartite counsel in *Foreign Affairs*, the journal of the CFR, in 1970. The three regions of the US, the Common Market and Japan represented 70% of the world's trade. In his book *Between Two Ages* (1970) Brzezinski had called for "limitations on national sovereignty".

92. Rivera, *op. cit.*, p. 190.

93. Rivera, *op. cit.*, p. 190.

94. There is a single-source claim, not sufficiently substantiated to my satisfaction, that the most controversial and disputed of these organizations, known as the Committee of 300, controls all the groups. Dr John Coleman is an ex-intelligence officer with MI6 who encountered all the hidden organizations during his career. He wrote *Conspirators' Hierarchy: The Story of the Committee of 300* in 1992. He and George Armstrong, an authority on the Rothschilds (in *The Rothschild Money Trust* – p25), hold that on Mayer Amschel Rothschild's death his descendants were faced with the task of managing the greatest estate the world has ever known, and that by the 1890s this had grown to enormous proportions. Armstrong believes that Thomas Herzl, the founder of the Zionist movement to establish a Jewish homeland and intimate friend of Lord Rothschild, was in the Rothschilds' employ, and that he was asked to draw up a plan to cope with the administration of such vast power. Herzl helped to establish a Secret Committee of 300 to manage the huge estate. (Armstrong believes the 300 double up as the 300 Elders mentioned in *The Protocols of the Elders of Zion*, which may have been written by Herzl.)

The authoritative Quigley worryingly does not mention the Committee of 300. According to Coleman, the Committee of 300 is the power that established the Round Table through MI6 (Coleman, *op. cit.*, p. 152); controls the Bilderberg Group (Coleman, *op. cit.*, p. 207), which is directed by the RIIA; and controls and manages the British and US governments through the RIIA and the CFR. He claims that the Club of Rome is an additional foreign policy arm of the Round Table/Committee of 300 (Coleman, *op. cit.*, p. 101), and that besides presenting reports to the British government, MI6 is also the Committee of 300's secret intelligence arm.

According to Coleman, the structure of the Committee of 300 may have evolved from the British East India Company, a British commercial and political organization incorporated in 1600 that worked as an agent of British imperialism in India as it traded in East-Indian spices, cotton, silks and eventually opium. The Committee goes back to the 1830s or 1840s, but did not take its present form until 1897, the year Milner (then High Commissioner of South Africa) began to build up his body of assistants ("Milner's Kindergarten"), as described in detail by Quigley in *The Anglo-American Establishment*.

According to Coleman, on the death of Queen Victoria the royal families of Europe – the families of the monarchs of Britain, the Netherlands and Denmark and the noble, aristocratic families of Italy – decided to go into business with leaders of corporate enterprise, "commoners," to gain world-wide control and rule the world. The 300 are the members of this 'firm' that seeks to control world events through the influence of the likes of the Rothschilds. Coleman claims that the Knights of the Garter are the inner circle of this Committee – the ceiling of the Throne Room in Buckingham Palace is covered in Garter stars. Coleman holds that the Rothschild estates are managed to neutralize Britain's loss of her American Empire. To make up for, or even reverse, the loss of the American Empire was one of the Round Table's aims. Coleman claims that the Bilderberg Group is the foreign policy arm of the Committee of 300, and that the Council on Foreign Relations has a secret Anglophile agenda; that Britain is at the forefront of its decisions and policy-making.

Is Coleman a credible witness? Or is the Committee of 300 just another name for the Round Table, or perhaps Rhodes's original secret society out of which the Round Table grew? Rivera says that the Round Table is sometimes called the "Committee of 300" and "Olympians"; and Daniel makes no mention of the Committee – he only refers to the Round Table. One of Coleman's claims is very hard to believe. He says that the Committee of 300 is headed by the Queen; and that it runs the US as if the War of Independence had not happened. Bush Jr.'s decisions to go to war in Afghanistan and Iraq were surely taken with the US's considerations in mind, not on London's direction. If we are sceptical of this claim, we should also be wary of going with Coleman's inside knowledge and seeing the Committee of 300 as the most powerful of all the organizations we have been considering. See Coleman, *op. cit.*, pp. 7–9, 13, 25, 52, 171, also, pp. 2–4, 39, 179, 203–4, 248, 253, 265.

4. The United States of All the Americas

1. Booklets on sale at the State House, Philadelphia: *The History of the American Revolution, Highlights of the Important Battles and Documents of Freedom;* and Richard Morris, *The Framing of the Federal Constitution.*

2. 1951 Masonic edition of the *Holy Bible,* quoted in Still, *op. cit.,* p. 61. However, Paul Bessel maintains that only nine of the 56 who signed the Declaration of Independence were Freemasons, and that only 13 of the 39 who signed the US Constitution were Freemasons. See: http://bessel.org/declmas.htm. In the case of those who signed the US Constitution, the information, Bessel states, comes from a booklet by Bro. Ronald E. Heaton, *Masonic Membership of the Signers of the Constitution of the United States,* published by the Masonic Service Association (1962,1986). This dissenting view comes from a Masonic source, which may be seeking to disguise the level of Masonic involvement in these two documents.

3. Daniel, *op. cit.,* pp. 688–9, 709.

4. Daniel, *op. cit.,* pp. 166, 686–7.

5. According to the legend found in Plato's *Critias,* the antediluvian Atlantis was ruled in harmony by a cooperative commonwealth of 10 kings. Freemasonry calls for a one-world government to be patterned after the Atlantic League of ten kings. It will have ten regions and will lead mankind to universal happiness. Bacon's philosophical Atlantis in his utopian novel *New Atlantis* was Masonic.

6. Rev. J. R. Church, *Guardians of the Grail,* pp. 163–4, quoted in Daniel, *op. cit.,* p. 166.

7. Daniel, *op. cit.,* p. 688.

8. Allen E. Roberts, *G. Washington: Master Mason,* quoting records at the George Washington Masonic National Memorial, Shooters Hill, Alexandria, Virginia. Records of the Lodge at Fredericksburg show that George Washington was initiated into that Lodge as an entered apprentice on November 4, 1752, and was raised to the degree of Master Mason on August 4, 1753. He was elected Grand Master of Masons of the American Colonies in 1779 but did not serve due to the war. He was elected Worshipful Master by the Lodge at Alexandria, Virginia, no. 39, in 1788 and served until his death eleven years later. General Lafayette presented Washington with a Masonic apron made by the Marquis's wife in 1784.

9. See J. B. Campbell, 'Our Masonic Constitution': http://www.freemasonrywatch.org/masonicconstitution.html, who quotes Henry Clausen, *Masons Who Helped Shape Our Nation,* pp. 14–16: "The significance of Freemasonry's influence on the Constitution cannot be overstated." And, p. 82: "Since the Masonic federal system of organization was the only pattern for effective organization operating in each of the original Thirteen Colonies, it was natural that patriotic Brethren should turn to the organizational base of the Craft for a model. Regardless of the other forces that affected the formation of the Constitution during the Constitutional Convention in 1787, the fact remains that the federalism created is identical to the federalism of the Grand Lodge system of Masonic government created in Anderson's Constitutions of 1723."

10. Edward Decker, *Freemasonry: Satan's Door to America,* quoted in Daniel, *op. cit.,* p. 707.

11. See note 10; Roberts, *op. cit.*, pp. 134–40. On September 18, 1793 George Washington, in full Masonic regalia and surrounded by brother Master Masons, laid the cornerstone of the Capitol building in Washington.

12. Raymond E. Capt, *Our Great Seal: The Symbols of our Heritage and our Destiny*, p. 11; quoted in Daniel, *op. cit.*, p. 708.

13. Daniel, *op. cit.*, p. 686.

14. Daniel, *op. cit.*, pp. 163–4, 708–13; Robert Hieronimus, *America's Secret Destiny*, pp. 63–92.

15. Daniel, *op. cit.*, p. 709. Congress rejected the ideas of the first committee in January 1777. A second committee was formed in 1780. Its proposals were also rejected. A third committee was formed on May 4, 1782 and the images on the present Seal were adopted on June 20, 1782. For a full account, see Hieronimus, *op. cit.*, pp. 48–56. These pages show the images recommended by all three committees.

16. Daniel, *op. cit.*, p. 165.

17. Daniel, *op. cit.*, pp. 164–5; pp. 715–6 (Atlantis).

18. Still, *op. cit.*, p. 65; Daniel, *op. cit.*, pp. 713–4.

19. Still, *op. cit.*, p. 67.

20. For the Glory Cloud, see Daniel, *op. cit.*, pp. 715–6. For the Star of David being used by Kabbalists and Jewish communities (first of all in Prague), see *Encyclopaedia Britannica*.

21. Daniel, *op. cit.*, p. 709. The single eye representing the sun-god Osiris was used by Egyptians. The symbol was adopted by the Priory of Sion and then by Freemasonry.

22. Daniel, *op. cit.*, pp. 164–5.

23. Capt, *op. cit.*, p. 39; quoted in Daniel, *op. cit.*, pp. 174–5.

24. Capt, *op. cit.*; quoted in Daniel, *op. cit.*, p. 175.

25. Daniel, *op. cit.*, pp. 163–5.

26. Daniel, *op. cit.*, pp. 688–93.

27. See Free Trade Area of Americas: http://www.itcilo.it/english/actrav/telearn/global/ilo/blokit/ftaa.htm//Introduction%2oand%20Countries%20Involved.

28. Quoted in: http://www.newswithviews.com/Vcon/joan5.htm.

29. See *American Free Press*, February 3, 2003, p. 3: "Rockefeller men plot to oust Venezuelan populist." Gustavo Cisneros, a Venezuelan billionaire, was identified by sources such as *Newsweek*, local Venezuelan publications and analysts as one of the protagonists and financiers of the attempted *coup* against President Chavez, which took the form of a general strike and lock-out on April 11, 2002. See: http://www.venezuelananalysis.com/news.pht?newsno-1183 – a website of women protesting against the presentation by Kissinger of a US award to Cisneros. The previous November Chavez had passed 50

laws, including the Hydro Carbon Law, which raised the costs of those running the state-owned energy monopoly of Venezuela, Petroleos de Venezuela (PDVFA). The aim of the attempted *coup* was to restore internationalist control of Venezuelan oil. See *Venezuela: The Great Oil Grab: Target Hugo Chavez*, http://www.informationclearinghouse.info/article5078.hgm. Cisneros was then the founding member of the International Advisory Board of the CFR in New York, a former director of the International Advisory Committee of the Chase Manhattan Bank, a Director and Trustee of the Rockefeller University in New York and founding member of the Advisory Committee for the David Rockefeller Center for Latin American Studies at Harvard University, Rockefeller University Fund. He was also director of the Chairman's Council of the Americas Society and owned one of the largest privately held broadcast, media, technology and telecommunications organizations in the world, with over 70 companies operating in 39 countries. See: http://www.giic.org/commissioners/bio/bio_cisneros.asp.

30. To the politicians and diplomats of the Round Table, the plan was to establish a one-world government. To Freemasons, the plan is to re-establish a one-world government that (Freemasons claim) was partly destroyed with Atlantis and finally destroyed by God at Babylon. The plan is to rebuild a new Atlantis based on the New World, the USA. The constitution of the USA parallels that of the Masonic federal system of government. By spreading the federal constitution of the USA throughout the world, Freemasonry will be spreading its own federal system of government. The plan has motivated numerous revolutions, including the French and Russian revolutions, as I have shown in *The Secret History of the West*. This is a very longstanding plan and can be found in the thinking of Victor Hugo, Lenin and Stalin. See pages 70 and 85. Early Round Table activity joined the five colonies in Australia into the Commonwealth of Australia in 1901 and the four colonies in South Africa into the Union of South Africa in 1910. See Quigley, *Tragedy and Hope*, p. 133. For decades, the CFR journal *Foreign Affairs* promoted the creation of blocs through articles entitled "Toward European Integration," "Toward Unity in Africa," "Toward a Caribbean Federation." See Perloff, *op. cit.*, p. 86. Roberto Ducci, in a *Foreign Affairs* article in 1964, called for wider political units "to keep the peace in their respective areas: NATO in the North Atlantic and the Council of Europe in the European regions, OAS in the Americas, OAU in Africa, SEATO in Southeast Asia." *Foreign Affairs*, April 1964, pp. 389–90, quoted in Perloff, *op. cit.*, pp. 85–6. For the United States of Africa, see *Le Monde diplomatique*: http://mondediplo.com/2000.09/12africa.

31. US Trade Representative: www.ustr.gov/regions/

32. See the New Nation: //nation.ittefaq.com/artman/publish/article_6837.shtml on SAFTA and the coming Asian Economic Community. On China, see: http://www.csis.org/pubs/prospectus/02fall_douglas.htm. See ch 15, *The United States of the World*. See: http://wsws.org/articles/2001/jan2001/oil-j03.shtml.

33. Article in *Sunday Times*, March 14, 2004, "Giants of the East Vie for Russia's Oil."

34. See *Ten Zones* section in ch 15.

5. Hitler: A Failed One-World Revolution?

1. General Albert Pike, a Grand Orient Freemason who initiated the southern revolt in the American Civil War, wrote this letter to the European revolutionary Mazzini. His letter of August 15, 1871 can be found in Myron Fagan, *The Illuminati*, audio cassette, rec 1967 (transcribed from two audio cassettes by Sons of Liberty, 1985), 8. This letter used to be on display in the British Museum Library in London, and is catalogued. In 1949 an appendage to this letter surfaced in the British Museum. In it Pike goes on to say that a first world war would enable Communism to destroy the Tsar's government in Russia and establish atheism. A second world war would follow the rise of Fascism and set Britain against Germany. Communist Russia would then destroy governments and religion and advance Zionism in a third world war (i.e. the Cold War). A fourth world war would begin out of the conflicts between Zionists and the Arabs and bring the world into final conflict out of which a one-world Masonic dictatorship would arise that would rule the world. A forgery? The ramblings of a lunatic? We don't know. And in a way it doesn't matter. This is what many people believe.

2. Carroll Quigley, *The Invisible Government*; quoted in Sutton, *Wall Street and the Rise of Hitler*, p. 24.

3. Sutton, *Wall Street and the Rise of Hitler, op. cit.*, p. 24.

4. Rivera, *op. cit.*, p. 112.

5. Rivera, *op. cit.*, p. 112.

6. Rivera, *op. cit.*, p. 112.

7. Rivera, *op. cit.*, p. 111.

8. See: http://www.bebeyond.com/cgi-bin/BBs.pl?ID-p%2B%CZeXBv6%3A%5EO%7Df& theme-Dreams. Sutton, *Wall Street and the Rise of Hitler, op. cit.*, p. 43.

9. Sutton, *Wall Street and the Rise of Hitler, op. cit.*, p. 15; Rivera, *op. cit.*, p. 111. Reported by William Dodd, the US Ambassador to Germany, to President Roosevelt on October 19, 1936.

10. Sutton, *Wall Street and the Rise of Hitler, op. cit.*, pp. 108–9; Perloff, *op. cit.*, p. 48.

11. Sutton, *Wall Street and the Rise of Hitler, op. cit.*, pp. 55–62. International General Electric owned 30% of German General Electric, which had four American directors. On p. 56 of his book Sutton reproduces the original transfer slip dated March 2, 1933 from German General Electric to Delbrück, Schickler Bank in Berlin, with instructions to pay 60,000 RM to a fund administered by Schacht and Hess, which was used to elect Hitler in March 1933. This was Nuremburg Military Tribunal document no. 391–395.

12. Josephson, *The Strange Death of Franklin D. Roosevelt, op. cit.*, pp. 184–5; Josephson, *Rockefeller "Internationalist", op. cit.*, p. 379; Sutton, *op. cit.*, p. 43.

13. Josephson, *Rockefeller "Internationalist", op. cit.*, p. 379.

14. Josephson, *The Strange Death of Franklin D. Roosevelt, op. cit.*, pp. 184–5, *Rockefeller "Internationalist", op. cit.*, p379; Sutton, *Wall Street and the Rise of Hitler, op. cit.*, pp. 155–8;

Mullins, *op. cit.*, p. 94.

15. Mullins, *op. cit.*, p. 153.

16. See 15.

17. Sutton, *Wall Street and the Rise of Hitler*, pp. 108, 118–120.

18. Josephson, *The Strange Death of Franklin D. Roosevelt, op. cit.*, p. 185; Josephson, *Rockefeller "Internationalist", op. cit.*, p. 379.

19. Daniel, *op. cit.*, p. 580, quoting Higham, *op. cit.*, p. 57. In 1939 "Rockefellers" Standard Oil of New Jersey sold I. G. Farbenindustrie $20,000 worth of petroleum products, including aviation benzene for use in Germany's war-effort. See Sutton, *Wall Street and the Rise of Hitler, op. cit.*, p. 35.

20. Mullins, *op. cit.*, p. 93; Daniel, *op. cit.*, p. 580.

21. Daniel, *op. cit.*, p. 580.

22. Mullins, *op. cit.*, p. 93.

23. Josephson, *The Strange Death of Franklin D. Roosevelt, op. cit.*, p. 185.

24. Sutton, *Wall Street and the Rise of Hitler, op. cit.*, p. 79 and ch 7. Sutton explores in detail who financed Hitler. He concludes that in February-March 1933 Edsel B. Ford, C. E. Mitchell, Walter Teagle and Paul Warburg of American I. G. Farben through their German source I. G. Farbenindustrie gave 400,000 RM to the intermediary or agent 'Nationale Treuhand', while from 1932 to 1944 Walter Teagle, J. A. Moffett and W. S. Farish (Chairman) of Standard Oil of New Jersey through their German source Emil Helffrich of German-American Petroleum Co., gave funds to Heinrich Himmler's SS via Keppler's Circle. During the same period Sosthenes Behn of ITT through its German source Kurt von Schröder, Mix and Genest Lorenz gave funds to Heinrich Himmler's SS via Keppler's Circle (p. 105).

25. Mullins, *op. cit.*, p. 93: "To lure Hitler into World War II, it was necessary to guarantee him adequate supplies of such necessities as ball-bearings and oil." Mullins was a disciple of Pound's; his book, *The World Order*, was published by the "Ezra Pound Institute of Civilization." Mullins was reflecting Pound's view. In conversation with me he said that Pound was the source of all his ideas regarding Rockefellers and Rothschilds.

26. Mullins, *op. cit.*, p. 93. See also Webster G. Tarpley and Anton Chaitkin, *George Bush: The Unauthorised Biography*, ch 3: http://www.tarpley.net/bush3.htm: "Farish owns and boards the studs which mate with the Queen's mares. That is her public rationale when she comes to America and stays in Farish's house." Also for Farish's links to Bush Sr.

27. Sutton, *Wall Street and the Rise of Hitler, op. cit.*, p. 81. The newly merged company was called Schröder, Rockefeller & Co, Inc. at 48 Wall Street. John D. Rockefeller's nephew Avery Rockefeller became vice-president and director of the new firm.

28. See John Loftus and Mark Aarons, *The Secret War against the Jews*, p. 168.

29. See note 28.

30. Sutton, *Wall Street and the Rise of Hitler, op. cit.*, p. 99 ("By 1919 Krupp was already

giving financial aid to one of the reactionary political groups which sowed the seed of the present Nazi ideology") and pp. 59–62. Sutton calls Krupp "another Hitler supporter." "Rothschilds" (see note 33) indirect funding was through J. P. Morgans, who controlled General Motors. The Nazis granted tax-exempt status to General Motors' subsidiary Opel in 1936, and General Motors reinvested the resulting profits in German industry.

31. Sutton, *Wall Street and the Rise of Hitler, op. cit.*, p. 109.

32. Schacht's father was cashier for the Berlin branch of Equitable Assurance. Sutton, *Wall Street and the Rise of Hitler, op. cit.*, p. 109.

33. Sutton, *Wall Street and the Rise of Hitler, op. cit.*, p. 31: "American companies associated with the Morgan-Rockefeller International investment bankers ... were intimately related to the growth of Nazi industry ... General Motors, Ford, General Electric, DuPont and the handful of US companies intimately involved with the development of Nazi Germany were – except for the Ford Motor Company – controlled by the Wall Street élite – the J. P. Morgan firm, the Rockefeller Chase Bank and to a lesser extent the Warburg Manhattan bank." On p. 160 Sutton states that there is "evidence which suggests co-operation with the Wehrmacht (Ford Motor Company, Chase bank, Morgan bank)." Morgan and Co. were owned and controlled by Rothschilds.

   Also: "The Standard Oil group of companies, in which the Rockefeller family owned a one-quarter (and controlling) interest, was of critical assistance in helping Nazi Germany prepare for World War II" (p. 67). "The financing of Hitler and his SS street thugs came in part from affiliates or subsidiaries of US firms, including Henry Ford in 1922, payments by I. G. Farben and General Electric in 1933, followed by the Standard Oil of New Jersey and ITT subsidiary payments to Heinrich Himmler up to 1944" (p. 163).

34. Sutton, *Wall Street and the Rise of Hitler, op. cit.*, p. 166 states that international bankers including Hjalmar Schacht, Bernard Baruch, Owen Young and Gerard Swope and international banks that included J. P. Morgan, Guaranty Trust and Chase Bank backed the Bolshevik Revolution and profited from the new Soviet Union; backed Roosevelt and profited from New Deal socialism; and backed Hitler and profited from German rearmament in the 1930s. See Rivera, *op. cit.*, pp. 111–2.

35. See Quigley, *The Anglo-American Establishment, op. cit.*, ch 12 for a full account of this time.

36. Martin Gilbert, *Churchill: A Life*, Minerva, p. 71. Churchill wanted to be a correspondent at the war between Turkey and Greece in 1897. He asked his mother to find a newspaper, saying: "Lord Rothschild would be the person to arrange this for me as he knows everyone." His mother made the arrangement, but the Turks defeated the Greeks before his ship reached Italy.

37. John Charmley, *The End of Glory*, p. 336.

38. Charmley, *op. cit.*, p. 336.

39. Michael McLaughlin, *For Those Who Cannot Speak*: "With bankruptcy looming in 1938, Churchill (then a member of UK parliament) knew he would be forced to vacate his seat there and he would also lose his beloved home, Chartwell. Fortunately for him, Jewish millionaire Henry Strakosch advanced the aging politician a £150,000 loan and became his 'advisor,' reviving his political career." See http://www.aijf.org/p11.html.

Also see http://www.heretical.com/miscella/churchil.html on how Strakosch became Churchill's advisor and confidant but "miraculously managed to avoid the spotlight of publicity." For the "interest-free" see note 42.

40. Douglas Reed, *Controversy of Zion*, p. 330; quoted in Griffin, *Descent into Slavery?*, *op. cit.*, p. 143.

41. Griffin, *Descent into Slavery?*, *op. cit.*, pp. 143–4.

42. "1944 February 1. *The Times* of London discloses that the last will and testament of Austrian-born Sir Henry Strakosch had converted 'interest free' loans to Winston Churchill and Lord Simon into gifts. Simon had received £10,000, and Churchill twice as much. Strakosch was a multi-millionaire who made his fortune in gold mining in South Africa." See http://www.fair-trade-usa.com/kronos/timebase/00798–201–00000a.html.

43. The Saudi-Arabian scenario has been stated by Dr. Peter Beter, general counsel for the Export Import Bank of Washington and a candidate for the governorship of West Virginia, who worked with Emmanuel Josephson, in his audiotapes. His theme is that "Rockefellers" wanted the British oil concessions in Saudi Arabia, and twice used Germany as a threat that would make Britain surrender Saudi-Arabian oil; first during the First World War and then during the Second World War. "Nelson Rockefeller also stepped into active planning for World War II. The war was to be used both to take over the Saudi-Arabian oil interests of Great Britain and also to crush Japan, which was trying to open up vast Chinese oilfields that the Rockefeller interests had suppressed for years for monopolistic purposes." See: http://www.bebeyond.com/cgi-bin/BBs.pl?ID-p%2B%CZeXBv6%3A%5EO%7Df&theme-Dreams. See note 46 in ch 2, Chevron.

The joint company, Standard Oil of California and the Texas Company (Texaco) was owned by Caltex. The operating company, a subsidiary, was the Arabian-American Oil Company, called Aramco, formed in January 1944. See Josephson, *Rockefeller "Internationalist"*, *op. cit.*, p. 388. Some oil was found in January 1936. Commercial production began on March 3, 1938. See Chevron: http://www.chevron.com.learning_center/history/topic/explorepg2.asp.

44. Josephson, *The Strange Death of Franklin D. Roosevelt*, *op. cit.*, p184; and Blood and Oil – A Middle East Primer for UE Members: http://dupagepiece.home.att.net/history2.html, p.1. For the blocking by the British, see note 46.

45. In 1935 Anglo-Persian Oil Co. was renamed Anglo-Iranian Oil Co., which was renamed British Petroleum in 1954. See note 52.

46. See: http://www.bebeyond.com/cgi-bin/BBs.pl?ID-p%2B%CZeXBv6%3A%5EO%7Df&theme-Dreams. Blood and Oil – "A Middle East Primer for UE Members": http://dupagepiece.home.att.net/history2.html

47. Josephson, *Rockefeller "Internationalist"*, *op. cit.*, p. 375.

48. Josephson, *Rockefeller "Internationalist"*, *op. cit.*, p. 380. Josephson, *The Strange Death of Franklin D. Roosevelt*, *op. cit.*, p. 185: 'The plan was to build Hitler up as a menace to England, and smash the British Empire if necessary to gain control of its oil reserves and other resources. The best way to dismantle the British Empire was for Churchill to promise to de-colonize. Roosevelt, mindful of American pacifism and isolationism,

could plead that American public opinion would approve a British anti-colonialist posture. The costs of the war would be shifted to the US taxpayer by the device of Lend-Lease. It fell to Attlee, Churchill's replacement as Prime Minister after the war, to deliver de-colonization.' See Josephson, *The Strange Death of Franklin D. Roosevelt, op. cit.*, p. 186: "From the start of his Administration, F. D. R. spared no effort to foment war ... The full extent of Roosevelt's treachery ... will not be known until the exchanges between Roosevelt and his distant cousin Winston Churchill are published. Of special interest would be the full text of the letter in which Churchill stated 'Between us we can divide the world.'" For the context of an agreement to de-colonize, see note 52. See note 51.

49. Some 2,000 barges were assembled in German, Belgian, and French harbors. The objective of Operation Sea Lion was to land 160,000 German soldiers along a 40–mile coastal stretch of south-east England. The plan was abandoned on October 12, 1940, and replaced by the Blitz. See: http://www.spartacus.schoolnet.co.uk/2WWsealoin.htm (*sic*)

50. In 1944 Roosevelt received Lord Halifax at the White House and showed him a sketch he had made of the Middle East. He said, "Persian oil is yours. We share the oil of Iraq and Kuwait. As for Saudi-Arabian oil, it's ours." Quoted in Daniel Yergin, *The Prize: The Epic Quest for Oil, Money and Power*, see: http://wat.ncf.ca/our-magazine/links/issue51/articles/51–04–05.pdf. Also see Josephson, *The Strange Death of Franklin D. Roosevelt, op. cit.*, pp184–5; and *The "Federal" Reserve Conspiracy and Rockefeller, op. cit.*, p. 75. See note 51.

51. Roosevelt and Churchill were cousins. Both were descended from Viscount Anthony Browne III (1526–1592); Churchill from his son, the 3rd Earl of Southampton's (Shakespeare's patron's) father and Roosevelt from his brother, Hon. Anthony Browne IV. Churchill and Roosevelt were 11th cousins one time removed. Their kinship may have made Churchill more trusting than he might otherwise have been. See: http://users.legacyfamilytree.com/USPresidents/fdr.church.htm. See note 52 for the circumstances surrounding the agreement and deal which may have included a promise to de-colonize. On June 4, 1940, Churchill made his "we shall fight on the beaches" speech. Evidence of the agreement can be found in it: "We shall go on to the end ... ; until ... the New World, with all its power and might, steps forth to the rescue and the liberation of the Old." See Gilbert, *op. cit.*, p. 656. See note 48.

52. The evacuation of Dunkirk took place between May 27 and June 3, 1940. In that time 224,318 British and 111,172 French troops were evacuated to Britain. See Gilbert, *op. cit.*, p. 654. In January 1940 Roosevelt requested $2b from Congress for US defense in the fiscal year 1941. On May 16, 1940 he requested a further $1.182b. On May 31, 1940 he requested a further $1,277,741,170. On July 10, 1940 he requested a further $4,848,171,957. See: http://www.ibiblio.org/pha/7–2–188/188–18.html. On January 8, 1941 Roosevelt's emissary Harry Hopkins met Churchill in London. Even as they talked Roosevelt announced that the US would build what Britain needed and then lease it to her, with payments to be delayed until after the war. But first Britain must pay all the debts she could in gold and sell all her commercial assets in the US. The transfer of Saudi Arabian oilfields and disposal of British colonies were presumably within the deal, although kept secret. Churchill agreed to sell Britain's gold and assets to the Syndicate in return for US help against Hitler.

53. In April 1941 the US Roosevelt administration loaned King Saud $6m at Aramco's

insistence. Aramco also advanced the King royalties. In 1941–2 the White House channeled $10m to King Saud as part of a $42.5m wartime loan to Britain. In February 1943 Roosevelt authorized direct Lend-Lease aid to the Saud family, and over the next two years delivered $18m in goods and services to him. See: http://wat.ncf.ca/our-magazine/links/issue51/articles/51-04-05.pdf. Josephson, *The Strange Death of Franklin D. Roosevelt, op. cit.*, p. 219.

54. Blood and Oil – A Middle East Primer for UE Members: http://dupagepiece.home.att.net/history2.html, p. 3.

55. Dhahran Airport was built with public funds. See: http://www.mises.org/econsense/ch93.asp.

56. King Saud met Roosevelt on the USS *Quincy* in Egypt's Great Bitter Lake. The meeting initiated the transfer of the region from the British to the US sphere of influence, and from 1946 Saud was under US rather than British protection. Residents in the Middle East saw the change as thousands of Americans and their families arrived on the Hasa coast of Arabia where the US government had assisted Aramco in building Saudi Arabia's first major refinery as an emergency war measure and where a US Air Force base was under construction at Dhahran. See: http://wat.ncf.ca/our-magazine/links/issue51/articles/51-04-05.pdf. Elizabeth Schulte, "A brief history Petro-Politics": http://www.deeperwants.com/cul1/homeworlds/journal/archives/001051.thml.

57. Blood and Oil – A Middle East Primer for UE Members: http://dupagepiece.home.att.net/history2.html, p. 3.

58. Josephson, *The Strange Death of Franklin D. Roosevelt, op. cit.*, p. 189: "The world was amazed at Hitler's failure to make the easy, simple crossing of the English Channel, that could have been made in a few hours. Had there been known the Dunkirk deal between the Rockefeller-Standard Oil interests and the British, the situation would have been understood more readily. For it was common knowledge that as a result of the victory of the I. G. Farbenindustrie (the German Dye Trust) in its feud with the Steel Trust for the control of Nazi Germany, the Rockefeller-Standard Oil interests had a powerful voice in the domination of the creature Hitler. He was ordered to turn aside from England and attack Germany's ally, Russia." Also Josephson, *Rockefeller "Internationalist", op. cit.*, p. 380: 'Though Hitler could have crossed the channel in a matter of hours, and invaded England, some force deterred him and caused him to turn against Germany's ally, Soviet Russia, in a suicidal invasion attempt. The role played by the Rockefeller and I. G. interests in influencing this decision has yet to be fathomed. But it is clear that since they dominated Hitler and the Nazi party, they did play a role.'

59. See note 58. Sutton, *Wall Street and the Rise of Hitler, op. cit.*, p. 33: "On the eve of World War II the German chemical complex of I. G. Farben was the largest chemical manufacturing enterprise in the world, with extraordinary political and economic power and influence with the Hitlerian Nazi state. I. G. has been aptly described as 'a state within a state' .... Without the capital supplied by Wall Street, there would have been no I. G. Farben in the first place and almost certainly no Adolf Hitler and World War II." I. G. Farben cooperated with Standard Oil. See Sutton for documentary primary source evidence that Hitler was financed by the Syndicate. Also see note 48.

60. *Barbarossa, the Axis and the Allies*, ed. by John Erickson and David Dilks, pp. 256–8.

61. Nigel Pennick, *Hitler's Secret Sciences*, p. 25. For the swastika on a flag on Liebenfels' temple overlooking the Danube, see Suster, *Hitler: Black Magician*, p. 39. Rivera, *op. cit.*, p. 110.

62. Daniel, *op. cit.*, p. 571. Under his given name Lanz – he changed his name to von Liebenfels later – von Liebenfels had taught in a Benedictine cloister school from 1890 to 1900. Hitler (who was born in 1889) attended the same school for the last half of that decade.

63. Suster, *op. cit.*, p. 48.

64. See note 75.

65. Pennick, *op. cit.*, p. 28. The Thule Society was founded by Baron von Sebottendorff in 1912. Daniel, *op. cit.*, p. 573; Rivera, *op. cit.*, p. 110.

66. Pennick, *op. cit.*, pp. 28–9.

67. Pennick, *op. cit.*, p. 91. Also, Suster, *op. cit.*, p100: "Black magic consists of using this energy for material gain, or, above all, for the pursuit of power. By this definition, the Thule Group pursued black magic."

68. Pennick, *op. cit.*, p. 26. Also p. 175, on Hitler's pact with higher powers, involving a release of "bio-electrical energy – vril." See also Sklar, *The Nazis and the Occult*, p. 107, on vril as an *élan vital*, which Hitler manipulated.

69. Pennick, *op. cit.*, p. 151. I have visited the Externsteine and Irminsul and can testify to their atmosphere.

70. Pennick, *op. cit.*, pp. 158–160. As part of my research I have visited Schloss Wewelsburg's crypt.

71. Pennick, *op. cit.*, p. 159; Graber, *History of the SS*, p. 87.

72. Pennick, *op. cit.*, p. 18.

73. Rivera, *op. cit.*, p. 111.

74. *Volkisch* occultism, the study of German nationalist, racist, and occult folklore, was founded by Guido von List, a white-bearded magus whose symbol was the swastika and whose championing of the Aryan Germans influenced the Thule Group. See Suster, *op. cit.*, pp. 38, 46.

75. Hitler was sentenced to five years in prison after the failed *putsch* of November 8, 1923. He arrived at the fortress of Landsberg on April 1, 1924 and was released on December 20, 1924. See: http://www.hitler.org/writings/prison. Eckart met Hitler after one of his beer-hall speeches, took him to the Thule Society and gave him lodging in his house in Obersalzburg, high above the plot that would later contain the Berghof, Hitler's residence during the Second World War. He announced Hitler as the Führer to the German people in an article in August 1921. See Daniel, *op. cit.*, pp. 574–5. Also Rivera, *op. cit.*, p. 110.

76. I rely on my own research and visits to all these places. See also Pennick, *op. cit.*, p. 146.

77. The Syndicate controlled Hitler through funding and supply of raw materials for the war, via I. G. Farben/I. G. Farbenindustrie. They also had links with the plotters who attempted to assassinate Hitler on July 20, 1944, on the initiative of von Stauffenberg. The date for the plot was originally set as September 28, 1938, but was cancelled when news reached Berlin that Chamberlain was travelling to Munich. The intellectual leader of the war time conspirators, Helmuth von Moltke and Adam von Trott zu Solz, a prominent plotter, were both close to the Milner Group – see Quigley, *The Anglo-American Establishment, op. cit.*, pp288–290 and 315 (where they are listed as members of the Round Table). The Stauffenberg plot could have been a failed attempt by the Syndicate to replace Hitler.

78. Franciszek Piper in *Auschwitz, How Many Perished*, pp. 7–10, covers the testimony of SS men and camp workers. The consensus puts the number of Jews killed at between 4.5 and 5.5 million. According to the camp commander Hoess told the International Military Tribunal in Nuremberg that at least 2.5 million died in Auschwitz-Birkenau alone, but after his extradition to Poland he changed parts of his testimony and put the figure at 1.13 million before he was hanged. Raul Hilberg in *The Destruction of the European Jews* (three-volume 2003 edition) arrives at 5.1 million Jews killed during the Holocaust, with under 1 million killed at Auschwitz-Birkenau. See: http://www.literaturehistoryhub.com/Destruction_of_the_european_jews_084190909105.html.

79. For I. G. Farben's manufacturing of Zyklon B gas, see Perloff, *op. cit.*, p. 47. Two German firms, Tesch/Stabenow and Degesch, produced granular Zyklon B after they acquired the patent from Farben. Tesch supplied two tons a month, and Degesch three quarters of a ton. See: www.nizkor.org/faqs/auschwitz-faq-06.html. After the war the directors of both firms denied knowing that their products were being used on humans. The prosecutors found letters from Tesch offering to supply the gas crystals and advising on how to use the ventilating equipment. Hoess, the Auschwitz camp commander, testified that the Tesch directors sold him enough to annihilate 2 million people. Two Tesch partners were hanged in 1946; the director of Degesch was sentenced to five years in prison.

80. The BIS was set up under Morgan banker Owen D. Young's plan to provide the Allies with reparations to be paid by Germany for the First World War. With Rockefeller banker Gates W. McGarrah (formerly of Chase National Bank and the Federal Reserve Bank) as its first president, it soon turned into a channel for American and British funds to reach Hitler. By the outbreak of the Second World War the BIS was "completely under Hitler's control" (Charles Higham). Its directors included Hermann Schmitz, head of I. G. Farben; Baron Kurt von Schröder, head of J. H. Stein Bank of Cologne (financier of the Gestapo); and two of Hitler's personal appointees, Dr Walther Funk of the Reichsbank and Emil Puhl, vice-president of the Reichsbank (receiver of gold from conquered nations). The president of the Nazi-controlled BIS was an American, Harrington McKittrick. See Charles Higham, *Trading with the Enemy, How the Allied Multinationals Supplied Nazi Germany Throughout World War Two*: http://www.bilderberg.org/bis.htm.

81. Montagu Norman, Governor of the Bank of England, was an enthusiastic supporter of Hitler.

82. Norman Livergood, *The New US-British Oil Imperialism*: http://www.hermes-press.com/impintro1.htm.

83. The *Encyclopaedia Britannica* states the total deaths in the Second World War as 35,813,000. However, more detailed research involving Soviet records revealed after the collapse of the USSR in *Barbarossa, The Axis and the Allies, op. cit.*, shows that 49 million Soviet people died in Russia after Operation Barbarossa alone. According to this work, a conservative estimate of the total number of dead in the Second World War is between just under 36 million (including 18 million Russians) to 67 million; and a higher estimate is between 60 and 90 million. The numbers killed rose colossally after von Stauffenberg's plot, and if the known figures of those killed to mid-1944 are put against the higher estimate, then 30 million is not an unreasonable figure for those killed on a higher estimate (which is merited by post-Soviet research) during the final year.

84. The Syndicate's switch to Stalin first revealed itself when Eisenhower, in conjunction with Gen. Marshall, rejected Field Marshal Montgomery's plan made in late 1944 to take Berlin. Eisenhower and those above him used delaying tactics to allow Stalin to reach Berlin before the Allies. Before that efforts were made, as part of the war effort, to ensure that the USSR was not defeated by Germany, and that invading Nazi troops were beaten back. There was nothing strange about this policy; Churchill's Britain also wanted its ally Stalin to survive. See next paragraph.

   Stalin was saved when, with Hitler and his army only 37 miles from Moscow on October 24, 1941, the US entered the war in response to Japan's attack on Pearl Harbor. In so far as the Syndicate was responsible for intriguing the attack on Pearl Harbor, the Syndicate was responsible for saving Stalin – and siding with Stalin against Hitler. Evidence for Roosevelt's pro-Russian policy surfaced in the spring of 1943, when a faction within the German secret service offered to assassinate Hitler and surrender so long as Soviet troops ceased their advance. Roosevelt refused and postponed a planned US invasion of Europe. The effect of this decision was to give Stalin more time to advance. See Rivera, *op. cit.*, p. 112.

85. Roosevelt, whose Cabinet included many Rockefeller nominees, appointed Eisenhower Supreme Commander in Europe on December 24, 1943. He had no battle experience or experience of handling hundreds of thousands of troops in the field. He had been promoted above some 150 more experienced soldiers. In a speech when opening a part in New York, founded by Bernard Baruch in honor of his father, Eisenhower said: "Twenty-five years ago, as a young and unknown Major, I took the wisest step in my life – I consulted Mr Baruch." See A. K. Chesterton, *The New Unhappy Lords*, p. 36. Baruch was advisor to several presidents and influenced Roosevelt throughout his political life. Eisenhower and Marshall were both acting in CFR and Rockefellerite interests. Roosevelt was a Rockefeller puppet in so far as he owed his presidency to the intriguing of Col. House who made sure he followed a Rockefellerite agenda. House masterminded the election of Roosevelt – and then vanished from the political scene. (Griffin, *Descent into Slavery?, op. cit.*, pp. 137–8.) Roosevelt was a Wall Street creation. See Griffin, *Descent into Slavery?, op. cit.*, p. 134. Baruch took over House's role. For Eisenhower see Griffin, *Descent into Slavery?, op. cit.*, pp. 156–8.

   For Roosevelt as Rockefeller puppet, see: http://www.bebeyond.com/cgi-bin/BBs. pl?ID-p%2B%CZeXBv6%3A%5EO%7Df&theme-Dreams: "Nelson Rockefeller made sure that President Roosevelt's preparations for the war were coordinated precisely with the Rockefeller machinations overseas, including Hitler's build-up on the one hand and the plotting of the Pearl Harbor on the other." This is a quotation from Dr Peter Beter's audiotapes on the theme that the Second World War was instigated by "Rockefellers" as an "extortion plot" to help the Rockefeller oil cartel take Saudi-Arabian oil rights away from the British by creating Nazi Germany as a threat until the British gave in. Beter's website: http://wwwetext.org/Politics/Beter.Audio.Letter/dbalo1.

86. For Montgomery's urgings regarding a drive on Berlin, see Read and Fisher, *The Fall of Berlin*, pp. 179–81, 195, 270–2. I give a full account of his urgings in my verse play, *The Warlords*.

87. The I. G. Farben Building was used as the headquarters of the American Forces in Europe from May 26, 1945. On September 19, 1945 Eisenhower signed Proclamation No. 2 there (declaring which parts of Germany would be in the American Zone). He stayed in the I. G. Farben Building until the end of 1945. See: http://www.empgx.uni-frankfurt.de/history–poelzig.htm.

88. Norman Livergood, *The New US-British Oil Imperialism*: http://www.hermes-press.com/impintro1.htm, p. 4.

89. The first BIS president was Gates W. McGarrah, formerly of the Chase National Bank and the Federal Reserve Bank.

6. The Two States: The Cold War

1. The "balance of terror" (a play on Sir Robert Walpole's "balance of power" of 1741) was otherwise known as the doctrine of mutually assured destruction (MAD). The US had an overkill capability of destroying the Soviet Union 30 times over, and the Soviet Union of destroying the United States 20 times over. Although the US was more powerful, an equilibrium was established because people can only die once. See "A new balance of terror," http://weekly.ahram.org.eg/2002/579/op3.htm.

2. See the heading "West European De-colonization," para. 1, in ch 6.

3. See notes 85 and 86 in ch 5.

4. Rev. Jim Shaw, *The Deadly Deception*, quoted by Still, *op. cit.*, pp. 170–171; Daniel, *op. cit.*, pp. 486, 499. Roosevelt was a 32nd-degree Mason, a Knight Templar; Churchill was a 3rd-degree English Mason as early as 1919; and Stalin was a Rosicrucian Martinist Freemason – see Daniel, *op. cit.*, p. 572, quoting Baigent, Leigh, and Lincoln, *The Messianic Legacy*, p. 187, where it is asserted that Stalin lived in 1899 or 1900 with the family of George Gurdjieff. In 1900 Stalin is believed to have lived for a year in Georgia with Gurdjieff, the teacher of Tibetan mysteries, who initiated him into Martinist Freemasonry. The authors' source, Webb in *The Harmonious Circle*, p. 45, claims that "Stalin's daughter fled to the USA and joined a Gurdjieff group there" (Webb p. 425). In the course of a five-hour discussion with Svetlana Stalin I asked her if she realized that her father was a Martinist Rosicrucian, and she said, "No, I had no idea." Rosicrucian Martinism was a front for the Priory of Sion, see Daniel, *op. cit.*, p. 378.

5. Confirmed by the author during research for *Overlord*, bk 7, which states that all members of the US delegation's negotiating team were Freemasons (lines 2,764–6) and that all present in the first Plenary session – 10 Americans, 8 British and 10 Russians – were Freemasons (lines 2,959–2,962). Research from numerous books about the Second World War.

6. At one level Stalin's purge in the 1930s was to remove his political opponents and strengthen his dictatorial power. At another level it reflected the interests of the Freemasonic allegiance and reduced the influence of the Grand Orient Templar Freemasonry in favour of his own Sionist Rosicrucianism.

7. Wilgus, *The Illuminoids*, pp. 202–4, quoted in Daniel, *op. cit.*, pp. 551–2, 629 (where Pasvolsky's name is misprinted).

8. The CFR's "Commonwealth of Free Nations" drew on the concept of the British Commonwealth of Nations, a concept first drafted in the statute of Westminster, 1931. The CFR proposal was that a Commonwealth of Nations should act as a League of Nations/United Nations.

9. Hoopes and Brinkley, *FDR and the Creation of the UN*, pp. 45–6. Churchill was staying at the White House, and Roosevelt burst into his bedroom while Churchill was in the bath and secured his approval for the name "United Nations" that he had just thought up. See Devine, *Second Chance*, pp. 47–8.

10. Hoopes and Brinkley, *op. cit.*, pp. 88–91.

11. Hoopes and Brinkley, *op. cit.*, pp. 130–2. For Hiss as a Soviet spy, see Perloff, *op. cit.*, p. 70; Rivera, *op. cit.*, p. 166.

12. Josephson, *Rockefeller "Internationalist"*, *op. cit.*, p. 237. For the writing of the UN charter, see Josephson, *Rockefeller "Internationalist"*, *op. cit.*, p. 391: "Ch 13, The Council on Foreign Relations, 'Foreign Office' of the Rockefeller Empire." Josephson refers to the CFR as the Rockefeller Foreign Office several times. Perloff, *op. cit.*, p. 64, says of the CFR, "It worked in secret and was underwritten by the Rockefeller Foundation." Hence the nickname. Gary Allen, *None Dare Call It Conspiracy*, p. 83.

13. Hoopes and Brinkley, *op. cit.*, p. 176.

14. Perloff, *op. cit.*, p. 64; Rivera, *op. cit.*, p. 93.

15. Rivera, *op. cit.*, p. 94. The Ford Foundation contributed $1.5m.

16. Kennedy's administration had 63 CFR members out of 82; Carter's had over 70, and 20 members of the Trilateral Commission; Nixon's had 110 CFR members in government appointments; and Reagan's had more than 80 members of the CFR or Trilateral Commission or both. Up to 1988 14 Secretaries of State were members of the CFR, 14 Treasury Secretaries and 11 Defense Secretaries. Three Secretaries of State were past Chairmen of the Rockefeller Foundation: John Foster Dulles under Eisenhower; Dean Rusk under Kennedy; and Cyrus Vance under Carter. Nixon chose Kissinger who had had a long and close association with the Rockefellers, having worked for Nelson Rockefeller, although he had never been Chairman of the Rockefeller Foundation. For citings in order, see Perloff, *op. cit.*, pp. 111, 145, 158–9, 168; 7; 104, 110, 158; 145.

17. Rivera, *op. cit.*, p. 93.

18. Hoopes and Brinkley, *op. cit.*, pp. 202–3. Truman announced his plan for a UN on June 23, and personally delivered the Charter to the Senate less than a week later.

19. Rivera, *op. cit.*, p. 166; Perloff, *op. cit.*, p. 72. Rockefeller presented a check to Trygve Lie, first Secretary General of the UN. The $65m to build the UN building on the land was raised as an interest-free "loan" from the American taxpayer.

20. Perloff, *op. cit.*, p. 43.

21. Rivera, *op. cit.*, p. 166.

22. Quoted in Rivera, *op. cit.*, p. 166.

23. Rivera, *op. cit.*, pp. 166–7.

24. Hoopes and Brinkley, *op. cit.*, p. 175.

25. See note 24.

26. Hoopes and Brinkley, *op. cit.*, pp. 114–7.

27. Coleman, *Diplomacy by Deception*, *op. cit.*, p138.

28. Coleman, *Diplomacy by Deception*, *op. cit.*, p138.

29. Churchill, speech at Fulton, Missouri in 1946.

30. Quoted in Brian Crozier, *Soviet Imperialism, How to Contain It*, p. 23.

31. The Baruch Plan was presented to the UN Atomic Energy Commission on June 14, 1946. He proposed that all atomic energy should be placed under an international Atomic Development Authority and that the manufacture of atomic bombs should stop, i.e. the US would be left as the sole atomic power. See: http://www.nuclearfiles.org/ redocuments/1946/460614.baruch.html.

32. Jasper, *Global Tyranny...Step by Step, The United Nations and the Emerging New World Order,* p. 239.

33. Jasper, *op. cit.,* p. 241. Marshall had conferred at length with Monnet at the Paris Peace Conference.

34. The Marshall Plan transferred $13b from the US taxpayer to the Economic Co-operation Administration. This was linked to purchases of particular US goods and services. US firms increased their sales to European consumers, who made their purchases free of charge.

35. "In 1946–1947 lawyer Charles M. Spofford headed a (CRF study) group with banker David Rockefeller as secretary, on reconstruction in Western Europe; in 1947–1948 that body was retitled the Marshall Plan" (Shoup and Minter, *Imperial Brain Trust,* p. 35). The Rockefeller involvement can be gauged from David Rockefeller's involvement as secretary. It was originally to have been called the Truman Plan; it was named the Marshall Plan because Gen. Marshall, Chief of Staff during the war, could attract bipartisan congressional support. Perloff, *op. cit.,* p. 82. For David Rockefeller, see Jasper, *op. cit.,* p. 241. Gen. Marshall unveiled the plan in a speech at Harvard University on June 5, 1947.

36. For $13b see comment on Marshall's address of June 5, 1947: http://www.hpol.org/ marshall. Also Jeffrey Tucker, "The Marshall Plan Myth": http://www.mises.org/freemarket_detail.asp?control=120&sortorder=articledate.

37. Perloff, *op. cit.,* p. 72.

38. Hitler had spoken of a new world order under his rule. F. S. Marvin had written a book entitled *New World Order,* which was published in 1932. The CFR worked for world government and therefore a new world order. For the optimistic mood within the CFR and the US after the Second World War, see Perloff, *op. cit.,* ch 5.

39. For the 37,000 tied down, see BBC News, March 11, 2004: http://news.bbc.co.uk/1/hi/world/asia-pacific/country_profiles/1123668.stm. Michael McLaughlin, *For Those Who Cannot Speak.* Also: http://www.heretical.com/miscella/ churchil.html.

40. Josephson, *Rockefeller "Internationalist",* *op. cit.,* p. 419; Josephson, *The "Federal" Reserve Conspiracy and Rockefeller, op. cit.,* p. 135.

41. Mao, *Memorandum on a New Program for World Revolution,* March 1953; quoted in Rivera, *op. cit.,* p. 135.

42. See note 40. Josephson, *The "Federal" Reserve Conspiracy and Rockefeller, op. cit.,* p. 293. See: http://www.fair-trade-usa.com/kronos/timebase/00798–201–00000a.html, quoting *The Times* of London. Krushchev's arms arrived in Egypt in September 1955.

43. See ch 2, note 84.

44. Disraeli visited Baron Lionel Rothschild on November 14, 1875 to ask him to buy the Suez Canal. See Morton, *op. cit.*, pp. 149–152. For a full account of the events behind the collusion between Israel, France and Great Britain, see Wint and Calvocoressi, *Middle East Crisis, op. cit.*, p. 66; and pp. 66–9 for the other facts in this paragraph and the previous paragraph.

45. *Suez 1956*: http://history.acusd.edu/gen/text/suez.html (many end notes), p. 4.

46. See note 45.

47. See note 45. Eden went to his grave condemning Dulles for abandoning him after the Suez invasion. There is no record of any promise Dulles made to Eden. However, technically Dulles began the Suez crisis by reneging (on July 19, 1956) on his offer to fund the Aswan dam.

48. Quoted in "World Conquest through World Government": http://world.std.com/obi/Rants/Protocols/The_Protocols_of_The_Learned_Elders_of_Zion.

49. Churchill may have agreed to de-colonize in return for US involvement in the Second World War after Dunkirk (see notes 50–52 in ch 5). The Attlee government may have been honoring this secret promise. Whether or not the decision to de-colonize was taken in 1940–41, de-colonization was inevitable after Suez in 1956. De-colonization had long been an aim of the Round Table, where self-government was being advanced for India as early as 1909 and Curtis proposed changing the name "British Empire" to "Commonwealth of Nations" in a book published in 1916. See Quigley, *Tragedy and Hope, op. cit.*, pp144, 164–5. The Rothschilds, first funders of the Round Table, may have initiated the decision to speed up de-colonization in early 1957 and have inspired the Earl of Gosford's statement. They certainly went along with it. Ferguson (*op. cit.*, pp. 816–7) points out that the Rothschilds backed British Empire-building when it could be achieved without precipitating conflict with other European powers, and preferred "multi-national imperialism" if conflict threatened. 1957 was a time when they could be expect to prefer "multi-national imperialism," i.e. in Europe's case, a United States of Europe.

    For Macmillan as a member of the RIIA, see Mullins, *op. cit.*, p. 51. The 1934 list of members of RIIA included Macmillan's name. He was an MP from 1924 to 1929 and from 1931 to 1964. Whatever help he gave the RIIA was on top of his work as an MP.

    Macmillan's "winds of change" speech (as it became known) was delivered twice, first in Accra, then in Cape Town a few weeks later. The wording suggests an intention to de-colonize rather than a lament at hostility towards the colonies: "Ever since the break-up of the Roman Empire, one of the constant factors of political life has been the emergence of the independent nations. The wind of change is blowing through this continent and whether we like it or not this growth of national consciousness is a political fact. We must all accept this fact and our national policies must take account of it." A nation seeking to retain hold of its colonies would have hushed these sentiments up rather than deliver them twice in different parts of Africa. See: http://www.edencamp.co.uk/hut13/.

50. For the facts in the previous paragraph of the text, see *Foreign Office Files for Cuba* (Public Record Office Class FP371), "Part 3: The Cuban Missile Crisis, 1962": http://www.adam-

matthew-publications.co.uk/collect/p428.htm, pp. 1–2. Josephson, *The "Federal" Reserve Conspiracy and Rockefeller, op. cit.,* p. 238: "Though Catholic by birth, he was by education and training ... inclined ... to the Rockefeller brand of Marxism, and to Sovietism. He obtained his education at two Rockefeller subsidized ... institutions ... He sat at the feet of 'Fabian' propagandists, Harold Laski and John Maynard Keynes ... Following his inauguration as President Kennedy's first act was to appoint to his cabinet a clutch of Rockefeller 'Liberals' or Reds. And his next move was to hustle to Vienna for the purpose of rendering homage to the conspirators' Soviet agent, Krushchev. This he followed up by delivering Cuba to the Soviets as a missile base, while belatedly pretending to block its takeover."

In 1956 the Rockefeller Brothers Fund had commissioned a project to consider America's military preparedness and foreign policy. Under first Nelson and then Laurance Rockefeller, the panel produced six reports, the most important of which was *International Security: The Military Aspect*, which was prepared under the direction of Henry Kissinger (then Associated Director of the Center for International Affairs). After the Russians successfully tested the first intercontinental ballistic missile (ICBM) the Rockefellers (in conjunction with a certain Gatler) produced reports urging an expansion of missile programs, and an increase in deterrents in conventional forces. "Rockefellers" wrote the blueprint for an acceleration in the arms race that would increase America's debt to the Syndicate's banks. The reports were implemented when J. F. Kennedy took office in January 1961.

51. Josephson, *The "Federal" Reserve Conspiracy and Rockefeller, op. cit.,* p. 238, is critical of Kennedy. Kennedy, he says, sent GIs into a "trap" in Vietnam, where they were surrounded by the Communist population. The French had been driven from Indo-China in order to gain control of the oilfields in the China coastal shelf. But Pope Paul VI had urged the withdrawal of US troops. Josephson remarks, "It is incredible that any one of the faith would favor the slaughter of the Catholic refugees in Vietnam that would certainly follow the withdrawal of (US) troops there, as demanded by Pope Paul." As a Catholic, he was bound to listen to the Pope's view. Kennedy was known to have wanted to withdraw US troops from Vietnam by 1965. And the Syndicate may have thought him unreliable. Also Daniel, *op. cit.,* p. 632: "Vice-President Lyndon Johnson was told by Hoover why JFK had to be killed – that he had de-escalated the Vietnam War."

52. The film was shown at the Global Conspiracy conference at Wembley Arena on January 9–10, 1992.

53. See note 52. William Cooper announced from the platform that the showing of the film was putting his life in danger. Cooper announced that the driver was reported to have died in 1985, but said he might not in fact be dead. He attributed Jackie Kennedy's silence about the driver to her concern for her children.

54. Daniel, *op. cit.,* pp. 243, 632. Warren was 33rd-degree Grand Master of the Grand Lodge of California in the 1920s.

55. Daniel, *op. cit.,* pp. 549, 626.

56. See note 50.

57. President Kennedy signed Executive Order no. 11110 on June 4, 1963. He was assassinated five months later. After his death no more "silver certificates" (i.e. certificates against

silver bullion, silver for standard silver dollars in the Treasury) were issued. See: http://
www.thetruthseker.co.uk/print.asp?ID=1279 and link to the Executive Order on: http://
www.john-f-kennedy.net/executiveorder11110.htm. Kennedy had printed $4.3b of non-
interest-bearing money, which threatened to abolish the Fed. After his death Johnson
recalled the debt-free notes. Kennedy, like Lincoln before him, tried to create interest-
free money. Both men were assassinated, perhaps in consequence. See Dr Ken Matto,
"The Federal Reserve: History of Lies, Thievery, and Deceit", in *Gold is Money*: http://
www.goldismoney.info/forums/showthread.php?t=4021.

58. For the Moscow crowds during David Rockefeller's visits, see Mullins, *op. cit.*, pp. 80–1.
    The speech by Krushchev is quoted in John Cotter, *A Study in Syncretism*, Canadian
    Intelligence Publications, 1979, p. 105.

59. See Capt. Victor de Kayville, April 3, 1934, quoting official information from Russia
    in 1920, http://www.compuserb.com/jewrus01.htm. Also two articles in the *Catholic
    Herald*, 1933: http://theunjustmedia.comUnjustmedia%20Archive/March%202004/
    march%2019%202004.htm and http://www.stormfront.org/posterity/13texan/q201–
    250.htm.

60. Through Gen. Marshall, the Syndicate had supported the replacement of Chiang by Mao
    in China. US/Syndicate policy at Yalta and Potsdam in 1945 was summarized by Owen
    Lattimore: "The problem was how to allow them (China) to fall without making it look
    as if the United States had pushed them." "Rockefellers" had backed Mao, and the Sino-
    Soviet Pact cemented their work on pipelining out Soviet and Chinese oil. When the
    feud between Krushchev and Mao caused trade between the USSR and China to break
    down, "Rockefellers" interests were damaged. "David Rockefeller's personally opened
    Hong Kong branch of his Chase Manhattan Bank got no business or profits from that
    trade. The press openly discussed the advantage for restoring that trade, of deposing both
    Krushchev and Mao Tse Tung, the two stumbling blocks." Josephson, *The "Federal" Reserve
    Conspiracy and Rockefeller, op. cit.*, p. 292. To restore profits to the Hong Kong branch of his
    bank, David Rockefeller expected both Krushchev and Mao to restore their trade.

61. Josephson, *The "Federal" Reserve Conspiracy and Rockefeller, op. cit.*, p. 292.

62. Until the 1930s, Rockefellers supplied kerosene for Chinese lamps and through the
    ruling Soong family made sure that no competitors drilled for oil in any part of China.
    They therefore had an effective monopoly rather than a monopoly by right of the kind
    Elizabeth I granted Sir Walter Raleigh on all exports from the New World in the 1590s.
    In 1931 Japan invaded China's north-eastern Manchurian provinces to control their oil.
    "Rockefellers" wanted the Second World War so that Japan's challenge to China could be
    destroyed. Since 1945 "Rockefellers" have been the key player in the extraction of China's
    oil, but have no longer enjoyed an effective monopoly. See note 32 to ch 4. See Josephson,
    Rockefeller "Internationalist", op. cit., pp. 381–2. By the 1920s, the Socony-Vacuum-
    Standard Oil subsidiaries had a virtual monopoly of the market for oil/kerosene for the
    lamps of China. The companies managed it so that very little oil was produced in China.
    They were in collaboration with the Soong family and the Nationalist government.

63. For the background to this, see Josephson, *Rockefeller "Internationalist", op. cit.*, pp. 382–6:
    "The (Japanese) proceeded to seize China ... They could not forget the role played by the
    'Rockefeller'-Standard Oil crowd in the cancellation of the concessions. They avenged

themselves ... by destroying 'Rockefeller'-Standard Oil property first ... To accomplish the destruction of Japan, it was necessary to bring the American Army to the rescue of their property in China. But it would have been futile for the 'Rockefeller'-Standard Oil interests to ask Congress to declare war on Japan because it was destroying their property in China ... If, however, Japan could be induced to attack the US – that would be a different story ... The appointment of Joseph Grew, nephew of John Pierpont Morgan, as Ambassador to Japan was dictated. The plan was to induce the Japs to attack the United States ... The conspirators were impatiently waiting and working to bring about an attack on the United States that would force Congress to declare officially the war that Roosevelt already was waging unofficially ... Rockefeller's Institute of Pacific Relations agents working under Sorge precipitated the Japanese attack on Pearl Harbor that the conspirators sought in order to bring the US into the war ... As early as October 1941 the conspirators knew that the Japanese definitely planned an attack on Pearl Harbor."

The principal "Rockefellerite" in Truman's war cabinet was the Secretary of the Department of War, Henry Stimson. The Stimson Center was later funded by the Rockefeller Foundation – see http://www.stimson.org/?SN=AB2001120454. When Stimson, a member of the CFR, went to Washington in 1940 as Secretary of War he took with him John McCloy as Assistant Secretary of War of the CFR. Before 1940 McCloy had been a member of the law firm Cravath, Gersdorff, Swaine and Wood, which had represented I. G. Farben and its affiliates, Rockefellerite enterprises. He became High Commissioner in post-war Germany.

64. The development of the atomic bomb took place at the Rockefeller-owned University of Chicago. Enrico Fermi was awarded a Rockefeller Fellowship to help develop the atomic bomb. See http://www.reformation.org/pharaoh-rockefeller.html under the heading "Rockefeller financed the atomic bomb." Truman made the decision to use the atomic bomb against Japan between July 17 and 24, 1945. On July 17 Stimson flew to Potsdam and gave Truman full details of the successful atomic test. Truman immediately called in Gen. Marshall, Byrnes, Leahy, Gen. Arnold and Admiral King to review military strategy in the light of the successful test. Stimson was the focal point of the meeting. On July 24 The War Department, i.e. Stimson's department, was "given orders" to instruct Gen. Spaatz that the first bomb would be dropped as soon after August 3 as weather permitted. The key figures in the decision to drop the first atomic bomb were Stimson and Truman. Truman had not heard of the bomb when he took over the presidency on Roosevelt's death; Stimson told Truman about the new weapon on April 12, 1945. For a timeline for the decision to use the atomic bomb, see Nuclearfiles.org, http://www.nuclearfiles.org/redocuments/1957/570529–chronology.html. Also "Atomic Bomb: Decision," http://www.dannen.com/decision/index.html. The Hungarian-born scientist Dr. Leo Szilard opposed the use of the bomb, felt that Truman and those immediately below him gave insufficient study to all the alternatives to using the atomic bomb: "They thought only in terms of our having to end the war by military means." See "President Truman Did Not Understand," http://www.peak.org/~danneng/decision/usnews.html. Stimson was as much a Syndicate pawn as Marshall, both of whom manipulated an inexperienced and pliant president.

Stimson had already done war work for "Rockefellers"/the IPR. He had been behind the events that led up to Pearl Harbor. He wrote in his diary after meeting President Roosevelt: "We face the delicate question of the diplomatic fencing to be done so as to be sure Japan is put into the wrong and make the first bad move – overt move." After a later meeting he wrote: "The question was how we should maneuver them (the Japanese) into the position of firing the first shot." Quoted in Perloff, *op. cit.*, pp. 66–7.

65. Josephson, *The "Federal" Reserve Conspiracy and Rockefeller, op. cit.*, p. 292.

66. Josephson, *The "Federal" Reserve Conspiracy and Rockefeller, op. cit.*, p. 292.

67. Josephson, *The "Federal" Reserve Conspiracy and Rockefeller, op. cit.*, p. 292. Also Allen and Abraham, *None Dare Call It Conspiracy, op. cit.*, p. 107: "Would it not be more accurate to define the Communists as Rockefeller agents? Indicative of this was a strange event which occurred in October of 1964. David Rockefeller, President of the Chase Manhattan Bank and chairman of the board of the Council on Foreign Relations, took a vacation in the Soviet Union ... A few days after Rockefeller ended his 'vacation' in the Kremlin, Nikita Krushchev was recalled from a vacation at a Black Sea resort to learn that he had been fired ... Krushchev was the absolute dictator of the Soviet government and, more important, head of the Communist Party which ran the USSR. Who has the power to fire the man who was supposedly the absolute dictator? Did David Rockefeller journey to the Soviet Union to fire an employee? Obviously the position of premier in the Soviet Union is a figurehead with the true power residing elsewhere. Perhaps in New York." At first sight this passage is extremely far-fetched. It all hinges on the identity of the mysterious Council of Elders and their whereabouts. Presumably they have continued to exist after 1989 and are in control of Putin?

68. See note 58.

69. Robert Gaylon Ross Sr., *Who's Who of the Elite*, pp. 224–233.

70. Norman Livergood, *The New US-British Oil Imperialism*: http://www.hermes-press.com/impintro1.htm, pp. 7–8.

71. See note 70.

72. Marshall Douglas Smith, *Black Gold Hot Gold*, ch 3, quoted in Norman Livergood, *The New US-British Oil Imperialism*, pp. 8–9.

73. Andrew Rotter, *The Causes of the Vietnam War*: http://www.english.uiuc.edu/maps/vietnam/causes.htm.

74. See note 73.

75. See note 73.

76. Josephson, *The "Federal" Reserve Conspiracy and Rockefeller, op. cit.*, pp. 284–5, 183.

77. See note 76.

78. See note 76.

79. For the $50m aluminum plant (to produce aluminum for jet planes), see Rivera, *op. cit.*, p. 69. The Rockefeller-Eaton "axis" also built two synthetic rubber plants worth $200m (i.e. tire factories for trucks). Also see Allen and Abraham, *None Dare Call It Conspiracy, op. cit.*, p. 104. On October 20, 1969 IBEC (International Basic Economy Corporation) announced that N. M. Rothschild and Sons of London had entered into partnership with the firm, according to Allen and Abraham, *None Dare Call It Conspiracy, op. cit.*, p. 104. See also Rivera, *op. cit.*, p. 69.

80. See note 76: "Soviet Premier Brezhnev exultantly announced that Soviet Russia would be enabled thereby to increase her support of her satellites, the Vietnamese, ... ordering us to withdraw our GIs from Vietnam or have them face extermination."

81. Rivera, *op. cit.*, p. 140.

82. *The Encyclopaedia Britannica*, "History of Vietnam."

83. Rivera, *op. cit.*, p. 140.

84. Norman Livergood, *The New US-British Oil Imperialism*: http://www.hermes-press.com/impintro1.htm, p. 9.

85. Norman Livergood, *The New US-British Oil Imperialism*: http://www.hermes-press.com/impintro1.htm, pp. 9–10.

86. See note 84.

87. Josephson, *The "Federal" Reserve Conspiracy and Rockefeller, op. cit.*, pp. 292–3. Josephson says "The Arabs had been armed by the Soviets" and writes of "the Rockefeller control of Soviet Russia." Josephson writes that the Rockefeller-Eaton arms production company supplied deliberately defective arms to the Arabs. These were apparently adequate to destroy Israel, and duped Nasser into launching his embargo which began the war, so that Nasser, "grown too big for his breeches," (i.e. by trying to raise Arab profits from Rockefeller oil) would be cut down to size and destroyed. Josephson says: "The tanks were designed to lose their treads after traveling a few miles; and the missiles were set to travel in circles." The story beggars credulity, and should perhaps be treated sceptically.

88. Josephson, *The "Federal" Reserve Conspiracy and Rockefeller, op. cit.*, pp. 292–3.

89. Josephson, *The "Federal" Reserve Conspiracy and Rockefeller, op. cit.*, pp. 292–3.

90. On the Soviet Fleet, see "How Six Day war almost led to Armageddon," *Guardian*: http://www.guardian.co.uk/print/0,3858,4027859–103681,00.html.

91. Guevara's "Message to the *Tricontinental*" was written in Cuba in 1966 before he left for Bolivia. It was addressed to the Organization of Solidarity with the Peoples of Asia, Africa and Latin America, and appeared in April 1967 in the organization's magazine *Tricontinental*. Under Guevara's title: "Create two, three ... many Vietnams, that is the watchword." The seven-paragraph article mentions revolutionary activity in the Far East (Vietnam, Laos, Cambodia, Indonesia), Middle East and Africa (Guinea) and focuses on Latin America: Guatemala, Colombia, Venezuela, Bolivia and Brazil. The article was republished in *The Militant*, October 14, 1996: http://www.themilitant/com/1996/6036/6036_33.html.
    Bolivia had long been "Rockefellerite" territory. Standard Oil of New Jersey found oil in Bolivia in 1927. In 1937 Standard Oil of Bolivia was confiscated by the military Toro government. The US petroleum companies were not invited back into Bolivia until the overthrow of the military regime in 1952.

92. For OPEC's rebellion and quadrupling of the price of crude oil, see "Oil a Powerful and Profitable Business": http://home.clear.net.nz/pages/wpnz/spt20.oooil.htm. For Yamani and Carlos, see BBC News: http://news.bbc.co.uk/2/hi/middle_east/3055760.stm.

93. Perloff, *op. cit.*, p. 145; Kutz, *op. cit.*, p. 6.

94. Perloff, *op. cit.*, p. 145.

7. The United States of Europe and Russia

1. Quoted in Rivera, *op. cit.*, p. 174.

2. See Lenin, *Collected Works*, vol. 21, pp. 339–43: ttp://www.marx2mao.org/Lenin/USE15. html.

3. See text for ch 6, note 32.

4. Rivera, *op. cit.*, p. 174.

5. The Round Table began as supporters of a Federation of the English-speaking world, but by the Second World War they had progressed to advocating a union between England and France, and idea of Monnet's that greatly interested Toynbee and the RIIA; see Jenkins, *op. cit.*, pp. 61–7, "Franco-Anglo Union." Monnet worked with the CFR while he was Roosevelt's personal advisor on Europe during the Second World War, especially when he and the CFR were devising the European Recovery Program, which became the Marshall Plan. The first Bilderberg Group meeting of 1954 focused on a united Europe as the leader of one of three world blocs. "The CFR," wrote du Berrier, "saw the Common Market from the first as a regional government to which more and more nations would be added until the world government which the UN had failed to bring about would be realized." Quoted in Jasper, *op. cit.*, p. 250. As the CFR has been Rockefeller-dominated, Rockefellers can be seen to be behind the coming United States of Europe. The expansion of the EU to include Russia and the ex-Soviet republics was on the agenda for the 2003 meeting of the Bilderberg Group. See ch 14.

6. See *Sunday Telegraph*, November 3, 2002, article by Christopher Booker, "A Superstate Half a Century in the Making." Also, Jasper, *op. cit.*, pp. 249–50.

7. Victor, Lord Rothschild, was head of Heath's policy unit for four years and "allegedly head of an unnamed subversive organization designed to manipulate the introduction of a Federal Europe." See: http://educate-yourself.org/nwo/brotherhoodpart2.shtml. In the mid-1980s he was rumored to be the "5th man" in the KGB spy ring of Cambridge Apostles (Burgess, Maclean, Philby, and Blunt). He certainly tipped off Philby, causing him to flee to the Soviet Union.

8. For Kissinger, see *Spotlight*, May 29, 1989. Also see Norris McWhirter and Rodney Atkinson, *The Destruction of the Nation-State*: "Perhaps the Bilderbergers' greatest *coup* was the removal from office of Margaret Thatcher in November 1990 which had been planned at a meeting on the island of La Toja off the Atlantic coast of Spain on the weekend of 11th May 1989 ... Britain's Prime Minister, as we know, said 'No, No, No' to the new Euro-fascism but within two years the Bilderberg plan had prevailed. A democratically elected Prime Minister had been dismissed without a general election and an international cabal had conspired to destroy a nation's leader" (pp. 20–21). Also, *Spotlight*, May 29, 1989: "Sources inside the secret society of international financiers and political leaders said their clandestine meeting this year emphasized the need to bring down Mrs. Thatcher because of her refusal to yield British sovereignty to the European super-state that is to emerge in 1992 ... Political leaders in Britain who participated in the Bilderberg meeting were instructed to attack Mrs Thatcher politically in an effort to bend the 'Iron Lady's' will." Website for both quotations: http://www.gwb.com.au/2000/

multi/bild1.htm.

The British politician Paddy Ashdown was at the 1989 Bilderberg meeting, and records in his diary that the afternoons of Friday May 12 and Saturday May 13 were dominated by discussions on Europe. On the Saturday: "In afternoon a long discussion on monetary union in Europe. Nearly everybody attacked Mrs. Thatcher, even her closest admirers. The only exception was Cecil Parkinson, who put up a spirited loyal defence but didn't make any sense and had his leg pulled by everyone else." *The Ashdown Diaries*, vol. 1, published by Penguin, 2000, http://www.bilderberg.org/bilder.htm. He does not report Kissinger's attack.

9. Michael Heseltine was the first to rebel and was spoken of as Thatcher's successor. To block Heseltine's succession, Thatcher "touched" John Major. As a result many MPs voted for Major. Heseltine was a pro-European and the most dominant figure outside Thatcher's immediate circle. He was surely "Rothschildites" first choice.

10. *Spotlight*, July 17, 1995, p. 5: "The Bilderberg Group was outraged when Major, who had been put in power because Margaret Thatcher had protected British sovereignty (*Spotlight*, May 29, 1989), tried to appease 'Euro-rebels' by suggesting 'the time may never be right' for a common European currency ... Major, finding himself in political quicksand, quickly recanted and again supports the common currency. Despite being a tool of the Bilderbergers since taking office, his momentary slip brought outrage, and Bilderberg influence forced Major to resign as party leader and stand for election. But the only challenger to emerge was John Redwood, a Thatcherite who bitterly opposes surrendering British sovereignty to the European Union, so the Bilderberg Group was forced to embrace its Prodigal Son again." Major astonished ministers in his government by voting for the Maastricht Treaty. (One minister told me he was expecting Major to vote against.) The Syndicate evidently expected him to deliver progress towards a united Europe. His small majority impeded this, and he was replaced by Blair following a general election.

11. The British Prime Minister is always a "Rothschildite." Sir Evelyn de Rothschild agreed to fund Blair's campaign for the 2005 general election. See the last section of ch 14.

12. These constitutional changes were to create regions in the coming United States of Europe.

13. The plan to split England into 8 European regions was formulated under Major's premiership. Some 170 local government officers from Eastern region were summoned to a secret conference, a report on which was leaked to me in 1998. See Prescott's regional commission in 1996, in the next paragraph. All the regions in the coming United States of Europe are to have tax-raising powers. A White Paper published on May 9, 2002 envisaged that regional assemblies would receive most of their money directly from Whitehall, but that they would be able to raise extra cash to cover estimated running costs of £25m a year by levying a precept on council tax. See: http://www.telegraph. co.uk/news/main.jhtml?xml=/news/2002/05/10/nreg10.xml. This arrangement is a kind of "half-way house". When fully fledged, regional assemblies are to have tax-raising powers. See Lord Stoddart of Swindon, House of Lords on March 20, 2003: "If they are not to have tax-raising powers, they would be inferior to Scotland ... The fact that they would consider themselves to be inferior, as Wales is now doing, would mean that they would press for tax-raising powers. If they are to be significant regional entities, they

probably need tax-raising powers." See: http://www.parliament.the-stationery-office. co.uk/pa/1d199900/ldhansrd/pdvn/lds03/text/30320–10.htm.

14. See the European Union's own website: http://www.cor.eu.int/en/index.html, 'Commit-tee of the Regions' and 'Activities of the European Union, Summaries of Legislation': http://europa.eu.int/scadplus/leg/en/lvb/g24215.htm. Also see "Regional Assemblies. co.uk" for the case against Regional Assemblies for England.

15. Brown gave the Bank of England the right to decide interest rates. The Bank of England has been linked to the Rothschilds since the Battle of Waterloo, see ch 2.

16. See BBC News: http://news.bbc.co.uk/1/hi/business/2744115.stm. Optimists claimed that a record £34b deficit for 2002 was not the biggest deficit as a share of GDP and below the deficit/GDP levels of the late 1980s.

17. Heath was told that British fishing interests would have to be sacrificed if Britain was to join the Common Market. He agreed to this. See: http://www.bobdoust.co.uk/curouk. htm.

18. Alistair McConnachie, *Sovereignty*, January 2003, http://www.sovereignty.org.uk/ features/articles/fishing6.html, holds that the "conservation crisis" argument is a convenient excuse for the severe cutbacks on the British – predominantly Scottish – fleet, which make increasing room for Spain and others. The French have been allowed to fish for 25 days per month, whereas Scottish whitefish trawlers will only be allowed to fish for up to 15 days a month, with quotas cut by 45%. For the Brussels plan to assist the "poorer" nations of Ireland and Spain to construct boats which will be able to catch more fish, confining North Sea British boats to nine days' fishing per month instead of the previous 15, see: http://www.bfors.com/mediacentre/dossiers/display.asp?IDNO=943.

19. See Dr Richard North, "Towards a British Agricultural Policy": http://www.users.dircon. co.uk/~iits/newalliance/britfarm.hdm.

20. See BBC News: http://news.bbc.co.uk/1/hi/business/3534519.stm. With the closure of the Selby pit complex later in 2004 there would be only nine working pits left in the UK. There were 180,000 miners in 1984; in early 2004 there were 6,000 in 12 working pits.
    There is a case for seeing the miners' strike, which was linked with the Communist Party of Great Britain and the USSR, as a Soviet-based "Rockefellerite" attempt to intrigue a revolution in Britain through the use of flying pickets in order to seize and control North-Sea oil.

21. Decommissioning commenced on the following dates for these nuclear power stations in the UK: Windscale (1981); Berkeley (1988–89); Hunterston A and Winfrith (1990); Trawsfyndd (1993); Dounreay (1994); Hinkley Point A (2000); and Bradwell (2002). Decommissioning was due to take place on Dungeness A and Sizewell A (2006). There were 12 other nuclear power stations in the UK waiting to hear their fate. See: http:// www.iee.org/Policy/Areas/EnvEnergy/Nucdec.pdf.

22. *Daily Mail*, October 24, 2003, reports "a suggestion by the German defence ministry that Britain hands control of its nuclear weapons to Europe." For Germany's wish to create a fully fledged European army, see *Daily Telegraph*, October 24, 2003. See: http:// www.kc3.co.uk/~dt/eu_army.htm.

23. For Franco-German proposals for a planning headquarters for a European army outside NATO, see *EU Weekly News*, November 30, 2003. Also, Chirac's determination to create an EU military HQ separate from NATO, *International Herald Tribune*, October 22, 2003. For reports on both articles, see: http://www.kc3.co.uk/~dt/eu_army.htm.

24. For one of the reports that the German military high command want to create a fully fledged European army reporting to a European Union government and financed by the European Parliament, see: http://www.telegraph.co.uk/news/main.jhtml?xml=/news/2003/10/24/weu24.xml. The report revealed a memorandum written by senior German army officials on the future of European defense. Blair had denied that there were any plans to create a unified EU military force.

25. See BBC News, October 29, 2002: http://news.bbc.co.uk/1/hi/programmes/newsnight/archive/2372175.stm.

26. There was considerable speculation in the informed press that Blair would move from being Prime Minister of the UK to President of Europe.

27. Widely reported in the British press. For example the *Daily Telegraph*, Thursday October 16, 2003, front-page headlined story: "The Queen is growing more concerned about Tony Blair's plans to sign a European constitution that she fears could undermine her role as sovereign. The *Daily Telegraph* has learnt that Buckingham Palance has asked for documents highlighting the constitutional implications of the EU's plans to be sent to her advisors ... It is believed that the Palace's concerns focus on whether the Queen's supreme authority as the guardian of the British constitution, asserted through the sovereignty of Parliament, could be altered or undermined by article 10 of the draft text." Article 10 states: "The constitution and law adopted by the union's institutions in exercising competences conferred on it shall have primacy over the law of the member states." The caption under a photo of the Queen stated: "Sources say she has sought independent advice on the EU plans." The Queen was said to be unhappy with plans to get rid of the Lord Chancellor's role as part of constitutional reform (see two paras below). See http://news.bbc.co.uk/1/hi/uk_politics/3499702.stm.

28. Buckingham Palace stated, "We will be consulted in due course." For the removal of "Crown" from the Crown Prosecution Service, see BBC News, http://news.bbc.co.uk/1/hi/uk_politics/3529125.stm. Blair denied the change was a snub to the Queen. However Her Majesty's Prison Service was also renamed the National Offender Management Service, and Conservatives claimed Labour had a republican agenda.

   See *Portman Papers*, October 2002, p. 12. A constitutional expert David Bourne argues that the UK of England, Northern Ireland, Scotland and Wales, the basis of the Throne of the Queen, is not the same as the UK within the EU in which England (nine regions), Northern Ireland, Scotland and Wales (one region each) make up 12 regions. Within the EU England is not a state, region, or administrative unit of the EU and therefore has no status or existence within the EU. Therefore the Throne of Great Britain and Northern Ireland does not exist. On this argument the Queen became an ordinary European citizen when the Maastricht Treaty was signed. The root cause of this situation was the signing of the Treaty of Rome and the passing of the European Communities Act 1972, which, according to Judge Morgan surrendered British sovereignty to the EU. It was asserted in *Portman Papers*, October 2001, "Since John Major established offices to vet the Queen's mail ... she does not get to know anything the politicians do not want her to know." And: "Unless the Queen can be made to retract the Treaty of Accession (signed around January 17, 1972), which she will not do, then England is no more."

29. On April 9, 2001 in Sunderland, district Judge Bruce Morgan found Steve Thoburn, a market greengrocer, guilty of selling bananas by the pound. He said Britain now operated under a "new legal order." The 1972 European Communities Act intentionally surrendered parliament's sovereignty to the primacy of European law and the European courts. "Every national court must now set aside any national law which conflicts with Community law." He said that all the commentators on the British legal system represent "yesteryear" and now only describe a "none-binding historical perspective." See http://users.aol.com/footrule/bananas.htm. Also, see note 28.

30. Widely reported in the British press. Sir John Kerr was listed as a participant at the Trilateral Commission's 2002 meeting at the Ritz Carlton Hotel, Washington. See *American Free Press*, April 22, 2002. See http://www.guardian.co.uk/eu/story/0.7369.1102711.00.html for Gisela Stuart's attack on Sir John Kerr for refusing to produce some key legal texts in English, or doing so at the last minute. In the House of Lords, Lord Hurd, disagreeing with Gisela Stuart's remarks, said that the picture Stuart painted was of "a constitution, parts of which she describes as utter nonsense, being railroaded through with minimal debate by Giscard d'Estaing and a narrow clique." See http://www.parliament.the-stationery-office.co.uk/pa/1d199900/ldhansrd/pdvn/lds03/text/31210-07.htm.

31. See *The European Spider's Web.... Welcome to Hitler's Europe, 50 years on!*: http://iaehv.nl/users/lightnet/world/awaken/spider.html.

32. Letwin was reported to have acted as go-between. He visited Davis, who was next door to him, and came away with a message for Howard that Davis would not be standing. He contributed to giving Howard a clear run by establishing that, or fixing that his main rival, Davis, would not be opposing him.

33. See note 32.

34. The UK has recorded a current account deficit in every year between 1984 and 2003. Since Britain's accession in 1973, its visible trade with other EU members has been in deficit for every year except two. Cumulatively there has been an adverse balance of £94.123b from 1973 to 1994. See table below:

Year	Exports	Imports	Balance
1973	3,739	5,138	−1,399
1974	5,546	7,680	−2,134
1975	6,227	8,734	−2,507
1976	8,936	11,194	−2,258
1977	11,674	13,606	−1,932
1978	13,348	15,863	−2,515
1979	18,084	20,767	−2,683
1980	21,467	20,709	+758
1981	21,938	21,899	+39
1982	24,267	25,590	−1,323
1983	27,955	30,799	−2,844
1984	32,961	36,427	−3,466
1985	37,899	40,460	−2,561
1986	34,725	43,584	−8,859

Year	Exports	Imports	Balance
1987	38,880	48,537	−9,657
1988	40,678	54,440	−13,762
1989	47,025	62,422	−15,397
1990	54,193	64,089	−9,896
1991	58,684	59,215	−531
1992	60,569	64,017	−3,448
1993	64,165	68,156	−3,991
1994	70,750	74,507	−3,757

Deficit during the period: −94,123

Invisible trade (sea and air transport, travel, financial, and other services) has shown a surplus over the same period of £21.318b. From 1985 to 1994, the UK had an overall trade deficit with other EU members of £89b; contributed $30b to the EU budget; lost at least £68b as a result of ERM membership between October 1990 and September 1992; and paid 8% of its GDP to meet Brussels directives. For all the figures in this note, see http://www.bullen.demon.co.uk/cibbb3.htm. These figures are an informed commentator's reflection of the Treasury Pink Book: B. Burkitt, University of Bradford, at this website. They are less authoritative than Treasury Pink Book data as they are an interpretation. Also see note 36.

35. Figure widely reported in the British press. The September deficit (£3.9b) reflected a £63m gap in the trade in oil, the first time since August 1991 that the UK imported more oil than it exported. See BBC News: http://news.bbc.co.uk/1/hi/business/3260045.stm; and *Guardian* website for November 11, 2003: http://money.guardian.co.uk/print/

36. According to the Treasury Pink Book 2003, the British current account balance with the EU showed a record deficit of £15.5b in 2002. See http://www.statistics.gov.uk/downloads/theme_economy/Pink_Book_2003.pdf. While the UK has consistently had a trade deficit with the member states of the EU, it has had a current account surplus with the USA every year since 1992, and had a record surplus of £12.2b in 2002. For the £27.323b, see the following table of Britain's payments to and receipts from the EU:

Year	Payments	Receipts (£ million)	Balance
1973	187	83	−104
1974	186	153	−33
1975	350	400	+50
1976	474	299	−175
1977	750	376	−374
1978	1,364	533	−831
1979	1,606	658	−948
1980	1,767	1,062	−705
1981	2,174	1,777	−397
1982	2,862	2,259	−603
1983	2,976	2,328	−648
1984	3,201	2,545	−656
1985	3,759	1,914	−1,845
1986	2,792	2,216	−576
1987	4,049	2,345	−1,704
1988	3,525	2,183	−1,342
1989	4,431	2,116	−2,315

Year	Payments	Receipts (£ million)	Balance
1990	4,658	2,183	−2,475
1991	3,308	2,766	−542
1992	4,856	2,823	−2,033
1993	5,442	3,291	−2,151
1994	5,462	3,254	−2,208
1995	7,682	3,665	−4,017
1996	6,721	4,373	−2,348
1997	6,258	4,661	−1,597
1998	8,712	4,115	−4,597
1999	7,117	3,479	−3,638
2000	8,433	4,241	−4,192
Total	63,991	36,668	−27,323

For the other calculation, see the following table of gross and net contributions to the EU:

1999 Figures in £ m at current prices	2000	2001
Gross contributions by Britain to the EU	10,524	10,719	9,557
Abatement	3,176	2,084	4,560
Gross contribution	7,446	8,635	4,997
Receipts from EU			
Agricultural support	2,747	2,916	2,830
Regional & social support	719	1,975	1,439
	3,466	4,781	4,268
Net contribution to EU	3,882	3,854	729

Both these tables can be found on: http://www.bullen.demon.co.uk/indy54.htm. These figures, by B. Burkitt, University of Bradford, are less authoritative than the Treasury Pink Book data; they represent an informed commentator's reflection of the Treasury Pink Book.

37. Once the new European constitution has been ratified by all 25 member states, British oil and gas will be under the jurisdiction and allocation of Brussels. Oil and natural gas exploration will be tendered out and many contracts can be expected to go to American-owned multinationals.

38. A word-of-mouth claim to the author from a well-placed witness in the independence movement.

39. In 1984 besides traveling to London Gorbachev visited Paris, where he was initiated into French Grand Orient Freemasonry. Daniel, *op. cit.*, pp. 518–9.

40. Otto von Habsburg held the Sionist title "King of Jerusalem." See Church, *op. cit.*, pp. 215–231; and Baigent et al., *The Holy Blood and the Holy Grail*, p. 409. Quoted in Daniel, *op. cit.*, p. 346. John Coleman, *Black Nobility Unmasked*, audio cassette, 1984; quoted in Daniel, *op. cit.*, p. 472.

41. Daniel, *op. cit.*, p. 516. By 1989 there were reports from France that Gorbachev planned to reopen Masonic lodges inside the Soviet Union and satellite states. See Texe Marrs, "Gorbachev and Masonry," *Flashpoint*, September 1990, p. 2: "Both of the top Masonic organizations in France, the Grand Orient ... and the Grand Lodge ... are now working

on this high priority project."

42. Texe Marrs, "Gorbachev and Masonry," *Flashpoint*, September 1990, p. 2; quoted in Daniel, *op. cit.*, p. 472.

43. Georgia Anne Geye, "After six years, Mikhail Gorbachev left office and achieved greatness," *Longview News Journal*, January 1, 1992, p. 4-A; quoted in Daniel, *op. cit.*, p. 519.

44. See Christopher Story, *The European Union Collective* for exploration of the ideas in this paragraph.

45. Malachi Martin, *Interview with the New American*, September 6, 1997. See: http:// kenraggio.com/Krpn-Gorbachev_PresidumtoPresidio.htm: "As early as April of 1991, (Gorbachev's) American friends and sponsors had set up the non profit nucleus for that (Gorbachev) Foundation, calling it the Tamalpais Institute of San Francisco ... (in) May of that year (they held) a fund-raising dinner at New York's Waldorf-Astoria. There, in the presence of Henry Kissinger, officials of the Rockefeller Brothers Fund, the Carnegie Endowment for International Peace, the Ford Foundation and the Pew and Mellon Funds all pitched in with a guarantee to supply the Gorbachev Foundation with its start up bankroll of $3.05 million." Before Gorbachev left office, plans for his future role were in hand. Malachi Martin states in the same interview: "It is my opinion ... that the USSR didn't disintegrate naturally but was ordered to collapse. Gorbachev was told to vacate his powerbase, and also to inform other leaders of the Soviet bloc nations to do likewise. Those orders came from the Capstone." For the Capstone, see note 4 in ch 14.

46. The Forum was convened in San Francisco on September 27, 1995. See http://www. crossroad.2to/text/articles/gorb10–95.html. For Brzezinski's words, see http://www. cipherwar.com/info/tools/new_world_order.htm.

47. *Spotlight*, April 22, 1996, pp. 4–5. A photo accompanying a full article shows Russian Prime Minister Viktor Chernomyrdin speaking to the media after meeting with leaders of major Russian commercial banks at the Moscow Interbank currency exchange. The caption states: "Sources have told *The Spotlight* Chernomyrdin and David Rockefeller are secret partners in Russian energy combines." For the "give-away prices," compare the "price worth" (authorized capital stock) with the "price paid" for the various assets. Of the Gazprom deal, the article states: "The lucky partners behind this bargain buy are reportedly David Rockefeller and Chernomyrdin, who made the deal through a syndicate front." Lukoil and United Energy Systems were sold to unidentified Western speculators/international investors. Chase Manhattan Bank was mentioned in the same paragraph as Lukoil. Neither the financial details nor the identity of the winning bidders for the state property auctions were officially made public in Russia.

48. See note 47.

49. Gazprom, a state gas concern, was privatized in February 1993. In February 2003 the company's authorized capital stock totaled $3.72b. The Russian government owned 38.37% of the shares and foreign shareholders owned 11.5% of the shares. 44.3% of the shares were divided among 500,000 companies and private shareholders.

50. The Rothschilds supported Rhodes to form De Beers; see Gorden Le Sueur (Rhodes' confidential secretary), *Cecil Rhodes, The Man and His Work*, p. 10. Edmond de Rothschild

owned 10% in De Beers mining in South Africa. See http://www.whale.tp/b/sp/ rothschild.html#35. In addition to Chase Manhattan's link with "Rothschilds" through the Bilderberg Group, De Beers was linked with "Rockefellers" through the CFR, which De Beers supported. See http://www.ewtn.com/library/BUSINESS/ANTDEBRS.HTM.

51. See Robert E. Ebel, "The History and Politics of Chechen Oil," *Caspian Crossroads Magazine*: http://ourworld.compuserve.com/homepages/usazerb/3.htm.

52. Yugoslavia was "kicked out" of the IMF in 1992 and cut off from the World Bank in 1993 for its role in the Balkan wars and its refusal to pay back loans. See http://news.bbc. co.uk/1/hi/world/europe/1080895.stm.

53. See Karen Talbot, "Former Yugoslavia: The Name of the Game is Oil!": http://icpj.org/ yugoslavia.html.

54. See http://www.btinternet.com/~nlpwessex/Documents/balkansUSbackterrorism.htm for Gen. Jackson (quoted in *Italian Daily*, April 13, 1999), p. 6, and for 750,000 barrels a day (*Guardian*, February 15, 2001), p. 4. Also see note 53.

55. See note 53.

56. See note 53.

57. See note 53. Also Michel Chossudovsky, "America at War in Macedonia": Emperor'sClothes. com.

58. For further details, see Norris McWhirter and Rodney Atkinson, *Treason at Maastricht*, pp. 118–125.

8. The United States of the Middle East

1. Arnold Toynbee, *America and the World Revolution*, lectures delivered at the University of Pennsylvania in 1961.

2. See http://www.eurorealist.co.uk/eurorealist/NWOchronology/part2.html, which gives a chronology for the development of the New World Order from 1962 to 1996. Adolf Hitler had said, "National Socialism will use its own revolution for the establishing of a new world order." Nelson Rockefeller had been echoing Hitler. Rockefeller's 1968 speech was made to the International Platform Association at the Sheraton Park Hotel in New York. See http://www.100777.com/node/view/22.

3. The March 30, 1989 opening date is on the Louvre's own website, http://www.louvre. or.jp/louvre/presse/en/activities/archives/anniv.htm. The Louvre pyramid and the new Opera Bastille together commemorated the 200th Anniversary of the French Revolution, see http://www.parisianhotels.net/history/htm.

4. Daniel, *op. cit.*, p. 670.

5. Daniel, *op. cit.*, p. 675. The windowpanes of the pyramid are of triangular glass, and there are said to be 666 in all (*Insight Magazine*, July 3, 1989). In fact, there are 673 – see note 13 in ch 15.

6. Speech to a joint session of Congress, September 11, 1990; quoted in Daniel, *op. cit.*, p. 705.

7. Answer to a question about punishing Saddam Hussein for invading Kuwait on the way to Brussels; quoted in Daniel, *op. cit.*, pp. 705–6.

8. The quotations in this paragraph are in Daniel, *op. cit.*, p. 706.

9. Quoted in Daniel, *op. cit.*, p. 706.

10. Daniel, *op. cit.*, p. 705.

11. Mark Curtis, *The Ambiguities of Power*; quoted in "Oil a powerful and profitable business," *The Spark*, September 20, 2000,: http://home.clear.net.nz/pages/wpnz/spt20.oooil. htm.

12. See note 11.

13. See Dan Armstrong, *The Third World War (Unpayable Debt and the International Credit Cartel)*: http://quixote-quest.org/resources/Feedback/WWWIII_globalecon_042300. html.

14. See note 11.

15. Norman Livergood "The New US-British Oil Imperialism": http://www.hermes-press. com/impintro1.htm.

16. See note 15.

17. Antony Sutton and Patrick M. Wood in *Trilaterals Over Washington*, vol. ii, p173, state: "The Shah was induced to invest his funds (estimates range from $1/_2$b to $25b) with Chase Manhattan." According to Jack Anderson, a syndicated columnist, in December

1979 "Rockefellers" helped plan the August 1953 CIA *coup* in Iran that installed the Shah, who, out of gratitude, deposited huge somes of cash in the Chase Manhattan bank. See http://www.wealth4freedom.com/wns/sprpt/rockefeller.htm. David Rockefeller's bank profited from the Shah's deposits. When the Shah was ousted in January 1979, Khomeini's government ordered $6b to be withdrawn from Chase Manhattan bank. Rockefeller and Kissinger were appalled by Carter's treatment of the Shah, who had to move from Egypt to Morocco to Mexico to the US to Panama, before returning to Egypt to die in 1980. See http://www.consortiumnews.com/archive/xfile4.html.

18. See note 17.

19. See note 15.

20. See note 15.

21. The Shah was later of the view (in several interviews) that President Carter wanted his removal. Carter was "Rockefellers" nominee, and so it is likely that reports of the 1979 Bilderberg Group's meeting endorsing Khomeini are correct. "Rockefellers" and Kissinger believed the Shah was badly treated, being drummed from pillar to post by Carter when ill, but they were still responsible for contributing to the change, which they no doubt soon regretted. See http://www.consortiumnews.com/archive/xfile4.html.

22. The transfer was made electronically to the Bank of England under Executive Order no. 12277 signed by Jimmy Carter, on January 23, 1981. The Bank of England then made the transfer to Iran.

23. The planned pipeline seems to have been through Afghanistan and Pakistan to the coast, whence the oil could be shipped. This would have replaced the flow of Russian oil through Iran, which Khomeini had stopped. See notes 15 and 16.

24. See note 15.

25. See note 16 in ch 6; Perloff, *op. cit.*, p. 158; Rivera, *op. cit.*, p. 200. Jimmy Carter's career took off after he had dinner with David Rockefeller in London in the autumn of 1973. See Rivera, *op. cit.*, p. 198.

26. Engdahl, *op. cit.*, pp. 190–1.

27. See note 23.

28. Coleman, *Diplomacy by Deception*, pp. 36–7.

29. See note 15. Coleman, *Diplomacy by Deception, op. cit.*, p. 37.

30. Coleman, *Diplomacy by Deception, op. cit.*, pp. 38, 43.

31. Coleman, *Diplomacy by Deception, op. cit.*, p. 40.

32. "Oil sector to have vital role in rebuilding of Iraq": http://www.gasandoil.com/goc/company/cnm31818.htm.

33. See Richard Sale, UPI intelligence correspondent, "Saddam key in early CIA plot," http://www.upi.com/view.cfm?StoryID=20030410–070214–6557r. Sale claims that Saddam was part of a CIA-authorized six-man assassination squad.

34. For the 3 million figure see Anna Badkhen, *San Francisco Chronicle*, April 2, 2003,

http://www.redding.com/hold/20030402hold059.shtml. For the 2 million figure, see David Pryce-Jones, *National Review*, April 21, 2003, http://www.findarticles.com/cf_0/m1282/7_55/99624005/p1/article.jhtml: "Ruling a population of some 22m, he himself is already responsible for the death of between 1and 2m of them, almost literally decimation, with another 4m driven into exile." Other sources suggest a truer figure is 2 million. For the $500m worth of arms a year, see http://www.thirdworldtraveler.com/Iraq/SlowMotionHolocaust_Iraq.html.

35. At the Shah's request, Saddam had forced Khomeini to leave Najaf, where he was subverting the Shah's regime in 1978. In power, Khomeini targeted the Shi'ites in Iraq. Eying Iranian and Iraqi oil, the Syndicate-backed US and British governments sided with Saddam against Iran's clerical extremism. All through the summer of 1980, newspapers carried reports that Iraq was planning an attack on Iran "to teach Khomeini a lesson." According to Anthony Parsons (then UK Permanent Representative to the UN), in *Cold War to Hot Peace*, p45, no one at the UN tried to prevent war between Iraq and Iran. Khomeini had taken hostage the staff of the American Embassy in Tehran, and there was no sympathy with Iran – rather, covert encouragement of Iraq, including Western supply of arms to Saddam. After Saddam abrogated the 1975 agreement with Iran, the Security Council did not meet for some days. A senior Iraqi official spoke of a *blitzkrieg* that would last only a few days. See Engdahl, *op. cit.*, p. 238: "Washington had secretly encouraged Saddam Hussein to invade Iran in 1980, falsely feeding him intelligence data indicating early success."

36. Kissinger said this in 1984, see: http://www.technocracyinc.org/periodicals/natechnocrat/v2–3/oilandblood.html. For the £500m, see: http://www.thirdworldtraveler.com/Ronald_Reagan/Irangate/Israel_TICC.html.

37. In August 1985 the Israeli government approached the US and offered to act as an intermediary by shipping 508 American-made TOW anti-tank missiles to Iran in exchange for the release of the Rev. Benjamin Weir, an American hostage held by Iranian sympathizers in Lebanon. In January 1986 Reagan approved a plan whereby an American intermediary would sell arms to Iran in exchange for the release of the hostages, with profits funneled to the Contras ($30m) – the Iran-Contra Affair. See http://en.wikipedia.org/wiki/Iran-Contra_Affair. Also http://encarta.msn.com/encyclopedia_761573296/iran_contra_affair.html for the $30m. Also http://www.consortiumnews.com/archive/collin10.html for Gen. Colin Powell's role in supplying Saddam Hussein's military with American-designed equipment that boosted Iraq's air mobility.

38. Engdahl, *op. cit.*, p. 238.

39. Coleman, *Diplomacy by Deception, op. cit.*, p. 46.

40. Coleman, *Diplomacy by Deception, op. cit.*, p. 46. See p52 for the $5.5b. Coleman gives the loan figure as $2.1b whereas Engdahl, *op. cit.*, p239 gives it as $2.3b.

41. Coleman, *Diplomacy by Deception, op. cit.*, p. 47.

42. See http://www.firethistime.org/contempchrono.htm.

43. See note 42.

44. In 1988 Iraq owed around $65b to various creditors, mainly Kuwait and Saudi Arabia. See

Engdahl, *op. cit.*, p. 238. For the $17b debt see http://www.odiousdebts.org/odiousdebts/index.cfm?DFP=content&ContentID=6996. For Iraq's complaint that Kuwait was stealing Iraqi oil by slant-drilling, see http://www.deoxy.org/wc/wc-consp.htm. Also see http://www.thirdworldtraveler.com/Iraq/SlowMotionHolocaust_Iraq.html. See note 57 for slant-drilling.

45. Coleman, *Diplomacy by Deception, op. cit.*, p. 49. The $500m due in May 1990 was a separate loan from the $365m loaned in 1983.

46. Coleman, *Diplomacy by Deception, op. cit.*, p. 49. See Robert Gates, director, CIA: 'Testimony Before the House Armed Services Committee Defence Policy Panel', March 27, 1992: http://www.fas.org/irp/congress/1992_hr/h920327g.htm for a retrospective look at Iraq after the Gulf War: "We believe Iraq also retains some mobile Scud missile launchers and as many as several hundred missiles." Gates's attitude to Saddam before the war is apparent.

47. Coleman, *Diplomacy by Deception, op. cit.*, pp. 49–50.

48. Coleman, *Diplomacy by Deception, op. cit.*, p. 50.

49. See http://www.thirdworldtraveler.com/Iraq/SlowMotionHolocaust_Iraq.html. Coleman, *Diplomacy by Deception, op. cit.*, p. 50.

50. Coleman, *Diplomacy by Deception, op. cit.*, p. 50.

51. Coleman, *Diplomacy by Deception, op. cit.*, p. 51.

52. Coleman, *Diplomacy by Deception, op. cit.*, p. 51.

53. Coleman, *Diplomacy by Deception, op. cit.*, p. 51.

54. For the $61b figure, see BBC News, February 7, 2003: http://news.bbc.co.uk/1/hi/business/2737057.stm. This BBC website claims that the US was reimbursed for about 90% of its costs by its allies, including South Korea. Also see: http://www.prudentbear.com/archive_comm_article.asp?category=International+Perspective&content_idx=31358 for the $7b figure. This website claims that Japan contributed $13b, while Saudi Arabia, the UAE, Kuwait, Germany and other American allies contributed a total of $54.1b.

55. See http://www.firethistime.org/contempchrono.htm.

56. See http://www.firethistime.org/contempchrono.htm for all the figures. The Soviet Union received $1b from Saudi Arabia and $4b in loans and emergency aid from Saudi, Kuwait and UAE. China received a loan of $140m. The US paid the UN $187m, half the debt it owned the UN in unpaid dues. See the same website for the 52–47 vote and the number of men.

57. See http://www.csun.edu/~vcmthoom/iraqkuwait.html. For the 90%/10% ownership of the Rumaila oilfields see http://www.thirdworldtraveler.com/Iraq/SlowMotionHolocaust_Iraq.html.

58. A billionaire assisting the Rothschilds in supplying money to the Bank of England told me in a face-to-face meeting that he had seen the figure of $2b on a screen, and that the entry made it clear that the payment was to stop the war. I have no reason to doubt

that he was telling the truth, but his story must remain a "rumor" in the absence of documentary substantiation.

59. See note 57.

60. See Perloff, *op. cit.*, pp. 94–5. The Declaration was written by Henry Steele Commager of the CFR and sponsored by the World Affairs Council of Philadelphia.

9. The Middle East Rebellion

1. In Latin, "*Qui desiderat pacem, praeparet bellum.*" Vegetius, *De Re Mil.* 3, pol. (fourth century AD).

2. See Peter L. Bergen, *Holy War Inc: Inside the Secret World of Osama bin Laden*, pp. 49–50, for these details of SBG's trading. Bergen assembles his information from IPR Strategic Business Information, July 12, 2000: www.saudi-binladen-group.com/news.htm; www. middle-east-online.com/English, April 24, 2001; agence France-presse, September 14, 1998; *Washington Times*, September 15, 1998. By the mid 1990s, SBG was worth $5b. See Chris Blackhorst, *The Independent on Sunday*, September 16, 2001, p. 7 for some details in previous para. which came from unprecedented access to private dossiers, friends, and family. Bergen states that Osama was his father's seventeenth son; it has also been stated that he was the seventh son. I have gone with Bergen, whose research is impressive.

3. The Carlyle Group and its management of FBG were covered in several issues of the *American Free Press* and summarized in *Portman Papers*, January 2003, p. 12, which presents the involvement of Bush Sr. and Major.

4. Bergen, *op. cit.*, pp. 48–9; *American Free Press*, October 15, 2001, pp. 1, 3. Also *Daily Mail*, September 24, 2001, pp. 3–4.

5. Bergen, *op. cit.*, p. 49; see note 4.

6. See note 4.

7. See "Al-Qaeda's origins and links," http://news.bbc.co.uk/1/hi/world/1670089.stm. Al-Qaeda, meaning 'the Base', was created in 1989 as Soviet forces withdrew from Afghanistan and Osma bin Laden and his associates sought new jihads. Bergen, *op. cit.*, pp. 55, 204–9; Blackhorst, *The Independent on Sunday*, September 16, 2001.

8. See note 7.

9. Bergen, *op. cit.*, pp. 82–3. Al-Themar was located at its Al-Damazine farms.

10. See Sherman H. Skolnick, "America's Reichstag Fire," for this allegation: http://www. world-action.co.uk/reichstag.html: "It is a serious mistake ... to blame the Emergency all on Osama bin Laden ... Bin Laden is reportedly in the Mid-East Construction business. His reputed partners? The family of Sharon Percy Rockefeller."

11. See note 7.

12. See note 7. Also "Inside Al-Qaeda's Secret World," *Washington Post*, December 23, 2001, http://www.washingtonpost.comac2/wp-dyn/a17716–2001Dec22?language=printer, which states that bin Laden became an important benefactor to the Taliban: "By some US accounts he gave $100m to the Taliban over five years." For the view that Osama had "a few million at most," see Blackhorst, *The Independent on Sunday*, September 16, 2001. For the $35m figure and the loss of $150m in 1996, see Bergen, *op. cit.*, pp. 104–5, serialised in the *Daily Telegraph*, November 12, 2001, p. 15.

13. See http://www.telegraph.co.uk/news/main.jhtml?xml=/news/2001/12/02/wkando2. xml.

14. For bin Laden's poppy revenues see Adam Robinson, *Bin Laden: Behind the Mask of Terror.*

15. See *Irish Examiner*, "Atta met bin Laden at Afghan camp in '99'," September 11, 2002, http://archives.tem.ie/irishexaminer/2002/09/11/story578692886.asp.

16. For the $800,000 a month, see Jason Burke, the *Observer*, September 23, 2001, pp15–16. For the $1b from heroin deals, see Simon Reeve, *The New Jackals*, extracted in the British press, e.g. *News of the World*, September 16, 2001. Also see note 14.

17. Mick Fielding, *Sunday Times*. For the $200m Saudi deal with bin Laden, see http://www.foxnews.com/story/0,2933,61257,00.html. The $1 trillion lawsuit was filed in August 2002 by the 900 relatives of September 11 victims against members of the Saudi royal family, Saudi banks and Islamic charities, alleging funding of al-Qaeda terrorist training in Afghanistan. Saudi-Arabian princes are alleged to have paid bin Laden and the Taliban $200m to spare targets in Saudi Arabia.

18. Mullah Omar changed the name of Afghanistan to the Islamic Emirate of Afghanistan on October 27, 1997. See http://www.ace.unsw.edu.au/PEOPLE/rmjc/fotw/flags/af_talib.html. It has been reported in the British press that bin Laden demanded the change of name, but there is scanty documentary evidence. The *Sunday Telegraph*, September 16, 2001. See also "Bin Laden British cell planned gas attack on European Parliament," http://www.papillionsartpalace.com/binladenB.htm.

19. Article in *Sunday Times*, June 2, 2002, p. 21.

20. Many of the facts in this section were taken from press reports that appeared during the duration of the war. For Omar being in mountains near Baghran, see: http://www.time.com/time/world/article/0,8599,191890,00.html.

21. For reference to 1683, see Christopher Hitchens, "Why the suicide killers chose September 11," *Guardian*, October 3, 2001, http://www.guardian.co.uk/Archive/Article/0,4273,4269059,00.html.

22. Many of the facts in the rest of this chapter were taken from press reports that appeared during the duration of the war.

23. See biographical details of Kofi Annan, http://abcnews.go.com/reference/bio5/annan.htm

24. See BBC News, "The cost of the Iraq war: One year on," April 8, 2004, http://news.bbc.co.uk/1/hi/business/3603923.stm, which reports that the US Congress had, by April 2004, allocated $162b on invading and then rebuilding Iraq. The US military operations so far cost $143b, projected military operations $150b-300b. Reconstruction so far cost $33b; projected reconstruction was $50b-100b. Extra security would cost $40b-80b. The cost of the occupation would be more than double the cost of the war, adding $150b-300b to the initial $162b.

But see *American Free Press*, June 23, 2003, p. 9, "The unbearable cost of running Iraq." The plan presumably assumed that savings in US expenditure on oil and subsidies to Israel would recoup the war losses – and guarantee a flow of oil for the next 150 years. In the event, the turbulent situation in Iraq promised a long and costly entanglement, with troops forced to remain indefinitely, with escalating costs of reconstruction. Interest payments (to the Federal Reserve/Syndicate) on the cost of the war would be borne by the next two or three generations, and this in a time of mounting debt and deficits.

25. *The Times*, December 11, 2002, p. 3.

10. Doubts on September 11

1. Spenser, *The Faerie Queene*, bkv, cxxxviii.

2. Many of the facts in this chapter were taken from press reports that appeared during the duration of the war.

3. Widely reported in the Western Press. For example by William Lowther in Washington, *Daily Mail*, May 18, 2002, headlined "US had plan to topple bin Laden before Sept 11." The plan to remove bin Laden, dated September 10, 2001, was drawn up by White House foreign policy advisors after weeks of warnings of an imminent terrorist attack. It was "placed on Condoleezza Rice's desk for Bush to review." Lowther wrote: "The White House said it recommended thwarting bin Laden 'through work with the Northern Alliance to dismantle al-Qaeda and the Taliban.' The memo outlined a £140m CIA programme to arm the Northern Alliance and other anti-Taliban forces."

   Also see section headed *CIA? How much did the CIA know in advance?* below. On April 8, 2004, Condoleezza Rice, when questioned by the congressional hearing, held that Bush Jr. did take al-Qaeda seriously and that although there was a warning on 6 August that al-Qaeda wanted to attack America it was not specific and no one appreciated the scale of the coming attack in the absence of specific information. The Presidential Daily Briefing of August 6, 2001 reported "patterns of suspicious activity in this country consistent with preparations for hijackings or other types of attacks, including recent surveillance of federal buildings in New York". Its publication marked the first time in US history that a sitting president published one of his daily intelligence briefings. The plan on her desk on September 10 may have been a response to the warning of August 6. Rice denied having seen any reports about al-Qaeda using a plane as a weapon until after September 11. See: http://www.guardian.co.uk/uslatest/story/0%2C1282%2c-3963357%2C00.html.

   According to the *American Free Press* of November 11, 2002, p. 14, the US government said it was a "bizarre coincidence" that a US intelligence agency had planned a mock plane-into-building crash on September 11 – that a training 'exercise' was overlaid with a lethal scheme. In the same way Yitzhak Rabin, the former Israeli prime minister, was assassinated during a security exercise. The target of the US exercise was the National Reconnaissance Office building, which was set to conduct an emergency drill in which a simulated plane from Dulles International Airport four miles away crashed into it. A plane heading towards a tall building might have been thought to be taking part in the exercise. It was very convenient for those involved in the planning of the September-11 attacks that this exercise was scheduled on the same day.

4. See *American Free Press*, November 5, 2001, p. 1, "Evidence Planted?" Also *American Free Press*, December 24, 2001, p. 12, "Were the 9–11 hijackers really Arabs? Maybe not."

5. For the figures ($500,000 and $100,000), see David Rose, "The Iraqi Connection," in the *Observer*, November 11, 2001, pp. 15–16, which also deals with Atta's meeting with al-Ani. Bin Laden is alleged (by Parisoula Lampsos, one of Saddam's six mistresses) to have visited Saddam in the 1980s and again in the 1990s. Bin Laden's deputy Ayman al-Zawahiri is alleged to have dined with Saddam in 1998, after which bin Laden recruits received advance weapon training under Saddam's son, Uday, and 400 "Afghan Arabs" were sent to fight Kurds. Saudis from bin Laden's Wahhabi sect were housed in the

foreigners' camp at Salman Pak, Baghdad. Such meetings may be significant; on the other hand, they may have no more significance than gossip.

6. Roger Cohen, "World Trade Center – History Commentary": http://www.greatbuildings. com/buildings/World_Trade_Center_History.html. The New York Legislature created a World Trade Corporation in 1946 to explore the possibilities for a Trade Center in Manhattan. The idea was shelved when the Corporation focused on the New York waterfront. David Rockefeller revived the idea. From his 60–story headquarters of the Chase Manhattan Bank, he proposed the formation of the Downtown-Lower Manhattan Association, which retained an architectural partnership to make drawings. Rockefeller sent a DLMA report to Mayor Wagner and his own brother Nelson, New York's Governor; also to New Jersey Governor Robert Meyner. The Port Authority of New York and New Jersey took up David Rockefeller's suggestion that they should be involved. David Rockefeller insisted that the Trade Center should be in Lower Manhattan and be built by the Port Authority, and when eventually the Port Authority sought a major tenant Governor Rockefeller announced a consolidation of state offices in 1.9m square feet of space in the Trade Center. David and Nelson Rockefeller were crucial to the building of the World Trade Center. The Port Authority could not have built the Twin Towers without the two brothers, after whom they were jokingly nicknamed. Hence the informal dedication of the Twin Towers to them. In an interview with the *Daily Telegraph* of November 18, 2002, p. 15, David Rockefeller said, "I watched them go up and, unfortunately, I also watched them go down."

7. Sherman H. Skolnick, *US Government Prior Knowledge of Emergency, 9.11.2001,* www.skolnicksreport.com/pkem.html.

11. Doubts on Iraq: A Military Strategy?

1. See Christopher Bollyn, *American Free Press*, December 30, 2002, pp. 1, 7 for the PNAC plan and all the PNAC figures in this paragraph, including a Pentagon spokesman's statement that $17.5b of the initial $40b allocation went to defense. For the source for the $40b and $17.5b, described as "about $18b," provided in the fiscal year of 2002, see http://www.csbaonline.org/4Publications/Archive/B.20020124.us_Funding_for_Hom/B.20020124.us_Funding_for_Hom.htm.

   For Pearle's resignation and its link to the bankrupt Global Crossing telecommunications firm, which was set to pay him $725,000 for lobbying work he had done, see *American Free Press*, April 7, 2003, p. 10.

2. See *Disarmament Diplomacy*: www.acronym.org.uk for all the defence budget figures in this paragraph. Many facts in this chapter were reported in the Western press.

3. For the scrapping of Lukoil's $3.7b deal, see Michael Bunter, "Iraq: The Petroleum Exploration and Production Handbook": http://www.gasandoil.com/goc/company/cnm35000.htm. For the $20b, see Livergood, "The New US-British Oil Imperialism," *op. cit.*: http://www.hermes-press.com/impintro1.htm.

4. See BBC News: http://news.bbc.co.uk/1/hi/world/europe/320234.stm.

5. For the $3 trillion Israel costs the US taxpayer each year, see *American Free Press*, June 16, 2003, p. 17. The Mosul-Haifa pipeline originates near Kirkuk. Its reopening would benefit Israel, cutting the country's fuel costs by 25% and turning Haifa into "the Rotterdam of the Middle East." It would provide the US with cheap reliable access to Iraq's cheap, high quality oil. It would harm Turkey, for since the fall of Saddam, a large part of Iraq's oil exports were transported through Turkey to the Mediterranean. Turkey collected transit fees. See: http://www.cooperativeresearch.org/wot/iraq/mosulhaifapipeline.html. In 1997 Chalabi was introduced to Richard Perle, then undersecretary of defense for international security. The two have been close since then. See: http://www.prospect.org/prints/v13/21/dreyfuss-r.html.

12. The Pay-off

1. Rivera, *op. cit.*, pp. 182–3. Many of the facts in this chapter were reported in the Western press.

2. Afghanistan has 91 minerals, metals and gems at 1,407 documented potential mining sites. Its minerals include gold, silver, uranium, beryllium, copper, chrome, lead, zinc, manganese, iron and nickel. Beryllium is used in the nuclear industry infusion reactors and in constructing nuclear military weapons. It is in demand in the aerospace, energy, defense, nuclear, automotive, medical, and electronics industries. Afghan gemstones include an abundance of the following: lapis lazuli, amethyst, beryl, ruby, emerald, sapphire, alabaster, tourmaline, jade, and quartz. Rubies and sapphires are used in lasers for advanced weapons and military targeting systems.

3. See: http://www.newsfrombabylon.com/article.php?sid-69. Also see: http://www. hermes-press.com/impintrol.htm.

4. See note 3.

5. Christopher Andersen, *George & Laura*, a tongue-in-cheek but well-researched look at the Bushes. Extracted in *Daily Mail*, February 5, 2003.

6. See note 5.

7. See note 5.

8. The $80b figure is approximate. It includes $70b requested for the development of new weapons systems, $7.8b for research, development and testing, including the development of a minimal missile defense system in Alaska, and a number of other requests. These amounts are within the US defense budget for 2003 and following years. Ultimately, as with all federal deficits, the Federal Reserve System footed the bill, to the benefit of the Syndicate.

   See U.S. Gov Info/Resources, www.usgovinfo.about.com/library/weekly.

   The Pentagon requested $7.7b for missile defense spending in 2004. The total program, spanning several years, has been estimated at $80b. The initial capabilities include: up to 20 ground-based interceptors capable of intercepting and destroying ICBMs in mid-air located at Fort Greely, Alaska (16 interceptors) and Vandenberg Air Force Base, California (four interceptors); up to 20 sea-based interceptors on existing Aegis ships to intercept ICBMs in the first few minutes after they are launched; air-transportable Patriot Advanced capability-3 (PAC-3) systems to intercept short and medium-range ballistic missiles; land, sea and space-based sencors, including existing early warning satellites, upgraded radar now located at Shemya, Alaska, a new sea-based X-band radar, upgraded existing early warning radars in the UK and Greenland and use of radars and other sensors now on Aegis cruisers and destroyers. There will be additional ground-and-sea-based interceptors and PAC-3 units; a Theater High Altitude Area Defence System to intercept short and medium range missiles at high altitude; Airborne Laser aircraft to destroy ballistic missiles in the boost phase; and other interceptors, radars, sensors and space-based defences with kinetic energy (hit to kill) interceptors and advanced target-tracking satellites. See *Disarmanent Diplomacy*, www.acronym.org.uk, issue no 69, Feb-March 2003, News Review, put out by the Acronym Institute.

9. US Gov Info/Resources, see: http://usgovinfo.about.com/library/weekly/aso20402b. htm for all the figures in this paragraph.

10. The CIA analysis and news of China's hundred long-range missiles were covered in the London *Times* of January 10, 2002. China acquired the primary ports on the Atlantic and Pacific coasts of the Panama Canal through the Hong Kong Co-based Hutchison Whampoa Ltd., whose chairman Li Ka-shing was a business partner of the Riady family, friendly to both Clinton and Beijing's ruling *élite*. See: http://www.insightmag.com/news/199/12/27/Symposium/Q.Should.Congress.B.Concerned.About.China.And. The.Panama.Canal–208357.shtml. The Atlantic port is named Cristobal, the Pacific port Balboa. Hutchison Whampoa, under Article 2.8, is allowed to transfer contract rights to any third party registered in Panama and can extend its leases until 2047. Clinton admitted that China would control the Panama Canal after December 31, 1999. See: http://www.rense.com/general10/chinn.htm. See this same website for details of Hutchison Whampoa's dredging and expansion of the port at Freetown on the island of Grand Bahama, 60 miles from Florida, to enable it to handle the largest container ships in the world. Hutchison is building a massive naval facility there. The Bahamas port is the largest container terminal in the world. For China's leasing of the Longbeach Naval Station in California, see: http://www.nationaudio.com/News/EastAfrican/29102001/Business/Business13.html. News of the Panama and Bahamas arrangements was carried in the *American Free Press*.

11. See: http://globalpublicmedia.com/SECTIONS/ENERGYoil.north-korea.php.

13. The United States of Africa

1. *"Ex Africa semper aliquid novi."* Pliny, (AD 23–79), *Historia naturalis.*

2. See BBC News, 'United States of Africa?', July 11, 2000,: http://news.bbc.co.uk.1.hi/world/africa/829060/stm, which covers Gaddafi's role in the 2000 meeting.

3. Interestingly, according to a British press report Gaddafi drew a circle in sand and put a point in the middle to demonstrate his view of dictatorial democracy: the Leader as point surrounded by the people, an equidistant circle. The point within a circle is a well-known Illuminatist Masonic symbol. What was Gaddafi doing drawing an Illuminatist symbol in the Libyan sand?

4. The number of Rwandan refugees is variously given as 1.1 million – see Pan African Movement: http://www.panafricanmovement.org/Banyamul.htm; 1.2 million – see UN HCR: http://www.unhcr.ch; and 2 million – see Amnesty International: http://www.oneworld.org/amnesty/reports/rwa_bur/1.html. For a clear account of the tangled events that led up to Lumumba's murder, see Griffin, *Fourth Reich of the Rich, op. cit.,* pp. 148–151. For Ché Guevara's role in installing Lumumba, see the *Militant* article covered in note 91 of ch 6.

5. *Daily Telegraph* report, April 6, 2004, p. 14.

6. See: http://print.infoplease.com/ipa/AO198161.html.

7. See: http://www.mbendi.co.za/indy/oilg/af/zr/p0005.htm.

8. For the 2.5 million figure, see: http://print.infoplease.com/ipa/AO198161.html, p. 3, para 3.

9. See Mark Fineman, "The Oil Factor in Somalia," January 18, 1993: http://www.netnomad.com/fineman.html.

10. See note 9.

11. See: http://www.gasandoil.com/goc/company/cna11088.htm. Also *The Somaliland Times*: http://www.somalilandtimes.net/Archive/39/3902.htm.

12. The oil reserves in Nigeria are thought to have been inflated as oil companies' estimates of untapped reserves attract tax breaks from the Nigerian government. A system designed to encourage exploration has resulted in a systematic overstatement of Nigerian reserves, according to reports in the British press in March 2004.

13. See Smith, "Technological Capability in Oil Refining in Sierra Leone": http://web.idrc.ca/en/ev-30786-201-1-DO TOPIC.html.

14. See BBC News, "Britain's Role in Sierra Leone," September 10, 2000: http://news.bbc.co.uk/1/hi/special_report/1999/01/99/sierra_leone/91060.stm.

15. Monica Moorhead, "Why Bush Wants Troops in Liberia": http://www.iacenter.org/liberia_bush.htm, p. 3.

14. The Syndicate Today

1. Perhaps through the creation of the Committee of 300 in the 1890s; see ch 3, note 94.

2. Churchill visited Baruch in 1929 and wrote to him again in 1939. See ch 5, note 40.

3. Details of all the Bilderberg meetings described below were revealed in *The Spotlight* and its successor *The American Free Press*.

4. Armstrong, *op. cit.*, pp. 26–34, identifies five Rothschild "monarchs": King Rothschild I (Amschel); King Rothschild II, (Nathan, 1812–1836); King Rothschild III (Baron James, 1836–1868); King Rothschild IV (Baron Alphonse D.); and King Rothschild V or VI (Jeroboam Rothschild, alias Georges Mandel). In the nineteenth century the Rothschild "monarchs" were said to be wealthier than all the crown heads of Europe put together.

5. It is reported that "Rothschilds" are the capstone of the Masonic pyramid with a Council of Five. In 1992 it included Guy de Rothschild, Evelyn de Rothschild, George Schultz, Robert Roosa (a Rockefellerite from George Bush Sr.'s family firm of Brown Brothers Harriman, leaving one position unfilled. Averill Harriman and Victor, Lord Rothschild occupied seats before they died. See Mullins, *The World Order, op. cit.*, p. 273. It is also reported that beneath the Council of Five, who rule the world for "Rothschilds" is a private priesthood, a Council of 13 called the Grand Druid Council. See John Todd, *The Illuminati and Witchcraft*, lectures given at a Bible Baptist church, Elkton, Md, USA, in the autumn of 1978. Coleman, *Conspirators' Hierarchy: op. cit.* Near this is the Order of the Golden Dawn, which has always been Rothschilds' private coven. This structure is entirely Freemasonic.

6. The "Rothschildite" Council of Five has a rival, which also claims to run the world. The Templar Freemasons (Order of the Temple) call themselves a "Secret Brotherhood" and are headed by a "Rockefellerite" Council of Nine. See Texe Marrs, *Dark Majesty, The Secret Brotherhood and the Magic of A Thousand Points of Light*, Living Truth Publishers, 1992, pp. 18, 28–31, which mention most of the names in the rest of this note. The Nine are represented by the nine tail feathers of the hybrid eagle-phoenix on the obverse of America's Great Seal. They are reputed to possess more power and authority than any other body in history. They do not want to be named. Marrs reports that in the mid-1980s the nine men included: George Bush Sr.; David Rockefeller; Zbigniew Brzezinski; Averell Harriman (who died in 1986); Henry Kissinger; Brent Scowcroft; and Mikhail Gorbachev. The unfilled places may have been held at different times by Victor, Lord Rothschild (who died in 1990); Lord Carrington, then Chairman of the Bilderberg Group; the Head of the Priory of Sion; and even Pope John Paul II, who planned for the Vatican to become the leading global authority in the New World Order and described Bush Sr. as a "servant of the Council of Wise Men" (another name for the Council of Nine) – see Malachi Martin, *The Keys of This Blood*. The publisher was then located in Rockefeller Center.

7. See ch 3, note 94.

8. In the Rainbow portrait, Elizabeth I's cloak is scattered with eyes and ears, suggesting her claims to a French ambassador to know everything that happened in her kingdom. See Alan Haynes, *Invisible Powers. The Elizabethan Secret Service, 1570–1603*, p. xii, for the

portrait, which hangs in Hatfield House, see http://jack-of-all-trades.ca/meandmine/ ab16.html. Hatfield House was the seat of the Cecils, the most notable of whom was Lord Burleigh, Elizabeth I's spymaster. In the twentieth century "double-O" meant "license to kill." For example, "In *Casino Royale*, Bond earns his double-O designation – his license to kill – by shooting a Japanese cipher expert at the Rockefeller Center in New York" (Stephen Dorril, *MI6, Fifty Years of Special Operations*, p. 610). Bond's designation was "license to kill – 7," and the Tudor pattern has been overlaid.

9. See ch 1, note 21.

10. See gold-eagle: http://www.gold-eagle.com/editorials_99/goldfinger062999.html.

11. "Rockefellers" used to be financially dependent on the "Rothschilds," who could at one time have asked the US government to pay back a tranche of stock indebtedness to Federal Reserve banks, which by 2004 had increased to around $7.5 trillion. Over the years there appears to have been a shift to "Rockefellers." According to Standard and Poor, 53% of the shares in the Federal Reserve System are owned by the Rockefeller banking group; 8% are held by the Bank of Japan; and nine other shareholders own some 4% each: the Rothschild Bank, London; the Rothschild Bank, Berlin, Lazard Brothers Banks of Paris; Israel Moses Seif Banks of Italy; the Warburg Bank of Hamburg; the Warburg Bank of Amsterdam; Lehman Brothers Banks of New York; Kuhn, Loeb Bank of New York; and Goldman Sachs Bank of New York. On this view Rothschilds own no more than 10% of the Federal Reserve System shares. To sum up, Americans own 66%, Europeans 26% and Japanese 8%. See note 9.

The above list was adopted in 1991 by Gary Kah (in his book *En Route to Global Occupation*). However, the Federal Reserve Act of 1913 requires that all nationally chartered banks should buy stock in their regional Federal Reserve Bank, thereby becoming "member banks." Member stock can only be held by banks and is related to size, the largest banks holding the largest stock. The law does not permit non-Americans and non-bank firms to own shares in any Federal Reserve Bank. The New York Federal Reserve Bank itself reported that on June 30, 1997 the top eight stockholders were the following US-owned, nationally or state-chartered banks: Chase Manhattan Bank; Citibank; Morgan Guaranty Trust Company; Fleet Bank; Bankers Trust; Bank of New York; Marine Midland Bank; Summit Bank. If the same principle governs the Federal Reserve System, then there could not be European and Japanese ownership. See Dr. Edward Flaherty, "Do Foreigners Own the Federal Reserve?": http://www.alphalink. com.au/~noelmcd/lostlink/own.htm for all the facts in this paragraph.

It has been claimed by (Kah and Thomas D. Schauf) that huge profits from the Federal Reserve System and Federal Reserve Bank of New York have been diverted to non-Americans through dividends paid to stockholders, that non-Americans may own American banks. Kah holds that Rockefellers and their allies direct America's fiscal and monetary policies through the Treasury Department and the Federal Reserve System, making US economic policies synonymous with their own.

The truth is, the Syndicate is fully in charge of both the above lists of owners. Chase Manhattan and Morgans are names that keep cropping up in relation to the Syndicate. The Federal Reserve System is a privately operated system, with a net profit in 1995 of $23.9b. Of this, 97.9% was paid to the Treasury; the Federal Reserve Banks kept $283m, and paid $231m to the Federal Reserve System's stockholders as dividends. There is still room for enormous Rockefeller/Syndicate influence. See Thomas D. Schauf, "The

Federal Reserve is Privately Owned": http://www.worldnewsstand.net/today/articles/
fedprivatelyowned.htm.

12. See ch 2, note 21. For the higher figure of $14–15 trillion, see *American Free Press*, March
    17, 2003, pp. 10–11. Also see Pastor Sheldon Emry, "Billions for the Bankers, Debt for
    the People": http://www.libertydollar.us/money-control-in-america.html where the 1918
    figure is dated as 1910, and the 1974 figure 1981.

13. Federal Reserve Bank of New York press release February 3, 2003: http://www.
    newyorkfed.org/newsevents/news/research/2003/rp020205.html.

14. Compare ch 11, note 2. These marginally higher figures reflect an upward revision. For
    the 50,000 figure see: http://www.kambiahospital.org.uk/information_about/sierra_
    leone.htm.

15. Krieg, *July 4th 2016, The Last Independence Day, op. cit.* Many facts in the rest of this
    chapter were reported in the Western press.

16. A campaign has begun to amend the American constitution to allow a person who was
    not native-born to become president. Its purpose is to allow the Austrian-born Arnold
    Schwarzenegger, new Republican Governor of California, to be elected as president. It
    has been revealed (in the *American Free Press* of November 24, 2003) that Lord Rothschild
    is behind the campaign. One member of the Rothschild family is thus promoting the
    Democrat Hillary Clinton, another member the Republican Schwarzenegger.

15. The United States of the World

1. BBC News: http://news.bbc.co.uk/1/hi/world/europe/2005658.stm.

2. See Griffin, *Fourth Reich of the Rich, op. cit.*, pp. 159–162, which show pictures of Zeus in the UN lobby and of the meditation room shaped like a pyramid laid on its side.

3. The plan is usefully reprinted in Stan Deyo's *The Cosmic Conspiracy* (1992 edition), pp. 197–200.

4. There are oil reasons for the inclusion of Mexico. Oil was an issue in Mexico in 1912, when civil war broke out, as a result of which Gen. Obregon gained control of Mexico City and installed Venustiano Carranza as President. ("Rockefellers" Standard Oil had run guns and money to Carranza, and had given him $100,000 in cash and fuel credits.) He produced a constitution that maintained that oil was a resource of the Mexican people, which came as a shock to Standard Oil and Lord Cowdray's companies. A tax was imposed on American companies trading in Mexican oil. Cowdray sold his shares to Royal Dutch Shell, and following fighting Carranza was killed and replaced as President by Gen. Obregon, who, though supported by the US, taxed all oil exports 60%. Obregon was assassinated in 1928. The Mexican government then cancelled the 1918 decrees that declared Mexican oil a resource of the Mexican people, and by 1936 17 foreign companies were pumping Mexican oil. In 1936 Pres. Cardenas nationalized the subsoil rights of Standard Oil and other American and British companies, including Royal Dutch, which now opposed Cardenas. They boycotted Mexican oil, and Cardenas sent oil to Germany, Italy and Spain. In 1947 there was a settlement, and in 1970 a further settlement at the instigation of the CFR in which President Nixon and the Mexican President settled all past oil disputes. In fact America continues to export Mexican oil. The North American Free Trade Agreement (NAFTA) would allow oil to pass from Mexico to the United States.

5. See ch 4, for a more detailed view of the American Union.

6. See ch 4 for details of the United States of Europe, the United States of the Middle East and the United States of Africa.

7. See ch 4 for details of the Asian-Pacific Union, which is being prepared through various trade organizations.

8. Mullins, *op. cit.*, pp. 56–7. Belgium raised five major loans between 1830 and 1844 totaling some 300m francs, almost all of which were underwritten by the Rothschilds. See Ferguson, *op. cit.*, pp. 411–2.

9. Many facts in the rest of this chapter have been taken from reports in the Western press.

10. Martin Taylor, Honorary Secretary-General of the Bilderberg Group, in conversation with Nicholas Hagger.

11. Krieg, *July 4th 2016, The Last Independence Day, op. cit.*

12. Daniel, *op. cit.*, pp. 346, 670.

13. For the 673, see the Louvre website, http://www.louvre.or.jp/louvre/presse/en/activities/

archives/anniv.htm. For the view that there are 666 panes of glass, see Daniel, *op. cit.*, p. 675, quoting Helle Bering-Jensen, "Glass tipped atop a National Treasure," *Insight*, July 3, 1989, pp. 58–9. I have gone with the Louvre's own website. The seven additional panes may be a compromise between the Council of 5 and the Council of 9 – see notes 5 and 6 in ch 14. Between 1989 and 1999 over 50 million people visited the Louvre pyramid.

14. *Global 2000 Report to the President* (British Library book reference no. X.520/29289).

15. *Global Future: Time to Act, Report to the President on Global Resources, Environment and Population* (British Library book reference no. AS410/130, held in Boston Spa), made recommendations to the US government on the basis of the *Global 2000 Report*.

16. *Executive Intelligence Review's Special Report* by Vin Berg.

Recently revealed Defense Intelligence Agency (DIA) reports show that UN sanctions would put the Iraqi civilian population at risk. A report of January 1991 stated that the banning of chemicals and equipment would make drinking water unsafe, resulting in epidemics. A second DIA report listed lack of water, electrical and waste disposal systems, and distribution of preventative medicines, as likely causes of epidemics in urban areas. It predicted child diseases. The third report dated March 1991 noted an increase in gastrointestinal and respiratory diseases in children and that drinkable water had been reduced to 5% of prewar supplies. See "Genocide as Practical Policy" in "Slow Motion Holocaust" by Stephanie Reich, *Covert Action Quarterly*, Spring 2002, http://www.thirdworldtraveler.com/Iraq/SlowMotionHolocaust_Iraq.html, which argues that the US attack on Iraq's civilian population was "deliberate and calculated."

17. In 1991 the UN made the American Cyrus Vance the UN Secretary-General's Personal Envoy to Yugoslavia and entrusted him with the task of bringing about a cease-fire and introducing a UN peacekeeping force into Croatia at the end of the fighting. The UN then appointed him and the British Lord Owen as "Co-Chairmen of the Steering Committee," to be joint UN/EC negotiators. Vance and Owen were unable to secure a peaceful settlement for a long while. It is interesting that Vance, who was so identified with population control in 1980–1 should be entrusted with stopping the killing in former Yugoslavia in 1991–3.

18. *Executive Intelligence Review's Special Report, op. cit.*, p. 1.

It is worth considering the context of contrived depopulation. According to census records recently discovered in the Kremlin, Hitler's operation Barbarossa resulted in 49 million Soviet dead alone – see *Barbarossa, The Axis and the Allies*, ed. by John Erickson and David Dilks, pp. 256–8, which puts up the numbers killed in the Second World war from 36 to 60 million (including 18 million Soviets) to 67 to 90 million. Bearing in mind that the Second World War figures are higher than shown, and that we are not including recent genocides such as the 4 million killed in the Great Lakes regions of the Congo, we can list the 32 worst atrocities of the twentieth century as follows (see http://users.erols.com/mwhite28/atrox.htm):

	Death Toll	Event	Dates
1	50,000,000*	Second World War (Some overlap w/Stalin. Includes Sino-Japanese War and Holocaust. Doesn't incl. post-war German expulsions)	1937–45
2	48,250,000	China: Mao Zedong's regime (incl. famine)	1949–76
3	20,000,000	USSR: Stalin's regime (incl. WW2–era atrocities)	1924–53
4	15,000,000	First World War (incl. Armenian massacres)	1914–18
5	8,800,000	Russian Civil War	1918–21
6	4,000,000	China: Warlord & Nationalist Era	1917–37
7	3,000,000	Congo Free State [n.1]	1900–08
8	2,800,000	Korean War	1950–53
9	2,700,000	2nd Indochina War (incl. Laos & Cambodia)	1960–75
10	2,500,000	Chinese Civil War	1945–49
11	2,100,000	German Expulsions after WW2	1945–47
12	1,900,000	Second Sudanese Civil War	1983–
13	1,700,000	Congolese Civil War	1998–
14	1,650,000	Cambodia: Khmer Rouge Regime	1975–79
15	1,400,000	Afghanistan: Civil War	1980–
15	1,400,000	Ethiopian Civil Wars	1962–92
17	1,250,000	Mexican Revolution	1910–20
18	1,250,000	East Pakistan: Massacres	1971
19	1,000,000	Iran–Iraq War	1980–88
19	1,000,000	Nigeria: Biafran revolt	1967–70
21	800,000	Mozambique: Civil War	1976–92
21	800,000	Rwandan Massacres	1994
23	650,000	French–Algerian War	1954–62
24	600,000	First Indochina War	1945–54
25	500,000	India–Pakistan Partition	1947
25	500,000	Indonesia: Massacre of Communists	1965–67
25	500,000	Angolan Civil War	1975–94
25	500,000	First Sudanese Civil War	1955–72
25	500,000	Decline of the Amazonian Indians	1900–99
30	365,000	Spanish Civil War	1936–39
31	350,000	Somalia: Civil War	1991–
32	Unknown	North Korea: Communist Regime	1948–

*See note 83 in ch 5 for more accurate figures.

We can get a feel for specific genocides that have contributed to depopulation during the twentieth century: (see Genocide Watch, http://www.genocide.org/genocidetable.htm):

NATION	YEARS OF EPISODES SINCE 1945	CUMULATIVE CIVILIAN DEATH TOLL AFRICA	MAJOR KILLERS	MAIN DIVISIONS	STAGE in 2002
Burundi	1959 – 1962 1972 1988 1993 – 1995 1996 – present	50,000 Hutus 150,000 Hutus 25,000 Hutus 50,000 Tutsis, 100,000 Hutus 2001: 5,000	Tutsi government Tutsi army Tutsi army Hutu rebels Tutsi army	Ethnic, political	7 – Genocidal massacres
Sudan	1956 – 1972, 1983 – present	2 million Nuer, Dinka, Christians, Nuba, southerners 2001: 10,000 2004: 300,000?	Khartoum gov't NIF government, militias, rebels	Political, religious, racial, ethnic	7 – Politicide, Genocide
Democratic Republic of the Congo	1945 – 1960 1960 – 1965 1977 – 1979, 1984 1994 – 1997 1998 – 2002	1,000s Africans 1,000s civil war 1,000s civil war 80,000 Hutus, Banyamulenge, 10,000 Hema,Lendu 2 million (civil war) 2001: 80,000	Colonial forces Rebels, army Rebels, army Kabila/ Rwandan army, Ugandan, Rwandan armies, rebels, DRCongo & allied armies	Racial, colonial, economic Political, ethnic	7 – Politicide, Genocidal massacres
Côte d'Ivoire	1998 – present	100s Bambara, Senoufo, Bété, Burkinabe	Gov't police, rebels	Ethnic, national, Religious, political	7 – Massacres
Algeria	1954 – 1963 1991 – present	160,000 OAS, Harkis, settlers 50,000 Berbers 2001: 5,000	French legions, OAS, rebels Islamic Armed Group (GIA)	Colonial Religious, political	7 – Massacres
Liberia	1990 – 2000 2001 – present	100,000 Krahn, Gio, Mano, etc. 2001: 1,000s	Doe gov't army, Taylor rebels Gov't, rebels	Political, ethnic	7 – Politicide
Uganda	1972 – 1979, 1980 – 1986 1994 – present	300,000 Acholi, Lango, Karamoja 250,000 Baganda, Banyarwanda 1,000s LRA foes 2001: 100s	Amin gov't army, police Obote gov't army, police Lord's Resistance Army	Political, ethnic, religious	7 – Massacres
Nigeria	1966 – 1970, 1972 – 2000 (sporadic) 2001 – present	1 million Ibos Tiv, Hausa, Yoruba Ogoni, others 2001: 1,000s	Nigerian army Ethnic mobs Nigerian army, police	Political, ethnic, religious	6 – Preparation

NATION	YEARS OF EPISODES SINCE 1945	CUMULATIVE CIVILIAN DEATH TOLL	MAJOR KILLERS	MAIN DIVISIONS	STAGE in 2002
Zimbabwe	1982 – 84, 1998 – present	20,000 Ndebele, MDC, white farmers 2001: 100s	Gov't army 5th Brigade, ZANU-PF militias	Ethnic, political	6 – Preparation
Somalia	1988 – present	100,000 Somalis, Isaaq clan 2001: 100s	Warlord/clan militias	Political, clan	6 – Preparation
Sierra Leone	1991 – present	100,000 (civil war) 2001: 1000s	Revolutionary United Front, other militias	Political, ethnic	5 – Polarization
Rwanda	1959 – 1963, 1993 1994 1995 – present	10,000s Tutsi 800,000 Tutsi 1,000s Hutus 2001: 100s	Hutu gov't Hutu Power gov't *Interahamwe* Rwandan gov't	Ethnic, political	5 – Polarization
Congo-Brazzaville	1959 – 1968 1997 – 2000	5,000 Gov't foes 1,000s (civil war)	Gov't army, police, rebels	Colonial Political, ethnic	5 – Polarization
Central African Republic	1966 – 1979 2001	2,000 Bokassa foes	Gov't army, police	Political, ethnic	5 – Polarization
Ethiopia	1945 – 1974 1974 – 1979 1994 – 2000	150,000 Oromo, Eritreans, Somali 750,000 Class enemies, Oromo 10,000s (war with Eritrea)	Selassie monarchy Derg communists Army	National, religious, ethnic	5 – Polarization
Eritrea	1960s - 2000	10,000s Eritreans (independence war with Ethiopia)	Ethiopian armies, police	National, religious, ethnic	4 – Organization
Equatorial Guinea	1975 – 1979	50,000 Bubi, Nguema foes	Macias Nguema regime	Political, ethnic	4 – Organization
Senegal – Casamance	1990 – 2001	1,000 Diola (civil war)	Senegalese army, rebels	Political, ethnic	4 – Organization
Kenya	1952 – 1960 1991 – 1993	1,500 Kikuyu, colonials 1,000s Nilotics	Colonial forces MauMau Kikuyu Ethnic militias	Ethnic, political	4 – Organization
Angola	1961 – 1962 1975 – present	40,000 Kongo, 500,000 Umbundu, Ovimbundu 2001: 5,000	Colonial army Gov't, UNITA armies, allies	Colonial Political, ethnic	4 – Organization
Chad	1965 – 1996	10,000s southern Saras, civil war	Gov't army, Libyan army, rebels	Ethnic, racial, religious, political	4 – Organization

NATION	YEARS OF EPISODES SINCE 1945	CUMULATIVE CIVILIAN DEATH TOLL	MAJOR KILLERS	MAIN DIVISIONS	STAGE in 2002
Morocco- Western Sahara	1976 – present	1,000s: Sahrawis	Moroccan army, Polisario rebels	Political, ethnic	4 – Organization
Mali	1990 – 1993	1,000 Touaregs	Malian army, Touareg rebels	Ethnic, political	4 – Organization
Mozambique	1975 – 1994	1 million by MPLA, Renamo	Renamo, MPLA	Political, ethnic	4 – Organization
Madagascar	1947 – 1948	50,000 Malagasy nationalists	French colonial forces	National, racial, political, ethnic	4 – Organization
South Africa	1987 – 1996; 1996 – present	1,000s Zulus, Xhosa, ANC Boer farmers	Gov't police, ethnic militias; ethnic militias	Racial, political, ethnic	4 – Organization
Botswana	1990 – present	100s Kūng, Caprivi Namibians	Gov't police	Economic, political, ethnic	4 – Organization
Egypt	sporadic	100s Copts	Moslem funda-mentalists	Religious, political	4 – Organization
AMERICAS					
Colombia	1948 – 1958; 1975 – present	150,000; 10,000s; 2001: 1,000s	Political parties; Marxists, rightist death squads, drug cartels	Political; Political, narcotics cartels	7 – Politicide
Venezuela	1945 – 1970s,	1,000s Yanomami	Settlers, miners	Racial, ethnic	5 – Polarization
Brazil	1945 – 1964; 1964 – 1965 sporadic massacres	300,000 Vargas foes, Indians; 1,000s: Kayapo, Yanomami, etc.	Gov't police, settler militias; Settlers, miners	Political, economic, racial, ethnic	4 – Organization
Guatemala	1950s –1980s	200,000 Mayans	Gov't army, death squads	Racial, ethnic, political	4 – Organization
Cuba	1945 – 1959; 1959 – present	100s rebels; 75,000 "counter – revolutionaries"	Rightist gov'ts; Castro gov't	Political	4 – Organization
Argentina	1976 – 1980	20,000 leftists	Army, police	Racial, ethnic; Political	4 – Organization
Chile	1973 – 1976	10,000s leftists	Army, police	Political	4 – Organization
Nicaragua	1970 – 1979; 1980 – 1989	1,000s Sandinistas; 10,000s Contras	Gov't army; Sandinista army	Political	4 – Organization
El Salvador	1980 – 1992	10,000s leftists	Army, militias	Political	4 – Organization
Paraguay	1945 – 1962; 1962 – 1974	1000s Indians 1000 Aché Indians	Army, settlers Settlers	Racial, ethnic	4 – Organization

NATION	YEARS OF EPISODES SINCE 1945	CUMULATIVE CIVILIAN DEATH TOLL	MAJOR KILLERS	MAIN DIVISIONS	STAGE in 2002
Mexico Chiapas	1945 – 2001	10,000s Indians, gov't foes 10,000s Mayans	Army, police	Ethnic, political	4 – Organization
ASIA					
North Korea	1949 – present	2 million + 2001: 10,000s	Gov't, army, police	Political, class	7 – Politicide
India Kashmir	1947, 1949 – present (sporadic) 1947 – present	100,000s Moslems, Hindus 2001: 100s 2001: 1,000s	RSS mobs Moslem mobs Rebels, police	National, religious, ethnic, political	7 – Politicide, genocidal massacres
Peoples Republic of China	1949 – 1977 1977 – present	35 million "class enemies," religious minorities, Uighurs Moslems, Christians 2001: 1,000s	Maoist communist gov't, PRC army, Red Guards, police executions	Political, national, class, economic, ethnic, religious	7 – Politicide
Sri Lanka	1983 – present	1000s Tamil and Sinhalese civilians 2001: 100s	Anti-Tamil mobs Tamil Tiger rebels	Ethnic, national, political, religious	7 – Politicide genocidal massacres
Burma (Myanmar)	1945 – 1948 1948 – 1962 1962 – 1978 1979 – present	1,000s rebels 15,000 rebels, govt 100,000 Shan, Moslems, Karen, Christians 2001: 100s	Burma Ind Move U Nu govt, rebels Burmese gov't SLORC gov't	Ethnic, political, religious	7 – Politicide, genocidal massacres
Indonesia	1965 1966 – present	500,000 communist 10,000s: Aceh 1,000s: Irian Jaya 1,000s: Moluccas 1,000s: Sulewesi 2001: high 1000s	Suharto gov't Suharto gov't & successors Laskar Jihad Laskar Jihad	Political, ethnic Religious, political Political, religious, ethnic, national	7 – Politicide, genocidal massacres
Philippines	1972 – present	1,000s pro-gov't officials, separatists, communists	Marxists, gov't Army, Moros, Abu Sayyef	Political, religious	7 – Political massacres (by terrorists)
Nepal	1996 – present	2,600 anti-Maoists 2001: 100s	Maoist rebels	Political	7 – Political massacres

NATION	YEARS OF EPISODES SINCE 1945	CUMULATIVE CIVILIAN DEATH TOLL	MAJOR KILLERS	MAIN DIVISIONS	STAGE in 2002
Afghanistan	1978 – 1993	700,000 (civil war) 50,000+	Soviets Mujahadin	Political, national, religious, ethnic	6 – Preparation
	1993 – 1996	30,000 (civil war)	Warlords		
	1996 – 2001	50,000+ Tajiks, Uzbeks, Hazara 10,000+	Taliban, Al Queda		
	2001 – present	2001: 10,000s	NorthernAlliance Anti-Taliban		
Uzbekistan Fergana Valley	1991 – present	1,000s 2001: 100s	Moslem funda-mentalists	Political, religious	6 – Preparation
Pakistan East Pakistan: (now Bangladesh) West Pakistan	1947 1971 1973 – 1977 1978 – present	61,000 Hindus 1,500,000 Bengalis & Hindus Sindhis 2001: 100s	Moslem mobs West Pakistani army Army	Political, national, ethnic, religious	6 – Preparation
Tibet	1959 – 1990s	1,600,000 Tibetan Buddhists 2001: 100s	PRC communist Chinese gov't	National, political, religious, ethnic	5 – Polarization
Azerbaijan	1988 – 1994	10,000s Azeris & Armenians	Azeri & Armenian armies	Ethnic, political, religious national	5 – Polarization
Cambodia	1945 – 1966 1966 – 1975 1968 – 1975 1975 – 1979 1979 – 1993 1993 – present	5,000 king's foes 15,000 Vietnamese 360,000 pro-gov't 1.7 – 2.2 million class enemies, Cham Moslems, city people, Vietnamese, Eastern Zone 230,000 (civil war) 1,000s gov't foes 2001: 100s	Royal gov't Lon Nol gov't Khmer Rouge Khmer Rouge Samrin govt,KR Hun Sen gov't	Political, class, ethnic, religious, national	5 – Polarization
French Vietnam South Vietnam North Vietnam	1945 – 1953 1954 – 1975 1954 – 1975	10,000s leftists 90,000 leftists 1 million class enemies, minorities	French colonials South Viet gov't North Viet gov't	Political, class, ethnic, national	4 – Organization
Peoples Democratic Republic Vietnam	1975 – present	10,000s boat people, reeducated	Vietnamese gov't		

NATION	YEARS OF EPISODES SINCE 1945	CUMULATIVE CIVILIAN DEATH TOLL	MAJOR KILLERS	MAIN DIVISIONS	STAGE in 2002
Laos	1945 – 1960 1960 – 1975 1975 – present	10,000s leftists 100,000 anti-communists, Hmong 2001: 100s	Royalists, French Pathet Lao Peoples Democratic Republic	Political, ethnic	4 - Organization
East Timor	1965 – 2000	200,000 Timorese	Indonesian army, militias	Political, ethnic, national, religious	4 – Organization
EUROPE					
Russia –Chechnya	1943 – 1957 1994 – present	50,000 Chechens 2001: 1,000s	USSR army Russian Army	Ethnic, national, religious, political	7 – Politicide, massacres
Yugoslavia: Kosovo	1998 – 2001	10,000 Albanian Kosovars, 100s Serbs	Yugoslav Army KosovoLibArmy	Ethnic, religious, national, political	5 – Polarization
Yugoslavia Croatia Serbia, Bosnia (including 1941–1945 relevant to later conflicts)	1941 – 1945 1941 – 1945 1945 – 1987 1993 – 2001	650,000 Serbs 100,000 Croats, Moslems 1 million Tito foes 1,000s dissidents	Croatian Fascists (Ustashi) Serb Partisans (Chetniks) Tito gov't Milosevic gov't	Political, ethnic, national, religious	8 – Denial 5 – Polarization
Macedonia	1999 – 2001	100s Albanians, Macedonians	Albanian rebels, Macedonia gov't	Political, ethnic	5 – Polarization
Bosnia	1992 – 1998	200,000 Moslems, Croats, Serbs	Bosnian Serbs, Croats, Moslems	Ethnic, religious, national, political	5 – Polarization (partition)
Georgia: Abkhasia	1993 – present	100s Abkhasians 2001: under 100	Georgian army, separatist rebels	National, ethnic, political	5 – Polarization
Northern Ireland	1964 – present	3000 Catholics, Protestants 2001: under 100	Irish Republic Army, Protestant extremists	Religious, class, political, national	5 – Polarization
Croatia	1991 – 1995	50,000 Serbs, Bosnian Moslems	Croat army, militias	Ethnic, national, religious, political	4 - Organization
USSR (State no longer exists.)	1945 – 1953 1945 – 1947	15 million "class enemies" 1 million repatriated Soviet nationals 6 million dissidents	Soviet police, army, NKVD NKVD, KGB secret police	Political, national, ethnic, religious	Not applicable (State no longer exists.)
USSR national minorities, esp. in Crimea, Dagestan Ingushetia	1954 – 1991 1945 – 1991	400,000 Karachai, Meshketians, Balkar Crimean Tatars, Ingushi	Red Army, Secret police	Political, national, religious	4 – Organization

NATION	YEARS OF EPISODES SINCE 1945	CUMULATIVE CIVILIAN DEATH TOLL	MAJOR KILLERS	MAIN DIVISIONS	STAGE in 2002
		MIDDLE EAST			
Israel – Palestine	1948 – 1955, 1956, 1967, 1973, 1987 – 1993	1,000s Israelis, 1,000s Palestinians	Irgun, Arab terrorists, Israeli army, police, Fatah, Hamas	National, religious, ethnic, political	7 – Politicide, massacres
		1,162 Palestinians			
		160 Israelis			
	2000 – present	2001: 240 Israelis, 777 Palestinians			
Iraq	1961 – present	190,000 Kurds, Shiites, Kuwaitis 2001: 1,000s	Iraqi army, presidential guard	Political, ethnic, national, religious	8 – Denial 7 – Genocide Politicide
Turkey	1984 – present	10,000s Kurds 2001: 100s	Turkish army	Ethnic, religious, national, political	8 – Denial 6 – Preparation
Syria	1981 – 1982	21,000 Kurds, Sunni Moslems	Syrian army, police	Political, religious, national	5 – Polarization
Iran	1953 – 1978 1978 – 1992	26,000 Shah foes 60,000 Kurds, monarchists, Bahai	Secret police, Iranian army, revolution guards	Religious, ethnic, political, national	5 – Polarization
Cyprus	1963 – 1967	2,000 Turks, Greek Cypriots	Greek Cypriots Turks	Political, religious, ethnic, national	5 – Polarization (partition)
Lebanon	1974 – 1991	55,000 Christians, Moslems, Druze	Religious militias Hezbollah, Phalangists	Religious, political	5 – Polarization

We can list some specific post-cold-War conflicts in terms of those killed or made refugees as follows:
Order:

Conflict	Date	Killed	Refugees
Somalia	1991–1993	400,000	1 million (1988–94)
Liberia	1989–1996	150,000	700,000 / 750,000
Sierra Leone	1991–1999	50,000	2 million
Burundi	1993	200,000	800,000
Rwanda	1994	800,000	1.2–2 million
Congo	1998–2002	2 million	unknown
Croatia	1991–5	50,000	500,000
Bosnia	1992–5	250,000	4 million (2 million wounded)
Total		3.9 million	10.2m / 8m

It is instructive to look at the wider picture, the world refugee problem. By 1999 the UN High Commission for Refugees listed 21.5 million refugees and internally displaced persons as being of concern. This increased to 21.8 million by 2001. The great majority come from four continents:

Continent	Refugees (millions)	
	1999	2001
Africa	6.2	6.07
Asia	7.47	8.45
Europe	6.2	5.572
North America	1.3	1.047
Others	0.661	
Total	21.17	21.8

These refugees represent 1 in 280 of the world's population.

There are a further 30 million internally displaced persons who are of less concern, making 50 million in all who have been forced to flee from their homes, 1 in 120 of the world's population.

Some figures are immediately striking:

Country	Refugees
Palestine	3.2 million
Afghanistan	2.6 million
Iran	1.9 million
Iraq	631,000
Bosnia/ Herzegovina	597,000
Somalia	525,000
Burundi	517,000
Liberia	437,000
Sudan	351,000
Croatia	342,000
Sierra Leone	328,000
Vietnam	317,000
Total	11.745 million

In the post-war world things were just as bad:

Date	Peoples	Refugees
1945	Ethnic Germans	12.5 million
1945	"Displaced people' from Germany	1.1 million
1945–61	East Germans	3.7 million
c.1948	Arabs from Palestine Jewish sources	419,000
c.1948	Arabs from Palestine Arab sources	1–2 million*
1949	Chinese to Taiwan	2 million
1949	Chinese elsewhere inc. Hong Kong	2.065 million
1947	Hindus from Pakistan/Moslems from India	18 million
by 1960 Moslems from India		9 million
1971	From Bangladesh	10 million
1967	Arab-Israeli war displaced	4 million
1971	Tibetans	760,000
By mid-1972 South Vietnamese		4.5 million
By 1954 North Vietnamese		900,000
Total (highest figures counted)		70.525 million

Genocide and refugeedom were perennial problems in the twentieth century. We do well to ponder how many of the conflicts that led to such misery could have been avoided – and how many were desired from afar.

19. *Executive Intelligence Review's Special Report, op. cit.,* p. 27.

20. See: http://english.peopledaily.com.cn/features/populationpaper/populations.html.

21. IIASA Data – UN Population Projection, 1998 Revision: http://www.iiasa.ac.nt/ Research/LUC/ChinaFood/data/pop/pop_7.htm.

22. David Keys, *Catastrophe,* p. x ("Aims and Caveats"). 500 million were made homeless or displaced in the same disasters.

23. Term used by Coleman in *Conspirator's Hierarchy* (pp. 4, 22, 26, 65, 164) in quotation marks, taken from the Global Reports. For the prominence of the phrase "useless eaters," see Paula Demers, "Eliminate the Useless Eaters," http://www.conceptual.net. au/~jackc/useless.htm, a response to Coleman's *Global 2000: A Blueprint for Global Genocide.*

Epilogue

1. See: http://www.worldnetdaily.com/news/article.asp?_ID=18797. For the Charter's address to the governments of the world, calling on them to be more open and accountable, see Charter 99: http://www.charter99.org/html/thecharter.htm.

2. See World Federalist Association: http://www.wfa.org/issues/.

3. The Commission on Global Governance proposed that the UN should provide: global taxation; a standing UN army; an Economic Security Council; UN authority over the global commons; an end to the veto of Security Council permanent members; a new Court of Criminal Justice (achieved in July 1998 in Rome); binding verdicts of the International Court of Justice; and increased authority for the UN Secretary General. The Commission is not an official body of the UN but is endorsed by the UN Secretary General and funded through two UN trust funds, nine national governments and several foundations. See: http://www.sovereignty.net/p/gov/gganalysis.htm.

4. The Inter-Parliamentary Union was established in 1889 and its members (over 130 national parliaments) support the UN and work in close co-operation with it. See: http://www.ipu.org/english/whatipu.htm.

5. See my epic poem, *Overlord*, for a clash between these two New World Orders: Satan's, championed by Hitler; and Christ's, championed by Eisenhower, during the Second World War. In my poem Satan's/Hitler's New World Order leads to the horrors of Auschwitz.

6. We have seen that Arnold Toynbee was the interpreter for the Luciferian New World Order. My work *The Fire and the Stones*, a study of 25 civilizations, can be seen as an attempt, in a more modest way, to counterbalance Toynbee's *A Study of History*; to act as spiritual interpreter for the Universalist New World Order and perform a function similar – indeed, equivalent – to Toynbee's.

7. Albert Pike's Instructions, issued on July 14, 1889 to the 23 Supreme Councils of Freemasons of the world, recorded by A. C. De La Rive in *La Femme et l'Enfant dans la Franc-Maçonnerie Universelle* (p. 588), quoted in Lady Queenborough, *Occult Theocrasy*, pp. 220-1: "To you Sovereign Grand Instructors General, we say this, that you may repeat it to the Brethren of the 32nd, 31st and 30th degrees: 'The Masonic religion should be, by all of us initiates of the high degrees, maintained in the purity of the Luciferian doctrine. If Lucifer were not God, would Adonay (The God of the Christians) ... calumniate him? Yes, Lucifer is God, and unfortunately Adonay is also God. For the eternal law is that there is no light without shade, no beauty without ugliness, no white without black, for the absolute can only exist as two Gods: darkness being necessary for light to serve as its foil as the pedestal is necessary to the statue, and the brake to the locomotive ... The doctrine of Satanism is a heresy; and the true and pure philosophic religion is the belief in Lucifer, the equal of Adonay; but Lucifer, God of Light and God of Good is struggling for humanity against Adonay, the God of Darkness and Evil.'"

That message was to be given to all Freemasons of 30th degree and above in an initiative organized by Pike and Mazzini. Pike was then Sovereign Grand Commander of the Ancient and Accepted Scottish Rite of Freemasonry; Mazzini was head of the Grand Orient Lodges. A "super rite" was created following Mazzini's letter to Pike of January

22, 1870, a kind of supreme council of all Freemasons who were to be entrusted with the supreme knowledge that Lucifer was the God of Freemasonry. Pike's Instructions can be found in many books published in the twentieth century, including Still, *New World Order, op. cit.*, p. 31 ("Though few Masons know it, the god of Masonry is Lucifer"); Griffin, *Fourth Reich of the Rich, op. cit.*, p. 70; and Texe Marrs, *Dark Majesty, op. cit.*, ch 12. Many books assert that the plan for the New World Order is centered in Illuminated (i.e. Luciferian) Masonry, and have associated the New World Order leaders with the worship of Lucifer, for example Ralph Epperson, *The New World Order*, pp. 293–5 ("George Bush [Sr.] is going to the Great Pyramid in the year 1999 to bring in the millennium reign of Lucifer, a period called the New Age, or the New World Order"); and Pat Robertson, *The New World Order*, p. 37 ("a new order for the human race under the domination of Lucifer"). Also Coleman, *Conspirators' Hierarchy: The Story of the Committee of 300, op. cit.*, p. 21 ("The Olympians ... who have, like Lucifer their god, set themselves above our true God").

8. See Walter Hannah, *Darkness Visible*, p. 109 (*Explanation of the First Degree Tracing-Board*) and 173 (*Address of the Third Chair; the Historical Lecture*). For 'On', see p. 182 (*Address of the First Chair; Mystical Lecture*). Covered in Hagger, *The Fire and the Stones, op. cit.*, pp. 283–4.

9. See note 7.

10. See Daniel, *op. cit.*, pp. 705, 817 for Bush Sr. Templar Freemason – like Bush Jr, a member of the Order of Skull and Bones, and p. 801 for Clinton, English Sionist Freemason, and p. 632 for Ford; p. 706 for David Rockefeller and John D. Rockefeller IV, both members of the Lucis Trust (formerly Lucifer Publishing Co.); and p. 44 for 33rd-degree Freemasons Dole and Jackson. Also p. 550. Founding members of the CFR with no record of being Masons included J. P. Morgan and John D. Rockefeller I, but his sons embraced the Freemasonic New World Order. For all in the list, including those not mentioned above (Gingrich, Gore, and Perot) see Christopher Bollyn in the *American Free Press*, December 16 and 23, 2002: "Archbishop: Freemasonry contrary to Christianity" (on an interview with Britain's Archbishop of Canterbury, Dr. Rowan Williams).

11. Still, *op. cit.*, p. 31.

12. J. M. Church, *Guardians of the Grail*, p. 25. Quoted near the end of Hagger's *The Secret History of the West*.

13. See note 12.

14. Pei's pyramid, which symbolizes the United States of Europe as well as the United States of the World is reputed to include, among its 673 triangular window panes, 666 to reflect the 666 districts or counties of the United States of Europe. See note 5 in ch 8, and note 13 in ch 15.

15. See: http://home.iae.nl/users/lightnet/creator/markbeast.htm.

16. Clarence Hewitt, *The Seer of Babylon*, p. v.

17. Hewitt, *op. cit.*, pp. iv-v.

18. Hewitt, *op. cit.*, p. iv.

19. Hewitt, *op. cit.*, p. v.

20. Hewitt, *op. cit.*, pp. v-vi.

21. Hewitt, *op. cit.*, p. vi

22. Hewitt, *op. cit.*, p. vi.

23. The 12 stars do not correspond with the number of nations in the European Union. They are drawn from the image in Revelation, 12:1, of a woman clothed with the sun with 12 stars on her head for a crown: Semiramis. See Hewitt, *op. cit.*, pp. iv-vi.

24. Illustrated in Icke, *Alice in Wonderland and the World Trade Center Disaster*, p. 8.

25. Icke, *op. cit.*, pp. 7–8.

26. Icke, *op. cit.*, p. 7. The evidence suggests that the September 11 attacks on the Twin Towers were bin Laden's work. The question is, did the Syndicate/CIA know in advance that they had been planned? The Twin Towers may have been designed (with David Rockefeller's input – see ch 10, note 6) with a Masonic model in mind: the Twin Pillars of Atlantis built, according to Masons, by "the children of Lamech," which were erected at the entrance to Solomon's Temple in Jerusalem – Boaz "on the left" and Jachin "on the right" (1 Kings, 7:21; 2 Chronicles, 3:17). See Icke, *op. cit.*, p. 8. There can be no suggestion that the Syndicate ordered the attacks, but it is worth pointing out in passing that the Twin Towers, when set on fire, may have had a significance to occultists. Two smoking pillars constitute an altar, between which (if you take up an appropriate position) stands the Masonic Statue of Liberty/Semiramis with her torch. The torching of the two buildings could (to occultists), be construed as constituting a human sacrifice to Semiramis, bride of Lucifer, or perhaps to Lucifer himself as Moloch-Satan, to whom smoke went via the sky together with the energies of sacrificial victims. Moloch, the god of the anti-Roman Carthaginians, was a god to whom humans were sacrificed. Moloch is the owl-god whose graven image stood in Bohemian Grove, near Santa Rosa, California, where Jon Ronson claims to have seen men reputed to be world leaders dressed in robes and hoods, burning effigies. See his extraordinary account in *Them*, p. 301. The Bohemian Club of California is reputed to be a center for the inner élite of Templar Scottish Rite Freemasonry, whose members include former Secretaries of State George Shultz and Henry Kissinger. It hosted a televised extravaganza on February 3, 1983 in honor of the Queen, who sat on high watching two dancers who wore coned huge hats portraying Babylon (a ziggurat) and London (Big Ben), and a voice bellowed, "Oh Queen, you have traversed the ages from Babylon to London!" See Daniel, *op. cit.*, p. 663. All this is far too preposterous and far-fetched to include in the text – the implication is that the Syndicate torched the Twin Towers in an occult ritual – but such things are being said and written, and mention needs to be made of them.

27. Icke, *op. cit.*, p. 7.

28. After Noah's Flood Lucifer/Satan set up his headquarters in Babylon – see Daniel, *op. cit.*, p. 55. The *York Manuscript* states that Freemasonry originated at Babylon: "At ye makeing of ye toure of Babell there was Masonrie first much esteemed of, and the King of Babilon yt was called Nimrod was a Mason himselfe and loved well Masons" (Mackey's *Encyclopedia*, vol. ii, "Nimrod"). The Tower of Babel at Babylon was the first attempt at creating a world government. See Daniel, *op. cit.*, pp. 640, 20–1. Masons claim that God

destroyed Lucifer's/Satan's one-world government at Babylon by destroying the Tower of Babel. See Daniel, *op. cit.*, p. 43.

29. The whore of Babylon, Semiramis, and the Tower of Babel built by her husband Nimrod, the first priest to Baal, to "turn men from the fear of God" (Josephus, *Antiquities of the Jews*, bk 1, 4:2,3) became symbols in a mystery religion that survived into Roman times, long after Babylon itself had been destroyed. Modern occultists/Freemasons, relating to this mystery religion pilloried by St. John in Revelation, have shown an interest in Iraq as it contains ruins that evoke the mystery religion. For occult interest in Babylon, see Daniel, vol. ii on how the rituals of ancient Babylonian religions are identical to those of Freemasonry.

30. Woodrow, *Babylon Mystery Religion*, pp. 2–4.

31. Hagger, *The Fire and the Stones, op. cit.*, pp. 26–7. For sacred marriage see Kramer, *Cuneiform Inscriptions*, pp. 101ff and Chiera, *Sumerian Ritual Texts*, iv 14ff. These are dealt with in E. O. James, *The Ancient Gods*, pp. 304–5.

32. The tussle remains to turn the world into "Rockefellers" Templar universal republic or "Rothschilds" Sionist universal monarchy under the descendants of the King of Jerusalem.

Appendices

1. Hagger, *The Fire and the Stones, op. cit.*

2. See Krieg, *op. cit.*

3. Francis Fukuyama, *The End of History and the Last Man.*

4. Pierre Lellouche, *Le Nouveau Monde – de L'ordre de Yalta aux chaos des nations*, Grasset, 1992.

5. Hagger, *The Fire and the Stones, op. cit.*, pp. 703–15.

6. Immanuel Wallerstein, "The United States and the World 'Crisis'," in Boswell and Bergesen, eds, *America's Changing Role in the World System*, p. 17.

7. Paul Kennedy, *The Rise and Fall of the Great Powers*, pp. 514–35.

8. Charles Wolf, *America's Decline: Illusion or Reality?*, p. 22.

9. Joseph S. Nye Jr., *Bound to Lead, The Changing Nature of American Power*, pp. 233–7.

BIBLIOGRAPHY

Allen, Gary, *None Dare Call it Conspiracy*, Concord Press, 1972.

Allen, Gary, *The Rockefeller File*, USA: Buccaneer Books Inc., 1998.

Ambrose, Stephen E., *Rise to Globalism, American Foreign Policy since 1938*, Penguin, London, 1971.

Andersen, Christopher, *George and Laura: Portrait of an American Marriage*, Avon Books, 2003.

Armstrong, George, *The Rothschild Money Trust*, Omni Publications, California, 1940.

Baigent, Michael, Leigh, Richard and Lincoln, Henry, *The Messianic Legacy*, Corgi Books, 1986.

Berg, Vin, *Executive Intelligence Review's Special Report – Global 2000: Blueprint for Genocide*, London, August 1982.

Bergen, Peter L., *Holy War Inc: Inside the Secret World of Osama bin Laden*, Weidenfeld and Nicolson, London, 2001/Phoenix 2002.

Bobbitt, Philip, *The Shield of Achilles*, Allen Lane, London, 2002.

Boswell, Terry and Bergesen, Albert, eds, *America's Changing Role in the World System*, Greenwood Press, 1987.

Brzezinski, Zbigniew, *Between Two Ages*, 1973.

Brisard, Jean-Charles and Dasquie, Guillaume, *Bin Laden, la Verité Interdite*, France.

Burnham, James, *The Struggle for the World*, Jonathan Cape, London, 1947.

Bushrui, Suheil; Ayman, Iraj and Laszlo, Ervin, *Transition to a Global Society*, Oneworld, 1993.

Capell, Frank, *Henry Kissinger, Soviet Agent*, Criminal Politics magazine, 1992.

Capt, Raymond E., *Our Great Seal: The Symbols of our Heritage and our Destiny*, Thousand Oaks, CA: Artisan Sales, 1979.

Charmley, John, *Churchill: The End of Glory*, Hodder & Stoughton, London, 1993.

Chiera, *Sumerian Ritual Texts*, London, 1924.

Chernow, Ron, *Titan, The Life of John D. Rockefeller Sr*, Little, Brown, 1998.

Chesterton, A. K., *The New Unhappy Lords*, Britons Pub. Co. 1972.

Church, J. M., *Guardians of the Grail*, Oklahoma City, OK: Prophecy Publications, 1989.

Churchill, Winston, *The World Crisis*, (5 vols), Centenary Collected Edition, 1923–31.

CIA, *Foreign Missile Developments and the Ballistic Missile Threat Through 2015*.

Clinton, Hillary, *Living History, Memoirs*, Headline, London, 2003.

Coleman, Dr. John, *Conspirators' Hierarchy: The Story of the Committee of 300*, America West Publishers, PO Box 2208, Carson City, NV 89702, 1992.

Coleman, Dr. John, *Diplomacy by Deception*, Joseph Publishing Co, Nevada, 1993.

Coleman, Dr. John, *Global 2000: A Blueprint for Global Genocide*, 2533 North Carson Street, Carson City, NV 89706, 1992.

Collier, Peter with Horovitz, David, *The Roosevelts, An American Saga*, André Deutsch, London, 1995.

Corti, Count Egon Caesar, *The Rise of the House of Rothschild*, Western Islands, USA, 1928, 1972.

Cotter, John, *A Study in Syncretism*, Canadian Intelligence Publications, 1979.

Crompton, Piers, *The Broken Cross, The Hidden Hand in the Vatican*, Veritas, 1984.

Crozier, Brian, *Soviet Imperialism, How to Contain It*, Temple Smith, London, 1978.

Dale, John, *The Prince and the Paranormal, The Psychic Bloodline of the Royal Family*, W. H. Allen, London, 1987.

Dall, Curtis, *My Exploited Father-in-Law*, Action Associates, Washington DC, 1970.

Daniel, John, *Scarlet and the Beast, A History of the War between English and French Freemasonry*, vol. i, Jon Kregel, USA, 1995.

Darwin, Charles, *On the Origin of Species*, Broadview Press, 2003.

De La Rive, A. C., *La Femme at l'Enfant dans la Franc-Maçonnerie Universelle*, France.

De Pincins, Vicomte Leon, *The Secret Powers behind Revolution*, G S G & Associates Pub.

Devine, Robert, *Second Chance: The Triumph of Internationalism in America During World War II*, New York: Atheneum, 1967.

Deyo, Stan, *The Cosmic Conspiracy*, West Australian Texas Trading, 1992.

Dillon, Mgr George, *Grand Orient Freemasonry Unmasked as the Secret Power behind Communism*, 1885, distr. Bloomfield Books, England.

Dorril, Stephen, *MI6, Fifty Years of Special Operations*, Fourth Estate, London, 2000.

Drosnin, Michael, *The Bible Code II*, Phoenix, London, 2003.

Eliot, Gil, *Twentieth Century Book of the Dead*, Allen Lane, London, 1972.

Engdahl, F. William, *A Century of War, Anglo-American Oil Politics and the New World Order*, Dr. Böttiger Verlags-GmbH, 1992.

Epperson, Ralph, *The New World Order*, Publius Press, 1991.

Epperson, Ralph, *The Unseen Hand*, Publius Press, 1985.

Erickson, John and Dilks, David, ed., *Barbarossa, the Axis and the Allies*, Edinburgh University Press, 1994.

Eringer, Robert, *The Global Manipulators*, Pentacle Books, London, 1980.

Ferguson, Niall, *The World's Banker, The History of the House of Rothschild*, Weidenfeld and Nicolson, London, 1998.

Fukuyama, Francis, *The End of History and the Last Man*, Hamish Hamilton, London, 1992.

Garrison, Col. Ely, *Roosevelt, Wilson and the Federal Reserve Act*, The Christopher Publishing House, Boston, 1931.

Gilbert, Martin, *Churchill: A Life*, Minerva, 1991.

Global 2000 Report to the President, Penguin, London, 1982.

Global Future: Time to Act, Report to the President on Global Resources, Environment and Population, Council on Environmental Quality, Department of State, January 1981.

Goulevitch, Arsene, de, *Czarism and the Revolution*.

Griffin, Des, *Descent into Slavery*, Emissary Publications, USA, 1991.

Griffin, Des, *Fourth Reich of the Rich*, Emissary Publications, USA, 1993.

Griffin, G. Edward, *The Creature from Jekyll Island*, Appleton W. I.: American Opinion Publishing Inc, 1994.

Guarino, Nick, *The Wall Street Underground*.

Gunaratna, Rohan, *Inside al-Qaeda: Global Network of Terror*. Berkley Publishing Group, 2003.

Hagger, Nicholas, *Overlord*, Element, 1994–6.

Hagger, Nicholas, *The Fire and the Stones*, Element, 1991.

Hagger, Nicholas, *The Secret History of the West*, John Hunt, due for publication 2005.

Hannah, Walter, *Darkness Visible*, Augustine, London 1852.

Harvey, Robert, *Global Disorder*, Constable and Robinson, London, 2003.

Hayes, Stephen F., *The Connection: How al-Qaeda's Collaboration with Saddam Hussein Has Endangered America*, HarperCollins, 2004.

Heikal, Mohammed, *The Return of the Ayatollah*, André Deutsch, London, 1981.

Hewitt, Clarence H., *The Seer of Babylon*, Lamp Trimmers, USA, 1948, 1944.

Hilaire Du Berrier Reports, Monaco, September 1991.

Higham, Charles, *Trading with the Enemy*, New York: Dell, 1983.

Hilberg, Raul, *The Destruction of the European Jews*, Holmes & Meier Publishing, 1985.

Hitchens, Peter, *The Trial of Henry Kissinger*, Verso, 2001.

Hitler, Adolf, *Mein Kampf*, London, 1939.

Hoopes, Townsend and Brinkley, Douglas, *FDR and the Creation of the UN*, Yale University Press, 1997.

House, Edward Mandell, *Philip Dru: Administrator*, Indypublish.com., 2003.

Hufschmid, Eric, *Painful Questions: An Analysis of the September 11th Attack*.

Hull, Cordell, *Memoirs of Cordell Hull*, Macmillan, New York, 1948.

Huntington, Samuel, *The Clash of Civilizations and the Remaking of World Order*, Simon and Schuster, 1996.

Hurley, Andrew J., *Israel and the New World Order*, Fithian Press, USA, 1991.

Huxley, Aldous, *Brave New World*, Penguin, 1932.

Icke, David, *Alice in Wonderland and the World Trade Center Disaster*, Bridge of Love,

2002.

International Security: The Military Aspect, Center for International Affairs, Washington, 1956.

James, E. O., *The Ancient Gods*, Weidenfold and Nicolson, London, 1962.

Jasper, William F., *Global Tyranny...Step by Step, The United Nations and the Emerging New World Order*, Western Islands, USA, 1992.

Jenkins, Lindsay, *Britain Held Hostage, The Coming Euro-Dictatorship*, Orange State Press, Washington, 1997.

Josephson, Emanuel M., *Rockefeller "Internationalist", The Man who Misrules the World*, Chedney Press, New York, 1952.

Josephson, Emanuel M., *The "Federal" Reserve Conspiracy and Rockefeller*, Chedney Press, New York, 1968.

Josephson, Emanuel M., *The Strange Death of Franklin D. Roosevelt*, Chedney Press, New York, 1948.

Josephson, Emanuel M., *The Truth About Rockefeller, Public Enemy no. 1*, Chedney Press, 1964.

Kagan, Robert, *Paradise and Power*, Atlantic, 2003.

Kah, Gary H., *En Route to Global Occupation*, Huntingdon House Publishers, 1992.

Kennedy, Paul, *The Rise and Fall of the Great Powers*, Unwin Hyman, London, 1988.

Keys, David, *Catastrophe*, Arrow Books, 2000 (first published 1999).

King, Dr. Alexander and Schneider, Bertrand, *The First Global Revolution, A Report by the Council of the Club of Rome*, Simon and Schuster, 1992.

Kissinger, Henry, *Diplomacy*, Simon and Schuster, 1994.

Knightley, Phillip, *The Master Spy: The Story of Kim Philby*, Random House Inc., 1989.

Kramer, S.M., *Cuneiform Inscriptions*, Oxford, UK, 1923.

Krieg, Dr Adrian, *July 4th, 2016, The Last Independence Day*, Hallberg, 2000.

Krieg, Dr Adrian, *The Sartori and the New Mandarins*, Hallberg, 1997.

Kutz, Myer, *Rockefeller Power*, Pinnacle Books, New York, 1974.

Lash, J. P., *Roosevelt and Churchill 1939–41: The Partnership that Saved the West*, New York, 1976.

Le Sueur, Gorden, *Cecil Rhodes, The Man and His Work*, London: John Murray, 1913.

Lellouche, Pierre, *Le Nouveau Monde – de L'ordre de Yalta aux chaos des nations*, Grasset, 1992.

Livesey, Roy, *Understanding the New World Order*, New Wine Press, 1989.

Loftus, John and Aarons, Mark, *The Secret War Against the Jews*, St Martin's Press, New York, 1994.

McForan, Dr Desmond, *The World Held Hostage, The War Waged by International Terrorism*, Oak-Tree Books, London, 1986.

McLaughlin, Michael, *For Those Who Cannot Speak*, Historical Review Press, 1979.

McWhirter, Norris and Atkinson, Rodney, *Treason at Maastricht*, Compuprint Publishing, London, 1994.

Marrs, Texe, *Dark Majesty, The Secret Brotherhood and the Magic of A Thousand Points of Light*, Living Truth Publishers, 1992.

Martin, Malachi, *The Keys of This Blood*, Touchstone, New York, 1990.

Marx, Karl, *A World Without Jews*, 1844.

Meadows, Dennis, and others, *The Limits to Growth*, Universe Book, New York, 1972.

Mesarovic, Mihajlo, *Mankind at the Turning Point: The Second Report to the Club of Rome*, Penguin, 1975.

Mesarovic, Mihajlo and Pestel, Eduard, *Regionalized and Adaptive Model of the Global World System, Report on the Progress in the Strategy for Survival Project of the Club of Rome*, September 17, 1973.

Morton, Frederic, *The Rothschilds, A Family Portrait*, Atheneum, New York, 1962.

Mowrer, Edgar Ansell, *Germany Puts the Clock Bac*, Penguin, 1938.

Muller, Robert, *The Birth of a Global Civilization*, World Happiness and Co-Operation, USA, 1991.

Mullins, Eustace, *The Secrets of the Federal Reserve*, Bankers Research Institute, US 1991.

Mullins, Eustace, *The World Order, Our Secret Rulers*, Ezra Pound Institute of Civilization, PO Box 1105, Staunton, VA 24401, 2nd ed, 1992.

Nye, Joseph S. Jr., *Bound to Lead, The Changing Nature of American Power*, Basic Books, US, 1990.

O'Connor, Harvey, *The Empire of Oil*, Monthly Review Press, New York, 1955.

Orwell, George, *1984*, Heinemann Educational Books, 1977.

Parsons, Anthony, *From Cold War to Hot Peace, UN Interventions 1947–1994*, Michael Joseph, London, 1995.

Perloff, James, *The Shadows of Power, The Council on Foreign Relations and the American Decline*, Western Islands, USA, 1988.

Pestel, Eduard, *Beyond the Limits to Growth*, Universe Book, New York, 1989.

Plumme, William Robert, *The Untold History, How the British East India Company's 'pre-Fabian' Philosophical Radicals set up Capitalism and its antithesis Communism*, The Committee for the Restoration of the Republic, 1964.

PNAC, *Rebuilding America's Defenses: Strategies, Forces and Resources for a New Century*.

Pool, James and Pool, Suzanne, *Who Financed Hitler, The Secret Funding of Hitler's Rise to Power 1919–1933*, The Dial Press, New York, 1978.

Pound, Ezra, *America, Roosevelt and the Cause of the Present War*, London 1951

Queenborough, Lady, *Occult Theocrasy*, Emissary Publications, 1933.

Quigley, Carroll, *Anglo-American Establishment*, Emissary Publications, USA, 1981.

Quigley, Carroll, *The Invisible Government*, Boston: Western Islands, 1962.

Quigley, Carroll, *Tragedy and Hope*, Macmillan, New York, 1966.

Read, Anthony and Fisher, David, *The Fall of Berlin*, Pimlico, 1992.

Reed, Douglas, *Controversy of Zion*.

Rivera, David Allen, *Final Warning, A History of the New World Order*, Rivera Enterprises, 1984, 1994.

Roberts, Glyn, *The Most Powerful Man in the World*, Covici, Friede, 1938.

Robertson, Pat, *The New World Order*, Word, USA, 1991.

Robinson, Adam, *Bin Laden: Behind the Mask of Terror*, Mainstream, UK, 2001.

Rockefeller, David, *Memoirs*, Random House, New York, 2002.

Ronson, Jon, *Them, Adventures with Extremists*, Picador/Macmillan, London, 2001.

Ross, Robert Gaylon Sr., *Who's Who of the Elite*, RIE, HCR1, Box 516, Spicewood, Texas 78669–9549, 1995.

Sampietro, Luciano, *Nostradamus, The Final Prophecies*, Souvenir Press, 2002.

Shaw, Bernard, *Fabian Essays in Socialism*, London, 1899.

Shoup, Laurence and Minter, William, *Imperial Brain Trust: Council on Foreign Relations and United States Foreign Policy*, Monthly Rev. 1978

Simpson, Clive, *The Lusitania*, Little Brown, Boston, 1972.

Sklar, Dusty, *The Nazis and the Occult*, Dorset Press, New York, 1977.

Skolnick, Sherman H., *US Government Prior Knowledge of Emergency, 9.11.2001*, www.skolnicksreport.com/pkem.html.

Spengler, Oswald, *Decline of the West*, Oxford University Press.

Springmeier, Fritz, *The Top 13 Illuminati Bloodlines*, Springmeier, 1995.

Still, William T., *New World Order: The Ancient Plan of Secret Societies*, Huntington House, USA.

Story, Christopher, *The European Union Collective, Enemy of its Member States*, Edward Harle, 2002.

Stuart, James Gibb, *Hidden Menace to World Peace*, Ossian, UK, 1993.

Sutton, Antony C., *America's Secret Establishment*, Emissary Publications, USA, 1986.

Sutton, Antony C., *Two Faces of George Bush*, Veritas, Australia, 1988.

Sutton, Antony C., *Wall Street and the Bolshevik Revolution*, Veritas, 1981.

Sutton, Antony C., *Wall Street and the Rise of Hitler*, Bloomfield Books, London, 1976.

Sutton, Antony C. and Wood, Patrick M, *Trilaterals Over Washington*, vol II, Scottsdale, Arizona: The August Corporation, 1981.

Tarbell, Ida, *The History of the Standard Oil Company*, two volumes, New York: McClure, Phillips, 1904, updated and reissued in two volumes in 1931.

The Protocols of the Meetings of the Learned Elders of Zion, tr. by Victor E. Marsdon, Eyre and Spottiswoode, London, December 1921.

Thomas, Gordon, *Seeds of Fire: China and the Story Behind the Attack on America*, Dandelion Books, 2001.

Todd, John, *The Illuminati and Witchcraft*, lectures given at a Bible Baptist church, Elkton, Md, USA, 1978.

Toynbee, Arnold, *A Study of History*, 12 vols, Oxford University Press, 1934 to 1961.

Walker, Gen. Sir Walter, *The Next Domino?* Covenant Books, London, 1980.

Wells, H. G., *The New World Order, Whether it is Attainable, How it can be Attained, and What Sort of World a World at Peace Will Have to Be*, Alfred A. Knopf, New York, 1940.

Wilgus, Neal, *The Illuminoids*, New York,: Pocket Books, 1978.

Wilson, Derek, *Rothschild, A Story of Wealth and Power*, Mandarin, London, 1988.

Wint, Guy and Calvocoressi, Peter, *Middle East Crisis*, Penguin, London, 1957.

Wolf, Charles, *America's Decline: Illusion or Reality?*, Wall Street Journal, May 12, 1988.

Woodrow, Ralph Edward, *Babylon Mystery Religion Ancient and Modern*, Ralph Woodrow, 1966.

Wormser, René, *Foundations, Their Power and Influence*, Devin Adair, New York, 1958.

Yergin, Daniel, *The Prize: The Epic Quest for Oil, Money and Power*, Simon & Schuster, 1991.

Zimmern, Alfred, *The League of Nations and the Rule of Law*, Wm Gaunt & Sons, 1998.

Zumwalt, Admiral Elmo R. Jr., *My Watch: A Memoir*.

Dailies/Weeklies/Monthlies Consulted (Issues Cited)

The Spotlight
The American Free Press
Portman Papers
Jerusalem Post
Fire Engineering
Le Figaro
New York Times
Sunday Times
Washington Post
Post-Dispatch
Hansard
Pakistan Observer
London Times
London Daily Telegraph
Round Table
Daily Mail
Sun
AP
London's Independent on Sunday
The Mail on Sunday
Wall Street Journal
Morning Star
Sunday Telegraph Magazine
US News and World Report
London's Observer
Vanity Fair
London's *Al Qub*
Guardian